FROM BRADMAN TO BORDER

AUSTRALIAN

C·R·I·C·K·E·T·1948–1989

This book concludes Jack Pollard's four volume history of Australian Cricket. Other books in the series are:

The Formative Years of Australian Cricket (1803–93)
The Turbulent Years of Australian Cricket (1893–1917)
The Bradman Years, Australian Cricket (1918–48)

The four volumes should be read in conjunction with Ross Dundas' book on Australian cricket statistics
Highest, Most and Best.

Other recent books by Jack Pollard

Australian Fishing (ed., 1989, revised edition)
The Pictorial History of Australian Cricket (1990, 3rd edition)
When Stumps Were Drawn (ed., 1985)
Australian Rugby Union: The Game and the Players (1984)
Tribute to Lillee and Chappell (1984)
Australian Cricket: The Game and the Players (1988, revised edition)
Australian Horse Racing (1988)
The Pictorial History of Australian Horse Racing (1989, enlarged 3rd edition)
Six and Out (ed., 1990, enlarged 7th edition)

FROM BRADMAN TO BORDER

AUSTRALIAN

C·R·I·C·K·E·T·1948–1989

JACK POLLARD

ANGUS
& ROBERTSON

A division of HarperCollins*Publishers*

Contents

Introduction

In the 42 years covered by this book Australian cricket has moved through two of the most difficult periods in its history—the revolt by 28 players, who were to form the nucleus and provide the leadership for the Packer breakaway, and the rebel tours of South Africa. Each time leading players defied the expressed wishes of the Australian Cricket Board.

The South African tours wrecked the Board's efforts to rebuild a powerful Test team, but the Board wisely chose to let them proceed rather than become involved in costly litigation. In answer to the Packer revolt, the Board negotiated a settlement on behalf of the whole cricket world which ushered in a period of undreamed-of financial prosperity for Australian cricket. The Board had acted with caution in dealing with these crises, just as it did in 1912 when six notable players refused to join the team to England unless they were allowed to pick their manager.

The cricketers who have found their way into the pages of cricket history up to the start of the 1989–90 Australian season—the deadline for this fourth volume—were invariably honest, decent citizens. One was shot by a lover he rejected, but there were no murderers among them and very few villains. Some of them were unable to find peace in life after cricket and drifted in and out of jobs eagerly awaiting the next team reunion. A handful dabbled in politics. Most were devoted family men, usually disappointed in their hopes that their sons would emulate their deeds on the field. Very few became

rich, although television seems likely to change that. Bob Cowper, the Australian left-handed batsman now reputed to be worth more than $100 million, is a notable exception. Before Cowper began playing the stock market, Warwick Armstrong was probably Australia's richest cricketer. Armstrong, who married into a wealthy family, left £90,000 on his death in 1947, a sum that was a fortune by Australian standards of the time, though one suspects he made more of it out of selling whisky than playing cricket!

Among the 347 players to reach Test status in the 113 years of big cricket covered in my four volumes there have been some who had outstanding leadership qualities, and who should have become influential cricket administrators. Unfortunately, most of these men were discouraged by the tortuous system of holding elections first to appoint delegates to district clubs then further ballots to win places on State association committees and ultimately appointment to the Australian Cricket Board.

There have been notable exceptions. Sir Donald Bradman gave long and distinguished service to the game as a selector, State delegate, and Board chairman after his playing days ended. Sam Loxton injected a lot of commonsense to Victorian Cricket Association meetings as the Prahran club's delegate. Alan Davidson has been president of the New South Wales Cricket Association since 1970. Overall, however, far too few of our Test players have risked club ballots.

Since the Packer settlement much of the old distrust of cricket's administration, which dated back to the Board's broken promises in its formative years, has disappeared. More and more States appear to be seconding former star players to coaching and development committees without forcing them to submit to election. Western Australia's list of former Test and State players who in some way are helping the game to prosper is particularly impressive.

Over the years the Australian Test team has

periodically put in disappointing performances. Critics who blame this on poor administration should remember that since international cricket began Australia has beaten all the countries with whom she plays the game more often than the others have defeated Australia. Australia remains the world's strongest cricket nation on a Tests won-and-lost basis, even if it is occasionally beaten by countries to which it helped introduce big cricket. The 1980s were particularly disappointing, with Australia winning only 27 of the 97 Tests played, losing 34, drawing 35 and tying one. But the frustrations of this decade were all thrust aside by the four-nil defeat of England by Border's 1989 side.

The first Australian tours to India, Pakistan, South Africa, and the West Indies are all painstakingly covered in this history, and they show how eagerly young players in those countries set themselves to match the Australians' skills. Australia's first series in the West Indies in 1955 saw an Australian innings of 8 for 758 declared in which five Australians scored centuries. It was not long before the West Indians themselves would be handing out severe defeats.

Australians themselves had learned from the skilful English players who made the first tours of Australia. England has remained Australia's foremost rival, and no victory over the West Indies, Pakistan or any other cricket nation is ever as sweet as a win over England.

My major difficulty in completing the story of Australian cricket with the fourth volume has been the proliferation of overseas tours in the past decade. It is not uncommon for Australia to visit three countries in a year now and to entertain three countries at home. The advent of full-time professional cricketers who no longer have to depend on other jobs for a living has produced programmes that are the despair of cricket historians. Condensation in a form that was never considered in the years of restricted overseas tours has become essential. In the first volume of this history I devoted most of a chapter

to Australia's trip across America in 1878. In this volume I take the Australians from Australia to England in a sentence.

Much of the period under review has been dominated by the activities of Kerry Packer. Although he no longer controls the television network for which he fought so hard to secure exclusive cricket broadcast rights, the changes he introduced remain a major influence on the conduct of all our big matches. The crowd participation he encouraged has affected the atmosphere at the games. Originally, he wanted spectators to parade around inside the fences as they do during intervals in New Zealand and at the Eton–Harrow matches at Lord's. He has had to be satisfied with hundreds of banners— some of them ingenious, with coloured clothing for one-day matches, and with spectators imitating the warm-up routines of Merv Hughes.

The players' higher rates of pay, the Australian Cricket Board's big share of tour profits, and even tour itineraries are now all influenced by PBL Sports, the company Packer created. The role television plays in Australian cricket continues to expand, with the public accustomed to witnessing captains tossing, batsmen reaching a century, bowlers taking vital wickets, all without attending the ground. And Packer's men have proven they can sell everything from spanners to motor cars.

All of this began in 1977 and as Australian cricket entered the 1990s, television's grip on it shows no signs of easing. On the field, aware of their television audience as well as the big prizemoney on offer, players try for bigger sixes, more spectacular catches, and risk physical damage to cut off boundaries. Packer won his fight for television rights and in the process he changed the conduct of the game.

Photographer Jack Hickes' award-winning picture of the record crowd at Headingley in 1948 for the England–Australia Test captioned "The crowd within and the crowd without."

The Greats of '48

Australia in England 1948;
Bradman's last Test

The euphoria of victory in a brutal war had not faded among Britons who saw the twentieth Australian cricket team's 1948 tour as another demonstration of the Empire's superior way of life. Like the parades by the Empire's battle heroes, nobody wanted to miss the spectacle of Englishmen facing Australians in the most British of all games. People lined footpaths for hundreds of yards in streets leading to grounds at which the Australians appeared, and when Bradman played there were "House Full" signs. Those locked out gathered outside the Australians' hotels just to get a glimpse of him. Inside buzzing grounds those lucky enough to get seats were determined to celebrate, concentrating on every ball, applauding every good pick-up, every good throw, and rewarding dismissals with a volley of applause.

This was an audience still locked into austerity, sustained by twelve pennyworth of meat a week and able to buy only one suit a

An historic moment for Australian cricket. Bradman bowled for a duck in his last Test innings when he needed only four runs to average more than 100 in Tests. Even the bowler Eric Hollies was sorry.

year with food and clothing ration coupons. Newspapers were limited to four pages daily by newsprint shortages. Bomb damage at Old Trafford had been repaired, but lines with up to 400 people in them snaked back from the few available toilets. At The Oval the pitch and outfield had been resurfaced after use as a wartime camp for German prisoners. Before the Tests began, Bradman and Keith Johnson made a presentation of food they had brought with them for the British people and the mayor of Adelaide appealed to Australians to keep sending the parcels of food they had started posting to Britain during the war.

The Australian team had just the right blend to face 34 matches under these conditions, a fun-loving, well-groomed, unfailingly courteous outfit that played exciting cricket and knew how to enjoy a party. They were as good at looking after crippled kids and pensioners as they were at winning matches—chivalrous players eager to share their enjoyment of Australia's greatest cricket tour. They laughed their way through the longest train trips, and remained attentive through the most boring mayoral speeches. They were also the only Australian team to tour England without defeat.

Before the team was announced, Sid Barnes asked Don Bradman, whom he called George, if Bradman would tour. "If you go, George, then I'll go, too," he said. Once the tour began Barnes kept his team-mates alert with rapid-fire quips and wisecracks and close-catching practice when a wicket fell, the showman in him responding to crowds eager for surprises.

Bradman risked his reputation when he agreed to captain the side. At 39 the muscle spasms that worried him throughout the war years needed regular treatment. The rib injury that forced him to retire on 57 in his last Test appearance in Australia also troubled him. He had watched the sad failure of Wally Hammond at 43 when Hammond managed only 168 runs at 21.00 in the 1946–47 series in Australia. He

knew that only Warren Bardsley, 43 in 1926, Syd Gregory, 42 in 1912, Warwick Armstrong, 41 in 1921, Arthur Mailey, 40 in 1926, and Charlie Macartney, 39 in 1926, had toured England at a more mature age.

Some critics considered his final flourish foolhardy, but Bradman believed he owed it to English cricket fans and they were so overjoyed by the tour they sent the Australians up to 1000 letters a day. The Eagle Star insurance company lent Bradman a secretary who typed through the day while he was at the cricket, providing his answer to every letter. Like his players, Bradman devoted himself to daily sessions signing autographs.

Bradman had recovered from the bankruptcy of his employer Harry Hodgetts in 1942 and become successful in the stockbroking business. He was elected to the Adelaide Stock Exchange in May 1943. His difficulties with the Australian Cricket Board, which in 1938 had seen him write his letter of resignation from the Australian captaincy—fortunately, on the advice of Dr Rowley Pope, not delivered—had been brief. Once the Board withdrew objections to his wife joining him in England, normal relations had been resumed and he was appointed to the Board in 1946.

Since he had first come off the concrete pitches of country towns in 1928–29 to play Test cricket, he had won a unique place in the Australian community. He had become a symbol of recovery in the Depression years, a prize example of success despite humble origins, and his country's major headline-winner overseas. Failure in England in 1948 would have tarnished it all, but after he decided to go and forget the huge fees he could have commanded in the press box, he began encouraging his players and slowly the idea developed that they could make the first unbeaten tour of England.

His carefully chosen team was short of players with experience of wet pitches and overcast skies, but, like English sides with good pace bowlers,

The 1948 Australian team, the only side to go through an England tour without defeat: (L to R) (back) R. N. Harvey, D. Tallon, D. T. A. Ring, I. W. Johnson, R. R. Lindwall, R. A. Saggers, W. A. Johnston, S. J. E. Loxton, K. R. Miller, E. R. Toshack; (front) A. R. Morris, C. L. McCool, A. L. Hassett, D. G. Bradman (captain), W. A. Brown, S. G. Barnes, R. A. Hamence.

was assisted by an experimental rule that allowed a new ball to be taken every 55 overs. This rule virtually denied spinners a major role in the Tests. Even the most aggressive England batsmen could be contained with pace until a new ball came due. Of the 17 players in the Australian team, only Bradman, Hassett, Barnes and Brown had previously toured England, although Miller had had invaluable experience there in services cricket. Only three of the side, Harvey, Barnes and Toshack, had not served in the forces, and team discipline showed on the rare days that defeat threatened. The team was: D. G. Bradman, 39, A. L. Hassett, 34, A. R. Morris, 26, W. A. Brown, 35, S. G. Barnes, 32, S. J. E. Loxton, 27, R. N. Harvey, 19, K. R. Miller, 28, I. W. Johnson, 29, R. A. Hamence, 32, C. L. McCool, 32, R. R. Lindwall, 27, D. Tallon, 32, R. A. Saggers, 31, D. T. A. Ring, 30, W. A. Johnston, 26, E. R. Toshack, 30, with Bill Ferguson scorer. Keith Johnson beat the only other candidate, former Western Australian batsman A. C. Randell, for the manager's job.

Aware of the technique of England's leading batsmen, Bradman used Toshack—a tall, swarthy bush bowler of unique method, known to teammates as "The Black Prince"—particularly well. His stock left-arm delivery cut towards the leg but he varied it with finger spin and drifters, and a splendidly concealed fast one, all delivered over the wicket. Bradman had first seen Toshack in a 1934 match staged to open a turf wicket in the New South Wales country town Cowra. Toshack was one of five children born in the western town of Cobar whose mother and father died before the children reached their teens. A frugal life in the bush was enriched by the cricket Ernie Toshack played in the Grenfell district with Les and Stan McCabe. He could not afford to go to Sydney to play, but won a place in the State Colts in 1938 before a ruptured appendix almost killed him. Bradman made a careful study of the field Toshack needed, usually giving him four men on the off, including a slip, and five on the leg side, but when the pitch was damp or turning he moved in a leg slip and pushed Sid Barnes up to short leg.

Toshack only scraped into the team after five specialists examined his knee. With Queenslander Len Johnson on standby, two Melbourne doctors ruled Toshack unfit but three in Sydney took a more charitable view. The Board allowed him to tour on the majority verdict. More certain of his footwork was the team's "baby", Neil Harvey, at 19 the only player under 26, a quick-witted left-hander impervious to tension, an apprentice fitter and turner, and the fourth son of ex-coalminer Horace Harvey to play Shield cricket.

The all-round strength of the team meant fine cricketers like Bruce Dooland, George Tribe, Fred Freer, Geff Noblet, Jack Pettiford, Len Johnson, Ken Meuleman and Des Fothergill could be left behind. Notable performers Jack Walsh and Vic Jackson had made their debuts in English county cricket before the war and in 1946 Cec Pepper had commenced his long career in the Lancashire League. Others like Bill Alley, Ken Grieves, Jock Livingston and Jack McMahon lost hope of breaking into such a powerful side, took solace in the Lancashire League, and transferred from there to county cricket.

The batting was immensely strong, starting with superb openers Barnes and Morris, so effective a pair that Test selectors had to drop Brown, who had a famous double century at Lord's in 1938 behind him and was to score eight tour centuries batting down the order. Bradman, Hassett and Miller followed, with Loxton the ideal middle order hitter to exploit tired bowling. Harvey fought his way into the Tests only when Barnes was hurt. Ian Johnson, Lindwall and Tallon had all made first-class hundreds. Tallon was a majestic wicket-keeper, whom Bradman conceded was under-rated by selectors in 1938, and Saggers his polished deputy.

The Australian Board of Control instructed Tallon to have his tonsils removed following the team's medical examination. Some of the others still carried sallow complexions from war years in New Guinea where anti-malaria atabrine tablets were obligatory. Barnes, the world's best short-leg fieldsman, had a tan he got from sunlamps, Miller, the finest slips field, a surfer's sheen. The team boasted some exciting throwing arms. All the bowlers were safe catchers.

The bowling fell largely on the charismatic duo Raymond Russell Lindwall, ex-army signalman of Irish–Swedish extraction with the silken run-up and body action that propelled bouncers at the throat, and Keith Ross Miller, strapping ex-Mosquito pilot, horse fancier and admirer of beautiful women, who bowled a nasty faster ball from a short run. As a pair, they were so hostile that McCool, who had taken 18 wickets against England two years earlier, was not picked for Tests and Ring bowled only in the Fifth Test. With gangling Colac farmer, Bill Johnston, the bowler, Bradman worked hardest, returning and bowling spin after starting with fast-medium deliveries, the variety in the bowling never gave batsmen any easy periods. Loxton's brisk medium-pacers and Ian Johnson's flighted off spin could be used to attack or confine until a new ball became due.

The team benefited from a month at sea in the *Strathaird*, interrupted by matches against Tasmania in Hobart and Launceston. Throughout the voyage Bradman worked on speeches he would make later at tour dinners. At Perth from 13 to 16 March, 1948, Bradman made a chanceless 115, his eighth century in that Australian summer. The daring shot-making of his youth had gone, but he was harder to get out, playing closer to his body, concentrating intensely. In the one-day match at Colombo the female curator produced a pitch that was two yards short when measured by Ian Johnson, a problem the bowlers solved by moving the stumps.

At Bombay the big crowds who flocked to the quayside just to catch a glimpse of Bradman were a revelation to players like Bill Johnston from Ondit, a two-building town comprising the school and post office in western Victoria. With Bradman in charge they were in for some glittering welcomes. Swimming and deck games improved Bradman's fitness but at no stage of the tour was he 100 per cent fit. A century and a double century against Hammond's team in 1946–47, and three centuries and a double century against India in 1947–48 had prepared him for his final curtain, but he still had to be careful not to strain his physique.

For a fee of 250 guineas per match, the BBC radioed descriptions of the tour across the world in a hook-up that created hundreds of all-night parties in Australia and caused power failures in New Zealand. Overnight, Hampshire policeman-turned-poet John Arlott and unashamed Empire-lover Alan McGilvray became celebrities. Bill Ferguson sustained his record of never having lost a bag since he began scoring for Australian teams in 1905. Fergie travelled first-class for the first time, but still had to earn a few shillings in commission attending to the team's laundry. He did the job so well there was never a mud or grass stain on players' creams.

Cities, villages and hotels ran up flags to celebrate the Australians' presence. Tour lunches and dinners had a warmth and bonhomie later tours lost, with Bradman in sparkling speech-making form. His players' grooming was widely admired, all 17 at ease in dinner suits and unconcerned when functions demanded black tie. Even on railway stations people congregated to get a look at them.

After negotiating a big crowd at Paddington station to get to the first match at Worcester from 28 to 30 April, Bradman and Morris gave the tour the ideal start by scoring centuries in cold, cheerless weather. On that beautiful, unenclosed field with the cathedral in the background, Morris drove imperiously for 138. Bradman, with 40 photographers following him

Bradman on his way to a century against Worcestershire in 1948. On three previous visits he had made double centuries, but this time a rib injury forced him to give his innings away.

to the crease, threw his hand away after reaching 107, already troubled by his rib injury, letting a double century go as he frequently did on the tour, content to let his record against Worcestershire read: 236 in 1930, 206 in 1934 258 in 1938, and 107 in 1948.

Miller hit 38 of his 50 not out from three sixes and five fours, lifting Australia's total to 6 for 462 declared, enough to secure victory by an innings and 17 runs. But Miller's form at the nets was patchy so Bradman sent him in after the first wicket fell against Leicestershire in that match from 1 to 4 May, hoping a long innings would adjust Miller's timing. Miller responded with 202 not out, and Australia won by an innings and 171 runs, Johnson's spin providing match figures of 9 for 92.

Australia were in trouble at 6 for 31 in the fourth innings of the third match against Yorkshire, chasing 63 to win in front of workers from Bradford's woollen mills, with Loxton unfit to bat. Harvey was dropped at short leg before he went to 18 not out, winning the match with a towering six. Tallon, on 17 not out, leapt for joy at the other end.

Harvey's cavalier handling of Yorkshire's bowling in a crisis was vivid in the memory when he sprinted round the outfield at The Oval against Surrey to hold a catch baseball-fashion over his head. Set to take a long look at Bedser, son of a Woking bricklayer, Barnes made 176, Bradman 146, Hassett 110 in Australia's 632 between 8 and 10 May. Forty overs from Bedser, who joined Surrey in 1938 on the same day as his twin brother Eric, yielded 4 for 104. Australia then dismissed Surrey for 141 and 195 to win by an innings and 296 runs. Johnson had 5 for 53 in Surrey's first knock, Johnston 4 for 40 in the second.

At Southend on a sunny Saturday, 15 May, Australia scored an incredible 148 runs an hour while Bradman was at the crease. His 187 in 124 minutes was the fastest first-class innings of his career, and his team's 721 the highest ever total for six hours' first-class cricket. Barnes and Brown began with 145 in 95 minutes before Barnes was out hit wicket for 79. Bradman and Brown then added 219 in only 90 minutes for the second wicket. In the midst of this prolific run-getting, Miller went in and was

Sid Barnes, who told umpire Alec Skelding he should umpire with a blindman's aid of a dog and a cane, emphasises his point by handing a dog that strayed on to the field to Skelding during Australia's 1948 tour of England.

comprehensively beaten and bowled first ball for a duck.

To the delight of holidaymakers crammed into the ground Bradman hit 32 fours and a five before he threw his innings away. Hamence made a brisk 46 before Loxton and Saggers put on 166 in 65 minutes. Loxton's 120 included 14 fours and a six, Saggers' 104 nine fours. The last four batsmen sacrificed their wickets in the chase to 700. Essex managed only 83 and 187 to lose by an innings and 451 runs in less than two days. Toshack's 10.5 overs yielded 5 for 31 in the first innings, and Johnson had another good bag with 6 for 37 in the second innings.

For Australia's first appearance at Lord's, on 22 May, crowds four abreast reached back half a mile from every turnstile. Opposed to an MCC XI that included Edrich and Compton, who had made 18 centuries in the previous summer, the Australians suffered an early setback when Morris was out at 11, but Barnes and Bradman shared a 160-run stand to initiate another match-winning score. Barnes hit 12 fours in his 81, Bradman 11 fours in his 98, before the regal batting of Miller produced three sixes and 20 fours in a glorious 163. With Bradman calling for quick runs, Johnson joined the fun with three sixes and eight fours, adding 155 in 105 minutes with Miller. Laker was hammered for nine sixes in taking 3 for 127, and at that stage of his career there was a suggestion that he bowled badly when punished, but any bowler would have looked ragged in the face of such batting.

Australia's performance in dismissing MCC for 189 and 205 to win by an innings and 158 runs was soured by charges that fielding Barnes so close to the bat was unsporting. Bradman chose not to answer this, leaving it to the umpires to adjudicate.

Lord's had changed. Amateurs and professionals not only shared a dressing-room, but took the field together by the amateur route through the Long Room. The professionals' gate of pre-war days had disappeared.

The Honourable Lionel Hallam, the third Baron Tennyson, son of a former Governor-General of Australia, claimed that when he went to the Australians' room during this match, Bradman refused to see him. Lord Tennyson, a Regency figure whose calls for discipline in his staff were not apparent in his own bulging waistline or ruddy complexion, said Bradman was "a mannerless little man". English critics such as E. W. Swanton agreed that Bradman was right in accepting the room attendant's advice not to see his lordship. Tennyson had shown, in a visit to the English room, that he had lunched too well. On a later visit, Lord Tennyson's son apologised for what his father had done and invited Bradman to dinner.

On the eve of the first Test Lindwall worked himself into peak form with a match-winning display against Sussex at Hove from 5 to 7 June. He took 6 for 34 in Sussex's first innings of 86 and 5 for 25 in their second knock of 138. Australia's 5 for 549 declared included 184 from Morris, 109 by Bradman and 100 not out from Harvey. Australia won by an innings and 325 runs.

Bradman's century took him past Warren Bardsley's record for most runs by an Australian on English tours. Bradman reached 7927 runs in 94 innings compared with Bardsley's 7866 runs in 175 innings. Bradman passed 1000 runs for the tour in the first Test at Trent Bridge between 10 and 15 June, which Australia won by eight wickets, despite a brave England display.

Miller, the least mechanical of bowlers, started England's woes by bowling Hutton with a delivery of fearsome pace. By tea England were 8 for 74, despite the absence from the Australian attack of Lindwall, who tore a groin muscle after 13 overs and did not bowl again in the match. Johnston proved a worthy replacement, wrecking England's middle order with left-arm deliveries that swung, varied in pace, and occasionally nipped through, but never deviated from a perfect length.

Taking leave from my duties as turf editor of the *Sheffield Telegraph*, I was struck by the powers of endurance of a flautist who accompanied the England collapse with a wide repertoire of tunes and danced an authentic hornpipe as Surrey team-mates Bedser and Laker set about reviving England's innings. Their drives and pulls and educated edges produced 89 runs in 73 minutes after tea. Laker was on 63 when he nicked a Miller fireball to Tallon, and England were all out for 165. Splay-footed William Arras Johnston, loose-limbed to a point where the wrist bones virtually uncoupled, finished with 5 for 36 in his first Test in England. Apart from Johnston's pumping elbows, my memory of this Test retains the image of an astonishing Miller slips catch which ended with both his feet in the air above his head as he sent Hardstaff back for a duck.

Australia pressed home their advantage in an atmosphere of high tension on the second day. Bradman, more subdued than in any of his 27 other Test centuries against Yardley's leg-side attack, left for 138. Then Hassett found a highly competent partner in Lindwall and followed the stand of 120 with Bradman with a further 107 with Lindwall. Young at one stage sent down 11 overs without conceding a run in a 60-over stint that yielded 1 for 79. Hassett made 137, Lindwall 42.

Faced with a 344-run deficit, England had scored five when Washbrook was out trying to hook a bouncer for the second time in the match. Seventy minutes of pressure cricket followed Edrich's dismissal at 39. The Australian bowlers hurled themselves into an onslaught on Hutton and Compton and at one stage Miller let fly five bouncers in eight balls at Hutton, one of which struck Hutton high on his left arm. England's batting matched the high standard of the bowling and in the last 70 minutes of the second day Hutton and Compton added 82 runs.

Watching the continuing excitement of this session I felt drained when it was over, but one man in the Members' stand found the energy to boisterously hoot Miller as he went up the steps. Miller went to the man and lifted him by the coat from the ground. "What are you booing at?" he asked. The man was too surprised to answer and Miller put him down, laughing. The Australians believed Hutton had never been in any danger on an easy-paced pitch but had aroused the crowd with his mannerisms. Others took up the member's hooting and the result was one of the most hostile demonstrations against a bowler even seasoned players like Bradman had known. One spectator shouted: "You wouldn't do that if we had Larwood."

That night the Notts' secretary, H. A. Brown, called on Keith Johnson and apologised to him for the behaviour of the crowd. On Monday, before play began, Brown broadcast an appeal to the crowd to leave conduct of the game to the umpires and deplored the demonstration against Miller on Saturday. English newspapers reported that the member involved in the altercation with Miller had been expelled from the Notts club. Miller's success brought him dozens of calls and letters from old air force mates, all of them giving names of racehorses or greyhounds worth betting on.

Bad light and a storm interrupted play, but on resumption Miller bowled Hutton for the second time in the match, with a ball that broke back. Compton batted pluckily through the day and at stumps England were one run ahead with four wickets left.

On the last day, when Compton was 184, Miller unleashed a short bouncer which reared shoulder-high. Compton shaped to hook, changed his mind, and in trying to get his head out of the way, stepped on his stumps, a tragic end to a brave innings. Compton had defied the Australians for 6 hours 50 minutes, often in bad light, and hit 19 fours. Johnston, forced by Lindwall's injury to bowl 84 overs, had the best match return, 9 for 183. Set to score 98 to win, Australia got them for the loss of Morris and

The debonair racegoer Keith Miller about to leave his London hotel for Royal Ascot. His major disappointment in life was that he grew too big to become a jockey.

Bradman. Bradman's duck was his first in a Test in England and after 13 minutes his slowest duck anywhere.

Barnes thought the game was over when he cracked a square cut for four to bring the scores level. He snatched a stump and raced to the pavilion, only to be recalled from halfway up the steps by shouts from spectators. When Hassett made the winning hit, Barnes was unlucky in the scramble for souvenirs.

Hassett, a model vice-captain throughout the tour, took over the captaincy and the limelight for the match against Northants from 16 to 18 June at Northampton, where the Australians stocked up on footwear from local factories. Hassett topscored in Australia's first innings of 8 for 352 declared with 127, and his bowlers disposed of Northants for 119 and 169 to give

Australia victory by an innings and 64 runs. Australia struggled beneath murky clouds at Bramall Lane, set among Sheffield's steel mills, from 19 to 22 June against Yorkshire. Barnes was out for a duck to the third ball of the match, before Brown's immense skill against the sharp swing of Coxon and Aspinall took him to 113. Toshack's 7 for 81 gave Australia an honourable draw over a Yorkshire side that dropped seven catches. Despite the cold 51,824 attended Bramall Lane to see Bradman, whereas only 12,128 saw Yorkshire play Australia six weeks earlier when Bradman did not appear.

At Lord's from 24 to 29 June 132,000 people paid £43,000 to see champagne cricket in the second Test and beat all previous attendance and gate records for the ground but I got the impression that they could have been trebled if Lord's had had the space. Barnes backed himself at 15-to-1 with £8 to get a century. He offered to double the bets when Hutton caught him at short leg off Bedser before he had scored (the first of Hutton's three successive catches in that position). Barnes had no takers and while newspapers suggested the Bedser–Hutton leg trap was the answer to Bradman, Barnes won his bet in the second innings.

Bradman won the toss for the first time in a test in England and by the end of the first day Australia had lost 7 for 258, an admirable English effort given that Morris had made a chanceless 105. Yardley erred when the second day began by not introducing Doug Wright, whose kicking leg breaks from that strange loping, arms-outstretched approach run were regarded by the Australians as the most difficult spin bowling in England. The last three Australian wickets added 92, Tallon leading the way with 53.

In the dressing-room Miller told Bradman he was unable to bowl at the start of England's innings because of a back injury that originated in a wartime plane crash. Out on the field when Bradman tossed him the ball, Miller returned

it, disappointed that his back would not allow him to bowl on a pitch always helpful to pace bowlers. Some onlookers claimed Miller flouted Bradman's orders, but Miller told me: "There was nothing to it. I really wanted to bowl because you could get wickets at Lord's bowling under-arm, but I was forced to give Don the ball back because my back was too crook."

England's chances of taking advantage of Miller's absence went in the 45 minutes before lunch. Lindwall launched a magnificent pace attack with Johnston, ably supported by Johnson's off spin. Washbrook, Edrich and Horace Dollery, the Reading soccer star, went cheaply before Yardley and Compton staged a recovery at 4 for 46. They had put on 87 when Johnston, with the new ball, induced an edge from Compton with an outswinger from his wide arm-swing. Miller took the catch close to the grass, and was applauded all round the ground.

Bradman used only four bowlers, but Lindwall's blistering speed appeared to demoralise all the batsmen and England were out for 215. Australia extended their 135-run advantage with brilliant batting. Barnes and Morris put on 122 for the first wicket, Bradman and Barnes 174 for the second wicket. After reaching his cherished century, Barnes had a dip, hitting Laker for two successive sixes in an over that cost 21 runs. Yardley had Barnes caught on the boundary for 141 and bowled Hassett next ball, but when the momentary joy this created ebbed, Bradman (89) and Miller (74) continued the punishment of uninspired bowling. Australia's lead was 595 when Bradman declared with three wickets in hand.

On a rain-heavy pitch Bradman then produced trump-card Toshack in conditions ideal for him. Miller caught Compton low down in the slips before he and Toshack both took two wickets in an over. Toshack's 5 for 40 from 20.1 overs, bowling to two short legs and a silly mid-off, fully justified the gamble with his bad knee.

English critics were so concerned by the one-sidedness of Australia's two Test wins they began questioning the entire structure of English cricket. In county teams junior professionals still carried the bags for amateurs and senior pros, even lugging all the team's gear to railway stations. Amateurs travelled first-class and it was a rare county captain who went back to second-class to play cards with his pros on long train trips. At Nottingham, Australian Bruce Dooland was rebuked by a committeeman for calling his captain by his Christian name. Gloucestershire captain Basil Allen apologised when one of his pros called an opposing batsman by his nickname. At The Oval, after his discharge as Major Gover, Alf Gover was denied service in the Surrey tea room as Alf Gover, professional cricketer.

The theorising on the reasons for the poor condition of English cricket continued when Australia beat Surrey by ten wickets between 30 June and 2 July, and Gloucestershire by an innings and 363 runs at Bristol from 3 to 6 July. Australia's 7 for 774 was the season's highest score and its best-ever against a county. Morris was in glorious form as he made a century before lunch and a further century between lunch and tea. When he was out for 290, he had hit 42 fours and a six. Harvey contributed a breezy 95 and Loxton included four sixes in his 159 not out. Johnson, 6 for 68 and 5 for 32, and Ring with 5 for 47 in the second innings, were the match-winning bowlers. Only left-handed Cornishman Jack Crapp, 100 not out in Gloucestershire's first innings, offered any resistance.

Manchester's history of wet pitches gave loyal Englishmen more hope than their selectors for the third Test at Old Trafford from 8 to 13 July. Hutton, Wright, Coxon and Laker were dropped for Indian born George Emmett, left-arm tweaker Jack Young, fiery redhead Dick Pollard and the nuggetty in-form Jack Crapp. The ruthlessness of Hutton's omission ten years after his world record 364 surprised English fans and the hundreds of Australians who invested their savings to attend the Tests.

Johnston's yorker thudded into Washbrook's stumps in the first half hour and when Barnes snapped up Emmett close in, England were in early trouble. Before they could settle, Lindwall let loose a barrage of bouncers against Edrich and Compton. After taking a heavy blow on the arm, Compton swung lustily at a "no-ball" bouncer. The ball flew off the edge into his eyebrow. Compton staggered and was led from the field, with Miller stemming the heavy flow of blood from the cut. While Compton's eyebrow was stitched, Edrich and Crapp defended desperately. Only one run came in a 25-minute period and after two hours England were 2 for 57. Compton and Edrich, Miller and Lindwall, were great mates, duellists who relished the contest.

Bradman, Johnson and Miller help the stunned and bleeding Denis Compton from the field after he played a high ball up onto his forehead at Manchester in 1948. Compton later returned to make a brave century.

Cheers for Crapp's six off Johnson followed by three fours had barely subsided when the new ball came due. Within a few minutes, Crapp was lbw, Dollery hit over Johnston's swinging yorker, and Edrich snicked a rising flier from Lindwall. Edrich's 32 had taken 185 minutes but it had given Compton time to rest. Now he resumed at 5 for 119 to play a truly heroic innings of 145 not out, which, with dogged support from the England tail, lifted the score to 363.

Fielding only two paces from the bat, Barnes was careless in not spotting that Ian Johnson had returned to the bowling crease in place of the mechanically accurate Toshack. Johnson tried to tempt Dick Pollard, England's No. 10, but over-pitched and Pollard smashed the ball into Barnes' kidneys with sickening force. Four burly policemen carried Barnes away and he was rushed in an ambulance to hospital. No bones were broken but the bruising was extensive and deep. When Morris and Toshack visited Barnes that night in hospital, Barnes said: "You almost got me killed, Tosh, bowling that rubbish!" He was shocked to learn that Toshack had not delivered the ball responsible for his injury. "A man would have caught it, if he hadn't turned his back on it," he said as the truth got home.

Having omitted regular opener Bill Brown from their team, Australia used Ian Johnson as a stopgap opener in place of Barnes, but he and Bradman were both out with the score 13. Dogged batting by Morris, Hassett, Miller and Loxton, followed by some splendid driving by Tallon and Lindwall, avoided the follow-on but did not prevent England leading by 142 runs on the first innings. Barnes went out to bat after Australia slumped to 5 for 139 but sank to the ground in pain after half an hour and had to be helped off. He remained in hospital for ten days. The last six Australian wickets fell for 95 and for the first time since 1938 they appeared in danger of defeat.

Miller responded to the threat with 14 of the fastest overs of the tour. They failed to

Four burly Lancashire bobbies carry Sid Barnes from the field after he had been struck in the kidneys while fielding in the 1948 Test at Manchester.

produce a wicket. Without Barnes to worry about at short leg, Washbrook and Edrich put on 124 after Emmett had gone when the first ball he received produced a dazzling catch by Tallon off Lindwall. Edrich was run out for 53 by a brilliant Morris throw, Compton taken in the slips for a duck by Miller, but at 3 for 174 and 316 runs in front, England were in a strong position with two days left.

Lindwall set the trap to exploit Washbrook's eagerness to hook. Twice Washbrook lofted the ball straight into the hands of Hassett at deep square leg. The normally proficient Hassett dropped both catches. Hassett then delighted the crowd by borrowing a helmet from a policeman patrolling the boundary. With the helmet upended between his hands, he motioned to Lindwall he was ready for a third attempt.

With Washbrook on 85 not out, rain intervened. There was no play on the fourth day and none before lunch on the fifth day, when England declared. Australia were 1 for 92 when further rain brought a disappointing end to a match of sensations. The total attendance of 133,740 was higher than at Lord's a fortnight earlier. Every England–Australia Test at Manchester since 1905 had ended in stalemate because of rain.

Forced by injuries to replace Barnes and Tallon for the fourth Test at Leeds from 22 to 27 July, Australia brought in Harvey and Saggers for their first Tests in England. The confusion of the England selectors continued when they included Hutton, Keith Cranston and Laker in place of Dollery, Emmett and Young, and left Yardley without a recognised slow bowler to partner Laker.

This was one of the finest cricket matches ever played. There were records galore as the advantage swung from one side to the other until the final hour of the fifth day, deepening the disappointment of those locked out when the "House Full" signs went up each day.

Washbrook discarded his lofted hook shot to bat for 5 hours 20 minutes on the first day. After Hutton was out for 81 at 168, Washbrook (143) added 100 with Edrich, who next day went on to 111. The surprise in England's innings was Bedser's 79. Sent in as a nightwatchman, he helped Edrich put on 155 before he gave Johnson a return catch. With England 2 for 423, Australia staged a stunning recovery to have England out for 496.

Hassett and Morris lacked assurance as Australia's openers. Morris was out at 13 and early on the third morning Pollard had Hassett and Bradman out in three balls. At 3 for 68, Australia were in trouble when 19-year-old Harvey joined Miller. Harvey played and missed at successive deliveries before Miller called him to mid-pitch, put his arm around Harvey's shoulder, and told him to concentrate on middling

a few before he started playing his shots. Miller farmed the bowling cleverly and proceeded to provide a thrilling example, straight driving Laker with tremendous power. There have been few more exciting sights in cricket than Miller in his prime on the front foot and this day he was at his best. In just over 90 minutes they added 121 with majestic stroke-play. After boosting Harvey's confidence by twice hitting Laker into the crowd, Miller was out for 58 to his sole mistake in an innings as valuable as most hundreds.

He had set the tempo for Australia's response. Harvey and Loxton maintained it, adding 105 in 95 minutes. Harvey's 112, which included 17 fours, did not contain a rash shot until he reached 100, and made him the first Australian left-hander to get a century on his Test debut in England. At 93, Loxton, who had hit 5 sixes, tried to hit Yardley over the grandstand with an enormous hoick and was bowled. In the dressing-room, Bob Menzies, the once and future Australian Prime Minister, chided Loxton for missing a century. "We all make mistakes, sir," said Sam. "I'd guess you've made a few."

Despite the exhilarating fight back, Australia remained 141 runs behind with eight wickets down. Then Bill Johnston defended dourly while Lindwall dispatched half-volleys and pull shots with thrilling force at the other end. Toshack's knee had finally given up and when Johnston was out he stayed on the field as Toshack's runner. The ninth wicket put on 48, the tenth 55 through some hilarious running between wickets. The ever-smiling Johnston did his running from a position so far out the umpires made marks with their boot studs in line with the batting creases. Out among England's fieldsmen, Johnston's long legs snatched quick singles and converted twos into threes as Australia edged to within 38 runs of England's total. Finally Lindwall, who appeared certain of a century, edged Bedser to Crapp in the gully when he was 77.

Hutton and Washbrook opened England's

Sam Loxton congratulates Neil Harvey on his first century in England at Leeds in 1948. Loxton made 93, which included 5 sixes.

second innings with their second century partnership of the match, a world record. Both were out at 129. Edrich and Compton then put on 103 at better than a run a minute. A minor collapse followed but in the final session Evans and Laker punished the bowling and England ended the fourth day 400 runs ahead with two wickets left.

Yardley surprised experts by batting for five minutes on the fifth morning so that the heavy roller could be used before play began to help break up the pitch and increase the chances of it taking spin. Three runs came in the two overs England batted, and Australia were left to score 404 runs in 345 minutes to win the Test and clinch the series. Despite the size of the task, Bradman told his men to go for the runs, confident as ever that aggression would prevail.

No team in Test history had scored 400 runs to win in the fourth innings but Bradman's team was far from pessimistic about the challenge although the pitch took spin and the ball lifted and turned sharply. Yardley had Laker and stopgap left-arm spinner Compton on quickly, but Morris and Hassett moved smartly to 57 before Hassett was caught and bowled driving Compton. Bradman joined Morris, who had been badly missed at 32 when Evans should have stumped him. The applause that followed Bradman all the way to the crease came from normally partisan Yorkshire spectators appreciative of his prodigious scoring on the ground since 1930 (334, 304, 103, 16, and 33) but the difficulty of the task he faced was clear when he took guard in holes worn by the bowlers' following through.

Luck favoured Morris and Bradman as they continually pierced the field and at lunch Australia were 1 for 121. Here Yardley's lack of a second specialist spinner helped swing the match Australia's way. Compton had Bradman missed at 59 but tired badly. Morris recognised Compton as a danger because Bradman didn't always pick Compton's googly and launched a determined assault under which Compton wilted. Evans added to England's frustrations with mistakes behind the stumps, missing a difficult stumping of Bradman when he was 108. Laker dropped Morris when he was 126 and England did not break the stand until Australia reached 358.

Morris batted 4 hours 50 minutes for 182 and hit 33 fours, often lofting the ball over fieldsmen positioned close in for catches. Bradman scored freely with Miller as his partner and then Harvey, who made the winning hit with 15 minutes to spare. Bradman's 173 not out included 29 fours and not one three. It was his twenty-ninth and last Test century and his fourth in six innings at Leeds. His stand with Morris had yielded 301 and given Australia the Ashes and her sixth win over England in nine Tests since Hitler's war. When he was 145, he completed 5000 runs against

England, the only batsman ever to do so. Bradman maintained the required 70 runs an hour rate for the 217 minutes he was at the crease to give Australia a seven-wicket victory. No wonder the Test attendance and receipts records that had been broken at Trent Bridge and Lord's were again surpassed. The crowd aggregate was 158,000, receipts £34,000.

Despite hectic celebrations before play began next morning, with champagne generously provided by their opponents, the Australians ran up 456 in the first innings of their match against Derbyshire from 28 to 30 July at Derby. Brown shared century stands with Bradman and Miller on the way to his 140. McCool's length was astray in Derbyshire's first innings of 240, but when they followed on, 216 behind, his improved accuracy gave him 6 for 77 and Australia won by an innings and 34 runs. Barnes, in his first match since his third Test injury, did not field at short leg.

Ray Robinson was fascinated by the regular confrontations between Miller and Neville Cardus. Miller would whistle a few bars and challenge Cardus to identify the piece.

"That's a Rossini overture, Keith", Cardus would say.

"No, Neville, that's from Beethoven's Eroica."

"But Keith, you were whistling up with the violins. That piece comes down with the cellos." The only disagreement Lindwall, a jazz lover, and Miller, a classical buff, ever had was over which type of music should be played in rooms they shared.

With Toshack hobbling about on crutches, Bradman and Keith Johnson cabled the Board of Control for permission to have his knee operated on in London. The Board asked how much it would cost. The operation went ahead without an answer being sent.

At Manchester from 7 to 10 August Bradman generously played in Washbrook's benefit match but disappointed fans by scoring only 28 on a green pitch in the first innings. He made amends in his second knock by scoring 133 not out, his best score at Old Trafford. On the third morning he made over 100 of those runs before lunch, the eighth time in all that he achieved the feat, and the fourth time in England. To ensure a third-day gate, he did not enforce the follow-on and delayed his declaration until Lancashire had only 2 hours 45 minutes batting. Australia needed three wickets to win when the last over began but Roberts resisted six fearsome balls from Lindwall.

The fifth Test at The Oval from 14 to 18 August started an hour late because of rain but was virtually decided by the first lunch break when England were 4 for 29. Lindwall bowled with wonderful control and accuracy to take 6 for 20. Bill Johnston, by then a great crowd favourite, and Miller also exploited the humid atmosphere to have England out for 52, their lowest score this century and the second lowest in all Tests. Bradman's amazing memory recalled Compton hooking in the air in 1938 and this time he meticulously positioned Morris for the catch at square leg. Morris and Barnes put on 117 before Barnes was caught by Evans off 37-year-old Hollies. Barnes rushed from the field to film Bradman's innings.

One of the most emotional scenes in cricket followed as Bradman moved to the crease for what proved his last Test knock. He needed just four runs for an aggregate of 7000 runs in 52 Tests and a career average of 100. But he was unaware of this as the capacity crowd stood to clap him from the moment he came into view. The applause continued with every person in the crowd deeply moved as Yardley led the England team in three boisterous cheers. Yardley shook Bradman's hand and reluctantly the crowd sat down as Bradman took guard against Hollies, the son of a noted lob bowler, who, with the Ashes decided, said he would rather play for Warwickshire, still a county championship hope. The Warwickshire committee had persuaded Hollies to play in the Test.

Fast bowler Ray Lindwall acknowledges a great catch by wicket-keeper Don Tallon to dismiss Hutton. The catch gave Lindwall 6 for 20 for the innings of only 52. Hutton made 30 of them.

did well to dismiss Australia for 389 on the Monday. Morris made 196 before he ran himself out. Reg Simpson, fielding as a substitute for Watkins, beat Morris with a throw from third man as he needlessly tried for a sharp run. Morris hit 16 fours in an innings of the highest class during which his hooking and off-driving repeatedly eluded fieldsmen. Hutton made a subdued 64 in England's innings of 188. They never appeared likely to force Australia to bat again from the moment Lindwall jagged back a ball from the off to scatter Edrich's stumps. Lindwall hit the stumps seven times in a Test Australia won by an innings and 149 runs, his match bag of 9 for 70 confirming his niche among the great fast bowlers.

By winning the rubber 4–nil, with one drawn, the Australians earned generous applause for their spirited, entertaining cricket from thousands who gathered in front of the bomb-scarred pavilion. *The People* newspaper launched a Bradman Shilling Fund for cricket lovers to send Bradman home with their gratitude. No individual donations of more than one shilling were accepted but the money that poured in bought Bradman a small solid silver replica of the Warwick Vase, which came from Hadrian's villa in Rome and was installed at Warwick Castle. The surplus, at Bradman's request, went towards the installation of concrete wickets in English parks.

Bradman farewelled English cricket sprinting from the field after hitting three centuries in four matches, disappearing each time almost before umpires gave him out or crowds could engulf him. He made 65 against Kent at Canterbury, where Australia won by an innings and 186 runs between 21 and 23 August; 150 against the Gentlemen at Lord's where Australia's 5 for 610 got them home by an innings and 81 runs between 25 and 27 August, Bradman's 40th birthday; and 143 against South of England at Hastings, where Australia played a draw between 1 and 3 September. At Scarborough in another drawn match he made 153 against Leveson

Bradman survived the first ball but touched the second, a googly, onto his stumps just firmly enough to dislodge the off bail. His Test career had ended in anti-climax. He turned and walked from the field before a hushed and stunned crowd which only moments earlier had been so vociferous. Some spectators blamed tears aroused by the unbridled warmth of his reception, but Bradman refuted this and praised Hollies, who was good enough to take 100 wickets in a season 14 times, for producing a very good ball. In the dressing-room Barnes, still with pads on, told Bradman he had filmed the entire innings.

With Australia 2 for 153 and 101 runs ahead, the dampness in the pitch dried on the Sunday rest day and on a perfect batting surface England

Gower's XI from 8 to 10 September. He was in a happy, relaxed mood in these innings but still scored virtually at will, and all who saw him were struck by his enjoyment of it all. In his last match in Britain, against Scotland at Aberdeen on 17 and 18 September, he hit 123 not out.

With more people locked outside the ground than inside, his 150 in his final appearance at Lord's against the Gentlemen, was outshone by Hassett's 200, but it was Bradman who received all the cheers. H. D. G. ("Shrimp") Leveson Gower (whose selection of three bouncer bowlers, Farnes, Bowes and Nichols, for the 1938 festival match at Scarborough so angered Bradman) called to the crowd from the Lord's balcony for three cheers for Bradman's players. More than 6000 Londoners moved up to the Lord's pavilion to enjoy the last moments of a tour in which Australia had completely outplayed England.

The Australians won half their 34 matches with an innings to spare, two by ten wickets, one by nine wickets, two by eight wickets, and one by 409 runs. Eleven batsmen between them made 50 centuries. Hamence just missed joining them when run out on 99 against Somerset. Seven of the 17 players made 1000 runs on tour, Loxton finishing 27 short when he had his nose broken in the final match at Scarborough. The Australians failed to make 200 only twice and exceeded 350 in 24 innings. Australia's share of the profits, £75,000, more than doubled the Board of Control's previous best cheque from an English tour.

At Scarborough, in their last first-class matches before two light-hearted games in Scotland, footmen served the English

Don Bradman strolling in the grounds of Balmoral Castle with King George VI. Bradman was criticised for putting his hands in his pockets, but said that the King had told all the players to relax.

professionals tea on the field while the Australians and their amateur opponents took refreshments in a marquee. Bradman headed the first-class averages with 2428 runs at 89.92 and 11 centuries. Brown made eight centuries but played in only two Tests. Bill Johnston was the only bowler to take more than 100 wickets—and without ever losing his temper. To Bill O'Reilly Johnston's even temper was his great weakness. His 102 victims cost 16.42 each, but Lindwall finished ahead of Johnston's bowling average with 86 wickets at 15.68. Toshack appeared in only 10 of the 34 matches, but did what he was chosen to do in Tests. Only seven batsmen made centuries against the Australians.

Australian sportswriters were bemused by the idolatry of Bradman on a tour which saw dignitaries queuing to welcome him, hotels rolling out red carpets, and even small cities celebrating the team's arrival. To them Bradman was a prince among cricketers, a view King George VI shared when he invited the Australians to Balmoral Castle to relax and enjoy themselves. Bradman was criticised for strolling across the lawns at Balmoral next to the King with his hands in his pockets, criticism that looked cheap when Bradman was knighted for his services to cricket only three months later.

The son of Lord Gowrie, president of the MCC, who as Sir Alexander Hore-Ruthven was Governor of South Australia during the Bodyline series, said his father lobbied determinedly to overcome misgivings at Buckingham Palace about awarding knighthoods to sportsmen. Lionel Tennyson said the honour to Bradman belittled knighthoods, a laughable reaction from a man who inherited his own title, and a view not shared by the thousands who in letters and through the warmth of their applause paid tribute to the greatest cricketer they had seen. Bradman valued his privacy so much he questioned the Governor of South Australia about what was involved in accepting the knighthood.

The Horse Trader

Domestic cricket 1948-50; Australia tours South Africa and New Zealand 1949-50

Although all their expenses were paid, most of the 1948 team lost money by touring England despite the Australian Board of Control's £800 tour bonus. Some lost their jobs and had to look for work when they returned home. Others lost seniority in their job or missed out on promotion. One or two had to rely on relatives meeting mortgage payments while they were away. The days of big money contracts for endorsing bats and other items had not arrived, and probably only Barnes profited from their tour trading.

All bar Sidney George Barnes would have sacrificed his life's savings, however, for the privilege of joining such a tour, for they were aware they had been part of the most successful campaign ever undertaken by an Australian cricket team. Barnes, the only player concerned about financial rewards, was a throwback to Australia's greedy nineteenth-century tourists, but along with his team-mates he received a silver cigarette case and the £150 good behaviour money which the Board withheld from the tour bonus until they arrived home.

Incident-prone Sid Barnes snicks a ball between wicket-keeper Tallon and first slip in a New South Wales v. Queensland Shield match. The ball sailed harmlessly between the fieldsmen.

Throughout the seven-month tour Barnes indulged in an array of money-making ventures designed to compensate for the shortfall in the Board's payments. Arthur Morris, Barnes' roommate for most of the tour, finally asked Toshack to move in with Barnes because Morris could not get enough sleep. "I remember one occasion when tradesmen dropped a load of goods in our room," said Morris. "Half an hour later I was just dozing off when another group arrived to carry the goods away."

Barnes traded in rolls of suiting, autographed bats, cashmere sweaters, Harris tweed sports coats, Savile Row suits, all still scarce in Australia three years after the war ended, and his favourite tartan socks. He spent hours making a movie of the trip to show paying customers in Australia, but at Balmoral Castle and at Lord's was careful to ask Lord Gowrie for permission before filming the King with the Australian players. Each time Lord Gowrie said: "Go ahead. I'm sure His Majesty would like it." But at Lord's film rights to the ground had been sold and an official tried to stop Barnes, who ignored him. Barnes sustained his habit of making money by showing his film commercially when he returned home.

Barnes spent the early months of the war in the Armoured Division before it had any tanks. He was discharged to produce mosquito oil repellent, needed by servicemen in New Guinea, in a yard he operated with his brother and golfer Norman von Nida. Despite the demands of this protected occupation, he found time to sell Jan Vok liqueurs by the crate, give exhibition bouts with Olympic wrestler Eddie Scarf for paying customers, and trade in everything from hard-to-get luxury cars to ocean-going tugs. When US servicemen came to Sydney on leave he bought one of the motor cruisers they had used to ferry General Macarthur round the Pacific. He was at a dinner dance in the Blue Mountains when Eddie Scarf bet him the price of their meal he could not get a dance with a stunning redhead. Twelve months later Barnes married the girl,

Alison Edward, daughter of a Sydney University professor of theology. At the end of the war family commitments made him feel the eight-year break in Anglo–Australian Tests had cheated him of his destiny and robbed him of his big money-making years.

Barnes began his post-war cricket as New South Wales' captain and showed his acumen in the very first match, from 23 to 26 November 1945, by jumping the fence to prevent the Gabba groundsman cutting the grass which had slowed down many of his team's scoring shots on the previous day. Rival captain Bill Brown conceded that Barnes was right, as he invariably was when arguments arose over points of cricket law. Barnes made 200 in that game and followed with 115 against South Australia in Adelaide between 15 and 17 December, 146 against Victoria in Melbourne between 22 and 26 December, 154 against Queensland in Sydney from 31 December to 2 January, and 102 against the Australian Services at Sydney from 4 to 8 January. But even in such devastating form he lost the State captaincy within a few matches because of his sniping at administrators.

Barnes scoffed at the 30 shillings a day players received for Sheffield Shield games and the £1 a day paid Billy Brown's team in New Zealand. He said the Australian Board's blazer, with no coat-of-arms and only the initials "A.B.C." on it was the worst he had seen and soon traded it for an expensive Harris tweed jacket. New Zealand officials aroused the attention of Barnes and his team-mates when they told them they had offered to pay a tour bonus but the Australian Board had rejected the idea. Barnes had averaged 50 an innings in five New Zealand matches, and with 107 against Auckland at Eden Park between 1 and 5 March 1947, felt he deserved a bonus.

To make up for his lost years he reshaped his batting style, eliminating all the risky shots, refusing to get on to the front foot until he scored 40, and introducing a little side-step that brought him squarer behind the ball than other batsmen.

Much of the daring disappeared from his batting along with his brilliant pre-war hooking skill. Author Ray Robinson said Barnes became so obsessed with safety he was easily the hardest batsman in the world to get out between 1945 and 1948, even though at times Barnes walled himself up inside his run-making factory.

An argument with a policeman over where he could park his car at the Sydney Cricket Ground, followed by a row with a turnstile attendant in Melbourne, where he jumped over the gate after leaving his ticket in his hotel, made Barnes think he was out of favour with the Australian Board and might not get a place in the 1948 side to England. So he went off to England at the expense of a wine and spirit firm who wanted to introduce their goods there. This enabled him to play Lancashire League cricket in 1947 with Burnley and install his wife and family with her relatives in Scotland. He left his family in Scotland while he returned home to score enough runs to force his way into the 1948 side, but he had to give Bradman and the Board an assurance his wife would not travel with the team but would remain in Scotland. For Barnes, selection was a licence for unrestrained trading.

Before the *Strathaird* left Sydney on the voyage the 1948 team joined in Fremantle, Barnes loaded half a ton of food and trunk loads of cherry brandy to sell in England. One of the brandy bottles broke and he had to explain to a policeman summoned by the crew that it was brandy, not blood, leaking from his trunk.

Barnes was the only player in the 1948 side to provide his autograph with a rubber stamp instead of writing it. He paid a boy two bottles of ginger beer to stamp 5000 autographs. He was the only major member of the 1948 team omitted from a tobacco company's calendar on the tour. The company offered £5 a player and Barnes wanted £50. He was as tough physically as he was at bargaining with Yorkshire mill-owners over how many signed bats he should give them

for a roll of tweed that brought a high price in Australia. His black-haired body glowed with superb health whether he was bowling top-spinners, keeping wicket, fielding at short leg or throwing from the outfield with one hand while the other was protected from the cold inside his trouser pocket, all of which he did with effortless skill. When he showed the film of himself writhing on the turf after being hit by Pollard's rustic swing in the Manchester Test, he commented: "Would have killed an ordinary man," and one had to agree. Only the kidney injury suffered in that incident prevented his becoming one of *Wisden*'s five cricketers of the year, all of whom were his team-mates.

Barnes normally took umpires' decisions calmly but he was very angry about umpire Alec Skelding giving him out lbw in one 1948 match. Skelding could not miss hearing Barnes' comments about him being blind and before their next match together Skelding sent Barnes a note saying he would bring three pairs of glasses, one for lbws, one for run outs and one for catches, but added that he would be forced to leave his dog at the gate. Barnes got square when a tan and white terrier appeared on the field. He gathered it up and handed it to Skelding. "Here's your dog, Alec. Must have got away from the gate-keeper."

Barnes made only one appearance in the 1948–49 Australian season before selectors shocked cricket fans by excluding him from the Kippax–Oldfield testimonial match in Sydney from 25 February to 1 March. This misguided piece of selection brought the match more publicity than the fact that it was Bradman's final Sydney match. Kippax and Oldfield received £3015 each. Arthur Morris' XI made 581, 63 of them from Morris, 217 from Jack Moroney and 53 from Bradman. Hassett's XI scored 204 and 437 (Hassett 159) and Morris' side won by eight wickets.

Barnes' omission from that match, a final trial for Australia's 1949–50 South African tour, followed his announcement that he could not afford to go on the tour because the Australian Board of Control paid players only £450 out-of-pocket expenses, which he said was niggardly. The South African Cricket Board paid English players £600 each for their South African tour in 1948–49 and were prepared to pay at least as much to the Australians, then the world's top team, but the Australian Board settled for £450. Twelve weeks earlier Barnes' clowning in Bradman's testimonial match brought similar controversy. In a match studded with brilliant cricket played from 3 to 7 December, Bradman's XI tied with Hassett's XI, leaving Bradman richer by £9342 when donations from the State associations, £450 from the Melbourne Cricket Club, and £728 from Melbourne Cricket Club members were added to gate takings. Barnes enlivened proceedings by taking guard with a toy bat about eight inches long. The umpire was reluctant to give Barnes guard but did so on Barnes' insistence that it was legal.

He played a ball from Ian Johnson down the leg side for a single with the toy bat before handing it to the umpire and resuming with his normal bat. For the next hour he batted brilliantly to reach 89 before he was caught by Tallon off Ring. The match produced 1672 runs, including 100 in the last hour, 91 of which were scored by Tallon, who finished on 146 not out, bringing the scores level with two from the last ball of play. When Bradman explained that the extra run fieldsmen tried to get Tallon to take would have won the game, Tallon said: "Honest! Were the scores level, fair dinkum? A man should've taken the risk but I thought they were playing me for a sucker."

Lindwall, who always preferred batting to bowling, scored 104 in 84 minutes on the first day, including 160 in 84 minutes with Saggers. This took Hassett's XI to 406 and set the stage for Bradman to bat on the Saturday. At 97 Bradman hit the ball right into the hands of McCool in the outfield but McCool dropped the

The impish Sid Barnes, as he takes block with a toy bat during Bradman's Testimonial match in Melbourne.

catch. Bradman went on to 123, his 117th and last first-class century. Ken Meuleman also made a century to give Bradman's XI a first innings lead of 28. Hassett then joined the century-makers with 102 in his team's second innings of 430. A fast 104 by Morris plus Tallon's final hour splurge took Bradman's side to 402 and tied the game.

The 1948–49 Sheffield Shield matches, all well attended, provided two curious incidents. At Sydney in the match between Victoria and New South Wales from 28 January to 1 February, heavily ferruled stumps were used in place of the normal dome-topped type and the bails failed to move three times when the ball hit the stumps. Jim Burke survived when the Victorian left-arm bowler Harry Lambert hit his stumps, Bill Donaldson when leg-spinner Doug Ring hit his wicket, and Ron Saggers when he played on against Bill Johnston. Newspapers were still discussing these unprecedented events when South Australian Geff Noblet was out chasing a ball that had been called a wide. Facing Western Australia's slow left-arm bowler Tom O'Dwyer in the match at Adelaide Oval between 28 and 31 January, 1949, Noblet was given out "hit wicket", when he knocked over his stumps, swinging wildly with the bat.

Curiosity-seekers had another windfall when one-legged cricketer Athol Connors, playing for the New Lambton club in the Newcastle City and Suburban competition, gave cricket's law-makers a problem. Connors, who lost a leg as a child in a coalfields accident, fell foul of an umpire for the first time in the match with Awaba when he stopped a shot with his crutch. The umpire awarded four, taking the view that the crutch was an obstacle. Connors' club-mates argued that the crutch was Connors' second leg and he was entitled to stop a ball with it in the same way that players with wooden legs are not penalised by stopping balls with them.

New South Wales won the Shield for the twenty-third time by winning all their seven matches, four outright and three on the first innings, but this expected win was completely overshadowed by Bradman's decision to make yet another appearance for South Australia against Victoria in Adelaide from 4 to 8 March 1949. This was a generous move to boost attendance for a match set aside as the benefit of former South Australian and Test all-rounder Arthur Richardson. Bradman's presence had the desired effect although he twisted his ankle fielding in the first innings and retired from the match. This left Bradman with career figures which read:

Innings	Not Outs	Centuries	Runs	Average
338	43	117	28,067	95.14

This meant that Bradman scored a century at an average of slightly better than every third

time he batted. Over his entire career he maintained an average scoring rate of 42 runs an hour. According to the English county court judge, B. J. Wakley, who devoted an entire book to the statistics of Bradman's career, 74 of Bradman's 117 first-class centuries were chanceless and a further 20 were chanceless up to 100. Bradman gave his hand away 46 times.

In 1989, Bradman's 452 not out for New South Wales against Queensland in 1929–30 in Sydney was still the highest first-class innings on turf, although it has been surpassed on matting. He had six innings of more than 300 runs and 37 over 200. He was out bowled 78 times (or 26 per cent of his dismissals), was caught 174 times, was leg-before-wicket 27 times, stumped 11 times, hit wicket once, and run out four times. Wakley calculated that he hit 44 sixes, 7 fives, and 2586 fours, which gave him a total of 10,643 in boundaries. He made only 16 ducks, 6 first ball, 3 second ball, with 7 of them in his 52 Tests.

All the bowlers who dismissed him more than five times rank among cricket's greatest exponents of their craft. Grimmett dismissed him ten times, but Bradman scored 1709 runs in his 27 innings against Grimmett, averaging 62.29, including six centuries. Verity also had him out ten times, including eight Test dismissals, but Bradman scored 2895 runs in innings against him, averaging 74.23, with ten centuries. Alec Bedser dismissed him eight times, including six times in Tests and at one time English critics claimed Bedser had Bradman's measure, but Bradman played 19 innings against him, scored 1487 runs with six centuries and averaged 92.93. What gave sportswriters the mistaken impression that Bedser could get Bradman out when required was that six of the eight dismissals occurred in successive innings and included three in succession on the 1948 tour when Bradman was caught at short leg off in-swingers. Larwood had Bradman out seven times, but Bradman made 2009 runs against him with seven centuries, average 87.34. Tate also dismissed Bradman seven times, but Bradman got seven centuries against him, too, scoring 2024 runs at 88.00. O'Reilly dismissed Bradman six times, Bradman scoring four centuries and averaging 86.21 against him.

Bradman was one of the selectors—with E. A. Dwyer and J. Ryder—who picked the Australian team to tour South Africa in 1949–50. This time Toshack was not considered, though he had not retired. Barnes, Brown and the New South Wales batsman Bill Donaldson were not available. The team was: A. L. Hassett, R. N. Harvey, I. W. Johnson, W. A. Johnston, S. J. Loxton, R. R. Lindwall, J. Moroney, A. R. Morris, R. A. Saggers, A. K. Walker, K. A. Archer, D. Tallon, C. L. McCool and G. Noblet, with E. A. Dwyer as manager.

Hassett won the captaincy only when the last telegram arrived in the Australian Board's telegraphic vote, which author Ray Robinson said prevented a disgusting act of ingratitude. Morris' appointment as vice-captain showed there had been strong support for him within the Board despite his lack of leadership experience. Once again Hassett's notable achievements with the Services team had been devalued.

The omission of Miller from the team aroused howls of dismay, and was attributed in some newspapers to Bradman's anger over bouncers Miller bowled at him in the Kippax–Oldfield testimonial match. English critics had said after Australia's 1948 tour that given Miller England would have won because England had no bowler who could bounce Bradman. Miller was restored to the team after leading New South Wales to two Shield wins while the Australians were at sea. Bill Johnston misread an Afrikaans traffic sign and was injured in a car smash and Miller, who was considering tempting Lancashire League offers, was immediately flown over as a replacement. He played a major role in all five Tests. Both Bradman and Dwyer claimed they originally voted for Miller's inclusion, which caused Miller to comment: "Somebody's telling lies." Tallon withdrew from the team six weeks

Two contrasting Australian captains: Don Bradman, who led Australia from 1936 until 1948, left, and Lindsay Hassett, who carried on the job from 1949 to 1953. Hassett was a noted prankster, Bradman more reticent and subdued.

before it left. His replacement, South Australian Gil Langley, broke a finger after six matches, leaving Saggers to capably perform the Test job.

Hassett impressed from the start with his unobtrusive but commanding personality. There was a warmth and a sense of fun in him that Bradman had lacked, though he was just as ruthless in pressing home an advantage. He, too, had changed from the dashing batsman of pre-war cricket, but unlike Barnes the changes in his technique had come subconsciously without any anger over the lost years. His seniority now demanded a more subdued batting style that added solidity to Australian innings and he had fewer chances to attack at the age of 36 than he had had in his twenties, but he remained a batsman of consummate skill. Australian officials who had forgotten his splendid work with the Services side were agreeably surprised by the rare artfulness of his captaincy.

The newcomers to the Australian team included the New South Wales left-arm fast bowler Alan Walker, who after a fine tour of Britain and France with the 1947–48 Wallabies as a Rugby centre had made rapid advances in first-class cricket. Walker was a product of Saturday morning coaching classes at Manly Oval organised by two lovable, cricket-wise old characters, Les Gwynne and George Lowe. At Sydney Grammar School he concentrated on left-arm spin until the school's pace bowler broke down and he had to take over. Walker was an extremely wristy bowler who approached the crease with his left arm cocked behind his left ear, and there was always discussion about the fairness of his delivery, although he was never no-balled.

Another Great Public Schools graduate in the Australian side was the right-hand opening batsman Jack Moroney, a prolific scorer for Petersham–Marrickville in Sydney grade cricket whose weekly centuries cried out for recognition. He made his debut for New South Wales in 1945–46 and in the 1948–49 season made 122 against Queensland in Brisbane and 100 not out against Victoria to finish with an aggregate of 655 runs at 72.77 in Shield matches. He was a slow, sometimes clumsy fieldsman, but with a bat his powers of concentration developed at St. Joseph's College, Hunters Hill, were impressive.

Room-mates throughout the tour were the other newcomers Ken Archer and Geff Noblet. Archer was a Queensland opening batsman rated among the best fieldsmen produced in Australia, with a throwing arm that had attracted offers from American baseball clubs. He had not made a first-class century but in 1948–49 made 523 runs for Queensland at 43.58 and looked the only rival to Moroney for Barnes' Test place. Noblet could

either open the bowling with medium-pace deliveries that swung sharply or bowl off spinners that turned on the hardest pitches. His action started with a hop and ended with a pronounced flick of his hand as he went through the delivery stride. There were allegations that he threw but in eight years of first-class cricket umpires never called him for throwing.

The Australians played the first of their 21 first-class matches against Natal from 28 to 31 October at Durban. During the match an eye specialist whose rooms adjoined the team's hotel offered all the players a free examination. Neil Harvey, who had trouble reading figures on most scoreboards, took advantage of this offer and found his long sight was poor although he had no difficulty picking up even the fastest deliveries at close range. Years later when he started to wear glasses he found he enjoyed the games more because he knew what the scores were. The weakness did not prevent Harvey scoring four centuries in the Tests and heading the Australian Test averages with 660 runs at 132.00. In all first-class matches Harvey averaged 76.30.

Dismissed for 144 in their first innings, Natal escaped with a draw thanks to a second innings stand of 122 for the third wicket by Dudley Nourse and Ossie Dawson. Nourse made 104 not out, Dawson 61, which allowed Natal to deny the Australians a win although Morris had made 153 and Moroney 106 in Australia's second innings of 2 for 280 declared, after a first innings of 275.

Australia had their first tour win at Benoni between 5 and 7 November, defeating North-East Transvaal by ten wickets. This was entirely due to some superb batting by Hassett (100) and Harvey (100) in Australia's innings of 4 for 331 declared. Two splendid off-spin bowling displays brought Johnson 4 for 44 and 4 for 58 and had North-East Transvaal out for 135 and 214. McCool proved an ideal foil for Johnson, his leg spinners producing a match bag of 5 for 55.

Australia needed all of Johnson's bowling skill

Neil Harvey, who was so short-sighted he could not see scoreboards and follow the scoring. His short-sightedness did not prevent him scoring 23 Test centuries, but he enjoyed matches more at the end of his career when he wore glasses.

in the match with Transvaal at Johannesburg from 10 to 13 December, which they won by only 15 runs after a thrilling finish. On a pitch that took spin from the start, Athol Rowan's right-arm off spinners baffled all the Australians and gave Rowan a match analysis of 15 for 68. Australia made only 84 in the first innings, Athol Rowan giving Transvaal a 41-run lead by scoring 31 in a total of 9 declared for 125. Rowan followed his 9 for 19 in Australia's first innings with 6 for 49 in the second knock of 109, leaving Transvaal to score 69 to win. In a drama-charged atmosphere, Johnson flighted and spun the ball so well Transvaal collapsed for only 53. Although he was overshadowed by Rowan's figures, Johnson's 6 for 22 in the last innings swung the match, and gave him a further handsome match bag of 9 for 38.

Australia had five wins and three draws before the first Test at Johannesburg from 24 to 28 December, which began sensationally when openers Moroney and Morris were both out for ducks. This was Morris's first duck in 102 first-class innings and he confessed later that he was under the spell of a gorgeous Afrikaans girl at the time. Cuan McCarthy's first ball brushed his glove and was caught by Hugh Tayfield at first slip. "The umpire gave me not out, but in my befuddled state, I walked", said Morris. "I'd given myself out, letting down my team and my special fan, and made a fool of the umpire."

From 2 for 2, Australia rallied to score 413, Hassett contributing 112, Loxton 101, his first Test century, and the reliable Ian Johnson 66. Eric Rowan saved South Africa from disgrace by making 60 in their first innings of 137. Miller in his second appearance of the tour took 5 for 40. Johnston continued South Africa's embarrassment in the second innings, taking 6 for 44 in a total of 191, which gave Australia victory by an innings and 85 runs.

South Africa lost all hope of victory in the second Test at Cape Town from 31 December to 4 January after only a day's play, by which time Australia were 4 for 312. Harvey made 178, Moroney 87, Miller 58, Hassett 57 and Australia declared at 7 for 526. Only Eric Rowan (67) and Dudley Nourse (65) could handle McCool's leg breaks in South Africa's response of 278. McCool had 5 for 41. Lindwall took over as the destroyer when South Africa followed on, taking 5 for 32 in a total of 333, but it was McCool who had South Africa's top-scorer, Nourse, out for 114. This eight-wicket win took Australia to 2-nil in the series.

Australia's marvellous winning sequence continued in the third Test at Durban between 20 and 24 January in one of the cleverest pieces of captaincy in Australian cricket history. After a defiant innings of 143 by Eric Rowan, which took South Africa to 311, Australia were caught on a pitch that took spin after overnight rain,

Miller at full stretch following through. His original omission from the Australian team to tour South Africa in 1949–50 rates as one of the greatest of selection blunders. He later joined the team as a reinforcement when Bill Johnston was injured in a car accident.

and struggled to 75 in reply. Tayfield took 7 for 23 in the Australian innings when 18 wickets fell for 146 on the second day. South African captain Dudley Nourse had all the Sunday rest day to decide whether to enforce the follow-on and on Monday morning decided to bat again, probably thinking further rain was likely. Hassett asked his bowlers for an all-out assault on Nourse, and after he had made 27 Ian Johnson had him caught by McCool.

Hassett decided to keep the South Africans in while the pitch dried out without allowing them to score too many runs. After Lindwall had accounted for Eric Rowan, Ian Johnson and Bill Johnston dismissed South Africa's top order batsmen. At 6 for 90, the Australians cut off the boundaries, lengthened their approach runs and

made sure even singles took a long time. The South Africans scored only nine runs for the loss of their last four wickets and took far too long about it, but they still left Australia a difficult period to bat at the end of the day. Mann and Tayfield made the ball pop and turn sharply and at stumps Australia were 3 for 80, a superb effort considering every ball had to be carefully watched.

Australia wanted 256 to win with seven wickets left when the last day began. Harvey completely changed his natural, free-flowing style and adopted a dogged technique. The wicket improved with every over as Harvey batted for 5 hours 30 minutes without error. Helped first by Loxton and later by McCool, Harvey got Australia home by five wickets with 25 minutes to spare. Australia lost only two wickets on the last day and Harvey's 151 not out remains one of the most remarkable displays in all cricket of patience combined with skill. He put on 145 for the fifth wicket with Loxton and 106 unfinished with McCool.

Australia's memorable victory clinched the series and brought Nourse heated criticism for not enforcing the follow-on when he had Australia out for 75 in their first innings. But the guile of the Australians in prolonging South Africa's second innings without conceding them too many runs was a wet weather classic.

The fourth Test at Johannesburg from 10 to 14 February produced a further demonstration of Australia's batting strength when Morris and Moroney put on 214 for the first wicket. Morris, 111, hit a six and 9 fours, Moroney 13 fours in his 118. Miller followed with 84, Hassett 53, and Harvey 56 not out, in a total of 8 declared for 465. South Africa replied with 352, recovering from 6 for 148. With all chance of a result gone, Moroney made his second century of the match, 101 not out, and Harvey scored an even 100 and the game petered out with Australia on 2 for 259 in their second innings.

The power and depth of Australia's batting

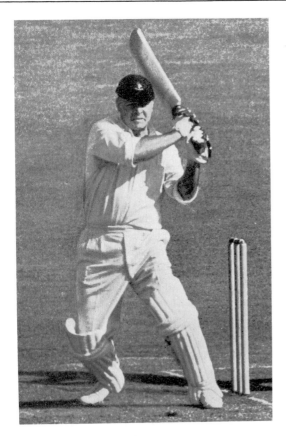

The great South African batsman Dudley Nourse, who found the Australian team of 1949–50 too well-balanced for his ill-balanced side.

took them to 7 for 549 declared in the first innings of the fifth Test from 3 to 6 March at Port Elizabeth. This remains Australia's highest score against South Africa. Morris made 157, Harvey 116 and Hassett 167, his best score of the tour, as South Africa missed several catches. All the Australian bowlers worried the Springboks who were twice out for under 200. Their scores of 158 and 132 gave Australia victory by an innings and 259 runs and a 4–nil margin in the series. Geff Noblet took 3 for 21 in his Test debut in South Africa's first innings.

Australia wound up the tour undefeated by playing a draw against Western Province from 10 to 13 March at Cape Town, where Morris scored 103 and McCool 100 not out, and by winning the match against a South Africa XI by an innings and 88 runs at Johannesburg, where Lindwall, Miller and Johnston had their opponents out for 49 and 90. Of the 21 first-class matches played, Australia won 14 and four were drawn.

Morris and Harvey both scored eight first-class centuries but Harvey had a higher aggregate and better average with 1526 runs at 76.30 compared to Morris's 1411 at 58.79. The Australians made 33 centuries in their 21 matches, and had only four centuries scored against them. Moroney's 1331 runs at 55.45 included seven centuries, Hassett's 889 runs at 68.38, four centuries. Of the bowlers, Ian Johnson took most wickets with 79 at 16.82 but Bill Johnston topped the averages with 56 wickets at 13.75. The fielding was brilliant throughout, with the throwing of Archer and Harvey awesome and the acrobatic catching of Miller the kind that swings matches.

The Australians' 4–nil win in the Test series matched the margin by their Australian predecessors in 1935–36, and left the South Africans without a win in 28 Tests. The Australians returned home in the *Athenic* on 31 March 1950, following operations on Noblet and Hassett at a South African nursing home to remove tonsils that worried them throughout the tour. Noblet lost when they tossed to see who would go into the operating theatre first. The Australians were beyond doubt the finest side in the world, but with seven of them over 30 years old their time on top would be short.

The team arrived home aware they faced keen competition for their Test places despite the continued exodus of talented new players to England. There was an eagerness to travel and seek experience among young players and there were changes in public attitudes the older men in charge of Australian cricket failed to recognise. Swimming, tennis, golf and surfing were challenging for support each summer, and the gambling sports were increasingly popular now

One of the rich personalities of Australian cricket, Big Bill Johnston. He was so loose jointed his limbs always looked likely to become uncoupled.

that wartime restrictions had gone.

Partition of India and creation of the new nation of Pakistan had been completed and the South Africa the Australians had just toured was moving quickly to become a republic. The Empire that had made Australian cricket a focus of national aspirations was breaking up but diehards Syd Smith, Jack Hutcheon, "Scouty" Macmillan, Aubrey Oxlade and Bill Jeanes, all of whom had been in cricket administration for half a century, held zealously to their old ideas.

An exception was Harold Heydon. He resigned as secretary of the New South Wales Cricket Association while the Australians were in South Africa, after 24 years in a job he took so seriously he sometimes slept on a camp bed in his office rather than go home. Syd Smith remained as president at what would have been an appropriate time to retire after 50 years in office when Heydon's successor Alan Barnes took

over. In Melbourne the Victorian Cricket Association secretary Harry Brereton was soon to hand over to Jack Ledward. The youthful Les Truman was rapidly enlarging cricket's support in Perth after a year as secretary of the Western Australian Cricket Association. Generally, though, the old-timers held on to positions they considered socially uplifting at a time when new ideas and younger, more imaginative administrators were needed.

With the Test players absent in South Africa, New South Wales retained the Sheffield Shield in 1949–50. Paddington all-rounder Ronnie James took over as captain after two matches, when Miller was called to South Africa, and handled the task commendably, heading his team's averages and taking some fine catches close in. Victoria beat New South Wales outright in Melbourne over Christmas 1949 after trailing by seven runs on the first innings. Two 19-year-old batsmen, Jimmy Burke and Richie Benaud, rescued New South Wales with a fifth wicket stand that produced 138 runs in 135 minutes. Burke continued stubbornly for six hours for 162 not out. Fast bowler Tom Brooks took 6 for 78 in Victoria's first innings. The New South Wales collapse for 123 in the second innings came from some baffling bowling by unorthodox spinner Jack Iverson, 34, an ex-Ninth Division sergeant, in his first season for Victoria.

Iverson's special ball was the delivery he let go with the middle finger of his bowling hand tucked in behind the ball. He had learned control of this delivery flicking table tennis balls at fellow servicemen in New Guinea and later found he could do it on a full length cricket pitch. He used the middle finger to propel the ball and by changing the position of his thumb he could bowl off breaks or leg breaks with little discernible change in his action. He graduated so quickly from the Brighton Club's thirds in sub-district cricket to Melbourne first grade he was innocent of the procedures of the game for a time and looked surprised when umpires asked if he wanted to take guard when he batted. He took 3 for 21 in New South Wales' second innings in this match and 46 wickets at an average of only 16.60 in the Shield season. Collingwood players who had seen Iverson take 7 for 6 against them in the 1948–49 premiership were not surprised.

The win gave Victoria a chance of winning the Shield but when they travelled north to Sydney they failed badly, losing what was virtually a Shield final by 196 runs to New South Wales between 27 and 30 January. Victoria dropped six catches on the first day, which enabled New South Wales to reach 312. Alan Davidson showed the rich promise of his left-arm swing bowling by taking 5 for 28 in Victoria's first innings of 123. Iverson bowled with commendable control in New South Wales' second innings of 142. But his 6 for 30 was not supported by Victoria's batsmen against excellent New South Wales bowling. Three weeks after his eighteenth birthday, Graeme Hole took six wickets in the match but made only 29 runs in his two innings. With their chance of taking the Shield gone, the Victorians gave a lethargic display against Queensland, who beat them by two wickets thanks to 58 not out in the final innings by Don Tallon.

Western Australia, continuing in the competition on a restricted basis in which they met other States only once, performed admirably. They defeated Queensland in Brisbane after centuries from Wally Driver (109) and Lester Charlesworth (122) between 11 to 15 November and South Australia in Perth from 27 to 31 January, then narrowly failed to score the 412 needed to beat Victoria between 25 and 29 November in Perth, where Ron Frankish made 104. The Perth postman Charlie Puckett, concentrating on medium-pace off breaks, took 32 wickets at 18.87 in the four matches. The other medium-pacers to stand out were Davidson and Len Johnson, who was yet again the mainstay

of Queensland's bowling.

The surprise of the season was the batting of bespectacled giant Bob McLean for South Australia. Chosen as a slow bowler, he was promoted from tailender to opener against Queensland in Adelaide from 24 to 28 December and scored 213. He took 5 hours 15 minutes to reach 100 on the first day and on the second day continued for a further 3 hours 13 minutes. He hit 22 fours. He went in first wicket down in Melbourne against Victoria between 30 December and 3 January and scored 135, finishing the season with 660 runs at an average of 50.76, a higher aggregate than any other batsman in the competition.

Towards the end of the 1949–50 summer Australia sent a team of 14 players to New Zealand for a 14-match tour under the captaincy of Bill Brown. They were undefeated and won ten matches, eight of them by an innings, and although their batting did not reach the standard of the Test side the bowling was exceptionally powerful. Only Brown, Tallon and the 28-year-old Victorian right-hander Roy Howard made centuries in the five first-class matches against steady, accurate bowling but against a low standard of batting the bowlers created havoc. This culminated in the second-class match against Wairarapa when Davidson took all ten wickets for 29 runs. The Australian team was: W. A. Brown, P. L. Ridings, J. W. Burke, A. K. Davidson, W. G. Driver, L. D. Duldig, R. Howard, J. B. Iverson, L. J. Johnson, K. D. Meuleman, C. W. Puckett, D. T. Ring, S. G. Sismey, D. Tallon. Victorian George Davies was manager, W. Watts scorer.

The major match of the tour against a full-strength New Zealand XI from 17 to 20 March, at Carisbrook, Dunedin, was drawn after a tense finish. With 15 minutes left, and only one second innings wicket to fall New Zealand needed just one run to avert an innings defeat. Wally Hadlee and G. F. Cresswell played out time.

Australia dismissed New Zealand for 231, largely because of Ring's 7 for 88. Australia replied with 299 following 116 by Tallon, who included 7 sixes and 8 fours in his score. Davidson sent Bert Sutcliffe back with his first ball and New Zealand lost 7 for 42. Hadlee hung on grimly, with New Zealand 9 for 76 at the close.

New Zealand newspapers said the tour was designed to assist their rising young cricketers, but the Australian bowlers were so destructive it probably did more to boost Aussie confidence for the England tour of Australia the following summer. Iverson had some amazing figures, including 6 for 8 and 5 for 14 in Australia's innings defeat of Southland. There was apprehension among the younger players when the team returned home to find compulsory military service was about to start.

Midway through 1950 the Marylebone Cricket Club announced from Lord's that it had invited 40-year-old Frederick Richard Brown, who had been missing from international cricket since he toured Australia with Jardine's team in 1932–33 to captain England in Australia. This completed one of cricket's most astonishing comebacks for Brown, who looked like a country publican with his ruddy face and jolly manner, had spent three years in prisoner-of-war camps after being captured at Tobruk. Not long after his team's tour began a Sydney barrow boy was heard shouting: "Beaut lettuces, beaut lettuces! Hearts as big as Freddie Brown's."

Iverson the Juggler

England tour Australia while a Commonwealth XI tours India 1950–51; Victoria wins the Sheffield Shield

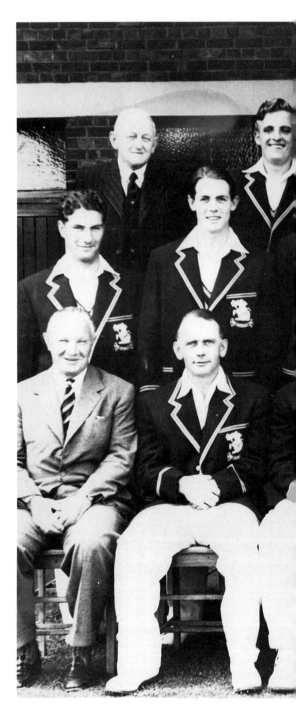

The Marylebone Cricket Club were having trouble finding a captain to bring the twenty-fifth England team to Australia in the southern summer of 1950–51 until the Gentlemen met the Players at Lord's six months before the tour started. Norman Yardley, whose sportsmanship had been so impressive against Australia in 1948, and George Mann, the captain of champion county Surrey, both declined the trip for business reasons. Yardley offered Brown captaincy of the Gentlemen's XI saying, "I've already captained the Gentlemen. It's time someone else had the honour. Give it to Freddie Brown—he hasn't done it before."

Selectors accepted Yardley's recommendation and Brown scored a pugnacious century, slamming 122 runs off the best bowlers in England

The 1950–51 England team to Australia: (L to R) (back) W. Ferguson (scorer), R. Berry, A. J. McIntyre, T. E. Bailey, W. G. A. Parkhouse, W. E. Hollies; (centre) J. G. Dewes, D. S. Sheppard, J. J. Warr, A. V. Bedser, D. B. Close, R. T. Simpson, D. V. P. Wright; (front) Brigadier M. A. Green (manager), C. Washbrook, D. C. S. Compton, F. R. Brown (captain), L. Hutton, T. G. Evans, J. A. Nash (manager).

in 120 minutes. He hit a six and 14 fours, hustling to 50 in 45 minutes, and 100 out of 109 scored while he was at the crease in 100 minutes. The innings proved that Brown's age did not hinder his run-getting. He was sitting in his bath with a large whisky and soda when Walter Robins came in and said: "I think the selectors want you to take the side to Australia." Next day Brown was officially appointed England's sixth captain since the Second World War.

Genial, companionable, 188 centimetres tall and weighing 89 kilograms, Brown had the ideal background for the job. He was born in 1910 in Peru, where he learned to play cricket in early family games. His father was a competent player, his brother played for his university and his sister toured Australia with the England side in 1948–49. Freddie's first school was St Piran's at Maidenhead in Berkshire, where South African Test star Major Aubrey Faulkner was a master. Faulkner, one of the first exponents of medium-paced googlies, had a talent for developing youngsters and Brown was one of his most promising students. He represented The Leys school at golf, squash and as a Rugby five-eighth. When he went up to Cambridge he won Blues for cricket and hockey in 1930 and 1931.

The Nawab of Pataudi made 238 not out for Oxford in the first innings of the match against Cambridge in 1931, but Brown was impressive with his right-arm leg breaks, finishing with 5 for 153 from 43.5 overs. He dismissed Pataudi for 4 in the second innings, in which his figures were 2 for 18. Although Oxford won by eight wickets, Brown's display earned him an invitation to play for the Gentlemen that season against the Players. He made his Test debut for England at The Oval shortly afterwards against New Zealand. He joined Surrey in 1931 and in 1932 he played in the only Test against India.

Brown made a tremendous impact on the hierarchy at Lord's by performing the double in his first full season of county cricket in 1932. Although he had forced his way into Test cricket

as a bowler, his all-round ability showed in his brilliant catching and in his century before lunch at The Oval in an innings of 212, in which he hit 7 sixes and 15 fours. Three of his sixes landed outside the ground.

These exploits earned him selection in Jardine's team to tour Australia in 1932–33, but he was scarcely required as England unleashed their Bodyline attack with Larwood and Voce. He formed a club known as the "Rabbits" on that tour with Maurice Tate and George Duckworth, with members asked to wear ties with a rabbit emblem.

Whenever he was in full practice Brown was one of England's most competent amateurs but he did not play Test cricket again until 1937 when he was picked to play in the second Test against New Zealand at Old Trafford. He had played in six Tests altogether when he joined the RASC as a lieutenant at the outbreak of war. After distinguished service in Crete, he played in services cricket matches involving Australians Lindsay Hassett and Cec Pepper in the Middle East. He was captured by Rommel's Afrika Korps at Tobruk and had lost 30 kilograms in weight when he was repatriated after three years in prison camps. He played in only one match for Surrey in the first three seasons after the war. In 1948, he played for a Yorkshire colliery team.

Brown became captain of Northamptonshire in 1949 and lifted them from last to sixth in two seasons. He was recalled to Test cricket, after an absence of 12 years, to captain England against New Zealand in 1949 in two of the four Tests, which were restricted to three days' play. All were drawn, which brought pleas from Brown to give New Zealanders a fair go by extending their Tests to four or five days.

England gave this gutsy antique the touring team he wanted. Having defied advancing years himself, Brown opted for youth, rejecting seasoned performers like Ikin, Edrich, Langridge, Gimblett, Watson, and Robertson for untried kids of limited resource with the bat and an adherence to mechanical orthodoxy with the ball. Worse still, they fielded like a village team and among half the side there was intense competition over who would prove the poorest catcher. Australians found Brown a companionable John Bull type who looked like a Toby jug with his pink cheeks, the inevitable pipe and knotted kerchief. His team: L. Hutton, C. Washbrook, R. T. Simpson, D. C. S. Compton, W. G. A. Parkhouse, J. G. Dewes, A. J. W. McIntyre, T. G. Evans, T. E. Bailey, A. V. Bedser, D. V. P. Wright, D. B. Close, W. E. Hollies, D. S. Sheppard, J. J. Warr and R. Berry, with Brigadier Michael Green and J. A. Nash as joint managers.

Compton was doubtful until shortly before the team sailed for Australia in the *Stratheden* on 14 September 1950 because of a knee injury, aggravated by playing soccer on the wing for Arsenal. Washbrook declined the original invitation but was allowed to fly out and join the team after they arrived. After the third Test Brown phoned Lord's for two bowlers to replace the injured Bailey and Wright. Bailey had fractured a thumb, Wright had torn a groin muscle. J. B. Statham and R. Tattersall were flown out to play in a country match on 24 January. Tattersall's absence from the original side had been widely condemned, but Bill Edrich was just as glaring an omission.

Seven of the 19 players England used on the tour were under 26. All-rounder Brian Close had become England's youngest-ever Test player when he appeared against New Zealand in 1949 at 18 years 149 days. Bob Berry had looked a very limited left-arm finger-spinner in his two Tests at home against the West Indies. Gilbert Parkhouse had yet to show he could score as heavily in Tests as he did for Glamorgan. John Warr had no Test experience and no fire in his belly. David Sheppard and John Dewes had not carried into big cricket the promise they had shown at Cambridge University, but in the English tradition their prestigious university backgrounds won them places.

After a one-day romp at Colombo, where Hutton damaged a finger and McIntyre made 104 against Ceylon, the Englishmen landed in Fremantle on 9 October. They began the serious part of their tour against Western Australia at the WACA ground from 20 to 24 October. At 3 for 45, Dewes (94) joined Compton (106) in a 163-run stand. A vigorous 108 not out from Close lifted England to 9 for 434 declared. Western Australia's 236 in reply included 59 by Carmody and 60 by Wally Langdon. Only Wright looked dangerous among England's bowlers, and his consistent length, googlies, and leg spin brought 7 for 60. The match petered out in a draw, with Western Australia on 4 for 207 and lacking the time to score the 319 wanted to win.

At Adelaide from 27 to 31 October, a sporting declaration by Phil Ridings left England 185 to win in 95 minutes and they got them with 15 minutes to spare. Hamence made 114 in South Australia's first innings of 350, Hutton 126 and Simpson 119 in England's 9 for 351. Ridings could have shut the game down but after a pugnacious 70 not out by Lance Duldig declared at 3 for 185 to set up the exciting finish. Washbrook and Simpson made 131 of the runs required in an hour, before Evans hit five of the last six balls for boundaries to clinch England's win.

Compton became the first professional to captain England in Australia since the days of Arthur Shrewsbury, in the 1880s, when he took over from the injured Brown for the match with Victoria in Melbourne from 3 to 8 November. He celebrated this honour with his second successive century, scoring 107 after early difficulties against Iverson. Victoria replied to England's 9 for 306 declared with 331, a total that looked unlikely when Victoria were 5 for 89. Roy Howard and Doug Ring swung the game against deteriorating England bowling by scoring 120 in 80 minutes. Howard made 139 to back up his promising form the previous summer in New Zealand, Ring 75. By arrangement, there was no play on 7 November, while the players went to the Melbourne Cup, and rain next day forced a draw.

On a perfect Sydney pitch New South Wales heroes Morris and Miller savaged the mediocre England attack in a drawn match from 10 to 14 November. Morris made 168 and Miller included 3 sixes and 15 fours in his 214. Facing a New South Wales total of 3 for 509 declared, England were saved by Hutton (112), Compton (92) and Washbrook (50 and 53 not out). Fred Johnston worried all the touring batsmen with his leg spinners and England were out for 339. New South Wales declared at 2 for 140 in the second innings, leaving England to score 311 to win at two runs a minute. England took up the challenge and scored 143 in 89 minutes before rain ended it.

There was so little character in England's cricket in the ten matches leading up to the first Test at the 'Gabba from 1 to 5 December nobody could have forecast the thrilling series that followed. Only Compton, whose batting average from seven first-class innings stood at 100.50, appeared a threat to Australia's outstanding side, but he turned out one of the failures of the rubber, a shadow of the heroic figure who had thwarted Australia so often in 1948. Australia introduced 185-centimetre, 100-kilogram Jack Iverson, who at 35 had never seen a Test match, and had never thought of playing cricket at all until 1946, when the efforts of some blind cricketers in a Melbourne park inspired him to have a go himself.

Batting first on a splendid 'Gabba pitch, Australia were bundled out for 228, with Bailey and Bedser improving dramatically on previous displays. From the fourth ball of the match Hutton caught Moroney at short leg for a duck before Australia had scored. But the catches that humbled Australia were both taken by Evans— one to dismiss Harvey for 74 after he leg glanced from the meat of the bat, the other the reward for a headlong dive down the pitch when Loxton edged a ball from Brown that bounded forward from Evans' gloves. Bedser seldom bowled a

Harvey plays a classical leg-glance on his way to another fine innings.

wayward ball and beat Hassett with one that swung sharply from the leg to hit the off stump to finish with 4 for 45.

Iverson's innocence of Australian team procedures was obvious when happy-go-lucky Bill Johnston snicked the ball through slips in his customary style and set sail for the bowler's end. When he arrived there Iverson had not moved so Bill took a quick look at the ball and decided there was time to make it to the striker's end before the deep third man fieldsman cut the shot off. When he got back to where he had started from, he watched the fieldsman accidentally kick the ball several metres round the edge of the boundary. So Bill set off again with those huge galumphing strides.

In mid-pitch, Johnston found Iverson alongside him, but before they crossed Iverson panicked and they both ended up again at the bowler's end. The third man fieldsman was still struggling to pick up the ball so Johnston decided to try to make the striker's end. Iverson decided at that moment to assuage his guilt and he, too, set out for the striker's end, the two of them running together. But as he neared the striker's end the sight of the ball hurtling towards the wicket-keeper frightened Iverson and he turned and scuttled back to the non-striker's end. The umpires decided that no runs had been scored. Johnston said later that his shots through the slips were always worth two, neglecting to say that he played it by trying to drive firmly through mid-off.

England opened with Simpson and Washbrook, reserving Hutton to strengthen the middle order. A successful light appeal ended an exciting first day, and an overnight storm washed out Saturday's play and prevented a start until half an hour before lunch on Monday. For 28 runs, Simpson and Washbrook batted skilfully against deliveries that reared head-high or kept very low, and it quickly became clear that England's major task was to avoid the follow-on. They did this by struggling to 7 for 68 with fieldsmen encircling the batsmen from a few yards away.

Brown's declaration, when he was still 150 runs behind, put Australia in on the treacherous pitch. Justification of this gamble came quickly when Moroney was out to the first ball he faced for the second time in the match. Moroney's first ball pair had reporters digging into record books trying to find a precedent while they watched the fun in the middle. Morris and Loxton followed Moroney, both without scoring. From 3 for 0, Australia progressed to 4 for 12, 5 for 19, 6 for 31 and 7 for 32 before Hassett declared and invited England to bat again.

"I remember that I went out on to the field and waved my arms after being dismissed for a hard-earned three," Hassett recalled later. "Freddie Brown looked at me nonplussed and wanted to know what was going on. I simply told him it was his move. England had to score 193 to win and to do so had to bat through the 70 minutes remaining that day without losing more than two or three wickets. With more rain unlikely, they stood a good chance of making the runs next day on a pitch that would have dried during the night, provided they had the bulk of their batting intact for the last day."

Lindwall shattered England's hopes by scattering Simpson's stumps with the first ball of the innings. Dewes and Washbrook departed half an hour later and in the last ten minutes the England batsmen panicked. Reserve wicket-keeper Arthur McIntyre, picked as a batsman, was run out attempting a foolish fourth run, and three wickets fell in two overs to batsmen chasing runs instead of preserving their wickets at all costs.

The pitch had lost most of its spite when England resumed on the last day, chasing 163 for a win with four wickets left, but Hassett pushed his fieldsmen in close to the bat to hide the truth from the batsmen. Evans helped Hutton put on 16 before he popped a catch to Loxton, fielding near the bat, off Johnston. Compton came in and played precisely the same shot off the next ball, expecting lift that was not there. Hutton continued his wonderful display of clever batting on a pitch that was rapidly drying out. From 8 for 46, he and Brown took the score to 77 before Brown misread Iverson and was caught by Loxton. Wright helped Hutton add 45 for the last wicket before Wright was out trying to hook the last ball before lunch. Hutton was unbeaten on 62 in a total of 122.

England were entitled to feel they had been unlucky in a match Australia won by 70 runs despite their dismal first-innings batting, but bold captaincy by Hassett and clever exploitation of the conditions by his bowlers and fieldsmen took full advantage of a classic Brisbane "sticky".

England's bowlers took heavy punishment in the drawn match with an Australian XI at Sydney from 15 to 19 December. Morris (100) and Ken Archer (81) shared an opening stand of 170. Run-making was so easy the normally good-tempered Morris found his dismissal by England's worst bowler and catcher hard to accept. "It's unbelievable!" said Morris, throwing down his bat as he unpadded. "Caught Warr, bowled Berry! People will think it's a misprint." At that stage Warr had not only dropped his catches but shown ineptitude in tackling them that usually aroused guffaws.

Miller and Lindwall hammered the bowling for a further 144 runs before Burke cast a pall over proceedings in scoring 128. He stirred from his lethargy twice to hit sixes but did not hit a four until he passed 100, causing a suffering spectator to yell: "Burke, I wish I was a pigeon and you were a statue." Compton worsened his knee injury scoring 115 when England were batting and had to withdraw from the approaching Test. Walker's 5 for 60 forced

Trevor Bailey dives a metre to his left to hold a low catch in the gully to dismiss Lindsay Hassett in the Melbourne Test in December, 1950.

England to follow on but time ran out when they had reached 3 for 173 in their second knock.

Ken Archer won the opening batsman's spot ahead of Jimmy Burke for the second Test from 22 to 27 December in Melbourne. The teams had both Christmas Day and Sunday off and repaid this recognition of their need for rest by providing one of the most thrilling of all Test matches. *Wisden* said that lack of nerve and experience in a crisis again cost England victory.

England enjoyed another wonderful first day on a pitch that had been covered for days against heavy rain in an atmosphere ideal for the swing of Bailey and Bedser. Bailey took 4 for 40, Bedser 4 for 37, and only some inaccurate bowling by Wright that allowed Hassett to make 52 enabled Australia to reach 194 right on stumps. England missed a marvellous chance to gain a winning position with some inept batting on the second day, despite vastly improved conditions. At 6 for 61 Brown played a pugnacious knock for 62 while Bailey defended, and when Evans added a brave 49 England scraped to a three-run lead.

Australia went ahead by taking 14 runs from Bailey's opening over in their second innings. In the two rest days that followed, a fierce sun beat down on the pitch, opening up cracks that

made batting difficult, increasing the tendency of the ball to keep low. Bailey and Bedser bowled splendidly but it was Wright, dropping on to a length immediately, who took the first wicket by trapping Morris lbw. Archer and Harvey stayed until lunch but at 99 Archer was caught in the gully. Harvey was run out when he backed up too far and Washbrook threw down the stumps at the bowler's end. Miller fell to Bailey's inswinger and Australia slumped to 4 for 126.

At this stage Brown came on, bowling medium-pace cutters instead of his customary leg spin, and gave England what appeared a winning advantage by taking four successive wickets, Hassett, Loxton, Lindwall and Tallon. His 4 for 26 saw Australia all out for 181, leaving England 179 to win. Lindwall bowled very fast for the last hour, but Iverson and Johnson took the wickets by dismissing Washbrook and Bailey before stumps. Lindwall bowled Simpson early on the fourth morning. With two days to play, the rest of the England batsmen decided to dig in. Only Hutton was ready to play strokes and, when he mis-hit Johnston to mid-wicket after 2 hours 40 minutes batting for 40 runs, the remaining batsmen brought about their own downfall through excessive caution. Bedser at No. 10 picked up runs so easily, his team-mates' lack of aggression was heart-breaking for their supporters. Wright held out while 16 runs were added for the last wicket but when Johnston had him lbw to end England's innings on 150, Australia's winning margin was 28 runs. For the first time since 1896 neither England nor Australia reached 200 in the four innings.

The great fast bowler Harold Larwood, who had migrated to Australia in 1950, was among a big gathering of ex-Test players who watched England's defeat. Larwood was taken to the Supreme Court Hotel to verify that a pair of boots hanging in the bar labelled "Harold Larwood's boots" were genuine. "They're mine all right—I can see where I dragged off the toecap", said Larwood.

Neither side could curb the high scoring in the return game between England and New South Wales in Sydney from 30 December to 3 January. Facing an England attack that lacked Bailey and Bedser, Morris hooked successive balls from Hollies into the crowd. His 105 should have set the stage for a huge score but after Miller went for 98 only de Courcy handled the threadbare attack with composure. Relieved to have New South Wales out for only 333, England made 8 for 553 in reply, Hutton contributing 150, Simpson 259, Parkhouse 92. Simpson batted five minutes short of nine hours in the highest score by an England batsman against New South Wales, but left little time to prevent a draw. Surprise of the match was the form of Warr, who collected match figures of 6 for 92 and troubled all batsmen.

Australia clinched the rubber by defeating England in the third Test at Sydney by an innings and 13 runs between 5 and 9 January. Restored to his opening spot, Hutton made 62 but Miller dismissed him and Compton in three deliveries and England had to be satisfied with a first day score of 5 for 211. Next morning the defiant Brown hit seven boundaries inside an hour before he was bowled swinging hard at Lindwall. England's problems multiplied when a rising ball fractured Bailey's thumb and Wright tore a leg muscle as he was run out. Miller's 4 for 37, and strong support from Lindwall, Johnston and Johnson had restricted England to 290 on a perfect batting wicket.

Weakened by their injuries, England held Australia's batsmen in check until Johnson joined Miller after tea on the second day. They added 106 before stumps and 150 altogether to take Australia to 426 and a lead of 136. With the pitch wearing, Hassett brought Iverson on for two long spells. He got Hutton, Washbrook and Simpson in the first, and Brown, Bedser and Warr in the second, to take 6 for 27 and finish England off. Only Compton, ball skills intact, played Iverson confidently but just when he appeared to have emerged from his series slump he hit

ABOVE: 'Keeper Tallon turns to see Ian Johnson
knock up a snick from Hutton in Sydney. Tallon dived
forward and completed the catch.

RIGHT: Miller executes a superb square cut. This was
some of the batting that thrilled crowds in the 1950–51
summer.

a simple half volley into Johnson's hands. The
freakish spin and high bounce secured by Iverson
had England's batsmen in shock, and ended Fleet
Street claims that accounts of his juggling were
an Australian confidence trick.

England won their two matches in Tasmania
in mid-January, defeating Tasmania in Hobart
by nine wickets, thanks to excellent bowling by
Warr (7 for 86) and Bedser (8 for 86). At
Launceston they beat a Combined XI for whom
Graeme Hole scored 105, by ten wickets, largely
through 142 from Compton and 112 by
Washbrook. Arthur Morris twice failed against
Bedser.

Splendid bowling by Noblet and McLean held
England to scores of 211 and 220 in the match

against South Australia from 27 to 31 January at Adelaide Oval, but that was enough to win by 152 runs. Noblet had 5 for 56 and 3 for 50, McLean 2 for 52 and 5 for 68. No South Australian reached 50 in innings of 126 and 153, Doug Wright finishing with match figures of 7 for 96.

Mel McInnes, a controversial umpire in 16 Tests, made his debut in international cricket in this match and felt compelled to no-ball Wright three balls in succession for over-stepping. He was wondering if Wright would ever speak to him again and re-examining the no-ball law in his mind when Wright approached and said: "Can't we be friends?"

Australia's winning sequence stretched to 25 Tests in the fourth Test at Adelaide from 2 to 8 February, after Jimmy Burke scored a century in his Test debut, aged 20 years 240 days. Morris recovered from his run of failures by scoring 206 in Australia's first innings of 371. England could manage only 272 in response, despite 156

A magnificent drive through the covers by Hutton off Iverson brings another boundary for a great batsman.

not out from Hutton who batted through a complete innings for the first time in Australia. He was the only English batsman to master Iverson. Consistent batting right down the list took Australia to 8 for 403 declared in the second innings. Harvey made 68, Miller 99, Burke 101 not out. Set 503 to win, England surrendered for 228 against a varied, persistently accurate attack that did not wilt in intense heat.

The return match between Victoria and England at Melbourne from 10 to 14 February never appeared likely to provide a result on an easy batting wicket. There were 20 fours and a five and some delightful leg-glides and cuts in Hassett's 232. Ring again demonstrated his batting skill in a stand of 166 with Hassett, scoring 74, and Victoria made 441. Compton opened for England in a bid to regain form, but he scratched about for 20. Hutton, 128, and Bailey, 125, took England to 414. England used eight bowlers in Victoria's second innings of 234 and were 136 at the end.

In the fifth Test at Melbourne from 23 to 28 February Morris and Hassett took Australia

to 1 for 111 before Freddie Brown took the ball. He had not wanted to bowl because of his injuries from the fourth day of the Adelaide Test but was compelled to do so when Bailey twisted an ankle. In 17 balls he dismissed Morris, Harvey and Miller without conceding a run. Hole came in for his Test debut, a tall, erect 20-year-old of impressive grace, with the immediate task of preventing a hat-trick after Harvey and Miller were out from successive balls.

When Australia seemed likely to recover through a Hassett century, Hutton scooped up a great one-handed slips catch wide to his right. Hassett had made 92. Bedser then took the new ball and with the swing in the air of the red cherry plus the added nip in the pitch bowled Hole and overwhelmed the tail. Chasing Australia's 217, England coasted to 3 for 204 because of splendid batting by Hutton and Reg Simpson. Lindwall and Miller then combined in the most devastating spell of fast bowling in the series to sweep aside all England's middle order. Simpson alone withstood the onslaught and when Tattersall joined him at 9 for 246, he produced a series of strokes as breathtaking in their execution as they were defiant.

In the next hour Simpson scored 64 runs while Tattersall made 10 and the last-wicket partnership took England to 320 and a lead of 103. Six of Simpson's fours came in his last 64. His 156 not out had taken 5 hours 40 minutes but had saved England when collapse threatened and given them the advantage.

With their long-standing supremacy under threat, the Australians lost two wickets for six runs against some superb Bedser bowling. Harvey and Hassett added 81 before Wright produced a match-winning spell. He restrained Harvey until he had him lbw and, after Brown had caught and bowled Miller for the second time in the match, came on at the start of the fifth morning and bowled Hassett with a perfectly pitched leg break. Hole carried on for 63 before he was bowled by Bailey. The last five Australian

The pitch for the final day's play in the fifth Test at Melbourne showed numerous cracks but it played truly. England broke their long run of failures against Australia with a win.

wickets put on only 55 runs.

Hutton calmly resisted an all-out Australian effort to deny England the 95 runs needed to win, batting with great certainty for 60 not out, giving England a deserved victory by eight wickets. The innings crowned a triumphant tour for Hutton, who scored 533 runs in the five Tests at an average of 88.83 and made five centuries on the trip. Bedser's ten wickets in the fifth Test

the series as the friendliest they had experienced between cricket's oldest rivals. Australia had badly missed Barnes, who accepted a lucrative offer to write on the series for newspapers, and neither Burke nor Ken Archer could remedy the weakness in Australia's batting that his absence exposed. Miller, however, had answered a concerted attack on his leg stump with several long, calm innings that lacked the big hitting spectators craved but were invaluable to his side. The mediocre standard of the Tests attracted smaller crowds than in past years and England's tour profit of £3842 sterling was only a tenth of that raised in 1946–47.

Hassett's disappointment over Australia's defeat was tempered by Victoria's triumph in the Sheffield Shield for the first time since 1946–47. He was always intensely loyal to his state and proud of its great record against touring sides and other states. At Brisbane, before the first Test against Freddie Brown's team, he angered Miller by removing Iverson from the bowling crease when Miller's turn came to bat at practice. When Australia fielded, Hassett ordered Miller from his special spot in the slips to silly point. The normally placid Morris erupted at Hassett's protection of Iverson. "It's a bloody disgrace that interstate considerations should be taken to such lengths when we are all representing Australia," Morris told Hassett.

Their irritation was strong enough for Miller and Morris to confer on the best way of dealing with Iverson's bowling. Neither could be certain of reading him correctly but he was such a cricket innocent they agreed to try and worry him into inaccuracy. Miller suggested taking guard wide of the stumps. The Shield competition that season of 1950–51 came down to a keen duel between Victoria and New South Wales. The Melbourne match was honoured by a superb hand of 179 from Hassett, whose gnome-like figure swayed inside and away from kicking deliveries from Miller, Lindwall and Walker as he glided them

gave him 30 wickets from the series at an average of only 16.06 but left him annoyed with the MCC's tour selectors: "If we had had some of the old hands instead of kids like Dewes, Sheppard, Close, Parkhouse and Berry, England would've walked it in", said Bedser. Miller was Australia's best batsman with 350 runs in the Tests at 43.75, but Hassett scored most runs with 366 at 40.66. Iverson topped the Australian bowling averages with 21 wickets at 15.23.

The fifth Test provided England with their first win against Australia since 1938 and sent them off for a four-match visit to New Zealand in high spirits. Both Hassett and Brown acclaimed

Rival captains Lindsay Hassett and Freddie Brown toast each other after the 1950–51 series, one of the friendliest tours in the long history of Australia v. England Tests.

away for fours. The power with which his drives hit the fence was eloquent testimony to the footwork and timing in his 168-centimetre, 63-kilogram frame.

The long-awaited contest between Iverson and the New South Wales batting heroes did not eventuate because Morris, Moroney, Miller and Burke were out cheaply and only a fighting 95 not out by Lindwall got New South Wales to within 28 runs of Victoria's 374. Miller's bat got caught in his pad and he fell to Loxton for a duck. At Sydney, however, Miller and Morris harassed Iverson right out of his rhythm and his 20 overs cost 108 runs. Morris made 182, Miller 83, and New South Wales won by 179 runs on the first innings. Miller gave the match additional spite by bowling a barrage of bouncers at his former South Melbourne clubmate, Ian Johnson.

Both Victoria and New South Wales were unbeaten by other states but Victoria took the Shield by beating South Australia outright in both Adelaide and Melbourne, whereas New South Wales only took first innings points in Adelaide. Harvey probably won the Shield for Victoria when he made 146 in the second innings against New South Wales in Sydney, denying New South Wales outright points.

Miller ended the season with an average of 121 despite two ducks. When New South Wales wanted 225 in 131 minutes to beat Queensland outright in Sydney, Miller (138 not out) and Morris (78 not out) scored the runs in an unbroken stand. In the other match against Queensland, in Brisbane, Miller made 201 not out in a knock that produced 5 sixes.

Bowlers who could not win a Test place dominated the Shield matches. McCool took 30 wickets for Queensland and another leg-break specialist, Fred Johnston, had 29 for New South Wales. Burly left-arm medium-pacer Alan Davidson could not win a regular berth in a New South Wales side boasting a surfeit of fast bowlers, after starting the season with 7 for 49 against Queensland. Western Australia, still restricted to only four Shield matches in the season (two home and two away), did well to finish third behind Victoria and New South Wales. Brilliant displays by Harry Price and Alan Edwards gave them a thrilling win over Queensland in Perth. Price took 5 for 68 and 5 for 49, removing McCool, Toovey and Chapman in one over when Queensland seemed set to win in the final innings. Edwards hit centuries in each innings, 103 and 105. Western Australia's right-arm medium-pacer Ron Frankish was no-balled for throwing by umpire Andy Barlow in the match with Victoria at Melbourne. He immediately slowed his pace and did not infringe again.

While the England–Australia Tests and the Sheffield Shield competition were under way in Australia, three talented Australian cricketers, Bruce Dooland, Ken Grieves and George Tribe, toured India with a Commonwealth XI captained by West Indian all-rounder Frank Worrell. The Commonwealth XI were unbeaten in 27 matches, with 13 won and 14 drawn. Dooland, renowned for resourceful leg spin, surprised by scoring three centuries on the tour, including two in the unofficial Tests. He made 830 runs at 39.52 and took 60 wickets at 24.66 on the tour. Grieves, a lanky, skilful ex-soccer goalie and champion slips fieldsman, hit two centuries in compiling 1193 runs at 42.60. Tribe took 76 wickets at 21.30 with his left-arm spinners, but all the bowling honours went to the frail little West Indian rubber ball, Sonny Ramadhin, who followed his shock success in England in 1950 by taking 79 wickets at 19.65. The Commonwealth XI won two of the five "Tests", and played a draw against Ceylon.

Ramadhin's triumph on hard, unhelpful pitches in India demonstrated that his bowling with Alf Valentine during the West Indies' 3–1 victory over England had been no fluke. Indeed the West Indies had defeated England in such convincing fashion, with a team of crowd-pleasing stroke-makers and clever bowlers, cricket buffs looked on the 1951–52 Australia–West Indies series as a virtual world championship, with the players who brought Calypso music to Lord's, "those two little friends of mine, Ramadhin and Valentine", at the centre of discussions.

The Australian Board of Control put the tour together quickly after the West Indies accepted their invitation to tour after the West Indian success in England. The lack of planning for the tour was to benefit Australia more than their opponents. The tour was insured against any losses caused by interruptions to the itinerary by the war in Korea, in which Australia was among the 15 United Nations countries supporting the United States.

The Board in Court

West Indies tour Australia 1951-52;
Barnes faces court;
South Africa in Australia 1952-53

The 1951–52 season saw Australian cricket in an earthy, argumentative mood. Hardly a day passed without newspapers offering lovers of the game unsophisticated jibes from administrators and players about each other's endeavours. It all culminated in a celebrated court case that brought Australian cricket's administration into disrepute. Even Lindsay Hassett, the master diplomat skilled in avoiding controversy, joined the fray in a Melbourne speech: "The West Indies have suffered from sheer stupidity in the organisation of their tour of Australia." The West Indies' itinerary gave them only one first-class match before the Tests which would decide who was the world's best team.

The West Indies side, the second from the Caribbean to visit Australia, included an array of match-winning cricketers, almost all of whom failed to show their best form. The famous Three Ws—1.9 metre, 95 kilogram Clyde Leopold

Australia needed 38 to win the fourth Test against the West Indies in 1951–52. To the delight of the Melbourne crowd, Johnston and Ring got them by a mixture of frantic running between wickets and lofted hitting. Here they make the winning run.

Walcott, the vigorous wicket-keeper-batsman, Frank Mortimore Maglinne Worrell, the gifted all-rounder, and Everton de Courcy Weekes, the quick-footed destroyer of bowlers—showed only glimpses of the form that had been so devastating in England in 1950. The pace bowlers found most pitches so unresponsive they failed to provide support for the spinners Ramadhin and Valentine, who were forced to bowl overlong spells. The West Indian team was: J. D. C. Goddard, 32, (captain), F. M. M. Worrell, 27, C. L. Walcott, 25, E. de C. Weekes, 26, R. E. Marshall, 21, J. B. Stollmeyer, 30, R. J. Christiani, 31, K. Rickards, 28, D. St. E. Atkinson, 25, S.

Ramadhin, 21, A. L. Valentine, 21, J. Trim, 36, P. E. Jones, 34, A. F. Rae, 29, G. E. Gomez, 32, S. C. Guillen, 27, W. Ferguson, 34, with Cyril Merry as manager.

The West Indies' tour began in Sydney on 20 October with a one-day match for the benefit of veteran scorer Bill Ferguson which raised £560. Worrell made 130 not out in an innings of 5 for 251 declared and Ramadhin then spun out a Combined XI for 120, taking 5 for 28. A one-day match at Canberra on 22 October between the Prime Minister's XI and the West Indies was curtailed by rain after Wilf Ferguson took 7 for 94 for the West Indies.

The limitation of the West Indies' attack without Ramadhin and Valentine was shown in the initial first-class match of the tour at the 'Gabba from 3 to 7 November. McCool swung the game Queensland's way by taking 6 for 83, bundling the West Indies out for 198. "Mick" Harvey (90), "Slasher" Mackay (79) and the Queensland captain Aub Carrigan (169) all scored

The 1951–52 West Indies team in Australia: (L to R) (back) S. Ramadhin, K. Rickards, D. St. E. Atkinson, S. C. Guillen, J. Trim, W. Ferguson; (centre) C. A. Merry (manager), A. F. Rae, A. L. Valentine, C. L. Walcott, P. E. Jones, R. E. Marshall, W. Ferguson (scorer); (front) R. J. Christiani, F. M. M. Worrell, G. E. Gomez, J. D. C. Goddard (captain), J. B. Stollmeyer, E. de C. Weekes.

The powerful Everton Weekes at the nets in Sydney.

freely in Queensland's innings of 455. Gomez, Marshall and Goddard restrained the batsmen but Ferguson conceded 156 runs in taking one wicket. The left-arm spinner "Mick" Raymer turned the ball awkwardly in West Indies' second innings of 282. Gomez, 97 not out, deserved a century but could find nobody to stay with him. Raymer had 6 for 69 and Queensland made the 29 runs needed to win without loss.

On this skimpy preparation the West Indies went in to the first Test from 9 to 14 November at the 'Gabba with their hopes resting heavily on Ramadhin and Valentine. Only Goddard handled the bouncers from Australia's fast bowlers with any confidence. Worrell, Weekes, Christiani and Marshall began well but showed concern when Miller, Lindwall and Johnston got

the ball up around their ears. Goddard's 45 was the closest any West Indian got to comfort in a total of 216.

With Australia chasing such a small score, Goddard threw Ramadhin and Valentine into the attack quickly. After rubbing the ball on the pitch to remove the shine, they bowled 129.7 of the 150.4 overs sent down by their team in the match. Initially honours went to bespectacled, tall, slim left-arm "magic fingers" Valentine. All the early batsmen were puzzled until Miller began using his exceptional reach to play forward. Missed catches, five of them in half an hour off Valentine, and sloppy ground fielding enabled Australia to take a first innings lead of 10 runs.

Classy batting in the second innings restored West Indian hopes, Weekes hitting out all round the wicket for 70, Gomez collecting a more subdued 55. Ring's 6 for 80, with his leg spinners, in a total of 245 encouraged Goddard to bring on Ramadhin and Valentine early when Australia began the chase for 236 to win. They sent down more than 80 overs between them in the innings. At 5 for 149 Australia appeared vulnerable but a sixth-wicket stand by Lindwall and Hole set up Australia's victory by three wickets. Gil Langley, an untidy-looking wicket-keeper from the Sturt club in Adelaide, whose hands were more disciplined than his shirt-tail, managed seven dismissals in his Test debut.

At Sydney from 16 to 20 November, the West Indies encountered further trouble. Leading by 105 runs on the first innings, New South Wales pressed home their advantage in an onslaught that enabled them to declare at 3 for 274. Moroney flogged the ragged bowling and, helped by fielding errors, finished on 166 not out. Left to score 380 runs in 405 minutes, the West Indies made 355 in a splendid attempt to get the runs but were thwarted by another fine spell from Miller. His 8 wickets for 63 runs in the match and some outstanding catching proved decisive, New South Wales winning by 24 runs.

The West Indies held a strong position against Victoria in Melbourne between 23 and 27 November when rain denied them the chance of their first win in a first-class match. West Indies took a first-innings lead of 35 runs thanks to a return to form by frail, 1.6 metre Ramadhin, who bowled in a cap, shirt-sleeves buttoned at the wrist, and troubled all batsmen. Stollmeyer was only five short of his century when the rain arrived, leaving the match drawn.

The second Test at Sydney from 30 November to 5 December turned on a dropped catch behind the stumps by Walcott off Hassett. After scoring 362 against an attack liberally sprinkled with bouncers, the West Indies had Australia 2 for 27 when Hassett escaped. Miller and Hassett then put on 235, at that time an Australian record for any wicket against the West Indies. Hassett (132) and Miller (129) subdued the bowling to such an extent that Lindwall (48) and Ring (65) gathered easy runs and lifted Australia to 517.

Despite Australia's lead of 155, the West Indies still had a chance to avert defeat, but a merciless barrage of bouncers from Miller and Lindwall removed all the top order batsmen. At one stage Lindwall bowled 15 bouncers in 40 balls at Weekes. Stollmeyer was hit on the head and Rae badly bruised as catches were picked up behind the wicket from unnecessary deflections. Weekes (56) hit some stinging cover drives and a dramatic hook but when he was out only a dogged 57 not out by Goddard held up Australia, which lost three wickets scoring the 136 needed to win.

Untidy fielding and bowling brought further defeats at Adelaide from 7 to 11 December against South Australia and at Perth from 14 to 18 December against Western Australia, who still required 48 runs to win when their ninth wicket fell in the fourth innings. Christiani fumbled away a run-out chance before Wally Edwards (73) made the necessary runs.

A curious administrative mix-up cost Phil Ridings a chance of playing in the third Test at Adelaide from 22 to 25 December. Hassett pulled a muscle at practice and selectors named Ridings to replace him, but Australian Board of Control members could not be contacted in time to approve and Hassett had to act as twelfth man. Morris took over the captaincy and no sooner had he won the toss and chosen to bat than the ball began to pop up or skid through low. Goddard gave medium-pacer Worrell the spearhead role and he took 6 for 38, dismissing Australia for 82, their lowest total against West Indies to that time.

The sodden pitch was ideal for Johnston, who took 6 for 62 and had West Indies out for 105, a lead of only 23 runs. Morris juggled the batting order to protect his senior batsmen but lost both stopgap opener Johnson and Noblet (who batted at No. 3), before the end of a day in which 22 wickets fell. Burke, chosen as opener at the expense of Archer, found himself batting at No. 9 in this innings.

The pitch dried out overnight and Ring went on to topscore with 67 before he was run out. Australia's total of 255—with Valentine's 6 for 102 a reward for excellent bowling—gave West Indies 233 to score to win. At 4 for 141, Australia still had a chance but faltered badly in the field. Gomez and Christiani were dropped, Gomez three times, and they were together when the target was reached. This was only Australia's second defeat in 29 Tests since the Second World War. A more varied attack, supported by flawless fielding and a desire to play strokes despite the conditions, had triumphed.

Australia clinched the series by winning the fourth Test in Melbourne from 31 December to 3 January when Johnston and Ring put on 38 runs in a last-wicket stand in the final innings. Earlier in the match, Worrell (108) and Hassett (102) had made centuries but this was all forgotten when the Australian last pair got together. Amid great excitement, Ring outsmarted the opposition by lofting the ball over fieldsmen positioned for catches, preventing the series going to a deciding fifth Test. When Hassett asked Johnston if he felt nervous knowing the series rested on him, Bill said: "Nervous? Don't be silly. How could I be nervous when I knew we had no hope?" Johnston defended while Ring swung lustily and they went off together with souvenir stumps, laughing unrestrainedly at a totally unlikely victory.

Hassett left the West Indies 297 to score in 210 minutes to win at Melbourne in the match against Victoria. The West Indians accepted the challenge and won by four wickets. Rae scored 171 in the West Indies' first innings of 327 in reply to Victoria's 387, and in the second innings bright centuries from Walcott (105) and Christiani (107 not out) enabled the West Indies to win with two minutes to spare.

The Australian part of the West Indies' tour ended with a 202-run defeat in the fifth Test at Sydney from 25 to 29 January. The West Indies appeared to have command when they dismissed

Johnston and Ring leave the field with souvenir stumps after their match-winning, last-wicket stand. Both came from the Richmond club in Melbourne.

Australia for 116, with the former schoolboy champions Colin McDonald and George Thoms going out to open for Australia. They put on 39 before Gomez bowled Thoms, the first of his seven wickets in the innings for 55 runs. This turned out the highest stand of a day in which 19 wickets fell. Miller and Lindwall completely upset the West Indians' composure with persistent bouncers and had them out for 78. Miller's 7.6 overs yielded 5 for 26.

McDonald and Thoms managed 55 runs at their second attempt but Hassett and McDonald had to wear the attack down before Miller and Hole hit out and lifted Australia's total to 377, a lead of 416. Rae, suffering from influenza, left his sick bed to open the West Indies' final innings with Stollmeyer and they resisted a fiery opening from Miller and Lindwall. Rae went to a spectacular catch by Harvey, leaving his team-mates to endure a furious, bouncer-laden attack from Miller and Lindwall. Stollmeyer (104) alone avoided miscueing against bouncers as seven wickets fell for 24 runs at the other end. Lindwall and Miller had seven wickets apiece in the match, which ended with Benaud taking his first Test wicket by bowling Valentine.

The West Indies' fielding never allowed them to match Australia, who excelled at sustaining pressure, and they had no bowlers fast enough to retaliate to Australia's bouncer barrage. Of the 22 games played, the West Indies won 9, lost 8, and drew 5, Australia repeating the 4–1 Test margin of the previous series against the West Indies in 1930–31.

Only Walcott scored 1000 runs on the tour, 1098 at 49.90 in first class matches, but Weekes was the polished stylist of the side. His 557 runs at 27.85 without a century were sad figures for a batsman of such class. Valentine and Ramadhin bowled their spinning fingers raw, Valentine taking most wickets, 61 at 23.83, with 24 at 28.79 in the Tests, Ramadhin 46 at 27.67.

The West Indies gave the clear impression that as gifted as they were they could be forced into mistakes in a crisis, a condition they were able to shake off on later tours of Australia. They went through the New Zealand part of their tour undefeated and won the Christchurch match so handsomely when Ramadhin took 9 for 125 that the high price they had paid in Australia for dropped catches was even more obvious.

Umpires twice intervened that summer in Sheffield Shield matches to prevent persistent use of short-pitched deliveries. Umpire H. McKinnon warned New South Wales bowlers in the Victoria–New South Wales match after Victorian batsmen showed resentment over the use of the bouncer. Umpire H. Elphinston warned Alan Walker for intimidatory bowling in the Sydney match between South Australia and New South Wales after Bruce Bowley was struck on the head when he ducked into a ball he believed shorter than it proved.

Following criticism of Australia's fast bowling tactics in the Tests, these incidents led to a discussion on the use of bouncers at a meeting of the New South Wales Cricket Association. Speakers in this debate said ill-feeling had been created among the players and warned of the risk of serious injuries if bouncers continued to be over-used. Nobody at the meeting wanted to prevent fast bowlers bowling occasional bouncers, but all delegates urged restriction on their frequent use.

At a later meeting the New South Wales Cricket Association decided to ask the Australian Board of Control to change the laws relating to intimidatory bowling to give the umpire at the bowler's end power to intervene. This move from the state that had most of Australia's fast bowlers petered out at Board level.

The mystery of the season was the continued omission of Barnes from the Test team. He played in all the Shield matches and captained New South Wales when Morris and Miller were absent, made two splendid centuries, and trained with all his old enthusiasm. At Melbourne in the match against Victoria from 7 to 11 December he made 107 in an opening stand of 210 with Morris (210) and at Sydney against Queensland from 29 December to 1 January he gave a brilliant display in scoring 128, including 213 for the first wicket with Burke. Barnes' 401 runs at 44.55 played an important part in New South Wales regaining the Shield. Australia tried six opening batsmen in the Tests without calling on him.

New South Wales officials apparently sensed Barnes was blacklisted from Australian teams when they asked him to bat in the middle of the order to give younger batsmen their chance in the top order. Ian Craig became the youngest player ever to appear in the Shield when he played for New South Wales against South Australia in Sydney from 16 to 19 February at 16 years and 8 months. Craig, who had earned his selection with a string of fine displays for the Mosman club in district cricket, showed exceptional poise

A splendid portrait of the legendary Australian left-hander Arthur Morris, who started his cricket career as a spin bowler.

way home from matches in which he was their scorer. de Courcy was from the Newcastle district, Davidson from the small village of Lisarow, a few miles from Gosford, New South Wales, where he had learned the game on a pitch he dug out for himself on the side of the hill.

The Australian Board of Control's treatment of Barnes attracted nationwide headlines in December 1951 when, for the first time in its history, the Board referred back to the selectors the team for a Test match because of objections to one player. Everybody knew the player was Barnes, who had just scored 107 against Victoria in Melbourne. Indeed the Board chairman, Aubrey Oxlade, apologised to Barnes in Stan McCabe's sports store in Sydney for the "scandalous thing that has occurred", although he would not confirm to newspapers that Barnes was the player to whom Board members objected in the side for the third Test with the West Indies.

For weeks rumour-mongers had a field day while newspapers paraded reasons for the Board's ban on Barnes. It was alleged he had lampooned the Board in his commentary for his movie on the 1948 tour; had disobeyed manager Keith Johnson's instructions not to film the royal family meeting the 1948 team; had been drunk on tour; had stolen from other players' pockets in the dressingroom. One well-known doctor even alleged Barnes had stolen a car on the 1948 tour, sold it, and forced the Board to reimburse the owner. None of these charges were ever substantiated.

Board members remained tight-lipped while Barnes' fellow Test players and celebrities like Dr H. V. Evatt defended him. Finally Barnes decided to seek help from leading barrister Jack Shand. In February 1952, Barnes issued a statement approved by Shand which he said was the only way to dispose of the rumours, but this failed to extract from the Board an explanation of the ban.

The autocrats appeared to have won the day

in scoring 91. His sedate innings was in marked contrast to the free hitting of other youngsters, Benaud, Flockton, de Courcy and Davidson, in the New South Wales side.

Benaud went to Parramatta Boys' High School and learned the game from his schoolteacher father Louis, a descendant of a French family who migrated to Australia in a sailing ship from La Rochelle. Lou Benaud, a leg-break bowler, was one of the few players ever to take all 20 wickets in a match. The younger Benaud showed his strength of character early by overcoming the effects of a fractured skull, sustained trying to hook Melbourne fast bowler Jack ("Dasher") Daniel, while playing for New South Wales *v.* Victoria in a second XI match in 1949. Flockton had overcome impoverished beginnings in his native Paddington, whose club members fed him on the and even those who had voted for Barnes' selection in the Test team were ready to let the affair fizzle out when a Mr Jacob L. Raith wrote a letter to the Sydney *Daily Mirror* in which he said: "It must be abundantly clear to all that the Board would not have excluded Mr Barnes from an Australian Eleven capriciously but only for a matter of a sufficiently serious nature. In declining to meet his request to publish reasons, the Board may be acting kindly towards him." Raith added that he wholeheartedly supported the Board and advised Barnes to let the matter drop. Barnes immediately sued Raith for libel.

Raith, who had never met Barnes, defended the case on the grounds of truth and public benefit, but after members of the Board of Control and the Australian selector Edmund Dwyer had been examined Raith's counsel, Mr J. Smyth, QC, admitted that seldom in the history of libel actions had such a plea failed so completely and utterly. Board secretary Bill Jeanes, chairman Aubrey Oxlade, and Board member Keith Johnson, manager of the 1948 team in England, all failed to provide justification for Barnes' exclusion from the Test team. Under cross-examination they presented a very poor picture of the administration of Australian cricket.

Jeanes initially tried to deny Judge Lloyd's District Court access to Board reports on the ground that they were confidential and personal papers, property of the Board. Judge Lloyd ordered that they be produced. When counsel examined the Board documents, Shand told Barnes: "You were put out of the Australian team for taking films during the 1948 tour of England."

Oxlade told the court that he, Frank Cush, and Sir Donald Bradman had voted to keep Barnes in the Test side, although there were small things in Barnes' past he regarded as childish. Things like jumping a stile in Melbourne, taking films in England, and bowing to the crowd after taking his cap off. He agreed that jumping a

turnstile was not a cardinal sin but said it was undignified.

Johnson came in for a particularly torrid time. He agreed that he voted against Barnes' inclusion in the Australian team (to play the West Indies) and would do so again. But he had not reprimanded Barnes once on the 1948 tour and agreed that the verbal report he gave the Board in addition to his written report on Barnes was wrong.

Smyth in his summing up to the jury said that neither his client, Raith, nor he had the slightest idea of what Barnes was charged with nor could they get this information from the Board. "You can see now why the Board was so reluctant to help us, why the Board was so anxious that none of its records should be available to the court for the purpose of assisting the defendant," said Smyth, who added:

Gentlemen, in assessing what damages you think are proper to be awarded to Barnes, all I ask is that there is not reflected against my client by your verdict the contempt that you and every decent citizen must feel for those members of the Board who, upon such silly, trivial grounds, excluded Barnes from the Australian Eleven. I exclude from all my remarks and condemnation, Mr Oxlade, Sir Donald Bradman, and Mr Cush.

We hear it said solemnly by this Board of so-called responsible citizens that six years ago Barnes jumped over a stile. Then he does the dreadful thing of taking off his cap and bowing to the crowd, to the great embarrassment of the Board. Did you ever hear such tommy rot? ... My client foolishly, as it turns out, believed that this Board was an impartial body of cricket administrators. You can well imagine what Mr Raith thinks of those gentlemen now.

The case ended with Barnes, who had never sought financial gain in launching the case, accepting Raith's admission that had he known the true facts he would never have written the letter of support for the Board. Raith paid Barnes' taxed costs. Barnes' counsel Jack Shand

Concerned New South Wales Cricket Association officials at the Sid Barnes court case in 1952: (L to R) Frank Cush, "Chappie" Dwyer, Keith Johnson, Alan Barnes and Aubrey Oxlade.

commended Raith for his courage in withdrawing when the facts were known and for clearing Barnes' name.

Barnes had won a handsome victory and immediately began a daily programme of exercises, roadwork and long workouts in the nets to get himself fit for the 1953 tour of England, rejecting numerous offers to write on that tour for newspapers. For weeks he went to Chatswood Oval for daily practice, knowing that he had to make some big scores to force his way into the Australian team for the 1952–53 matches against the visiting South Africans.

The season started badly when Morris was sacked as New South Wales captain, while he was away in Hong Kong, without any reason being given. Miller had strong claims to the job but even he could not feel happy about receiving the captaincy with Morris out of the country.

Barnes failed in the Brisbane and Sydney matches against Queensland in late October and early November but he produced a commanding knock of 152 in what was virtually a Test trial

against Victoria in Melbourne from 21 to 25 November. He made this century in vintage Barnes style after dropping to first wicket down to give Sid Carroll a shot at the Test opener's job. Against a Victorian attack in which all five bowlers used later won Test honours, Barnes square cut savagely, drove with authority, responding to a wonderful crowd reception when he went to the crease.

Barnes was not picked in Australia's team to play South Africa in the first Test and he said then that the Board had had its revenge over his win in the courts. At 36 he gave up the struggle. He went to the New South Wales selectors in Adelaide, Morris, Miller and Lindwall, and suggested he drop out in favour of Flockton or one of the up-and-coming New South Wales youngsters. The selectors should never have agreed if they had wanted New South Wales to field its best team. They erred even further when they entered into discussions with Barnes about the role of a perfect twelfth man.

Barnes went out on the field in a lounge suit, sporting a red carnation in the buttonhole, carrying an iced towel, a comb, and a mirror for the players to straighten their hair, a scent spray and a portable radio. The interlude was extended because Barnes had so much

Sid Barnes, as he undertakes his duties as twelfth man for New South Wales by producing iced towels, cigars, a portable radio and scent.

paraphernalia he did not take out enough drinks and an attendant had to be sent to get more. Far from being unaware of Barnes' intentions, the New South Wales team manager, Cyril Jago, helped him take the radio out.

By his defection, Barnes caused Ray Lindwall to go in as an opening batsman, and although he made 70 South Australia won by three wickets. Noblet turned the match with his 6 for 39 and 3 for 45, but Favell's 105 in the South Australian second innings proved invaluable.

Favell had played for Sydney's St George Club at 18 and switched to South Australia when he was 22. He, like Barnes, was a marvellous hooker and cutter, but did not have Barnes' problems with an obdurate, unforgiving Australian Board of Control. To the Board, Barnes' pranks as twelfth man in Adelaide were simply confirmation that he was unfit to represent Australia.

Barnes stopped practising and in his last first-class match watched 17-year-old Ian Craig score 213 not out for New South Wales against the touring South Africans between 1 and 5 January in Sydney. Barnes batted at No. 9 and made 18, after which he moved to the press box as a representative of the London *Daily Express* at a much higher salary than the Australian Board of Control's big-match fees. The press box was badly in need of new blood because the occupants had been almost unanimously astray in forecasts on the South Africans' performance. Some had even suggested the tour be cancelled as cricket in South Africa was in decline and their team could expect only crushing defeats in Australia.

The Australian Board of Control, disappointed by the financial failure of the West Indian tour the previous summer, informed South African administrators that it feared public response to the tour would be poor and cause heavy losses. The South African Board of Control accepted this news with a pledge that it would bear losses up to £10,000 on the tour, which it regarded as an educational venture for its young players.

The South Africans had made remarkable improvement since the 1949–50 series against Australia and at Trent Bridge in 1951 had defeated England by 71 runs in their first victory in 28 Tests. The captaincy of John Erskine Cheetham had transformed them from a demoralised outfit into a hard-working unit in which every player unselfishly devoted his energies to the task of winning. They were among the finest fielding teams ever to visit Australia, the outcome of hours spent on calisthenics suggested by Rugby boss, Dr Danie Craven. Their gathering and throwing, coupled with spectacular catching, often atoned for their lapses in batting or bowling. The team was: J. E. Cheetham, 32, R. A. McLean, 22, D. J. McGlew, 23, W. R. Endean, 28, H. J. Keith, 25, K. J. Funston, 27, G. A. S. Innes, 21, A. R. A. Murray, 30, J. H. B. Waite, 22, J. C. Watkins, 29, P. N. F. Mansell, 32, E. B. Norton, 33, H. J. Tayfield, 24, M. G. Melle, 22, E. R. H. Fuller, 21, with Ken Viljoen, 42, as manager. Eric Rowan was informed by letter in October 1951 that following incidents on the 1951 tour of England he would not be considered for the Australian tour. Clive van Ryneveld was unavailable and Cuan McCarthy, studying at Cambridge, was available but was not selected.

Australians were amazed when Cheetham and Viljoen devoted four hours a day to fielding practice in the fortnight before the South Africans' first match in Perth. They kept it up for the entire four months of the tour and, despite the absence of established stars like the Rowans, "Tufty" Mann and Dudley Nourse, ended with a better record in Tests than any team in Australia since Douglas Jardine's MCC side in 1932–33 and went home with a profit of £3000, having achieved the biggest upset in years.

They began with a draw against Western Australia in Perth from 24 to 28 October 1952. "Sticker" McGlew batted all the first day and eight hours in all to score 182 before he was run out. Only Percy Mansell batted with any freedom in South Africa's total of 9 for 427 declared. Western Australia were just as cautious and captain Wally Langdon was catcalled for taking five hours to reach 120. The match against South Australia in Adelaide from 31 October to 4 November was also drawn. South Africa escaped defeat through a second innings sixth-

The South African team in Australia in 1952–53: (L to R) (back) H. J. Tayfield, J. C. Watkins, A. R. A. Murray, M. G. Melle; (centre) W. Ferguson (scorer), K. J. Funston, H. J. Keith, E. B. Norton, G. A. S. Innes, E. R. Fuller; (front) J. H. B. Waite, P. N. F. Mansell, J. E. Cheetham (captain), K. G. Viljoen (manager), D. J. McGlew, W. R. Endean, R. A. McLean.

wicket stand of 112 by Cheetham and Headley Keith.

A hat-trick by Tayfield in Melbourne against Victoria was not enough to produce a result from 7 to 11 November. Ring, captaining Victoria in Hassett's absence, made 56 out of Victoria's first innings of 138. Spinners Iverson, Johnson and Ring then had South Africa out for 113. At 3 for 124 in their second innings, Victoria looked in a strong position but Tayfield took five wickets in 15 balls, including his hat-trick, to finish with 7 for 71 and have Victoria out for 159. Rain upset South Africa's bid for the 184 needed to win.

New South Wales defeated South Africa at Sydney from 14 to 18 November thanks to Lindwall, who took 5 for 30 after Miller won the toss and sent the visitors in. A fine double by Endean (77 and 95) failed to save South Africa in a match in which Tayfield captured a further nine wickets. He was established as a master of off spin by the time South Africa played another draw from 28 November to 2 December against Queensland at the 'Gabba. His habit of stubbing his toe before every delivery and kissing his cap before each over captivated spectators.

The South Africans fought grimly for ascendancy for the first four days of the first Test at Brisbane between 5 and 10 December. Watkins and Melle launched a spirited fast-medium attack on the first day that was backed by inspired fielding. Only a third-wicket stand between Harvey and Hassett worth 155 runs broke South Africa's control of the game, but when Hassett went for 55, four wickets fell for 35 runs against the new ball. Harvey had to bat at his best to make 109. Melle took 6 for 71, Watkins 4 for 41 in Australia's innings of 280. The South Africans dealt with Australia's pace bowlers comfortably enough but few played Ring's leg breaks confidently and his 6 for 72 had South Africa out for 221.

Harvey, McDonald and Lindwall gave chances that were missed in Australia's second

innings of 277. Miller was unfit to bowl when South Africa set out for the 337 runs needed to win, and by the end of the fourth day South Africa wanted 187 with eight wickets in hand. South Africa's batting broke down against a wonderful spell by Lindwall on the last day, the last five wickets falling for 31 runs. Lindwall took 5 for 60.

South Africa had their first win over Australia for 42 years in the second Test at Melbourne from 24 to 30 December, turning in a performance that had critics comparing them with the great fielding sides. To achieve it they had to overcome a miserable start. At 3 for 27 the innings appeared in tatters and at 7 for 126 Australia had a clear advantage, but the total reached 227 through a defiant 51 from Murray.

The fielding when Australia batted gave spectacular support to the off spin of Tayfield and the leg breaks of Mansell. Typical of the South African display was Tayfield's catch to dismiss Morris when a powerful drive bounced off Cheetham, fielding at silly mid-off. Tayfield spun round, chased after the ball and scooped it up with a full-length dive. Cheetham and McGlew held breathtaking catches and Endean dragged down a fierce drive by Miller when the ball was within inches of passing over the iron fence for six, the best of his 29 tour catches.

"Endless" Endean then defied spirited Australian bowling for seven and a half hours without offering a chance. His 162 not out helped give South Africa a total of 388 and a lead of 372 although his batting was stodgy and his runs came mainly from deflections. Miller completed the double of 1000 runs and 100 wickets in Tests when he had Waite caught by Hole. Further high class bowling from Tayfield so restricted Australia's scoring he had one period on nine overs without conceding a run during which he dismissed Miller, Langley and Hole. His 13 wickets in the match for 165 runs came from his unflagging accuracy and tigerish fielding.

Ian Craig became the youngest Australian at

17 to score a double century against a touring team when he made 213 not out for New South Wales against the South Africans in Sydney from 1 to 5 January 1953. Craig's timing and stylish stroke play even overshadowed Miller's batting in their seventh-wicket stand of 159. After dismissing South Africa for 196, New South Wales declared at 7 for 416. Against tight, varied bowling South Africa salvaged a draw.

The technical efficiency of the Australians reasserted itself in the third Test at Sydney from 9 to 13 January. Lindwall again swept aside South African resistance in the first innings with his wonderful control of pace and late swing. From 0 for 53, South Africa were all out for 173. With a lineup so strong that no place could be found for Craig, Australia went to a 270-run lead when Harvey made 190. His 168-run fourth wicket stand with Miller thrilled spectators and was a record for Australia against South Africa. South Africa lost all chance of forcing Australia to bat again when Lindwall dismissed both openers in his first three overs. Tayfield could not bat because of a fractured thumb and Australia won by an innings and 38 runs.

South Africa retained their hopes of levelling the series by forcing a draw in the fourth Test at Adelaide from 24 to 29 January. McDonald (154), Hassett (163), Harvey (84) and Hole (59) took Australia to a first innings total of 530. The second-wicket partnership of 275 by McDonald and Hassett was the highest for any wicket by Australia against South Africa. South Africa's chances of saving the match increased when Miller and Lindwall sustained injuries, and with a score of 387 they avoided the follow-on by six runs. Harvey scored his seventh century in nine Tests against South Africa, 116 out of a total of 3 for 233 declared in Australia's second innings. Left to score 377 in 235 minutes, South Africa batted steadily to end on 6 for 177.

Headley Keith played his way into the fifth Test with innings of 111 and 113 not out in the drawn match with Victoria from 31 January to 4 February, in Melbourne. South Africa made 401 and 228, Victoria 260 and 0 for 21, Mansell taking 6 for 53 in Victoria's first innings.

Although the series was undecided, the Australian selectors took the surprise step of resting both Lindwall and Miller from the fifth Test between 6 and 12 February in Melbourne, bringing in the large Queensland Rugby star and right-arm medium-pace bowler Ron Archer with Ian Craig, at 17 years 239 days the youngest Australian to appear in Test cricket. The selectors were mindful of the big work load Lindwall and Miller would soon have to face in England.

Australia appeared to have avoided any chance of defeat by scoring 520 in their first innings, Morris contributing 99, Harvey 205, his first double century in Tests. He batted for just short of five hours, but was often outshone by Craig in his fourth wicket stand of 148. Craig made 53. Waite (64), Watkins (92), McLean (81), Cheetham (66) and Mansell (52) all batted bravely in South Africa's 435 in reply. Craig again showed impressive temperament as wickets fell at the other end in Australia's second innings. His 47 gave him an even 100 runs for the match, Fuller's 5 for 66 restricting Australia to 209. This left South Africa to score 297 to win, which they achieved with steady, efficient batting. Near the end McLean produced some lovely drives, cuts and pulls and put on 76 of an unbroken fifth wicket stand with Keith. It was only the third time in cricket history that a team had won despite having 500 runs scored against them.

South Africa had squared the series at two Tests apiece against all the odds, considering the difficulty they had against the States. The Australians scored six centuries to one in the Tests, had a more experienced lineup, and the most dangerous bowlers, Lindwall and Miller. But by sheer strength of character the South Africans had put together their greatest cricket triumph. They had also shown that Australian supremacy in world cricket, dating back to 1938, would be at risk in England in 1953.

Australia
in Decline

Australia loses the Ashes 1953

The 1953 Australian team, the twenty-first to tour England, was chosen amid disquiet over the treatment of New South Wales's Edmund Alfred ("Chappie") Dwyer, who was unceremoniously sacked from the Test selection panel he had served since 1931. Dwyer was then 59, seasoned in the wiles of cricketers, well-liked, a man of probity who had been a team-mate of Trumper and Noble and as a selector was the first to spot Stan McCabe's talent. His dismissal left New South Wales, the strongest State, without a representative on the national selection committee, and was widely attributed to his support for Sid Barnes the previous year.

Bradman was also missing from the selection panel because of his commitment to cover the tour for the London *Daily Mail*. Billy Brown, Phil Ridings and Jack Ryder picked the team knowing that the 38-year-old spinners Jack Iverson and Colin McCool were unavailable. Unhappily, the Board named as manager Victorian George Davies, whose lack of discipline virtually left Hassett to run the tour.

Old traditions took a long time to die in English cricket. Here the professionals are served tea on the pitch in the Scarborough festival match at the end of the 1953 tour. The Australians and their amateur opponents had theirs in the marquee.

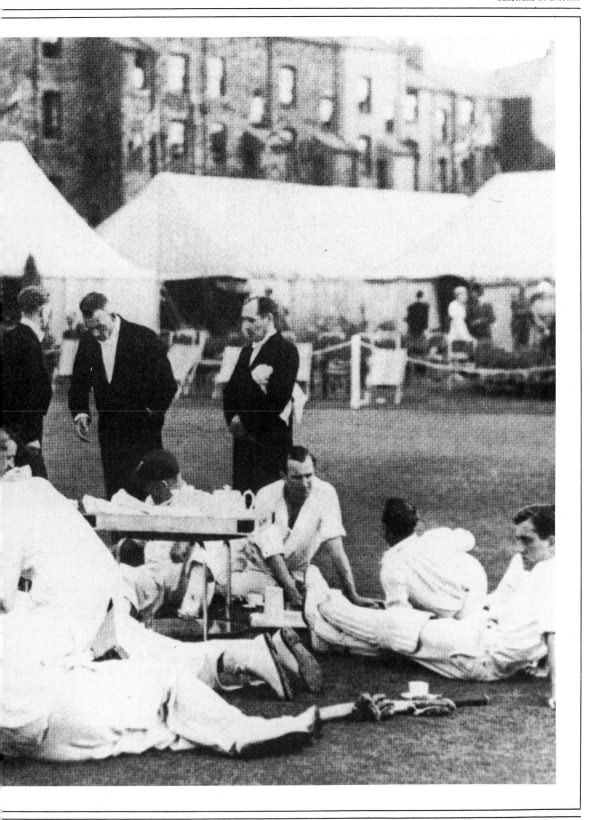

Iverson's withdrawal ended a brief, much-discussed career in big cricket that covered 34 matches, 18 of them for Victoria, and brought him 157 wickets at 19.22. He introduced a new bowling technique to cricket applicable only to bowlers with long fingers, and in four seasons took five wickets in an innings nine times and ten wickets in a match once. Young cricketers with small hands tore finger ligaments trying to emulate his methods. His supporters rightly claimed he won Test matches for Australia, though Miller and Morris believed he lost interest after they hammered him in Sydney. McCool

Only a few weeks after completing the thrilling series against South Africa, Australia sent the following team to England in 1953: (L to R) (back) R. R. Lindwall, A. K. Davidson, D. T. Ring, J. C. Hill, G. R. Langley; (centre) G. B. Hole, R. G. Archer, W. A. Johnston, K. R. Miller, R. Benaud, D. Tallon; (front) I. D. Craig, J. H. de Courcy, A. L. Hassett (captain), G. Davies (manager), A. R. Morris, R. N. Harvey, C. C. McDonald.

went to East Lancashire with a good record in his 14 Tests and the justifiable conviction that selectors were unfriendly to leg spinners. In 1956 he began a successful career with Somerset.

The Board initially decided to take 16 players but when it was realised the team would be away for eight months added Ian Craig to the party as seventeenth man. Barnes, whose inclusion would have vastly improved the side, followed the team's 39 matches as a journalist and became its most savage critic. Barnes and Bradman together in the press box aroused some friendly banter but it did not sidetrack Bradman from producing assessments of each day's play that remain models of their kind.

The team was A. L. Hassett, 39, A. R. Morris, 31, R. G. Archer, 19, R. Benaud, 22, I. D. Craig, 17, A. K. Davidson, 23, J. H. de Courcy, 26, R. N. Harvey, 24, J. C. Hill, 29, G. B. Hole, 22, W. A. Johnston, 31, G. R. Langley, 33, R. R. Lindwall, 31, C. C. McDonald 24, K. R. Miller, 33, D. T. Ring, 34, D. Tallon, 37.

The team included a group of seasoned Test players but clearly depended on some of the youngsters attaining Test class. The major surprise was the inclusion of Victorian spinner of brisk pace, Jack Hill, whose leg break seldom turned but whose top spinner bounced awkwardly high. He had been a valuable member of the Victorian team since his debut in 1945–46. In 1952–53 his 21 wickets at 18.33 had included figures of 7 for 51 against South Australia in Melbourne, a performance that encouraged the view he would do well on English pitches. He was an outstanding Australian Rules footballer whose career was cut short when he twice fractured his skull playing for the St Kilda club, which he captained.

The Australians arrived in England at a time when pitches at home were protected against rain and they were unsettled when the ball turned or lifted on wet wickets. The senior players were among the notable failures on rain-soaked pitches and their lack of sound technique affected the younger players. But on dry pitches the team played attractive, enjoyable cricket and only two of the side did not get a chance in Tests.

A fortnight after their arrival in England the team took part in a 13-a-side match for the Duke of Edinburgh's playing fields charity on 26 April at East Molesey, where the object was to try and hit the ball right out of the ground and across a stream onto Tagg's Island. Miller came the closest with one of his blows splashing water up onto the island. Bill Johnston strained his right knee, an injury that worried him throughout the tour.

The serious part of the tour began at Worcester from 29 April to 1 May with the match against Worcestershire. Right-hand batsman Don Kenyon became the first player for the county to make a century against Australia when he scored 122 in Worcestershire's innings of 7 for 333 declared. Australia looked to be in trouble at 3 for 28 but Miller upheld the Australian tradition of scoring double centuries at Worcester with an innings of 220 not out. Apart from hitting a six and 18 fours and occupying the crease for 6 hours 15 minutes Miller gave invaluable advice on English conditions to Hole (112), Benaud (44) and Archer (108) and Australia declared at 7 for 542. Only ten wickets fell in the three days.

Australia had their first win in the second match, from 2 to 4 May against Leicestershire. Harvey led the way with 202 not out in Australia's 8 for 443 declared. He hit 27 fours but was outpaced by Davidson (63) in their stand of 117 in an hour. Australia then dismissed Leicestershire twice in a day for 109 and 180 to win by an innings and 154 runs. Ring took nine wickets in the match for 123 runs.

At Bradford, against the only county that had troubled them in 1948, Australia overwhelmed Yorkshire by an innings and 94 runs from May 6 to 8. Miller hit a six and 20 fours in his 159 not out and shared stands of 143 with de Courcy (53) and 152 with Benaud (97). Benaud completed an outstanding double by starting the Yorkshire slide with his leg breaks. Yorkshire managed only 145 and 214, Jack Hill cleaning up the tail with his top spinners.

Australia's dominant form was attracting big crowds to grounds that were in better shape than in 1948. At The Oval, I found it hard among the press of spectators to get a glimpse of Australia's demolition of Surrey, whom they put out for 58 and 122. Archer's explosive action produced swing and lift that nonplussed batsmen as much as Lindwall's pace and he had match figures of 6 for 26 and 5 for 35. Australia's scoring was curbed by craftsmanlike bowling from Bedser and Lock, whose action immediately raised doubts among the Australians, but Harvey's 66 took them to 256, enough to win without batting twice.

At Lord's against the MCC from 16 to 19 May, Lindwall celebrated his return to the home of cricket by dismissing Simpson, Sheppard and Compton in his first five overs. Ring completed

Richie Benaud, who made his Test debut in the fifth Test against the West Indies in 1951–52 at Sydney, proved a fine attacking batsman, adept on the drives.

of Queen Elizabeth II in London. Bad light and a hailstorm upset what Australians regarded as an important match. Dooland topscored with 69 in Notts' 208, which included a first ball duck by Sri Lankan Gamini Goonesena that took him six minutes to achieve, such were the long walks involved. Hole, Hassett, Miller and Davidson all delighted the audience with their batting but Australia's appeal against the light at 6 for 290 disgusted them. Notts secretary Harry Brown did not conceal his anger as the Australians rushed for the London train.

By the seaside at Hove from 3 to 5 June the last Sussex batsmen James and Webb thwarted an exciting Australian effort to win. Australia began with a score of 325, McDonald producing his first big innings of the tour before he was run out for 106. Harvey helped him put on 149. Sheppard and John Langridge added 112 but when they went Sussex folded up for 218. Leading by 107, the Australians scored at better than a run a minute before declaring at 1 for 259, with 240 minutes left. At 9 for 174, an Australian win looked certain but James and Webb defied the bowling for 40 minutes. Hill's eight wickets cost only 78 runs.

Barbados all-rounder Roy Marshall single-handedly delayed an Australian victory over Hampshire from 6 to 8 June at Southampton. After Harvey had made a brilliant 109, Marshall took 4 for 69 with his off breaks to have Australia out for 268. Hampshire managed only 131 in reply, Johnston taking 5 for 75. Australia then rushed on 169 runs for the loss of five wickets before declaring 306 ahead. Marshall's 71 was the only show of defiance in Hampshire's second knock of 148, Australia winning by 158 runs.

Bedser gave Hutton, the first professional appointed England's regular leader, a good start to his captaincy by uprooting Hole's middle stump with the first ball of his second over in the first Test at Trent Bridge from 11 to 16 June. At 3 for 237 a big Australian score appeared likely, but when Hassett went for 115 and Miller

the rout. With MCC out for 80, Australia struggled against Bailey and Moss but achieved a lead of 99. The dour Bailey held up Australia long enough on the last day to indicate he would be troublesome in the Tests. Ring's match bag was 6 for 52. Rain forced a draw.

Lancashire gave the Australians a tough match at Manchester from 27 to 29 May, until rain again ended proceedings. Harvey struggled to find his timing in his first 50 but then breezed to 103, out of 298, the second 50 taking only an hour. Nigel Howard's 78 was a sober effort but enough to take Lancashire to 9 for 232 after they had lost 4 for 59.

By courtesy of the Notts club the match against Nottinghamshire at Trent Bridge was restricted to two days, 30 May and 1 June, to allow the Australians to watch the coronation for 55 the last six batsmen added only six runs in a total of 249. Bedser bowled his last four victims in taking 7 for 55.

After his customary warm-up callisthenics, Lindwall countered Bedser's display with a masterly mix of swing and high speed bowling, and with energetic support from Davidson and Hill had England out for 144. Lindwall's 5 for 57 included three wickets while the England score remained on 17. Australia held every catch offered and the ground fielding was quite wonderful.

Hassett got the only ball that popped awkwardly in Australia's second innings but it spread suspicion about the pitch through the team when short leg took a simple catch off his glove. From 1 for 44, Australia collapsed to be all out for 123, Bedser's 7 for 44 giving him 14 for 99 in the match and making him the highest England wicket-taker in Tests against Australia, surpassing the 189 wickets by S. F. Barnes, who was in the crowd.

Australia's innings included some reckless hitting from Davidson and Tallon who blazed away after Tallon misheard captain Hassett's instructions to appeal against the light. Rain washed out the match with England requiring 109 to win with nine wickets in hand. The four-day attendance of 86,000 and receipts of £29,261 were a Trent Bridge record.

At Chesterfield from 17 to 19 June Australia had an engrossing encounter with that happy Derbyshire extrovert Cliff Gladwin, whose right-arm in-dippers yielded 5 for 84 and 4 for 59 and made me wonder why he was not an automatic selection in England Test teams. He had support from an outstanding young off spinner, Edwin Smith, but rain washed out the last day with Derbyshire on 1 for 17 needing 275 to win.

The second Test at Lord's from 25 to 30 June produced a world record gate for a cricket match of £57,716 and one of cricket's classic rearguard stands. Lord's was only half full at the start of this partnership between Bailey and Watson, because England's chances appeared hopeless, but as word spread around London that they were still batting taxis kept disgorging spectators all around the ground entrances.

The match was conducted during the closing days of the trial of one of England's most notorious murderers, John Christie, who was charged with killing ten people and stuffing their bodies under the floorboards of his house in Rillington Place. When Christie was sentenced to death and was being led away to the cells, he turned to a warder and asked: "What's the score?"

Australia dropped Hill for Ring, and Tallon for Langley, ending the Test career of the player many consider the greatest wicket-keeper Australia had produced. Tallon had begun his Test career at 30 but in his 21-Test reign as Australia's Test 'keeper dismissed 58 batsmen, 50 of them caught, and eight stumped. Bradman rated him inferior only to Les Ames, of Kent, as wicket-keeper-batsman, but even Ames's admirers agreed Tallon was the faster stumper. The slight deafness that prevented him hearing snicks or his captain's instructions hastened his replacement by Langley for this Test, and sent him back to his general store in Bundaberg.

Australia appeared to have the match won when Lindwall's 2 sixes and 5 fours in an innings of 50 extended their lead to 342, going into the last innings. Lindwall improved Australia's prospects by removing Kenyon and Hutton before stumps, and when Graveney went to a brilliant diving catch by Langley, England were in an apparently hopeless position at 3 for 12 with a day to play. In the last over Watson gave a catch to short leg that was dropped.

Sid Barnes later alleged the Australians celebrated prematurely that night by attending the musical *Guys and Dolls*, followed by a backstage party, and a session at the Cafe de Paris. "It was a night of great celebration and carnival and so the Australians sauntered on to

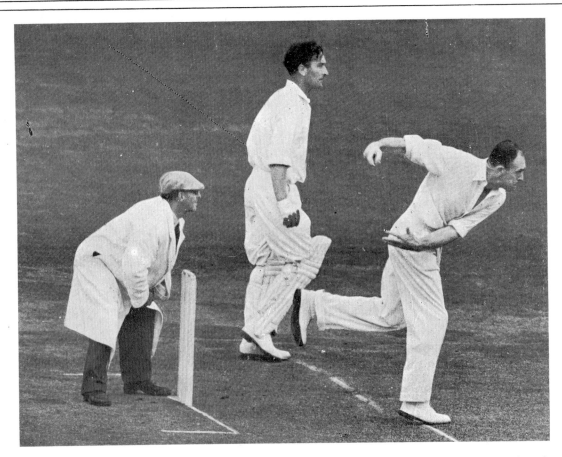

Big Bill Johnston bowling against England in 1953 when he delighted all cricket lovers by heading the tour batting averages, going in last every time he batted. He was only out once.

the field for the last day, physically tired, mentally tired, and indeed a little piqued that what could have been a day of leisure was interrupted for an hour or so while they disposed of the remaining England batsmen," wrote Barnes in his book, *Eyes on the Ashes*.

The pitch was crumbling and taking spin but by lunch only Compton had been dismissed, leaving Bailey and Watson together in their celebrated partnership. Both hit the ball with the full face of straight but dead bats as Lindwall, Miller and Johnston went through their repertoires. Hassett could not risk giving his spinners Benaud and Ring long spells for fear

the batsmen would exploit their uncertain length and direction and go for the runs.

The stand finally ended at 5.50 when Watson, after 5 hours 45 minutes nicked a googly from Ring to Hole at slip. He had made 109. Bailey tried a cover drive soon afterwards and was caught for 71 after 4 hours 15 minutes. With six wickets down, there were still 35 minutes left but instead of defending Brown hit out boldly, ending Australian hopes of a win with a flurry of lusty blows. The ball fell in the gaps until he had made 28 and the Test was safe, and as stumps were drawn amid wild applause England were on 7 for 282, still 61 runs short of victory. Seldom in the history of Test cricket had a dropped catch been as costly as that which allowed Watson to escape near the end of the fourth day.

Freddie Brown could not restrain his

merriment when a young fast bowler named Frank Tyson had McDonald lbw and then uprooted Hole's stumps with the third and fourth balls of a fierce opening over in the Australians' match from 4 to 6 July against Northamptonshire. Brown, who had watched Lindwall and Miller dust English batsmen for years, chuckled as Tyson administered bruises and obvious discomfort to the Australians. Three men were out for 10 before the left-handers Morris and Harvey restored the innings with a fourth-wicket stand of 175.

Harvey in his seventh century of the tour hit 18 fours with strokes to every corner of the field. Morris was content to let Harvey's 118 overshadow his patient 80. Expatriate Australian Test bowler George Tribe took 5 for 97, in an innings of 323, three of his victims losing their stumps when they played the wrong way at his famous "Chinaman" or left-hand wrist-spinner's googly. Australia's bowling, fielding and catching reached a very high standard when they bundled the previously unbeaten Northants out for 141 and 120. Archer had 7 for 56 in the first innings, Ring 5 for 46 in the second, Australia winning by an innings and 62 runs.

Rain restricted the third Test at Manchester between 9 and 14 July to 13 hours 50 minutes instead of the allotted 30 hours. This probably would have been enough for England to win had Godfrey Evans held an easy catch from Neil Harvey standing back to Bailey, when Harvey was 4. Australia were 3 for 48 at the time after Hassett had been bowled and both Morris and Miller had played on. Harvey survived and helped lift the total to 256 by scoring 122 before Evans brilliantly caught him down the leg side. Hole (66) and de Courcy (41) took Australia, after stoppages, to 318 on the third day. Many thought Hassett should have declared to get England in on the damp pitch.

England had to fight hard to avoid the follow-on on the fifth day with the sixth wicket falling and 20 still needed. But Simpson, Bailey and Evans played some excellent strokes to lift the

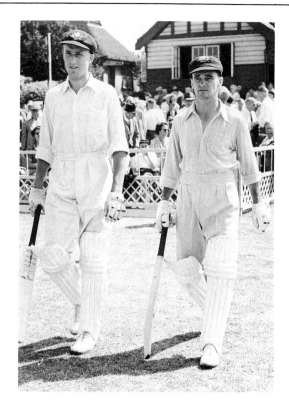

Graeme Hole and Jim de Courcy resume batting after lunch in Australia's match at Southend against Essex in 1953. On their first tour both did well in county matches but disappointed in Tests.

total to 276, which would have been unobtainable had the Australians not bowled so short. Laker and Wardle showed where to pitch the ball on such a vile wicket when Australia batted, and eight batsmen were out for 35 runs before time ran out. Wardle took four wickets from five overs for only seven runs in the last half hour.

The first match between Australia and Holland took place on 16 July when a Test-strength Australian side comprising Hassett, Morris, McDonald, Harvey, Miller, de Courcy, Benaud, Archer, Davidson, Ring, and Tallon appeared at The Hague. The Archives Committee of the Royal Netherlands Cricket Association told me this was Australia's initial match on the European Continent. Australia batted first and scored 279, aided by 70 from

Morris and 66 by McDonald. Holland struggled for three hours to make 122 in reply, leaving Australia winners by 157 runs on the first innings.

The continued failure of Craig, the team's baby, attracted more publicity in the drawn match at Lord's from 18 to 21 July against Middlesex. Only Bill Edrich held up Australia as Middlesex were put out for 150. Rather than tire his players by chasing a win just before the next Test, Hassett used Australia's innings for batting practice. Everyone benefited except Craig, whose 2 was the only failure in Australia's top order. De Courcy hit five sixes and six fours to topscore with 74, scoring 70 of the 102 runs he put on with Benaud. When the Queen met the players in front of the Lord's pavilion she asked Craig: "Is this your first trip to England?" Craig: "Yes, Your Majesty, and unless my batting improves it will be my last."

Rain that seeped through the covers during two days of heavy showers worried both captains at the start of the fourth Test at Leeds from 23 to 28 July. Bradman and Jardine, antagonists in the infamous Bodyline series, sat unsmilingly side-by-side in the press box as Hutton spun the coin and Hassett called correctly. Hutton threw the coin away in disgust, causing a wild scramble among schoolboys, but Hassett refused to be bluffed and sent England in. Lindwall uprooted Hutton's stumps with the second ball, and although Graveney stayed 3 hours 15 minutes for 55, England's misfortunes multiplied. Simpson took a nasty blow on the elbow and had to retire. Umpire Frank Lee disallowed an lbw appeal against Watson, but the ball rolled off Watson's ankle onto the stumps, dislodging a bail. Then Bailey wrenched his knee vainly trying to avoid being run out.

England's 7 for 142 from 96 overs was the lowest ever for a day's play in England. Australia finished England off for 167, Lindwall leading the bowlers yet again with 5 for 54. Morris, Hassett and Miller were out for 84 when Harvey and Hole came together and took Australia into the lead by doubling the score. The tail faltered but a 48-run stand for the last wicket by Archer and Langley carried Australia to a lead of 99 with three days left. Bedser's 6 for 95 had retrieved a potentially dangerous position for England and taken him past Clarrie Grimmett's world record of 216 wickets in Tests.

More rain converted the England innings into a struggle for survival and the skill of the Middlesex pair, Edrich and Compton, was matched against the alarming pace of Miller, Lindwall and Archer in a wonderful duel. Slowly the batsmen cleared the deficit, adding 77 in 150 minutes. At 139, Edrich fell for 64 to a magnificent gully catch by de Courcy.

Then Miller swung the match Australia's way in two deliveries, with Watson caught off his glove from the first and Simpson taken in the slips from the second. Bailey avoided the hat-trick but at 171 England were only 72 ahead with half her side out. Amid a volley of bouncers, heavy showers came to England's aid, ending the day's play with only six more runs added.

Next morning Compton's thumb was so swollen he could not grip the bat but defiant innings by Bailey and Laker allowed him to remain in the pavilion for treatment until after lunch. "Barnacle" Bailey had perfected a dead bat pendulum stroke that he could play for over after over. Compton made only a single when he went in after lunch but the 25 minutes he took to do it was important. England fought desperately for time as Lock stayed 40 minutes with Bailey and Bedser a further 45 minutes.

Australia wanted 177 to win in 115 minutes when Bailey was last out for 38. Lindwall's 89 six-ball overs or 534 deliveries was the longest ever match stint by a fast bowler in England–Australia Tests and produced 8 for 158. When the renowned hitter Davidson joined Hole, with 66 wanted in 45 minutes and seven wickets left, England's time-wasting seemed to have gone astray.

But Bailey went back to a long approach

run and by bowling wide of the leg stump slowed the scoring. Forced to go for big hits, Hole swung Bailey high. On the square-leg fence Graveney pulled down what otherwise would have been a six. Only 12 overs were bowled in the final 45 minutes, which de Courcy enlivened with six off Bedser, and Australia finished 30 short of the target. The draw left England still without a victory over Australia at Leeds, with the series to be decided in the fifth Test. The fourth Test had been watched by a further 151,000 spectators and drew a gate of £48,313 sterling.

The grim, evenly-matched fight for the Ashes had already made this the most financially successful tour known to cricket, with only the small size of the grounds limiting the crowds and the takings. Off the field Hassett's wonderful blend of sparkling speechmaking, impish pranks, and deflation of the pompous had also made it the most enjoyable for the Australians and their opponents. In the art of making friends for himself and for Australian cricket, there has never been anybody like him. He could waltz with a duchess as enthusiastically as he conducted community singing. He persuaded one mayor to get up on a table wearing his chain and robes of office and give his players a demonstration of the Charleston, then enjoying a worldwide comeback.

The distinction between amateurs and professionals in teams the Australians met always amused Hassett but he never uttered a word of criticism. At The Oval, where the Australians played Surrey from 29 to 31 July, the amateur captain Stuart Surridge and his heir-apparent, Peter May, changed in the amateurs' room upstairs in the pavilion. The pros were downstairs. There the seniors, Bedser, Laker, Lock, and McIntyre had their gear laid out for them by the trainee junior pros, Micky Stewart and Ken Barrington. When Surrey travelled it was the job of Stewart, Barrington and the masseur Sandy Tait to get 12 huge cricket bags to the relevant railway station and ensure they

got to the ground at the end of the trip. Hassett stayed with his team, resisting invitations to use captains' dressing-rooms, and Bill Ferguson looked after their bags.

Surrey did well on the first day, when David Fletcher made 78 and May (56) joined him in a 128 stand. Bill Johnston, in his return to the Australian side after a month's absence with his knee trouble, took three quick wickets next morning on a pitch affected by overnight rain. Surridge immediately declared, with the score on 8 for 209, hoping to catch Australia on a spiteful pitch. But Hassett's use of the roller took the malice from the pitch and Australia settled to a day of sustained stroke-play that took them to 327 and a lead of 118. Rain washed out the last day with Australia well placed to force a win. Harvey (113), Morris (67) and Hassett (67) forced Surridge to use seven bowlers.

Morris took over the Australian captaincy for the match from 1 to 4 August at Swansea, where Glamorgan needed 123 to avoid an innings defeat following Australia's 386. They got them thanks to a 125-run partnership by Wilfred Wooller and Bernard Muncer. Morris settled for a draw with Glamorgan on 7 for 188.

Hassett endured the undreamt-of experience of being heckled by 20,000 spectators, when he refused the challenge of scoring 166 in 170 minutes on a pitch taking spin in the final innings of the match against Warwickshire at Birmingham from 5 to 7 August.

Spectators wanted an exciting chase for runs by Australia but Hassett, aware of his side's inexperience against spin on turning pitches, immediately settled down to dogged defence. Hollies' mixture of leg breaks and googlies had brought him 5 for 45 in the first innings. Hassett was still there on 21 not out and Australia on 5 for 53 when the match ended in a draw, having set ground takings and attendance records.

Morris was the most confirmed bachelor in the Australian team when a few of them went backstage after watching the Crazy Gang show

The famous scene at The Oval in 1953 when England regained The Ashes which Australia had held since 1934 in England. The crowd gathered like this in front of the pavilion waiting for captains Hassett and Hutton to come out and speak to them.

Ring Out the Bells at the Victoria Palace in London. There he fell in love with showgirl Valerie Hudson, who had begun dancing at the Windmill Theatre as a teenager in wartime, a redhead whose beauty turned heads whenever she entered a room.

Arthur and Valerie were deciding about their future when Hassett made a decision about Frank Chester and sent an objection to Lord's against Chester standing in the crucial fifth Test from

15 to 19 August. Chester, the best known English umpire, had puzzled the Australians with strange decisions through the tour. Umpires Frank Lee and Dai Davies were given the Test.

All-night queues among the decaying Victorian tenements surrounding The Oval did not deter 26,300 people from watching Hassett win the toss for the fifth time in the rubber. Trueman was generously applauded on his debut against Australia and he responded with a fiery first over in which he had an appeal for caught behind against Morris disallowed. Trueman's approach run was so long his first five overs took 45 minutes.

Bedser dismissed Morris for the 18th time in post-war Tests when Morris did not offer a

stroke at an inswinger and was ruled lbw. Miller went lbw to Bailey and Australia were 2 for 41. Rain in the lunch break gave spite to the pitch which Bedser and Trueman used to send back Hassett and Harvey. A ten-minute delay for rain broke de Courcy's concentration and immediately play resumed he edged a catch to Evans. Archer became Bedser's 39th wicket of the series, surpassing Maurice Tate's record haul against Australia back in 1924–25.

Lindwall saved the innings from disaster by adding 47 with Davidson, 38 with Langley, and 30 with Johnston in a display studded with off drives that took him to 62. Five dropped catches helped Australia reach 275.

After England led by 31 on the first innings,

showers laid the dust, but when hot sun fell on the drying pitch Laker and Lock proved match-winners. Lock bowled Harvey off his pads and made Morris miss with his shuffle shot. Laker had Hassett and Hole lbw and Miller superbly caught by Trueman at short leg. From 1 for 59, Australia collapsed to 6 for 85.

The most belligerent batting of the innings came from Archer and Davidson, who both hit magnificent sixes, adding 50 so quickly England were forced to review their tactics. Both Laker and Lock changed their fields, Laker bowling down the leg side with only three men on the off, Lock outside the off stump with only three on the leg side. This slowed the scoring and accounted for the last four wickets for only 31 runs. Laker took 4 for 75, Lock 5 for 45 in Australia's 162.

Miller gave umpire Lee a tip for the races as England set out after the 132 needed to win. When Lee rejected an lbw appeal, Miller said: "No more tips for you, Frank." Lindwall bowled 21 fine overs but England moved remorselessly towards the target through steady batting by Edrich and May. When only nine runs were wanted, Hassett went on to bowl with Morris, and just before three o'clock on the fourth day Compton hit Morris for four to win the match.

Before the ball reached the boundary hordes of running, laughing people engulfed Edrich, Compton and the Australians and converted even such a drab and colourless field as The Oval into a joyful place. England's eight-wicket win gave her the Ashes for the first time since 1932–33 and followed a summer of celebrations for the Coronation and Hillary's first conquest of Everest. Hutton, the first modern professional to captain England through a series, became the first Test captain to succeed after losing all five tosses.

Despite his team's misgivings over Lock's part in Australia losing the Ashes, after holding them for 18 years and 362 days, Hassett accepted umpires Lee and Davies' view that Lock was not a chucker, graciously joining Hutton in speeches to the thousands in front of the pavilion. The MCC and the Australian Board of Control had agreed to extend the match if needed to ensure a result but ultimately England won inside four days, largely because of Australia's lack of a top-class spinner.

The six first-class matches that followed the fifth Test and the two non-first-class matches in Scotland were an anticlimax, but for the whole tour huge crowds watched the Australians. The Oval Test had drawn 115,000 people and receipts of £37,000, and while the counties could not match that, their treasurers were still happy.

At a time when many young English cricketers were forced to do National Service,

Len Hutton guides Lindsay Hassett's hand as he cuts the victory cake after the final Test of the 1953 series. England regained the Ashes after 20 years.

Miller and de Courcy reserved the highest scores of their careers for the match against the Combined Services at Kingston on 5 and 7 September. Australia won by an innings and 261 runs with a day to spare. Miller reached 262 not out, de Courcy 204, heavily punishing Fred Trueman in Australia's innings of 4 for 592. Hill's 6 for 34 were the best figures as the Services were bundled out for 161 and 170. Colin Ingleby-Mackenzie made 66, claiming later he was only chosen when his father, an admiral, ordered a subordinate to pick him.

"After the game there was a kind of disciplinary tribunal headed by an air vice-marshal," said Ingleby-Mackenzie. "We were all given a rocket for losing in two days but the real bollocking was directed at Freddie Trueman, who was told his performance was appalling. To this he gave the immortal reply, 'Well sir, firstly I knew there was really not much chance of shifting those two on that wicket, and second I was appalled when they put that bloody Major Parnaby at short-leg. I'm supposed to be a specialist fieldsman there for England and yet you expect me to give way to an old gentleman like that.' At this the air vice-marshal gave Fred a further rocket and said: 'You will never play for Combined Services again.' 'Too bloody right,' said Fred, 'I'm being demobbed tomorrow.' "

The final first-class match of the tour provided more heroics for spectators, with Australia beating T. N. Pearce's XI at Scarborough from 9 to 11 September by two wickets. Hutton made 102 in the third innings to set Australia 320 to win in 220 minutes. Benaud opened and virtually won the match by scoring 135 out of 209 in 110 minutes. He scratched around until a comment by Hutton that he was batting to protect his average angered him. He proceeded to hit 11 sixes and 9 fours, including 4 sixes in succession from Tattersall. Benaud's first century in England included 102 in boundaries, and dominated a match that produced 34 sixes.

A record 1,494,979 people paid £226,000 to watch the 80 days' play on the tour. Aggregate attendance at the five Tests was 270,650. The Australian Board of Control received £A134,898 from the tour. This was more than double the profit from the 1948 tour by Bradman's unbeaten side. The team won 16 of their 33 first-class matches, drew 16 and lost only the fifth Test.

The side's batting strength was apparent in their record of scoring 30 centuries while only seven were scored against them. Harvey scored ten centuries, five more than the next best total of five 100s by Hassett. Harvey also headed the batting aggregates with 2040 runs at 65.80. Miller, with 1433 runs at 51.17, Hassett, 1236 at 44.14, de Courcy, 1214 at 41.86, Morris, 1302 at 38.29, and Hole, 1118 at 33.87, all scored 1000 runs on the tour. Harvey also headed the bowling averages with four wickets at 10.75, but of the frontline bowlers Lindwall was the best with 85 wickets at 16.40.

The statistical star of the tour, however, was Bill Johnston, who was once out in scoring 102 runs and finished with 102 as his batting average. Johnston's effort in taking 75 wickets at 20.54 in the 16 matches he was restricted to by his injured knee was even more remarkable. The prospect of such a batting dunce as Johnston heading the batting averages was the reason Hassett jumped the fence to remind players that Johnston should remain not out in the final matches. The feat brought more laughter to a happy tour. The rival players were so friendly that when the Australians sailed for home in September Tony Lock promised Jack Hill he would name his first child after Hill if it was a boy. Hill said he would do the same.

Who's For Captain?

Domestic cricket 1953-55;
New Zealand and England in
Australia 1954-55

Hassett's retirement after the 1953 tour of England aroused the fervent hope among every red-blooded Australian cricket fan that Keith Miller would be given Test captaincy. He was the nation's finest player, the embodiment of the aggressive spirit that had made Australian cricket supreme, and one of the few in the game's history who could influence the result in two or three overs through his batting, bowling or catching. His sophistication was shown in his love of classical music and his acceptance by the aristocracy was there for all to see in the photographs of him in his top hat at Epsom and Royal Ascot.

The Australian Board of Control remained unmoved by the wishes of cricket followers or the need to revitalise the fortunes of a declining Test team by appointing Miller to lead it. The

The 1954–55 England side to Australia: (L to R)
(back) G. Duckworth (scorer), K. V. Andrew, P. J.
Loader, T. W. Graveney, F. H. Tyson, H. W.
Dalton (masseur); (centre) J. H. Wardle, R. T.
Simpson, J. V. Wilson, R. Appleyard, J. McConnon,
J. B. Statham, M. C. Cowdrey, C. G. Howard
(manager); (front) T. E. Bailey, W. J. Edrich,
P. B. H. May, L. Hutton (captain), D. C. S. Compton,
A. V. Bedser, T. G. Evans.

Board's hidebound attitude had been shown on the 1953 tour when, after the failure of the spinners in big games, it did not call up Bruce Dooland, Jack Walsh, or George Tribe to do the job. Other cricket nations did so: the West Indies got players to drop League commitments and had Worrell and Ramadhin quit Commonwealth teams to join their tours in India. But the Australian Board showed no desire to field its best national team.

There was no overseas tour of Australia in the summer of 1953–54 and no need to elect a new Test captain. This gave the Victorian members of the Board, then chaired by South Australian Roy Middleton, time to air their reservations about Miller.

He was, it seemed, a captain of unorthodox methods, given to telling his New South Wales team to "spread out", instead of informing each man where he should field. He had gone on the field for a Shield match in Adelaide with 13 players and been forced to tell two to "nick off" when umpires informed him of this. He had once thanked the mayor of a country town on behalf of the New South Wales players for lavish hospitality and then asked the players where they were. Nobody mentioned that he was the biggest drawcard since Bradman and that people who normally did not attend big cricket went along just to see him flick his mop of black hair into place.

Miller gave a further demonstration of his eminence by scoring two separate centuries in Hassett's testimonial match at Melbourne from 15 to 19 January, 1954. The bowlers tried to answer the crowd's hunger for boundaries and 20 sixes and 189 fours were hit during the match. Craig hit 4 sixes off five balls from Johnson and put on 50 in eight minutes with Carmody.

Morris' XI began with 562, with Craig's 106 the highest of six innings over 50. Hassett's XI responded with 415, Miller (100) and Hassett (126), heading the run-makers. Morris' side made 399 in their second innings, Hole adding 97 to

his first innings of 72. Lindwall clean-bowled Hassett for three in Hassett's final first-class innings. Miller's 101 took Hassett's XI to 425, leaving Morris' XI winners by 121 runs.

Hassett went out of first-class cricket with a cheque for £5503, comprising £3503 taken through the gate at this match plus £2000 in donations. "I've had no practice in handling cheques for £5000," he told Prime Minister Bob Menzies as he received the money. Despite losing the best years of his career through war, he scored 16,890 runs at 58.24 in first-class cricket, made 59 centuries, 23 of them for Victoria, and held 170 catches. In 43 Tests he scored 3073 runs at 46.56, with ten centuries. He played four Tests by the age of 24, the rest after he turned 33. At 1.67 metres and a few beers either side of 63 kilograms, Hassett was the finest player of fast bowling among cricket's smaller men. He was seldom hit by bouncers and he had an uncanny ability to sway under or away from the most vicious kickers.

His 18 first-class wickets at 39.05 included one for which he did not get proper recognition. On England's 1938 tour of England when, after weeks of verbal pressure, Bradman relented and gave him the ball at Nottingham, Hassett's first delivery to Walter Keeton started about half a metre outside the off stump and drifted further out in the cross breeze. "It was the kind of ball Keeton had probably not encountered since his pre-school days," said Hassett. "He lunged at it and just managed to reach it with the end of the bat and it flew to Fleetwood-Smith at second slip, where it lodged, jammed between his legs. Some smart character in Australia received the cable 'Keeton caught Fleetwood-Smith bowled Hassett 0', reckoned it was a mistake, and changed it for the Australian papers to 'Keeton caught Hassett bowled Fleetwood-Smith 0'."

Hassett won 14 of his 24 Tests as Australia's captain and had only four losses. Author Ray Robinson calculated that in Hassett's last 20 Tests

Australia's first wicket fell 26 times before the score reached 30. This forced Hassett to subdue his natural shot-making and finally forced him to undertake the opener's job. Noted English critic Robertson-Glasgow said: "Hassett's greatest performances concerned the heart of the game rather than its arithmetic. He proved that Test matches, win or lose, can still be fun as well as good finance."

Australian cricket badly needed the £A134,898 received as her share of profits from the 1953 tour of England by Hassett's team, for many of the first-class matches staged within Australia lost money. The West Indian tour in 1950–51 had produced a loss and the South African tour in 1952–53 had made only a small profit despite providing thrills galore. Attractive Sheffield Shield matches usually showed a profit in Sydney and Melbourne, but in Brisbane, Adelaide and Perth too many matches were held at a loss. The public's delight at the revival of international cricket in 1946–47, when 846,942 attended the England–Australia series, had quickly faded. Increased popularity of other sports such as tennis, which in the 1950s drew huge crowds to Davis Cup matches, had seen a decline in the average daily attendance at Shield matches from 6021 between the wars to 3836 in a nation that had doubled its population and expanded its major domestic cricket competition from 39 to 61 playing days.

The 1950s were boom years for the Australian economy but years of stagnation for cricket. Cash distributions from state associations to district clubs were too small to fund the running of a club. Clubs had to rely more on membership fees and their own fund-raising activities to survive. With clubs pressing for larger shares of the income from tours, the state associations had to spend much of their money moving Shield teams around the states. In Brisbane, Adelaide and Perth the state associations—not the state governments—paid for ground improvements.

The biggest disappointment was that income from matches involving Western Australia had not improved after they won the Shield in their first year. The public appeal of the Western Australian team had dwindled, sometimes because of unimaginative selections, and in Perth WACA Ground memberships had not risen as expected. After six years in the competition on a restricted basis, Western Australia found that eastern states were not prepared to fund the extra matches that would improve her team's performance. There was bitterness in Perth because other states would not give Western Australia full Shield membership but the figures supported the other states' view that they could not afford it. The Western Australian Cricket Association was deeply concerned about its finances, when Sir Donald Bradman began to look for a solution in the early 1950s.

The Australian Board of Control's need for tight financial housekeeping offered little opportunity to assist junior or schools cricket and made it an administration preoccupied with overseas tours. Social cricketers such as those who played on Sydney's Centennial Park or Moore Park, the churches' cricket association in Melbourne or the Brisbane business houses competition, had little contact with state associations and none at all with the Board. The Board's contact with the vast majority of cricketers in action around Australia was so remote the players naturally believed the Board was unconcerned with the overall strength of the game. For thousands of social players with no prospect of playing state or Test cricket their control came from the local council or the curators who pegged down their matting. After 50 years of administering Australian cricket, the men who sat on the Board of Control were virtually unknown figures, with Bradman the notable exception.

One cricketer with no wish to sit on committees was Keith Miller, who captained New South Wales to regain the Sheffield Shield in the 1953–54 season. New South Wales' sole defeat was against Victoria in Sydney from 29 January to 2 February, when Collingwood left-arm fast-medium bowler 33-year-old Harry Lambert took 6 for 55 in a spirited display. Lambert's coup had New South Wales out for 182, enough to give Victoria a first innings lead of 52 runs. Miller revived his team's hopes with a fighting 143 sprinkled with majestic strokes off the front foot, but in the final innings Ray Harvey made a splendid 106 not out to win the match for Victoria by five wickets.

New South Wales successfully tried the Bankstown-Canterbury club's right-hander Ronnie Briggs as Arthur Morris' opening partner. They frequently provided starts that led to big scores when the hitters like Miller, Benaud and Davidson came in against disheartened attacks. Briggs made 136 in an aggressive performance against South Australia from 19 to 23 February, which led to a five-wicket victory.

Queensland fielded some outstanding youngsters in Brian Flynn, Peter Burge and Jim Bratchford to support "Possum" Raymer, the Archer brothers, competent new wicket-keeper Wally Grout, long serving medium-pacer Len Johnson and the eccentric Ken ("Slasher") Mackay, who had been in the side since the first season after the Second World War. Mackay, whose Brisbane fans were used to his unorthodoxy, batted for 9 hours 45 minutes to score 223 against Victoria in Brisbane from 22 to 26 January, which enabled Queensland to beat Victoria on the first innings by 274 runs. Ron Archer made 114 in Queensland's innings of 561, his highest Shield score. Jeff Hallebone frustrated Queensland hopes of an outright victory by scoring 143 not out in Victoria's second innings. He hit 6 sixes off left-hand spinner Raymer.

New South Wales selectors angered all fair-minded cricket followers by excluding champion fast bowler Ray Lindwall from the team for the last match of the Shield programme against South Australia in Sydney from 19 to 23 February. Lindwall had announced his intention of moving

to Queensland the following season. By omitting him the selectors deprived a player who had given the New South Wales side 50 matches of wholehearted effort a farewell appearance for his native State.

Five of the young players who toured England in 1953 showed lasting benefit from that tour. Benaud played an innings of rare power and immense concentration to score 158 against Queensland in Brisbane from 13 to 17 November, after taking 5 for 88 in Queensland's first innings. de Courcy averaged 50.62 an innings. Hole (226) and McDonald (229) both produced their highest scores to that time in first-class cricket. Ron Archer advanced with every appearance.

For the first time in years spin bowlers were among the most successful with the ball. Ian Johnson, dropped from the Australian team that toured England in 1953, showed glimpses of his best form for Victoria, taking 37 wickets at 16.37 apiece. Benaud was New South Wales' highest wicket-taker with 30 wickets at 27.70 and none worked harder at the practice nets. Brian Flynn, who went to Ray Lindwall's old school in Sydney, Marist Brothers, Darlinghurst, took 27 wickets at 30.22 for Queensland.

Johnson had taken over from Hassett as Victoria's captain and at 35 figured he would give it one more season when he went to a 1953 New Year's Eve party. He had taken only one wicket for 119 runs in two matches to that time and was not looking forward to next day's match against South Australia. At 2.30 a.m. Hassett backed him into a corner and roasted Johnson for his lack of effort. Johnson got annoyed and refuted this, which in turn stung Hassett, who said: "You know you're not getting stuck into it. You're just coasting. If you've got any brains at all you'll get stuck right into it. If you do you'll be captain of Australia next year. There's no one else who could do the job as well if you get into it and show some form."

Hassett's words needled Johnson, who said that every ball he bowled from then on was

Ian Johnson, who took over the Victorian captaincy in 1953 from Lindsay Hassett. He later became Australian captain, the fifth from the South Melbourne club.

century, against South Australia.

Victoria were without two valuable players, Sam Loxton and Jack Iverson, who were away with fellow Australians Ken Meuleman and Ben Barnett playing for the Commonwealth team in India. Loxton's bustling, no-nonsense style was as useful to Ben Barnett's XI as it had been through the year to Wesley College, Prahran, Victoria and Australia. His all-out aggression compensated for his lack of style and few batsmen could hit longer sixes. Nobody bowled bouncers to Sam without risking threats that they would wear Sam's bat around their ears.

The Commonwealth team's travelling was conducted solely by train and over four months and 21 matches Barnett had to call on 20 players. Iverson was one of the replacements, flown in when Worrell, Ramadhin, Simpson, Crapp, Fletcher and McConnon went home. The Indian batsmen were repeatedly bamboozled by Iverson's methods and in six matches he took 27 wickets at 22.48, beating the bat so often the Australians could only regret his failure to win a place in the 1953 team to England. Meuleman scored three centuries for the Commonwealth team, two of them in the unofficial Tests and with 1158 runs at 52.63 was the only batsman to pass 1000 runs on the tour.

The Commonwealth XI won only 3 of their 21 matches, lost 5 and left 13 drawn. Their wins included the third of the five unofficial Tests, when Iverson took 4 for 78 and 6 for 47 only a few days after arriving from Australia.

New Zealand played three first-class matches in Australia in March 1954, on their way home from a disappointing long tour of South Africa, who had stretched the New Zealanders' Test record to 31 matches without a win and won the Tests 4–nil. At Perth from 5 to 9 March New Zealand defeated Western Australia by 184 runs because of a hard-hitting 142 by left-hander Bert Sutcliffe. This took New Zealand to a first innings lead of 125. Centuries by Lawrie Miller (142) and Sutcliffe (149) paved the way to an

spurred on by what Hassett had said. It finished up his best-ever season, and after taking 4 for 59 and 4 for 21 against South Australia, 5 for 97 against Queensland, 3 for 44 against New South Wales, 2 for 36 against Western Australia and 6 for 85 and 6 for 99 against Western Australia he began to think he might get back into the Australian side. Through the winter he set himself a tough training programme.

On the other side of Australia success had also stirred the ambitions of a young Perth mathematics master, John Rutherford, who in Sydney from 6 to 9 February made 55 stylish runs before team-mate Patrick McCarthy slammed the New South Wales bowlers all over the park to score 98. Two months earlier in Perth Rutherford had made 121, his initial Shield eight-wicket win over South Australia in Adelaide from 12 to 16 March. Colin Pinch made 130, Langley 160 not out and John Drennan took 5 for 83 for South Australia.

A brilliant innings by John Reid, who hit 26 fours in his 160, opened the New Zealanders' match against Victoria from 19 to 23 March in Melbourne. Reid put on 173 in 120 minutes with Miller (60). Victoria replied to New Zealand's 367 with a free-hitting display that produced 423 in better than even time, Hallebone topscoring with 99. Sutcliffe (117) and Reid (64) added 149 in 90 minutes in New Zealand's second innings of 312. Set to score 257 in 120 minutes to win, the Victorians simply played out time.

Bill Jeanes resigned as secretary of the Australian Board of Control early in 1954 after 27 years in the job, and in September that year a hard-working, tactful Victorian, Jack Ledward, took over. Ledward had played 21 matches for Victoria between 1934 and 1938 and had made two first-class centuries. He had been secretary of the Victorian Cricket Association since 1951. His appointment put administration of Australian cricket firmly in the hands of the Victorians, which was probably why Hassett realised Johnson would raise the votes required for the Australian captaincy provided he performed well on the field.

Bushfires, the Queen's visit, the centenary of the Melbourne Cricket Ground, and the defection of the Russian spy Vladimir Petrov dominated the front pages of the Australian press. But the sports pages debated the claims of Miller and Morris for the Test captaincy, with Johnson only occasionally named as a long shot. One player with a keen interest in the discussion was Bob Simpson, a cadet journalist born in Australia of Scottish parents, who had made his debut for New South Wales in 1952 at the age of 16. Simpson had fielded in the 1953–54 season as a substitute for New South Wales. When he asked Miller where he should field, Miller looked puzzled for a moment and then said "Go there",

and pointed to the slips. It was not considered ethical for a twelfth man to occupy a catching position, but Miller took little heed of protocol.

Simpson, who had always previously fielded on the drives, spent the next 13 summers in the slips and built a reputation as one of the greatest slips fieldsmen of all time after catching Neil Harvey and Harry Lambert in the half hour he was on the ground that day. Miller knew a good slips fieldsman when he saw one and the following season Simpson took 15 of the 16 slips catches that came his way for New South Wales.

The twenty-sixth England team to tour Australia, which was announced on 27 July 1954, retained the professional Len Hutton as captain but had amateur Peter May as vice-captain. Australians could scarcely believe the omission of Laker, Lock and Trueman, the destroyers in the decisive fifth Test in 1953, but looked forward to watching "Typhoon" Tyson, the Durham University graduate who could quote freely from Shakespeare or other great poets. Compton was doubtful for a time because of his recurring knee injury but was allowed to remain at home for treatment while the team travelled out in the *Orsova*, flying out to join the tour later. Yorkshire batsman John Wilson, who regularly made 1000 runs in an English season, was added to the team in case Compton broke down. The team was L. Hutton, 38, P. B. H. May, 24, R. T. Simpson, 34, W. J. Edrich, 38, T. E. Bailey, 30, M. C. Cowdrey, 21, D. C. S. Compton, 36, A. V. Bedser, 36, T. G. Evans, 33, J. H. Wardle 31, J. B. Statham, 24, T. W. Graveney, 27, R. Appleyard, 30, J. McConnon, 31, P. J. Loader, 24, F. H. Tyson, 24, K. V. Andrew, 24, J. V. Wilson, 33, with the former Lancashire wicket-keeper George Duckworth as scorer and baggage-master and Geoffrey Howard as manager.

The Marylebone Cricket Club hesitated before giving the captaincy to Hutton, who in 1953–54 had led England to a 2–2 draw in the

West Indies, before deciding that May was not ready for the job. Hutton was the first professional to take an MCC team to Australia since the club had become responsible for overseas tours in 1903–04. He handled the job warily and even among his players was monosyllabic, and his clothes were as conservative as his speeches, but he helped change attitudes towards professionals which once had caused Lord Hawke to comment: "I pray God that no professional will ever captain England."

England beat Western Australia at Perth between 15 and 19 October by seven wickets. Hutton sent Western Australia in to bat on a hard, true pitch, but Statham quickly vindicated this decision by taking 6 for 23 to tumble the state side out for 103. Hutton batted for four hours before retiring with a strained leg muscle on 145 and MCC reached 321. Only a determined 109 by Meuleman in Western Australia's second innings of 255 forced England to bat again.

South Australia seemed certain to beat England at Adelaide between 29 October and 2 November, but collapsed after lunch on the last day when they only wanted 74, with seven wickets left. Tyson started the rout by bowling Favell. Appleyard followed up with four wickets for five runs and England won by 21 runs. Compton made 113 only two days after arriving by plane from London in England's first innings.

Rain put an early end to the match between England and an Australian XI at Melbourne from 5 to 10 November after Ian Johnson had underlined his return to form by taking 6 for 66 in England's innings of 205. At Sydney, Cowdrey hit a century in each innings of a drawn match against New South Wales from 12 to 16 November. Hutton was in grand form and after scoring 102 in the first innings was out for 87 in the second because of an astonishing catch by Simpson, who dived full length to reach a full-blooded back cut. Hutton watched Simpson's dive in disbelief. Willie Watson, a short, stylish opener from the St George club, made 155 for

Len Hutton, who became the first regular professional captain of England, when he brought the 1954–1955 team to Australia. Professionals like Jack Hobbs had previously only filled in for injured amateur captains.

New South Wales, his first century at any level of cricket.

The Board of Control ended speculation about the Australian captaincy by appointing Ian Johnson to lead the side for the first Test at the 'Gabba from 26 November to 1 December. This was Johnson's 29th Test but only his 13th first-class match as captain. Rejecting the idea that Australian cricket cried out for the adventurous captaincy Miller would have provided, the Board gave the job to a player quite unlikely to have a prolonged stay in the Test team. Johnson had been unable to win a place in the previous nine

Tests played by Australia, and had failed to earn selection for the 1953 tour of England.

Johnson was the South Melbourne club's sixth Australian Test captain, following Blackham, Harry Trott, Armstrong, Woodfull and Hassett, but he took over the job without the Australia-wide support enjoyed by the others. Understandably, cricket fans in other States suggested his appointment was due to his family influence. He was the son of long-serving Melbourne official and selector, William Johnson, the North Melbourne wine-and-spirit grocer, who picked Australian teams with Bradman before the Second World War. Trevor Bailey claimed Johnson threw every ball but said English umpires would not no-ball him because he had not been called in his own country. Sid Barnes greeted Johnson's appointment by branding him "Australia's non-playing captain", a jibe he repeated whenever Johnson failed with bat or ball.

With the Brisbane pitch covered against rain, for the first time, Hutton gambled and lost when he put Australia in. He was the first to do so in Australia since Johnny Douglas in 1911–12. Australia showed how wrong Hutton was in counting on four fast bowlers—Bailey, Bedser, Statham and Tyson—by declaring at 8 for 601. England dropped 11 catches, which allowed Morris to reach 153 and Harvey 162. Evans retired with sunstroke. Bedser, who had shingles and should not have played, had seven catches dropped and finished with 1 for 131. Compton broke a bone in his left hand on the fence while fielding. He batted last in each innings, holding the bat in one hand. England collapsed for 190 and 257 to Miller and Lindwall supported by Johnson and Benaud, leaving Australia winners by an innings and 154 runs.

After a drawn match with Victoria from 10 to 14 December in Melbourne, England entered the second Test three days later on a grassy Sydney pitch in fine shape. All their batsmen were in form and strongman Tyson's experiment

in cutting his run to 15 steps was producing blistering pace. He began with six shuffling steps, followed by ten long strides, and his 6 for 68 against Victoria was the best analysis at that stage of his career.

Reports circulated that Compton had been involved in a punch-up when he appeared at the SCG with a very black eye. Compton put the record straight by explaining that he had tripped and hit a garden tap at an outdoor party at the South Yarra home of importer Bill Gluth.

Neither Johnson nor Miller could play because of injury and Morris, who had only just married Valerie Hudson, took over the captaincy of a side that included Davidson and Burke. England made four changes, bringing in Evans for Andrew, Graveney for Compton, Wardle for Simpson and Appleyard for Bedser, who was dropped after dismissing 236 batsmen in 51 Tests. Bedser was not told of his exclusion but discovered it when he read the team sheet pinned on the dressing-room wall on the morning of the match. "Funny bloke, Hutton," Bedser later told sportswriter Frank Keating. "When I was ill on that tour, I was in the next room but he never once popped in."

Morris, in his second match as Australian captain, won the toss and sent England in, aware that the pitch would be at its liveliest on the first day and that Tyson and Statham would be more hostile on it than an Australian attack without Miller. Lindwall was below his best because of liver trouble, but showed Archer and Davidson the way by bowling to a full length and swinging the ball either way. England were out for 154 after last pair, Wardle and Statham, added 43.

England bowled at a disgraceful rate of only 85 balls an hour on the second day, but the 51.6 overs bowled proved enough to dismiss Australia for 228, after an innings that had looked more promising than that at 2 for 100.

Trailing by 74, England lost 3 for 55 in their second innings before May and Cowdrey put on

116 and at stumps were 4 for 204. This was a marvellous flourish by two young amateurs who hit every loose ball for four and were not afraid to dispatch half-volleys. Archer and Lindwall took charge with the new ball and five more wickets fell for 46 runs during which Tyson was knocked out by a Lindwall bouncer that he turned his back on. Morris stuck with his pace bowlers as Appleyard and Statham put on 46 runs in 50 minutes in a last-wicket stand that took England to 296, but Australia's task of scoring 223 to win in the last innings did not look difficult.

Following a precautionary X-ray at hospital Tyson bowled at a pace far in excess of what the ageing Lindwall had achieved to give openers Favell and Morris an anxious time. Just before tea on the fourth day Statham beat Morris with four balls in the last over and had him leg before with the seventh. On the fifth day strong winds blew in from Botany Bay, behind Tyson's back, and he bowled at astounding pace, yorking Burke and Hole in his second over. Statham, beating into the wind, supported him admirably and from 4 for 102 Australia were all out for 184, giving England victory by 38 runs. Tyson had taken 4 for 45 and 6 for 85, match figures 10 for 130 from 31.4 overs.

The mood within the England team had changed dramatically when Johnson returned as Australia's captain for the third Test in Melbourne from 31 December to 5 January. Miller immediately showed his displeasure over Australia's defeat at Sydney with a magnificent opening spell. At lunch on the first morning his figures were: 9 overs, 8 maidens, 5 runs, 3 wickets. Only two scoring strokes had been made against him as he sent back Hutton, Edrich and Compton. Lindwall got May for a duck and England were 4 for 41.

For two hours Bailey and Cowdrey held out this malevolent pace bowling while they added 74 runs, after which the two men of Kent, Cowdrey and Evans, combined to put on 54. The last four wickets fell for 22 runs. Cowdrey's 102

Les Favell, a no-nonsense opening batsman whose ability to hook and cut made him an Adelaide Oval favourite. He toured every cricket nation except England with Australian teams.

was an innings beyond praise against bowling of such hostility that England's total was restricted to 191.

Next day the grim contest between bat and ball unfolded as the bowlers again rescued England. Statham and Tyson got the openers Favell and Morris, Miller fell to a wonderful diving catch by Evans, and Hole was beaten for pace by a full toss. Len Maddocks, deputising as wicket-keeper for the injured Langley, went to the crease at 6 for 115 and by sensible batting remained until stumps when Australia were 8 for 188. England had bowled only 54 overs in the day compared with 67.6 by Australia the previous day. Spectators hooted when Hutton held three conferences with Statham in one over.

Apart from England's painfully slow over-rate the Australian batsmen endured periodic shooters that had previously been unknown so early on the second day on Melbourne's traditionally hard wicket. The players blamed it on soaring temperatures. When cracks appeared on it on Saturday afternoon, ground staff blamed an outside contractor who had been called in to help prepare the Test pitch. Throughout the Sunday rest day Australia sweltered under a heat wave and temperatures reached 116 degrees Fahrenheit. Bushfires in Victoria's western districts destroyed 14 homes and on the Melbourne Cricket Ground, where the temperature was more than 41°C (106°F), the ground staff pondered over what to do about the cracks that now looked like bringing the match to a quick end. Thousands slept on the beaches to escape the heat on Melbourne's hottest recorded night.

On Monday morning when Ian Johnson and his deputy Arthur Morris inspected the pitch to decide on which roller to use they were shocked to discover the scarred, cracked pitch was smooth and clean like a fresh wicket. Johnson scratched the edge with his boots and said: "This pitch has been watered, Arthur." They agreed to remain silent about what they had seen but reported it to Board of Control secretary Jack Ledward.

Players from both teams were amazed that cracks in the pitch, which should have widened in Sunday's heat, were smaller than on Saturday. By midday cables were on their way to Fleet Street. The *Daily Express* said: "Has anyone been monkeying with the pitch? If so, it is an illegal and horrifying act. We could have one of Test cricket's major scandals on our hands."

Sitting in the press box covering the match for the Melbourne *Age*, former Victorian captain Percy Beames knew what had happened to the pitch. Jack House, a crony from Beames' years as an Australian Rules footballer, had watered the pitch for fear it would not last out the match. For hours Beames agonised over his loyalty to his friend and the loyalty he owed his paper. Finally the *Age* disclosed that the pitch had been illegally watered without naming the culprit.

Vernon Ransford, secretary of the Melbourne Cricket Club, said he was confident that neither Jack House, who had charge of the preparation of the pitch, nor the curator, Bill Vanthoff, or any of their staff had watered the pitch. Security guards had stood watch over the pitch from the time it was vacated on Saturday afternoon until play began on Monday. Neither they nor the cleaners working in the stands saw anyone watering the wicket. Ransford added: "The honour of the Melbourne Cricket Club is at stake. I am bewildered and worried. I intend to confer with the Melbourne Cricket Club president Dr McClelland about an inquiry."

The captains agreed to continue the match while inquiries were under way. Members of the Board of Control discussed whether they should offer to replay the Test if Australia won. Statutory declarations from House and Vanthoff swearing that the pitch had not been watered were produced, along with a scientific opinion that the pitch had sweated under the covers and then dried to a hard crust. The VCA and Melbourne Cricket Club inquiry later "emphatically denied" the watering claim, but nobody who inspected the pitch ever took the denials seriously.

The shooters that had bedevilled Australia's batsmen disappeared when England began its second innings and after Hutton and Edrich had cleared the arrears May played a masterly knock for 91. Bailey held the middle order together for 165 minutes and Wardle and Evans profited from some hefty swings, leaving England on 279, and Australia to score 240 to win. At the end of the fourth day Australia were 2 for 75.

The experts predicted that Appleyard's spin would be Australia's big problem on the fifth morning, but Tyson and Statham made nonsense of that by sweeping aside the Australian batsmen in only 75 minutes, the last eight wickets falling for 35 runs. Tyson's 6.3 overs brought 6 for 16, Statham's 6 overs 2 for 19 and England won by 128 runs. All of the Australian batsmen agreed that in taking 9 for 95 in the match Tyson bowled faster than any bowler they had ever encountered. With England 2–1 up, Hutton was asked if he had any protest to make about the watering of the pitch. "Actually, I think it helped us," he said.

The fourth Test at Adelaide from 28 January to 2 February provided another stirring contest. McDonald, who replaced Favell, gave Australia a 59-run start with Morris, in temperatures around 38° C (100° F), which restricted Statham and Tyson to short spells. Steady, accurate bowling had Australia on 8 for 229 when Maddocks and Johnson put on 92 for the ninth wicket. Maddocks followed his 47 in Melbourne with 69 not out in Australia's 323.

England took an 18-run first innings lead by scoring 341 after a tense duel between Hutton, Cowdrey and Compton and the leg spin of Benaud and the off spin of Johnson. Hutton and Cowdrey put on 99 in 165 minutes before Hutton was out to a freakish catch at short leg for 80.

Hutton gave Statham only two overs when Australia batted a second time, and on a pitch unfavourable to pace he brought on Appleyard, who exploited the worn patches caused by the bowlers' footmarks to dismiss Morris, Burke and Harvey in six overs. Appleyard appeared so dominant newspapers forecast that he would be unplayable next day, but Appleyard did not bowl another ball. Instead Statham and Tyson routed the Australians, the last six wickets falling for 42 runs. *Wisden* noted that in 90 minutes before

lunch Statham and Tyson won the match without bowling a single bouncer.

Set to score only 94 to win, England stumbled momentarily against some fearsome bowling by Miller, who dismissed Hutton, Edrich and Cowdrey in three overs for 12 runs. Then Miller held a spectacular catch to get rid of May with 41 runs still required. But without Lindwall, who missed the match through injury, Miller lacked the support needed to bring off a total collapse. Bailey steadied the innings with Compton and England won by five wickets.

Assessing England's first series win in Australia since the 1932–33 Bodyline tour, Hutton said the variable bounce from Australian pitches had made fast bowlers very difficult to face. He praised spectators' patience when England bowled so few overs in a day. "Fast bowlers must take their time, and as youngsters they needed my help in placing their fields," he said.

The Keith-Miller-for-Test-captain lobby gained strength when New South Wales brought off the major surprise of the season by defeating England in Sydney from 18 to 22 February by 45 runs. Left to score 315 to win, England managed 269 in the final innings against a varied and enthusiastic attack splendidly handled by Miller. When May and Hutton looked threatening in a 77-run stand, Miller put the issue beyond doubt by uprooting May's stumps.

Appalling floods which caused lives to be lost and did millions of pounds of damage delayed the start of the fifth Test in Sydney from 25 February to 3 March, until after lunch on the fourth day and cut the MCC tour profits by around £8000. The delay gave England's long list of injured players time to recover but in the 13 hours available a draw was inevitable.

Australia introduced Willie Watson and Peter Burge to Test cricket. Both had been named among the 16 players due to go off to the West Indies a week after the Test ended. Graveney became the 100th player to score a century in England–Australia Tests with his innings of 111 in England's total of 371. Bailey allowed himself to be bowled for 72 to give Lindwall 100 wickets in Tests against England. Australia's 221 in reply enabled England to enforce the follow-on for the first time since 1938 when Hutton made his 364 at The Oval. Time ran out with Australia 6 for 118 in the second innings, but by then Tyson's 28 Test wickets at 20.82 had made him a national hero. England's 22 matches in Australia attracted 1,108,923 spectators who paid £A185,203 to watch them. They lost only two matches, scored 17 centuries and had only four scored against them.

England went off to New Zealand for four matches, including two Tests which they won, leaving critics condemning the Australian Test side as the worst since 1912, when six famous players refused to join the tour to England on the Board's terms. Arthur Morris defended Australia's performance in an article he wrote headed "Blame the Yawns on Hutton", which said:

> *England's time-wasting tactics are best defined as the art of doing anything one can think of to interrupt the normal progress of a cricket match. Meandering between overs, unnecessary field changing, mid-wicket conferences as often as possible, the bowler waiting for the ball to be returned before leisurely walking back to start his run, dawdling from one position to another. The aim of the tactics is to provoke the opposition to take risks, to irritate and tempt the most patient batsmen into errors.*

Morris named Bailey as willing accessory to Hutton's time-wasting policy and added:

> *If there were 22 Trevor Baileys playing in a match, who would ever go and watch it? There would never be any more tours if the money had to come from such matches.*

New South Wales won the Sheffield Shield in a summer in which this competition took second place to England's tour, with the

Neil Harvey, who made most runs (1009) in the 1954–55 Shield season.

programme cut from 16 to 9 matches. Western Australia played only two matches, both against South Australia, and the other States four each in a move to reduce financial losses. Rising young players had their opportunities severely reduced and the task of State and Australian selectors became more complicated.

John Rutherford headed the Shield averages by scoring a century for Western Australia in both their matches against South Australia. Rutherford averaged 68.40, whereas Neil Harvey who made most runs (1009) averaged 45.80. Pat Crawford, the New South Wales right-arm fast bowling discovery, headed the Shield bowling averages with 35 wickets at 12.96.

Keith Miller's captaincy of New South Wales in their victory over England and his leadership in the State's fifth Shield win in nine post-war seasons earned him the vice-captaincy of the Australian team for the first-ever tour of the West Indies ahead of Morris, but it should have got him the captaincy. The Australians set off for the Caribbean knowing they had to rehabilitate themselves after the severe drubbing by England. Their captain, Ian Johnson, faced the biggest trial of all, with only nine first-class matches, including five Tests, in which to prove himself worthy of the job.

Caribbean Comeback

First Australian tour of the West
Indies 1955; domestic cricket
1955-56; Australia in England 1956

Cricket began in the group of beautiful islands
scattered across the Gulf of Mexico around the
same time it arrived in Australia. Clubs formed
by aristocratic plantation-owners and sustained
by large European coffee, sugar, and oil
companies date back at least to 1806 when St
Anne's Cricket Club was founded in Barbados.
But even after slavery was abolished in 1833 white
players dominated and usually led the islands'
teams.

Inter-island matches and occasional visits
from English teams under Lord Hawke and
Pelham Warner helped boost cricket's appeal and
improve its administration. In 1900, a West Indian
team was formed under the captaincy of H. B.
G. Austin, a middle-order batsman who was the
son of the Bishop of the West Indies, to visit
England for a series of non-first-class matches.
When Austin went off to fight for the Empire
in the Boer War, R. S. A. Warner, elder brother
of Pelham, took over the leadership.

One of the side was a coloured right-hand

*A fascinating shot of Ray Lindwall's umbrella field
during the first Test on the 1956 tour. He is bowling to
Peter Richardson who made 81 and 73 in his Test debut.*

batsman named Lebrun Samuel Constantine, know as "Old Con". On the morning the team left "Old Con" was found wandering about by friends who discovered he did not have the money to join the tour. They had a whip-round and chartered a launch that got him to the boat just as it moved out to sea. Constantine made the first West Indian century in England against MCC at Lord's.

Between the wars some notable players emerged from the islands, batsmen like George Challenor and the great George Headley, bowlers like George John and George Francis and all-rounder Learie Constantine, "Old Con's" son. They laid the foundations but it was not until after the Second World War that cricket took hold of the 20-odd-million people in the islands with an intensity that shaped their lives as well as their leisure. Finer points of cricket law, mannerisms of players, were the source of raging arguments.

By the time Ian Johnson, well briefed by the Department of Foreign Affairs, took the first Australian team there in 1955 for three months of island-hopping, black and coloured men had largely replaced whites in West Indian teams and were supported by fervent, vociferous crowds to whom cricket was a second religion. The Australians had a marvellous time by joining them in the bar every chance they got, even though the grounds were little better than Australian suburban council fields.

Bottle-throwing spectators, upset by umpiring decisions, had given Hutton's MCC team a torrid time the previous year, making white West Indians fear for the future of international tours. Attacks on the families of umpires, Fred Trueman's over-reaction to crowd abuse, the no-balling of Tony Lock for throwing, all contributed to a tour of unsurpassed rancour. Fraternisation with the blacks upset many wealthy whites in the islands but for Johnson's players it turned out to be the way to prevent disturbances.

Johnson found himself in a similar position to Bill Woodfull in 1934 when Woodfull had to re-establish goodwill lost in the Bodyline tour. Unlike the cautious, reticent Woodfull, he met the challenge by taking coloured pressmen into his confidence and sharing the problems with them from the moment the Australians arrived in Kingston, Jamaica, for the start of the tour. Johnson said:

As we reached the airport reception centre we were besieged by a crowd of English reporters who had flown out to witness what they thought would be a holocaust. They were plying us with questions when I spotted a group of West Indian pressmen about a cricket pitch away.

I grabbed Keith Miller and whispered that the West Indians were more important to us than the Poms, who were just after sensation. The West Indian reporters conveyed our friendliness to their readers and told them to forget the White Australia policy. We were off to a wonderful start.

The crowds were extremely volatile. They'd laugh their heads off one minute and next be crying for your blood. The important thing was when they abused you not to show resentment. You had to laugh with them, not at them. By doing so you could change their hot temper to genuine friendship. The tour was the most successful ever undertaken by an Australian team and it was certainly the most enjoyable any of us were ever on.

The team was chosen by Bradman, Jack Ryder and Dudley Seddon, who were largely unaware of conditions in the West Indies, but concentrated on picking a well-balanced outfit. They were fortunate in their appointment of T. J. Burge, Peter Burge's father, as manager, for his long experience in dealing with cricketers and officials in Queensland proved invaluable. The team was I. W. Johnson (captain), 36, K. R. Miller (vice-captain), 35, R. G. Archer, 21, R. Benaud, 24, P. J. P Burge, 22, A. K. Davidson, 25, L. E. Favell, 25, R. N. Harvey, 26, J. C. Hill, 31, W. A. Johnston, 33, G. R. Langley, 35, R. R. Lindwall,

33, C. C. McDonald, 26, L. V. Maddocks, 28, A. R. Morris, 33, W. J. Watson, 24.

On the lovely island of Jamaica before cricket's most hyperactive fans Australia took command from the start of the first Test from 26 to 31 March at Sabina Park, Kingston. McDonald and Morris began with a stand of 102, Harvey (133) scored his 13th Test century, and Miller chimed in with a powerful 147 on a pitch so hard and well-rolled it threw up reflections. Harvey's stand with Miller put on 224 for the third wicket. Chasing Australia's 9 for 515 declared, Clyde Walcott gave a plucky display in scoring 108 for the West Indies, but they could not recover from losing 5 for 101.

Following on 256 behind, the West Indies fared well while John Holt and Collie Smith were at the crease. Smith, a happy, laughing figure, hooked and drove with a freedom that was instinctive to make a century (104) in his Test debut, which included 14 fours. Holt left the scene without complaint when he was given out caught behind by Maddocks off Benaud. A year earlier when Holt was given out lbw to Statham in the Test on the same pitch against England, spectators assaulted umpire Perry Burke's wife and child in protest at the decision.

With the last six West Indians departing for only 66 runs, Australia scored the 20 runs needed to win for the loss of Morris's wicket. All the Australian pace bowlers relished the fast brown pitch and the hot sun, but Benaud struck the most telling blow when he caught and bowled Weekes.

As the players left the field after this match, Johnson picked up a tiny barefoot brown boy and carried him off the field in his arms, talking with him about the game. The Jamaicans were delighted, pressing near to eavesdrop.

Clyde Walcott became the first West Indian to score a century in each innings of a Test in the drawn second Test at Port of Spain, Trinidad, from 11 to 16 April. The gates had to be closed before this match started, with every tree and every seat in the stand packed with talkative fans. The crowd of 28,000 was the biggest ever to watch a match in the West Indies to that time. On the second day Weekes, right back to his best, helped Walcott put on 242, a record for any West Indian wicket in Tests against Australia. Weekes hit a six and 24 fours in his 139, Walcott 17 fours in 126 and West Indies reached 382. Lindwall's remarkable competitive qualities enable him to survive this mauling to finish with 6 for 95. The last five wickets fell for 27 runs, four of them to Lindwall.

McDonald and Morris retaliated with an opening stand of 191 for Australia, with the West Indies trying nine bowlers, including the 18-year-old Garfield St Aubrun Sobers who was playing his second Test after his debut at 17 against England. McDonald made 110, Morris 111 before Harvey completed his second century of the series, 133. Archer and Johnson then savaged the West Indian bowling in a display of hitting that carried Australia to a lead of 218, Johnson declaring at nine for 600. Archer's 84 included a six and 12 fours.

The West Indies took the lead for the loss of only two wickets. Walcott hit another bold century in just under two hours, adding 127 with Weekes, who was 87 not out when time ran out. Walcott's 110 included 13 fours. This was the first Test played on grass in Trinidad, where Tests previously had been played on jute matting, and it produced 1255 runs for the loss of 23 wickets.

Johnson had the satisfaction of clinching an eight-wicket win for his team in the third Test, from 26 to 29 April at the Bourda ground, Georgetown, British Guiana, with a canny bowling performance in the final innings. His 7 for 44 from 22.2 overs were the best figures for a Test on the ground to that time, and made the rubber safe.

West Indies succumbed to Australia's pace bowlers to be 5 for 86 at lunch on the first day. Weekes tried hard to revive the innings, but when he left for 81 Benaud caused another slump by

Two brilliant West Indian players the Australians encountered for the first time on the 1955 tour by the West Indies, Garfield Sobers (left) and Lance Gibbs. Both were to break many records.

taking four wickets from 23 deliveries for 15 runs. Australia lost half their wickets in passing the West Indies' 182 and only a hard-hitting 68 from Benaud brought a 75-run lead. Three wickets fell for 25 runs when West Indies batted again and a 125-run stand by Walcott and Worrell was not enough to save them.

The fourth Test at Bridgetown in Barbados from 14 to 20 May saw brilliant batting from both sides and some tense moments in the Australian dressing-room. Australia made the game safe by scoring 668 in the first innings after a breezy opening stand of 108 by McDonald and Favell. Miller hit 22 fours in his 137, adding 206 for the sixth wicket with Archer, who was

bowled by Worrell just two short of his century. Lindwall then hit his second Test century, 118, with two sixes and 15 fours.

West Indies slumped to 6 for 146 and an Australian win appeared likely when Miller dismissed Weekes and Collie Smith in one over. Johnson immediately took Miller off, one of the worst bowling changes ever. Atkinson and Depeiza put on a Test record of 347 for the seventh wicket. Atkinson made 219, including a six and 26 fours, Depeiza 122.

At one point during this stand Lindwall was reluctant to bowl when Johnson offered him the ball. Miller intervened and said, "If he doesn't want to bowl, he shouldn't have to." Annoyed at this, Johnson insisted on his captain's right to say who bowled. In the dressing room at the end of an unproductive day, Miller told Johnson he could not captain a team of schoolboys. Understandably Johnson objected to being rebuked in front of his side and he offered to settle the disagreement with Miller outside with his fists. Other players stepped between them and after tempers cooled Johnson and Miller returned to their hotel in the same car.

When Australia batted a second time, with

a lead of 158, Holt at third slip dropped McDonald and Lindwall off Tom Dewdney, and Archer off Worrell before they had scored. Spectators were so angry at Holt's clumsiness he needed police protection when the players came off. The courts had just sentenced popular cricketer Leslie Hylton to death for the murder of his wife in a case followed throughout the West Indies and next morning a placard appeared at the ground "Save Hylton, Hang Holt".

Favell batted cleverly for 53 and Johnson showed no after-effects of his altercation with Miller in scoring 57 to lift Australia to 249 and the West Indian target to 408 with only 230 minutes left. West Indies were 6 for 234 thanks to Walcott's 83 when an eventful match petered out in a draw.

On one flight between islands Johnson persuaded the pilot to let him take the controls. Although Johnson was an experienced pilot, the Board of Control were not amused when reports of this flight reached Melbourne. They fired back a cable to manager Burge, who was ill in bed, instructing him to prevent team members piloting aircraft. Henceforth a clause appeared in Board contracts for overseas tours banning players from flying any aircraft in which they travelled. Visions of insurance claims the Board would attract in the event of a crash were enough to give Board members apoplexy.

Australia completed a triumphant tour with a magnificent batting display in the fifth Test at Kingston, where the total of 8 for 758 declared was the second highest in international history. The West Indies began badly, losing 2 for 13, but recovered to reach 357 through a fighting 155 by Walcott. Five Australians made centuries after a similarly poor start. From 2 for 7, McDonald and Harvey put on 295 for the third wicket. McDonald made 127 but Harvey stayed until he had 204 and Australia was ahead. Miller (109), Archer (128) and Benaud (121) then flogged a tired attack before Johnson declared when Benaud was out, having reached his century in

only 78 minutes and hitting a total of 2 sixes and 15 fours.

With Australia 401 ahead, three West Indies wickets fell for 65 runs before Walcott checked the collapse by scoring his second century (110) of the match and his fifth in the rubber. He had stylish support from Sobers who stayed while 179 runs were added but Australia won by an innings and 82 runs. Miller followed his century by taking 8 for 165 with the ball.

The Australians scored 15 centuries on the tour, with Miller and Harvey contributing three each in the Tests. They had 13 centuries scored against them, including five by Walcott, and two each by Smith and Weekes. Harvey had a Test average of 108.33 and his 204 was the highest score on either side. Walcott averaged 82.70. The difference in the teams was clearly shown in the bowling statistics. Australia had five bowlers who took 11 wickets or more, the West Indies only one, Atkinson (with 13 victims at 35.30), who secured more than ten wickets. Four Australians scored more than 500 runs in the nine first-class matches. Hill topped the first-class bowling averages for Australia with 18 wickets at 21.11, but Lindwall took most wickets, 28 at 28.85.

The first-ever West Indian tour by Australia was a triumph for Ian Johnson, who apart from leading an unbeaten team set new ground rules for captains. He took his players out to meet the local people and at official receptions and lunches was reminiscent of Hassett at his best. On the field he turned in solid performances with both bat and ball, averaging 47.75 an innings in the Tests and taking 14 wickets at 29.00, including the match-winning 7 for 33 in the third Test, and was even able to shrug off his dressing-room clash with Miller. He said:

I come from a tough school, having been brought up on Victoria versus New South Wales matches. These matches are the toughest in the world, bitter affairs in which bumpers fly and curses are exchanged. Nobody is spared, but as soon as stumps are drawn both teams gather in one or other of the dressing rooms, drink a few beers together, and laugh about what has taken place. The players remain the best of cobbers until play starts the next morning. Then the gloves come off, the bitterness and intensity start all over again. We enjoy it.

Johnson received very little praise at home for his showing in the West Indies and his former team-mate Sid Barnes became the most scathing of a group of critics scornful of Johnson's prowess as a player. Johnson took it all without complaint, knowing that having Barnes as your critic was probably helpful among the true power-brokers of Australian cricket.

For Arthur Morris, one of Johnson's co-selectors on the West Indian tour, the homecoming brought tragic news. While he was away, his wife of less than a year had been diagnosed as having cancer. She had not told him, for fear of upsetting his cricket, but on hearing the news Morris retired from cricket, electing to accept an offer to cover the 1956 Australian tour of England for a London newspaper. Valerie Morris died 18 months later.

Morris had begun in Sydney grade cricket as a left-arm spin bowler but in 46 Tests he had opened for Australia in 77 of his 79 innings, scoring 3533 runs at 46.48, and bowled only 111 balls for two wickets and 50 runs. He ranks with Clem Hill, Joe Darling, Vernon Ransford, Neil Harvey, Bill Lawry and Allan Border among the greatest Australian left-handed batsmen, and is still the only Australian to score a century in each innings of his initial first-class match. In all first-class matches he made 12,614 runs at 53.67 and scored 46 centuries, 12 of them in Tests. Above all, he is remembered for his unflappable temperament and his goodwill to his fellow cricketers. There are no nasty stories about Morris, only sympathy for his ill-luck in losing four years out of his career during the war and the tragedy that forced his retirement at 33.

Aubrey Oxlade died in Sydney in September

1955, a few days before he was due to be re-elected for another term as chairman of the Australian Board of Control. He had been a member of the Manly club in Sydney since 1905, of the New South Wales Cricket Association since 1910, had served on the NSWCA's executive committee for 45 years, and was awarded the CBE in 1934 for his role in settling the Bodyline crisis. Frank Cush was appointed chairman of the Board in Oxlade's place and the talkative Sydney Queen's Counsel Syd Webb was appointed to fill the vacancy on the New South Wales executive.

The 1955–56 season in Australia was devoted

Former schoolmates in the then impoverished Sydney suburb of Waterloo — one-time Governor-General Sir William McKell, right, and legendary spin bowler Arthur Mailey. Seen here relaxing on the Sydney Hill during Mailey's testimonial match in 1956.

solely to the Sheffield Shield competition without interference from an overseas team. The Melbourne Cricket Ground was closed so that it could be prepared for the 1956 Olympic Games and Melbourne's Shield matches were held at St Kilda Oval.

New South Wales sustained their splendid winning sequence by winning the Sheffield Shield for the third successive year. They won two of their seven matches outright, three on the first innings and had one draw, conceding first innings points only to Queensland, who had their first success in Sydney for 20 years under the captaincy of Lindwall. Queensland did New South Wales a favour by beating Victoria on the first innings in Brisbane, which put Victoria out of the reckoning for the Shield.

Miller again dominated the headlines. At Sydney in the match against South Australia between 18 and 21 November he threw the ball to Davidson to open the bowling on the second morning after New South Wales had declared at 8 for 215. Miller felt that the breeze from the Randwick end, which he liked to use to swing the ball, was missing. Before Davidson could mark out his run, a breeze sprang up which ruffled Miller's famous mop of black hair. He immediately called for the ball and in a sustained spell of accuracy and late swing took seven wickets for 12 runs, the best ever bowling analysis in a Shield match.

Davidson, who had had the ball in his hand ready to bowl, did not deliver a ball and South Australia were dismissed for 27, the lowest total in an inter-state match for 72 years and the smallest ever Shield total. Three of the four batsmen Miller clean-bowled—Favell, Hole and Langley—were Test players.

Mainly because of 69 by the former New South Wales batsman Colin Pinch, South Australia made 252 in their second innings, with Benaud taking 6 for 76, but New South Wales only needed 65 to win outright. Benaud was highly impressive throughout the summer,

spending long hours at the practice nets to consolidate the improvement he had made over the previous two years with both bat and ball.

Miller fell while running between wickets in the match against Queensland in Sydney between 31 December and 4 January and pulled a back muscle. The injury and the fact that he would be expected to carry a big workload in England in 1956 caused selectors to rest him from the testimonial match for Arthur Mailey and Johnny Taylor at Sydney from 13 to 17 January, between sides captained by Johnson and Lindwall. This was the official trial for the 1956 tour of England and resulted in Mailey and Taylor receiving £A3590 each. Mailey wore a lounge suit as he sent down a ball to Taylor during a lunch break. The ball knocked down Taylor's stumps. "Probably should always have bowled with a coat on," said Mailey as he came off.

This was a happy occasion for patrons of the famous Sydney Hill, with Mailey and his former schoolmaster Billy McKell, later Governor-General of Australia, sprawled out among them on the grass. Mailey pointed to a spot where he and McKell had climbed through a hole in the wall to get in free when they were barefoot boys. Here through the years between the wars Australia's most celebrated cricket spectator, Stephen Harold Gasgoigne, otherwise known as "Yabba", had held court. "Yabba" died in 1942 at the age of 64, a horny-handed man who could skin a rabbit in less time than it took Miller to run in to bowl. His voice remains a poignant memory for it carried from the midst of the beer-swilling pie-eaters on the Hill right across the ground and could be clearly heard in the Members' Stand.

John Rutherford made a long journey to play in the Mailey-Taylor testimonial, finding his way to Perth airport with difficulty after a car smash and treating his cuts and bruises on the 3000-mile flight, to stake his claim in the touring team. He made 113, the most significant of his six first-class centuries, and it made him the first Western

The 1956 Australian team to England: (L to R) (back) N. Gorman (baggage master), I. D. Craig, K. D. Mackay, J. W. Burke, W. P. A. Crawford, P. J. P. Burge, L. V. Maddocks, J. W. Rutherford, J. W. Wilson, A. James (masseur); (front) W. J. Dowling (manager), R. G. Archer, G. R. Langley, R. R. Lindwall, I. W. Johnson (captain), K. R. Miller, R. N. Harvey, R. Benaud, C. C. McDonald, W. L. Rush (assistant manager), (inset) A. K. Davidson.

Australian to be chosen for an Australian touring team.

The twenty-second Australian team to England undertook one of the longest tours on record from 1 April to 8 November 1956. They played two matches in Tasmania and one in Perth before an itinerary of 31 matches in England, and on the way home visited India and Pakistan for four more Tests. Morris accompanied the team as a commentator, using the fees from this to pay for his wife's medical bills. Miller hesitated for weeks about touring because of his painful back injury but finally decided to go. Pat Crawford accepted an offer to play Lancashire League cricket in 1956, but pulled out of that agreement when he won selection in the touring party, which was I. W. Johnson (captain), 37,

K. R. Miller (vice-captain), 36, R. G. Archer, 22, R. Benaud, 25, P. J. P. Burge, 23, G. R. Langley, 36, R. R. Lindwall, 34, C. C. McDonald, 27, J. W. Burke, 25, I. D. Craig, 20, W. P. A. Crawford, 22, A. K. Davidson, 26, R. N. Harvey, 27, K. D. Mackay, 29, L. V. Maddocks, 29, J. W. Rutherford, 26, and J. W. Wilson, 33, with Bill Dowling as manager and Norman Gorman as scorer–baggage master.

Despite his success in the West Indies the previous year Johnson faced big problems as leader of a team that combined fading heroes and youngsters who had not managed the jump from Shield to Test cricket. The spinners in the team lacked Test quality and it was evident from the start that Australia would have to depend on pace bowling to win important matches. Everyone who mixed with the team was struck by the low morale and spirit compared with that of the 1948 and 1953 sides to England. The nub of the problem was that Johnson in the twilight of his career was not worth his place in the side as a player.

The advantage Australia enjoyed when their captains were chosen on ability and English team captains because they went to the right schools and universities, had gone. Peter May, who had succeeded Hutton as England's captain, had gone to the right schools but he was also a brilliant player. Hutton had quit at 39 with 120 first-class centuries behind him, but he never did qualify to have his initials printed with his name in some English papers and as a pro was never honoured with the captaincy of Yorkshire though he had led England 23 times.

The infectious friendliness of English crowds and players so obvious in 1948 had disappeared. County teams no longer fielded their strongest possible teams against Australia, often resting star players so they could concentrate on county championship matches, but advance bookings for the Tests were still heavy and showed no decline in interest. With a team that included six players on their first tour, Johnson could not be blamed for not chasing early wins. He tried instead to give every man a chance and to play his key men into form for the Tests.

Miller swings a ball to leg for Australia against Sussex at Hove in 1956. Many believed he should have captained the side in place of Johnson who was well past his best.

Australia made an ideal start to the tour by dismissing Worcestershire for 90 at Worcester. For the rest of the three days, 2 to 4 May, Australia outplayed Worcestershire, taking a 348 lead by scoring 438 in the first tour innings, and then sweeping aside the early batsmen in Worcestershire's second innings. With defeat imminent at 5 for 99, Peter Richardson led a long Worcestershire fight-back by batting 5 hours 20 minutes for 130 not out. Three wickets in the last 20 minutes was not enough to give Australia victory and the match ended in a draw with Worcestershire on 9 for 231.

Johnson drew severe criticism in the second tour match from 5 to 8 May against Leicestershire by using the whole of the last two days for batting practice. His bowlers had Leicestershire out for 298 on the first day, but Johnson made no attempt to force a win. Australia used up the remaining time in scoring 6 for 694. Burke made 123, Mackay 58, Miller 281 not out, Burge 99, and Archer 88, and after lunch on the third day, when no declaration came, the crowd hooted Johnson all round the ground. Miller's innings was the highest of his career and took six and a half hours. He hit 1 six, 1 five, and 35 fours.

Surrey became the first county for 44 years to beat Australia between 16 and 18 May at The Oval. Johnson acknowledged Surrey's superiority by presenting the Surrey captain Stuart Surridge with his cap. The match evolved into an intriguing duel between the off spin of Laker and the off spin of Johnson.

Jumping in his delivery stride to gain added height from his extended arm action, Laker dug the ball into the pitch too sharply for the Australians to play him on the half-volley, and took all ten wickets for 88 runs in Australia's first innings of 259. This was the first time a bowler had taken all ten wickets against Australia since 1878 when another Surrey player, Edward D'Oyley Barratt, did it for the Players.

Johnson bowled for most of the Surrey innings of 347, but it was soon clear that his technique of looping the ball up at the batsman, well flighted though deliveries were, did not achieve the results that Laker managed. Johnson's 60.3 overs brought 6 for 168 with the Surrey top-order batsmen able to pick the balls to punish. Laker took 16 from one Johnson over, including a six and two fours.

In Australia's second innings, the last nine wickets added only 51 runs. Lock took the first six wickets for 40 runs and finished with 7 for 49, turning the ball at a brisk pace and occasionally getting one to lift awkwardly. Surrey's smart catching hastened Australia's collapse for 107. Surrey took 55 minutes to make the 20 runs needed for an historic victory.

Mackay and Rutherford got lost in the pavilion when they left the Australian dressing room to open against the MCC at Lord's between 26 and 29 May. They walked up and down corridors and through doors without finding their way to the field. Finally they spotted daylight and got out on to the ground several minutes late by jumping the fence about 40 metres from the players' gate.

Mackay was out at 4 but Rutherford stayed to help Harvey put on 282 for the second wicket. Rutherford was out for 98, but Harvey went on to 225, including 2 sixes and 33 fours. Most of the batsmen who followed threw away their wickets chasing quick runs and Australia slumped from 5 for 381 to all out for 413. Fred Titmus, the Middlesex off spinner who had taken 191 county wickets at 16.31 the previous year, again demonstrated Australia's weakness against spin by taking 5 for 130 from 45.1 overs. Archer dismissed Simpson, Milton, Graveney and Cowdrey for 57 runs before rain ended the match, with MCC on 9 for 203. Archer, Davidson and Lindwall were all injured in this match and at one time Australia fielded three substitutes.

Australia reached the first Test at Nottingham from 7 to 12 June without a win over any of the first-class counties. Rain prevented a result despite two England declarations. Peter Richardson topscored in

John Rutherford and Ken Mackay finally get onto the field after losing their way in the labyrinth of corridors and rooms in the Lord's pavilion. They had to jump the fence.

England's innings of 217 with 81 in his Test debut, but apart from May, who made 73, the other batsmen disappointed against clever bowling by Miller, Archer and Davidson, who chipped an ankle bone in his tenth over. Laker, Lock and Appleyard shared the wickets in Australia's innings of 148, giving England a 69-run lead. A 151-run opening stand by Richardson (73) and Cowdrey (81) enabled England to declare at 3 for 188, but Australia never tried to score the 258 required to win in 240 minutes, and were content to survive.

The expatriate Australians Jock Livingston, George Tribe and John Manning combined with opening batsman Dennis Brookes to give Australia a hard time at Northampton from 13 to 15 June in the match with Northants. Brookes'

144 not out and a lovely 85 by Livingston allowed Northants to declare at 3 for 339. Tribe and Manning both had batsmen playing and missing with their left-arm spinners in Australia's innings of 314. Northants' second innings yielded 171, all but fifty of them scored by Livingston, Tribe and Manning. Left to score 197 in 78 minutes to win, Australia abandoned the attempt after losing four wickets.

Australia had her first Test win in England since 1948 by outplaying England with a fine team performance in the second Test from 21 to 26 June at Lord's. England were handicapped by the continued absence of Tyson through injury, but Statham was fit to join Trueman and Wardle replaced Lock. Mackay and Crawford made their Test debuts for Australia in place of Lindwall and Davidson, both injured.

Benaud's famous gully catch that dismissed Colin Cowdrey in the Lord's Test in 1956 off the bowling of "Slasher" Mackay.

Bad light interrupted play on the first day but three missed catches, all by May, allowed Australia to reach 3 for 180 by stumps. Next morning, with Statham and Trueman bowling very fast, the last seven Australian wickets fell for 105 runs. McDonald (78) and Burke (65) had looked an impressive opening pair but when they left only the gum-chewing Mackay, who took 160 minutes for his 38, showed sustained resistance.

Benaud, developing rapidly into a cricketer of stature, held a remarkable catch in the gully to dismiss Cowdrey and give Mackay his first Test victim. Benaud threw his hand up as he lost his footing to hold a full-blooded cut. When Johnson tried spin, Benaud sent back May and Evans. Miller and Archer returned with the new ball to finish off the innings for 171.

Leading by 114, Australia never lost their grip on the match, despite a lion-hearted effort from Trueman. Benaud produced a stirring show of judicious hitting. His 97 and a handy 31 from

Mackay lifted the total to 257 and set England 372 to win. Miller and Archer again combined to cut through the England batting, with May's 53 the only score over 30, and Australia won by 185 runs. Miller finished with 5 for 72 and 5 for 80. Langley set a Test record with nine dismissals in the match, five of them in England's second innings. Evans dismissed seven batsmen for England in a match that saw 21 wickets fall to catches behind the stumps.

At Bristol from 30 June to 2 July Australia secured a badly needed win by defeating Gloucestershire by an innings and 48 runs. The victory belonged to Jack Wilson, who took 12 for 61 on a sandy pitch ideal for his full-length spinners. Australia had struggled to make 216 against hostile spin from "Bomber" Wells before dismissing Gloucestershire for 44 and 124. Only Jack Crapp, with 35 in the second innings, made more than 20 for the losers.

Groundsmen raise a cloud of dust from an under-prepared pitch during the 1956 Test at Manchester in which Jim Laker took 19 wickets. Laker bowled superbly but the pitch was a disgrace.

Jimmy Burke scored two centuries against Somerset at Taunton between 4 and 6 July but the pitch was too good to produce a result. Burke's first innings of 138 took Australia to 5 declared for 340. Somerset replied with 275, thanks to former Australian Test star Colin McCool's 90. Australia declared in their second innings at 1 for 236 after Burke had made 125 not out and Craig 100 not out. McCool made up for his near-miss in the first innings by scoring 116 in Somerset's second innings of 5 for 234, giving both Johnson and Wilson a hammering. He hit 14 fours and 4 sixes.

Miller could not bowl in the third Test at Leeds from 12 to 17 July because of a knee injury. Lindwall returned, although his fitness was suspect, and Maddocks replaced the injured Langley. England gambled heavily by recalling Washbrook, who had not played in a Test since 1950–51 and was now 41. His appearance brought heavy criticism of the selectors but it was quickly silenced when Washbrook joined May at 3 for 17 on the first morning after Archer dismissed Richardson, Cowdrey and Oakman.

Four days before the match the Headingley

pitch had been under water, but as Washbrook and May put on 187 in 287 minutes it looked ideal for batting. Miller's inability to bowl assisted the recovery. May was on 101 when he hit a ball from Johnson to backward square leg where Lindwall dived and held up the ball, indicating he had caught it. May left immediately. Washbrook, who made 98 of England's 325, later asked May if he thought the ball had carried to the fieldsman. May replied, "I could not be sure but as the fieldsman was Lindwall I walked."

Bare patches had started to appear on the pitch when Australia batted and May quickly brought on Laker and Lock. Six wickets fell for 69 runs, 41 of them to Burke, before Miller and Benaud took the score to 142. The last three wickets added only one run. Following-on 182 behind, Australia relied on Miller's experience of turning wickets and Harvey's natural skill. Miller (26) batted for 2 hours 15 minutes, relying often on his exceptional reach, Harvey (69) for 4 hours 30 minutes, but once they left, England ran out winners by an innings and 42 runs. Laker had taken 5 for 58 and 6 for 55, Lock 4 for 41 and 3 for 40.

Australia journeyed to Manchester for the fourth Test with their vulnerability to spin exposed to all cricket buffs. It was a cruel period for Australian cricket, with the techniques that succeeded on sun-drenched, heavily rolled pitches sadly inadequate. England batted first on a strip that was studded with arid patches, despite persistent recent rain. At the first lunch break the groundsman created a small dust storm when he swept the pitch. Richardson and Cowdrey put on 174 for the first wicket, Sheppard and May 93, and at stumps England were 3 for 307. They carried on to 459, with Johnson's 47 overs costing 151 runs, a high price for four wickets on such a pitch.

Laker and Lock were in action 20 minutes after the start of Australia's innings and took 15 minutes to warm up. Eighty minutes later Australia were all out. After an opening stand of 48 by McDonald (32) and Burke (22), Australia managed a total of only 84 runs. Lock had Burke caught in the gully by Cowdrey but the other nine wickets all went to Laker, whose 16.4 overs cost 37 runs.

The ball turned on a strip that blatantly assisted spin, but after his ten wickets in an innings in the Surrey match Laker had a psychological advantage over the Australians that was more important. Harvey hit a full toss straight into mid-wicket's hands after McDonald retired with knee problems early in Australia's second innings. Next day only 45 minutes play was possible, Australia losing Burke to a fine leg-side catch by Lock. On the Monday Craig and McDonald survived 19.2 overs. On the last day overnight rain gave the batsmen some respite from sharp spin until lunch, with Craig and McDonald together after batting for four hours.

The sun beat down on the pitch through the interval and when play resumed Laker had Craig lbw. Mackay, Miller and Archer went without scoring, Mackay without offering a stroke as he padded up to successive deliveries. McDonald went in the first over after tea for 89 after batting for 5 hours 37 minutes, and Laker took the last three wickets to finish with 10 for 53 and 19 for 90 in the match. Lock had bowled 55 overs in the second innings for 69 runs without taking a wicket and all 19 Laker wickets had fallen at the same end.

England won the match by an innings and 170 runs, retained the Ashes and ended an era for Australian cricket in emphatic style. The decline was complete. The players with records stretching back before the Second World War had done an outstanding job, but the time had come to rebuild Australia's national team.

Australia on the Mat

The 1956 Australians return home via
Pakistan and India;
domestic cricket 1956-57; Australia
tours New Zealand 1957

The Australian Board of Control were not overly
concerned at the fundamental weaknesses in
technique Laker exposed in their national team.
They were more interested in the 1956 tour's
financial return, which remained respectable at
£42,000, although only half the amount achieved
by Hassett's team three years earlier. When
financial forecasts fell below expectations, the
Board simply reduced cash distributions to the
State associations.

Australia had enjoyed a wonderful run since
the humiliation at The Oval in 1938 and in the
rapidly changing world of cricket still had the
best record of all nations who played the game.
Past experience had shown Australian cricket to
be remarkably resilient, with brilliant young
players emerging when needed.

The Board stuck with their policies by fining
Lindwall £50 and Miller £100 for syndicating

*Jim Laker's field in 1956 to left-hander Ken Mackay
shows how England benefitted from the sharply turning
Manchester pitch. Cowdrey, Oakman (who is about to
catch Mackay), Lock and May are all within a few
metres of the bat. The 'keeper is Evans.*

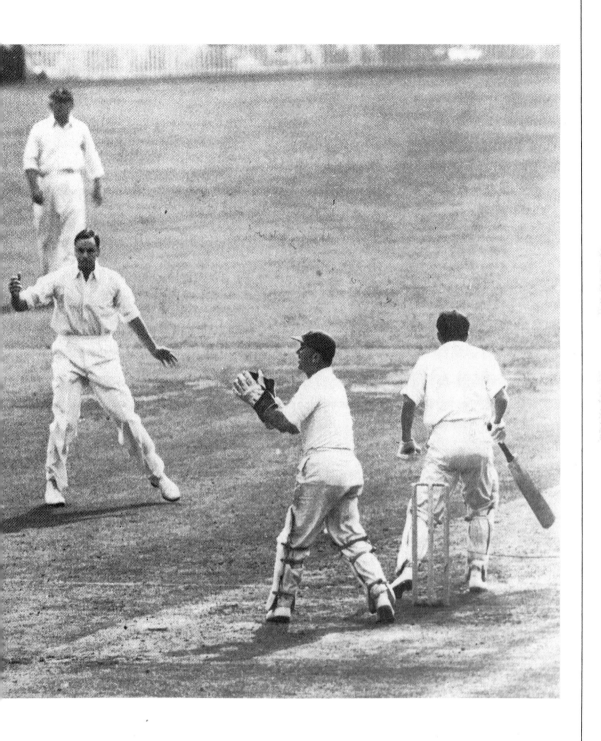

articles on the tour before they returned home, and barely giving a passing thought to how valuable Bruce Dooland, George Tribe, Jack Walsh, Colin McCool and others playing for English clubs would have been to the Test side. They were completely unperturbed that the Test team did not contain Australia's best cricketers.

There was no concern that cricket was losing its dominance in sports broadcasts with more and more stations expanding their coverage of tennis, surfing and golf. At a time when there was a boom in home tennis courts and a big increase in tennis coaching classes, the best cricket officials could provide as a counter was free admission to children after 4 p.m. at their grounds. The *Courier Mail*'s photographer who went to the 'Gabba to take photographs the day before a match was thrown out and a fashion writer from the same paper was denied entrance to the Members' Stand.

Fifty years after its formation, the Board had no national junior development programme, no plans to ensure coaches were qualified and no plans to develop its own grounds. Coaching in schools was left to masters seconded to the job by their headmasters, and in district clubs the fathers of small boys were often recruited to coach and organise travel for their sons' teams. Capital city ground improvements were left to State associations.

Australians took to the car as their main means of transport to Test match grounds in the 1950s, discarding trams and buses, but parking facilities at the grounds remained primitive. Most had to park in the back streets of nearby suburbs and walk to the ground. The marvel of it all was that so many continued to play the game despite such supine administration. The charm of the game still enthralled and people still appreciated that the game's standards of behaviour were a model for all of life.

James Charles Laker, born in 1922 at Frizinghall, Yorkshire, joined Surrey as a professional and became part of the fine team that was to win the English county championship for seven successive seasons from 1952. In what will always be known as "Laker's match", here are the main records he set at Manchester against Ian Johnson's Australian team:

- *His 19 wickets in the Test was a record for any first-class match, eclipsing the previous best of 17 wickets, which had been achieved 20 times.*

- *He produced a result in a Manchester Test for the first time since 1905.*

- *He became the first bowler to take all ten wickets in a Test innings, and the first to take all ten wickets twice in a season.*

- *By adding 19 wickets to the 20 he had taken in the three Tests previously played that summer, he equalled Alec Bedser's record of 39 victims in an England–Australia series, a figure he was to lift to 46 wickets by the end of the series, and which remains the record.*

Laker's feat did not pass without controversy. A group of Australian sportswriters obtained a signed affidavit from the groundsman in which he admitted that he had instructions to prepare a pitch that would take spin. The doyen of English cricket writers, E. W. Swanton, even urged an inquiry into English wicket preparation. Australian newspapers published photographs of Old Trafford groundsmen sweeping the pitch, resembling what Ray Robinson called "dim figures in a Sahara sand storm".

Johnson agreed that, in a summer in which Australia had only two good wickets to bat on in ten Test innings, something sinister had occurred; but he left it to reporters to speculate on groundsmen receiving instructions from Lord's about pitches that nullified Miller and Lindwall's pace and assisted Laker and Lock's spin. "When all the controversy and the side issues of the match are forgotten, Laker's wonderful bowling will remain," Johnson said.

Two things almost deprived Laker of his record-breaking ten wickets in Australia's second innings. Tony Lock repeatedly beat the bat during the innings but failed to get an edge, and rain that had interrupted the match held off just long enough for Laker to trap Len Maddocks lbw as his tenth victim. That night heavy rain fell across Manchester and next day not a single ball was bowled in any of England's first-class matches.

One of the days washed out was the first day of Australia's return match against Surrey, scheduled from 1 to 3 August at The Oval, with Australia due to face Laker and Lock again. When play began on the second day, Laker troubled all the batsmen except the left-hander Davidson, who was re-appearing after damaging his ankle in the first Test. Davidson showed surprising footwork for a bulky man and he hit both Laker and Lock for sixes and included 6 fours in a 50-minute innings of 44.

Despite Davidson's knock, Australia made only 143. Miller then deprived Surrey of whatever chance they had of repeating their earlier win over Australia by taking 5 for 84 in 35 fiery overs. After another interruption for rain, Surrey declared at 9 for 181, 38 runs ahead. Burke and Craig had no difficulty playing out time for a draw. Laker had added 5 for 58 to his season's bag.

Australia won their next three matches in succession in sunny weather on firm pitches. They defeated Glamorgan by an innings and 11 runs from 4 to 7 August at Swansea, where Mackay made 163 not out, Archer 148 and Wilson took 5 for 88 in the final innings; Warwickshire by an innings and 127 runs from 8 to 10 August at Birmingham, where Burke made 194, Harvey 145, and Benaud's match figures were 11 for 75; and Derbyshire by 57 runs from 11 to 14 August at Derby, where Lindwall had 7 for 40 in the first innings and Miller 5 for 29 in the second innings.

Rain forced a draw against Lancashire at Old Trafford from 15 to 17 August. Another swashbuckling innings by Davidson when Australia were bogged down set up a win from 18 to 21 August at Southend over Essex, who were beaten with 20 minutes to spare by an innings and 12 runs. Essex made 154 and 183, Australia 349. Davidson's 75 in a stand of 125 for the seventh wicket gave Australia their 195-run first innings lead.

The critics frequently told Johnson he was a passenger but he never raised the subject of his own place at meetings with fellow selectors Langley and Miller. Davidson returned for Mackay and Langley for Maddocks when the team for the fifth Test at The Oval between 23 and 28 August was named. Although England had retained the Ashes, Australia could have shared the series with a win.

Lindwall thrilled Australian supporters when he had Cowdrey caught behind off a late in-swinger to the fifth ball of the Test. But within twenty minutes rain flooded the ground and prevented any play for three days. Compton, back after an operation to remove his right knee cap, shared a 156-run stand with May when play resumed. From 3 for 221, England were out for 247, with Compton contributing 94, May 83.

Further rain upset Australia's first innings and on a treacherous pitch Johnson adopted stalling tactics. He was booed when he walked to the other end to pat down patches his partner had already flattened. Then he stopped play when sawdust blew out of the bowler's footmarks. Benaud joined in by repeatedly asking for the same block. Burke asked umpires about the light when a shaft of sunshine reflected from a stand. But it was Harvey who saved Australia by personally taking all the strike when Laker bowled. He kept it up for 2 hours 30 minutes and when the pitch improved, Miller and Benaud added 48, Miller and Lindwall 43, and Australia did well to get to within 45 runs of England's score.

Langley, who had aroused laughter when he split his pants and had the split closed with a large safety pin, went to hospital when a ball from Archer kicked viciously off a full length

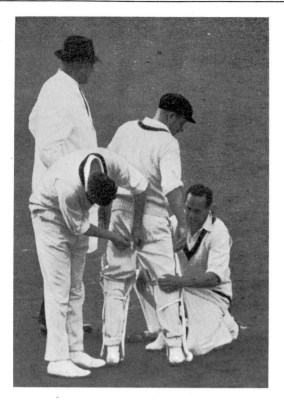

Miller and Johnson do some repair work on 'keeper Langley's trousers at Lord's in 1956, saving his dignity with a safety pin.

and hit him on the head. Davidson and Archer reverted to spinners but neither they nor Johnson and Burke were accurate and England declared their second innings closed at 3 for 182. Left to score 228 in 120 minutes to win, Australia opted for survival and the match was drawn with Australia on 5 for 27. Laker's 3 for 8 in the second

innings after his 4 for 80 in the first gave him 46 wickets in the Tests and 63 in seven matches against Australia that summer.

Australia were held to a draw by Scotland at Glasgow on 12 and 13 September because of a spectacular hundred by the Reverend J. A. Aitchison, the first Scotsman to make a century against Australia since John Kerr, of Greenock, made 147 in 1921. Kerr was in the crowd that watched Aitchison play strokes to every corner of the ground. The Australians were wholehearted in their applause for what they rated the best century against them all summer. Aitchison had five previous centuries for Scotland to his credit, including one against South Africa in 1947.

Johnson's Australian team had found victory harder to achieve than any side since 1926, when Herbie Collins' tourists surrendered the Ashes. *Wisden* published the table below to demonstrate the point.

None of these teams had the bad luck with injuries encountered by Johnson's team, which at one stage had 12 players in bandages, during the wettest English summer in memory. The idea of using Miller mainly as a batsman had to be scrapped when Davidson chipped an ankle bone and Lindwall pulled a leg muscle in the first Test. The effect of the weather and the injuries was shown in the batting statistics, with Australia completing a Test series for the first time without one batsman scoring a century.

Ten of the team made a total of 17 first-

Year	Captain	Played	Won	Drawn	Lost	Tie
1921	W. W. Armstrong	33	21	10	2	—
1926	H. L. Collins	33	9	23	1	—
1930	W. M. Woodfull	31	11	18	1	1
1934	W. M. Woodfull	30	13	16	1	—
1938	D. G. Bradman	30	15	12	2	—
1948	D. G. Bradman	31	23	8	0	—
1953	A. L. Hassett	31	16	16	1	—
1956	I. W. Johnson	31	9	19	3	—

class centuries but only Burke, McDonald and Mackay scored 1000 runs on the tour. Harvey was the biggest disappointment, with 976 runs in first-class matches at 31.48, compared with his aggregate of 2040 in 1953 at 65.80. In 1953, he made ten centuries, in 1956 two.

Mackay headed the Australian batting averages with 1103 runs at 52.52, but he also brought disgrace on Australian batsmanship when he attempted to play Laker in the Manchester Test without using his bat, reasoning that he could survive by continually padding up. Arthur Mailey was so disgusted at this he left the team and returned to London to visit friends. "They are too bad to watch," said Mailey.

Miller topped the bowling averages with 50 wickets at 19.60, but Archer took most wickets with 61 at 22.18. They also were the best bowlers in the Tests, Miller taking 21 wickets at 22.23, Archer 18 at 25.05. Their lack of support was shown in the fact that no other bowler took 10 Test wickets. Johnson's six Test wickets cost 50.50 apiece. The Australian slow bowlers took only 14 wickets between them in the Tests, whereas Laker and Lock took 61.

Langley lacked polish as a wicket-keeper but he caught everything that came his way and finished the tour with 47 victims from 39 catches and 8 stumpings. His efficient deputy, Len Maddocks, managed 39 dismissals from 27 catches and 12 stumpings. The best all-round performance came from Archer, who hit one century in averaging 30.90 with the bat and held 25 catches, as well as taking most wickets.

Benaud played the highest Test innings with his 97 at Lord's but his other eight Test knocks realised only 103 runs and his leg-spin bowling was a long way from Test quality, although on a tour in which 43 days were upset by rain many of the pitches should have suited him.

Most of the team holidayed on the Continent for a month before they gathered on 8 October at Ciampano airport in Rome for brief visits to Pakistan and India. They reached Karachi on 9 October and three days' practice proved insufficient to make the change from grass to matting pitches. They were further hindered by their spiked boots in a period before ripple soles.

Pakistan, the junior member of the Imperial Cricket Conference, had only existed since August 1947, when it was established from a division of India, with East and West Pakistan separated by about 1600 kilometres of Indian territory. The Pakistan team for the first Test against Australia, played from 11 to 17 October, included Gul Mahomed, who had previously played eight Tests for India. But the danger for Australia was right-arm fast-medium bowler Fazal Mahmood, who two years earlier had taken 12 wickets against England at The Oval to set up a Pakistan win that shocked the cricket world. On the mat in Karachi, using a wind blowing in from the Arabian Sea, Fazal could be deadly.

He proved this on the first day by bundling a full-strength Australian team out for 80, taking 6 for 34 from 27 overs. Khan Mohammad, who two years earlier had been drafted into the Pakistan touring team in England from the Lancashire League, took 4 for 43 at the other end. They were the only bowlers used in an innings which saw the Australians floundering against swinging deliveries that cut and nipped from the mat. Miller topscored with 21, and only four batsmen reached double figures. Pakistan were 1 for 15 at stumps after a day that produced the fewest runs in Tests but captivated both players and spectators.

Neither Miller, Lindwall, Davidson nor Archer could use the mat as effectively as Fazal and it was Johnson who impressed most among the Australian bowlers. Pakistan were 5 for 70 when Wazir Mohammad and Abdul Hafeez Kardar, the father of Pakistani cricket, put on 104 runs in what proved the match-winning partnership. Johnson dismissed them both, Wazir for 67, Kardar for 69, and although the tail collapsed Pakistan made 199, a lead of 119. Johnson's 20.3 overs yielded 4 for 50. Lindwall's sole wicket at a cost of 40 runs was his 200th in Tests.

Fazal's accuracy continued in Australia's second innings, and he varied his swing with leg cutters and fast off breaks, and despite a partnership of 64 for the sixth wicket Australia were out for 187. This time Fazal took 7 for 80 to finish with match figures of 13 for 114. Pakistan crawled towards the 69 needed for an historic win and after 2 hours and 40 minutes were still six short. Next morning they reached their target for the loss of only one wicket and the entire Pakistan nation celebrated.

Miller bowled 12 overs without taking a wicket in Pakistan's second innings before his knee gave out and ended his Test career. He had appeared in 55 Tests, scoring 2958 runs at 36.97 and taking 170 wickets at 22.97, but the figures do not convey the immense value of the man to Australian cricket. He was a crowd pleaser without rival, a cricketer who could swing a match in 20 minutes. He scored 41 first-class centuries in compiling 14,183 first-class runs at 48.90, top score 281 not out, and took five wickets in an innings 16 times in dismissing 497 batsmen. He also held 136 catches, some of them among the most astonishing known to cricket.

English cricket writer Crawford White said after Australia won the first two post-war series against England: "The difference between the sides is one man—Keith Miller." Said distinguished broadcaster John Arlott: "If I had my choice of one player to win a match off the last ball, whether it required a six or a wicket, I would pick only one player—Keith Miller."

Ron Archer, heir apparent to the Australian captaincy, was another major casualty at Karachi, injuring his left knee so badly when his sprigs caught in the mat it ultimately ended his career. Bill Dowling in his manager's report on the tour praised Archer's intelligent application but he also paid tribute to the manner in which Ian Craig fought his way back into the Test side. Craig's potential as a leader impressed him.

Ron Archer not long before a knee injury forced his retirement. He had been hailed as another allrounder of Keith Miller's calibre and a likely Test captain.

Australia began their first-ever Test in India from 19 to 23 October on a grass pitch at the Corporation Stadium in Madras. India won the toss and batted, but were over-cautious against a mediocre attack that was minus Miller, Archer and Davidson, who were injured, and later, Lindwall who went off with a stomach ailment after he had bowled a few overs. They took a full day to reach 5 for 117. On the second day

Benaud took the last five wickets for 44 runs to finish with 7 for 72 and restrict India to 161.

Australia went to the front with only four wickets down, all the top-order batsmen performing well, and Johnson (73) and Crawford (34) putting on 87 for the ninth wicket in sparkling style. Langley and Johnson added a further 32 for the last wicket to increase Australia's lead to 158. Lindwall returned for India's second innings and gave a fine display of sustained pace bowling to take 7 for 43 and give Australia victory by an innings and 3 runs.

The second Test at the Brabourne Stadium in Bombay from 26 to 31 October was drawn after a successful rearguard action by India. They began with a first innings of 251, which would have been far fewer had Crawford not had to leave the field with a muscle strain after taking 3 for 28. Vijay Manjrekar (55) and Gulabrai Ramchand (109) steered India clear of disaster after four wickets had fallen for 74 runs.

Spectators scaled a two-metre fence to reach the playing area and drape a garland of flowers over Harvey's head when he completed his century in Australia's innings of 7 declared for 523. Harvey's brilliant 140 dominated a stand of 204 with Burke. Dogged and unadventurous, Burke carried on in a stand of 137 with Burge (83) and batted for eight hours before he was out for 161. Johnson declared with Australia 272 runs ahead.

Vinoo Mankad went at 31 to leave India in trouble, but Pankaj Roy, 79, and Polly Umrigar, who was continually heckled in his six hours at the crease for 78, saved India from an innings defeat. Lindwall, in his only Test as Australia's captain, tried eight bowlers without achieving the required breakthrough. Lindwall said:

The thing I remember most is being a captain without bowlers. Injuries kept Johnson, Miller and Archer out. Stomach trouble affected Davidson. Crawford strained a hip. Wilson pulled a muscle, and a fever made Benaud too ill to bowl for part of

the game. We had McDonald fielding as a substitute when he caught Ramchand for 109. Over 1000 runs were scored in the game but the bowlers could not average five wickets a day.

Johnson recovered to lead Australia in the third Test, from 2 to 6 November, on a pitch that took spin at Eden Gardens in Calcutta. Spinners took all but four of the 39 wickets that fell in the match and ended it a day and a half early. With Umrigar relying on off spinner Ghulam Ahmed and Mankad's left-arm spin, wickets fell steadily and India appeared in a strong position when Australia were out for 177, Ahmed taking 7 for 49.

Overnight rain produced an ideal surface for Benaud's leg breaks and his 6 for 52 had India out 41 runs short of Australia's total. Harvey stayed three hours for 69 in Australia's second innings of 9 declared for 189. Left to score 231 to win, India were all out for 136, the last five wickets falling for 15 runs. Benaud's 5 for 53 gave him a match analysis of 11 for 105. Burke's off breaks from a highly suspect action yielded 4 for 37, giving Australia the series by two matches to nil with one drawn. Benaud's 23 wickets at 16.86 in India were compensation for his disappointing showing in England, as were Harvey's 253 runs in the three Tests at 63.25.

Ian Johnson went out of Test cricket with 7 wins, 5 draws and 5 losses from his 17 Tests as Australian captain. In the last of his 45 Tests he completed the double, 109 wickets at 29.19 and 1000 runs at 18.51, which took him into an exclusive group. He also took 30 Test catches. He played 189 first-class matches, taking 619 wickets at 23.30 and scoring 4905 runs, including centuries for Victoria against Queensland and for Australia against Somerset. Not long after he arrived home he took over as secretary of the Melbourne Cricket Club, beating 44 other applicants for the job previously held by Vernon Ransford.

The younger members of the Australian team

Australian wicket-keeper Gil Langley after his election as speaker to the South Australian Parliament.

went straight into the 1956–57 season when they arrived home, with the first two Sheffield Shield matches played before they returned. A record number of 20 matches were staged in the Shield competition, with Western Australia playing a full programme of matches for the first time since it was admitted to interstate cricket in 1947–48. Players in all five states were aware of the opportunities for Test selection in a rebuilt Australian side.

Apart from the retirement of Johnson and Miller, Ron Archer's future was in doubt with his right knee frequently needing to be drained of fluid and a fast bowler's backache persisting. Before the season ended Gil Langley chose the South Australia versus New South Wales match in Adelaide to mark his retirement at the age of 37. There were doubts, too, about Lindwall's ability to retain his Test spot at the age of 35, after moving to Queensland.

Langley's 19 dismissals in the Tests against England in 1956 was more than the previous best for such a series by Godfrey Evans in 1953, and was achieved in only three Tests. Injuries deprived Langley of the all-time record when a five-Test series record of 23 dismissals by South African John Waite was made against New Zealand in 1954. He averaged nearly four dismissals per Test—96 in 26 Tests. None of the other great 'keepers average three per Test. His batting brought him 3236 first-class runs at 25.68, with four centuries, including 100 in his final match, when New South Wales players cheered him from the field.

Bradman had meetings with the Western Australian Cricket Association's international and interstate committee and exchanged numerous letters with its members, notably Alf Randell and Mr Justice Jackson, which led to Western Australia's acceptance as a full member of the Sheffield Shield competition. The interstate conference of Shield states granted full Shield status on condition that Western Australia paid other states £550 each time they visited Perth. This amount was calculated as half the cost of sending a team from Adelaide to Perth, and meant that instead of finishing what were known as their southern tours with a match in Adelaide, the eastern states would instead go on and play Western Australia in Perth.

It was an ingenious solution to a difficult, complex problem. Western Australia still had to finance a tour to all states for an estimated £3200 each year at a time when it continually hovered close to its overdraft limit, but the additional matches that full Shield membership provided gave her players the chance to lift their playing standards. The other states were not happy about it. Queensland in particular was in parlous financial shape, but they went along with the scheme because of the distinction of its proposer.

The New South Wales Cricket Association never tried to collect the £550 when its teams went to Perth, but the other states did. The opportunity Western Australia's admission to full Shield membership presented for a more equitable representation of the states on the Board of Control was lost. New South Wales, Victoria and South Australia retained three members, Queensland two, and Western Australia one. Although it had been a fully fledged Shield state for more than 30 years, Queensland again failed to get three representatives on to the Board.

New South Wales and Victoria were not prepared to give smaller states more voting power because they also wanted to ensure other states did not receive a bigger share of profits from overseas tours. New South Wales claimed its higher share was justified because of the larger numbers of players it provided for Australian teams and because it had more cricketers to look after. Rather than look to the Board for more revenue as a result of its full Shield status, Western Australia had to concentrate on attracting bigger crowds in Perth and to increasing ground membership at the WACA.

The 1956–57 Shield matches were supplemented by a testimonial match in Sydney for Bill O'Reilly and Stan McCabe, which the Board of Control sanctioned as an official trial for Australia's tour of New Zealand at the end of the season. The teams were a blend of Test players and promising youngsters captained by Neil Harvey and Ray Lindwall, but at the last moment Ian Craig dropped out through illness

Spin bowler Peter Philpott dives wide to take a spectacular one hand catch to dismiss Laurie Sawle in a Sheffield Shield match between New South Wales and Western Australia in 1957 in Sydney.

and Jimmy Burke because of injury. Just 1233 runs were scored between 5 and 9 January, with Harvey's XI winning by seven wickets. More than 35,000 attended and McCabe and O'Reilly each received £A3750, after expenses of £A2300 had been deducted. The match gave Sydney fans their first look at Ian Meckiff, from the South Melbourne club, a left-arm bowler of considerable pace, which he achieved through double-jointed shoulders and very thin wrists.

The depressing results on the 1956 tour of England convinced Board of Control members it was time for a fresh approach in choosing Test team leaders, overlooking senior players such as Lindwall and Harvey, and giving youth a chance. The message went down the line when Ian Craig became New South Wales captain at the age of 21. He was still getting over the shock of beating Benaud for the job when New South Wales played Victoria from 22 to 27 December in Melbourne. Meckiff topscored with 55 in Victoria's first innings of 244 before Jimmy Burke put together one of his patient, irksome centuries, batting through the New South Wales innings of 281 for 132 not out. Then leg spinner Jack Treanor put New South Wales into a winning position by taking 5 for 36. Lindsay Hassett's nephew John Shaw seemed likely to get Victoria out of trouble but at 52 he was stumped off Treanor by Ossie Lambert and Victoria succumbed for 197. Chasing 161 to win on a drying pitch, New South Wales appeared beaten at 7 for 70 after hostile spells by Meckiff and Kline.

Craig, who had been in bed with tonsillitis when the innings began, went in and batted for half an hour. Pale and weak, he made 24 runs, partnering Benaud, who made 63, in a thrilling effort to get the runs. Burke had retired with a broken finger but when the ninth wicket fell, re-entered. The scores were level when Meckiff made Burke his fourth victim of the innings and produced the first tie in the 100-year history of interstate cricket. Kline finished with 6 for 57, Meckiff 4 for 64.

The two points from that tie proved vital to New South Wales, who edged out Queensland by 25 points to 24 to win the Sheffield Shield for the fourth successive season. Craig's courage in the 75-run eighth-wicket stand during which his throat was so sore he could not call loudly enough for Benaud to hear, won wide acclaim. In the return match against Victoria in Sydney from 26 to 30 January, a stubborn fourth-wicket stand by Craig and Sid Carroll averted outright defeat after New South Wales had been headed on the first innings. The point saved prevented Queensland winning the Shield for the first time, for they would have won on percentages had they finished level with New South Wales.

Queensland, captained by Lindwall, had defeated New South Wales in Sydney for the second year running. "Slasher" Mackay batted for almost six and a half hours for 169 before Grout hit out strongly for 119 not out, his first Shield century. Queensland also defeated Victoria in Melbourne for the first time since 1939 and later beat Victoria on the first innings in Brisbane. Burge made 135 against Victoria in Melbourne and 210 in Brisbane.

Western Australia celebrated their admission to full Shield membership by defeating South Australia in Adelaide and followed with their first outright success over Victoria at St Kilda. Ken Meuleman made 243 against South Australia, the highest score in a first-class match in Perth, and had several high-scoring partnerships with Barry Shepherd in scoring 779 runs at 70.81. But Western Australia still lost all their four Perth matches. South Australia finished at the bottom of the Shield ladder although Les Favell scored a century in each innings against New South Wales in Sydney and Colin Pinch repeated this achievement against Western Australia in Perth.

Queensland's two members of the Board of Control both died in 1957. Peter Burge's father, J. T. Burge, died in Brisbane while Peter was batting in the New Zealand tour trial in Sydney, and Jack Hutcheon, president of the QCA for

The aggressive new face of Australian cricket. Richie Benaud batting in Sydney with Alan Davidson after the debacle in England in 1956 shows the spirit that led to a revival.

30 years and a member of the Board for 38 years, died in Brisbane, aged 75.

At the end of the Australian season a team of 14 players made a 12-match tour of New Zealand under the captaincy of Ian Craig. The team was hailed as the youngest from any cricket nation ever sent overseas, with Norman O'Neill the youngest at 19 and Neil Harvey the oldest at 28. They were unbeaten, winning five of their seven first-class matches and leaving two drawn.

The team was I. D. Craig (captain), 22, R. N. Harvey, 28, P. J. P. Burge, 25, R. Benaud, 26, N. C. O'Neill, 19, R. B. Simpson, 21, L. E. Favell, 28, J. W. Martin, 26, J. Drennan, 28, R. A. Gaunt, 23, B. N. Jarman, 21, L. F. Kline, 23, W. J. Watson, 26, I. Meckiff, 22.

They took time to become accustomed to the slow pace of damp New Zealand pitches but played with increased assurance as the tour progressed and towards the end showed more harmony than Australia had known for several seasons. Craig, modest and unassuming, was quickly accepted by players aware he had not sought the captaincy ahead of Harvey or Benaud, who had not got on with Ian Johnson in England.

*"Billy" Watson, who was overshadowed on the 1957
New Zealand tour by the heavy scoring of Harvey
O'Neill, Craig and Burge. A family bereavement ended
his career soon afterwards.*

The first representative match of the tour
against New Zealand between 1 and 4 March
at Christchurch was drawn. New Zealand led

by 52 on the first innings by scoring 268 in reply
to Australia's 216. Australia recovered through
splendid batting by Harvey (84) and Craig (123
not out), and Craig declared at 3 for 284. Set
to score 233 in 140 minutes, New Zealand did
not try for the runs.

New Zealand had the best of the second
representative match from 8 to 11 March at
Wellington. Following his seven-wicket bag in
the first match between the countries Harry Cave
took 3 for 28 and 5 for 46 with his right-arm
medium-pacers.

Australia began with 215, only Favell (62)
and Burge (67) resisting for long. Sutcliffe
showed why he was rated among the world's
best left-handers with an innings of 107 in New
Zealand's 249. Benaud, 6 for 79, troubled all the
New Zealand batsmen except Sutcliffe. Wickets
fell frequently in Australia's second innings but
at 6 for 146 and Australia only 112 ahead the
last three hours were washed out.

Outstanding displays by Norm O'Neill and
Johnny Martin led to Australia's best win of the
tour over New Zealand from 29 March to 1 April
at Auckland. New Zealand were dismissed for
198 with Meckiff, Drennan, Benaud and Martin
all worrying the batsmen. Favell (65) and Craig
(57) set the stage for a powerful innings of 102
not out by O'Neill which included 13 fours.
Martin's well-flighted left-arm spinners baffled
all the batsmen except John Reid (54) in New
Zealand's second innings of 161. Martin's 6 for
46 meant that Australia only had to score 10 runs
in their second innings to secure a ten wicket
victory.

The only disappointment in a valuable tour
for Australia's crop of rising young players was
wicket-keeper Barry Jarman, whose frequent
fumbling suggested selectors erred in not
preferring Grout. Benaud was the most
impressive Australian, emerging as a top-class
all-rounder and justifying the selectors' patience
with him. The Australians scored five centuries
on the tour and had only one scored against them.

South Australian John Drennan, whose 22 wickets in major matches on the 1957 New Zealand tour, cost only 12.50 apiece.

named as manager, had a heart attack a few days before the team's departure on 7 October. C. J. R. Howard, of Bulawayo, took over as temporary manager until Jack Norton, president of the New South Wales Cricketers' Club who had managed Craig's team in New Zealand, could join the side.

The main surprises in the team were the absence of Norman O'Neill, Ray Gaunt and Ray Lindwall, whom the selectors judged to be past his best at 36. The selectors preferred Sydney-born Bobby Simpson to O'Neill following Simpson's brilliant catching and consistent all-round proficiency for Western Australia. Simpson, son of a former Stenhousemuir soccer player who worked on the printing floor for Frank Packer's *Daily Telegraph*, bowled leg spinners and batted down the order. Meckiff and Drennan were preferred to Gaunt, but when they were injured he flew over as a replacement. Mackay was the oldest player in the team at 32, Jarman the youngest at 21, 14 days younger than Simpson. The team, selected by Sir Donald Bradman, Jack Ryder and Dudley Seddon, was I. D. Craig (captain), 21, R. N. Harvey (vice-captain), 29, R. Benaud, 26, P. J. P. Burge, 25, J. W. Burke, 27, A. K. Davidson, 28, J. Drennan, 25, L. E. Favell, 27, A. T. W. Grout, 30, B. N. Jarman, 21, L. F. Kline, 22, K. D. Mackay, 32, C. C. McDonald, 29, I. Meckiff, 22, R. B. Simpson, 21.

They left Australia on 7 October 1957, flying to Johannesburg via Perth and the Cocos Islands, faced with restoring Australia's sagging cricket prestige against a South African side that contained most of the players who had shared the previous series in Australia and included two fast bowlers, Neil Adcock and Peter Heine, who were every bit as fast and hostile as Tyson and Statham and had a habit of bruising opposing batsmen with a liberal supply of bouncers. Adcock had sent New Zealanders Bert Sutcliffe and Laurie Miller to hospital before they had scored in 1953–54.

O'Neill headed the batting averages with 218 runs at 72.66, Meckiff the bowling averages with 20 wickets at 10.85. Craig's leadership was calm and friction-free.

The players had only been home from New Zealand for a month when the Board of Control announced the team for the 22-match tour of South Africa in the southern summer of 1957–58. Archer was in the original party of 15 players but the thigh injury sustained in Pakistan forced his retirement and gave Ken Mackay a chance to redeem himself. South Australian Jack Jantke,

Speedy Recovery

Australia tours South Africa 1957-58; domestic cricket 1957-58; Australia regains the Ashes 1958-59

Ian David Craig, the 27th Australian cricket captain, first son of a banker, was born on 12 June 1935 at Yass in southern New South Wales. He played centrefield for Australia's best schoolboy baseball team at the age of 13, captained North Sydney Boys' High School at Rugby, and was vice-captain of the cricket team led by all-rounder Peter Philpott. He played for Mosman Cricket Club at 13 and at 16 scored a first grade century for the club.

The former Test selector Edmund Dwyer had him promoted to the state team before Craig finished his first season in first grade. At 16 years 249 days, he was the youngest ever to play for the state but his elder sister Helen said she could always get him out in the backyard. He made 90 on debut and in his ninth match for the state made 213 not out, although he weighed less than 64 kilograms and was only 172 centimetres tall, passing 200 by going down on one knee and sweeping South African Hugh Tayfield to the

A group of Australians just before they flew to South Africa in 1957–58 (L to R): Les Favell, Ken Mackay, Neil Harvey, Bob Simpson, and Alan Davidson, with a toy kangaroo provided by a Qantas official.

square leg fence. At 17 years 207 days, he was the youngest player in the world to score a double century in first-class cricket, 117 days younger than Hanif Mohammad when he made 203 not out for Pakistan against Bombay.

The stylish, authoritative manner of his batting in that innings left Australians expecting huge scores from him every time he batted. With each failure, the pressure for him to produce a big score mounted and when he went to England six weeks short of his 18th birthday in 1953 as the youngest player Australia had ever sent overseas he had to suffer the jibes of those relieved that he was not another Bradman.

Craig had to play a further 40 innings and wait 13 months before he scored his next century. He did it in Hassett's testimonial match in Melbourne when he hit Ian Johnson for four sixes in five deliveries. Army service and his studies as a pharmacist made him unavailable for big cricket during England's 1954–55 tour under Hutton, but he returned to England in 1956, the first player to make two tours before he was 21. His talents finally brought success in the second half of that tour after he scored 62 and 100 not out against Somerset.

Even those who criticised his appointment as New South Wales and Australian captain acknowledged that he did a good job in New Zealand. Meanwhile he completed his pharmacy course at Sydney University and received permission from the Board of Control to spend six months in England before the South African tour gaining experience with Boots pharmacy chain. He arrived from London by sea to take over the leadership of the 14 players who had flown in from Australia.

There were immediate difficulties, for nobody had foreseen the need to include Jack Jantke's briefcase containing all the tour arrangements with the team's luggage. The players objected to temporary manager Howard's dictatorial attitude and took over the management of their laundry and travel which

drew them closer together. For a fortnight while they awaited replacement manager Jack Norton the Australians followed an itinerary Craig put together in discussions with officials of the South African Cricket Association. He handled the welcoming speechmaking with composure beyond his years, supported by players desperately keen to regain Australia's leadership in world cricket.

After a draw in a warm-up match at Kitwe on 19 and 21 October against Northern Rhodesia, Australia made a wonderful start to the tour by winning the first four first-class matches. Craig made the initial first-class century of the tour with an innings of style and polish against Rhodesia from 25 to 29 October at Salisbury.

Ian Craig batting in his backyard in Mosman to the bowling of his brother Geoff.

Drennan's 5 for 53 helped dismiss Rhodesia for 210. Then Craig made 113, followed by 117 not out from Benaud and 100 not out by Davidson, who added 177 in 120 minutes in an unbroken seventh-wicket stand. Craig declared at 6 for 520, leaving Rhodesia to score 310 to avoid an innings defeat. Despite 139 from Paul Winslow, Rhodesia were out for 296, Benaud taking 6 for 93.

At Bulawayo Australia defeated a reconstructed Rhodesian team from 1 to 4 November by ten wickets. Craig scored his second successive century (100) and Burke made 106. Powerful batting and steady, accurate bowling by a well balanced attack brought another one-sided win against Transvaal at Johannesburg from 8 to 12 November.

Harvey, in his first appearance after damaging his left hand at practice before the tour began, made 173 in the match against a South African XI from 15 to 19 November at Pretoria. Harvey and Craig (88) put on 195 before Burge went in and hammered the bowling in scoring 111 not out. This helped take Australia to 8 for 519 declared, a lead of 184. Davidson's pace and swing, coupled with the spin of Benaud, had the South African XI out for 154. The improvement of Mackay as a medium-pace bowler of such accuracy meant risks had to be taken to get him away, to the delight of the Australians.

Grout, Kline, Meckiff and Simpson made their debuts in the first Test from 23 to 28 December at the New Wanderers ground in Johannesburg. Simpson was picked because of his slips catching to Davidson's bowling, as much as for his batting, which still had not produced big scores. Without Harvey, their most experienced batsman, Australia had to fight hard all the way to emerge with an honourable draw. They found Adcock and Heine at their best after South Africa declared at 9 for 470, McGlew scoring 108, Goddard 90 and Waite 115. With South Africa 3 for 300, Craig asked Davidson: "What do we do now?" Instead of pointing out

that Craig should have known as captain, Davidson suggested tightening up the game and soon found himself bowling to a packed leg-side field.

At 6 for 177, Australia appeared certain to follow on, Heine having taken 4 for 37. Benaud (122) and Simpson (60) led a fine recovery to restrict South Africa's lead to 102. Heine's 6 for 58 might have been better had he not been forced to leave the field for treatment to a leg injury. Australia bounced back into the game by taking 4 for 19 in South Africa's second innings, Davidson claiming 3 for 11. But Waite and Endean put South Africa back in command with a fifth-wicket stand of 129, and although the tail folded up cheaply Australia were left to score 304 in 270 minutes. They did not try for the runs after Burke retired with damaged fingers and let Mackay bat for 225 minutes in his own peculiar style to make a draw certain.

Heine had to miss the second Test at Cape Town from 31 December to 3 January through injury and Harvey returned for Australia in place of Burge. On an easy pitch Burke batted for 578 minutes for 189, his highest Test score, adding 190 for the first wicket with McDonald (99). Then Burke and Mackay spent almost four hours scoring 130 runs, which took the match well into the second day and had the effect of breaking up the pitch. Australia took 11 wickets for 180 runs on the third day, forcing South Africa to follow on 240 behind. Davidson was lame but he managed to get McGlew for a duck at the start of South Africa's second innings.

Benaud and Kline then spun the ball cleverly to dismiss South Africa for 99 and give Australia victory by an innings and 141 runs. Benaud had nine wickets with 4 for 95 and 5 for 49. Kline took 3 for 29 and 3 for 18, ending the match, with a dramatic hat-trick by dismissing Fuller, Tayfield and Adcock. The last nine South African wickets fell for 82 runs despite a plucky 56 not out by opener John Goddard.

Craig was learning captaincy fast, giving

Davidson the new ball ahead of Meckiff to exploit the shine and not worrying if Benaud or Kline were hit for fours. The respect his players had for him and their green caps was shown in their brilliant fielding. On the rare occasions their returns strayed, Grout gave them a blast that earned him the nickname "Griz", short for grizzler.

Ron Gaunt, the thickset Western Australian right-arm fast-medium bowler who had been flown over to reinforce the team because of the injuries to Meckiff and Drennan, made his first appearance at Johannesburg between 10 and 15 January against Transvaal. Heavy rain and bad light brought repeated interruptions and Australia's first innings of 369 took until the third morning. Benaud and Kline then spun Transvaal out for 188. Following on 181 behind, Transvaal were saved by a defiant 57 from Ken Funston and were on 7 for 257 when time ran out.

Benaud, now the dominant personality on the tour, made 187 against Natal at Pietermaritzburg from 17 to 21 January, adding 224 in a display of powerful driving with Davidson (121). The Australians scored 589 in 536 minutes. Benaud followed his fine batting by capturing 5 for 71 in Natal's first innings of 288, but when they followed on 301 behind, all the bowlers encountered gutsy opposition from Goddard, whose 131 not out in five hours forced a draw.

South Africa's unnecessarily slow batting contributed to the draw in the third Test between 24 and 29 January at Durban. After Adcock and Heine bowled with sustained pace and fire to bundle Australia out for 163, McGlew scored the slowest century in history, taking 9 hours 5 minutes over his century and a further 30 minutes to reach 105. Waite was almost as slow in scoring 134. Neither Gaunt, in his Test debut, nor Davidson could get any life from the pitch and Benaud took over as mainstay of the attack, bowling 50.7 overs for his 5 for 114. Grout dismissed five batsmen in the innings, which lasted for 13 hours.

Trailing by 221 on the first innings, Australia were compelled to play for a draw and were 7 for 292 when time ran out.

Craig promoted Benaud from No. 7 to No. 4 in the batting order for the fourth Test from 7 to 12 February at Johannesburg. He was vindicated as Benaud produced the fastest century of the rubber, lifting the score from 2 for 52 to 3 for 210 in a 158-run third-wicket stand with Burke. After Burke was out for 81 and Benaud for 100, Australia slumped to 7 for 234 before Mackay and Davidson led a record recovery with an 81-run partnership. Mackay was 83 not out when the innings ended at 401.

In ideal batting conditions, only Funston shaped confidently against Benaud and Kline. His 70 was not enough to avoid the follow-on, however, and South Africa began their second innings 198 behind. Benaud, with 5 for 84, and Kline, 3 for 27, again troubled all the batsmen and although Funston (64 not out) found support from McGlew (70), the innings ended on 198. Two outstanding slips catches by Simpson sent back Goddard and Endean. Australia scored the single run needed to win by ten wickets and clinch the series.

In the fifth Test at St George's Park, Port Elizabeth, from 28 February to 4 March South Africa, batting first on a good pitch, managed only 214 against high-quality bowling by Davidson and Kline, who each took four wickets. Then Adcock and Heine, hampered in earlier Tests by influenza and leg strains, threw themselves into the attack on Australia's batsmen.

Adcock felled Burke with a ball that broke a rib and personally called for a stretcher to have him carried away. Altogether Adcock unleashed 15 chest- or head-high bumpers and Heine 10. After Benaud was flattened, Craig asked umpire W. Marais if the bowling resembled Bodyline. In the midst of the turmoil, Mackay batted patiently in his own unique style and from 6 for 199 helped lift the score to 291, finishing with an invaluable 77 not out.

Davidson, 5 for 38, and Benaud, 5 for 82, continued the high-level craftsmanship they had shown throughout the tour to dismiss South Africa for 144 in their second innings, leaving Australia to score 68 for a resounding win.

The humiliation of South Africa's batsmen did not please Adcock, whose first over against McDonald and Grout, substituting for the injured Burke, included three successive head-high bouncers which McDonald only narrowly avoided. Umpire W. Marais then appealed to Adcock's sense of sportsmanship over continuing with this form of attack, and as Adcock walked back to his mark his captain, Clive van Ryneveld, asked him to discontinue the bouncer attack.

Adcock replied by letting loose a fourth bouncer, outside the off stump, which McDonald edged to Tayfield in the slips. Non-striker Grout then asked if McDonald could be out under the laws relating to intimidatory bowling. Marais replied, "If the ball had been pitched in line with the batsman I'd have intervened." Fair-minded onlookers believed van Ryneveld should have taken Adcock off immediately but he allowed him to bowl a further three overs before relieving him. Grout remained calm and his 35 not out saw Australia safely to victory.

A drawn match at Cape Town from 8 to 11 March against South African Universities enabled Australia to complete the tour without defeat. The Australians scored 22 centuries in winning 11 of their 20 first-class matches, with nine drawn. Eight centuries were scored against them. Burke headed the batting averages with 1041 runs at 65.06, scoring four centuries. Davidson topped the bowling averages with 72 wickets at 15.13. But the outstanding player of the tour was Benaud, who made four centuries in compiling 817 runs at 51.06 and took 106 wickets at 19.40. Thirty of his wickets came in Tests, in which he took five wickets in an innings four times. Davidson was not far behind him with 813 runs at 54.20, including four centuries and 25 wickets in the Tests.

By winning the Test series 3–nil Craig's team had restored Australia's cricket prestige and built a young team into a slick unit, accomplished in all aspects of the game, but particularly impressive in the way senior players supported the newcomers. Craig had not carried on with his marvellous start by scoring more centuries but did reasonably well with 591 runs at 36.93 despite losing his stumps eight times in 16 innings on the tour.

The South Africans never achieved under van Ryneveld's captaincy the team spirit and fielding skill they reached under Goddard four years earlier in Australia and gave themselves an impossible task through their ponderous, often tediously slow batting. None of their bowlers gave Adcock and Heine support. Tayfield was completely frustrated by Mackay, who reversed his poor batting against Laker's off spin and made Tayfield pay a high price for his wicket in all eight innings they faced each other.

The series had been enlivened by Simpson's slips catching and the wonderful standard reached by the wicket-keepers Wally Grout and Jackie Waite. Grout not only set records but established himself as a handy batsman and a colourful personality. His courage under pressure matched the traditions of Australian Test wicket-keeping dating back to Jack Blackham, and like Blackham he had been shown as a player of sportsmanship and high principles. While Grout remained fit, Barry Jarman's Test aspirations would have to wait.

Craig's effort in reviving pride and confidence so soon after the disaster of Manchester was not only a tribute to his personal qualities but also a high compliment to his senior players. Harvey, Benaud, Favell, McDonald, Burke and Davidson were all entitled to feel upset at the appointment of such a youthful, untried Test player without captaincy experience. Instead they were unflagging in their encouragement and set out to reduce his problems by improving their own performances.

Ian Craig, who reigned briefly as Australian captain after the retirement of Ian Johnson, at the Sydney nets.

In Australia while they were away New South Wales won the Sheffield Shield competition for the fifth successive year. The competition was decided under a new points system which awarded ten points for an outright win if the winner led on the first innings and six points to outright winners who were behind on the first innings. The idea was to brighten up fourth days by encouraging teams already certain of first innings points to try for outright victory.

New South Wales captain Sid Carroll gave a good demonstration of the value of the new system by declaring on the last day of the match against South Australia from 10 to 14 January. South Australia had to score 237 runs in 195 minutes to win and they won by six wickets with 18 minutes to spare. Five and a quarter hours of play on the last day produced 420 runs. The match was a triumph for the new system and for Glenelg club's right-hand opening batsman Gavin Stevens, who made 164 and 111 in innings of smart stroke-play. O'Neill made a brilliant 125 in New South Wales' first innings and 1005 runs in the season at 83.75. He also headed the Shield bowling averages with 26 wickets at 20.42, bowling leg breaks with a very quick, snapping action.

When reliable Ossie Lambert was forced to withdraw from the New South Wales team at the start of the season, selectors picked Balmain's keeper Keith Herron to replace him. But an extensive search failed to locate Herron who was on holiday at a South Coast caravan park and the job was given to Doug Ford, the Newcastle-born keeper who played for Mosman. Ford did so well he held the job for 56 matches.

Lindwall, captaining Queensland, set a record for the highest number of wickets in Shield cricket by passing Ernie Jones' mark of 209 victims. Lindwall went to 210 wickets in his 54th Shield match, whereas Jones played in 38 matches between 1892 and 1906. One of the most colourful of all Shield cricketers, Walter Thomas Walmsley, at 42 the oldest player in the competition, hit a chanceless century against New South Wales in Brisbane between 25 and 29 October. His unbroken tenth-wicket stand of 105 with John Freeman was the best for Queensland in Shield cricket. Walmsley, born in Sydney where he was a stalwart of the Western Suburbs club, had moved to Queensland from

Tasmania, where he represented that State in 1947–48. He made a century against the 1948 Australians in Hobart and had played Lancashire League cricket for Stockport and Oldham.

Absence of the Test players gave several promising youngsters a chance to impress, among them red-haired Victorian slow left-arm bowler, Ian Quick, who took 32 wickets, including 6 for 45 against Western Australia in Melbourne between 8 and 12 November and 7 for 47 against Western Australia in Perth from 28 February to 4 March. Johnny Martin, the Petersham club's slow left-arm spinner, took 25 wickets for New South Wales, including 7 for 59 v South Australia in Adelaide from 19 to 22 December. Bruce Dooland, back in action for his native State after a distinguished five-season career in county cricket for Nottinghamshire, took 29 wickets, but was worried by a shoulder injury and retired at the end of the summer.

Dooland, born in Adelaide, learned to bowl on a concrete pitch laid down by his father in the family backyard, and progressed from Thebarton Central School to Adelaide High, to the West Torrens club, and finally at the age of 17 to the South Australian side. He took 1016 wickets in first-class cricket at 21.98 and scored 7141 runs at 24.37. He was one of the greatest leg spinners cricket has known but sadly for Australian cricket played for most of his career in England. He retired from county cricket at the same time as Doug Wright and Eric Hollies. Between them these three googly bowlers took more than 5000 wickets.

Sam Loxton, Liberal member of parliament for Prahran, captained Victoria in Neil Harvey's absence, and in one match lost sight of a mis-hit. "Better look for it in Hansard, Sam," a barracker yelled. When Sam, then 36, showed signs of weariness after a 12-over stint, a spectator bellowed: "Why don't you give up the game, Loxton? You're old enough to be my father." From leg-slip Sam hollered: "I've got a birth certificate!" At the end of the season Loxton

quit, to concentrate on politics. He made seven centuries for Victoria and 13 in all first-class matches, compiling 6249 runs at 36.97, and took 232 wickets at 25.73. His retirement left Victoria with a leadership problem as Neil Harvey moved to Sydney on his return from South Africa.

The 1957–58 Australian season was also notable for an experimental law limiting bowlers to two leg-side fieldsmen behind the stumps. The law, designed to give batsmen more chance to protect themselves against leg-side bouncers, worked well but at the end of the season the interstate conference decided by a margin of one vote to discontinue the experiment during the England team's Australian tour in 1958–59. There was no such law in the tour conditions and selectors wanted to judge Test team aspirants under the same laws that applied in the Tests.

There were dramatic developments in England before the MCC settled on a touring party. Laker originally declared himself unavailable but then changed his mind. The Yorkshire left-arm spinner Johnny Wardle was named in the original side of 17 players but had his invitation withdrawn after he wrote a series of articles in the *Daily Mail* criticising the administration of the Yorkshire club. To Australians the criticisms appeared justified as Yorkshire had allowed Test players Willie Watson, Bob Appleyard and Frank Lowson to leave the club. Watson became captain of Leicestershire, while Lowson and Appleyard left the game, both aged 33. Yorkshire decided that as Wardle had broken his contract with the club by writing the articles, he was not acceptable to play for them. MCC then dropped Wardle, who joined reporters covering the tour.

Sixteen players sailed from London in the *Iberia* without a replacement being named. Watson injured a knee during the voyage and required an operation. Instead of sending out replacements when the tour began, MCC hesitated until Raman Subba Row fractured a wrist just before the first Test at Brisbane. They then reinforced the side by flying out John Mortimore and Ted Dexter. The enlarged MCC party, the twenty-seventh English side to visit Australia, thus comprised P. B. H. May (captain), 28, M. C. Cowdrey (vice-captain), 26, T. E. Bailey, 34, E. R. Dexter, 23, T. G. Evans, 38, T. W. Graveney, 31, J. C. Laker, 36, P. J. Loader, 28, G. A. R. Lock, 29, C. A. Milton, 30, J. B. Mortimore, 25, P. E. Richardson, 27, J. B. Statham, 28, R. Swetman, 24, R. Subba Row, 26, F. S. Trueman, 26, F. H. Tyson, 28, W. Watson, 38, with F. R. Brown as manager, E. D. R. Eagar, assistant manager, and G. Duckworth as scorer and baggage-master.

Mortimore was a lower-order right-hand batsman who hit 1000 runs five times in an English season, and right-arm off-break bowler who formed a successful partnership with his former county partner David Allen. Swetman was the deputy wicket-keeper to Evans, a neat, slightly-built figure who at the time kept regularly for Surrey and knew Laker's and Lock's tricks well. Milton was a former England soccer player who played outside right for Arsenal and Bristol City, an opening batsman with a wide enough range of strokes for him to score 1000 runs in an English season 16 times. Subba Row was the London-born left-handed batsman who could open or fit in the middle order, an excellent fieldsman and useful leg-break bowler who had been a key man in an outstanding Cambridge University team. England's programme of 18 first-class matches plus four minor matches in Australia began at Perth with a draw against Western Australia from 17 to 21 October. Graveney made the first century of the tour with 177 not out in a total of 351. Trueman had Rutherford caught in slips with his first ball in Australia.

The Australian selectors rushed O'Neill into his first major encounter with a Test standard attack in the match between England and a Combined XI at Perth from 24 to 28 October. He produced an exciting all-round display, bowling and fielding splendidly and scoring a

Ted Dexter, swashbuckling right-hand batsman, on the first of his two tours to Australia in 1958–59. Australians saw too little of his stroke play as he was often forced to play defensive innings.

century (104) every bit as attractive as May's century (113) for England. May retired with an injured knee on 68 and completed his innings using a runner. Statham and Laker fully tested O'Neill but he hit 10 fours in his century, which took 280 minutes and gave him a long look at bowlers who had humbled Australia's batting heroes on previous tours. England made 349, the Combined XI 260, and England were 4 for 257 with Cowdrey 100 not out when time ran out.

Laker and Lock turned the ball disconcertingly to pave the way for England's nine-wicket win over South Australia from 31 October to 3 November at Adelaide Oval. England batsmen in turn showed concern at the left-arm spin from Johnny Martin, who had transferred from New South Wales to South Australia to further his Test hopes. Laker took 10 for 101, Lock 4 for 65 in South Australia's innings of 165 and 194. Martin had 7 for 110 in England's first innings of 245. England scored the 115 needed to win in the final innings for the loss of one wicket, thanks to the splendid batting of Milton (63 not out).

Milton continued this form against Victoria between 7 and 11 November in Melbourne with 116, which took England to 396. Following his success on Australia's South African tour Meckiff impressed all the England players with the pace he generated from a short approach, but the spinners Kline and Quick were punished. Victoria's first innings of 252 produced some very fast bowling from Statham (7 for 47), who hit the stumps four times. A workmanlike 78 not out from Graveney enabled England to set Victoria to score 294 in 255 minutes. Lock (6 for 74) bowled them to victory by 87 runs, taking the last two wickets with the sixth and seventh deliveries of the final over.

At Sydney against New South Wales between 14 and 18 November Burke (104) and Harvey (149) made centuries and O'Neill was 84 not out when Craig declared at 7 for 391. Spinners Benaud and Philpott had England out for 177 in their first innings but a dogged opening stand of 170 by Milton and Richardson in the second innings saved the game. Milton made 81, Richardson 87 and England were 6 for 356 when time expired. The Englishmen offered no complaints at the bowling of blond Mosman giant Gordon Rorke, who repeatedly slid yards up the pitch with his 16 stone balanced on the toe of his back foot. But Rorke's figures (1 for 15, and 0 for 25) cast no fears, whereas Benaud (5 for

Richie Benaud took a long time to mature as a leg-spin bowler, but from the time he took over the captaincy, following Craig's illness, he thrived on leadership and became a shrewder bowler.

48 and 2 for 84) looked a major threat for the Tests.

England then defeated a strong Australian XI in Sydney by 345 runs between 21 and 25 November. Two separate centuries by May—the second between lunch and tea on the third day—and outstanding bowling by Lock on the fourth morning gave the Australian selectors little guidance in what was organised as a Test trial. May made 140 out of 319 in England's first innings, and 114 out of 3 declared for 257 in the second. Lock pitched the ball in the rough created by the fast bowlers to take 6 for 19 in 11 overs and finish the match. England were in danger of defeat, however, in their very next game against Queensland in Brisbane from 28

November to 2 December, before rain washed out play halfway through the last day. Lindwall, showing his old control, gave Queensland a 59 run lead on the first innings with 5 for 57 and took two of the four wickets that fell in England's second innings for 71 runs before rain stopped play.

Still without a replacement for Wardle, with Subba Row out for the series, and Milton and Watson struggling to recover from injuries, England were in disarray just before the first Test. But their success in the previous series between the countries had been so emphatic they were still hot favourites for the first series shown on television in Australia. Australia brought in O'Neill for his first Test and Benaud took over the captaincy from Craig, troubled again by hepatitis.

Benaud's appointment was a shock to all who were aware of the outstanding job the team's senior player, Neil Harvey, had done on the South African tour. Harvey had never been in trouble with administrators, had experience captaining Victoria before he moved to Sydney, and as the side's most prolific run-maker deserved the captaincy. To his eternal credit, he gave Benaud wholehearted support and gave no outward show of disappointment.

Benaud's advance from a player who had done so little on two tours of England to Test captain staggered cricketers who had opposed him in his early years in Sydney grade cricket. From a batsman with a crouched, awkward stance in which he choked the bat handle, he had taken the stoop out of his stance, moved his grip up the handle, and learned to deal with all forms of bowling stylishly and confidently. With the ball he had improved through dedicated practice from a bowler dependent on top spin to a world-class leg spinner who could occasionally produce the flipper, or googly with top spin, he had learned from Bruce Dooland.

His marriage to attractive blonde Marcia Lavender had produced two sons and he had shown marked aptitude for journalism after his promotion from the accounts department of the Sydney *Sun*. From early instruction by noted cricket commentator Johnnie Moyes, he had graduated to the hurly-burly of Police Rounds where his crime stories were guided by a wise and tough senior writer named Noel Bailey.

From the start of his term as Australian captain Benaud adopted an open-handed policy which was a revelation to cricket writers. He shared his problems with them, hid nothing, and was ready to answer telephone calls at any hour because he understood deadline problems. He trusted everybody and the journalists responded by giving coverage that lifted cricket back to Australia's No. 1 sport.

One of his innovations was a Test eve dinner restricted to the players at which the tactics for the game could be discussed at length. At one of these the Australians decided to concentrate their pace attack on running the ball across right-handers, a strategy that depended on them holding their slips catches. Benaud was to follow Bill O'Reilly's advice and concentrate on leg breaks rather than a mixture of deliveries, a move that improved the accuracy of his stock ball.

The 'Gabba Test from 5 to 10 December 1958 was one of the dreariest ever played but it began a notable revival in Australian cricket, continuing the rebuilding work done so effectively by Craig's team in New Zealand and South Africa. Both Davidson and Meckiff had England's top order playing and missing. They took three wickets each, regularly finding the edges. England never recovered from the loss of two wickets at 16 and, with Grout dismissing four batsmen, were out for 134. Australia struggled to a lead of 52 through sound batting by McDonald (42) and some strong driving by O'Neill (34).

The turning point came on the fourth day when Graveney was run out and Cowdrey was given out after the catch just carried to Kline. Bailey then showed his complete disdain for spectators by batting 7 hours 30 minutes for 68. He scored off only 40 of the 425 balls he faced. The lack of run getting gave critics time to study the actions of Burke and Meckiff, who operated for a time at opposite ends. Most agreed that they were suspect and when England were out for 198 and Australia were set only 147 to win, the opinion that Australia's bowlers were throwing intensified. At 2 for 58, O'Neill came in and played an innings of delightful freedom, adding the 89 runs still wanted just before a heavy storm flooded the ground. Burke had matched Bailey for stubbornness in scoring 28, and O'Neill was 71 not out with 7 fours.

Trueman recovered from the back injury that kept him out of the first Test to figure in an exciting finish against South Australia in Adelaide between 24 and 29 December. Trueman took the ninth wicket with the last ball of the last over, following a spell in which he took three wickets for five runs. He had 9 for 79 in a drawn match, but the headlines in Fleet Street stories of the match went to South Australian suspect opening bowlers Peter Trethewey and Alan Hitchcock, who were labelled "Trethrowey and Pitchcox". One English paper informed readers that a spectator called "Strike one", after Hitchcock bowled the first ball of the match. Another said a spectator shouted: "Put Harvey on—he throws straighter."

England's anger over so many Australian bowlers allegedly throwing reached its peak in the second Test at Melbourne, from 31 December to 5 January, when Meckiff took 6 for 38 in the second England innings of 87, their lowest score in Australia since 1903–04. Meckiff certainly had a jerky approach and achieved his pace with a whipped arm swing, but his arm moved so quickly it was impossible to tell from the stands if he contravened the laws on chucking. This did not stop reporters branding him a cheat.

England were dismissed for 259 in their first innings after losing three wickets for seven runs,

Ian Meckiff, the most discussed bowler of his time. His left arm had a bend in it which could not be straightened. He had double-jointed shoulders and extremely thin wrists.

all to Davidson. England passed the 200 with only four wickets down but then lost six wickets for 39 runs. Harvey produced a brilliant knock to take Australia to 308, a lead of 49. Harvey scored more than half his side's total with 167, hitting 16 fours in his six hours batting.

England gave up all chance of winning by losing five wickets before hitting off the arrears. A succession of brilliant catches completed Meckiff's coup. Australia made the 39 needed to win for the loss of two wickets. The glorious uncertainty of cricket was intact. In only three matches, England and Australia's positions had been reversed. Australia's humiliation at Manchester in 1956 had been matched by England's dismissal and heavy defeat at Melbourne only 28 months later, with the charges of chucking strong in each match. The Melbourne match attracted 230,948 spectators and £A46,791 in receipts.

For reasons that escaped the most diligent research, the selectors replaced Kline with Slater for the third Test at Sydney from 9 to 15 January, apparently unaware of the mounting agitation in the press box over chucking. He had an unproductive match, which, sadly for such an enthusiastic cricketer, was his habit. Indeed in 77 first-class matches he never once took five wickets in an innings. But he did look promising in the first innings when he had May caught for 42 and trapped Dexter lbw without offering a stroke.

England lost their last four wickets for 29 runs to be all out for 219, to which Australia replied with 357 from a tenacious team batting effort, recovering well from crises, first with a 110-run stand from Favell and O'Neill and later a 115-run stand by Mackay and Davidson. Leading by 138, they had England 3 for 64 with a day and a half to play. Cowdrey (100 not out) and May (92) then staged a 182-run partnership that saved the game. Cowdrey was an hour in the nineties. England's declaration at 7 for 287 left no time for a result.

England had their first win in seven weeks when they beat Victoria at Melbourne from 17 to 21 January by nine wickets. This was almost entirely due to the batting of Cowdrey (85) and Watson (141), who put on 169 for the fourth wicket.

Laker pulled out of the fourth Test in Adelaide from 30 January to 5 February after a net trial and with his attack dependent on pace May put Australia in after winning the toss. McDonald was almost bowled first ball, pulled a thigh muscle at 137 and retired hurt at 149, resuming with Jimmy Burke as his runner when Australia were 7 for 407. Burke chose to run wide on the off side, which umpire Mel McInnes foolishly allowed although he could not see Burke. McInnes should have positioned Burke on the leg side where he could be seen. His

Mel McInnes, who umpired four Tests in the 1958–59 England v. Australia series. England's supporters were angered that he did not deal harshly with the bowling actions of Meckiff and Rorke.

oversight caused a blunder when McInnes gave McDonald out to a throw from the leg boundary by Statham to bowler Tyson. When he realised Burke was behind him, McInnes had to reverse his decision.

McDonald was finally out for 170. Evans broke a finger early in Australia's innings of 476 and later handed over the wicket-keeping to Graveney. England followed on after scoring 240, 84 of them from Cowdrey, and their second innings of 270 gave Australia the easy task of scoring 35 to win. Benaud proved the match-winning bowler with 5 for 91 and 4 for 82, and set an inspiring example in the field.

The Australians received little praise for winning back the Ashes from English critics interested mainly in the bowling of Rorke, who had replaced the injured Meckiff. In the London *Daily Express* Brian Chapman described him as "a honey of a chucker". Despite intense heat Rorke bowled 52.1 overs in the match and dismissed Cowdrey, May, Graveney, Watson and Lock for 101 runs. Wally Grout stirred him up when he appeared to be wilting by suggesting he might stand right up on the stumps to Rorke's bowling, an insult no fast bowler would accept without finding something extra.

Australia won the fifth Test, in Melbourne from 13 to 18 February, by nine wickets to complete a 4–nil sweep of the series. Benaud won the toss and sent England in against four fast bowlers, the suspect Rorke and Meckiff supporting Lindwall and Davidson. England managed only 205, to which Australia responded with 351. England's second innings of 214 left Australia with only 69 to win, McDonald rounding off a fine series by adding 51 not out to his first innings 133, during which he was given not out after dislodging a bail at 12. Lindwall achieved the record he had been chasing by passing Grimmett's 216 Test wickets. Grout equalled Tallon's record of 20 dismissals in a Test series. Bailey, in his last Test, made a pair.

There were many events in this argumentative series that angered cricket lovers. Time-wasting became so bad that England managed only 51 overs in a day during the Adelaide Test and crowds had to put up with days that produced less than 150 runs in five hours. The batting of Bailey and Burke in particular was painfully slow. Umpires' mistakes were too common, as was gamesmanship and dragging (where a fast bowler dragged his back foot a long way through the crease in his delivery stride before releasing the ball, thereby gaining an unfair advantage). Bowlers and batsmen ran along the pitch. Laker and Lock rubbed the new ball on the pitch without reproof from umpires. But even before the fifth Test it was clear Australia faced a problem of enormous proportions, such was the witch hunt conducted against jerkers and throwers.

At first the Australian Board of Control denied any problem with throwing existed because umpires had not called a single bowler. This only increased the controversy surrounding a tour watched by 1,130,000 people—50,000 more than saw England in 1954–55. Play was still barred on Sundays. The five Tests made a profit of £44,984, with the Australian players receiving £A85 per Test. The MCC were much more candid and admitted that the doubtful actions of certain bowlers were causing concern. Controversies over chucking had dogged cricket since bowlers changed from underarm to overarm but the worst of all disputes on the subject was about to dawn, with the careers of many players, some of them Australian, at risk.

Chuckers on Trial

Domestic cricket 1958-60; Australia victorious in Pakistan and India 1959-60; West Indies in Australia and the first tied Test 1960-61

By the end of the 1958–59 rubber in which Australia defeated England 4–nil, accusations that chuckers were ruining Test cricket were reaching a stage of hysteria. The high calibre of Benaud's Australian team was overlooked by English writers who claimed his side won the Ashes because they had more chuckers than England, whose chief exponent of chucking was Tony Lock with his faster ball. There was nothing new about controversial bowling actions, but for the first time the debate was enflamed by the powerful medium of television, which some reporters felt they had to outdo. Overnight they developed eyesight so keen they could tell from 70 metres away, amid a blur of swinging arms and shoulders, that Meckiff and Rorke jerked their wrists or fingers in breach of the law. Most Australians were bewildered by the fuss as Meckiff and Rorke were not as quick as Tyson had been on much faster pitches in 1954–55. The only misdemeanour that could be proved against

The first tie in Test cricket history came at Brisbane in the 1960–61 series between Australia and West Indies. This is the run out of Ian Meckiff that ended the match.

them in a series in which not one bowler was no-balled for throwing, was that Rorke bowled from 18 yards, Meckiff from 19 yards. Between them they took 25 Test wickets, but it was Benaud, Davidson and Lindwall who took more wickets than all the England bowlers put together and outbowled England. Meckiff topped the averages with 17 wickets at the low cost of 17.17 each from four Tests.

Ian Johnson tried to inject some sanity into the discussion by stressing in a Melbourne *Herald* article that if the law on throwing (Law 24) was interpreted as written, then Statham, Lock and Trueman should also be called for throwing. Johnson said: "Every pace bowler of quality gives the ball a violent jerk with his wrist and fingers. Leg-spinners who flick their wrists or off-spinners who jerk their shoulders, wrists and fingers to impart spin also breach the law."

This argument went unheard in London where umpire Frank Chester recalled that South African Cuan McCarthy threw the ball so blatantly at Trent Bridge in the 1951 Test against England that Chester sought official sanction for no-balling McCarthy. Chester said he had encountered a lack of support familiar to most umpires and decided not to "stick my neck out".

Confusion over throwing on cricket tours dated back to August 1880 when the second Australian team played Eighteen of Scarborough. Australian opener Alick Bannerman refused to face the bowling of Yorkshire amateur Joseph Frank because he "shied". Bannerman stood back and allowed a shy from Frank to hit his wicket without offering a stroke. This threw the match into confusion, with players leaving the field to debate the issue. When play resumed, Bannerman faced Frank and was caught at point from his third ball. Later in the innings Frank struck Fred Spofforth on the hand, breaking small bones and rendering him unfit for the first Test in England, from 6 to 8 September 1880.

In 1883 and 1884 respectively, Middlesex and Nottinghamshire refused to play against Lancashire because they included John Crossland and George Nash, who both had doubtful actions. In 1885, Kent also refused to play Lancashire when Lord Harris objected to Crossland's appearance. After he was no-balled for throwing for the Mansfield Town club at Sutton-in-Ashfield, Crossland demanded the umpire's removal. The opposing captain refused to comply and the game ended in confusion. That night Crossland hired a town crier to inform the public his delivery was fair. Haygarth's *Scores and Biographies* said Crossland could throw a cricket ball 100 yards "whilst standing in a tub", but did not explain the reason for standing in the tub or who put him there.

In the 1897–98 season Adelaide-born umpire Jim Phillips surprised the cricket world by no-balling countrymen Ernie Jones and Tom McKibbin for throwing. But they were not the only bowlers whose actions were under scrutiny and in 1901 a meeting of English county captains agreed not to bowl 14 players unanimously regarded as throwers.

Phillips wrote that the all-important part of the bowling action was the movement of the elbow joint, which was difficult to watch at the bowler's end but easy to study at square leg: "I am one of those who hold the opinion that to bowl a fair ball it is immaterial whether the arm is straight or at an angle so long as there is no perceptible movement of the elbow joint at the precise moment the ball leaves the bowler's hand."

Apart from Jones and McKibbin, Dave Gregory, Jack Marsh, Frank Pitcher, Ron Halcombe, Eddie Gilbert, Harold Cotton and Ron Cotton had all been no-balled for throwing in first-class matches and Tom Wills, playing for Victoria against New South Wales in 1892, has the "honour" of being the first bowler called in a first-class match in Australia.

The veteran Sydney representative bowler Bill Hunt claimed Gilbert did not know a throw from a legitimate ball. Angered that Gilbert had thrown him out, Hunt retaliated with a deliberate throw when Gilbert batted for Queensland against New South Wales. The throw scattered Gilbert's stumps but as he departed, he said: "Good ball, Bill."

Bradman urged that the problem be left to the umpires, who had the right to no-ball any bowler. Bradman favoured the *Oxford Dictionary* definition of a throw: "To deliver the ball with a sudden straightening of the elbow." All attempts to define a throw to the satisfaction of all cricket nations failed, however, and the noted English critic John Arlott said it was best left to barristers, not cricket officials or writers. Another London sports commentator Jim Manning suggested the problem was similar to defining the action of a trotter.

While the England tour was in progress, New South Wales continued their postwar domination of the Sheffield Shield competition by winning for the sixth successive season. Benaud captained the side in five matches, Sid Carroll in two and when he had apparently recovered from hepatitis, Ian Craig took charge. Selectors stuck with Craig ahead of Benaud for the match with Western Australia in Sydney from 7 to 11 November but after he had scored two ducks and added another in New South Wales' match against England, it became clear he had not fully recovered from his illness and he stood down for the rest of the summer.

This gave Benaud a chance to consolidate his claims to the state and Australian captaincy, which he did brilliantly. Indeed he seemed to bowl better under his own captaincy than for other leaders and the encouragement he gave newcomers Grahame Thomas, a gifted right-hand stroke-player, and Neil Marks, the aggressive left-hand son of the New South Wales batsman of the 1930s, Alex Marks, played a major part in their success. Thomas and Marks created a Shield record 332 for the sixth wicket against South Australia in Sydney from 5 to 9 December.

Marks ended on 180 not out and later made 103 against Victoria in Melbourne. Thomas made 189 and later 86 in a brisk 213-run stand with O'Neill against Victoria in Sydney.

South Australia remained on the bottom of the Shield table, although the right-hand batsman Gavin Stevens became the first batsman from his State to head the Shield averages since A. R. McLean in 1949–50. Stevens scored 859 runs at 85.90, including 259 not out against New South Wales in Sydney from 5 to 9 December, the highest individual Shield score since 1939–40. Other impressive newcomers were the South Australian John Lill, Victorian Bill Lawry, Queenslander Ray Reynolds, and the Western Australians Barry Shepherd and Murray Vernon.

In a season marred by the allegations about chucking, 193-centimetre tall Gordon Rorke won further headlines when he took six wickets for eight runs for New South Wales against Queensland in Sydney, which included a hat-trick. Branded a chucker, Jimmy Burke retired at 28 after 24 Tests. He made three Test centuries and five for New South Wales in scoring 7563 first-class runs at 45.01, wearing one of the baggiest of all green caps.

Burke also took 101 first-class wickets at 29.12, humorous figures to those who believed he was the worst of all the chuckers, delivering the ball with a flipped action from an arm bent so low only the fingers were above his head at the moment of delivery. Crowds jeered and laughed at his action but umpires remained silent, presumably because he was so innocuous. Having satisfied Test umpires, he was free to create mayhem in grade cricket because umpires refused to make fools of more illustrious colleagues. After surviving a New South Wales opening attack that included Rorke, Davidson, Pat Crawford and earlier, Alan Walker, most state batsmen were relieved to face Burke for a few overs, however obvious his cheating, and there was more than one whispered agreement not to protest at his methods.

The 1958–59 South Australian Sheffield Shield team celebrate with slow left-arm spinner Johnny Martin, second right in front, after he had taken 7 for 110 against England.

Benaud was rewarded for outbatting, outbowling and outmanoeuvring England with the captaincy of the Australian side that toured Pakistan and India between November 1959 and January 1960. Fiercely hot, Pakistan had quickly become established as one of the toughest of nations to tour, with food and drink fraught with danger for players who lived in each other's pockets and endured strict prohibition against alcohol. Selectors Bradman, Ryder and Seddon picked their best 15 players, seven with previous experience of Tests in India, and appointed the tough, experienced Sam Loxton as manager. The team was R. Benaud (captain), 29, P. J. P. Burge, 27, A. K. Davidson, 30, L. E. Favell, 30, A. T. W. Grout, 32, R. N. Harvey, 31, B. N. Jarman, 23, L. F. Kline, 25, R. R. Lindwall, 38, C. C. McDonald, 30, K. D. Mackay, 33, I. Meckiff, 24, N. C. O'Neill, 22, G. F. Rorke, 21, G. B. Stevens, 27.

Maddocks was originally named as the second wicket-keeper, but Jarman took his place when Maddocks withdrew. Dr Ian H. McDonald, a specialist in tropical diseases, the brother of Colin McDonald and a former Shield cricketer, went as official team doctor, but was the first one to have stomach trouble. Benaud, Davidson, Harvey, Burge, Lindwall, Mackay and McDonald had all been to India before, and Stevens was the only newcomer to international cricket.

There was little room for experimentation, with eight of the team's 11 matches Tests. A grass pitch was prepared for the opening match, a Test with Pakistan, but heavy rain forced the players onto a matting over clay pitch at Dacca Stadium, in a low swampy area of East Pakistan, from 13 to 18 November.

Benaud took the precaution of sending Kline to the ground two hours before play began each day to supervise the tension of the mat. Kline's only instructions were to ensure the mat was tight when Australia batted. The Australian team were encouraged when they arrived to hear Kline yelling ''Pull, you bastards'' to the Dacca ground staff.

Benaud sent Pakistan in and after three runs were scored Davidson had Ijaz Butt caught behind by Grout. Hanif Mohammad (66) figured in useful stands for the second and third wickets but after Hanif's dismissal Pakistan wickets fell regularly. From 3 for 145, they were all out for 200. Davidson had 4 for 42, Benaud 4 for 69. Australia also had trouble scoring on the mat which seemed to vary in tension when Pakistan batted and despite a superb hand by Harvey (96), only took a first innings lead due to Grout's 66 not out, which included 7 fours.

Fazal Mahmood again proved hostile for the Australians, taking 5 for 71 from 35.5 overs, which included 11 maidens. Mackay came on to give a splendid imitation of Fazal's methods in Pakistan's second innings, bowling medium-pace off breaks to a perfect length. His 6 for 42 swung the match Australia's way. Trailing by 25 runs, Pakistan reached only 134, leaving Australia 110 to win, which they scored for the loss of Favell and Harvey.

Australia became the first visiting country to win a Test series in Pakistan by winning the second Test in oppressive heat at Lahore from 21 to 26 November by seven wickets. This time they had Pakistan out on a grass pitch for 146 and 366. The mixture of pace from Meckiff and Davidson and spin from Benaud and Kline proved too much for all the Pakistani batsmen except Saeed Ahmed, who took six hours over 166. Australia gained a clear advantage through O'Neill's aggressive first innings of 134, which included 19 fours and lifted the total to 391. Set to score 122 in two hours to win, Australia got them with 12 minutes to spare, O'Neill adding

Lindsay Kline in the midst of his famous ''kangaroo hop'' just before delivery.

43 not out to his earlier triumph.

After defeating the President's XI by three wickets at Rawalpindi, 520 metres above sea level on a Himalayan plateau, between 28 and 30 November, Australia began the third Test, at the National Stadium in Karachi from 4 to 9 December, on the same matting pitch which three years earlier had produced the world's slowest ever day of Test cricket. Pakistan started this Test in confident style, assisted by a curator who kept loosening or tightening the mat according to Pakistan's need, but from 1 for 124 were all out for 287. Hanif made 51, Saeed Ahmed 91 and Ijaz Butt 58.

A last-wicket stand of 50 by Davidson and Lindwall kept Australia's deficit down to 30. Pakistan were again painfully slow in their second innings, declaring at 8 for 194 after eight hours batting. The fourth day, watched by President Eisenhower, the first United States President to watch Test cricket, produced only 104 runs for the loss of five Pakistani wickets. Left to make 225 to win in 120 minutes, Australia settled for a draw.

Benaud, who had bowled cleverly and with great stamina in Pakistan, took 3 for 0 and 5 for 76 in a match-winning display in the first Test against India from 12 to 16 December at Feroz Shah Kotla in Delhi. India scored 135 and 206, Australia 468 to win by an innings and 127 runs. Victory was achieved with more than a day to spare, which unhappy spectators greeted by jostling the umpires and throwing bottles onto the field. Harvey made 114, the amazing Mackay 78, and nine Australians contributed 20 or more.

At Green Park ground in Kanpur, in Uttar Pradesh, for the second Test between 19 and 24 December, India brought in the Ahmedabad off-spinner Jasubhai Patel just before the start of play on a newly-laid turf pitch. Patel took 14 wickets for 124 runs in the match, including 9 for 69 in Australia's first innings, achieved with a jerky action he said was due to a boyhood wrist injury. If Patel's action was legal, one can only wonder at why he played in only seven Tests.

India began with a laborious innings of 152, Davidson taking 5 for 31, Benaud 4 for 63. Australia had made 71 without loss when Patel got to work, clean-bowling five batsmen. With Australia ahead by 67 runs, Davidson then bowled Australia back into the match; unchanged from the start of the fourth day until 5.57 p.m., he took 7 for 93 from 57.3 overs.

There was tremendous excitement on the last day, when Australia needed 225 to win without Rorke, who had retired ill after bowling two overs in the first innings. McDonald (34), and Harvey (25), and Meckiff (14 not out) batted comfortably but the other seven batsmen made only 20 runs between them. Patel this time bowled 25.4 overs for his 5 for 55. Polly Umrigar supported him with 4 for 27 from 25 overs and amid ecstatic scenes India achieved her first win over Australia since the countries first met in 1947. Australia's 105 in the second innings remains the lowest in any Test against India.

Rorke went to hospital in serious trouble with gastroenteritis on Christmas Eve. He lost 8 kilograms and had to be flown home for treatment on 6 January. He was never the same again. One of the most controversial bowlers of all time, his freakish delivery slide caused changes to the law on dragging although few other pace bowlers could match his sleight-of-foot. His four Tests yielded only 10 wickets at 20.30, remarkable statistics considering his influence on the game.

Patel, hero of the previous Test, withdrew on the morning of the third Test, from 1 to 6 January at Brabourne stadium in Bombay, where the wicket had originally been laid out by Australian Frank Tarrant. His replacement Salim Durani could not bowl because of a cut finger and Polly Umrigar hurt his back after a few overs, further reducing India's attack. But the Australians could not exploit the weakened India bowling, taking too long to score 8 for 387 declared after India began with 289. O'Neill batted six hours for 163, Harvey close to five hours for 102. Nari Contractor followed his first innings 108 with a stubborn 43, making a draw certain in an opening stand of 95 with Pankaj Roy. India declared at 5 for 226 in their second innings, leaving Australia to score 129 in 25 minutes, which obviously they did not attempt.

Australia took a 2–1 lead in the series by winning the fourth Test at Madras between 13 and 17 January by an innings and 55 runs. Favell made 101—his only Test century—in Australia's first innings of 342, Mackay playing a sheet-anchor role for 89, his highest Test score. Benaud turned his leg break sharply when India batted and at one stage took four wickets for seven runs, finishing with 5 for 43. Following on 193 behind, India were never able to recover from the loss of their first two wickets for 11 runs.

Needing a win to share the rubber, India's hopes were shattered on the first day of the fifth Test, from 23 to 28 January at Eden Gardens in Calcutta, a large, swampy delta city on the Bay of Bengal. Lindwall, in his last Test, lifted his Australian record total to 228 wickets, breaking through India's middle-order batting by dismissing "Bapu" Nadkarni and Ramanath Kenny to have India reeling at 5 for 112. Davidson finished off the innings by removing "Ram" Ramchand and "Tiny" Desai. Chasing 194, Australia had little difficulty scoring 331 after a fourth-wicket stand of 150 by Burge (60) and O'Neill, whose 113 included 15 boundaries.

India batted feebly at the start of their second innings and at 5 for 123—requiring 137 to make Australia bat again—appeared destined for defeat. But Chandra Borde and Kenny hit freely on the final day to save the game. Set to score 203 to win, Australia made 2 for 121 to make sure of a draw and a series win.

With Rorke already invalided home, Stevens was in hospital in Madras during the last two tour matches. He was later diagnosed as having a rare form of hepatitis. Kline could not play in the fifth Test and flew home with what was found to be a sinus infection. All of the team suffered severe bouts of gastroenteritis that kept Dr McDonald busy.

O'Neill's full-blooded aggression dominated Australia's batting and he headed both the tour aggregate and averages with 941 runs in 10 matches at 85.54. Grout, with 364 runs at 52.00, was the only other batsman with an average better than 50 on a tour which saw Australians score ten centuries, four to O'Neill, two each to Favell and Harvey and one each to Burge

and Grout. Davidson headed Australia's bowling averages with 42 wickets at 18.59, but Benaud took most wickets with 49 at 20.65. They had confirmed their position as the world's best cricket team on a difficult tour that ended the Test aspirations of Gavin Stevens as well as Rorke and left most of the players 3 kilograms or more underweight.

They arrived home in time for the season's crucial Sheffield Shield match between New South Wales and Western Australia from 5 to 9 February in Sydney. Western Australia had won their match in Perth from 11 to 15 December by an innings and 105 runs with Simpson, benefiting from his move to Perth, scoring 236 not out, then the highest score in first-class cricket in the West, in an unbroken stand of 301 for the fifth wicket with Ken Meuleman (153 not out). Simpson, passed over for the Pakistan tour, had finished New South Wales off in that match by taking 5 for 45 with his leg breaks.

Benaud took over the New South Wales captaincy from Craig and made sure of victory in the Shield with a nine-wicket win. O'Neill batted with awesome power, making 175 and lifting New South Wales' score to 9 declared for 470. Simpson, who had held an incredible slips catch to dismiss Harvey at 15, played two splendid innings of 98 and 161 not out but his team-mates could not handle Benaud, who took 6 for 74 in both innings. With New South Wales chasing 28 to win outright in bad light and heavy rain, Western Australian captain Meuleman earned high praise by not appealing against the conditions. Simpson, who was on the field for all but 20 minutes of the four days' play, finished the season with 902 runs from six innings at an astonishing average of 300.66.

Flockton returned to the New South Wales team after an absence of six seasons, and finished third to Simpson and O'Neill in the Shield batting averages. His 264 not out against South Australia in Sydney between 8 and 12 January was the

The famous Norman O'Neill sweep shot shows him down on one knee. He sharpened his reflexes hitting a ball hanging from a backyard clothes line.

highest postwar score in Shield cricket and lifted him to 627 runs at 78.37 for the season.

Wally Grout celebrated his success in Pakistan by catching eight Western Australian batsmen in an innings between 12 and 16 February in Brisbane. This remains the highest number of catches in a first-class innings and the record for a wicket-keeper in one innings.

Experimental regulations on throwing and dragging operated through this season. At Sydney in the match against New South Wales Jack McLaughlin, who was not a regular bowler, was no-balled for throwing for Queensland. Umpire Jim Bowden, who called McLaughlin from square leg, did not repeat the call in the only over McLaughlin bowled. Without Rorke in operation, there was a marked decline in dragging, with pace bowlers at all levels of the game taking extreme care with their approach runs.

At the end of the Australian season Ian Craig led a 14-man team on a nine-match tour of New Zealand. The Australian Board of Control insisted on calling them a Second XI although the side included nine players who appeared in

Tests. None of the team had been to Pakistan, although the selectors probably regretted they had not sent Simpson there. The New Zealand tourists were I. D. Craig (captain), 24, R. B. Simpson, 24, L. V. Maddocks, 23, B. C. Booth, 26, J. H. Shaw, 28, J. Potter, 21, G. Thomas, 21, B. Fisher, 26, K. N. Slate, 24, I. W. Quick, 26, J. W. Martin, 28, J. C. Lill, 26, F. M. Misson, 21, and R. A. Gaunt, 25.

Predictably, the tour was dominated by Simpson, who scored 518 runs at 74.00, including a splendid 129 not out against New Zealand in one of the four representative matches. The only other Australian batsman to average more than 50 was wicket-keeper Maddocks, with 286 runs at 71.50. Of the bowlers, Misson and Gaunt found conditions similar to the north of England and once they adjusted to the heavy atmosphere and damp pitches troubled all batsmen. Misson headed the bowling averages with 17 wickets at 12.47, but Ian Quick took most wickets with left arm spin, 28 at 17.18. Simpson at slip was the most brilliant Australian fieldsman and a useful change bowler.

The first representative match at Wellington from 19 to 23 February and the second at Christchurch from 27 February to 2 March were drawn, Bert Sutcliffe supplying the highlight with an innings of 108 at Christchurch. Australia won the third representative match at Dunedin between 4 and 8 March by eight wickets, thanks to Simpson's 129 not out and lively bowling from Misson (4 for 35 and 4 for 40) and Gaunt (2 for 39 and 5 for 90). The fourth representative match at Auckland from 18 to 22 March was drawn. Australia made 381 largely because of Maddocks' 122 not out. New Zealand responded with 203, but Craig chose to bat a second time, declaring at 1 for 105. Set to score 284 to win, New Zealand were 8 for 149 when rain saved them.

The first Fijian cricket team to visit Australia since 1907–08 toured New South Wales country districts in 1959–60 and played two exhibition matches in Sydney. The Fijians' programme included 16 one-day or two-day matches, of which they won 10, lost 5, and left 1 drawn. The Fijians wore sulus on the field and usually were barefooted. The team comprised N. M. Uluiviti (captain), S. B. Snowsill, H. J. Apted, W. W. Apted, I. L. Bula, M. A. Dean, A. Driu, M. J. Fenn, P. Kubunavanua, I. Logavatu, P. Sigeva, I. V. Tabualevu, O. Tuidraki, and F. L. Valentine.

The Fijians attracted 9070 spectators to watch them defeat a New South Wales XI, whom they softened up by serving kava at the drinks break. One batsman, struck on his bare toes by an Alan Davidson yorker that would have crippled some batsmen in ripple soles, merely flexed his toes and batted on. Keith Miller ran two from a skied drive before a Fijian later identified as an Olympic sprinter caught it after running 50 yards round the outfield. The youngest Fijian, Freddie Valentine, dismissed Test players Burke, O'Neill, Benaud and Davidson with his off cutters. Right-hander Bill Apted batted through the Fijian first innings for 70 not out. Fiji scored 163 and 4 for 60 declared, the New South Wales XI 137 and 7 for 52, Fiji winning on the first innings.

The confessions of leading umpires all around the cricket world that they were reluctant to call chuckers without a guarantee that their futures would not be jeopardised brought quick reactions from officials. Umpires were assured of full support and suddenly no-balling of chuckers increased in all the cricket nations.

With Meckiff trying to modify his action, the most dramatic no-balling of a chucker occurred in the English summer of 1960 with the blond South African Geoffrey Merton Griffin the culprit. Like the majority of chuckers, Griffin had a physical defect after a schoolboy accident left him with a decided crook in his right elbow and a right arm he could not straighten.

At Lord's between 21 and 24 May in the match between South Africa and MCC, umpires Frank

Lee and John Langridge no-balled Griffin three times for throwing. A week later umpires T. J. Bartley and W. S. Copson called him eight times for the same offence in South Africa's match against Nottinghamshire. The South African manager Dudley Nourse and captain Jackie McGlew immediately decided to send Griffin to cricket coach Alf Gover to try and eliminate the trouble in an intensive three-day workout at the Spencer Cricket Club, Wandsworth. Griffin survived the Whitsun match with Glamorgan at Cardiff and the first Test at Edgbaston without being called, but the trouble re-emerged when he bowled against Hampshire at Southampton from 18 to 21 June.

Umpires J. H. Parks and Harry Elliott, both experienced former county players, called Griffin six times for throwing. Griffin's problems culminated in the second Test at Lord's between 23 and 27 June. After becoming the first South African bowler to take a Test hat-trick, the first ever achieved at Lord's, he was called 11 times for throwing by umpire Frank Lee. This made Griffin the first bowler ever called for throwing in a Test in England. Australian Ernie Jones, called for throwing against England in 1897–98 at Melbourne, and England's Tony Lock, called against the West Indies at Kingston, Jamaica, in 1953–54, were the only other bowlers no-balled for chucking in Tests.

After the Lord's Test ended in victory to England by an innings and 73 runs on the fourth day, the teams played an exhibition game. Griffin's only over in this match comprised 11 deliveries. Umpire Sid Buller watched Griffin from square leg, then crossed to point, before returning to square leg where he called Griffin four times. Griffin completed his over under-arm, having been called by seven first-class umpires a total of 28 times. Griffin retained his dignity throughout, continuing his career for several seasons with Rhodesia as a batsman.

South Africans were furious with Buller and consequently he did not umpire again in the Tests. But in December that year the English county captains expressed full confidence in him. He was then placed on a panel of umpires for the Test against Australia in 1961 and paid the fees lost for missing a Test with South Africa.

The no-balling of Griffin was on the front pages of London newspapers when Sir Donald Bradman and Board of Control chairman Bill Dowling arrived for the Imperial Cricket Conference at Lord's. Australia considered an agenda that included the throwing controversy so important they decided to send their senior administrators, rather than follow the normal procedure of being represented by the Board's London representative, Ben Barnett.

Dowling made no attempt to hide his concern over the unfairness of the criticism in Fleet Street of Meckiff, whose action had never been questioned by school, district cricket, state or Test umpires:

> *The attacks being made in England on Meckiff and Rorke amount to intimidation of umpires. They have been prejudged and condemned as throwers without ever having been seen in England. It is contrary to every principle of fair play that feeling should be whipped up and sportsmen condemned out of hand before ever appearing in a country.*

The conference agreed on a definition of a throw which in effect was a combination of English and Australian drafts on the subject:

> *A ball shall be deemed to have been thrown if, in the opinion of either umpire, the bowling arm having been bent at the elbow (whether the wrist be backward of the elbow or not), is suddenly straightened immediately prior to the instant of delivery. The bowler shall, nevertheless, be at liberty to use the wrist freely in the delivery action.*

The extraordinary whip in Ian Meckiff's left-arm action brought accusations of throwing only after he reached Test status. In this magic-eye sequence he has escaped being no-balled for dragging well past the stumps but even under the present front foot rule deserved to be called.

The definition was hailed by most critics as a brave attempt to solve a very difficult problem, but inadequate for legal purposes or as an instruction to umpires. To curb dragging, the conference agreed to introduce from September 1962 the front foot rule under which bowlers had to release the ball with their leading foot behind the batting crease. The conference gave umpires the power to take off bowlers guilty of time-wasting or excessive use of the bouncer.

By the time of the 1960 conference of cricket nations the Englishmen D. B. Pearson, G. A. R. Lock, K. J. Aldridge, H. J. Rhodes, E. M. Bryant, and D. W. White, South Africans C. N. McCarthy and G. M. Griffin, Australians J. W. Burke, G. F. Rorke, K. N. Slater, I Meckiff, and J. J. McLaughlin, and the West Indian C. Sayers had all been branded as chuckers by umpires or critics. Indeed the throwing controversy had so intensified it was seriously suggested that Australia's 1961 tour of England should be postponed to allow tempers to cool. Bradman on his return home from the London conference said:

> It is the most complex question in cricket history because it is not a matter of fact, but of opinion and interpretation. It is so involved that two men of equal goodwill and sincerity can take opposite views. I plead that a calm, patient attitude be exercised while we pursue and resolve the problem.

The goodwill Bradman sought came when the second West Indian team arrived for their 1960–61 tour of Australia under the captaincy of the Barbadan Frank Worrell, the first black captain of the West Indies and a man, as C. L. R. James emphasises, with remarkable perception of each player's contribution to the team effort. He had established himself as a gifted, consistent right-hand batsman and left-arm medium or slow bowler, a lithe, elegant stylist, but now at a time of flagging interest in cricket in Australia he faced his major test as a captain. The boredom Trevor Bailey and Jimmy Burke had inflicted on the

previous Test series in Australia, the incessant arguments over throwing and dragging, had Australian cricket in the doldrums when this West Indian team arrived: F. M. M. Worrell (captain), 36, C. C. Hunte, 28, F. C. M. Alexander, 32, A. L. Valentine, 30, R. B. Kanhai, 25, G. St A. Sobers, 24, J. L. Hendriks, 26, S. M. Nurse, 27, C. W. Smith, 28, J. S. Solomon, 30, P. D. Lashley, 23, W. W. Hall, 23, L. R. Gibbs, 26, C. Watson, 21, T. Dewdney, 27, S. Ramadhin, 31, with Gerry Gomez as manager.

The West Indians had played a grim series the previous southern summer in the West Indies against England, in which bowlers Hall and Watson were warned for intimidatory bowling and their over-use of bouncers was strongly criticised. Nine years before Lindwall and Miller had given Weekes, Walcott and Worrell a torrid time, frequently forcing them to duck under bouncers and this time they appeared well equipped to square accounts. Worrell wanted rebellious Jamaican fast bowler Roy Gilchrist in the team but the West Indian Cricket Board refused to consider him. Gilchrist had been sent home in disgrace from the West Indies' tour of India in 1959 for bowling "beamers" (full tosses at the head) against tail-enders. Manager Gomez insisted from the start that his bowlers would only use bouncers intelligently, and that they intended to play bright, adventurous cricket. Cynics who had suffered a decade of lifeless play were unconvinced.

The tour started disastrously for the visitors. After a warm-up match against a Western Australian Country XI at Bunbury, where Ramadhin had 3 for 1, Dewdney 3 for 10, they were defeated at the WACA by Western Australia between 28 October and 1 November. Bob Simpson virtually won the match single-handedly scoring 87 and 221 not out for Western Australia, who made 140 and 5 declared for 444. West Indies paid the penalty for a feeble first innings batting display, collapsing against Des Hoare (5 for 65) and Hugh Bevan (3 for 29) to be all out for 97. Sobers hit out aggressively in the second innings for 119 but five catches by wicket-keeper Bruce Buggins left the West Indies 95 short of their target.

The West Indies had their first win in Melbourne from 18 to 22 November, beating Victoria by an innings and 171 runs, after a masterly knock of 252 by Kanhai, who did not give a chance in six and a half hours batting. Ramadhin bamboozled the Victorians in both innings, taking 5 for 37 and 5 for 65.

At Sydney from 25 to 28 November Rorke found the front foot rule so difficult to adjust to he knocked over the stumps five times in his first five overs. The West Indies struggled against Davidson and the spin of Benaud and Martin, losing Worrell to injury in their first innings of 111. Harvey (109) and O'Neill (156 not out) then hammered all the West Indian bowlers to help New South Wales to 6 for 429 declared and a lead of 318. Benaud restricted the West Indies to 199 in their second innings by taking 5 for 31.

'Gabba fans watched in disbelief as "Slasher" Mackay, chewing furiously at his gum, rushed to 143 not out, scoring 62 runs in boundaries, to lift Queensland to 4 for 329 on 2 December. West Indies' response to Queensland's 431 included brilliant strokeplay by Kanhai, who made 75 out of 357. Rain washed out play on the final day.

The 500th Test match, from 9 to 14 December, began before a small 'Gabba crowd, understandable considering the drab cricket inflicted on Brisbanites two seasons earlier by England. Davidson induced edged catches from Smith, Hunte and Kanhai and just missed a fourth when Sobers slashed at a ball that flew to Benaud in the slips, only to glance off his hands to the boundary. West Indies were 3 for 65 when Worrell joined Sobers. Meckiff bowled with his front arm higher than previously but modifications to his action had lessened his hostility.

Garfield Sobers on his way to a brilliant 132 in the Brisbane tied Test. O'Neill countered with a dazzling 181 for Australia.

After his early let-off Sobers hit three fours in four balls from Benaud to reach his 50. Then he straight-drove Benaud for four to bring up the century stand with Worrell, who made 38 of them. Benaud brought on Mackay to slow the scoring and keep the game tight while Davidson and Meckiff rested, but after Sobers had heavily plundered three overs he had to take Mackay off and try Kline. When Sobers belted Kline over mid-wicket for four, Worrell called: "Enough of that. This is a Test match." The power of Sobers' shot-making was as thrilling as his eagerness to go for his strokes. He moved to 132 in 174 minutes before Meckiff bowled him a full-toss wide of the leg stump. The ball hit the back of his bat and dollied up for an easy catch to Kline at mid-on. All the Australians joined in the crowd's applause for a wonderful knock that included 21 fours.

From 4 for 239, the West Indies total reached

Australia *v*. Indies 1960–61 (First Test)

At Woolloongabba, Brisbane, 9, 10, 12, 13, 14 December
Result: Match Tied

West Indies

First Innings	
C. C. Hunte *c*. Benaud *b*. Davidson	24
C. W. Smith *c*. Grout *b*. Davidson	7
R. B. Kanhai *c*. Grout *b*. Davidson	15
G. St A. Sobers *c*. Kline *b*. Meckiff	132
F. M. M. Worrell *c*. Grout *b*. Davidson	65
J. S. Solomon hit wkt *b*. Simpson	65
P. D. Lashley *c*. Grout *b*. Kline	19
F. C. M. Alexander *c*. Davidson *b*. Kline	60
S. Ramadhin *c*. Harvey *b*. Davidson	12
W. W. Hall *st*. Grout *b*. Kline	50
A. L. Valentine *not out*	0
Extras (LB 3, W 1)	4
Total	453

Second Innings	
c. Simpson *b*. Mackay	39
c. O'Neill *b*. Davidson	6
c. Grout *b*. Davidson	54
b. Davidson	14
c. Grout *b*. Davidson	65
lbw *b*. Simpson	47
b. Davidson	0
b. Benaud	5
c. Harvey *b*. Simpson	6
b. Davidson	18
not out	7
(B 14, LB 7, W 2)	23
Total	284

Bowling

	Overs	Maidens	Runs	Wickets
Davidson	30	2	135	5
Meckiff	18	0	129	1
Mackay	3	0	15	0
Benaud	24	3	93	0
Simpson	8	0	25	1
Kline	17.6	6	52	3

Bowling

	Overs	Maidens	Runs	Wickets
Davidson	24.6	4	87	6
Meckiff	4	1	19	0
Mackay	21	7	52	1
Benaud	31	6	69	1
Simpson	7	2	18	2
Kline	4	0	14	0
O'Neill	1	0	2	0

Australia

First Innings		
C. C. McDonald *c.* Hunte *b.* Sobers	57	
R. B. Simpson *b.* Ramadhin	92	
R. N. Harvey *b.* Valentine	15	
N. C. O'Neill *c.* Valentine *b.* Hall	181	
L. E. Favell *run out*	45	
K. D. Mackay *b.* Sobers	35	
A. K. Davidson *c.* Alexander *b.* Hall	44	
R. Benaud *lbw b.* Hall	10	
A. T. W. Grout *lbw b.* Hall	4	
I. Meckiff *run out*	4	
L. F. Kline *not out*	3	
Extras (B 2, LB 8, W 1, NB 4)	15	
Total	505	

Second Innings		
b. Worrell	16	
c. sub (L. R. Gibbs) *b.* Hall	0	
c. Sobers *b.* Hall	5	
c. Alexander *b.* Hall	26	
c. Solomon *b.* Hall	7	
b. Ramadhin	28	
run out	80	
c. Alexander *b.* Hall	52	
run out	2	
run out	2	
not out	0	
(B 2, LB 9, NB 3)	14	
Total	232	

Bowling

	Overs	Maidens	Runs	Wickets
Hall	29.3	1	140	4
Worrell	30	0	93	0
Sobers	32	0	115	2
Valentine	24	6	82	1
Ramadhin	15	1	60	1

Bowling

	Overs	Maidens	Runs	Wickets
Hall	17.7	3	63	5
Worrell	16	3	41	1
Sobers	8	0	30	0
Valentine	10	4	27	0
Ramadhin	17	3	57	1

Fall of Wickets

Wkt	WI 1st	A 1st	WI 2nd	A 2nd
1st	23	84	13	1
2nd	42	138	88	7
3rd	65	194	114	49
4th	239	278	127	49
5th	243	381	210	57

Fall of Wickets

Wkt	WI 1st	A 1st	WI 2nd	A 2nd
6th	283	469	210	92
7th	347	484	241	226
8th	366	489	250	228
9th	452	496	253	232

Umpires: C. J. Egar and C. Hoy

453 with disciplined contributions from Worrell (65), Solomon (65), Alexander (60) and Hall (50). Davidson took the bowling honours with 5 for 135, Grout made four catches and a stumping, but Meckiff disappointed with 1 for 129.

Australia took a 52-run lead with a first innings of 505, but compared to the West Indies the stroke play of O'Neill's 181 and Simpson's 92 looked stultified. Batting with O'Neill, Mackay watched the ball instead of the crease

'Keeper Wally Grout appeals after Joe Solomon's cap dislodged a bail during the stroke. Solomon was given out hit wicket in this much-discussed incident in the first Test, 1960–61.

and ran one short. West Indies' second innings of 284 was held together by sensible batting from Kanhai (54), Worrell (65) and Solomon (47), with Davidson again troubling them all in taking 6 for 87.

Left to score 233 in 310 minutes, 45 an hour, Australia lost 5 for 57 to a spectacular spell by Hall, who repeatedly beat the bat with sheer pace. When the sixth wicket fell at 92, spectators from southern states headed for the airport or sped away in cars for the New South Wales border. Instead of settling for a draw, Benaud played each ball on its merits, interposing brilliant strokes with calm defence. Davidson was cheered when he hooked Ramadhin for six and when Hall

gave him a fierce head-high bouncer he pulled it for four. The running between wickets as they picked up singles and turned twos into threes was the ideal blend of judgement and nimble-footedness.

They were still together with only 7 runs wanted. Then dramatically the West Indian fieldsmen, who had thrown wildly throughout this stirring partnership, became deadly accurate. Davidson was run out for 80 when Joe Solomon hit the stumps from mid-wicket. Davidson's 11 for 222 and 124 runs made him the first player to score 100 and take ten wickets in a Test, a feat since matched only by Ian Botham and Imran Khan.

Six runs were needed with three wickets in hand when the last over began. A leg-bye resulted when Hall hit Grout in the ribs. Hall's second delivery was a bouncer which Benaud tried to hook but tickled to 'keeper Gerry Alexander. Meckiff played the third ball back to the bowler. They sneaked a single from the fourth as it thudded through to Alexander, which so disgusted Hall he pitched the ball at the stumps, forcing Valentine to scamper desperately at mid-off to prevent four overthrows. Grout skied the fifth ball, which looked a simple catch for Kanhai at square leg, but Hall swerved off his follow-through to hurl himself after it. Kanhai backed away from a collision and the ball bounced off Hall's hands as another run was taken. Meckiff hit the sixth ball high into the sun at square leg and the batsmen crossed twice before Hunte cut it off on the fence, wheeled and threw to the keeper as Grout finished a stride short of the run that would have given Australia victory.

Kline walked in to face the last two balls with the scores level. He played the seventh delivery with the élan of Jack Hobbs firmly towards square leg and Meckiff, backing up splendidly, raced down the pitch, only to be run out by a magnificent low throw from Solomon, who had only one stump to aim at. The West Indians leapt exuberantly in the air and clasped their heads for joy, but few knew the result.

The final over had lasted nine minutes and ended four minutes after scheduled stumps. The delight of the 4100 spectators and the players became rapturous as umpire Col Hoy announced history's first tied Test and the realisation of what had happened sank home. In the confused Australian dressing-room Meckiff said: "Fancy getting beat like that." Mackay kept asking who had won. Up in the Queensland Cricketers' Club a member asked Ray Lindwall if the tie was a record and Lindwall said: "I dunno, mate, but Bradman says it has never been done before and if Bradman says so nobody's going to argue."

Lucky Benaud

Record crowds for the rest of the Series; domestic cricket 1960-61; Australia tours England 1961

The new era the Brisbane tie ushered in was played out by cricketers far removed from the journeymen who dominated the early years of Australia's big cricket. Frank Worrell had to get time off from his university to tour in a team sprinkled with professional cricketers. The Australians drove their own cars to the grounds, Benaud in a smart red two-seater. None of them ironed their own flannels. Both teams had their own masseurs.

The players stayed at the best hotels, went by air from state to state, owned their own bats, kept their gear in their own cricket bags, and were accustomed to a daily round of television, radio and newspaper interviews. Long before the tour ended a few had book contracts in their luggage. Alan McGilvray had become such an important figure in the game through his radio broadcasts umpires made special signals to him in stands indicating if a batsman was out leg before wicket or caught behind.

The West Indian tour had none of the partisanship of the normal England–Australia

Frank Worrell gives the Frank Worrell trophy a shine before handing it to Richie Benaud after a wonderful series.

series. Spectators applauded exceptional cricket regardless of which side was responsible, and disliked seeing such entertaining players as the West Indians lose. Neither side feared defeat and the crowd recognised this when they called all 22 players onto the verandah of the 'Gabba pavilion.

New South Wales needed only two of the three days allotted to the return state match, 23 and 24 December, to beat the West Indies by an innings and 97 runs. O'Neill scored his third successive century (114), Craig made 83, Booth 87, Harvey 74, and Davidson 81 in a polished batting display for New South Wales on a pitch that disadvantaged bowlers. Chasing 468, the West Indies collapsed against a varied attack and followed on 305 runs behind. Hunte batted superbly for 105 in 110 minutes, hitting 18 fours, but against the spin of left-hander Johnny Martin and the wily Benaud his teammates folded for 208.

Martin, whose 45 wickets at 23.64 in 1959–60 was the highest number of wickets in Shield cricket for ten seasons, bowled himself into a Test spot, replacing Lindsay Kline for the second Test in Melbourne from 30 December to 3 January. Frank Misson replaced Ian Meckiff in the other Australian change.

Australia were 8 for 251 before Mackay (74) and Martin (55) put on 97. Chasing 348, the West Indies collapsed for 181 on the third day, with 123 of the runs coming from a third-wicket stand by Kanhai (84) and Nurse (70). Davidson followed his triumphs in Brisbane by taking 6 for 53.

Following on 167 behind, the West Indies' problems increased when Solomons was given out hit wicket when his cap fell onto his stumps and dislodged a bail. Hunte (110) and Alexander (72) added 87 for the sixth wicket but they could not make up for the loss of Kanhai, Sobers and Worrell in four balls from Martin. Hall at his fastest gave Australia a torrid time in scoring the 67 needed to win by seven wickets and was twice warned for excessive use of the bouncer.

Gibbs and Valentine formed a highly effective spin combination in the third Test at Sydney from 13 to 18 January, taking 16 wickets between them. Sobers moved slowly to 80 but after tea launched a brilliant assault on pace bowlers using the new ball, scoring at a run a minute to add a further 88. His 168 took West Indies to 339. Hall's pace accounted for Simpson and Harvey and despite a stubborn 71 by O'Neill Australia were out for 202 when three wickets fell in four balls to Gibbs.

Leading by 137, the West Indies stumbled when Davidson dismissed Hunte, Kanhai and Sobers for 22, but Worrell and Smith restored their advantage with a century stand in 67 minutes. The Australian attack took a battering from the West Indian tail when Davidson and Meckiff could not bowl because of injuries and Alexander made 108, the only century of his career. Australia had to score 464 in the final innings to win and when Harvey (85) and O'Neill (70) were together that looked possible. But from 2 for 191 Australia slumped to 7 for 209 and were all out for 241. On a helpful pitch Gibbs put the issue beyond doubt on the fifth morning by taking 4 for 2, to finish with match figures of 8 for 112. Valentine had 8 for 153. The West Indies win, by 222 runs, levelled the series and touched off a demand for seats to the Adelaide and Melbourne Tests that exceeded demand for football grand finals.

The Adelaide Test from 27 January to 1 February produced one of the most exciting rearguard actions in Australian cricket. With Davidson and Meckiff unavailable through injury, Australia opened the attack with blond Sydney physical fitness fanatic Frank Misson and strapping 190-centimetre Western Australian Des Hoare, who had impressive performances in Shield cricket behind him. All the Australians believed the West Indies erred in preferring an extra batsman instead of allowing Chester Watson, a bowler of genuine pace, to partner Hall.

At 3 for 91, Kanhai and Worrell put on 107

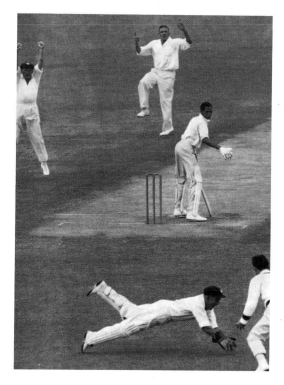

Wally Grout dives full length to brilliantly catch Lance Gibbs off Davidson in the third Test in Sydney in 1960–61.

in an hour of delightfully free batting. Kanhai reached a century in two hours and his 117 included 2 sixes and 11 fours. Worrell (71) and Alexander (63 not out) were severe on Kline but Benaud restricted the total to 393 by taking 5 for 96.

Dogged batting by McDonald (71) and Simpson (85) gave Australia hope before Gibbs achieved a hat-trick by dismissing Mackay, Grout and Misson. Australia slumped from 5 for 281 to 8 for 281. Benaud (77) received assistance from Hoare (35), lifting the total to 366. Kanhai's second century of the match (115) included a record second-wicket stand of 163 with Hunte (79) and allowed Worrell to declare at 6 for 432. Kanhai's willingness to hit was shown when he put the first ball of the fourth morning from Benaud into the crowd for six before most spectators had settled into their seats.

Set to score 460 to win in 390 minutes, Australia looked beaten when six wickets fell for 193. The last pair, Kline and Mackay, came together at 9 for 207 with 100 minutes left and no hope of reaching the target. Kline went straight to the crease from the practice nets, where Martin and O'Neill had got him out 11 times, seven of them bowled. The pair defended grimly, picking up 66 runs as Worrell relied on Hall and Gibbs to break the stand when Sobers' left-arm spin appeared more dangerous.

Mackay said he became more determined to bat out time when the West Indians started to walk off after Sobers caught him from a bump ball. Mackay and Kline stood their ground and when the West Indians claimed a catch, umpire Col Egar rejected the appeal. Mackay believed this was deliberate gamesmanship and settled down to enjoy the unusual experience of being applauded for slow scoring. Even when Worrell tried Joe Solomon, who had never bowled in a Test before, Mackay defended dourly and Solomon's three overs cost only one run.

The West Indians began hurrying through their overs and sprinting into position at the change of ends. Overs that normally took four minutes were completed in two minutes, with a loss of quality. At two minutes to six Worrell rushed through an over so fast a further over appeared likely. To prevent it, Mackay appealed to umpire Egar to remove spectators who had jumped the fence. Egar ordered them to play on as Worrell handed the ball to Hall for the last over.

Wesley Winfield Hall, 188 centimetres tall, heavily-muscled, gold teeth gleaming, had a long approach-run in which he moved with the steadily accelerating flow of a disciplined athlete. He was timed at 146 kilometres an hour and was just as fast at the end of a day as at the start. He was a tremendous crowd-pleaser in Australia but as he moved into the last over the Adelaide crowd fell silent. Facing him, "Slasher" Mackay was encouraged to see that the footmarks in the

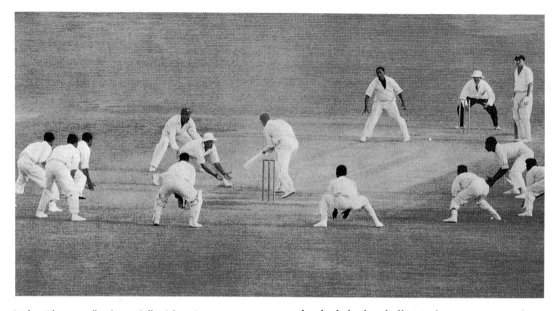

Lindsay Kline, normally a batting duffer, defying the West Indian bowlers in the thrilling last wicket stand with Ken Mackay that saved the fourth Test for Australia.

pitch were too wide for Hall to exploit.

The first ball travelled at fearsome pace and momentarily looked to have got through Mackay's defence but he jammed down on it at the last instant. The next two flashed past wide of the off stump. The fourth was on the middle stump and Mackay could have taken two as it raced past point but he declined to run. The fifth ball rocketed past the off stump and Mackay told himself Hall was wasting his shots. The sixth and seventh deliveries were right on the stumps, propelled with all Hall's force, but Mackay jabbed down on them. Hall lost his step as he stormed in for the last ball, rushed over the crease and banged the ball at his own feet in disgust. Umpire Hoy called "No-ball" but spectators did not hear him. Small boys swept over the ground, and policemen herded them back to the fence. Hall began again, only to have a small boy holding an autograph book clamber onto the field.

The over had taken ten minutes when Hall unleashed the last ball. Mackay saw it was short and decided to take it on the body rather than risk a snick. It smacked into Mackay's ribs well away from the bat and he staggered clear of the stumps, desperate to avoid falling on them, to force the draw. Kline and Mackay took an hour to get through back-slapping team-mates and spectators, accept the congratulations of the West Indians, and get into the shower. Mackay, who had resisted for four hours, was relieved to find the last-ball bruise was no worse than the handful inflicted on Col McDonald through the series. Next day at Brisbane airport press photographers took him into a toilet to take pictures of the multi-coloured bruise, by then as big as a soup plate. The *Courier-Mail* launched a "Bob in for Slasher" fund that realised more than £800.

Despite his plucky batting in Adelaide, Kline was dropped from the fifth Test at Melbourne from 10 to 15 February because he had not taken a wicket in 33 overs. Benaud sent the West Indians in when he won the toss and his judgement that a wet outfield would curb the score proved correct, although he must have had misgivings when the score reached 75 for the loss of only one wicket. Sobers, with 64, was the only West

"Slasher" Mackay, having seen a short delivery, deliberately lets the last ball of the drawn fourth Test in Adelaide strike him on the body rather than risk nicking a catch. This allowed Australia to go into the fifth Test with the series all square.

Indian to pass 50 and they were all out early on the second day for 292.

The second day attracted 90,800 spectators, still a world record. Even those clustered on the roofs of the stands applauded as Simpson (75) and McDonald (91) put on 146, the best opening stand by either side in the series. Sobers bowled unchanged for 41 eight ball overs, taking the ball at 0 for 124 and coming off at 9 for 335. He bowled slow at first, opened at a brisk medium-pace with the new ball on Monday, and returned to his slows for an hour, finishing with 5 for 120. By scoring 24, Davidson completed his 1000th Test run, to go with his 100 wickets, and reach the double after 34 Tests.

Unperturbed by a first-innings deficit of 64, the West Indies went for their strokes. Cammie Smith hooked the second ball of the innings for six and put on 50 in 50 minutes with Hunte. Kanhai scattered fieldsmen with some ferocious shots, going down on one knee to sweep and driving with such force he lost his footing. Australia gained the ascendancy early on the fourth day before Gerry Alexander defied them for two and a half hours in scoring 73.

The final innings began with Australia requiring 258 to win with cricket fans listening to their radios all round the world. Simpson thrilled them by scoring 18 runs in the first over and 24 from the first ten balls he faced. The West Indian spinners turned the ball sharply but Simpson played brilliantly until Gibbs bowled him for 92.

With three wickets in hand and four runs wanted, Grout back cut Valentine and the ball skimmed away towards the fence. There was an

An aerial view of the Melbourne Cricket Ground on the second day of the fifth Test when a world-record crowd of 90,800 watched. Australia went on to a tense, two-wicket win.

appeal and Grout's off bail was spotted on the ground with Alexander pointing at it. "Keep running," Mackay shouted to Grout. They ran two as Alexander appealed and pointed at the bail on the turf in front of the stumps. Umpire Egar at the bowler's end conferred with umpire Hoy at square leg as 41,000 people speculated on how the bail got there.

Egar said his view had been obscured by the bowler running in front of him. Hoy said that Grout's bat had not touched the stumps or Alexander's gloves. Egar then ruled not out. Alexander clutched his head in annoyance and Lashley and Solomon threw themselves on the the grass in disgust. Worrell immediately beckoned them to get up, but the West Indian players looked far from happy at the decision.

Some reports suggested Grout cut the ball onto his stumps, but Mackay's view was that Alexander had accidentally brushed the stumps with his pads or gloves as he turned to follow the path of the ball. "If Slash had told me I was out I would have walked," said Grout, who was caught by Smith going for the winning hit two balls later.

At 8 for 256, Martin joined Mackay and skied the ball for a single to bring the scores level. Police tried vainly to clear boys from inside the fence. Valentine bowled to Mackay who was beaten by a ball that spun back, missed the stumps, and also beat Alexander, providing Australia with a bye, to win its most exciting series. Australia had won the rubber 2–1, with 1 drawn and 1 tied.

Thousands of spectators invaded the ground and as the players sprinted for the dressing room the umpires grabbed both sets of stumps and headed after them. The traditional scramble for souvenirs had been banned but one small boy beat the ban by scooting away with the ball. Wes Hall pursued him and as the boy leapt the fence Hall reached him and said: "Mister Frank Worrell would like that ball!" With the huge Hall frame towering over him, the boy handed it over.

Almost 20,000 spectators gathered in front of the Grey Smith stand chanting for Worrell. An announcer appeared and said that Worrell was taking a shower but the crowd refused to go. Forty minutes after the match ended Worrell came out to present the Frank Worrell trophy to Richie Benaud. This perpetual trophy had been produced by the Australian Board of Control just before the match. Mounted on top of it were the balls used in the first tied Test. On one side there was a kangaroo and on the other West Indian palm trees.

Worrell made the presentation and then said he had his own gifts for Benaud. He handed over his cap, representing his scalp, his tie that was his neck, and his blazer that was his body. His legs were too feeble to offer anybody, he said. Most of the crowd realised they would never see Worrell again, and it was a sad moment as thousands of voices sang their farewell to him.

The tour of 22 matches had been watched by 956,018 people who paid £A213,530 for the privilege. Two days after play ended the West Indians were given a ticker-tape send-off as they drove in open cars through Melbourne streets bedecked in streamers and balloons. Players constantly leaned forward from their cars to shake hands with people who tossed them maroon and white streamers, the West Indian colours. Melbourne trams stopped and torn paper fluttered down from office buildings as the players moved to a civic reception at Melbourne Town Hall. Next morning Worrell wrote in the Melbourne *Herald* that it was the most touching tribute ever paid to a sporting team anywhere in the world.

"I can't tell you how overwhelmed the boys and I were," wrote Worrell. "The tears came easily to me in that extraordinary procession and I couldn't be bothered wiping them away. And I wasn't the only one. It was incredible."

The 1960–61 West Indian team in Australia was an outfit that bristled with entertainers, skilful cricketers with a happy, daring approach. Kanhai headed the first-class batting averages with 1093 runs at 64.29 in 11 matches, including four centuries. Alexander, with 734 runs at 52.42, was the only other player to average over fifty in a side with scant regard for averages. More to the point eight of the 16 players made more than 400 runs. Of the side's ten first-class centuries, Sobers' 132 in Brisbane and 168 in Sydney rank among the classic Test 100s.

Wes Hall captured the adulation of Australians with his marvellous athleticism, taking 21 wickets at 29.33 in the Tests and 40 wickets at 27.72 on the tour. His figures would have been better but for Simpson who scored two centuries and had six innings of 70 or more in eight matches against the West Indies. Ramadhin, displaced by Gibbs after two Tests, was past his prime but still terrorised country batsmen.

O'Neill scored most runs for Australia in the Tests, 522 at 52.20, though Burge headed him in the averages with 215 runs from two games at 53.75. O'Neill made the only Australian Test century, 181, and scored three of the nine centuries made against the tourists. The wicket-keepers, Alexander and Grout, reached a very high standard with Grout dismissing 23 batsmen and Alexander playing an innings of 50 or more in all five Tests.

Despite his absence through injury in the fourth Test, Davidson took 33 wickets, more than any other bowler on either side. Benaud's 23 Test wickets were costly at 33.86, although he bowled 95 overs more than any team-mate. Lack of a class spinner to partner Benaud remained an unsolved problem for Australia's selectors, neither Kline nor Martin measuring up. Meckiff's new action was a flop.

The West Indies took home £30,000, much of it earned in the dramatic final Test when 274,404 people paid £A48,749, the highest receipts for any match in Australia. They deserved the ecstatic welcome home they received in the Caribbean because they had given new vitality to all international cricket at a time when restrictive tactics originated by England were driving spectators away from the game.

The 1960–61 Sheffield Shield competition produced two outstanding young bowlers. Western Australia's giant fast-medium bowler Graham McKenzie, a trainee physical education instructor from the Claremont–Cottesloe club, surprised the West Indians with his pace from the pitch in their first Australian match and continued to show rare promise. Another 19-year-old, red-haired left-arm googly bowler David Sincock, paved the way for a shock South Australian win over New South Wales in Adelaide between 3 and 7 February that brought the Shield competition to a dramatic conclusion. Sincock took 6 for 52 in 13.1 overs, his victims including Booth, Thomas, Benaud and Martin. Benaud (119) and Flockton (84) bustled him off his length in the second innings, but by then Favell (87) and Lill (91) had capitalised on the advantage Sincock had given South Australia, who ran out winners by three wickets.

This defeat meant that New South Wales started their last match in Perth against Western Australia six points behind Victoria. With their sequence of seven successive Shield wins in danger, New South Wales scored 2 for 339 on the first day. Craig went on to 197, and Thomas also scored a century (113), which enabled Craig to declare at 6 for 549. Western Australia made 331 in their first innings but still followed on, and clever leg spin bundled them out for 158, giving New South Wales victory by an innings and 60 runs.

The West Indies receive a ticker-tape farewell from Melbourne fans delighted by their dashing cricket at the conclusion of the 1960–61 tour.

Meanwhile in Brisbane over the same weekend, 10 to 14 February, Queensland defeated Victoria on the first innings. Queensland scored 490, thanks to a fine 126 from Sam Trimble, and dismissed Victoria for 198. Following on, the Victorians, plumber Bill Lawry and schoolteacher Jack Potter, put on 237 for the second wicket to put outright victory out of Queensland's reach. Potter, a right-hander from the Fitzroy club in Melbourne, made 126. Northcote left-hander Lawry's 134, following his 266 earlier in the season against New South Wales, took his season's total to 813 runs, average 62.53. Craig had hoped his 197 in Perth would win him a place as an opener in the 1961 team to England but Lawry's 134 won him the spot.

Victoria's defeat gave New South Wales the Shield for a record eight successive seasons, but Victoria still had five players in the team for England after a wonderful season in which state teams often followed the West Indies' adventurous example. The dragging problem had been checked by diligent umpires and Brian Quigley was dropped from the South Australian side after umpire Col Egar twice called him for chucking in the match against Victoria.

Thirty-year-old Jim Clissold, playing for Sutherland against Ryde at Ryde Oval in Sydney's Municipal and Shires competition, won space among the Test headlines when he performed three hat-tricks in one day. Clissold took 6 for 50, including a hat-trick, in the first innings, and 7 for 15, with two hat-tricks, in the second innings.

The twenty-third Australian team to tour England included only one player new to touring, Lawry, although the experience of three players,

The 1961 Australian team in England: (L to R) (back) B. C. Booth, W. M. Lawry, F. M. Misson, R. A. Gaunt, G. D. McKenzie; (centre) A. James (masseur), J. Cameron (scorer), B. N. Jarman, I. W. Quick, R. C. Steele (treasurer), L. F. Kline, N. C. O'Neill, P. J. P. Burge, R. B. Simpson; (front) A. T. W. Grout, A. K. Davidson, R. Benaud (captain), S. G. Webb (manager), R. N. Harvey, C. C. McDonald, K. D. Mackay.

Booth, Misson and Quick, was limited to a brief New Zealand trip. All the others were seasoned campaigners with tours of South Africa, India, Pakistan and England behind them. Grout was lucky to pass the team's medical inspection as he had a history of blackouts, though fortunately not on the field. More than once Queensland team-mates had had to revive him when he passed out at practice. The team was chosen by Jack Ryder, Dudley Seddon and Sir Donald Bradman, who had just become chairman of the Australian Cricket Board in succession to Bill Dowling, and was managed by the Sydney Queen's Counsellor Syd Webb, with Victorian Ray Steele as treasurer, Jack Cameron as scorer and Arthur James as physiotherapist. The team was: R. Benaud (captain), 30, B. C. Booth, 27, P. J. P Burge, 29, A. K. Davidson, 31, W. M. Lawry, 24, K. D. Mackay, 35, C. C. McDonald, 32, G. D. McKenzie, 19, R. A. Gaunt, 27, A. T. W. Grout, 34, R. N. Harvey, 32, B. N. Jarman, 25, L. F. Kline, 26, F. M. Misson, 22, N. C. O'Neill, 24, I. W. Quick, 27, R. B. Simpson, 25.

The team, the last to go to England and back by sea, had played 311 Tests between them when they boarded the *Himalaya* in Fremantle on 29

March 1961, after winning their two warm-up matches in Tasmania and playing a draw against Western Australia in Perth. In England they faced opponents who had developed into a powerful combination thanks to the successful partnership of Peter May as captain on the field and "Gubby" Allen as his chairman of selectors. Allen had been particularly successful in bringing discipline to the England dressing room, for as former Glamorgan captain Wilf Wooller said: "Denis Compton, Godfrey Evans and Bill Edrich were all delightful characters, but they could be real blighters and laws unto themselves. This was where 'Gubby' was so good."

The team arrived at Tilbury on 21 April and from that first day Benaud's candour with the media won a big coverage. The Australians always tried to play entertaining cricket. They were ready to challenge the clock, never keen to settle for a draw, and in their moments of adversity took the bold way out.

The tour began under an agreement between Lord's and the Australian Board of Control for a truce against chuckers in the first five weeks. Both countries agreed that in this period any bowler in the Australian team's matches considered guilty of throwing should be reported to the Marylebone Cricket Club without umpires no-balling him. Without Meckiff, Slater, Burke, or Rorke in their lineup the Australians had little to worry about and the only bowler reported was Harold Rhodes of Derbyshire for his bowling at Lord's for MCC against Australia.

Australia took a grievous blow in the very first match when Benaud suffered a shoulder injury in cold and biting wind at Worcester. He was never completely fit for the rest of the tour. For the first two days, April 29 and 1 May, Worcestershire were on top and appeared likely to beat the Australians for the first time since 1912. Australia were 4 for 156 when Martin Horton ended the innings for the addition of only 21 more runs with his skilful off breaks. At their first encounter with a typical soft, slow-turning

English pitch, the Australians looked so perplexed the *Times* called them "refugees from reality".

With Benaud unable to bowl on the second day, Mackay took 4 for 14 to have Worcestershire out for 155. Jack Flavell and Len Coldwell bundled Australia out for 141 in their second innings, their right-arm medium pacers hitting the stumps eight times. Set to score 164 to win, Worcestershire were 0 for 10 on the last day, 2 May, and appeared set for an easy win with Horton batting well. Benaud, in great pain, bowled Horton round his legs and at 4 for 56 the match had turned Australia's way when rain washed out play.

The Australians had their first tour victory by four wickets with only seven minutes to spare against Lancashire at Old Trafford from 10 to 12 May. Before play began Lancashire captain Bob Barber offered Benaud and his vice-captain Neil Harvey use of the captains' spacious dressing room on top of the pavilion. Benaud thanked him and said: "If we accepted we'd be torn limb from limb by the rest of my team."

Peter Marner hit Kline for three sixes and had 11 fours in 87 and Jack Bond hit Simpson for 3 sixes in his 68 to take Lancashire to 7 declared for 310. Australia responded with centuries from Harvey (120) and Burge (101 not out) and a superb innings by O'Neill (74) to secure a 94-run lead. Lancashire tried to play out time for a draw until Bond hit two more sixes off Simpson. Left to score 113 in 95 minutes, the Australians handled the task comfortably.

On his first appearance in London, Lawry batted superbly against Surrey at The Oval between 13 and 16 May. His pulling, hooking and driving yielded 26 fours in a 270-minute innings for 165 that allowed Benaud to declare at 7 for 341. Australia's display in dismissing Surrey for 161 and 214 stemmed from a combination of fine fielding and controlled accuracy from six bowlers. They scored the 35 needed without loss to win by ten wickets, avenging Australia's 1956 defeat by Surrey.

Another enterprising declaration by Benaud set up Australia's 63-run win over MCC from 27 to 30 May. Lawry made 104 and O'Neill 122 in their first appearance at Lord's, which allowed Benaud to declare at 5 for 381. Cowdrey made 115 of MCC's 274 in reply. Lawry was 84 not out, Simpson 92 not out when Benaud deprived both of a century by declaring at 0 for 186 when Australia batted again. This gave MCC 294 to win in 240 minutes at a rate of 73 an hour. At 3 for 176 MCC had a good chance but the last five wickets fell for 67 runs, Benaud taking 5 for 67 to complete a personal triumph.

This was an important, morale-boosting win for Australia. In the week prior to the Lord's encounter, they had been unable to dispose of Glamorgan and Gloucestershire, but they had lifted their effort by easily disposing of the strongest side they would meet outside of the Tests. None of the Australians were aware that the Derbyshire fast bowler Harold Rhodes was reported for throwing in the 36 overs he bowled in the match. Rhodes, who had been called for throwing the previous season, took one of the five wickets that fell for 567 at a cost of 129 runs.

Tragedy struck in the match against Sussex at Hove from 3 to 6 June when O'Neill turned to throw from the boundary and wrenched a knee. Benaud gave his shoulder a trial by bowling 21.1 overs in Sussex's first innings of 336. Burge's aggression in scoring 158 with 25 fours and a six, followed by Misson's 6 for 75, left Australia with 245 to win. McDonald gave them a fine chance with 116 not out, but three wickets for two runs from 12 balls by left-arm spinner Ronald Bell halted the Australian charge. They finished nine runs short of victory with one wicket to fall and O'Neill, who had returned to London for treatment, unable to bat. Doctors who put his knee in plaster gave O'Neill no chance of playing in the first Test.

Benaud saw the Test series as the last contest between sides led by amateur-style captains prepared to go for victories rather than play for draws. Both sides had to regroup after the retirement of seasoned players and both had serious injury worries, but there were some memorable events in an entertaining rubber that carried on the revival of big cricket which the West Indies had started in Australia.

May did not recover from his groin strain in time for the first Test at wind-swept Edgbaston from 8 to 13 June and England were led by another establishment stalwart, Colin Cowdrey. Middlesex wicket-keeper John Murray took Godfrey Evans' place, and Subba Row played his first Test against Australia, who were making their first Test appearance in Birmingham since 1909. O'Neill made an amazing recovery to pass a fitness test before play began and Dexter satisfied "Gubby" Allen his knee was sound. Australia brought in Lawry to open in his first Test with McDonald and batted Simpson in the middle order.

England were all out for 195 after a slow first day. Harvey and O'Neill gave Australia the advantage with a third-wicket stand of 146. Later batsmen improved the position established by Harvey's 114 and O'Neill's 82, Simpson contributing 76, Mackay 64, Benaud 35 not out, to take the total to 516. Despite the first-innings lead of 321, Australia's prospects of a win disappeared when Dexter twice edged Davidson to second slip and was dropped each time by Mackay.

Rain delayed play until the last day, with England 215 behind on 1 for 106. Then Dexter and Subba Row took the score to 202, Subba Row including 14 fours in his maiden Test century (112). Dexter, all doubts over his concentration forgotten, went on batting splendidly with Barrington before he was stumped by Grout off Simpson for 180. Benaud was only able to bowl in pain for nine overs on the last day, which ended with the match drawn and England on 4 for 401.

In the Australian dressing room after the

match Benaud showed reporters how turning his right wrist was severely restricted. "My shoulder will only come right if I rest it," he said. "The only cure is heaps of rest." He tried to grin but it was so clear he faced a real crisis the Australian team's depression quickly spread.

The injury prevented Benaud playing in the second Test at Lord's from 22 to 26 June, giving McKenzie a chance to make his Test debut under Harvey's captaincy. Unpredictable bounce at the Members' End and a tendency for the ball to fizz through caused close examination of the grassless pitch which revealed constrained depressions and led to this Test becoming known

Fiery Fred Trueman bowled 34 overs for 118 runs in Australia's first innings during "The Battle of the Ridge" at Lord's in 1961. Most of the Australians took painful blows from him and Brian Statham.

as "The Battle of the Ridge".

There was a degree of journalistic licence in reports of this match because of an Australian Board of Control instruction, just before play began, barring Benaud from commenting to the press. Benaud had made regular headlines in the 14 matches Australia had played until then, which offended Syd Webb, who felt he was neglected as manager and had Benaud gagged. Instead of listening to Webb's uninformed waffling, the media treated the match like a military exercise.

The Melbourne pigeon-fancier Bill Lawry, always loyal to basic principles, was the hero. He went to the crease to open for Australia after watching batsmen flounder when Davidson and McKenzie made the ball kick and fly, bruising knuckles and ribs. England's score would have been much less than 206 if several catches had been held. Throwing off the torpor in which he had bowled for weeks, Davidson had 5 for 42.

Facing Trueman and Statham, Lawry showed he was prepared for a few bruises, with his position in the Australian side at stake. He batted for seven hours, absorbing some savage blows, playing and missing often, but refusing to let the pitch or the bowling of a great pair upset him. He added 95 for the fifth wicket with Burge who left for 46 with his right thigh purple with bruises. "I've never been so scared in my life," Burge told commentator Charles Fortune. "If I'd had the courage, I'd have run back to the pavilion and away from it all, but it needed more courage to run from it than it took to stay out there."

Mackay, Misson, and McKenzie all put on valuable runs, Mackay using a runner after taking a stunning blow on the instep. Lawry was eighth out for a chanceless 130, in which he hit 18 fours. His innings was hailed as a brave triumph over "the Ridge", and gave Australia a 134-run lead.

England's second innings saw the start of a great career as McKenzie, then only 20, took 5 for 37 in a memorable exhibition of fast-medium bowling. After Davidson had disposed of the troublesome Barrington (66), McKenzie took the last three wickets in 12 balls to end England's innings on 202, a lead of 69. Grout held five catches in the innings and eight in the match for the second time in his career.

High drama developed as Trueman and Statham exploited the brute of a pitch to have Australia reeling at 4 for 19. Then Burge came in to take a further pasting but defiantly hit off 37 of the last 52 runs to give Australia a five-wicket win and a 1–nil lead in the series. Crowds of 32,000 attended on two of the four days and the total attendance was 117,000. This was England's first defeat since February 1959 in Melbourne and ended a sequence of 18 matches without defeat. To Australians, it was Harvey's Test, the only time the great left-hander captained Australia in a Test.

An hour after the Test ended an army of experts moved out onto the Lord's pitch armed with surveyors' tripods and poles, micrometers and theodolites, followed by MCC chiefs "Gubby" Allen and R. W. V. Robins. From under an enormous golfing umbrella, topped with the MCC colours, they supervised the taking of levels and bearings. The experts' report said the pitch was built over "a little valley" containing not a ridge but pot-holes and corrugations, which made Harvey's assessment that it was not "a good cricket wicket" a notable understatement.

The third Test from 6 to 8 July at Headingley was also played on a peculiar pitch. This one had been treated by chemicals only a few weeks earlier. After the tea break Trueman took 5 for 16 in six overs on the whitish-green piebald strip. With the batsmen completely unable to assess how the ball would behave, Australia lost seven wickets for 21 runs in 50 minutes. A last-wicket stand of 29 by Davidson and McKenzie took the total to 237. Trueman's 22 overs yielded 5 for 58. English critics condemned Benaud for playing in this Test but with Misson and Gaunt unfit he had no alternative.

England's first innings of 299 featured another fine display from Cowdrey who was out for 93 when a loose ball flicked his glove as he tried to sweep McKenzie. A determined assault on Benaud by Lock lifted England's lead to 62. Australia never recovered from the loss of McDonald with four runs on the board in the second innings, four batsmen failing to score in an innings of 120. Trueman again found the strange pitch to his liking and after dismissing Harvey for 53 dropped his pace to bowl off-cutters from a short run, taking five wickets without conceding a run. Chasing 59 to win, England got them for the loss of two wickets. This eight-wicket win levelled the series at a win apiece, but on that scandalous pitch play lasted only three days, restricting the gate to £27,723 and attendance to 75,000. Trueman's match bag was 11 for 88. Benaud achieved a pair, Trueman twice knocking back his stumps.

The London *Daily Telegraph*'s E. W. Swanton said that E. W. ("Brian") Sellars and those under his supervision had shown they did not know how to prepare a Test match pitch. The Headingley groundsman Arthur Waite denied he had followed instructions in preparing the pitch. "The only people in a position to instruct me are those who pay my wages," said Waite, "and what they wanted was for the Test to go five full days so they could sell more pies and beer."

The Australians returned to London for a social match against Club Cricket Conference at Blackheath and a cocktail party at Clarence House as guests of the Queen Mother. Earlier, manager Syd Webb had found his pockets loaded with fish knives and dessert forks bearing a family crest after the side visited titled hosts in Kent. Webb had to return the family silver with his apologies. At Clarence House one of his pace bowlers said to the Queen Mother: "Ma'am, forgive me for mentioning it, but our manager has a habit of dropping items in his pockets that really worries us." But the Queen Mother said: "Don't worry. There truly isn't much around here for him to take."

"Slasher" Mackay's 168 against Middlesex at Lord's from 22 to 25 July took four hours and included a six and 27 fours. The Australians had just heard that South Africa had lost its membership of the Imperial Cricket Conference because it was no longer a member of the Commonwealth. Mackay's innings rescued Australia from 3 for 45, set her on the path to a 10-wicket win, and inspired this famous piece by former English Test spinner Ian Peebles:

To describe the innings in any technical detail is difficult in the extreme. The striker lifted the bat no higher than is his habit, which is not very high at all, but the ball came forth with that velocity that caused John Nyren to exclaim, 'Egad, she went as though she had been fired.' When Mackay cut, the effect is, in the words of the television copywriters, richer, creamier, delicious, refreshing. Most strokes were, however, largely of his own invention, one particularly fascinating when the half volley is half cut, half trapped, so that it spurts past cover like an apple pip playfully squeezed from finger and thumb.

The fourth Test at Old Trafford, from 27 July to 1 August, provided Australian cricket with a memorable victory. Benaud returned to captain the team aware that the amateurs who formed the backbone of England's batting, May, Cowdrey, Dexter and Subba Row, were all in splendid form. At the last moment Cowdrey withdrew because of a throat infection and Close took his place. Brian Booth, a tall, upright right-hand batsman who played hockey for Australia at the 1956 Olympics, replaced the injured McDonald. Booth, born at Bathurst in western New South Wales, joined the long list of players who have graduated to the Australian team from bush cricket.

Benaud elected to bat on a green pitch that assisted pace and swing. All the early Australian batsmen had a torrid time. O'Neill trod on his stumps dodging a Trueman bouncer after taking frequent blows on the thighs and torso from

Flavell. Only a hard-driving 74 from Lawry and a stubborn 46 from Booth lifted the Australian total to 190.

England gained the advantage when Pullar and May put on 111 for the third wicket, during which Mackay pulled a calf muscle. Keen Australian bowling and fielding forced England to graft for runs, but 95 from May and 78 from Barrington took them to a handy 177-run lead. Subba Row dropped Lawry at 25 when Australia batted again, which proved costly. Lawry and Simpson added 113 for the first wicket, Lawry going on to 102. Harvey was dropped twice in scoring 35. O'Neill again absorbed heavy knocks in his 67.

On the last day Australia slumped from 6 for 331 to 9 for 334 when David Allen took three for none in 15 balls. At that point Australia were only 157 ahead and England appeared to have the match won. Then Davidson and McKenzie joined in a last-wicket stand that produced 98 runs. Davidson hit Allen for 20 in an over, including two huge drives for six, and May had to take Allen off on a pitch that was tailor-made for him. Unable to exploit the rough as Allen had done, Trueman and Statham conceded easy runs, before Flavell bowled McKenzie for 32 with a fine delivery. Davidson walked off in triumph, 77 not out.

Quickly changing their boots, McKenzie and Davidson went back on the field to share the new ball, with England needing 256 to win in 230 minutes. At 1 for 40, Dexter unleashed a withering attack on the Australian bowling, driving with tremendous force and cutting and pulling strongly. He breezed to 76 in an 84-minute stand with Subba Row that yielded 110 runs and seemed to have made victory for England a formality.

Benaud realised there was no chance of containing England with their batsmen in this mood. Australia had to bowl them out and forget the draw. Benaud bowled round the wicket into Trueman's footmarks and in the twenty minutes

Bill Lawry acknowledges the applause of the England players after scoring his second Test century of the 1961 tour in the fourth Test at Old Trafford.

before tea got Dexter to tickle one to Grout. Next he bowled May round his legs with a ball that turned half a metre, had Close caught at backward square leg trying for a second six, and bowled the stubborn Subba Row. At 5 for 163, England wanted 93 with 85 minutes left. Benaud told Mackay, whose leg muscle was heavily bandaged, to close up one end while he worked on the footmarks, but Mackay exceeded his brief by trapping Barrington lbw. Then Simpson brought off two amazing slips catches to get rid of Murray and Allen, diving like a soccer goalie and skidding on his elbows each time.

Twenty minutes from stumps Flavell joined Statham and Benaud threw the old ball to Davidson to warm up for the new one. The new ball was not needed, for with his fourth delivery he knocked back Statham's off stump to give Australia a 54-run victory.

England's loss of her last nine wickets for 51 runs stunned English cricket supporters, some of whom blamed Close for his recklessness in going for big hits when steady stroke-play may have prevailed, but the highest traditions of the game had been preserved by two captains willing to go for a win.

Benaud's 5 for 12 in 25 balls, in what "Gubby" Allen called the only black day in his seven-year partnership with May, swung the game and gave him 6 for 70 in the innings. Neville Cardus called him "Lucky Benaud" because of the manner in which he had won the Ashes but he made his own luck. In 17 of his 28 Tests as captain Benaud lost the toss, but the myth about his luck remained deep-seated, particularly among the opponents fooled by his spinners. The Derbyshire and England fast bowler Harold Rhodes said: "If you put your head in a bucket of slops, Benordy, you'd come up with a mouthful of diamonds."

Boredom from the Bluebloods

Domestic cricket 1961-63;
England in Australia 1962-63

At the end of the 1961–62 season the Queensland Cricket Association suspended "Slasher" Mackay for two matches. The umpire's report on which the QCA acted said Mackay deliberately threw a ball while bowling in a Brisbane club match and that he made fools of umpires by taking guard a third of a metre outside the leg stump. This bizarre piece of administration resulted from a harmless prank after Mackay had played cricket non-stop for 18 months. Mackay felt the urge to celebrate his forthcoming rest with a last-ball-of-the-season throw and when he was no-balled for it he completed his over with his normal action. The umpires and Mackay considered the season closed, but a newspaper article on his throw stirred one umpire to report him, adding the charge about his comical guard, unaware that he *always* took guard outside leg stump on wet pitches, like the one they had that day.

Mackay was so angry at this ingratitude after

Officials of the New South Wales Cricket Association making their annual pilgrimage to Victor Trumper's grave. Here president Syd Smith lays a wreath.

toiling manfully for his country through two famous Test series that he fired in an indiscreet reply to the umpire's claims to the QCA. Reports circulated that he had abused the umpire in terms that would have made a wharf-labourer blush. In Sydney Sid Barnes recorded that Mackay had completely lost his temper. Finally Mackay had a meeting with the QCA executive who accepted that he had not uttered one rude word and reduced his suspension to one match, or two Saturdays of club cricket. The executive recognised the multitude of problems involved in punishing Mackay for his technical sins, as well as foreshadowing the laughter this would have caused at the QCA's expense around the cricket world.

People were often wrong about Kenneth Donald Mackay, a freak with a withered arm and a lion's heart, whose stubborn faith in his own eccentricity made him unique among Australian cricketers. The *Manchester Guardian* said: "Mackay is like the common cold. There is no cure for either."

For all his imperfections in technique, Mackay was gifted with amazing eyesight and reflexes that were to bring him 23 first-class centuries and a top score of 223. He went out to bat with pussy-foot strides as if concerned about bruising the turf. Commentators call it his Groucho Marx walk. When he arrived at the crease he viewed the surrounds with the suspicion of an infantryman in a minefield. He had dressed for this ordeal by attending to his left side first— his left sock, boot, batting glove and pad had to go on first and when he captained Queensland he always spun the coin with his left hand.

Few batsmen could use a fast pitch as efficiently as he did in England in 1961, trapping half-volleys with an almost imperceptible movement of the bat from which they spurted off in all directions until he dominated the scene. "Slasher does not hit the ball, he squirts it," said Peter May. Mackay's squirts, dabs and pushes, all of his own development, brought him 683

runs at 33.04 on this, his second tour of England. But his immense value to the Australian team came through his astonishing improvement as a bowler. From a quick and supple arm action, bowling from a low trajectory, he moved the ball just enough in English conditions to find the edges, and on pitches that helped his seaming he made the ball wobble appreciably. His capacity for work in a team with slim bowling resources was shown in his 273 overs in the Tests, 68 of them in England's second innings in the fifth Test. His 667.2 overs in first-class matches was 33 overs more than the next hardest worked bowler Alan Davidson.

Wisden reported that following Australia's Ashes-winning display in the fourth Test Surrey batted with an almost incredible lack of spirit in the tourists' next match at The Oval from 2 to 4 August. Mickey Stewart, captaining Surrey in the absence through injury of Peter May, sent Australia in. At 4 for 48, Benaud was dropped by Stewart at forward short leg. Benaud and Burge then put on 79, which helped lift Australia's score to 209.

Surrey collapsed for 79 to give Australia a lead of 130. Lawry and Simpson put on 92 for the first wicket before Australia faltered again against off spin, but Benaud's declaration at 9 for 225 left Surrey 356 to get to win. Only Barrington (68) reached double figures in Surrey's second innings, leaving Australia winners by 255 runs.

England left Trueman out of their team for the fifth Test at The Oval from 17 to 22 August, blaming him for the rough into which Benaud had pitched at Old Trafford. Cowdrey and Lock returned and for Australia Gaunt replaced the injured McKenzie. The Yorkshire newspapers pilloried England's selectors for fielding a team without a Yorkshireman. Gaunt looked far inferior to three years earlier in his only other Test—against South Africa at Durban—and he was lucky to finish with 3 for 53 in the England first innings of 256.

Australia started badly, losing Lawry and Harvey for 15. Superb footwork which enabled them to get down the pitch to drive and exhilarating running between wickets by both O'Neill and Burge produced the best batting of the rubber in a 123-run stand for the fourth wicket. Showing enterprise and sound technique, they scored at almost twice the rate England had achieved on the first day. When O'Neill left for 117 at 211, Booth continued the free scoring with his own stylish range of drives, cuts and pulls. Burge was finally bowled by Allen for 181, Booth caught by Subba Row off Lock for 71 and Australia reached 494. A fine 137 from Subba Row, a stubborn 83 from Barrington and injuries to Davidson and McKenzie allowed England to hold out for a draw. Mackay's effort in bowling 107 overs in the match again demonstrated the lack of depth in Australia's attack.

Australia completed the first-class part of the tour with four wins in five matches. Between 23 and 25 August they defeated Essex by five wickets at Southchurch Park, Southend, thanks to a sporting declaration by Trevor Bailey when Essex were still 44 runs behind with seven wickets in hand in their first innings. At Southampton from 26 to 29 August, they beat Hampshire by five wickets. Then they had a draw against the Gentlemen from 30 August to 1 September at Lord's, where Lawry hit his ninth century of the tour and his third on the ground, his 109 taking him past 2000 runs. They rounded off a triumphant tour by winning the festival matches during the first week of September at Hastings against Arthur Gilligan's XI and at Scarborough against T. N. Pearce's XI, both by three wickets. Simpson hit another century (121) at Scarborough, his sixth of the tour, at a run a minute. Four non-first-class matches against Minor Counties, Scotland and Ireland wound up a happy tour.

Despite his shoulder injury, Benaud had done his best to recapture in England the thrills and exciting finishes of the West Indies *v.* Australia

series the previous southern summer, but he had been hamstrung by dreadful pitches at Lord's and Leeds and by his unbalanced attack. In each of the five Tests the pitches were so lively the side batting second led on the first innings.

More people watched the tour at the grounds or on television than any previous tour, though the profit of £29,000 was the lowest since the war, partly because of the increase in county club members who provided no revenue for the tourists. The team won 13 of their 32 first-class matches, lost 1, and had 18 drawn. They scored 39 centuries in these matches and had 15 scored against them. Six of the 17 players scored 1000 runs and eight took 50 wickets or more.

Lawry was the surprise success of the tour after narrowly beating Ian Craig for a team berth. He headed both the Test and first-class averages, scoring 420 runs at 52.50 in the Tests and 2019 runs at 61.18 in 23 first-class appearances. O'Neill confirmed his high ranking among Australia's great batsmen with a classic century in the fifth Test at The Oval and had a shot-making brilliance his team-mates lacked but his overall value to his team was little ahead of Burge, Harvey and Simpson.

Davidson justified his rating as Australia's main strike bowler with 68 wickets at 22.30 on the tour and 23 wickets at 24.86 in the Tests and his 77 not out at Old Trafford contributed to Australia's dramatic win there. Benaud could not bowl in his normal style but still managed 61 tour wickets at 23.54 and 15 in Tests at 32.53. McKenzie was the notable improver among the bowlers, but Gaunt, Misson, Kline and Quick failed to capitalise on wonderful opportunities.

Wise-cracking wicket-keeper Wally Grout was criticised for intercepting catches headed for first slip but did not drop them and his 21 dismissals was a record for England–Australia Tests. He completed the tour with a magnificent record, having never appeared in a losing team since he came into Test cricket. Simpson was in a class by himself as a slips fieldsman, made

Wally Grout, known to team-mates as "The Griz,"
shows the style that won him a place among Australia's
great wicket-keepers.

1947 tour runs at 51.23 and, when Benaud was injured, supplied valuable leg spin, taking 51 wickets at 33.47. Surprisingly, Harvey took more catches than Simpson, 25 to 23, and his work in the covers remains unequalled by an Australian.

The striking feature of the entire tour was the total elimination of controversy over throwing and dragging. Much of this was due to long, patient behind-the-scenes work by Sir Donald Bradman and "Gubby" Allen but the captains played their part by omitting both subjects from their media conferences. Absence of both Rorke and Meckiff from the Australian team also helped diffuse the chucking and dragging rows.

At home the control of first-class cricket had settled firmly into the day-to-day administration of the Board of Control in Sydney through secretary Alan Barnes, guided by a constant stream of phone calls and letters from Board chairman, Sir Donald Bradman, in Adelaide. The financial position of the Queensland Cricket Association in 1962 gave them great anxiety and after five years of full membership Western

Australia's participation in the Sheffield Shield continued to disappoint. Eastern-state spectators simply did not support matches involving Western Australia and in Perth, Shield gates had not risen and ground membership of the WACA had not increased, as expected. Western Australia requested eastern-state teams to stay at cheaper hotels on their visits to Perth to cut costs but the nub of the problem was that the Western Australian team had failed to play crowd-pleasing cricket.

The excitement of the 1960–61 Tests series with the West Indies rubbed off onto the following Shield season, which attracted 363,360 spectators, the largest season aggregate since 1927–28 and the third-largest season total ever. The presence of the charismatic West Indians, Wes Hall (Queensland), Rohan Kanhai (Western Australia) and Garfield Sobers (South Australia) added to spectator interest in a domestic season without Tests. As Richard Cashman pointed out in his study of Australian cricket crowds, the Sheffield Shield was still viable in the 1960s because there were no visits by overseas teams in four of the ten summers.

New South Wales continued their winning sequence in the Shield during a season of exciting finishes when other captains followed Benaud's example, making sporting declarations that kept the last day's play under keen public scrutiny. Hall had some tense encounters with Australia's leading batsmen, taking 43 wickets for Queensland, Kanhai played some brilliant knocks for Western Australia and although Sobers did not do his talents justice early on, he played a superb innings of 251 and took 6 for 72 to bring about New South Wales' sole defeat. David Sincock, the young South Australian spinner who experts such as Clarrie Grimmett said should have gone to England instead of other left-arm bowlers Lindsay Kline or Ian Quick, proved a major crowd attraction.

New South Wales included seven players from the 1961 team in England, including Bob

This is the view batsmen regularly got of West Indian speedster Wes Hall after he returned to play for Queensland in 1961–62. He proved immensely popular but could not win Queensland the Sheffield Shield.

Simpson who had transferred back from Western Australia, but competition for places in the side was so keen that talented players like Ray Flockton or Grahame Thomas had to be relegated to twelfth man. The Benaud brand of cricket brought boom times to Sydney, where the biggest crowd since 1948 watched the Saturday's play in the match between New South Wales and South Australia (17,864). They were rewarded with a superb day's cricket in which 418 runs were scored and five wonderful catches were held. The last day of the Queensland v. New

South Wales match in Sydney produced record takings of £4533. In Adelaide 24,827 attended the New South Wales *v.* South Australia match, a postwar record for an interstate match.

Davidson had a remarkable season for New South Wales, heading the Shield bowling averages with 38 wickets at 14.34 and scoring two blazing centuries inside a week. In the second of these he made 106 against Victoria in Sydney, passing the century in a 59-run tenth-wicket stand with Doug Ford. Davidson hit with enormous power and farmed the strike so cleverly Ford faced only three balls while Davidson made 58 runs. The other run came from a leg-bye. Ian Craig, after a successful season as Simpson's opening partner, retired from first-class cricket after scoring 7328 runs at 37.96 with 15 centuries. His four overseas tours with Australian teams included two as captain. The success of Bill Lawry had thwarted his hopes of a comeback to Tests as an opener.

Barry Shepherd, a former schoolboy champion with Scotch College in Perth, headed the Shield batting averages with 777 runs at 64.75, including 212 not out against Queensland at Perth in which he hit 6 sixes and 20 fours. Stories of his uncompromising efforts to secure greater commitment from his players that filtered through to the eastern states demonstrated how passionately Shepherd wanted the Shield for his state. He saw it as the prize that would change everything and was prepared to threaten and cajole his players to get it.

The New Zealand team that toured South Africa in 1961–62 played three matches in Australia. They had a draw against Western Australia at Perth between 12 and 14 October on the forward journey on a lively bowlers' pitch. Hugh Bevan took 5 for 55 for Western Australia and Francis Cameron 7 for 27 for New Zealand. On the homeward journey New Zealand found David Sincock (6 for 54) and Neil Hawke (5 for 71) too much for them in the match with South Australia at Adelaide from 2 to 5 March,

Ian Craig, recovered from illness, made a brave attempt to regain his Australian Test spot as an opening batsman. Craig, shown hitting a four off Gaunt in Sydney, was thwarted by the success of Bill Lawry in the opening spot.

losing by five wickets after a blazing 109 by Les Favell. At Sydney from 9 to 12 March, New South Wales beat the New Zealanders by 59 runs, despite 127 by wicket-keeper Art Dick, who, in the South African series had, by dismissing 23 batsmen, equalled the world record.

In England the Duke of Norfolk went down to breakfast one morning at Arundel Castle to be

Norfolk brought to Australia was greeted as the best available by English cricket writers, although fast bowlers Trueman and Statham were, at 32, veterans under Australian conditions. The duke had Alec Bedser as his assistant manager, W. R. Watkins as scorer. The team was E. R. Dexter (captain), 27, M. C. Cowdrey (vice-captain), 29, D. A. Allen, 26, K. F. Barrington, 31, L. J. Coldwell, 29, T. W. Graveney, 35, R. Illingworth, 30, B. R. Knight, 24, J. D. F. Larter, 22, A. C. Smith, 26, F. J. Titmus, 29, J. T. Murray, 27, P. H. Parfitt, 26, G. Pullar, 27, J. B. Statham, 32, F. S. Trueman, 31, and the Reverend D. S. Sheppard, 33.

Six of them had played in the last Gentlemen versus Players match at Lord's from 18 to 20 July 1962, ten days before the touring team was announced. The long agonising in England over the morality of cricketers' status had been resolved by the Advisory County Cricket Committee, who ruled that henceforth all English cricketers should enjoy equal privileges and the terms "amateur" and "professional" be discarded.

Colin Cowdrey was named to captain the Gentlemen but withdrew with kidney trouble and Dexter took over. Sheppard showed his obvious class by scoring the only century of the match (112) and next day newspapers hailed him as the tourists' captain-elect, but the selectors named Dexter without commenting on whether Sheppard's vocation influenced the decision.

There was no alteration to the team before they flew to Aden on 27 September and joined *Canberra* for the voyage to Fremantle via Colombo. Dexter's boldness with the bat had not been emulated by his players in his captaincy of Sussex, which he had taken over in 1965, nor in his one season as England's leader in 1962 against Pakistan, whom England defeated 4-nil, but his strategical battle with Benaud was eagerly awaited by fans who hoped he would prove another Worrell.

England's preparation for the Tests in the

informed by his wife that he looked pale. "Funny you should say that, dear," he said, "the boys at the club have been suggesting that I should escape the winter and go out to Australia for some sun." The duchess approved this idea and urged her husband to try Australia. His club turned out to be the Marylebone Cricket Club and once he agreed to accompany the team to Australia England's premier nobleman had no trouble securing the manager's job, an appointment which set in motion the MCC's blue-blooded challenge for the Ashes.

The England team announced in August 1962 was captained by Ted Dexter, whose aristocratic manner had by then won him the soubriquet "Lord Ted". The team he and the Duke of spin around the states was unimpressive. From 19 to 22 October they defeated Western Australia in Perth by 10 wickets in the first tour match, but they were surprisingly beaten in the second match on the same ground by a Combined XI, for whom Bob Simpson scored 109 and 66 not out. The Combined XI won by ten wickets after England's batting folded for 157 in their first innings.

The team with which Richie Benaud played a drawn series against England in 1962–63: (L to R) (back) P. J. P. Burge, W. M. Lawry, G. D. McKenzie; (centre) B. C. Booth, B. K. Shepherd, N. C. O'Neill, B. N. Jarman; (front) R. B. Simpson, A. K. Davidson, R. Benaud, R. N. Harvey, K. D. Mackay. Both sides won a Test and three were drawn.

Draws followed in Adelaide against South Australia from 2 to 6 November and against an Australian XI from 9 to 13 November in Melbourne, where Barrington made 219 not out, Knight 108 and Dexter 102, only to have Simpson (130) and Shepherd (114) respond with centuries. They were defeated by an innings and 80 runs in Sydney between 16 and 19 November by the powerful New South Wales side. England scored 348 (Pullar 132) and 104 (Benaud 7 for 18), New South Wales 6 for 532 declared (O'Neill 143, Simpson 110). Mackay made 105 not out against them for Queensland between 23 and 27 November at the 'Gabba. England regained prestige by scoring 6 for 581 declared (Barrington 183 not out) in reply to Queensland's 7 for 433,

but it was clear that bowling, not batting, was their problem.

Benaud was six weeks past his 32nd birthday and already past his best as a leg spinner when the 1962–63 series began. From an approach run of one step and five paces he could still drop the ball on a soup plate with mechanical accuracy, but the spin he imparted with his smallish fingers in the three campaigns prior to injuring his shoulder in England had lost its bite. He was not helped by the slow pitches on which the series was played nor the failure of young spinners to reach a level where they could offer support. His batsmen were an accomplished, reliable lot with a goodly ration of pluck and his team outclassed England in the field, but too often it was left to Benaud and Davidson to get England out.

Trueman gave England a splendid start to the 'Gabba Test scheduled for 30 November to 5 December, the first played in Australia with six-hour days. But with Australia 6 for 208, England wilted in the sun, and with Booth scoring a polished 112 Australia reached 7 for 323 by stumps. Next day the batsmen not out overnight prospered, Mackay making 86, Benaud 51, and Australia totalled 404.

Dexter gave spectators a taste of the batting they craved by scoring his first 50 in 58 minutes but after he left for 70, the tedium of England's batting drove people to slow handclapping. Barrington took four hours for 78, poking about like an old professional making sure of his wages instead of celebrating his new status as a cricketer. Parfitt was just as scornful of the gallery in batting four hours for 80 as England limped to 389. Benaud's 42 overs yielded 6 for 115.

Dropped catches and feeble England ground fielding further lowered standards on the fourth day, which ended with Australia on 4 for 362. Lawry and Simpson, unchallenged as the opening pair following the retirement of the courageous McDonald, put on 136 for the first wicket. Lawry

made 98, Simpson 71, O'Neill 56, and Harvey 57.

Benaud declared at the start of the fifth morning, leaving England to score 378 in 360 minutes to win. Pullar and Sheppard gave England an encouraging start of 114 runs and Dexter hit so freely in mid-afternoon an England win appeared likely. But when Dexter was bowled by McKenzie for 99, England lost three wickets for four runs and from then on had to defend desperately to avoid defeat. Australia's lack of a top-class spinner to back up Benaud was painfully clear as his attack failed to dismiss tailenders, the match ending in a draw with England 6 for 278.

All the England top batsmen played themselves into form in the six matches between Tests, four of them second-class. England had a confidence-boosting win over Victoria in Melbourne despite 177 by Lawry, thanks to the neglected Len Coldwell's 6 for 49 in Victoria's second innings. At Adelaide Cowdrey enhanced his popularity with Australian crowds by scoring 307, the best score of his career, in the drawn game with South Australia.

The second Test in Melbourne from 29 December to 3 January was a tremendous tussle. Lawry and Simpson got Australia away to a reasonable start with a 62-run opening stand but at 111 Australia lost three wickets for one run and only sound batting by Davidson, Mackay and Benaud late in the innings helped the total to 316. England were in disarray at 2 for 19, facing a wonderful onslaught by Davidson, before a display of English batsmanship at its best by Dexter and Cowdrey added 175 in 198 minutes. Dexter went for 93 following his 99 in Brisbane, Cowdrey for 113. Davidson mopped up the tail to finish with 6 for 75 and limit England's lead to 15.

Australia were unlucky in their efforts to resist inspired fast bowling from Trueman and Statham, both Burge and Lawry falling to ankle-high shooters and only a chanceless century by

Bobby Simpson held some dazzling catches in his long career, but none better than this one to dismiss England captain Ted Dexter in the 1962–63 series in Australia. Dexter had reached 93 in the second Test in Melbourne.

Booth (103) lifted the second innings total to 248. Lawry's 57 took five hours but such was the calibre of the bowling nobody minded. Bandy-legged Trueman's 5 for 62 underlined English selectors' mistake in not sending him to Australia when he first came out of the Yorkshire coalmines. Few bowlers have had such powerful hips and back and fewer still could muster the contempt his glares showed for batsmen.

Sheppard had dropped important catches and scored a first innings duck when he opened England's chase for the 234 runs wanted for victory. He lost Pullar at five before Divine Providence intervened and he added 124 with Dexter. Australia had a chance when Dexter was run out for 52 but Cowdrey was dropped with

the score on 149 and Sheppard at 151, both behind the wicket, and England won by seven wickets without Australia taking a wicket on the final day. Sheppard was run out for 113.

When Prime Minister Bob Menzies presented Trueman with a pewter pot to commemorate his 5 for 62, the Duke of Norfolk thanked him but added: "You've undone months of disciplinary work with Trueman."

Australia brought in Shepherd and Guest for Burge and Mackay for the third Test in Sydney from 11 to 15 January. Public interest was so high all three Sydney television stations covered the game from 4 to 6 p.m., the period allowed local stations. Interstate channels covered the whole day's play. Australia contained England with some magnificent ground fielding in their first innings, with Pullar (53) and Cowdrey (85) both out pulling long-hops. From 7 for 221 overnight, Titmus and Trueman put on 51 for the eighth wicket. Simpson took 5 for 57 and Davidson 4 for 54 in an innings of 279.

Wicket-keeper Murray injured his shoulder diving to catch Lawry for 8 and had to be replaced by Parfitt. Australia's second wicket did not fall until 174 as Simpson and Harvey plundered the bowling; then Titmus, floating occasional balls and varying his pace, dismissed Harvey, Simpson, O'Neill and Booth in 51 balls at a cost of only five runs. Shepherd swung the balance back in Australia's favour with 71 not out, including a stand of 39 for the last wicket, which lifted Australia's total to 319 and a lead of 40. Titmus' 7 for 79 off 37 overs was a memorable display of controlled off-spin bowling.

Swinging the ball both ways very late at just above medium pace, Davidson won the match for Australia with a masterly 45-minute spell. Simpson showed equal genius in the slips. England lost wickets at 0, 20, 25, 37, 53 and 71 and at

Alan Davidson goes through his paces at the nets watched by selectors Don Bradman (dark glasses) and Dudley Seddon.

stumps were 6 for 86. Murray batted 100 minutes for three runs on the fourth morning but Australia's bowlers never lost their grip on the match. With England out for 104, Australia scored the 65 required to win for the loss of two wickets, completing a remarkable performance for Simpson, who scored 125 runs for once out, took five wickets, and held three magnificent slips catches. Davidson's match bag was 9 for 79.

After his disappointing form in Sydney, Guest was dropped for Mackay, which gave Benaud an extra batsman for the fourth Test at Adelaide from 25 to 30 January. England substituted Illingworth for Coldwell and in his first spell Illingworth sneaked a ball between Lawry's bat and pad to hit the stumps. Smith caught Simpson on the leg side to have Australia reeling at 2 for 16. Sheppard dropped another vital catch when he spilled a simple one from Harvey, who survived three chances before he settled down and went on to 154, O'Neill made an even 100 and Australia reached 393.

The greying Davidson pulled a hamstring muscle in the fourth over of England's first innings but McKenzie accepted the added responsibility admirably, bowling with exceptional lift and stamina. His 5 for 89 held England's score to 331, giving Australia a lead of 62. At the end of the fourth day Australia had increased this to 287 through sound batting by Simpson (71) and Booth (77), but with Davidson unfit Benaud had to bat on. Trailing by 355, England were at risk at 4 for 122 with 105 minutes left but Barrington made certain of a draw by scoring 132 not out.

This proved to be Mackay's last Test, for it was clear at 38 that the fast bowlers had the measure of even his unique range of strokes. His 37 Tests had produced 1507 runs at 33.48 with 13 scores over 50 but unhappily no centuries. He took 50 wickets at 34.42. When he retired at the end of that season he had made 10,823 first-class runs at 43.64 and taken 251 wickets

at 33.31. He made 23 first-class centuries, top score 223, and took five wickets in an innings seven times.

A draw against Victoria from 1 to 5 February at Melbourne attracted Fleet Street reporters because of the appearance of Meckiff, the centre of so much controversy on the previous England tour. He did not disappoint, taking 5 for 93 and worrying all the England batsmen except Graveney, who made a lovely 185. Jack Potter, a right-hand batsman with six seasons of first-class experience, scored 106 in Victoria's first innings of 307 in reply to England's 375. England declared at 5 for 218 in their second innings and Victoria had to hang on desperately to save the match, finishing on 9 for 188.

Light-hearted matches in Canberra against the Prime Minister's XI, and in Dubbo and Tamworth against country sides preceded the fifth Test in Sydney from 15 to 20 February, with the Ashes at stake. Commercial radio stations, who in lean years left cricket to the Australian Broadcasting Commission, informed their listeners that Neil Hawke had come in to strengthen Australia's bowling, in place of Mackay, and Burge had replaced Shepherd in the middle order.

This was a wretched match. England opened their batting with Cowdrey to counter the menace of Davidson, but the tactic failed when Davidson had him out at 5. Sheppard gave Hawke his first Test wicket at 39 and thereafter Dexter and Barrington batted ponderously, with Davidson wary of his hamstring and Hawke pitching too short. At the end of the first day England were 5 for 195. Barrington went on to a lacklustre 101, which included only 4 fours. Trueman batted 110 minutes for 30 and England's 321 took 9 hours 30 minutes.

Australia were equally inhibited after losing Lawry at 28. Simpson took two hours over 30. Only O'Neill appeared willing to play strokes and after he left for 73 Burge took 5 hours 30 minutes scoring 103. Australia led by 28 but by then the audience was insensible to such details and wondering why they had come.

England were daring enough to have their batsmen hit out in the second innings while Barrington blocked up one end, a policy that enabled them to set Australia 241 to win in 240 minutes. Australia followed the same strategy, using Lawry to close up one end, but, after four wickets fell for 70 runs, were content to close up the match and settle for a drawn series. Lawry batted 240 minutes for 45 runs, and understandably the rubber ended amid jeers and catcalls. A series that ended in stalemate made nonsense of the hopes for bright and innovative cricket and provided a dismal farewell to Test cricket for Neil Harvey and Alan Davidson. The confrontation of cricket's oldest rivals drove people away from big cricket vowing never to return.

The former professionals in the England team now had the status—but they did not have the money. And judged on their performance with Dexter's team in Australia they remained over-cautious and unwilling to adopt the carefree approach synonymous with amateurism that spectators wanted. Some of the England players moaned about their tour pay but the way they fielded they were not worth a penny more.

More interesting than the Tests was the Shield competition, in which Victoria broke New South Wales' nine-year supremacy. Competently led by Lawry, Victoria's batting and bowling had the depth to field a strong lineup when Lawry or Guest were on Test duty. Left-hander Bob Cowper, son of a Rugby international, headed the Shield batting averages with 813 runs at 101.62, but Victoria also benefited from the contributions of Ian Redpath, a right-handed

antique-collector from the South Melbourne club, who made 637 runs at 63.70 and Potter, who made 708 at 59.00. The bowling spoils were evenly shared between Guest (39 wickets at 18.28), Meckiff (47 at 19.61) and hard-working right-arm fast-medium bowler Alan Connolly (36 at 27.72). Ian Redpath's 261 against Queensland helped Victoria to 4 for 633 declared, their highest Shield score since 1927–28.

Meckiff's efforts to develop a bowling action that would satisfy umpires met severe setbacks in Victoria's match against South Australia in Adelaide from 11 to 15 January when he was no-balled for throwing by umpire J. M. Kierse standing at square leg, and in the match against Queensland at Brisbane from 1 to 5 March when umpire Bill Priem also no-balled him for throwing. Western Australia inflicted the only defeat of the season on Victoria because of Barry Shepherd's career-best of 219 at a run a minute, but the calling of Meckiff overshadowed even outstanding innings like this.

The 1960s introduced the mini-skirt and the Beatles and had seen a major uplift in South African playing skills and through the success of Shepherd and McKenzie it was no longer a novelty for a Western Australian to play for Australia, but the final act in the great chucking controversy still had to be played out.

The third Australian women's team to tour England had a happy trip in the northern summer of 1963, but lost one and drew two of the three Tests. Star of the tour was the 24-year-old Victorian Miriam Knee, who took 8 for 57 in one Test (5 for 35 and 3 for 22), and created an Australian women's Test record by sharing a sixth-wicket stand of 125 with Mary Allitt.

New Horizons

The chucking controversy;
South Africa in Australia 1963-64;
domestic cricket 1963-65;
Australia on tour 1964

Between December 1957 and December 1963, Ian Meckiff made three overseas tours with Australian teams and took 45 wickets in 18 Tests at 31.62. They are far from exceptional figures but during these six years he became the most controversial player in big cricket, the King of the Chuckers—an ogre who, according to the respected English cricket coach Alf Gover, did not bowl a single legal delivery.

From the time he took 6 for 38 against England in 1958 at Melbourne Meckiff shared the headlines with Soviet and American attempts to land a rocket on the moon. Englishmen could accept that they were not involved in the space race, but they could not accept Meckiff's domination of their Test batsmen. "It's ridiculous that a player with his action should be the agent of England's destruction," said Gover in the *Sunday Pictorial*. E. M. Wellings in the *Evening News* accused Meckiff of "blatantly throwing out England".

The Australian Cricket Board at its meeting in the Victorian Cricket Association's boardroom in 1963, with E. G. Macmillan in the chair, Board secretary Alan Barnes on MacMillan's left, alongside Sir Donald Bradman.

Australia's selectors had done their best to diffuse the chucking row by omitting Meckiff from the 1961 tour of England, despite the urgent need for an opening bowler partner for Davidson. Benaud had strongly defended Meckiff's action, following his Melbourne coup, in a press statement which said:

The Australian team is completely satisfied that Ian Meckiff's bowling delivery is fair and legitimate. I have studied his bowling from every position on the field and I am absolutely convinced his bowling conforms to the rules formulated by the MCC. So apparently are the umpires in New Zealand, South Africa, and Australia, where he has played his cricket.

Despite Benaud's strong support Meckiff came under heavy strain in the seasons that followed. His son Wayne was nicknamed "Chucker" by his schoolmates. His parents and wife were pestered by people who said Ian was a cheat. When he stood in a bunker playing golf—which he did right-handed—someone suggested he throw the ball out. The jest of friends, who jokingly called him "Chucker", caught on in clubs and pubs and got to a stage where he refused to go out. "The personal strain finally told on me and I had to seek medical advice," Meckiff said in his book *Thrown Out*.

The doctor told me the worry and tension I was under every time I bowled was affecting the nerve system in my stomach, and I have been under treatment for five months. The doctor also attributed most of the injuries, which were starting to become far too constant, to the tension I had built up inside me. During the whole of the chucking controversy I was unable to defend myself by answering my accusers because of my "no comment" contract with the Australian Board of Control.

Benaud was Australia's captain at the 'Gabba for the first Test against South Africa from 6 to 11 December 1963, when the throwing row came to an unsatisfactory climax. Although

Meckiff had been no-balled twice for throwing in Shield games at the end of the previous season, he had played two Shield games in the 1963–64 season without being called. But when Benaud threw the ball to him for the second over of South Africa's first innings, umpire Col Egar no-balled Meckiff from square leg for throwing his second, third, fifth and ninth deliveries.

By the time Meckiff delivered the twelfth ball of the over, everyone present knew his career was over, but many of the spectators were surprised that Benaud did not give Meckiff an over at the other end so that umpire Lou Rowan could pass judgment on him. Benaud accepted that he would be a bowler short for the rest of the match and did not bowl Meckiff again. Benaud said he accepted the umpire's decision, just as he had when Meckiff was not called.

At the start of the season the State associations, under instructions from the Australian Board of Control, had urged all umpires to deal firmly with bowlers whose legality they doubted and had promised full support. There is little doubt Meckiff was sacrificed to end the long-running controversy and the way it was done irked many cricket-lovers. During this Test, the crowd's objections to the calling of Meckiff were so noisy that extra police were sent to the 'Gabba and Egar went to and from the ground in a police car. At the close of the Test, umpire Egar was booed and spectators carried Meckiff shoulder-high from the ground. Meckiff retired from cricket to a public relations job for a Melbourne radio station.

In the Test, Australia had a first innings of 435 through Booth's 169 and Eddie Barlow became the only South African to score a century (114) in his initial Test against Australia, but the match ended in a tame draw when heavy rain fell after lunch on the last day.

Benaud relinquished the Australian captaincy after this Test but played under Bob Simpson in three of the four Tests that followed. Benaud had lost only four of his 27 Tests as Australian

The eventful first Test between South Africa and Australia at Brisbane in 1963 saw the end of Ian Meckiff's career. It also produced a bad injury for Australia's Brian Booth seen here at silly midoff stopping the drive, from Peter Van Der Merwe, that took two chips from his knuckles.

captain and had earned himself a place alongside Harry Trott, Joe Darling, Warwick Armstrong, Don Bradman and Lindsay Hassett as one of the finest of all Australian captains. His major contribution was in bringing big crowds back to cricket by providing entertaining play.

The fourth South African team to Australia included two sets of brothers, A. J. and D. B. Pithey and R. G. and P. M. Pollock. They lacked the fielding brilliance of Cheetham's 1952–53 side and dropped too many catches, but their matches attracted more than 500,000 people and the tour profit was more than £3000. The team was T. L. Goddard (captain), 32, E. J. Barlow, 23, K. C. Bland, 25, R. G. Pollock, 19, A. J. Pithey, 30,

D. T. Lindsay, 24, J. H. B. Waite, 33, P. R. Carlstein, 23, P. L. Van der Merwe, 26, W. S. Farrer, 27, D. B. Pithey, 27, P. M. Pollock, 22, C. G. Halse, 28, Dr M. A. Seymour, 27, J. T. Partridge, 31, with K. G. Viljoen as manager.

They had mixed fortunes in their first six matches in Australia, between 25 October and 3 December, winning three matches handsomely but losing twice, with the other match drawn. At Perth they won with more than a day to spare over Western Australia, who in a significant move had just appointed Tony Lock as state coach. They drew the second match at the WACA against a Combined XI after double centuries by Barlow (209) and Simpson (246) and centuries by Graeme Pollock (127) and Benaud (132). South Australia beat them by eight wickets in Adelaide following a 253-run fourth-wicket stand by Ian McLachlan (149) and Garfield Sobers (155), despite centuries from Lindsay (104) and Carlstein (123). At Melbourne they defeated an Australian XI by three wickets, thanks to another century by Barlow (112). At Sydney they beat New South Wales by an innings and 101 runs when Graeme Pollock scored a century (120) and Joe Partridge took 9 for 117. But in the last first-class match before the first Test Queensland beat them by an innings and 73 runs at the 'Gabba, Burge scoring 129 and a burly off-spinner, Tom Veivers, taking 7 for 129. This display earned Veivers a place in the first Test in which Australia also introduced the tall right-arm fast-medium bowler from South Melbourne, Alan Connolly.

Between 13 and 28 December, after the first Test, the South Africans played at Toowoomba, Lismore, Benalla, Launceston, Devonport, Hobart and Geelong. At Launceston a 249-run second-wicket stand by Barlow (161) and Tony Pithey (170 retired) paved the way to an innings and 147-run win over Tasmania. At Hobart a gale held up play for 20 minutes and Victorian Jack Potter scored a fine 123 not out for a Combined XI on the first day. On the second day Farrer (107) and Waite (115) scored centuries and lifted South Africa to a total of 6 for 445 declared. The match ended on the third day with the last Combined XI batsmen at the crease.

Just before the second Test in Melbourne from 1 to 6 January a man rang the South Melbourne police station and said: "Egar will get the Kennedy treatment at the Test." President John Kennedy had been assassinated in America seven weeks earlier. Again police drove Egar to and from the cricket ground throughout the five days of the Test and placed special guards on the MCG umpires' and players' rooms.

Keith Miller asked cricket fans to sympathise with Simpson who had to take over from the all-conquering Benaud with the "weakest team Australia has put into the field in donkeys' years". Simpson won the toss and sent South Africa in. Only the bespectacled Barlow (109) batted comfortably against McKenzie, Hawke and Connolly in the South African total of 274.

With his score on 4, Lawry hooked Partridge to the fence and, as he did, fell on his stumps.

Meckiff's retirement left Graham McKenzie as the spearhead of the Australian attack. He proved a willing workhorse, physically very strong and powerful, mentally eager for work and extremely determined.

Lawry sprawled on all fours amid the stumps and bails but umpire Lou Rowan concluded he had completed the shot when he broke the wicket and rejected South African appeals. Lawry went on to 157, adding 129 for the first wicket with Redpath in his Test debut, who missed a century by three runs. Shepherd added to Australia's heavy scoring with 96, which took the total to 447, a lead of 173. Tony Pithey (76) and Waite (77) tried hard to save the match but South Africa's second innings of 306 set Australia only 134 to win. With Seymour and Peter Pollock unable to bowl through injury, Australia won by eight wickets, Simpson hitting the winning run.

On the advice of his father Ian Redpath made his Test debut strictly as an amateur, refusing to accept the £85 match fee, the going rate at that time, which included £15 for expenses. His father was concerned that if Ian failed to make it as a Test cricketer he could be refused a place as a rover with Geelong Amateurs Australian Rules team. This had happened to St Kilda allrounder Bill Pearson after he played 14 matches for Victoria in 1936–37 and Redpath senior wanted to safeguard Ian against similar queries over his status. Pearson was welcomed back to amateur football only on condition that he return all the money he received by playing as a "professional" Sheffield Shield player. Redpath went two seasons, including three Tests, without accepting pay.

The third Test at Sydney from 10 to 15 January 1964, and the South Africans' match with the strong Victorian side at Melbourne, from 17 to 21 January, were both drawn after some brilliant batting by Graeme Pollock. By scoring 122 in the Test he became the youngest South African, at 19 years 318 days, to make a hundred in Test cricket and in the match against Victoria he scored 110. Goddard (194) also hit a century against Victoria, for whom Lawry made 187 not out in the second innings.

South Africa levelled the series at one win apiece by defeating Australia by ten wickets in the fourth Test at Adelaide from 24 to 29 January. This time Barlow became only the third South African to score a double century against Australia, with an innings of 201. His third-wicket stand of 341 with Graeme Pollock (175) remains the highest for any wicket by South Africa in Tests. South Africa's 595 gave them a first innings lead of 250. Australia fought hard to avoid defeat in their second innings but Barlow's 3 wickets for 6 runs set South Africa an easy task to win. From 5 for 301, Australia were all out for 331. Grout passed Bert Oldfield's wicket-keeping record of 130 dismissals when he dismissed Tony Pithey in this match.

South Africa had a wonderful chance to win their first series ever against Australia but were frustrated by a plucky last-wicket stand of 45 by Veivers and Hawke on the last day of the fifth Test in Sydney between 7 and 12 February. Booth made a fighting 102 in conditions that produced pronounced swing for Joe Partridge (7 for 91) in Australia's first innings of 311. South Africa took a 100-run lead with Colin Bland's 126 in 300 minutes and looked to have the game won when the ninth Australian second-innings wicket fell at 225. But the Veivers–Hawke stand lasted 75 minutes and gave South Africa only 85 minutes in which to score 171, which was beyond them.

Goddard's team won 5 of their 14 first-class matches in Australia, lost 3 and drew 6. They drew bigger crowds than any previous South African team but costs were so high they had a profit of only £3000. They visited more country centres than most tourists, with 13 of their Australian matches not considered first-class. Barlow, a bespectacled right-hand opening batsman built like Billy Bunter, scored six of their 19 first-class centuries, Graeme Pollock, a left-hander with a surgeon's delicacy of touch, five. They had 12 first-class centuries scored against them. They were the first South African side to break away from their previously dour, unattractive methods and play attacking strokes, but they were badly let down by their fielding, only Colin Bland with his brilliant throwing and Barlow in the slips showing consistency.

Only Booth (Test average 88.50) and Lawry (55.11) lived up to their reputations in an Australian team desperately short of strike bowlers. None of the Australians took more than McKenzie's 16 wickets (at 43.06) in the Tests, but bustling Peter Pollock (average per wicket 28.40) and sturdy seamer Joe Partridge (33.32) both took 25 wickets for South Africa.

Several Sheffield Shield matches were played concurrently with the Tests in what proved a fascinating 1963–64 domestic competition. Victoria, the Shield holder, remained a contender until the second-last match when they were defeated by an innings by South Australia, who thus clinched their first Shield win since 1952–53.

Les Favell captained South Australia with imagination, helped by the all-round brilliance of Sobers, the reliability of middle order batsmen Ian McLachlan and John Lill, the all-round success of young Glenelg star Ian Chappell, and leg-spinner Rex Sellers' 46 wickets at 26.63. Chappell, a grandson of former Test captain Vic Richardson and the eldest of three brothers whose cricket developed at Prince Alfred College, capped a splendid season by scoring 205 not out against Queensland at the 'Gabba. Sobers scored 973 runs at 74.84 and took 47 wickets at 27.59, in a magnificent all-round contribution to South Australia's success.

Batsmen were on top in a season when pace bowlers were unsettled by their first experience of the front foot rule, which compelled them to release the ball with their leading foot behind the bowling crease. Seven batsmen exceeded 1000 runs in the season with the new Test captain Simpson heading the first-class aggregates with 1436 runs.

Alan Barnes, secretary of the Australian Board of Control, was the New South Wales team manager in Brisbane when Peter Burge came in at the tea adjournment on the second day, on 180 not out. Burge had just completed stands of 110 for the third wicket and 190 for the fourth and as he collapsed into a chair Barnes asked if he felt like a cup of tea. "No, I'm stuffed and feel more like a double rum," said Burge. Barnes did not have any rum but he produced a bottle of whisky and Burge took a healthy swig. Revived, he went on to 283, the highest score by a Queenslander in first-class cricket, batting seven and a half hours and hitting 42 fours. But Barnes' men refused to give up and scored 661 to Queensland's 613 to win on the first innings, Simpson scoring 359, with 33 fours, and figuring in a stand of 241 with Booth, who made 121.

Simpson, now back from Perth with his Test status confirmed, made 247 not out against Western Australia in Sydney in his next match during which he put on 308, a record opening stand, with Grahame Thomas. When Western Australia went on to Brisbane, Burge made 205 not out against them. Sam Trimble made five centuries during the summer for Queensland, including 252 not out against New South Wales in Sydney and a century in each innings against Victoria in Brisbane.

Sir Donald Bradman, Jack Ryder and Dudley Seddon, who had taken over "Chappie" Dwyer's old spot as the New South Wales representative on the panel, selected the twenty-fourth Australian team to tour England, knowing that with the retirement of Benaud, Harvey and Davidson, a new era was about to begin. The team announced on 13 February 1964 was: R. B. Simpson (captain), 28, B. C. Booth (vice-captain), 30, P. J. P. Burge, 32, A. N. Connolly, 24, G. E. Corling, 22, R. M. Cowper, 23, A. T. W. Grout, 37, N. J. N. Hawke, 25, B. N. Jarman, 28, W. M. Lawry, 27, G. D. McKenzie, 22, J. W. Martin, 32, N. C. O'Neill, 27, J. T. Potter, 26, I. R. Redpath, 23, R. H. D. Sellers, 23, T. R. Veivers, 27, with R. C. Steele as manager, J. A. Ledward as assistant-manager, Dave Sherwood as scorer, and A. E. James as masseur.

Ian Chappell was unlucky to miss selection and the choice of Potter ahead of McLachlan was absurd. Corling was a surprise pick as one of the team's four fast-medium bowlers and became the team's youngest member, three weeks junior to McKenzie. Sellers, a tall, loose-limbed leg spinner born at Bulsar, India, received a letter from Prime Minister Bob Menzies just before the team sailed on the *Orcades*, granting him Australian citizenship. Soon after the team arrived in England Sellers found he could not grip the ball properly and he had to have a cyst removed from his spinning finger, which forced him to miss most of the tour.

The team was the last to go to England by

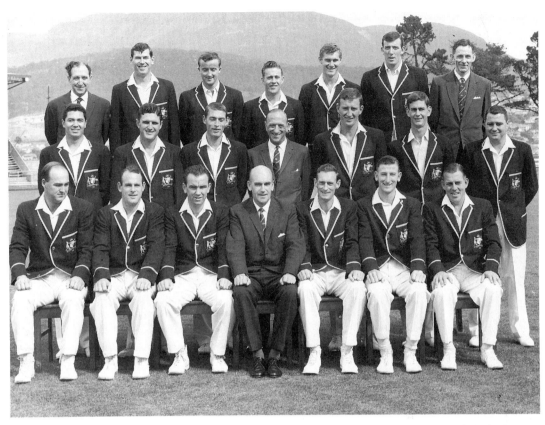

*Australia's Ashes-winning 1964 team to England,
photographed in Hobart: (L to R) (back) A. E. James
(masseur), N. J. N. Hawke, G. E. Corling, J. W.
Martin, R. M. Cowper, A. N. Connolly,
D. Sherwood (scorer); (centre) R. H. D. Sellers, T. R.
Veivers, J. T. Potter, J. A. Ledward (assistant
manager), G. D. McKenzie, I. R. Redpath, B. N.
Jarman; (front) P. J. P. Burge, N. C. O'Neill, R. B.
Simpson (captain), R. C. Steele (manager), B. C.
Booth, W. M. Lawry, A. T. W. Grout*

sea. On the way to England they played four
matches, two at the end of March against
Tasmania in Hobart and Launceston, which were
drawn, one against Western Australia in Perth
from 3 to 7 April, which they won by eight
wickets after Redpath had made 202, O'Neill 135,
and a one-day match in Colombo against Ceylon
on 15 April.

They found major changes in English cricket.
The traditional distinctions between professional
and amateur cricketers had been abolished, a one-
day competition had been introduced, and Sir
Pelham ("Plum") Warner, so often the centre
of drama involving Australian cricketers, had
died and had his ashes scattered over Lord's,
where he had influenced cricket administration
for more than half a century.

Between 29 April and 2 June they beat
Gloucestershire at Bristol by ten wickets,
Somerset at Taunton by 172 runs, MCC at Lord's
by nine wickets, and Oxford University at
Oxford by an innings and 120 runs. They then
played draws with Worcestershire at Worcester,
Surrey at The Oval, (Simpson 138, Booth 109
not out), Nottinghamshire at Trent Bridge
(Redpath 107, Cowper 113), Glamorgan at
Cardiff, (O'Neill 109), Cambridge University at
Cambridge, and Lancashire at Old Trafford. By
then it was clear they had major problems with
their bowling.

Rain interrupted four days of the first Test at Trent Bridge from 4 to 9 June, washing out nearly 15 hours of the scheduled playing time. Edrich reported unfit just before the match and England had to use Titmus as a stopgap opener. Titmus escaped being run out when Grout refused to break the wicket after the batsman collided with the bowler. Geoffrey Boycott, on his debut for England, became the first victim of another debutante, Grahame Corling, after scoring 48. Corling, a team-mate of Simpson's with the Western Suburbs club in Sydney, bowled with a stylish, high action, but was not as successful as the lion-hearted McKenzie, who had 5 for 53 in England's second innings. Dexter set Australia 242 to score in 195 minutes but rain intervened after 45 minutes.

Two further draws followed, the first at Derby against Derbyshire from 10 to 12 June, and the second at Sheffield against Yorkshire between 13 and 16 June, when O'Neill made 134 for Australia and Ken Taylor 160 for Yorkshire. Needing to score 159 to win, Australia defended desperately after losing 4 for 54.

Rain again prevented any chance of a result in the second Test at Lord's between 18 and 23 June, washing out the first two days and ending the match just after lunch on the fifth day. The takings still reached £54,615, £45,000 of it in advance bookings. Trueman took 5 for 48 in a heady display on the damp pitch in Australia's innings of 176. England gained a lead of 70 thanks to a 375-minute innings of 120 by John Edrich. Cool batting in the little time left gave Australia a draw.

Burge's form had been disappointing but he showed his class in the third Test at Headingley from 2 to 6 July with the innings that won the series. Australia were 7 for 178 in reply to England's 268 before Burge and Hawke added 105 in 99 minutes. Burge reached his century off the second-last ball of the day and Hawke was out to the last. Next morning Burge went on to 160 as England conceded a further 106 runs.

Burge batted for 5 hours 15 minutes and hit 24 fours.

Superb Australian catching reduced England's second innings to 229, leaving Australia to score 109 to win. They accomplished this for the loss of three wickets in the face of a fine spell by Titmus, whose 27 overs yielded 2 for 25. Australia owed much to McKenzie's stamina and persistent hostility in taking 7 for 127 in the match.

Australia upset spectators by making little effort to win the match against Leicestershire at Leicester from 8 to 10 July, but played an exciting draw with Hampshire at Southampton, where Henry Barnard (123) became the first Hampshire player to score a century against Australia for 30 years. Left to score 309 in the final innings, Hampshire were 8 for 279 and defending grimly against a ring of close-in fieldsmen when time expired.

Opening bowlers McKenzie and Hawke set up a 63-run win over Sussex at Hove from 15 to 17 July, twice breaking through the early batting. Parfitt (121) and Brearley (106 not out) hit centuries in the drawn match between Australia and Middlesex at Lord's between 18 and 21 July, which the tourists treated as a Test rehearsal for their batsmen. Booth made 132 and Burge 96, but injuries to McKenzie and Corling gave Australia no chance of forcing a result.

Australia retained the Ashes by drawing the fourth Test without ever trying to win, from 23 to 28 July at Old Trafford. Simpson kept England in the field until the third morning and England replied with equally tiresome batting, only 20 wickets falling in five days. Amid all the talk about entertaining cricket, many critics felt the match was a disgrace that could only drive those unfortunate enough to endure it away from the game.

Lawry and Simpson put on 201, a record for the first wicket against England, surpassing Warren Bardsley and Syd Gregory's 180 in 1909. After Lawry was out for 106, Simpson went on

Brian Booth, whose 29 Tests for Australia included five centuries. He was a graceful right-handed batsman who delayed his bid for Test honours to play hockey for Australia at the Melbourne Olympic Games.

to his first Test century in 30 appearances. Next day he made a further 156 and took his score to 265 not out, and on the third day he moved to 311 in 12 hours 42 minutes, the longest Test innings played in England, with 1 six and only 23 fours. He added 219 with Booth (98) for the fifth wicket and when he declared at 8 for 656 England had to make 457 to avoid the follow-on.

At stumps England were 2 for 162 and through

methods as painful as Simpson's they added a further 210 without loss on the fourth day. Dropped catches allowed Dexter to survive to 174 and Barrington to 256, his first century in England, after scoring nine Test hundreds abroad. Speculation that England might pass Australia's mammoth total ended when McKenzie burst through the tail to finish with 7 for 153 in an innings of 611. Veivers' 95.1 overs in this innings beat all previous endurance records for England–Australia matches and was only 17 balls short of the all-time record by Sonny Ramadhin for West Indies against England at Birmingham in 1957.

From 1 to 4 August at Swansea, Glamorgan had their first win over Australia since their recognition as a first-class county 43 years earlier. Glamorgan set up their victory before jubilant Welsh spectators by scoring 197 on a turning pitch and then dismissing half the Australian side for 21 by the end of the first day. A bold 51 from Veivers lifted the Australian total to 101. Veivers hit 6 sixes but slow left-arm spinner Jim Pressdee had the last laugh by taking 6 for 58 and giving Glamorgan a lead of 96. Glamorgan's second innings of 232 set Australia 329 to win. Lawry (64) and Veivers (54) were the only Australians to resist for long on the final day, Pressdee taking four more wickets to finish the match with 10 for 123. Off spinner Don Shepherd had 9 for 93 to complete a spinners' triumph.

The excitement of this defeat had barely subsided when Australia suffered their second tour defeat between 5 and 7 August at Birmingham against Warwickshire, after both sides had made sporting declarations. Bob Barber gave Warwickshire the edge by scoring 138 out of 384 in their first innings. Australia responded with 8 for 253, Lawry sending Warwickshire in again when Burge reached 100 not out. Mike Smith then declared at 1 for 63, leaving Australia to score 209 in 135 minutes to win. Potter (60) and Burge (53) gave them a fine chance to get the runs but later batsmen faltered. Australia needed 14 to win from the last over by local schoolteacher Roger Edmonds. He took two wickets and with Grout unfit to bat, Warwickshire won the game by nine runs with two balls to spare.

Australia recovered splendidly from these losses to beat Yorkshire at Bradford between 8 and 11 August by 81 runs. At 4 for 73, Booth rescued Australia with a magnificent 193 not out that contained 3 sixes and 24 fours. Yorkshire had to make 323 to win in the fourth innings and were out for 241 despite a stubborn 122 from Boycott, his first century against Australia.

Neil Hawke's 6 for 47 on a seamer's pitch enabled Australia to take an early advantage in the fifth Test at The Oval from 13 to 18 August by dismissing England for 182. Australia's batting on the second day was tedious to watch, Lawry batting 5 hours 15 minutes for 94. Booth continued in fine form with 74 for Australia to lead by 197, after Trueman had taken three wickets in four balls to become the first bowler with 300 Test victims. After Boycott had scored his maiden Test century (113), the final day was lost to rain with England 184 ahead on 4 for 381. Two wickets had fallen to McKenzie, who finished with 29 dismissals for the series, equalling the record for the most wickets taken by an Australian in England set by Clarrie Grimmett in 1930.

Barry Jarman made 105 in a drawn match with MCC at Lord's which started on the day after the Test, but Johnny Martin's three sixes won most applause. At Southend between 22 and 25 August Essex beat Australia by six wickets, following centuries by Gordon Barker (123) and Keith Fletcher (125). This was Essex's first win over Australia since 1905 and Australia's third and final loss of a disappointing tour, which they wound up with victories over Kent at Canterbury, Arthur Gilligan's XI at Hastings and T. N. Pearce's XI at Scarborough between 26 August and 8 September.

Australia concluded the tour with a 66-run

Barry Jarman, whose career was overshadowed by Wally Grout, was a fine team-man and a diligent worker at practice as this shot shows.

win over Sussex in a one-day match at Hove on 14 September. Burge (124 not out) and Booth (79 not out), with an unbroken 193-run stand for the fourth wicket, swung the match Australia's way. The win was significant at a time when limited-over cricket had just been introduced in England, as Sussex were the first winners of the Gillette Cup.

The Australians achieved their main mission by retaining the Ashes but had such obvious limitations in bowling they were fortunate to bring home a profit of £30,000. The five Tests were watched by 354,436 people and full receipts were £356,436, which was £23,582 down on 1963. The Australians scored 25 centuries but had 18 scored against them. Simpson headed the batting averages with 1714 runs at 57.13, Hawke the bowling averages with 83 wickets at 19.80.

McKenzie took most wickets, 88 at 22.45. Veivers, whom one London writer likened to a koala who had just emerged from sleeping in a gum tree, bowled a prodigious 754.3 overs, 226 of them maidens, but his 52 wickets cost 36.17 each. Apart from Simpson, O'Neill and Grout, the fielding did not reach the standard for which Australian teams are famous.

Simpson's team suffered the ignominy of defeat by The Netherlands in a one-day match played on matting at The Hague on 29 August. O'Neill topscored with 87 in Australia's innings of 197, only 11 days after they had defeated England for the Ashes. The Netherlands scored 7 for 201 in reply to win by three wickets. Marseille (77) and Vandervegt (33) put on 99 for the first wicket and tailender Onstein clubbed two huge sixes and a four in a knock of 24 not out that saw The Netherlands home. London columnist Jim Manning said it was the most staggering sporting result since America beat England at soccer in 1950. Potter, batting in black sandshoes, had his skull fractured in the match, an injury that compelled the management to fly him home without accompanying the team to India and Pakistan.

After a fortnight's holiday in Europe the Australians flew from London to Madras for the first of their four matches in India and Pakistan, all of them Tests. They defeated India by 139 runs at the Corporation Stadium between 2 and 7 October because of outstanding bowling by McKenzie and a splendid display of team batting in their second knock. McKenzie's match figures were 10 for 91. The Nawab of Pataudi emulated his father by scoring a century (128 not out) in his first innings against Australia.

India reversed this result by defeating Australia in the second Test from 10 to 15 October at Bombay after O'Neill fell ill with stomach pains soon after the start. He could not bat in either innings. Before a crowd of 42,000 India scored the 254 runs needed to win in the final innings with two wickets and half an hour to spare. Veivers bowled a further 91.4 overs in taking 6 for 150. Rain prevented play on the last two days of the third Test at Calcutta from 17 to 22 October and the series was left drawn.

Pakistan's preparations for the Test at Karachi between 24 and 29 October were likened to a military campaign by the Australians. They retained only five players from the team that toured England in 1962, introducing six men new to Tests, including Majid Khan, who later played for Cambridge University and Glamorgan, and Khalid Ibadulla, who had appeared for Warwickshire (and subsequently for Tasmania and Otago), and was called from England specially for the match.

Ibadulla became the first Pakistan batsman to make a century in his first Test with an innings of 166, which was part of a first-wicket stand of 249 with Abdul Kadir, which remains the Pakistan record for any wicket in Test cricket. Ibadulla was out off the last ball of the first day after 5 hours 30 minutes batting. He hit 20 fours. Australia broke through the middle order but Intikhab Alam (53) and Asif Iqbal (41) batted stylishly to lift Pakistan to 414, then their highest score against Australia. McKenzie took 6 for 69.

Simpson made a century in each innings for Australia, following 153 in the first innings of 352 with 115 in the second, which virtually made Australia safe from defeat. Australia appeared likely to make the 342 needed to win in 290 minutes, with the score at 2 for 173, but Redpath took 37 minutes to get off the mark and batted four hours in all for 40 runs and the match fizzled out in a draw.

Immediately after Australia's visit a Commonwealth team played six matches in Pakistan and their six matches were watched by more than half a million people, including 400,000 at the first three representative matches. The pitches were so easy only one match produced a result, with the Commonwealth XI beating the Governor's XI at Lyallpur, but in all the matches spectators saw a feast of bright batting from stars like Bill Alley, Rohan Kanhai, Tom Graveney and Basil Butcher.

Pakistan's intense desire to challenge the world's best cricket nations was further demonstrated on a short visit to Australia in the three weeks before Christmas 1964. They played dour, tough cricket in four drawn matches, showing rigid discipline, never taking risks or conceding an advantage, but always mindful of the laws of the game. Their application in strange conditions was so determined that rapid improvement looked inevitable.

They began with a draw against Queensland at the 'Gabba, where Grout made a breezy 117 that allowed Queensland to lead by 55 runs on the first innings. A fighting 126 by Mohammad Ilyas having prevented defeat, they set Queensland 315 to win in just over two hours, which they did not attempt. At Melbourne from 4 to 8 December in the initial Tests between the countries in Australia Hanif Mohammad, the most gifted of four famous brothers, kept wicket and captained the team, took five catches, and scored 104 and 93.

Australians, eager to study the batsman who had lifted Bradman's world record score from 452 to 499, were fascinated by his unerring judgement. His bat looked impassable as he completed his century but he was far too cautious in his second knock to leave Australia a reasonable last-innings target. Ian Chappell made his Test debut in this match and was the only failure in Australia's top order. McKenzie's match bag of 7 for 140 gave him 71 wickets in his 14 Tests during 1964.

Pakistan's caution annoyed spectators in the drawn match in Sydney against New South Wales. Doug Walters, in his second season with New South Wales at the age of 19, took 6 for 66 with his well controlled right-arm medium-pacers and only a stubborn 105 by Saeed Ahmed took Pakistan to a first innings total of 283. Centuries from Booth (115) and Thomas (125) took New South Wales to an 85-run lead but

the match died from painful Pakistani batting.

The Pakistanis' match with South Australia produced entertaining cricket until rain forced a draw. Ken Cunningham made his initial first-class century (120), before Mohammad Ilyas hit 17 fours in an impressive 154. Hanif Mohammad was on 110 not out when he declared with Pakistan 179 ahead. Favell's belligerent 71 took South Australia to 3 for 165 before the rain came, and the Pakistanis went off for 12 matches in New Zealand. Not long afterwards war broke out between Pakistan and India.

The Australian team to tour the West Indies in 1965 was announced on 13 January that year and some of the selected players dropped out of the exciting final matches in the Sheffield Shield competition. New South Wales recovered the Shield after two seasons with two unexpected wins from a patched-up team under stopgap captain Barry Rothwell.

At Adelaide from 5 to 9 February, they defeated South Australia on the first innings because of a record second-wicket stand of 378 runs in 307 minutes by left-hander Lynn Marks, whose 185 included 20 fours, and right-hander Doug Walters, who included a six and 23 fours in his 253. The previous best in the Shield was 334 by Bradman and Archie Jackson in Adelaide in 1930–31. Walters batted for 6 hours 42 minutes and became the youngest Australian to make a double century. South Australia played their West-Indies-bound trio in the match but New South Wales omitted their five tourists. South Australia replied to New South Wales' 9 for 601 declared with innings of 364 (Ian Chappell 122) and 8 for 298. Walters followed his brilliant batting with 7 for 63 in South Australia's first innings.

New South Wales then flew to Perth for the match with Western Australia, knowing that an outright win for either side could win them the Shield. A tense struggle ensued, with Walters again at the centre of events. Western Australia, led by Tony Lock, made 184 and 273, with Walters taking 2 for 44 and 5 for 92. New South Wales again relied heavily on Marks (75) and Walters (57) in their first innings of 9 for 302 declared. Walters was at the crease on 34 not out when New South Wales reached 5 for 156, to win by five wickets and win the Shield by two points from Victoria, whose two first innings losses to Western Australia were clear evidence of that State's improvement under Lock.

The match that ruined Victoria's Shield hopes was their outright loss to Queensland at Melbourne, from 11 to 15 December, when 14 wickets fell on the last day for 423 runs in the five hours' play. Queensland won by 41 runs after trailing by 71 runs on the first innings. Sam Trimble's 161 (19 fours) in Queensland's second innings enabled Burge to declare when he was out for 97 and Queensland were 5 for 332. This gave Victoria 262 to score in 160 minutes. They made a thrilling attempt to get the runs but four run-outs gave Queensland victory with 25 minutes to spare.

This was the first season in which Shield cricket was played on a Sunday. After years of opposition from church groups, the interstate conference gave the states the right to decide when they wanted Sunday play but only Queensland and Western Australia took advantage of the new rule, staging both their Perth and Brisbane matches on Sundays, with an immediate improvement in attendances.

Two bowlers were no-balled in Shield matches for throwing. Victorian right-arm fast-medium bowler Edward Illingworth was called from square leg by Test umpire Col Egar and by umpire John Ryan, in the Adelaide match against South Australia. Illingworth later satisfied umpires with his bowling for Victoria against Western Australia in Melbourne. Leading Sydney umpire Ted Wykes no-balled Keith Slater for throwing his faster ball during the Western Australia *v.* New South Wales match in Sydney.

Later in the match Wykes sent Tony Lock to the dressing room to remove excessive ointment from the fingers of his bowling hand.

Western Australia's improved showing brought sighs of relief from treasurers of state associations right round the country. Not only were attendances and ground membership at the WACA showing a sharp increase on previous seasons but spectators in other capital cities had begun to show more interest in watching the Western Australian team perform on their eastern visits.

Three Western Australians were included in the Australia team for the ten-match tour of the West Indies in 1965. The West Indies had never won a series against Australia, but this time their team included the feared fast bowler Charlie Griffith, who in 1962 at Barbados had knocked Indian captain Nari Contractor senseless, fracturing his skull so badly Contractor hovered near death for several days.

On the West Indies' 1964 tour of England Australian-born umpire Cec Pepper reported to Lord's that in one match in which he stood he would not have hesitated to no-ball Griffith for throwing if the game had not been an exhibition. That was the first year of the new front foot rule to eliminate dragging and Pepper said in his report that he had been asked by Trevor Bailey, who captained the home side in the exhibition, to take it easy on the West Indian bowlers, who had no experience of the front foot rule.

Pepper's report to the MCC was intended to be confidential but was leaked to the London *Daily Mail* not long before the Australians arrived in the West Indies. The Australians were aware that West Indian umpire Cortez Jordan had called Griffith for throwing in 1962. They also realised that the outcome of their clashes with the Hall–Griffith combination probably would decide what had been described as the unofficial world championship.

A Basic Flaw

Australia tours West Indies 1965;
domestic cricket 1965-66;
England tour Australia 1965-66;
Australia tours South
Africa 1966-67

The tendency to panic that had been characteristic of West Indian sides in the early encounters with Australia changed teams and the unease was now all in the Australian team. It centred on the legality of Charlie Griffith's bowling and in the six matches he played against them his presence cast a pall over the Australian dressing room.

Griffith was a big—188 centimetres tall—man who thudded along a 20-pace approach run and delivered the ball with his chest facing the batsman. His most controversial ball was his exceptionally fast yorker but the delivery that caused the damage, which followed him throughout his career, was his bouncer, the ball that had briefly threatened the life of Nari Contractor and caused Griffith to be no-balled for throwing in that match. To secure the bounce and extra pace, Griffith dipped his right shoulder

The Australian team to the West Indies in 1964–65:
(L to R) (back) S. C. Trimble, P. J. Allan, G. D.
McKenzie, B. K. Shepherd, N. J. N. Hawke, L. C.
Mayne, R. M. Cowper, D. J. Sincock, G. Thomas,
P. I. Philpott; (front) B. N. Jarman, W. M. Lawry,
R. B. Simpson (captain), R. Parish (manager), B. C.
Booth (vice-captain), N. C. O'Neill, A. T. W. Grout.

as he reached the crease and it was in the arm swing which followed that Griffith's action became suspect.

The Australian team that flew from Sydney on 13 February 1965 and on via San Francisco and New York to Kingston, lacked bowlers of the pace Griffith and Wes Hall generated. The team was also short of batsmen who could hook expertly enough to punish the bouncers that had become an integral part of West Indian cricket. Ian Chappell, then 22 and already a noted exponent of the hook, would have been handy instead of Trimble, who failed to win Test selection despite two tour centuries. Burge and Veivers were unavailable for the team which was chosen by Bradman, Ryder and Seddon and managed by Melbourne businessman Bob Parish. The team was R. B. Simpson (captain), 29, B. C. Booth (vice-captain), 31, P. J. Allan, 30, R. M. Cowper, 24, A. T. W. Grout, 37, N. J. N. Hawke, 26, W. M. Lawry, 28, B. N. Jarman, 29, G. D. McKenzie, 23, L. C. Mayne, 23, N. C. O'Neill, 28, P. I. Philpott, 30, B. K. Shepherd, 26, D. J. Sincock, 23, G. Thomas, 26, and S. C. Trimble, 30.

The selectors gambled on their pace bowlers Queenslander Peter Allan and Western Australian Laurie Mayne advancing to Test calibre to partner McKenzie and the South Australian Neil Hawke, who swung the ball at medium pace. The spin bowling was entrusted to freckle-faced David Sincock, who had returned to Adelaide after two seasons in Sydney, and the nomadic Sydney schoolteacher Peter Philpott, who had bowled leg breaks successfully for four seasons in the Lancashire League. Sincock had clinched his tour spot by taking 12 for 142 for South Australia against Victoria the previous November. Board of Control team announcements usually were made alphabetically and Philpott thought he had missed out when announcers went past the "P's" without naming him. His name was the last mentioned.

After a warm-up in a second-class match at

Laurie Mayne, the West Australian pace bowler who took eight wickets in his first Test at Kingston, Jamaica, in 1965. He was unable to repeat this fine start.

St Ann's Bay on 20 and 22 February against Jamaican Colts, Australia began the serious part of the tour with a handsome win over Jamaica, whom they beat by an innings and six runs between 24 and 27 February at Kingston. Simpson (111), Cowper (121), O'Neill (125) and Booth (89 not out) took Australia to 5 declared for 547. Jamaica replied with 340 and 201, Philpott taking 8 for 164.

On the eve of the Test series Ted Dexter, who had captained England against Griffith in 1963 and made no official complaint about his bowling, said the rubber would be meaningless if Griffith was allowed to bowl against Australia as he had done in England. In the West Indies, where cricket is what Clive Lloyd, the celebrated leader, calls the instrument of Caribbean cohesion, the captaincy of the national team was a bigger issue than Griffith's action. Unlike Australia, there are no challenging heroes to the West Indian Test captain, no jockeys, tennis players, surfers or golfers to rival the man who carries the region's hopes as no politician can.

After Worrell retired to become a Warden at the University of the West Indies after 51 Tests, 15 as captain, the logical candidates should have been Collie Smith, Conrad Hunte and Garfield Sobers. But Smith had died of injuries received in a 1959 car crash and when his body was flown back to Jamaica 60,000 people attended his funeral. Hunte ruined his claims by pressing his belief in the Moral Rearmament movement in the dressing room, a place where politics generally are taboo. So the job fell to Sobers, who had Worrell's unqualified support.

The reality of the Hall–Griffith menace emerged quickly in the first Test at Sabina Park, Jamaica, from 3 to 8 March when the West Indies had their first home win over Australia. The pitch produced erratic bounce but it is doubtful if Hall ever bowled faster. His 5 for 60 and 4 for 45, together with Griffith's 2 for 59 and 2 for 36, gave the West Indies a hold on the match they never lost.

Mayne, supporting his Claremont–Cottesloe clubmate McKenzie, had the splendid match figures of 8 for 99 from 41 overs, but nothing he bowled caused the alarm of Griffith's faster ball, which the Australians had difficulty sighting. Hunte (81) and Butcher (71) turned the match the West Indies' way with a 116-run third wicket stand in the second innings of 373. Left to score 396 in the final innings to win, the Australians found Hall and Griffith too fast for them, and in the West Indies islands thousands rejoiced. Sobers, in his first match as West Indian captain, took his 100th Test wicket when he dismissed Philpott in Australia's second innings of 216, the West Indies winning by 179 runs.

The Australians recovered well with an innings and 31-run win over the Leeward Islands at Basseterre, St Kitts, where Cowper's 188 and Allan's 5 for 33 swung the match. They then played draws against Trinidad Colts at Point-a-Pierre, and at Port of Spain against Trinidad after centuries from O'Neill (125) and Lawry (134 not out).

Australia's ground fielding and throwing were superb in the second Test at Port of Spain from 26 March to 1 April but dropped catches allowed the West Indians to reach 429 in their first innings. Both Butcher (117) and Sobers (69) were run out after some classic stroke play. Australia replied with 516, defying a sustained bouncer attack by Hall and Griffith. Courageous Cowper (143) and Booth (117) added 225 runs for the third wicket after O'Neill retired hurt. He was struck on the arm protecting his head from a Griffith bouncer. On a lifeless pitch part-time trundlers Simpson, Cowper and O'Neill had long spells of bowling in an inauspicious draw.

On his home pitch at Bourda, Georgetown, Butcher produced a brilliant knock of 157 which included three sixes and 22 fours in the drawn match between British Guyana and Australia from 7 to 10 April. Behind the scenes, while Butcher hammered Australia's bowlers, an angry dispute occurred over the appointment of umpires for the third Test at the ground. The Guyanese objected that a local was not appointed but finally dropped their threat to boycott the Test when Gerry Gomez, the former Test star and then Test selector, was named as umpire with H. B. de C. Jordan. Gomez held an umpire's certificate but had not previously umpired a first-class match.

Gomez showed his conscientiousness by ordering the re-marking of the creases before play began. Kanhai, in his prime, frustrated all the Australian bowlers except Hawke in a magnificent knock of 89 to take the West Indies to 355. Hall, Sobers, Griffith and Gibbs then bundled a dispirited Australia out cheaply twice (179 and 144). Although the West Indies disappointed by scoring only 180 in their second innings, they won by 212 runs. Gibbs' 9 for 82 included his 100th Test wicket but Hawke outdid him with 10 for 115, a record for any Test in Georgetown.

The great Everton Weekes came out of retirement to captain Barbados Colts against Australia at Bridgetown on 24 and 26 April. Weekes made 105 retired and figured in a 196-run stand with A. Bethel (157). Hawke took 8 for 98, fine figures even in a second-class match. Trimble made 164 not out in Australia's reply of 6 for 320.

Five individual centuries turned the match between Australia and Barbados at Bridgetown from 28 April to 1 May into a run feast that was always unlikely to provide a result. Simpson (117), O'Neill (101) and Thomas (110 not out) took Australia's first innings to 9 declared for 461. Barbados responded with the same total, R. Brancker (100) and Sobers (183 not out) providing the centuries. The match petered out with Australia on 1 for 189 in their second innings.

Twice well beaten and seemingly demoralised by Hall and Griffith's bouncers, Australia had all the best of the drawn fourth Test at Bridgetown's Kensington Oval between 5 and 11 May. Simpson and Lawry gave them the sound start they had been lacking by batting all the first day for 263 and became the first opening pair to score double centuries in the same Test. Australia's first wicket fell at 382, the second at 522. Cowper (102) added his century to Simpson's 201 and Lawry's 210 with what *Wisden* called disdainful ease and Australia declared at 6 for 650.

The West Indies were in immediate trouble when Bryan Davis went at 13 and Hunte had to leave the field after taking a ball in the face from Hawke. Kanhai responded to the crisis with a magnificent 129 before Nurse scored 201, the third double century of a match suffocated by runs. Simpson gambled by declaring at 4 for 175 in Australia's second innings and in a thrilling

conclusion the West Indies, with five wickets in hand, finished only 11 runs short of the winning target of 253, with eight fieldsmen on the boundary.

West Indies won their first rubber against Australia despite Australia's 10-wicket win in the fifth Test from 14 to 17 May. This created problems for officials who had sold tickets for the two days that now were not needed, but brought great joy to the Australian team who felt they had been victims of wretched umpiring throughout their tour. Kanhai made 121 in the West Indies' first innings but Australia still finished with a 70-run lead. McKenzie's 5 for 33 in the West Indies second innings of 131 included three clean-bowled dismissals in four deliveries and gave Australia only 63 to win, which they achieved without loss. A drawn match against Windward Islands at St George's, Grenada, completed the first-class matches on the tour but only started the recriminations.

Richie Benaud and Keith Miller questioned the legality of Griffith's action in their reports on the tour for Australian papers. Benaud took photographs from a variety of angles which showed Griffith's elbow bent, but not at the moment of delivery. Griffith argued that although he bent his arm in the delivery swing he straightened it by the instant of release. Miller was full of praise, however, for the brilliance of the West Indian strokeplay and condemned Australian attempts to blame Griffith's illegal action for the defeat.

Hall had led the Test bowling averages for the West Indies with 16 wickets at 28.37, Gibbs took 18 wickets at 30.83, and Griffith 15 wickets at 32.00. Neil Hawke was Australia's best bowler with 24 wickets at 21.83 and McKenzie took 18 wickets at 34.94. In all first-class matches Philpott's 49 wickets at 24.63 remain the highest number taken by an Australian on a West Indian tour.

Australia's major weakness was the failure to achieve good starts with the bat in four of

A photograph of Charlie Griffith just before he released the ball which experts said proved he threw. Griffith was called for excessive bouncers in the 1965 series with Australia, but not for throwing, which drew strong criticism from the Australians.

the five Tests. The left-handed Cowper made impressive improvement batting at No. 3 but the middle order repeatedly failed to resist Hall and Griffith. Gibbs and Sobers gave them no relief when they did weather the pace barrage.

Australia won 3 of their 10 first-class matches, lost 2 and drew 5. Conrad Hunte was the only batsman on either side to score more than 500 Test runs, averaging 61.11. Sobers came through his first series as captain a winner but had a highest score of only 69, which aroused speculation over whether leadership affected his batting.

The Australians made no official complaint about Griffith's action but the bitterness that simmered between the teams because of it surfaced the day after the tour ended when Norman O'Neill put his name to an article written for him by Sydney journalist Robert

Gray, in which he told readers of the London *Daily Mail* Griffith was a chucker. The article bitterly attacked Keith Miller, who responded with a pointed attack on O'Neill's "20-odd Test innings without a century". O'Neill's highest score in the series against the West Indies was 74 not out.

The Australian Board of Control fined O'Neill for writing the article, refusing to accept his argument that the tour had ended when it appeared. According to the Board, the tour ended when the team arrived home.

Griffith was adamant that his action was legal and his outspoken views of his critics were colourful enough to give him a rebellious, "bad boy of cricket" image. In England in 1966 umpire Arthur Fagg, the former Test opening batsman, no-balled him eight times for over-stepping and once for throwing in the West Indies match against Lancashire at Old Trafford. The call for throwing went unreported until the Lancashire players drew attention to it after the match. The call clearly depressed Griffith, who was nowhere near as effective on that tour as he had been earlier, and with 94 wickets at 28.54 in 28 Tests he fell six short of the 100-wicket mark that appeared to be at his mercy.

Michael Manley, Prime Minister of Jamaica from 1972 to 1980, in his *History of West Indian Cricket*, said:

> *To pounce upon a player who has passed through the ranks of school and youth cricket, club cricket and first-class cricket like the Shell Shield games in the West Indies and county cricket in England, only to be told on appearance in Tests that his action is wrong reveals a basic flaw in the organisation of the game internationally. A man like Griffith came close to greatness only to find himself recalled with doubt. He lives out his days under the bitter shadow that doubt has cast.*

One of the disappointments of the West Indian tour, Peter Allan, who appeared in only four matches, combined with Ross Duncan to provide a sensational opening to the 1965–66 Sheffield Shield competition. Allan took 4 for 32, Duncan 4 for 42 and they had New South Wales out for 108, which forced them to follow on. Grahame Thomas led a wonderful New South Wales recovery by scoring 182 out of a total of 450 and they won the match by 27 runs.

Allan's good form earned him a place in Australia's side for the first Test against Mike Smith's England team to Australia, along with 19-year-old Doug Walters, who learned to bat on an antbed pitch he and his family, mother included, used in between milking 150 cows a day on their Dungog dairy farm, 240 kilometres from Sydney.

The Englishmen had begun their tour in Perth with the avowed intention of eliminating the reputation for dullness left by the previous two MCC teams. The English team was the first to fly all the way to Australia and a number of their players started the tour with viral infections attributed to their rapid change to a different climate. They were captained by the former Oxford University and Leicestershire right-hander M. J. K. Smith, who had just scored 1607 runs at 44.63 for Warwickshire, a tall, bespectacled right-hander with exceptional powers of concentration who was a little past his best at 33. The team was M. J. K. Smith (captain), 33, M. C. Cowdrey, 33, K. F. Barrington, 35, F. J. Titmus, 33, J. M. Parks, 34, W. E. Russell, 29, B. R. Knight, 27, R. W. Barber, 30, J. H. Edrich, 28, G. Boycott, 25, J. T. Murray, 30, D. A. Allen, 30, P. H. Parfitt, 29, D. J. Brown, 23, K. Higgs, 28, I. J. Jones, 24, J. D. F. Larter, 25, with Billy Griffith as manager and Jack Ikin as assistant manager.

Griffith was given wide powers by the MCC and he persuaded some of the stolid batsmen in the side to attack more often. He and Ikin made a close study of batsmen's scoring rates and the over rates of the bowlers, but they could do little about the team's indifferent fielding. Knight was not in the original team but was summoned from

Doug Walters in 1965–66 when he forced his way into the Australian team with two centuries and two 80s in State matches. His career was to be sadly interrupted by Army service.

England as a reinforcement when injuries sidelined Larter and Brown. Jones had trouble throughout the tour because of his habit of following through down the pitch and was warned about it several times by umpires. Finally Dick Burgess banned him from bowling again in the match with New South Wales in Sydney.

Between 29 October and 26 November England won two and drew one of their first-class matches and were beaten by Victoria by 32 runs. Their first success came against Western Australia in Perth, where Peter Kelly scored centuries in each innings (119 and 108 not out) for the home side. Barber (126) and Parks (107 not out) made centuries for England, who got home by nine runs right on time. A rain-affected draw followed against a Combined XI on the same ground, Smith (112) and Barber (113) scoring centuries for England and Cowper (122 not out) a century for the Combined side. After a six-wicket win over South Australia in Adelaide, they suffered their first setback in Melbourne. Lawry batted for seven and a quarter hours in scoring 153 and 61 to set up the win for Victoria, whose team included two Cowpers, Bob and his elder brother David, who kept wicket.

England laid the foundation for an excellent win over New South Wales from 26 to 30 November with a first innings of 6 declared for 527. Barber made 90, Russell 93, Cowdrey 63, Smith 59, Parks 63, Titmus 80 not out, Allen 54 not out, and only Parfitt (16) failed to get a half-century. Walters made 129 in his first innings against England but on a pitch that helped spinners New South Wales managed only 288 and 240, and England needed only two runs to win by nine wickets. Russell (110) and Edrich (133) made centuries for England and Burge (114 not out) a century for Queensland in the drawn match played at the 'Gabba from 3 to 7 December.

Despite all the calls for brighter cricket, the Test series deteriorated to the familiar dull pattern with both sides afraid of losing. Doug Walters was the main success of the rubber, opening his Test career between 10 and 15 December with a lovely innings of 155 in the first Test at the 'Gabba, where rain curtailed the first day's play and washed out the second. Australia declared at 6 for 443 in the first innings following Walters' century and 166 from Lawry. England showed concern about Philpott's leg spin, but Parks (52) and Titmus (60) delayed the follow-on, 163 behind, until midway through the last day.

Walters was the ninth Australian to score a century in his Test debut, following in the steps of Charles Bannerman, Harry Graham, Reg Duff, Roger Hartigan, Herbie Collins, Bill Ponsford, Archie Jackson and, postwar, Jimmy Burke.

Brian Booth, captaining Australia in Simpson's absence through injury, sportingly allowed Boycott to paw a Philpott leg break away after a defensive shot, but warned him: "Do that again, matey, and you'll be out." Boycott apologised, but later in the same innings accepted an apology from Grout, who had appealed for a catch behind the stumps before realising he had hit the ground and not the ball.

Second-class matches at Canberra, Bathurst, Albury and Mount Gambier took England to Adelaide for the return match with South Australia over Christmas. Alan Shiell, a bus-driver's son from the East Torrens club who graduated from the Australian Schoolboys XI, made 202 not out with 2 sixes and 19 fours, which allowed Favell to declare at 7 for 459. England ended any chance of defeat by replying with 444, Smith (108) and Murray (110) supplying centuries. The runs continued as Ian Chappell made 113 not out in South Australia's second innings before Favell declared, leaving England to score 269 to win in 190 minutes. They got them with half an hour to spare for the loss of four wickets.

Simpson recovered from the broken wrist that had kept him out of the first Test to lead Australia in the second Test at Melbourne between 30 December and 4 January. Walters, just 20, scored 115 in Australia's second innings, his third century in as many matches against England. Burge (120) also made a century while Edrich (109) and Cowdrey (104) reached three figures for England in a boring draw, the 11th in 17 Tests between the countries. Fifteen of the 22 players bowled, with McKenzie's 5 for 135 in England's first innings the best figures.

The following week in Sydney, England defeated Australia by an innings and 93 runs. England began with an opening stand of 234 in 240 minutes between Boycott (84) and Barber, who reached his 100 off 147 balls and went on to 185. Edrich followed with 103 and despite spirited bowling by Hawke, who took 7 for 105, England reached 488.

Prime Minister Bob Menzies with the English and Australian players who appeared in a match in Canberra in 1965–66. The captains, Richie Benaud and Mike Smith are on either side of Menzies in the front row, with England manager Billy Griffith second on his left.

Simpson had chicken pox and Booth, who as Simpson's deputy had led Australia in 14 matches, took over again as captain. He found his batsmen struggling on a wearing pitch after a second-wicket stand of 81 by Thomas (51) and Cowper (60) and they followed on. The best stand produced 46 runs from Thomas and Lawry. Walters played the turning ball with exceptional skill for two hours in Australia's second innings. Titmus became a great crowd favourite in this, his 40th Test, during which he completed the double of 100 wickets and 1000 runs in Tests.

Nothing in the match surpassed Barber's batting, and having watched his clean, crisp strokeplay, I find it astonishing that this was his only Test century. Booth rushed from the field to open the English dressing-room door and as they came past applauded them all, but he had a special pat on the back for Barber. The gesture was in the best traditions of big cricket but earned Booth the reputation as a softie and he was dropped for the last two Tests.

English critics, apparently unaware that tour itineraries are agreed up to four years in advance, criticised the fact that England then had to play a New South Wales country side at Newcastle, and two matches in Tasmania before the fourth Test at Adelaide from 28 January to February 1. The implication that the programme was a plot was, of course, absurd, as the MCC had ample time to examine the itinerary and was only too ready to take the game to places starved of first-class cricket.

With Simpson fit, Australia made four changes for the fourth Test at Adelaide from 28 January to 1 February, with Booth, Cowper,

Philpott and Sincock dropped for Simpson, Veivers, Ian Chappell and Stackpole, who was selected as a leg spinner. Allan originally was preferred to McKenzie, but suffered a late injury. McKenzie was reinstated and on the first day gave a match-winning display, taking 6 for 48. Simpson (225) and Lawry (119) exploited the advantage this gave Australia with an opening partnership of 244 in 266 minutes, which remains the highest for the first wicket against England. Barrington's 102 in England's second innings was not enough to save England from defeat by an innings and 9 runs, Hawke taking 5 for 54.

Simpson continued his commanding form with a stand of 156 for the second wicket with Grahame Thomas for New South Wales against England in Sydney between 4 and 8 February. Simpson batted 200 minutes for 123, Thomas 170 minutes for 129, but on a good pitch neither side had the bowling resources to force a result.

England's first innings of 9 declared for 485 in the fifth Test at Melbourne from 11 to 16 February included the fastest century of the series from Barrington. His 115 included 2 sixes and 8 fours and he passed the century from 122 balls. England then squandered her strong position by bowling only 96 deliveries an hour when Australia batted. This gave Australia little chance of seeking a win and they were content to bat for most of the time that was left. Lawry took more than six hours to score 108, his fifth century of the season against England, and effectively killed the match by taking five and a half hours over the 212 he added for the third wicket with Cowper, who had replaced Burge in the side. Cowper took 310 minutes to reach 100, a further 225 minutes to make 200 and 727 minutes in all over 307, the only triple century in a Test in Australia. It was also the longest innings ever played in Australia, the longest against England, and the third-longest in all first-class cricket.

Instead of triumph, Cowper's innings provided a sour ending to a disappointing series with the public forgotten at the end by teams

Bob Cowper, who made 99 in the second Test at Melbourne in 1965–66, improved on this effort in the fifth Test in Melbourne when he made 307, the first triple century in a home Test by an Australia.

who hated to risk defeat. England won only five of their 15 first-class matches on the tour with the Tests even at one win apiece. They played entertainingly enough until the last three matches, which included two Tests, and it was their final efforts that earned them the rating as a mediocre outfit.

International cricket by then provided a bewildering kaleidoscope of touring teams, with seven countries submitting their national sides to frequent tours. Key players understandably tried to ease the burden of persistent absences from home by taking their families with them. There may have been substance in the view that Mike Smith was distracted from his responsibilities as England's captain by the presence of his wife and family in Australia.

Barrington headed England's batting averages with 946 runs at 67.56 in first-class matches, but Barber scored most runs with 1001 at 50.05. Barrington also topped the bowling averages with six wickets at 24.83 each but Titmus took most wickets with 36 at 30.80. England's batsmen scored 23 centuries in Australian first-class matches and had 21 scored against them. The umpiring in all States reached a high level with the Test pair, Col Egar and Lou Rowan, outstanding.

Brian Booth's omission from the last two Tests, after captaining Australia in the first and third Tests, brought a sad end to an international career that included 29 Tests. Booth, born at Perthville, 9 kilometres from Bathurst in an old gold-mining region of New South Wales, failed by one Test to qualify for the Provident Fund that provides a $50-a-Test retirement bonus once a player has reached 30 Tests. Ironically, he continued to play for New South Wales for a further three seasons and at one stage had played more matches for his State than any other player, 92. His career total of 11,265 runs included 26 centuries, average 45.42.

The damage injury did to Peter Allan's Test career was underlined in Melbourne early in January when he took all ten Victorian wickets for Queensland at a cost of 61 runs. He was the second bowler to achieve this feat in Shield cricket, emulating another pace bowler Tim Wall, who took all ten New South Wales wickets in 1932–33. But the bowler who made the biggest advance in 1965–66 was Neil Hawke, whose 49 wickets was the highest in all first-class matches.

Queenslander John ("Sandy") Morgan headed the Shield bowling averages in his first season of big cricket, taking five wickets in an innings in three of his five matches at the age of 20. Morgan's 25 wickets cost 19.20 each. Allan was second with 39 at 21.36. South Australian Donell Robins' 30 wickets at 29.30 included a hat-trick against New South Wales in Adelaide, the tenth in Shield cricket to that time. Johnny Martin gave up retirement plans to take 41 wickets at 31.49 for New South Wales, which took him to a total of 261 wickets, only five behind Benaud's record 266.

Five batsmen topped 1000 runs in the season and four made double centuries, Cowper's 307 in the fifth Test enabled him to head the first-class averages with 1418 runs at 74.63, just ahead of Lawry's 1445 at 72.25 and Walters' 1332 at 70.11. New South Wales retained the Shield despite the frequent absence of players on Test duty. Walters had the misfortune to be called up for two years Army service on 8 March 1966, and Graeme Watson replaced him in the Australian team to tour South Africa in the summer of 1966–67.

At the age of 86, Syd Smith retired from the presidency of the New South Wales Cricket Association, which he had held since 1935. Smith, who managed the 1921 and 1926 Australian teams to England, was succeeded as New South Wales president by E. C. McMillan, then chairman of the Australian Board of Control. Smith departed with New South Wales in possession of the Sheffield Shield for the 36th time.

The Australian team for South Africa, chosen by Bradman, Ryder and Seddon, was announced in February. The year before this tour the South Africans soundly beat England during a trip on which the Pollock brothers, Barlow, Lindsay, Bacher, Bland and van der Merwe played some wonderful cricket. Unable to test themselves against the West Indies because of apartheid, the South Africans wanted to beat Australia at least as heavily as the West Indies had done, to show they were the best side in the world. The Australian team was R. B. Simpson (captain), 30,

W. M. Lawry, 29, G. C. Becker, 30, I. M. Chappell, 23, R. M. Cowper, 26, N. J. N. Hawke, 27, J. M. Hubble, 24, G. D. McKenzie, 25, J. W. Martin, 35, I. R. Redpath, 25, D. A. Renneberg, 24, K. R. Stackpole, 26, H. B. Taber, 26, G. Thomas, 28, T. R. Veivers, 29, G. D. Watson, 21, with Bill Jacobs, the former Fitzroy batsman, as manager and M. MacLennan as baggageman–scorer.

The left-arm medium-pace bowler Jim Hubble, from the Subiaco–Fremantle club in Perth, was the surprise selection in a team for which Jarman was unavailable. O'Neill, Grout, Philpott and Burge had retired. The South Africans raised no objection to the inclusion of Grahame Thomas, who had Red Indian blood and was coloured under their laws, but Thomas had an uncomfortable tour which affected his form, although he was shown every courtesy. Hawke broke his right shoulder playing Australian Rules football and had to have it pinned before he was passed fit to tour.

The Australians faced a tour of 23 matches, 17 of them first-class, stretching from a warm-up at Bulawayo against a Matabeleland XI which started on 2 November 1966 to the fifth Test scheduled to end on 1 March 1967. They started well by beating Rhodesia at Salisbury from 5 to 8 November by eight wickets thanks to spinners Martin (5 for 26) and Chappell (5 for 53) and Redpath's 139 not out. But in the second match at Johannesburg, between 11 and 15 November, they lost for the first time in South Africa in 64 years when Transvaal defeated them by 76 runs. Ali Bacher's 235 and H. R. ("Tiger") Lance's 107 gave Australia 489 to score in the last innings in 400 minutes. They fought magnificently to reach 6 for 379 but their last four wickets went for 21 runs, the end coming with eight minutes left.

Far from being demoralised by this defeat, Australia compiled 9 declared for 504 against Western Province at Cape Town, to set up an innings and 108 runs win. This happened between 18 to 22 November, with Redpath (154) and Stackpole (138 not out) contributing centuries and Cowper taking 6 for 40 with his off spinners. Simpson square-cut the fourth-last ball of the match against Eastern Province to clinch a six-wicket win between 25 and 29 November at Port Elizabeth. Chappell made 113, Watson 118 not out, Hubble took 5 for 74 in an innings and Cowper five more valuable wickets. A 190-run defeat by a Combined XI at East London upset Australian morale before the first Test, despite a 67-run win over Natal in the second week of December.

South Africa recovered brilliantly from a horrendous start in the first Test at Johannesburg from 23 to 28 December. On the New Wanderers ground, that had been saturated by days of rain, South Africa were 5 for 41. Lance (44) and Lindsay (69) added 110 for the sixth wicket but South Africa managed only 199. McKenzie finished with 5 for 46, forcing the ball to hurry on before the pitch dried out.

Australia appeared in command when Simpson and Lawry put on 118 for the first wicket and they passed the South African total with nine wickets in hand. But three wickets fell for three runs and another 11 runs later Australia had slumped to 5 for 218. Thereafter every run was a struggle and Australia's first innings lead was only 126.

Dropped catches galore then allowed South Africa to reach their highest total in Tests, 620. Lindsay, dropped at 10, made 182 and van der Merwe, let off at 2, scored 76. Even then Australia seemed set to save the match until Simpson ran himself out on the final morning. An outstanding display of left-arm swing bowling by Trevor Goddard gave him 6 for 53 and took South Africa to a remarkable win by 233 runs. The 'keepers Lindsay and Taber (in his Test debut) had memorable matches, both dismissing eight batsmen.

After only three days rest Australia staged a praiseworthy comeback at Newlands, Cape

Town, between 31 December and 5 January. Simpson attacked the bowling confidently to score 153, his sixth Test century and his first against South Africa, and his assurance spread through the side. Redpath (54) and Chappell (49) carried the score along with entertaining strokeplay and when they left Stackpole (134) and Watson (50), in his first Test, added 128 runs in 95 minutes.

McKenzie again made an early breakthrough, dismissing Goddard, Barlow and Bacher for 41, and although Graeme Pollock made 209 in 350 minutes, the highest Test score at Cape Town, South Africa still finished 189 behind and had to follow on. McKenzie added to his first innings bag of 5 for 65 with 3 for 67 in South Africa's second innings but it was Simpson who captured the prized wicket when he bowled Graeme Pollock for 4. From 4 for 64, South Africa did well to reach 367, Lindsay topscoring with 81 and Peter Pollock, batting at No. 9, contributing 75 not out. Set to score 179 to win, Australia lost four wickets, Redpath producing 69 not out.

Australia's batsmen went on the rampage before the next Test. At East London, Chappell and Veivers put on 198 in only 84 minutes against Border from 7 to 10 January. Chappell's 164 included 26 fours and Veivers' 109, 3 sixes and 16 fours. The Border batsmen resisted grimly but Australia's total of 6 declared for 493 proved too big and Australia won by ten wickets. From 13 to 16 January, at Bloemfontein, Cowper made 201 not out in a total of 6 declared for 409, but Lawry did not enforce the follow-on when Orange Free State were out for 270, preferring to give his batsmen practice for the Test.

South Africa introduced two new players for the third Test at Durban between 20 and 25 January, Mike Procter and Pat Trimborn, both lively medium-pace bowlers, apparently hoping to curb Australia's batting stars. The move worked. Procter took 7 for 98 and Trimborn removed Cowper in the first innings and Simpson in the second. Simpson sent South Africa in when

he won the toss and his tactic appeared to succeed when Barlow was out to the first ball of the match, but a fine century by Lindsay, his second of the series, rescued his side and helped lift the total to 300.

Lawry had to have ten stitches inserted in a head wound when he mis-hit a bouncer from Pollock but returned to topscore with 44 in Australia's poor total of 147. Following on, Australia made 334. South Africa scored the 182 runs required to win with the loss of two wickets, Graeme Pollock and Bacher adding 127 unfinished.

Australia still had a chance of sharing the series in the fifth Test at Port Elizabeth, set down for 24 February to 1 March. Rain had saved them in the fourth Test at Johannesburg, from 3 to 8 February, when they were 41 runs short of an innings defeat with two wickets left; but Australia were rattled from the start of the fifth Test when Lawry was run out without facing a ball attempting a third run. Thereafter superb all-round cricket from Goddard proved the difference between the sides. Goddard made 74 and 59 and, taking 3 for 13 and 3 for 63, caused collapses in both Australian innings when Australia had fought their way past the pace bowlers. Graeme Pollock's 105 further demonstrated South Africa's superiority in a match in which only Cowper scored more than 50 for Australia.

South Africa won by seven wickets inside four days, to take the series 3–1, their first victory over Australia. Lindsay set a record for wicket-keepers by holding 24 catches in the series and Peter Pollock became the fourth South African to take 100 Test wickets. Only his opposite number Brian Taber justified his selection among Australia's newcomers to Test cricket. McKenzie was the only Australian bowler of Test quality, taking 24 wickets at 26.00, and the failure of Hawke and Renneberg to support him proved costly.

Australia won 7 of their 17 first-class matches,

lost 5 and drew 7. Simpson scored three of the 13 centuries collected by the Australians and topped the Test and first-class averages. Graeme Pollock and Dennis Lindsay both scored three centuries against Australia, who had 12 three-figure scores compiled against them. Indeed Lindsay's 606 runs at 86.57 in the Tests, together with his 24 catches, was arguably the best-ever effort by a wicket-keeper-batsman.

The tour made a profit of $75,000 but following the heavy defeat by the West Indies and the moderate showing against England, it left Australia with a great deal of rebuilding to do to regain a leading position in world cricket. South Africa on the other hand had confirmed her claims to a top position among the cricket nations with her team fast approaching world dominance.

Australia's Pinocchio

Domestic cricket 1966-69;
India and New Zealand tour Australia
1967-68; Australia's twenty-fifth
tour of England 1968;
West Indies in Australia 1968-69;
Australia tours India 1969-70

The Australian second team that toured New Zealand while the senior players were in South Africa included an unorthodox spinner who, in 1966–67 when Victoria won the Sheffield Shield, topped the bowling averages with 23 wickets at 18.22 from four matches in his initial first-class season. This was one of the most fascinating figures in Australia's cricket history, John William Gleeson, who tucked the middle finger of his bowling hand behind the ball and had batsmen misreading his breaks wherever he played.

Gleeson, born at Wingaree, near Kyogle, on a dairy farm, toured the world twice with the Emus, a group of Australian bush cricket addicts who put up their own money for overseas trips. He worked as a telephone linesman at Tamworth in north-eastern New South Wales, where he began experimenting with the bent-finger grip perfected by Jack Iverson. He started with table tennis balls on a table and later bowled old cricket

Former Test Captain Vic Richardson presents his grandson Ian Chappell with a "Cricketer of the Year" award in Adelaide in 1968–69.

balls at gum trees, trying to perfect the length with his unusual grip that he could achieve on a long table. Initially, he toured with the Emus as a wicket-keeper but on his second trip began to take wickets regularly with his spinners.

The fingers that he used to untangle telephone wires around the Tamworth district produced spin which caused a sensation in local cricket matches and attracted offers from the Western Suburbs and Balmain clubs in Sydney. Wests wanted him to live in Sydney but he preferred Balmain, who agreed simply to pay his air fares from Tamworth and back every weekend. In his first season he topped the Balmain bowling averages with 40 wickets at 17.03, which included a hat-trick against the Randwick club, and in his second season he won State selection.

Gleeson took eight wickets for New South Wales against Queensland in his third first-class match, with Peter Burge among his victims. He had nine more wickets in his next match, against South Australia in Sydney, with his spin baffling veterans Favell and Dansie. In eight matches in New Zealand he took 26 wickets at 28.61 on pitches unresponsive to spin.

Despite his bush background Gleeson was a far more worldly cricketer than Iverson. He used his bent finger grip with more subtlety, resorting to orthodox spinners to widen his range, but because of the high bounce he achieved with his grip special thought had to be given to his field, which some of his captains did not understand.

Gleeson made his Test debut against India at Adelaide from 23 to 28 December 1967, along with the classy young Victorian batsman Paul Sheahan, after playing in only five Sheffield Shield matches. They were brought into the Australian team largely to assess their skills at the international level before Bradman, Ryder and Neil Harvey, who had replaced Dudley Seddon on the national selection panel, sat down to pick the team to tour England in 1968.

The Indians brought a team completely lacking fast bowling for a nine-match tour designed to lift their standards. They were led by the Nawab of Pataudi, an heroic figure partially blind in one eye following a car accident while he was at Oxford University. He took over the captaincy at 21 from Nari Contractor. The team he brought to Australia in the summer of 1967–68 was Nawab of Pataudi jr, 21, R. F. Surti, 29, Abid Ali, 25, F. M. Engineer, 27, A. L. Wadekar, 24, V. Subramanya, 29, C. G. Borde, 31, E. A. S Prasanna, 25, R. G. Nadkarni, 33, D. N. Sardesai, 25, B. S. Bedi, 19, U. N. Kulkarni, 23, B. S. Chandrasekhar, 20, with Ghulam Ahmed as manager and A. N. Ghose as treasurer. M. L. Jaisimha, 26, arrived after eight matches had been played and appeared in the last two of the four Tests.

Cricket had been played in India since 1721 when sailors of a trading ship are said to have set up stumps at Cambay in the western region, but India's oldest club, the Calcutta Cricket Club, dates from 1792. They first sent a team overseas in 1886 when the Parsees won only one of their 28 matches in England. They first toured Australia in 1947–48 under the captaincy of Lala Amarnath. India's unhappy learning period in big cricket lasted until 1961–62, when they beat a touring England side led by Ted Dexter 2–nil. Since then success had eluded them.

In the month before the first Test they were beaten by an innings by both Western Australia in Perth and South Australia in Adelaide, and played draws with Victoria and Tasmania. Borde took over the captaincy for the Test, at Adelaide from 23 to 28 December 1967, when Pataudi was injured but, with an attack dependent solely on spin, could not contain Australia's batsmen, who made 335 and 369, with Cowper taking the honours by scoring 92 and 108. Engineer (89), Borde (69) and Surti (70) batted well in India's first innings but they could not handle the pace of McKenzie and Renneberg (5 for 39) in their second innings and lost by 146 runs.

The second Test at Melbourne from 30 December to 3 January produced two brave

Victorian left-hander Les Joslin in action during his only Test in 1967–68 against India. He toured England in 1968 but made only 344 runs at 21.50, spoiling a career that looked full of promise.

Brisbane, where Simpson handed over the Australian captaincy to Lawry for the third Test, between 19 and 24 January, Jaisimha gave a remarkable display only a few days after arriving. Without match practice and with little time in the nets, he made 74 and 101, the only Indian century of the series. His task was made easier by the absence of McKenzie who, with a big workload ahead of him in England that year, was rested from the last two Tests. Australia won the third Test by 39 runs.

After missing the third Test, Simpson returned to play in the fourth Test, at Sydney from 26 to 31 January, under Lawry's captaincy, playing what was thought to be his farewell match on his home field. Simpson failed with the bat but celebrated by taking 8 for 97 in the match with his leg spinners, including 5 for 59 in the second innings. Walters, who played in the last two Tests while on leave from the army, followed his 93 and 62 not out in the third Test with 94 not out in the fourth Test to head the series averages with 127.00. India, 49 behind on the first innings, fought back with an opening stand of 83 between Abid Ali and Engineer in their second innings, but brilliant slips catching eroded their bid and Simpson finished off their last three batsmen in seven balls to give Australia the match by 144 runs and the series 4-nil.

Cowper proved more penetrative with his right-arm spinners than Gleeson with his unorthodox turn, repeatedly chiming in with handy wickets, and made two centuries in the four Tests. Sheahan did not score a century but played some magnificent strokes and with three scores over 50 looked rich in promise. India were severely handicapped by the breakdown of the googly bowler Chandrasekhar, who missed two Tests, and failed to win any of their first-class matches but in Bedi and Prasanna they looked to have highly promising spinners.

innings from Pataudi, who was handicapped by a torn hamstring muscle. But his 75 and 85 and a patient 99 from the left-handed Wadekar could not save them from defeat by an innings and 4 runs against an Australian side that scored 529 after Simpson (109) and Lawry (100) put on 191 for the first wicket. Ian Chappell was dropped several times in scoring 151. McKenzie (10 for 151) and Renneberg (4 for 135) gave the other bowlers little to do.

Rain helped produce a draw against New South Wales and washed out the match with Queensland in the first half of January. At

A New Zealand team of 13 players toured Australia early in the summer for four first-class matches before returning home to play against India. This was only the second New Zealand team to visit Australia, although matches had been played against New Zealand teams travelling to or from South Africa and England. The New Zealanders did not win a match, losing by 24 runs to South Australia in Adelaide and playing a draw with Victoria in Melbourne at the end of November. Early in December they drew with Queensland in Brisbane and were beaten by 131 runs by New South Wales in Sydney, where Simpson made 137 not out batting down the order. Freeman advanced his claims for a spot in the team to England by taking 11 for 97 against them in Adelaide, including 8 for 47 in the second innings. Sheahan scored 161 against them in Melbourne. The sole New Zealand century on the tour came from Vic Pollard, who reached 125 against Queensland.

The major shock of the 1967–68 season came when Western Australia won the Sheffield Shield under the captaincy of Tony Lock, their first win since they were granted full membership in the competition. They had previously won the Shield in 1947–48 when they had a modified programme of only four matches. Immediately Western Australia had completed the win, Lock flew off to the Caribbean as a reinforcement for the England side.

Western Australia began by beating Victoria and New South Wales in Perth but lost their matches with South Australia, the first when Perth-born Ashley Mallett returned home to take 8 for 101 and the second when Greg Chappell, who was in his first season of first-class cricket, put on 215 for the sixth wicket with Barry Jarman. Chappell made 157, his initial first-class century.

Western Australia then had to wait six weeks before they made their trip east, which proved a triumph. They took full points from Queensland, New South Wales and Victoria. Former Test bowler Laurie Mayne returned to form a formidable opening attack with McKenzie

South Australian John Causby practising in the nets in 1967–68 for the match against Western Australia in Perth. Earlier that summer he made 137 in a 281 stand with Les Favell for the first wicket against New South Wales.

on this tour, which featured dominant batting by John Inverarity, whose two centuries on the trip took him to second place on the Shield batting averages with 59.59 behind Paul Sheahan (64.87) and won him a place in the team to England. New South Wales lost six of their eight matches but Simpson's 277 against Queensland was the highest score on the Sydney ground since Bradman's 452 not out in 1929–30.

Meanwhile in the West Indies England achieved miracles by defeating the side rated best in the world 1–nil in a torrid series. It sparked off a bottle-throwing riot in Kingston and a bouncer-war in Bridgetown when John Snow and the strapping Welshman Jeff Jones retaliated against a barrage of head-high deliveries. Bowling at a pace faster than either Hall or Griffith, Snow and Jones bowled frequent bouncers at the West Indians for more than an hour, leaving Kanhai battered and bruised. England won the series in the next Test at Port-of-Spain, with a team that included the coloured batsman Basil D'Oliveira, who had been barred from playing in his native Cape Town and had won his way into Test cricket via the Lancashire League and Worcestershire.

England's success in the West Indies boosted interest in Australia's twenty-fifth tour of England, one hundred years after the first Australian team's visit there, the all-Aboriginal side captained by the former Surrey professional Charles Lawrence. The team was chosen by Bradman, Ryder and Harvey, who left out Greg Chappell but were able to include Doug Walters at the last moment, after the completion of his army service. The team was W. M. Lawry (captain), 31, B. N. Jarman (vice-captain), 32, I. M. Chappell, 24, A. N. Connolly, 28, R. M. Cowper, 27, E. W. Freeman, 23, J. W. Gleeson, 29, N. J. N. Hawke, 29, R. J. Inverarity, 24, L. R. Joslin, 20, G. D. McKenzie, 26, A. A. Mallett, 22, I. R. Redpath, 27, D. A. Renneberg, 25, A. P. Sheahan, 20, H. B. Taber, 28, K. D. Walters, 22, with Bob Parish as manager, Les Truman as treasurer, Dave Sherwood as scorer-baggagemaster and Arthur James as masseur. The team was the youngest Australia had sent to England and it flew from Sydney on 24 April 1968 without Jarman, whose wife was expecting a baby. He joined the side later.

The first match at Worcester from 8 to 10 May was abandoned because of bad weather, the first time this had happened, and that set the pattern for a frustrating and totally disappointing tour. The next three matches, against Leicestershire, Lancashire and MCC, were drawn and it was not until the fifth match against Northants at Northampton between 22 and 24 May that the rain disappeared. Freeman, who

played wearing contact lenses, had a great match, taking 5 for 78 in Northants' first innings and scoring a century in 90 minutes. His 116 included 5 mighty sixes and 13 fours and was his initial first-class century. Mallett took 7 for 75 in Northants' second innings and Australia won by ten wickets.

Three Australians made centuries at Taunton at the end of May against Somerset, who included Greg Chappell and Bill Alley in their lineup. Ian Chappell's 147, Cowper's 148 and Redpath's 112 were all entertaining hands sprinkled with sixes but the last Somerset pair held out for a draw. Redpath had a further century (106) against Surrey at The Oval between 1 and 4 June but the weather again prevented a result.

McKenzie and Cowper bowled Australia to victory in the first Test at Old Trafford from 6 to 11 June by restricting England's first innings to 165, after solid batting by Lawry (81), Walters (81), Sheahan (88) and Chappell (73). Sheahan lost composure after running Chappell out and a century on debut in England was lost to them both. McKenzie had good support from Connolly, Gleeson and Cowper in England's second innings, Australia winning by 159 runs. Walters' 81 and 86 turned out his most productive Test batting in England.

Chappell's 202 at Birmingham against Warwickshire from 12 to 14 June allowed Jarman to declare on the last day and set a side that included noted stroke-makers like Amiss, Kanhai, Jameson and M. J. K. Smith 299 to win at 85 an hour. There was wild excitement as Warwickshire got to within 31 runs of the target and then had to hold on desperately in the last half hour to salvage a draw.

The 200th match between the countries attracted advance bookings of £73,000, or £14,000 more than the best takings for any previous cricket match in England, but rain at Lord's over the 20 to 25 June period cut playing time in half. Australia were dismissed for 78 in their first innings, their lowest total since South Africa

Unorthodox spinner Johnny Gleeson bowling in England in 1968 when he took 58 wickets. Many experts thought captain Bill Lawry failed to fully exploit Gleeson's bowling.

100 Tests at Edgbaston, where he made 104.

The fourth Test at Headingley between 25 and 30 July was the least affected by the weather of the Tests, but with Lawry absent through injury Jarman concentrated on avoiding defeat. He relied heavily on McKenzie, Connolly and Freeman to pin England down, apparently concerned about giving away runs by using the potentially more dangerous spin of Gleeson, Cowper and Chappell. England gave a dispirited display with the bat and with neither side deserving to win, the match petered out in a draw.

Glamorgan made history at Swansea early in August by defeating Australia by 79 runs, their second win on successive tours. Glamorgan held some remarkable catches and Sheahan lessened the severity of Australia's defeat by scoring a marvellous 137 on the last day, but by then most interest had gone from the tour.

With Australia certain of retaining the Ashes, although they had been outplayed in two of the draws, England won the fifth Test at The Oval from 22 to 27 August by 226 runs with five minutes to spare. Inverarity made a valiant effort to save Australia by batting throughout the final innings and was the last man out when he padded up to a ball from Underwood (7 for 50) and was ruled lbw. Edrich (164) and D'Oliveira (158) made centuries for an England team from which Barrington was omitted for slow scoring. Lawry showed what he thought of this by taking 350 minutes to make 135. When he was out caught behind by Knott he had a few well-chosen words with umpire Arthur Fagg about the decision.

On the second last day of the Test, news reached The Oval of the death in Sydney of the great Australian batsman Stan McCabe. He had tried to dispose of a dead possum and fallen down a cliff at the back of his home in the Sydney suburb of Mosman. He was 58. When news of his death was announced The Oval crowd went silent, removing their hats and standing up. On the field, the players stopped in their tracks. Jack

tumbled them out for 75 in 1949–50, but there was insufficient time for England to press home the advantage.

After a good win at Southend over Essex, when Renneberg took 8 for 72 and Lawry made 135, the Australians suffered their first defeat of the tour at Bramall Lane, Sheffield, where Yorkshire, captained by Fred Trueman, scored 9 declared for 355 and then had Australia out for 148 and 138 on a pitch responsive to both pace and spin. Trueman had 6 for 83 and Illingworth 8 for 67 in the match. This was Yorkshire's first win over Australia since 1902.

Between 6 and 23 July rain-affected draws followed against Nottinghamshire at Trent Bridge (where Harold Larwood watched play), England in the Edgbaston Test, against Gloucestershire at Bristol, and against Middlesex at Lord's. Cowdrey, who led England throughout the series, became the first player to appear in

Graham McKenzie falls to Derek Underwood for a duck in the fifth Test in the 1968 series, one of five wickets to fall to Underwood in the last hour. England won by 226 runs with five minutes left.

Fingleton, reporting the series for Australian newspapers, deplored the fact that the Australians did not wear black armbands in McCabe's memory for he had been, 'as Cardus said, the most knightly and gallant batsman since Trumper, who in his career hit 29 centuries in 11,951 first-class runs.

The fifth Test marked the beginning of the celebrated D'Oliveira affair. Basil D'Oliveira had come into the English side as a late replacement when Roger Prideaux withdrew but despite his 158, D'Oliveira was not included when the English team to tour South Africa in the following southern summer was announced.

When Tom Cartwright later declared himself unfit and withdrew, D'Oliveira replaced him. South African Prime Minister Vorster refused to accept the English team if it included D'Oliveira and the tour was cancelled.

Australia's bowlers gave their best display of the tour at Lord's between 31 August and 3 September, when Australia beat the Rest of the World by eight wickets. They tumbled out a side that included Hanif Mohammad, Eddie Barlow, Seymour Nurse, Graeme Pollock, Dennis Lindsay, Basil Butcher and the Nawab of Pataudi in just over two hours for 107 to set up the win. Connolly provided the decisive burst with 3 for 18. Redpath made 111 runs in the match for once out.

Australia won only 8 of their 25 first-class matches, lost 3, had 14 draws, (including 1 abandoned). They scored 13 centuries and had seven scored against them. Lawry topped the Test averages with 45.00 compared with Ian Chappell's 43.50 but in all first-class matches their positions were reversed, Chappell heading the list with 48.50 ahead of Lawry's 45.30. Gleeson took most wickets with 58 at 20.65 but Connolly finished on top in the bowling averages with 55 wickets at 20.29 apiece. Only Chappell and Redpath (1474 at 43.35) scored 1000 runs and Connolly and Gleeson were the only bowlers to take 50 wickets. The tour showed a profit of £40,000, largely because of advance bookings. The major disappointment of an exasperating tour was that the unquestioned talents of Sheahan and Walters did not flower. Only in the field did Australia match the great teams of the past.

Shortly after the team's return Australian cricket was once again saddened by news of Grout's death in November 1968 at the age of 41. His death came as no surprise to those who had shaded him from the sun when he blacked out at practice sessions at the 'Gabba. He had ignored the warning so that he could continue his career until the age of 37.

The Australians had only a month's rest before they began the 1968–69 Sheffield Shield competition and prepared to receive the fourth West Indian team to tour Australia, under the captaincy of Garfield Sobers.

A world Double Wicket championship sponsored by a cigarette company was played in Australia in October, 1968, and proved a flop with spectators although $20,000 prizemoney was attractive to the two-man teams involved. The championship was played over five rounds with semi-finals and finals in five States, mainly on showgrounds and venues where cricketers were strangers. Each player batted for eight overs, unless a batsman was out.

Famous England batsman Ken Barrington collapsed with a heart attack in the Melbourne round of the event and did not play first-class cricket again. Fred Trueman took his place. Colin

Elegant Victorian Paul Sheahan glances to leg on his first tour of England in 1968, a time when his brief periods of brilliance excited spectators and commentators alike.

Milburn played with Inverarity as his partner in Perth and with Ian Chappell in Adelaide. Curiously, the West Indian pair, Kanhai and Griffith, failed to win a match. Final placings were: G. S. Sobers and W. W. Hall, 9 points; R. G. Pollock and P. M. Pollock, 8; C. Milburn and partner, 6; W. M. Lawry and K. D. Walters, 5; B. L. D'Oliveira and F. S. Trueman, 5; R. B. Simpson and G. D. McKenzie, 2; J. D. Lindsay and T. L. Goddard, 2; R. B. Kanhai and C. C. Griffith, nil.

From the start of the season all the players who had toured England showed marked improvement and the West Indians' visit turned out one of Australian cricket's finest triumphs. The West Indian team was G. S. Sobers (captain),

32, R. B. Kanhai, 33, M. C. Carew, 31, B. F. Butcher, 35, C. H. Lloyd, 24, S. M. Nurse, 35, R. C. Fredericks, 26, D. A. J. Holford, 28, J. L. Hendricks, 25, G. S. Camacho, 23, T. M. Findlay, 25, L. A. King, 29, C. C. Griffith, 30, R. M. Edwards, 28, W. W. Hall, 31, L. R. Gibbs, 34, C. A. Davis, 24, with B. M. Gaskin as manager.

Honours were even for the first six weeks of the tour. Sobers gave the West Indies a fine start with an innings of 132, which set up a win over Western Australia between 26 and 29 October in Perth. Defeats followed at the hands of a Combined XI in Perth, where Ian Chappell made a magnificent 188 not out and Paul Sheahan 111 not out in an unbeaten fourth-wicket stand, and in Adelaide against South Australia, for whom Ian Chappell made 123 and fast bowler Kevin McCarthy 127 in a South Australian record stand of 171 for the eighth wicket. The match against Victoria in Melbourne was drawn. Then came a confidence-boosting win over New South Wales by nine wickets in Sydney, where Camacho hit 102 and Sobers 130. Fredericks (136) and Butcher produced centuries in the drawn match at the 'Gabba against Queensland, whose captain Sam Trimble made 177.

Sobers puzzled his supporters by leaving the team to conduct some business in Melbourne in the fortnight preceding the first Test at the 'Gabba. When he returned it was found that he was in pain with a piece of floating bone in his shoulder which stopped him using his back-of-the-hand deliveries, and he also had knee trouble.

The side that batted first had a decided advantage in the first Test at the 'Gabba from 6 to 10 December on a pitch that broke up as play progressed. The West Indies were well placed at 3 for 241 when Connolly destroyed the innings by dismissing Butcher, Sobers and Lloyd for three runs. Chasing 296, Australia were 1 for 217 when Sobers brought on Lloyd, who in 25 minutes had Lawry out for 105 and Chappell for 117. With the ball turning, Gibbs (5 for 88) and Holford (2 for 88) finished off the innings.

Dashing West Indian batsman Rohan Kanhai plays a delightful on drive during the 1968–69 series in Australia. Australia won the series 3–1.

The West Indies were again in trouble at 4 for 93 in their second innings and again it fell to Lloyd to rescue them. His 129 proved the match-winner. Left to score 366 to win, Australia succumbed to Sobers' versatile mix of swing and spin for 240.

Gleeson had troubled all the West Indian batsmen in taking seven wickets in this Test following his 5 for 92 against them for New South Wales. He mesmerised them again in the second Test between 26 and 30 December in Melbourne after McKenzie had taken 8 for 71 in the first innings. This time he took 5 for 61, restricting the West Indies to 280 in their second innings. A double century by Lawry (205) in 440 minutes and 165 from Ian Chappell, his fifth century in as many matches against the tourists, and 76 by

Walters took Australia to a total of 510, enough to provide victory by an innings and 30 runs.

Right on top now, with the West Indian veterans unable to produce the great feats of their youth, Australia won the third Test at Sydney from 3 to 8 January by ten wickets. West Indies began with 264 but then their bowling was flogged in an Australian innings of 547, in which Walters was the star with 118. Only 101 from Butcher compelled Australia to bat a second time.

The fourth Test, from 24 to 29 January in Adelaide, was the best of the rubber, producing the highest scoring of any Test in Australia. The West Indies again had trouble reading Gleeson in their first innings of 276, with Sobers supplying 110. Australia responded with 533, Walters also scoring 110. All the West Indian top players succeeded in their second innings of 616, Butcher collecting his second century of the series (118). Left to score 360 in 345 minutes, Australia received a fine start from Lawry (89), Stackpole (50) and Chappell (96) and at 3 for 304 looked a great chance.

Then Griffith started a string of run-outs by knocking over the stumps at the bowler's end with Redpath out of his ground. Griffith had given no warning. Walters (50), Freeman and Jarman were all run out in a mixture of bad calling and superb throwing. McKenzie and Gleeson went cheaply and the last pair, Sheahan and Connolly, had to face 26 deliveries, 16 of them bowled with the new ball by Sobers and Griffith. Australia survived, still 21 short of victory, leaving a thrilling match drawn.

The fifth Test was extended to the six days from 14 to 20 February in Sydney because the series had not been decided. Sobers won the toss, sent Australia in, and at 3 for 51 appeared to have been justified, particularly when Lawry was dropped by Nurse when he was on 44. But Lawry and Walters were not separated until the score reached 387 and their 336-run stand had lasted 405 minutes. Lawry hit 12 fours in his 151, Walters 24 fours in his 242, his highest Test score. Freeman

(56), Taber (48), and Gleeson (45) then took Australia to 619, the highest total ever made by a side put in to bat in a Test.

The West Indies lacked application in their first innings of 279, but Lawry did not enforce the follow-on. Instead he gave Redpath (132) and Walters (103) the chance at further runs and declared at 8 for 394, which gave the West Indies 735 to score in ten hours. Sobers (113) and Nurse (137) scored centuries but Gleeson dismissed them both, leaving Australia winners by 382 runs in the match and 3–1 in the series. The great West Indian team of the sixties had disintegrated, and the leadership of their most brilliant player had been found wanting, with him often travelling to matches by car while his players took trains or planes. Worst of all, the feared fast bowling partnership of Griffith and Hall had flopped, with Griffith playing in only three Tests, Hall in two.

Walters, who in the fifth Test became the first batsman to score a double century and a century in the same Test, headed the Australian batting averages with 699 runs in six innings at 116.50, followed by Lawry with 667 at 83.37 and Chappell 548 at 68.50. McKenzie took most wickets and topped the bowling averages with 30 wickets at 25.26. Gleeson's 26 wickets at 32.46 also played a major part in Australia's success. Taber had proved a fine wicket-keeper when he took over from Jarman after the fourth Test and the youthful Australians' fielding had made most of their opponents look like crocks. The West Indians went off to complete their tour with six matches in New Zealand and the Australians were hailed as the world champions.

Turning to the Sheffield Shield competition, cricket fans enjoyed some spectacular events. These included Colin Milburn's opening stand of 328 with Derek Chadwick for Western Australia against Queensland in Brisbane, when Milburn scored 181 between lunch and tea. Milburn, a roly-poly English opener of around 108 kilograms who had been brought into the

Western Australian side from the Northants county team, hit 4 sixes and 38 fours, some of the hits landing in surrounding streets.

With this kind of explosive batting, backed by Lock's captaincy and slow bowling guile (46 wickets), Western Australia led the Shield table by two points going into the last match between South Australia and New South Wales in Sydney. South Australia hustled New South Wales out for 110 to make sure of first innings points and following a brilliant 102 from Greg Chappell, swept on to an eight-wicket victory. This was South Australia's ninth Shield win and the third since World War II.

New South Wales were a shambles, after dominating the competition for years, but their wicket-keeper Brian Taber confirmed his rating as the best wicket-keeper in Australia by figuring in 12 dismissals in the match with South Australia at Adelaide. This equalled the world record set by Edward Pooley for Surrey *v.* Sussex in 1868 and equalled in 1938–39 by Don Tallon for Queensland *v.* New South Wales, and made Taber a certainty for the Australian tour of India and South Africa in 1969–70. Taber had taken over the New South Wales captaincy when Walters asked to be relieved of the job.

Australia originally planned to tour India and Pakistan, but when Pakistan cancelled their part of the tour the South Africans were delighted to provide substitute matches, as the projected England tour the previous year had been cancelled when the South African government refused to permit entry to Basil D'Oliveira. The tour began in Ceylon (now Sri Lanka), a rapidly advancing nation in world cricket, and shaped up as one of the most arduous ever undertaken by Australia. The team was the last chosen by Bradman, who had picked 14 touring sides since 1938. With the help of Phil Ridings and Neil Harvey, this was his side: W. M. Lawry (captain), 32, I. M. Chappell (vice-captain), 26, A. N. Connolly, 30, E. W. Freeman, 25, J. W. Gleeson, 31, J. T. Irvine, 26, R. C. Jordan, 32, G. D.

McKenzie, 28, A. A. Mallett, 24, L. C. Mayne, 27, I. R. Redpath, 28, A. P. Sheahan, 23, K. R. Stackpole, 29, H. B. Taber, 29, K. D. Walters, 23, with Fred Bennett as manager and D. MacFarlane as masseur.

Twelve members of the team flew to Colombo from Australia, but McKenzie, Mayne and Connolly flew from England and were held up in Calcutta, unable to secure a connecting flight for three days. The team played three one-day matches in Ceylon and one three-day match against All Ceylon, which was drawn. After a second-class match at Poona they began the first Test against India at Brabourne Stadium in Bombay, from 4 to 9 November, amid a public outcry against the omission of Venkataraghavan from the Indian side. Finally Subrato Guga agreed to stand down so that Venkat could play.

McKenzie had India at 3 for 42 before Mankad and Pataudi put on 146 for the fourth wicket, a record against Australia. Ashok Mankad, taller and heavier than his father, fell to McKenzie for 74, Pataudi to Gleeson for 95 and the innings folded up for 271. Stackpole in his initial Test against India scored 103 of Australia's 345 in reply. Gleeson, Connolly and Mallett then won the match by dismissing India for 137 in their second innings, Gleeson finishing with match figures of 7 for 108 from 67.4 overs, and collecting his 50th wicket in 15 Tests.

At 7 for 114 in this innings, Venkat tried to square-cut a ball from Connolly as it went through to wicket-keeper Taber. The bowler and 'keeper did not appeal but mid-on, silly-leg and second slip did and umpire Shambu Pan gave Venkat out. Venkat's hesitation and a radio commentator's criticism of the decision touched off a riot, in which spectators hurled soft-drink bottles, oranges and stones onto the field. As the match proceeded, demonstrators set fire to hessian around tennis courts behind the East Stand. Others heaped smashed chairs on the fire and set parts of two other stands alight. The scorer walked into the middle and said he could

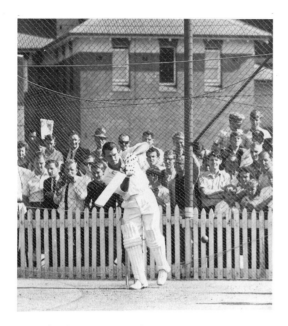

Even early in his career Doug Walters attracted a big following. Here at the Sydney nets in the start of the 1968–69 season he is watched by dozens of small boys.

not follow the match through the smoke but Lawry played on while the umpires suggested the scorer go to a smoke-free part of the ground.

Uproar continued, with bottles landing on the field, where they shattered, and at the fall of the ninth wicket on 125, play stopped. But following police advice the Australians remained on the field for 20 minutes while the riot squad cleared demonstrators from the stands and put out the fires. A flying bottle hit Gleeson behind the right ear as the Australians left the field and a wicker chair dropped from a balcony fell on Lawry. Bottled drinks were banned next day as Australia took the last Indian wicket and scored the 64 needed to win for the loss of two wickets.

Mallett took 10 wickets for 80 to pave the way for a victory over Central Zone between 11 and 13 November at Jaipur. At Kanpur, India brought in Gundappa Viswanath for his first Test and he scored a delightful debut century (137). Paul Sheahan also made his first Test hundred (114) and altogether the runs flowed too freely

to provide a result between 15 and 20 November. The tour had already developed into a captivating duel between India's spinners and the fleet-footed young Australian batsmen. Chappell showed his enthusiasm for the struggle with a superb 164, which included 4 sixes and 20 fours, in the drawn match against North Zone at Jullundur.

India won the third Test at Feroz Shah Kotla in New Delhi from 28 November to 2 December by seven wickets when the Indian spinners ruthlessly exploited a grassless pitch. Ian Chappell managed to hold together the Australian first innings with a chanceless 138, which helped take the score to 296 and give Australia a narrow first innings lead. But there was no denying Bedi and Prasanna in the second innings. Lawry became the sixth Australian to bat right through a completed innings, scoring 49 not out in 195 minutes but none of his teammates reached double figures in a total of 107.

India were left to score 181 runs in two days and reached the target with a day to spare through a 120-run unbeaten fourth-wicket stand by Wadekar (91 not out) and Viswanath (44 not out), who dealt cleverly with the Australian spinners. It was only India's third win over Australia.

The pressures of the tour deeply affected Lawry, who increasingly showed the strain of 15 years in big cricket. He was easily piqued by umpires' decisions and in the absence of Australian reporters became frustrated that his team's views were not aired. He had never cared for official functions but as the tour progressed he became more and more of a loner, seldom meeting opponents socially.

Before the fourth Test, at Eden Park Gardens, Calcutta, from 12 to 16 December, propagandists plastered posters on city walls claiming that Doug Walters had fought with the allies in Vietnam. The "Go Home Walters" posters disgusted the Australians who knew Walters' army service had never taken him out of Australia, but more than 3000 people demonstrated over the issue outside the Australians' hotel and the windows had to be boarded up. Army chiefs were called to conferences with the police and a unit of frontier riflemen placed on standby. At the Australians' practice police dispersed crowds who tried to interrupt proceedings by beating them with long staves. All around that huge stadium scalpers were paid five times the set price for seats to the cricket.

McKenzie bowled like a man inspired in India's first innings and his fieldsmen responded by catching all the flying snicks to have India out for 212. McKenzie, bowling well enough to take all ten and repeatedly beating the bat, took 6 for 67. There were 7 sixes in Australia's first innings total of 335 as a gifted lineup set out to hit Bedi and Prasanna off their length. Walters and Chappell and then Sheahan and Chappell joined in an exhilarating onslaught until Sheahan ran himself out. Chappell continued to 99 before he got a faint tickle to Bedi and Wadekar scooped up the slips catch.

After the third day's play, with Australia 123 ahead, people queued through the night to get seats. In the morning late arrivals tried to snatch tickets from the lucky ones and a stampede developed in which people fell and were trampled on. Police who tried to drag the fallen to safety were pelted with stones and soft drink bottles and a pitched battle followed. Six people were trampled to death, 100 injured, and 30 admitted to hospital. A mob who stoned the Australians' hotel had to be cleared away by baton-swinging police.

Australian Rules football star Eric Freeman bowled at a lively pace as India's second innings began and quickly sent back danger men Wadekar and Viswanath. Connolly joined in with cleverly disguised swing and cut and a lovely slower ball and India were out for 161. Freeman had 4 for 54 and Connolly 4 for 31. The crowd reacted with chants of "Shame Pataudi", fully aroused now by the heat and disappointment at India's display. From the top of the Ranji Stand bottles,

stones and refuse rained down on people in the lower deck, who swarmed onto the field to escape. Lawry and Stackpole stood at the crease while police tried to clear the field. In this period Lawry had a confrontation with an Indian photographer which drew this comment from Calcutta's *New Statesman*:

> Lawry did something that, to say the least, could be termed disgraceful. A photographer who wanted to get a close shot of Stackpole and Lawry brought upon himself the wrath of the Australian Pinocchio, Lawry, who could not keep his temper and struck the man with his bat. It was a horrible sight, and one that led one to wonder what Lawry thought himself to be.

Lawry denied striking the photographer with his bat and said that in trying to protect the pitch he pushed him with his hand. Stackpole said Lawry prodded the man with his bat so that the man fell and hurt himself on his camera. After 20 minutes delay, the Australians resumed batting, and five overs later Stackpole hit a full toss for four to give Australia victory by ten wickets. At the moment of defeat, sections of the crowd turned their ire on Pataudi. With people running about the field, Stackpole and Lawry told Pataudi to stay between them and they escorted him off, bats at the ready.

That night at the Australians' hotel McKenzie and Redpath, the mildest of men, were alleged to have assaulted Indian reporters during the team's celebration dinner. The truth was that when 20 pressmen turned up at the dinner they were told it was private and asked to leave. They retired to the hotel's liquor permit room and, later, men with cameras entered the room shared by Eric Freeman and Ashley Mallett. When they failed to respond to requests to leave, the 81-kilogram Freeman forcibly put them out. The big question was how the Australian Board of Control would react to the Australians' behaviour in the face of such extreme provocation and who they would blame for it.

Sacked Captain

Australia on tour 1969-70;
Victoria wins the Shield 1969-70;
England tours Australia 1970-71

On the team's way to Calcutta airport to fly to the next match at Bangalore, Indian peasants stoned the Australians' bus, smashing and cracking windows and badly frightening the players. One rock sailed through an open window and thudded into a seat inches from Johnny Gleeson. Groping about on the floor, the players were grateful to their driver who kept his foot down and eventually took them out of the stone-throwers' range. At the airport the police chief who had removed the escort which normally protected the team was badly shaken when he saw the state of their bus.

There was more stone-throwing at Bangalore, but this time it worked to Australia's advantage. South Zone had Australia in danger with eight wickets down for 53 runs, chasing 200 to win, when Gleeson joined Lawry with an hour to go. Prasanna had taken 6 for 9 in nine overs. Deprived of the victory they craved, the 20,000 spectators became more and more

The Western Australian pace attack in 1969–70, from left Bob Massie, Graham McKenzie and Dennis Lillee. All achieved notable Test figures.

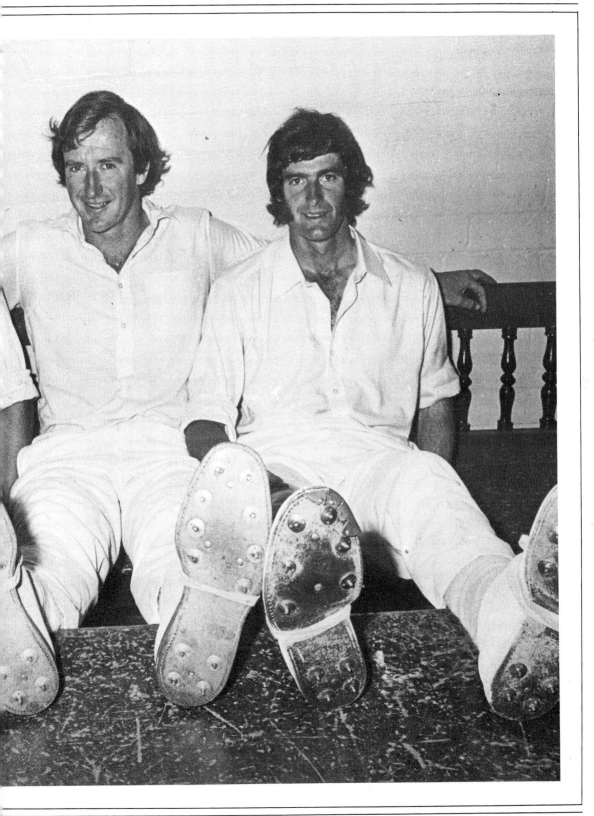

demonstrative as Lawry and Gleeson hung on. Lawry's time-wasting infuriated them. He patted down non-existent bumps on the pitch, stepped back from his stumps claiming to have been distracted by bright colours in a woman's sari as she walked by the sightboard, and collected scraps that nobody else could see from the pitch.

Ten minutes from time the crowd began pelting South Zone fieldsmen with coconut husks, apple cores and orange peel. Finally the barrage forced the umpires to call off the match five minutes early and Gleeson and Lawry sprinted from the ground with South Zone players and umpires. There were immediately calls for the remaining Test to be abandoned, but manager Fred Bennett accepted Indian advice that his players would not be in danger.

The fifth Test at Madras from 24 to 28 December resolved into a gripping duel between the Australian batsmen and the Indian spinners Bedi, Prasanna and Venkataraghavan, who between them delivered 726.3 of the 929.1 overs bowled in the five Tests and claimed 59 of the 70 wickets that fell to Indian bowlers. The Australians were clapped and cheered by crowds lining the streets on their way to and from the Chepauk ground. On the field only Lawry was singled out by hecklers. Their shouting, whistling and drum-beating forced him to protest to the umpires, who told him they were powerless to quieten the noise.

Fielding lapses saved Australia. Walters was dropped at 4 in the first innings and went on to 102 in a total of 258. After India had succumbed to Mallett (5 for 91) for 163, India's spinners had Australia 6 for 24 in the second innings before Redpath made 63 and took Australia to 153. Prasanna's 6 for 74 gave him match figures of 10 for 174. Set to score 249 to win, India again failed to handle Mallett, whose 5 for 53 gave him 10 for 144 in the match and 28 wickets in the five Tests at 19.10 apiece. Only Chappell, with 710 runs at 50.71, averaged more than 50 among Australia's batsmen in a series that turned

on Australia's safer catching. Taber was far superior to Engineer as wicket-keeper and finished the tour with 16 dismissals. Engineer missed stumping chances in the Madras Test against both Walters and Redpath which proved vital in India's defeat and gave Australia the rubber 3–1.

On the strength of Australia's showing in India and their 3–1 defeat of West Indies the previous summer, Lawry's confidence in his team on their arrival for a 12-week tour of South Africa was justified. But before the four Tests on this venture were over South African bowlers made nonsense of Lawry's assessment of Ian Chappell as "the best batsman in the world". Chappell made only 92 runs in eight innings in the Tests at an average of 11.50.

To prepare leading players for the Tests, following South Africa's three-year isolation from international cricket, the Currie Cup had been rescheduled to provide 22 warm-up matches. This gave South Africa's selectors time to study players' claims and provide new captain Dr Ali Bacher with a resourceful, balanced side.

Australia were not only humiliated on the field but their behaviour in defeat often saddened their fans. Long before South Africa completed a 4–nil thrashing of his team, Lawry disgusted team-mates and spectators alike with his vulgar hand signals. He rarely mixed with opposing players, avoided fraternising after each day's play, and became a virtual recluse in the team's hotel rooms. The Victorians in the team felt obliged to support their captain, but players from other states did not seek to disguise their disappointment in him. This in turn divided the team. They became demoralised by the failure of their top-order batsmen and the deplorable catching failures. The South African critic Geoffrey Chettle calculated that they dropped 70 chances in their 12 first-class matches, almost 30 of them in the four Tests, allowing the gifted batsmen Graeme Pollock and Barry Richards two or three reprieves.

Only four Australians reached international standard, batsmen Ian Redpath and Paul Sheahan and bowlers John Gleeson and Alan Connolly. Connolly laboured with skill and fine persistence to take 38 wickets in nine matches, including 6 for 47 in the fourth Test. Gleeson took 59 wickets in nine matches on pitches unfavourable to spin and in five matches took five wickets in an innings, with 10 for 105 against Griqualand West his best match figures. Graham McKenzie was listless throughout and took only one Test wicket at a cost of 333 runs.

Four South Africans averaged 50 or more in the Tests—Graeme Pollock (73.85), Richards (72.57), Barlow (51.42) and Irvine (50.42), whereas Redpath topped the Australian Test averages with 47.16. Mike Procter topped the South African Test bowling averages with 26 wickets at 13.57, compared with Connolly's 20 at 26.10 at the head of the Australian Test bowling table. The Australians managed seven centuries in their 12 first-class matches, but had 11 scored against them.

The Australians started their tour splendidly, winning two of the three matches before the first Test. They beat North-Eastern Transvaal at Pretoria between 6 and 8 January by ten wickets following a dashing 104 by Chappell and 86 not out from Lawry in a game that blacks and coloured people were barred from attending. At Kimberley from 10 to 12 January, they defeated Griqualand West by an innings and one run thanks to 157 not out from Lawry. Gleeson's 10 for 105 gave him 18 wickets in two matches. Then came a draw at Port Elizabeth against Eastern Province from 16 to 19 January, Lawry lifting his aggregate to 295 runs without being dismissed.

Eddie Barlow made his fourth century against Australia in the first Test at Newlands, Cape Town, from 22 to 27 January, giving South Africa an advantage they never lost. Chasing 382, Australia were dismissed for 164 against an enthusiastic, rampaging attack supported by some

Allrounder Eddie Barlow displays the verve that enabled South Africa to defeat Australia 4–nil in their last Test series before excommunication from Test cricket.

brilliant catching. Walters' 73 was his best knock in the series. Lawry (83) and Redpath (47 not out) tried hard to prevent defeat in Australia's second innings but had no support, South Africa winning by 170 runs. This was Australia's first defeat in 60 years of Test cricket at Newlands.

After a draw against Transvaal between 30 January and 2 February at Johannesburg, where Gleeson took a further seven wickets, Australia brought in Freeman for Mallett in the second Test at Kingsmead, Durban, from 5 to 10 February. Graeme Pollock's 274 in 417 minutes, which included a five and 43 fours, dominated the match. This was the highest score in Tests by a South African and followed a maiden Test century (140) by Richards. Pollock's sixth-wicket stand with Lance (61) produced 200 runs, a record for South Africa in any Test. South Africa's total of 9 declared for 622 was their highest score in Test cricket.

With victory out of the question, Australia put on 44 without loss but then slumped to 5 for 56 against some vigorous bowling. Sheahan batted admirably for 62 but Australia followed on 465 runs in arrears. Stackpole (71), Walters (74) and Redpath (74 not out) gave hope to Australia, but a three-wicket spell by Barlow gave South Africa victory by an innings and 129 runs with more than a day to spare, South Africa's biggest-ever winning margin.

South Africa's wins in the two remaining Tests were just as convincing. They won the third Test at the New Wanderers ground in Johannesburg from 19 to 24 February by 307 runs after a Barlow century (110) and another display of tight, hostile bowling backed by fine slips catching. They completed the humbling of Australia by winning the fourth Test from 5 to 10 March at St George's Park, Port Elizabeth, by 323 runs, the first time in their history South Africa had enjoyed a clean sweep. This time Barry Richards (81 and 126) and Brian Irvine (102) took the batting honours, and Procter the bowling honours (3 for 30 and 6 for 73). Connolly took his 100th Test wicket and Gleeson his 50th wicket of the tour, but both suffered from dropped catches.

The tour wound up with two matches in the middle of March. The first, against Western Province at Cape Town, was drawn after some free hitting by the Australians, with Stackpole and Redpath in a stand of 167 and Walters (109) collecting a century. Procter made 155, which included sixes off the last five deliveries of an over from Mallett. Chappell took over the captaincy for the last match, in which Australia defeated Orange Free State at Bloemfontein, following a blazing 152 from Redpath, who hit 6 sixes and 19 fours. Redpath and Chappell (71) added 121 for the second wicket in only 65 minutes.

Mike Procter, whose fine bowling helped to destroy a talented Australian batting lineup in 1969–70 in South Africa.

South Africa was excommunicated from international cricket at the end of the Australian tour, a sad event for the brilliant players who gave them such a wonderful triumph. For the Australians, a disappointing tour ended with some players avoiding each other and some of them kilograms underweight from the rigours of the Indian part of the tour.

Team manager Fred Bennett had the unenviable task of reporting to the Board of Control on a captain, hitherto a fine servant, who had petulantly challenged umpires' decisions throughout the long tour, thrown his cap on the ground, snatched the ball from an umpire, and kept up his ungentlemanly finger signs to crowds seething with disapproval. Lawry made only 193 runs in eight Test innings in South Africa at 24.12, which led to Keith Miller offering light-heartedly to come out of retirement and help Australia. "At least I could break in Lawry's bat," quipped Miller. Bennett did, however, ask the Board to pay the players a bonus of $500 each, knowing that the South African part of the tour had made a $250,000 profit. The Board turned this down.

While the Test side was in India and South Africa, the remaining Australian senior players had an exchange of visits with New Zealand. A 13-man New Zealand party captained by Graham Dowling played Tasmania, Victoria, and New South Wales and appeared in a one-day limited-over knockout competition in December and January. In February and March 1970 a 13-man Australian "B" team captained by Sam Trimble played eight matches in New Zealand, including three representative games.

The New Zealand team that visited Australia was G. T. Dowling (captain), B. E. Congdon, M. G. Burgess, R. O. Collinge, R. S. Cunis, D. R. Hadlee, B. F. Hastings, H. J. Howarth, B. W. Sinclair, B. R. Taylor, G. M. Turner, G. E. Vivian and K. J. Wadsworth, with B. J. Paterson as manager.

They began with a draw from 26 to 28 December 1969 at Hobart, where Turner had a splendid match, scoring 99 and 67. Kanhai made 108 not out for Tasmania. At Melbourne between 9 and 11 January they played a draw with Victoria, for whom Cowper scored 99. Vivian scored 137 not out for New Zealand. Burgess (91) took the batting honours in Sydney in the draw with New South Wales. New Zealand won the limited-over competition for the V&G trophy by beating Victoria by six wickets in the final at Melbourne on 1 January 1970.

The Australian "B" team that played in New Zealand the following month was S. C. Trimble (captain), 36, G. S. Chappell, 22, G. R. Davies, 24, R. J. Inverarity, 26, G. D. Watson, 25, A. Steele, 28, J. A. Maclean, 24, D. Chadwick, 29,

T. J. Jenner, 26, D. A. Renneberg, 28, A. L. Thomson, 25, D. K. Lillee, 21, and K. J. O'Keeffe, 21, with F. J. Bryant as manager.

The Australians won two matches and left six drawn. After a draw against Canterbury from 20 to 23 February at Lancaster Park, Christchurch, they defeated Otago by an innings and 50 runs from 26 to 28 February at Carisbrook, Dunedin, thanks to an outstanding all-round display by Inverarity, who made 108 and then took 5 for 28 with his left-arm slows in Otago's second innings. At McLean Park, Napier, they had another big win when they defeated a New Zealand Under-23 side by an innings and 20 runs. Lillee took 6 for 40 and 3 for 26 and Inverarity made 79.

John Inverarity made 117 in the first representative match with New Zealand from 6 to 10 March at Eden Park, Auckland, where rain robbed the Australians of a win when they were 58 runs short of victory with seven wickets left. Rain forced a tame draw in the second representative match at Lancaster Park, Christchurch, from 12 to 16 March. The best match of the tour came between 21 and 24 March at Pukekura Park, New Plymouth, where Geoff Davies scored 105 not out to rescue Australia from 6 for 73. Jenner took 8 for 131 in the match, which ended with Central Districts needing 23 runs to win with two wickets in hand.

Congdon made 128 out of New Zealand's 7 declared for 410 in the third representative match from 28 March to 1 April at Basin Reserve, Wellington. New Zealand's right-hand opening bowler Murray Webb was no-balled 20 times for overstepping on his run-up in Australia's innings and was badly mauled by the batsmen. Trimble went on to 213 in eight hours while wickets fell steadily at the other end. Bad light ended play early on the third day and rain washed out the final day to end an unsatisfactory tour. New Zealand lost $11,000 on the tour, which coupled with the $3500 lost on the earlier visit to Australia made it a disastrous summer.

Fiery Victorian fast bowler Alan ("Froggie") Thomson points an English batsman to the pavilion during the 1970–71 series in Australia.

The outstanding player for Australia was Greg Chappell, who scored 519 runs in 11 innings at 57.66, although Trimble's double century took him to a higher aggregate, 555 at 55.50. Jenner took most wickets with 32 from seven matches at 19.53 apiece, but Lillee, on his first overseas trip, headed the bowling averages with 16 dismissals at 18.50 each.

The disappointment of the New Zealand tour was Alan ("Froggy") Thomson, who took only 12 wickets on the trip at 29.88. Thomson was a bowler of absorbing interest whose wrong-foot action gave him exceptional bounce and puzzled batsmen encountering him for the first time. He had a difficult temperament but became a big crowd favourite in Melbourne from the time he made his state debut from the Fitzroy club in 1968–69. He led the Sheffield Shield wicket-takers while Australia's internationals were in India and South Africa with 49 wickets and took his total to 55 for the summer with six victims for Victoria against New Zealand. Lawry was known to have favoured Thomson had a reinforcement been required in South Africa.

Thomson played a big part in Victoria's winning of the Shield in 1969–70. At Brisbane, in the match between Victoria and Queensland from 30 January to 2 February, Thomson broke Tom Graveney's left arm with a high kicking delivery in Graveney's second match for Queensland. Victoria were well led by Cowper, whose side started with three outright wins and a first innings win from their first four matches. They faltered later but were never headed despite some outstanding performances around the states.

Greg Chappell topped the Shield batting aggregates with three centuries in his 856 runs at 65.84 and blossomed as a medium-pace bowler. Queensland produced an Aboriginal bowler of genuine pace in Ian King, from the Toombul club, who took 30 wickets at 28.36 and formed a successful opening attack with "Sandy" Morgan (30 wickets at 21.33) and Ross Duncan (24 at 31.70). Lillee, in his first season for Western Australia, proved a fearsome proposition, often failing to control deliveries of tremendous pace. His 32 wickets at 22.03 included eight batsmen who were caught behind by 'keeper Rodney Marsh, who was in his second season for the state.

In Brian Taber's absence with the Australian team, John Benaud captained New South Wales for six matches with much of the flair of his brother Richie. At Melbourne his 134 almost enabled New South Wales to turn a first innings deficit into outright victory. But the New South Wales Cricket Association disciplined Benaud for defying instructions that his team were not to wear cut-down ripple-soled shoes. Benaud was suspended indefinitely and did not go to Perth with his team.

The association executive suspended Benaud following a report from state selectors Stan

Sismey, Neil Harvey, Ernie Laidler, Sid Carroll and Jack Chegwyn, which partly blamed New South Wales' poor showing on players losing their footing in boots without sprigs. The Sydney *Daily Mirror* said 70-year-old executive chairman Syd Webb told them he had been congratulated at a Board of Control meeting in Melbourne for the way Benaud had been dealt with. Webb denied he said this and the association accepted his denial, but Richie Benaud resigned his Life Membership of the association because of its failure to check the story with the *Mirror* reporter, Pat Farrell. Not long afterwards Webb, deeply upset, resigned as chairman of the executive, a sad end to the administrative career of a man who had championed players' rights in the Sid Barnes case.

Powerfully built Tony Steele took over the captaincy for the matches in Adelaide and Perth. Steele's three centuries in the Shield competition allowed him to top the batting averages with 677 runs at 67.70 and won him a trip to New Zealand. Benaud's suspension was later lifted but the affair probably cost him a trip to New Zealand in Sam Trimble's team.

Les Favell, an entertaining shot-maker throughout a career lasting for 18 summers, retired at the end of the 1969–70 season. Favell toured all the cricket nations except England with Australian teams and finished his career with 8196 Shield runs, a total surpassed only by Bradman's 8926. He played in 19 Tests and his 12,379 first-class runs included 27 centuries.

One of his Australian team-mates, Alan Davidson, took over as NSWCA chairman in 1970 on the death of E. G. Macmillan. At 41, Davidson, the youngest-ever Association chairman, immediately set about boosting a coaching scheme similar to those starting up in the other states.

In England important changes were occurring in the administration of cricket. The Labour government decided it could not give financial assistance to an individual club but that its newly formed Sports Council could help a body known as the National Cricket Council. The government in turn paid the NCC £75,054 compensation for the cancellation of the 1970 tour of England by South Africa. The Council had expected £200,000.

The incessant demands on international players that had built up steadily with the advent of television meant little rest or opportunity to pursue another career and within a few months of returning from the exhausting tour of Ceylon, India and South Africa, Australia's leading cricketers found themselves applying for leave to play against the England team led by Ray Illingworth.

After 65 years of organising England's overseas tours the MCC handed that responsibility to the National Cricket Association, whose Test and County Cricket Board selectors A. V. Bedser, D. Kenyon, A. C. Smith and C. Washbrook picked the team and the captain to tour Australia, but were not asked to select the manager as David Clark had already been appointed by the MCC.

England had expected to prepare for this Australian tour with a series at home against South Africa, but when this was cancelled another was substituted against a Rest of the World team. Illingworth led England in these matches instead of Cowdrey, who was injured. Diehards in England wanted Cowdrey, the former amateur, to captain the team to Australia, rather than Illingworth the Yorkshire professional. Cowdrey clearly had higher credentials but the selectors stuck with Illingworth. The team was R. Illingworth (captain), M. C. Cowdrey (vice-captain), G. Boycott, J. H. Edrich, B. W. Luckhurst, B. L. D'Oliveira, A. P. E. Knott, J. H. Hampshire, K. W. R. Fletcher, J. A. Snow, R. W. Taylor, P. Lever, R. G. D. Willis, D. Wilson, K. Shuttleworth, A. Ward, D. R. Underwood, with B. Thomas as assistant to manager Clark.

Snow, the moody, intense, poetry-writing son

of a Sussex vicar, proved the most discussed figure in a team that would have benefited from the inclusion of A. W. Greig and R. N. S. Hobbs. Throughout the tour Snow proved a disputatious powderkeg of a bowler, arousing spectators and opposing batsmen with a liberal issue of bouncers that he could make kick viciously from a low arm action. He gave Australia's leading batsmen an awful shellacking.

The emphasis had changed from previous tours so there would be more major encounters for television. Instead of five Tests, six were originally scheduled. England began their tour in South Australia from 30 October to 2 November, rather than in Western Australia. Boycott immediately struck form with an innings of 173 and D'Oliveira made 103 not out that was welcomed, but all the praise for stroke-play belonged to Fletcher for his 70 and 80. Barry Richards helped South Australia respond to England's 9 declared for 451 with 9 declared for 649, to which he contributed 224.

A disaster followed for England in Melbourne where Victoria beat them by six wickets between 6 and 10 November. Thomson's unusual action should not have hoodwinked such experienced batsmen but his 6 for 80 and 3 for 101 had as big an influence on the arguments that followed. He greeted Illingworth with three bouncers in his first four balls, drawing a caution from umpire Bob Figgis. Lawry challenged this, arguing that Illingworth was not a "genuine tailender". The matches with New South Wales and Queensland were drawn. Trimble ruined the last first-class match before the Test series began by staying for nine hours while he scored 177. Boycott (124) and Edrich (120) responded in kind.

Australia's selectors sacked Taber in picking their team for the first Test at the 'Gabba from 27 November to 2 December, preferring Marsh in an amazing decision. Taber had done the job extremely well and shown that he could make valuable runs. Taber believed tablets he took to relieve a chest ailment that gave him a florid face helped spread the view that he was unwell. To drop him for a slow-moving man with legs like big tree logs upset all those concerned with selection justice.

This selection howler turned out not to matter too much because of an umpiring blunder which allowed Stackpole to continue when he was clearly run out at 18 in Australia's first innings. He went on to 207, a score only Bradman had exceeded in a Brisbane Test. From 3 for 418, Australia lost seven wickets in 47 minutes for 15 runs. Underwood dismissed Redpath, Sheahan and Walters in seven balls without conceding a run. Walters' 112 included many edges and mis-hits.

Marsh's wicket-keeping when England batted caused old Test players to laugh in disbelief. I remember standing in a group of former Test players whose unanimous view was that Marsh was the worst 'keeper they had ever seen play for Australia. His technique was so poor the label "Old Irongloves" swept the ground. His dismissal of four batsmen did nothing to pacify critics in the stands.

Luckhurst's 74 in his first Test produced the best batting of the England innings of 464, and he was unlucky to be run out by Knott's lapse in concentration within sight of a century. England's over rate was too tedious to secure a result despite Shuttleworth's second innings coup of 5 for 47. Australia were only 183 ahead but less than an hour remained when England began the fourth innings.

Test cricket arrived in Perth on 11 December 1970, when the second Test began at the WACA. Weeks of promotion attracted 85,000 spectators to watch the five days play, twice as many as had watched the previous Test in Brisbane. Gate receipts of around $50,000 were three times higher than in Brisbane.

Not all cricket was worthy of the occasion. Brian Luckhurst, a newcomer to Test cricket at the age of 31, dominated an opening stand of 171 with Geoff Boycott, square-cutting with

The controversial decision in the first Test at Brisbane in 1970–71, which allowed Keith Stackpole to escape when he appeared to have been clearly run out. He went on to score 207.

exquisite balance and timing. Defying a damaged thumb, Luckhurst went on to 131. This took England to 397, a total Australia appeared to have no prospect of reaching when Snow and Lever swept through the first three batsmen for 17 runs. At 5 for 107 Australia were still desperately placed when Greg Chappell, in his first Test, joined Redpath. They progressed slowly at first but at 240 Chappell unleashed a brilliant attack on the England bowling. His debut 108 was applauded for several minutes all around the ground. Redpath (171) was more subdued, uncertain against Snow's pace, but he kept going for eight hours and Australia gained a 43-run lead.

John Edrich held England's second innings together with a stubborn 115 not out, which allowed Illingworth to declare 244 runs ahead, with 145 minutes left. Lawry completely rejected this challenge. His second run completed his 5000 runs in Tests, his third 2000 runs against England,

but after 68 minutes he had made only 6. *Wisden* called his batting "craven", an apt description. As he had shown in the first Test, every spark of enterprise had gone from his makeup.

Umpire Rowan twice warned Snow for bowling too many short balls. Each time Snow argued the point, although he had Lawry and Redpath ducking and weaving. When Rowan took the first step towards preventing Snow from bowling, by reporting him to his captain, Illingworth said: "They're not bouncers!"

Impressed by the lift in standards Tony Lock had achieved in Western Australia, the Englishmen moved on to Adelaide for a tense struggle with the talented South Australian side between 18 and 21 December. The first South Australian wicket did not fall until 277, with Barry Richards scoring 146 and Ashley Woodcock 119, which allowed Ian Chappell to make an enterprising declaration at 2 for 297. All the English batsmen struggled against a purposeful attack and England trailed by 59 runs. They were rescued in South Australia's second innings by a superb spell from 196-centimetre Bob Willis, who had been flown out as a replacement for the injured Alan Ward. Greg Chappell produced another superb century, and Ian Chappell's second declaration of the match gave England 360 minutes to score 398, but after slumping to 3 for 29 they never seriously tried to win. Some lovely strokes from D'Oliveira late in the match lifted his own score to 162 not out and England to 3 for 336.

The third Test at Melbourne from 31 December to 3 January produced an argument that has gone on ever since. England won the toss and put Australia in but before the players took the field down came the rain. It continued until the third day, when the match was abandoned. A conference of members of the Australian Board of Control led by Sir Donald Bradman, the England team manager D. G. Clark, and the visiting MCC chiefs, Sir Cyril Hawker and G. O. Allen, in abandoning the

Greg Chappell during his debut century in Perth in 1970–71 at the age of 22. This was also the first Test staged at the WACA.

additional match even though they did not take the field. The argument has caused unfortunate differences in record books, with the 11 Australians chosen to play credited with one Test less in *Wisden* and books that follow the official definition of a Test than they do in publications that follow the Australian Board's ruling that because the toss was made the match occurred. I believe the Board is wrong and should reverse its ruling and fall into line with the accepted definition of a match.

The fourth Test at Sydney from 9 to 14 January 1971 gave England her biggest winning margin in runs since 1936–37. This was almost entirely due to the dogged batting of Boycott on a difficult pitch and the bowling of Snow, who made the ball lift viciously from a worn patch.

On the first day England reached 200 for the loss of only two wickets, before Mallett took 3 for 6. But England's tailenders rallied, lifting the total from 6 for 219 to 332. Redpath (64) and Walters (55) put on 99 for the third wicket in the only worthwhile stand in Australia's response of 236.

Boycott then methodically wore down the Australian bowling and sent spectators in search of refreshment. He ran out Edrich but had stands of 133 with D'Oliveira and 95 with Illingworth, adhering to a schedule that allowed Illingworth to give Australia nine hours for their second innings. After 6 hours 50 minutes batting in which Boycott avoided any semblance of a full-blooded stroke he left the scene unbeaten on 142 not out with 12 fours, mostly from deflections.

Neither McKenzie nor Connolly had been able to extract life from the pitch, but Snow was quite lethal when Australia began the chase for 416 runs. The first Australian wicket fell at 1, the fourth at 21 and the sixth at 66. Lawry (60 not out) batted stubbornly on to become the first Australian to bat right through an innings in Sydney, but Snow took 7 wickets for 40 and the innings totalled only 116, for England to win by 299 runs.

match agreed to substitute an additional Test, making seven in the rubber. A 40-over-a-side match was played on what would have been the last day of the third Test.

Statisticians argue that as not a single ball was bowled there was no play in the third Test and it does not count in the players' or umpires' records. But the Australian Board of Control ruled the Test should count and in fact paid Johnny Gleeson his Provident Fund entitlement for 30 Tests because he was named for this Test. Official Board of Control statistics always credit umpire Lou Rowan and Tom Brooks with an

English wicket-keeper Alan Knott leaps to touch a snick from Ian Chappell during 1970–71 series with England. Knott failed to hold the catch.

The fifth Test, at Melbourne from 21 to 26 January 1971, replaced England's return match with Victoria and a one-day match at Euroa. The match deteriorated into a bouncer war from the first over, when Snow bowled four at Stackpole, with umpire Max O'Connell unwilling to take action in his first Test. England dropped eight catches in Australia's first innings of 493, four of them by Cowdrey who returned to the side in place of Fletcher. He firstly missed Ian Chappell off Snow, before he scored, and then off D'Oliveira, when he was 14.

Chappell settled down to hit 12 fours in his 111. When Chappell reached 100, more than 2000 spectators invaded the pitch, defying Lou Rowan's attempts to keep them off the playing surface, stealing Cowdrey's white hat, a stump, and Chappell's cap. They were particularly offensive to the Englishmen, who had generously altered their itinerary to make the game possible, but Snow's provocations gave the crowd no chance to settle.

Lawry deprived Marsh of the chance to become the first Australian wicket-keeper to score a Test century when he declared Australia's first innings closed at 9 for 493, with Marsh on 92 not out. Marsh gave two chances in his sixties but clubbed the ball so hard in hitting 12 fours that most spectators felt it would only have taken two more heavy blows for him to achieve a unique place in the Australian game.

Australia established a lead of 101 by dismissing England for 392 after Thomson had England in trouble at 3 for 88. Thomson bowled five bouncers in two overs, the last one striking Luckhurst on the shoulder. Despite a broken finger in his left hand, Luckhurst made 109 in almost 330 minutes. He added 140 with

English bowler Bob Willis hands an injured seagull to a spectator during the 1970–71 Test in Adelaide. The bird recovered and a veterinarian later released it on an Adelaide beach.

D'Oliviera, whose 117 took 345 minutes. Batting at No. 8, Snow had to duck under bouncers from Thomson. Lawry's captaincy was sadly at fault when, despite Australia's lead, he allowed his batsmen to take 255 minutes to reach 4 for 169 in their second innings, far too slow a scoring rate to give Australia a chance to square the series.

Umpire Max O'Connell finally warned Snow over his over-use of the bouncer in Australia's second innings, when Snow bowled four at Walters. Running from point, Illingworth protested, arguing that Snow had bowled fewer than Thomson, who had not been cautioned. By then it was clear England had settled for a draw. Boycott and Edrich made little attempt to score the 271 needed in 240 minutes, plodding on to an unbeaten 161. For some reason this incensed the crowd, who kept up a barrage of abuse and banging of beer cans over the last 40 minutes. The umpires conferred but allowed play to continue amid the din, with the Australian spinners unable to break through in ideal conditions. Lawry gave Gleeson, who had proved a world-class spinner the previous summer in

South Africa, only three overs in this period, preferring to use O'Keeffe and Stackpole for 32 overs.

Dennis Lillee made his Test debut in the sixth Test at Adelaide from 29 January to 3 February, coming into the Australian team at the age of 21 in McKenzie's old spot. McKenzie's Test career had ended when he took only 1 for 139 in the fourth Test, a disappointing climax for the bowler who took 100 Test wickets faster than any Australian bowler—in 2 years 165 days—and had 246 Test wickets at 29.78. Lillee had to bowl through the stand of 107 for the first wicket by Boycott and Edrich and 169 for the second wicket by Edrich (130) and Fletcher (80) but finished with 5 for 84 despite dropped catches. There were a lot of wasted deliveries in his 28.3 overs but there was no denying his combativeness and fearsome pace. Boycott did not believe he was run out at 58 and refused manager David Clark's request to apologise to umpire Max O'Connell for disputing the decision.

Snow lacked the fire of earlier matches in Australia's innings of 235, enlivened only by 11 fours in 87 by Stackpole. Snow's listlessness probably influenced Illingworth in declining to enforce the follow-on. Boycott and Edrich put on another 103 for the first wicket and Boycott's 119, his sixth century of the tour, took him to within 18 runs of Hammond's 40-year record of 1571 runs on an Australian tour. Illingworth declared at 4 for 233, giving Australia 500 minutes to score 469 on a slow-paced pitch, a target they never attempted. Stackpole (136) and Ian

Chappell (104) took 315 minutes to put on 202 for the second wicket, and at the end Redpath dawdled for 120 minutes over 21 not out.

Before the match ended, the sacking of Lawry as Australian captain was announced. Aware of Lawry's poor behaviour on tour in India and South Africa, the Australian Cricket Board made no objection when selectors Bradman, Harvey and Loxton decided the Test team needed a more enterprising leader. Lawry thus became the first Australian captain dismissed during a series. Australia had not had a win in their last nine Tests and had suffered a humiliating four-nil drubbing in South Africa.

Lawry's Victorian team-mates were disgusted at the sacking and in the years that followed Paul Sheahan repeatedly condemned the injustice of it. Ian Chappell wrote many times that in taking over as Australia's captain he vowed he would never allow the Board to commit a similar act on him. The Board members have remained silent and the contents of Bennett's 1969–70 tour report have remained a secret, according to Board practice. The public assumed Lawry had paid the penalty for incidents on the India–South Africa tour. Nevertheless, the timing of Lawry's sacking was unfortunate. He deserved to lose the captaincy but not his place as a batsman. Only Bradman and Harvey had scored more Test runs than Lawry's 5234 at 47.15 when he was thrown out of Test cricket, having taken more than his share of bruises from Hall, Griffith, Trueman, Statham, Lever, Pollock, Willis and Snow at their fastest.

Barbarian Takeover

Domestic cricket 1970-72;
World XI tours Australia 1971-72;
Australia tours England 1972

Ian Michael Chappell had the breeding for the Australian captaincy. He was the eldest of three sons of Martin Chappell, who had headed the Adelaide district batting averages. His mother Jeanne was the daughter of Vic Richardson, who captained Australia on a South African tour and in four Tests, and both his brothers, Greg and Trevor, were destined to play Test cricket.

But somewhere between his move up from backyard toddler frolics to school matches with Prince Alfred's College (which had also produced earlier Australian captains Joe Darling and Clem Hill), on to club cricket for Glenelg and into the South Australian team under the venturesome leadership of Les Favell, he failed to acquire dignity. By the time he took over from Lawry he believed international cricketers were a persecuted breed. His courage, his cricket skills, and his innate sense of loyalty inspired devotion among his players few other Australian captains have enjoyed. But his foul tongue and flagrant

The Sydney Cricket Ground erupted when John Snow hit Terry Jenner with a bouncer in the seventh Test in 1970–71. The crowd's protests led to England walking from the field.

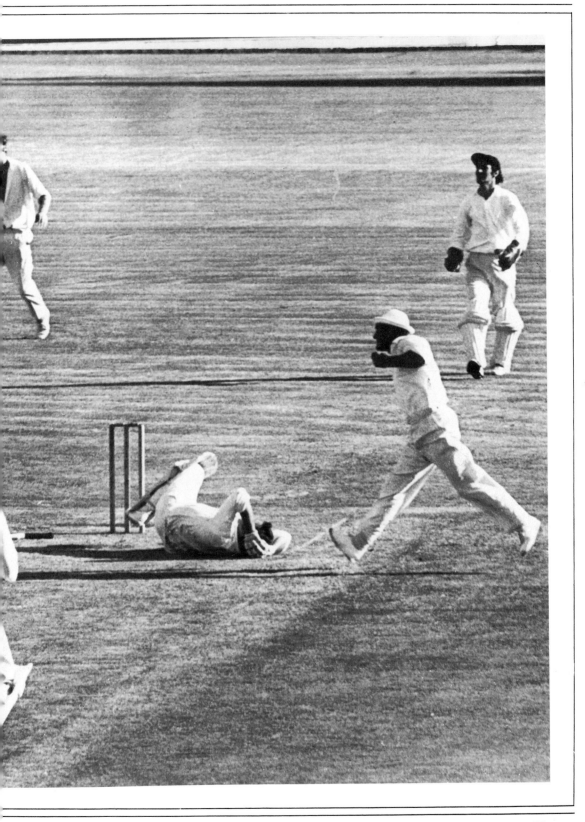

disregard for cricket's traditions attracted attention Australian cricket could have done without. New Zealand's great batsman Glenn Turner described the experience of sharing a dressing room with Ian Chappell as similar to a frontline stint in Vietnam. The respected English critic Robin Marlar said in the prestigious *World of Cricket* that history would find Ian one of cricket's "barbarians".

Chappell took over the captaincy for a match Australia had to win to share the series, the seventh Test at Sydney from 12 to 17 February 1971, with a team lacking frontline bowlers and seasoned batsmen. To deprive Chappell of a batsman of Lawry's experience and replace him, as Australia's opening batsman, with a 35-year-old left-hander of Ken Eastwood's limitations was reprehensible. McKenzie, Thomson and Duncan may not have done the job against competent opening batsmen, but to expect the lumbering, overweight Tony Dell to improve on their performances was fanciful thinking.

Without Boycott, who had broken his arm protecting his face against a McKenzie flier in a limited-over match four days earlier, England's batsmen took a pasting. Keith Fletcher could not avoid blows on the arm and chest in making 33 and Dell bruised D'Oliveira's torso before he bowled him. The crowd greeted Illingworth with unbridled hostility, blaming him through a surly undertone of booing for the bumper war. Illingworth remained unconcerned and was the only batsman to break up Chappell's close-in ring of fieldsmen, scoring 42 of his side's 184.

Snow took up the challenge England's position presented by bowling two short-pitched deliveries at Eastwood in his first over. Lever had Eastwood out in the next over and when Snow uprooted Stackpole's off stump, Australia were 2 for 13. Next day there was an election in New South Wales but there was more action at the cricket than at the polling booths. At 4 for 66 Redpath (59) and Walters (42) found themselves ducking under bouncers from Lever and Snow. After squatting under three in one over from Lever, Walters got one that bounced closer to Snow's feet than his own, but he survived long enough to put on 81 with Redpath. Greg Chappell then took Australia into the lead with spectators conducting a beer-can chorus against the slow scoring and the bouncers.

After a long spell Snow resumed and almost immediately let Chappell have a fiery bouncer. In his next over he had Jenner squirming away from two short-pitched deliveries, which prompted Illingworth to push in four leg-trap fieldsmen. Jenner knew they were waiting for a mis-hit from a bouncer and was ready for it but he could not get out of the way of a ball he tried to duck. It struck him a sickening blow on the left side of the head and as he went down in a heap the bouncer row that had been simmering for four months erupted. Illingworth was the first to reach him but the crowd cared nothing for his commiserations and hooted the Englishmen as Jenner was led away, blood oozing through his hair.

Before Snow bowled the next ball at the replacement batsman Dennis Lillee, umpire Rowan called to Snow, who ignored him and walked on towards his mark. "Just a minute, John," called Rowan, "I'm not impressed with your performance and am giving you a first warning." Rowan turned and signalled with one finger to his fellow umpire Tom Brooks at square leg. Snow whirled around and shouted: "That's the first bouncer I've bowled this over—your blokes have been bowling seven an over."

Illingworth scurried to the bowler's end to support Snow, the brimstone in him clear to the crowd. Rowan repeated his warning and immediately Snow let loose a tirade of abuse that would have had no place in his sonnets. The most impassioned booing I have ever heard at the Sydney ground accompanied Snow as he ran in to bowl the last ball of the over to Lillee, even those in the Members' Stand among the 30,000 spectators forgetting their good manners

The Chappell brothers just after Ian had taken over the Australian captaincy. Greg (centre) had begun his Test career with a brilliant century in Perth and Trevor (right) was consolidating his place in the South Australian Shield team.

to join in. Illingworth's loss of temper in disputing Rowan's actions had stirred them to a crescendo of hooting and, as the England players sat on the grass to take drinks, beer cans and oranges bounced onto the field.

The noisiest protests came from the north-east corner of the field and as an attendant finished clearing the cans into a gutter, Snow insisted on fielding down at the centre of the demonstration. Illingworth tried to get him to go instead to third man but Snow insisted on going to the fence at backward square leg. He

was greeted with taunts to which he responded with an obvious gesture. Boys leaned out to shake his hand but one drunk in an orange shirt grabbed Snow's shirt and hauled him against the pickets. Snow freed himself and moved about ten paces infield but a second wave of cans arrived, some of them landing near his feet. Willis ran in to support Snow, but could not refrain from shouting at the crowd.

More cans flew over the fence as Illingworth arrived to pull Snow away. Ignoring the umpires, he then waved his players from the field, apparently believing his first duty was to protect his men from the can-throwers. Bill Lawry, broadcasting the match, watched the Englishmen leave the field and immediately tried to collect a side-bet he had on the result with Richie Benaud. "Pay up, Benordy, England have forfeited," said Lawry. Several of the Englishmen apparently were also concerned at this possibility, as Illingworth had not informed the umpires of his intentions, and they were reluctant to leave the field.

The Australian batsmen remained at the pitch as Rowan and Tom Brooks, who was in his first season as a Test umpire, went after the Englishmen. As he passed through the gate Rowan spotted a former colleague Col Egar sitting in the Members' Stand. "You never had anything like this, pal," said Rowan, to which Egar replied: "Illingworth has forfeited the game."

Board of Control secretary Alan Barnes, highly distressed, accompanied Rowan and Brooks to the England dressing room, where Illingworth claimed the crowd were throwing bottles at his players. Rowan said the field would be cleared of cans and other debris, and England would then resume or forfeit the match. Back on the field, policemen herded spectators who had jumped onto the ground back over the fence and when ground staff had cleared the litter the match resumed.

John Edrich claimed the walk-off would not have occurred if it had not been for liquor, to which Rowan replied: "Don't tell me your bowlers have been drinking." The remaining 45 minutes play passed without incident. When the crowd left, groundsmen collected 40 cans from the gutters, most of them soft drink cans, which suggested they had been thrown by children. There were no bottles.

Jenner returned to contribute 30 runs to Australia's total of 264 and when England made 302 in their second knock Australia were left to score 223 on a pitch helpful to both pace and spin. Snow bowled Eastwood, who at the start of the summer could not win a place in the Victorian side, with his sixth ball but in the fifth over broke his hand on the boundary fence in attempting to catch Stackpole. Stackpole hit 2 sixes and 6 fours on the way to 67 before

Illingworth bowled him. None of the other batsmen stayed long after Illingworth lured Greg Chappell down the pitch and had him stumped by Knott. Lacking Boycott and, in the final stages, Snow, England accomplished a great victory by 62 runs to take the series 2–nil.

Additional Tests and improved receipts from television gave the Australian Board a profit of more than $125,000 on the tour, in which England lost only one of their 14 first-class matches. Boycott headed the Test averages with 93.85 and Australia's best batsman was Stackpole, who averaged 52.25. Snow took 31 Test wickets at 22.83 whereas the highest Australian wicket-taker was Gleeson with 14 at 43.21. England made 22 centuries and had 14 scored against them.

Barry Richards, the great South African batsman, dominated the Sheffield Shield competition during 1970–71 to an extent where he frequently overshadowed the events of England's argumentative tour. Richards headed the Australian batting averages for the season with 109.86, which included 224 in 360 minutes against England, and in 13 Shield innings made 1145 runs.

Richards' presence enriched the already powerful South Australian batting lineup and helped them regain the Shield from Victoria. In his fourth match for South Australia, in Perth against Western Australia from 20 to 23 November, Richards made 356 in 372 minutes, with 1 six and 48 fours. Ian Brayshaw, the rising young Claremont–Cottesloe club all-rounder, consoled himself when he dropped Richards at 160 with the thought that Richards could not get many more. Ken Eastwood ran second in the first-class averages, with 742 runs at 93.50 but demonstrated the big difference between Shield and Test cricket by his discomfort in his sole Test appearance.

The continued strong showing by Western Australia, who finished ahead of both New South Wales and Queensland on the Shield table, was a tribute to the coaching talents of Tony Lock, who retired at the end of the season. He had broken all wicket-taking records for Western Australia by taking 316 wickets at 24.50 and also held 85 catches. Alan Connolly also retired after this season, having taken an impressive 676 wickets in first-class cricket, 102 of them in Tests. More impressive was the fact that he sometimes bowled until there was blood inside his boots.

One-day cricket advanced in Australia with the England–Australia match in Melbourne, which attracted 46,000 spectators and a six-state, 40-over competition for the V&G trophy in which Tasmania joined the Shield states and England met the winners in Sydney. Western Australia won the final in Melbourne by scoring 170 runs compared with Queensland's 79, thanks to Graham McKenzie's 4 for 13. The match between Western Australia and England in Sydney had to be abandoned because of rain and at that stage limited-over cricket gave no sign that it would provide the financial bonanza for state treasurers that it had done for struggling English clubs since 1963.

One of the most gifted of all Australian cricketers, Leslie O'Brien Fleetwood-Smith, died a derelict in March 1971, after years on skid row. He was an expert on magpie calls, on imitating the whipbird and in producing unplayable deliveries when the mood struck him. He was generally regarded as the most prodigious spinner of the ball known to Australian cricket, but after he left big cricket showed a distaste for work, preferring the wine bars and parks where "metho" drinkers gathered. In April 1969, he was charged in Melbourne City Court with vagrancy, but the magistrate released him on a $20 good behaviour bond when old schoolmates from Xavier College and cricketers with whom he had played rallied to help. He appeared to have beaten his problems and settled to regular work when he fell ill, blaming too many parties and too many drinks.

In the Australian winter of 1971 Greg Chappell married Judy Donaldson in Sydney and the fifth South African Rugby team to visit the country provoked some of the ugliest demonstrations ever witnessed in Australia. The brilliance of the 26 Springbok footballers was forgotten when the team moved around the states accompanied by unprecedented violence as anti-apartheid protesters clashed with police. Hundreds of arrests were made in every major city. Courts and ambulance rooms were congested with battered and bleeding men and women who maintained their rage for seven weeks, forcing the Springboks to run the gauntlet of missiles, catcalls and smoke bombs. Gaols overflowed with protesters, the commercial airlines refused to handle the tourists, and the cost of drafting huge squads of police to string up barbed wire and protect the footballers ran into millions of dollars.

The Australian Board of Control for International Cricket, which had invited South Africa to tour Australia in 1971–72 as far back as 1967, appointed an emergency committee to report on whether the tour should proceed. The emergency committee, comprising Sir Donald Bradman, Syd Webb and Bob Parish, had two meetings and after considering its report a full Board meeting cancelled South Africa's invitation to tour. Board chairman Sir Donald Bradman telephoned the South African Cricket Association with the decision and then issued a statement which said:

> While there is substantial evidence that many Australians felt the tour should go on, the Board was equally aware of the widespread disapproval of the South African government's racial policy which restricted selection of the South African team . . . It weighed carefully the views expressed by responsible authorities, political leaders, union officials, church dignitaries, police commissioners, ground authorities, administrative officials and others . . . The Board wishes to commend the South African Cricket Association and its players for their courageous stand against their government's apartheid policy in cricket.

The South African team originally selected for the tour was Dr A. Bacher (captain), E. Barlow, H. Ackerman, D. Biggs, G. Chevalier, P. de Vaal, L. Irvine, D. Lindsay, G. Pollock, P. Pollock, M. Procter, C. Rice, B. Richards, P. Trimborn, and V. Van der Byl. The Board replaced their tour with a tour by a World XI involving two-limited over matches and 12 first-class matches including five five-day internationals against Australia, and matches against each state. There were also second-class matches in three country centres. The Board appointed Victorian Bill Jacobs, manager of the Australian team to South Africa in 1966–67, to manage the World XI, which comprised players from six countries: G. St A. Sobers, West Indies (captain), Intikhab Alam, Pakistan (vice-captain), H. M. Ackerman, South Africa, Asif Masood, Pakistan, B. S. Bedi, India, R. S. Cunis, New Zealand, F. M. Engineer, India, S. M. Gavaskar, India, N. Gifford, England, A. W. Greig, England, R. A. Hutton, England, R. B. Kanhai, West Indies, C. H. Lloyd, West Indies, R. W. Taylor, England, and Zaheer Abbas, Pakistan.

The Board called Greig, the South African-born son of a distinguished RAF pilot from Scotland, a South African but he had been living in England since 1966 and was to make his debut for England in 1972. Kanhai and Lloyd were both injured in the match against South Australia in Adelaide and late in December the Pollock brothers were flown in from South Africa to reinforce the World XI.

Sceptics who claimed that only teams with national prestige at stake produced tense cricket were proved wrong in a tour that provided brilliant, bruising cricket. After rain prevented a result in their first two matches, the tourists showed they were not interested in exhibition games. Their pride demanded that they should win and take home most of the prizemoney. At Melbourne in the match scheduled from 5 to 8 November, no play was possible against Victoria on the last two days. At Sydney in the match

South African Barry Richards hitting another boundary for Hampshire in 1972. He made a brilliant 73 against the touring Australians, but a record opening stand of 301 by Stackpole and Watson gave Australia victory.

with New South Wales from 12 to 15 November, Geoff Davies' 100 allowed Taber to close at 3 for 256 before Gavaskar made a lovely 95. Rain then intervened.

The Rest of the World defeated Queensland by 38 runs from 19 to 22 November at the 'Gabba due to centuries by Farokh Engineer (104) and Rohan Kanhai (121), and a match haul of 7 for 148 by Bedi, who had as many tricks as he had turbans. Opening batsman Alan Jones enjoyed the distinguished company by scoring 130, his sole century in 37 knocks for Queensland.

All chance of a result in the first big match between the World XI and Australia at the 'Gabba from 26 November to 1 December went when 686 minutes were lost to rain. In between showers Ian Chappell, adjusting his protector after every ball without trying to disguise it, made 145 and 106 in the two Australian innings, supported in the first by Stackpole (132). Left-handed opener Hylton Ackerman scored 112, Kanhai 101 for the World XI. One ball from Lillee smacked into Kanhai's ribs so hard he could not resume for several minutes, unable to conceal the pain. When he shaped up again, Lillee let fly another bouncer which Kanhai angrily hooked for four. Then he went off for an X-ray.

Australia took advantage of ideal conditions when they batted first in the second international at the WACA from 10 to 12 December, Walters contributing 125 to their 349 total. Lillee then emerged as a devastating new force in international cricket by taking 8 for 29 in 57 balls, only three of them bouncers. He dismissed Greig, Sobers and Hutton without cost in his sixth over, and later took the last three wickets without conceding a run. Four World XI batsmen were out for ducks in a score of 59. They never recovered, despite a pugnacious 118 from Kanhai, and were beaten by an innings and 111 runs. Lillee again made the ball bounce awkwardly in taking 4 for 63 in the second innings, for match figures of 12 for 92. From then on each incoming Australian batsman expected a bouncer from Greig, whose team-mates called it his "hullo ball".

Sobers, who had only played in Perth at the insistence of his team-mates, had to have two teeth cut out in Adelaide which specialists blamed for his focusing problems. His jaw was being stitched when Kanhai hurt a leg and Clive Lloyd fell on his shoulder injuring his spine, in the match with South Australia from 17 to 18 December in Adelaide, where South Australia beat the World XI by an innings and one run. Sobers followed the team to Launceston and before the stitches were removed batted for three hours for 134 not out to set up his team's eight-wicket win over Tasmania.

Manager Bill Jacobs later calculated that the World XI sustained 35 injuries, and at one stage it was difficult to get into the side's dressing room without stumbling on X-ray plates. About the time Clive Lloyd was flown back to England with two crushed vertebrae in the lower back, his career in jeopardy, Engineer was having pain-killing injections in a strained shoulder tendon to continue keeping wickets for the World XI against Australia in Melbourne from 1 to 6 January 1972. The Pollock brothers had been rushed into this match as reinforcements although neither had had a chance to recover from jet lag.

Australian opening batsman Graeme Watson was hit twice in this match. In the first innings he took a whack on the ear from Pollock and in the second innings a beamer from Greig fractured his nose and cheekbone. He was rushed to St Vincent's Hospital, where he was on the danger list until heart massage and transfusions of 40 pints of blood saved him.

Greg Chappell connected with a full-blooded sweep that cut Norman Gifford's leg from under him. Sobers made a catch off the rebound and Gifford was carried off. A fortnight passed before he could get a shoe on his swollen foot. In the Australian side John Benaud had to have a chipped knuckle strapped before each innings, but it kept getting in the way of rising deliveries. His batting fell below the standard of the previous season and the injury probably cost him a trip to England in 1972 with the Australian side.

The Melbourne clash between the World XI and Australia was the best match seen in Australia since the tied Test at Brisbane in 1960–61. When the World XI batted first on New Year's Day, Keith Stackpole held a snick off Lillee to have Sobers out for a duck in a total of 184. Lillee gave another stirring display in taking 5 for 48, and at one stage had the World XI 4 for 26.

Greg Chappell held the Australian innings together in the face of fine bowling from Greig and Sobers, with 115 not out collected in his now familiar elegant style. With Australia leading by 101, Sobers played one of the greatest innings ever seen in Melbourne. His 254 in 376 minutes contained 2 sixes and 33 fours and gave the World XI a 413-run lead. At the time Sobers was enduring jibes about preferring golf to net practice. Peter Pollock (54), his partner for three hours, said: "It was my greatest cricket experience. There can be no greater cricketer."

Doug Walters' 127 raised Australian hopes but in the end the steady, accurate spin of Intikhab Alam and Bishen Bedi prevailed. The World XI won by 97 runs in front of spectators who appreciated the 50 runs an hour scored against bowlers delivering 100 balls an hour in the very place where inert English batsmen and bowlers aroused beer-can protests only a season before.

The five-match series moved to Sydney, with the teams on one win apiece, for the fourth match between 8 and 13 January. Stackpole stressed his value as an aggressive opener with 104 and 95, Ian Chappell (119) and brother Greg (197 not out) had a long partnership, but again Bedi and Alam persisted in Australia's second innings total of 546. With Australia on top, thanks to Bob Massie's 7 for 76 with his medium-paced swing, rain prevented a result.

After one-day matches in Sydney and Melbourne and visits to Canberra and Newcastle, the World XI flew to Adelaide for the decisive fifth international from 28 January to 1 February. Australia's first innings slumped to 3 for 35, when John Benaud (99) and Greg Chappell (85) added 177. Both fell to Intikhab Alam but the World XI's star was Tony Greig, with 6 for 30.

An enterprising 136 from Graeme Pollock laid the foundation for the World XI's 367, which gave them a lead of 56. Bedi and Alam then gave the World XI a match-winning edge by bowling Australia out for 201. Ian Chappell's 111 not out, his fourth century of the series, was not enough to set the World XI a testing target and they scored the 146 needed for the loss of only one wicket, to take the match by nine wickets and the rubber 2–1. But the Australians

Asif Masood, Pakistan allrounder who proved one of the crowd-pleasers of the 1971–72 Australian tour by the World XI. The tour was rushed on when South Africa's visit had to be cancelled because of its apartheid policies.

won slightly more prizemoney—$7666 to $7333—because of their higher run rate, 4.34 against the World XI rate of 3.80 runs an over.

The World XI's pioneer multiracial tour was a major triumph for the Board of Control following the sad cancellation of the South African tour. More than 458,000 people watched their 16 matches, turning up in numbers that averaged 10,000 a match more than those on the previous South Africa tour in 1963–64. Although restricted by injuries, Kanhai topped the tour's first-class averages with 525 runs at 65.62. Tony Greig led the bowling averages with 26 wickets at 26.07, although both Intikhab Alam (38 at 30.92) and Bishen Bedi (36 at 29.58) took more wickets.

Greg Chappell (425 runs at 106.25), Ian Chappell (634 at 79.25), Walters (355 at 71.00) and Stackpole (490 at 54.88) all averaged more than fifty runs an innings for Australia in the five international matches. Lillee dominated the bowling figures, with 24 wickets at 20.08. The World XI scored 11 centuries on their tour and had 14 scored against them.

Western Australia won the Sheffield Shield for the third time in the 1971–72 season, when all Australia's leading players were available and eager to press claims for the forthcoming tour of England. They won by one point from South Australia under a new bonus points system which eliminated points for first innings wins. The win represented a triumph for Western Australian coaches Ken Meuleman, Peter Loader, Hugh Bevan, Wally Langdon, Laurie Mayne and Tony Lock, the man *Wisden* credited with changing the balance of power in Australian cricket. Crowds at Western Australia's last match against South Australia in Perth set a new record for the WACA of 25,000.

Western Australia's win stemmed from their great all-round depth, with every place in the side keenly contested, and the acumen of a selection panel who named the right combinations for each match. Ross Edwards, with four centuries in six matches, led the state's averages with 586 runs at 58.60, followed by Inverarity (641 at 53.41). The penetrative powers of their three new-ball bowlers, McKenzie (22 wickets at 22.31), Massie (22 at 24.28) and Lillee (24 at 18.75), accounted for 71 of the 128 wickets taken by Western Australia in the competition.

The interstate Colts matches attracted the interest of Sheffield Shield selectors and resulted in the selection of two interesting country cricketers in the New South Wales side. Gary Gilmour, who learned his cricket in the Newcastle district, made 106 and took three cheap wickets for New South Wales Colts against Victoria to win a place in the state senior side,

for which he scored 122 against South Australia in his initial first-class match. John Watkins, also from Newcastle, replaced the injured Gleeson for his Shield debut against South Australia. His 4 for 72 included the wickets of Ian and Greg Chappell. Western Australia's newfound prestige was recognised by selectors Neil Harvey, Sam Loxton and Phil Ridings, who included six players from that state when they named the twenty-sixth Australian team to tour England in 1972, under the management of Victorian Ray Steele.

In the absence of Lawry, still a great opener whatever his shortcomings as a captain, the selectors gambled on Bruce Francis's experience in the Lancashire League with Accrington in 1970 and in 1971 with Essex, (for whom he scored 1578 runs), to provide good starts with Stackpole. The alternative was to take Ashley Woodcock, a 25-year-old Adelaide physical training teacher and hope he would mature. The team was I. M. Chappell (captain), 28, D. J. Colley, 25, K. R. Stackpole, 31, G. S. Chappell, 23, R. Edwards, 29, B. C. Francis, 24, J. W. Gleeson, 34, J. R. Hammond, 22, R. J. Inverarity, 28, D. K. Lillee, 22, A. A. Mallett, 26, R. W. Marsh, 24, R. A. L. Massie, 25, A. P. Sheahan, 23, H. B. Taber, 32, K. D. Walters, 31, G. D. Watson, 27, with Fred Bennett as assistant manager, D. MacErlane as masseur, and Dave Sherwood as scorer.

Ian Chappell and Doug Walters were given permission to play in a double-wicket tournament in Jamaica and join the team in England. The main party flew from Sydney, via San Francisco, where 32 items of luggage were lost, and arrived in London on 19 April. Experts in Australia feared for a side whose four strike bowlers, Lillee, Colley, Massie and Hammond, had never been to England.

Just as Richie Benaud teams had set the fashion in hugging and back-slapping when opponents were dismissed, Chappell's long-haired side with their generous moustaches started the deterioration in dress standards, in the eyes of traditionalists. Ian's mauve safari suit

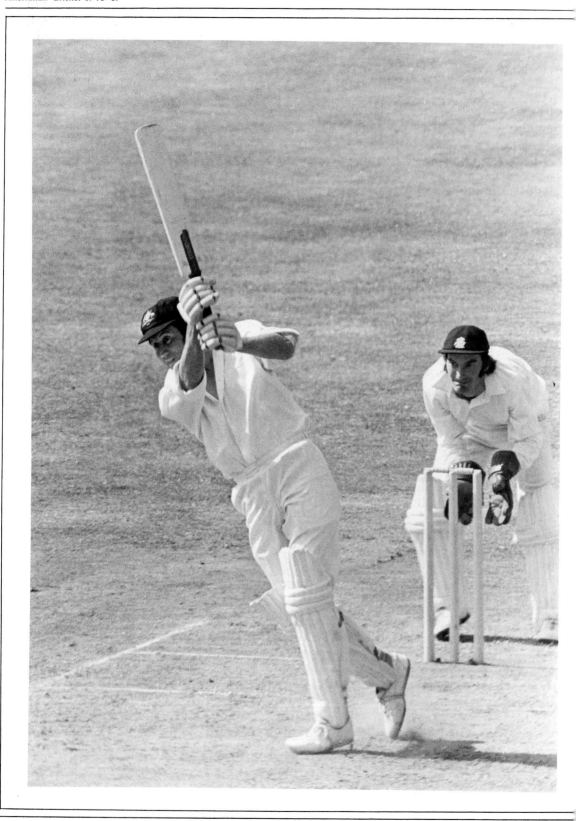

and vivid sports coats appalled old-timers at the team's receptions and when he appeared on the balcony at Lord's in a purple jump suit minus collar and tie, adherents almost had palpitations.

The Australian dressing room became a place where Doug Walters could indulge in cribbage and play his jokes with banknotes attached to a fishing line that recoiled into Doug's hand when he pressed the button. At the end of a day's play the team lingered over a few relaxing beers with guests like Mick Jagger and the camaraderie helped mould the side. Nobody cared about averages but they began to care a lot about winning.

The team's first five matches were rain-affected, and the third, against Yorkshire, was abandoned without a ball being bowled. After a disappointing preparation, Australia played the first Test from 8 to 13 June at Old Trafford on a seamer's pitch, and only Stackpole (53 and 67) found form against Arnold, Snow and Greig, although Marsh's 91 aroused most applause with its 4 sixes and 9 fours. England scored 249 and 234, Australia 142 and 252, giving England victory by 89 runs. Greig topscored for England in both innings in his first Test. Lillee's 6 for 66 in the second innings included the wickets of Illingworth, Snow and Gifford from four balls.

The second Test at Lord's from 22 to 26 June became known as "Massie's Match" when it ended just after lunch on the fourth day, but Australia's eight-wicket win would not have been possible but for a super-fine innings of 131, probably the best he ever played technically, from Greg Chappell. In humid conditions, Massie moved the ball late both ways in his Test debut, his swing puzzling England's highly experienced batsmen sufficiently for them to begin wondering about the shape of the ball and whether Massie

Ian Chappell moves down the pitch to drive at The Oval in 1972. He made 118 and Greg scored 113, the first instance of brothers scoring centuries in the same innings in Tests.

applied lip salve or hair cream to the ball. Massie had taken seven years since his first-class debut to find the chemistry that gave him 8 for 84 in England's first innings of 272 and 8 for 53 in the second innings of 116. His 16 for 137 remains a record for any bowler in his first Test and the best Test display at Lord's.

MCC chairman Freddie Brown invited Martin, Jeanne and Trevor Chappell to watch this match from his MCC president's box, where they found famous runner Sir Roger Bannister and his wife. At 6.30 one night, Lady Bannister said: "I thought you said the match finished at 6.30, Roger," to which Sir Roger replied: "Not in the middle of an over, dear."

Massie was supported by some brilliant catching. Marsh held five catches, four off Massie and one off Lillee. Greg and Ian Chappell in between sniping away at each other in a brotherly form of communication were magical in the slips. Lillee helped sustain the pressure on England's batsmen by taking four wickets and bowling at a pace that gave no respite at the other end. Only two years before this amazing display Massie had failed to win a contract in a try-out for Northamptonshire, and had spent the season with Kilmarnock in the Scottish League.

Australia's success broke a sequence of 15 Tests without a win and after splendid wins over Leicestershire (Massie 10 for 63) and Middlesex they went into the third Test at Trent Bridge from 13 to 18 July brimful of confidence. Stackpole, with a hard-hitting 114, helped Australia to a total of 315 despite Snow's 5 for 92. Lillee and Massie both took four wickets in England's innings of 189, which gave Australia a 126-run lead. Ross Edwards, already established as a superb cover fieldsman, then played the innings of his life, driving magnificently all over the off side for 170 not out. Chappell declared 450 ahead just after lunch on the fourth day, but England batted with such purpose only four wickets fell for 290 in the remaining day and a half. Chappell tried seven bowlers seeking the breakthrough that never came.

Chappell gambled on his bowlers' prowess in the final innings of the match against Sussex at Hove from 22 to 25 July, only to be frustrated by a sparkling innings from Gordon Greenidge. Australia began with 294. Sussex replied with 5 for 296, Greenidge scoring 99. Stackpole was on 154 not out when Chappell declared at 2 for 262, leaving Sussex to score 261 to win. They made it for the loss of only five wickets due to Greenidge's 125 not out.

The Headingley pitch for the fourth Test from 27 to 29 July was unrecognisable as a strip for an international match, and it was blamed

Greg Chappell brilliantly catches Basil D'Oliveira off the bowling of Mallett in the fifth Test at The Oval in 1972.

on a fungus. It could not have suited "Deadly Derek" Underwood better. A freak storm and weather that prevented the use of a heavy roller produced a pitch without grass that took spin on the first morning. Australia had valid reasons to refuse to play on it but the ever-diplomatic Ray Steele allowed what was laughably described as a Test to proceed. Australia made 146 and 136, England 263 and 1 for 21 to give England a 2–1 lead in the series. Underwood took 4 for 37 and 6 for 45 against batsmen who felt victims of sleight of hand.

A further loss at Northampton in the first week in August, after Bedi took 9 for 110, would have demoralised most teams, but in the fifth Test at The Oval, from 10 to 16 August, Australian cricket flowered. Gates were shut on full houses three days running in a Test that

yielded record takings and a splendid Australian win.

Watched by their younger brother Trevor and their parents, Ian and Greg Chappell both scored centuries after Lillee's 5 for 58 had helped put England out for 284. Ian's 118 and Greg's 113 and their stand of 201 for the third wicket gave Australia a 115-run lead. Lillee then took 5 for 123 to get England out for 356, before the ever-reliable Stackpole laid the foundations for Australia's five-wicket victory with a fine 79. Paul Sheahan and Marsh saw Australia home with an unbroken stand of 71, which meant that four of the five Tests had produced a result.

The Chappells had provided the first instance in Test history of brothers scoring hundreds in the same innings, and Ian had produced a winning team from nowhere. Marsh's 23 dismissals in the drawn series set an Australian record against England and permanently silenced his critics, who henceforth were in awe at his acrobatics.

A record 383,345 people paid £261,283 to watch the Tests, assuring Australia's state cricket associations of a handsome tour dividend. Many of those who attended were the jeans-clad generation responding to Chappell's free-wheeling style. Even raw recruits to cricket watching knew, however, these players were destined for greatness, and that this could develop into an all-conquering Australian team, careless dressing, sledging, and grumbling over tour payments notwithstanding.

Recognition for a Neighbour

Pakistan tours Australia 1972-73;
Australia tours West Indies 1973;
domestic cricket 1973-74;
Australia *v.* New Zealand 1973-74

On Australia's 1972 tour of England three limited-over internationals replaced the extra (sixth) Test previously agreed to by the two countries. England found a major sponsor in the Prudential Insurance group and all three matches attracted big crowds, who were captivated by the frantic action 55-over matches provided.

England won the first match at Old Trafford by six wickets, because of an innings of 103 from 134 balls in 161 minutes with 9 fours by Amiss, who thus had the honour of scoring the first century in international limited-over cricket. Australia won the second match at Lord's by five wickets, thanks to a 100-run stand in 78

The Australian team selected for the third Test against the West Indies in 1973: (L to R) (back) J. R. Watkins, T. J. Jenner, R. A. L. Massie, M. H. N. Walker, J. Benaud, K. J. O'Keeffe, J. R. Hammond, R. Edwards; (front) K. D. Walters, I. R. Redpath, I. M. Chappell (captain), W. Jacobs (manager), K. R. Stackpole (vice-captain), R. W. Marsh, G. S. Chappell. (D. K. Lillee, absent.)

minutes by Greg Chappell (48) and Keith Stackpole (52). England won overall by winning the third match at Edgbaston by two wickets.

These matches were the first true test of limited-over cricket at an international level, confirming the potential of this form of cricket which had been shown in the hastily staged one-day match at Melbourne in January 1971. On the ground where Test cricket had begun 94 years earlier, 46,000 spectators turned up to watch Australia beat England by five wickets in a 40-over game. This match had been quickly substituted for the washed-out third Test and even the most enthusiastic officials were amazed at the big crowd it attracted.

Success of limited-over cricket at the highest level followed the introduction of the Gillette Cup competition, which English county treasurers came to rely on. The most revolutionary change in international cricket this century came at a time when Australia's leading players were pressuring for more pay. Ross Edwards had lost his job with a Perth accountant by touring in 1972, and the bank balance of almost every man in the team suffered through going on a five-month tour for which the Australian Cricket Board paid them $2000 each.

Team manager Ray Steele heard the persistent claims for financial help but whatever he said at Board meetings did not change its hidebound attitude. The pressures international tours exerted on the players who had employers to satisfy never became a major discussion point for the Board, yet the Australian Board delayed introduction of its own provident fund. The honour of playing in a Test was sufficient added bonus to Australian players' tour and match payments, in the Board's eyes.

The Board was also highly conservative in its dealings with commercial television networks, who became increasingly irked at the huge profits they could see slipping away. By an arrangement between the Australian Broadcasting Commission and the British Broadcasting Commission the best of the fifth Test in 1972 was televised for the first time by satellite to Australia. This opened up tremendous opportunities for television networks, already impressed by the new audience Chappell's team had introduced to big cricket. But whenever networks such as the Packer family's Channel 9 organisation asked for discussions on television rights they were bluntly told the Australian Board was satisfied with the ABC radio and television coverage.

Success of one-day cricket increased the frustrations of commercial television stations. They recognised that the condensed form of the game offered exciting marketing opportunities by providing an immediate result. The 1972 Australian tour of England had attracted 15 million calls to the British telephone system's dial-a-score service from people who simply wanted to know who was winning.

Board members were worried about Ian Chappell's habit of adjusting his box between deliveries being exposed to millions on television, whereas commercial networks understood his jumpsuit and Afro hairdo brigade. Television had created big-occasion cricket. Matches old Australian players looked forward to in Hove, Taunton and Scarborough did not count. Nor did Lancashire's defeat of the 1972 Australians matter. The Australian Board of Control were dreadfully slow to recognise the impact of television despite the view of Bradman and other members that it was the most powerful medium ever invented. Nobody suggested that its fees provided the solution to their player-payment problems.

In their assessment of the 1972 Australian team's results in England, the Board saw that the profit amounted to $62,536 compared with $85,000 in 1968 and $87,600 in 1964, and that the team won 11, drew 10, and lost 5 of their 26 first-class matches. Stackpole headed the Test averages with 485 runs at 53.88. Greg Chappell, given no favours by his brother Ian, topped the first-class averages with 1206 runs at 70.00. Lillee headed the Test bowling averages with 31 wickets at 17.67, and in the first-class averages was one of the two bowlers to take 50 wickets, 53 at 22.58. Massie had 50 at 17.02.

The first players to arrive home after holidays in Europe flew in on 10 September. By 20 October they were involved in the Sheffield Shield competition and by 15 November the first matches of Pakistan's 1972-73 Australian tour had begun. With the Australian tour of the West Indies to follow between February and April 1973, the job strains and drain on the players' bank accounts was intolerable. At the beginning most of them would have played for Australia for nothing but they had done that and as most of them had married, they started to look for a fair return for their frequent absences.

New heroes had arisen from Pakistan's 112 million people to share the batting responsibilities carried for years by the Mohammad family—attractive stroke-players like Majid Khan, Asif Iqbal and Zaheer Abbas. The Mohammads were still represented in the touring team by Sadiq and Mushtaq, but the team was captained by shrewd, balding Intikhab Alam, whose spin bowling had been so impressive on the World XI's Australian tour. He led a team that had never won in Australia and had only one victory, at Karachi in 1956, to encourage them. The team was Intikhab Alam (captain), Asif Iqbal, Saeed Ahmed, Nasim-ul-Ghani, Majid Khan, Mushtaq Mohammad, Pervez Sajjad, Mohammad Ilyas, Salim Altaf, Wasim Bari, Asif Masood, Sarfraz Nawaz, Sadiq Mohammad, Talat Ali, Majid Usman and Masood Iqbal, with Wing Commander M. E. Z. Ghazali as manager.

Intikhab Alam said his batsmen were highly experienced against fast bowling, but in their first match in Perth, Western Australia defeated them by eight wickets between 18 and 21 November. Zaheer Abbas gave them an ideal start with an innings of 143 in a total of 357. But Marsh destroyed the Pakistan bowling by

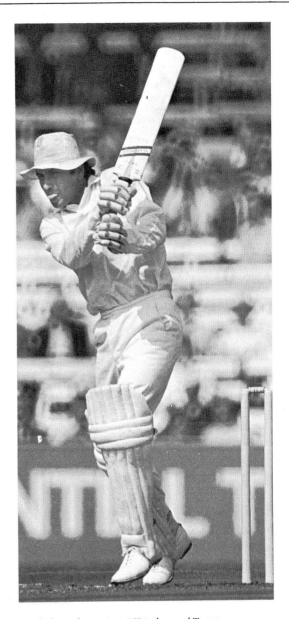

Majid Khan, whose majestic 158 in the second Test at Melbourne in 1972-73 failed to prevent an Australian victory. Sheahan and John Benaud responded with centuries for Australia.

scoring 236, the highest score of his career, which allowed Inverarity to declare at 6 for 398. Lillee then swung the match by taking 6 for 30, and with Wasim Bari unable to bat through injury, Pakistan were out for 133.

Further defeats by Victoria at the end of November and by Northern New South Wales early in December at Newcastle, where leg spinner John Watkins took 6 for 38, took Pakistan to the three-Test series against Australia with seemingly little hope of success. But the spirit Ian Chappell had aroused in the Australian team in England turned out to be badly needed. In two of the three Tests Australia was in a losing position and only a hair-raising mix of fighting cricket and strong nerves in a crisis enabled Australia to take the rubber.

The experiment of using Bruce Francis as an opener had failed in England and Ian Redpath shrugged off his omission from that team to form a productive pairing with Stackpole. Two exciting new-ball bowlers, 190-centimetre Max Walker, the Hobart-born wrong-foot bowler known as "Tangles", and the heavily muscled former javelin thrower Jeff Thomson, barred from soccer for life for flattening a referee, made their Test debuts at Melbourne.

Experts forecast that Lillee would be ineffective on the dusty Adelaide pitch in the first Test, from 22 to 27 December, but he managed 4 for 49 in Pakistan's first innings of 257, a gutsy effort by the Pakistanis who recovered from 6 for 104. Ian Chappell's 196, his highest Test score, was overshadowed by Marsh's historic 118 in Australia's 585 in reply. Marsh thus became the first Australian wicket-keeper to score a Test century. Mallett took 8 for 59 to give Australia victory, but Talat Ali, batting one-handed at No. 11 because of a thumb fractured by a ball from Lillee, won some prestige for Pakistan by taking the match into the last day.

At the end of the first day of the second Test, in Melbourne from 29 December to 3 January, Australia were looking comfortable on 4 for 349. Redpath had made 135 of these, Greg Chappell 116. Next day Marsh continued his wonderful batting with 74 and Australia declared at 5 for 441, a closure that gave the match life.

Pakistan reacted courageously with a score of 8 for 574, Sadiq Mohammad (137) and Majid Khan (158) inspiring team-mates. Thomson, bowling with what later was found to be a broken bone in his foot, suffered most with none for 100.

Australia's second innings of 425 included an elegant 127 from Paul Sheahan, and 142 from John Benaud, who had been told before he went in that he was not in the team for the next Test. Benaud's first Test century included 93 before lunch. His second-wicket stand with Sheahan was worth 233. On the last day, with Pakistan chasing 293 to win, both sides' fortunes fluctuated but three run-outs turned the match Australia's way.

Pakistan had the best of the third Test in Sydney from 6 to 11 January for all bar the final few hours. Watkins was completely overawed in his Test debut and had to be taken off after six wild overs in which he bowled several wides and appeared to have trouble landing on the pitch. Pakistan appeared to be so certain of winning on the fourth day that the Australians booked out of their motel, but Watkins and Massie had a ninth-wicket stand of 83, to take the match into the fifth day with Pakistan on 2 for 48 requiring a total of 159 to win and Zaheer still batting.

The score reached 2 for 83 on the fifth day before Lillee, who had a back strain, dismissed Zaheer. The big, lumbering frame of Walker then took control. He conceded only three runs from his last 30 deliveries and in that time took five wickets and won the match for Australia by 52 runs. His 6 for 15 took him to the head of the Australian bowling averages for the three Tests, with 12 wickets at 19.25. Ian Chappell headed the batting averages with 341 runs at 68.20.

Pakistan won only 2 of their 8 first-class matches on the tour and lost 5, with 1 drawn. They scored ten first-class centuries and had ten scored against them, and left for New Zealand with Australia 5–1 ahead after nine Tests between the countries.

batsman of stature, opting to concentrate on his teaching career.

The team was I. M. Chappell (captain), 29, K. R. Stackpole (vice-captain), 32, J. Benaud, 28, G. S. Chappell, 24, R. Edwards, 30, J. R. Hammond, 22, T. J. Jenner, 28, D. K. Lillee, 23, R. W. Marsh, 25, R. A. L. Massie, 25, K. J. O'Keeffe, 23, I. R. Redpath, 31, M. H. N. Walker, 24, K. D. Walters, 27, and J. R. Watkins, 29, with Bill Jacobs as manager.

In the three weeks between the announcement of the team and their departure, the players were peppered with letters from the Board of Control advising them on luggage arrangements, match fees and payments, when they would be required to wear dinner suits, what they could and could not say to the media, and the ban on wives accompanying them until after the last tour match. Their tour contracts stipulated that they could not pilot aircraft in which the team travelled and that they had to get the Board's approval of any manuscripts they might have with a publisher. There was also the customary stern warning that they had to pay for all their own alcohol.

This third Australian team to the West Indies had matured into a determined, resourceful outfit that would not accept defeat, led by a man with a tremendous liking for a crisis. They caught the West Indies at the end of an era, with Sobers, who had captained them since Frank Worrell retired, standing down after a cartilage operation. The only West Indian who could be certain of his Test place in a side that had failed to win a Test the previous summer against New Zealand, was Kanhai, the automatic choice as captain.

Manager Jacobs had some fun in the New South Wales Cricketers' Club before the Australians departed for the Caribbean by handing the Australian flag to Max Walker, insisting that he use all his bulk to protect it from vandals and thieves. Walker took the job in all innocence, knowing he had to prove himself

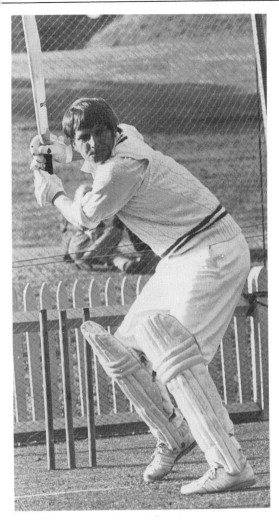

John Benaud, who won a place in the Australian team to the West Indies in 1973 after his impressive showing against Pakistan in Australia that summer.

A week before they left, the Australian team to tour the West Indies, chosen by Harvey, Loxton and Ridings, was announced. The selectors apparently considered the high full tosses and wides Watkins bowled in the Sydney Test were attributable to nerves, for they retained him in the side in front of the accomplished Gleeson, who could not find a place even with Mallett unavailable. Sheahan also withdrew from a tour he would dearly have liked to make, just as he was maturing into a Test on his first tour. Jacobs whispered to me: "The flag will disappear at the first match. One of those skin-and-bones urchins will go up and down the flagpole so fast big Max will never catch him."

All the newcomers in the team, unaware of West Indian cricket, were stunned by the excitement generated by their visit. Kingston airport echoed with cries of "Which one's Lillee?" and "Where's Massie?" and at their hotel after the drive past the grass huts and lean-tos, a resident reggae band beat out tunes of welcome. At the ground hundreds watched from trees, hanging by one arm with a bottle of rum in the other. When Ian Chappell walked out to toss on 3 February with Jamaican captain Maurice Foster, the crowd was dancing and jigging and flapping their arms to a background of steel bands, hammering on lids and metal grandstand girders.

Splendid centuries by Greg Chappell (106) and Laurence Rowe (149) delighted spectators who erupted into an enormous roar for every four and went delirious with joy over sixes. Walker lost the flag but he won the bowling honours with a match-winning 6 for 94 in Jamaica's second innings. Australia followed this five-wicket victory with a seven-wicket win over the President's XI at Montego Bay, where Clive Lloyd made a laboured return to big cricket after his long recuperation from his spinal injury.

Jeff Hammond's eight wickets at Montego Bay won him selection in the first Test at Kingston from 16 to 21 February as Australia's third pace bowler, a precaution the Australians were pleased they took when Lillee's back problems worsened. He completely lacked the fire he had shown in England and did not take a wicket in conceding 132 runs. Walker and Hammond took over the major workload but on a lifeless pitch could not force a result. Foster's 125 in his first Test knock enabled West Indies to match Australia's first innings total of 428, in which Marsh hit his own stumps when he was

on 97. Stackpole (142) had a 160-run opening stand with Redpath in Australia's second innings but by then a draw had become a formality.

Lillee took four wickets (including Viv Richards for 5) in the next match, against the Leeward Islands at St John's, Antigua, between 24 and 26 February, but complained of his back, and from then until the end of the tour made the rounds of doctors, who diagnosed muscular trouble or hair-line fractures to the vertebrae and forbade him from bowling. He was restricted to only five matches, but even that was more than Watkins, who was out of his class and made only four appearances. Massie was another failure, searching for swing that was impossible in the dry atmosphere, sending down full tosses and half volleys and unable to bowl an accurate line and length.

Hammond and Walker found Australia's hopes depending on them and they responded magnificently. Hammond, deprived of opportunities on the English tour, became a better bowler from the time he dismissed Kallicharran in the first Test, moving the ball away from the batsman with great consistency at a pace just short of express speed. In Walker he had an ideal partner, a bowler who never stopped attacking the stumps and forced batsmen to play. Both showed exceptional stamina in continuing for long spells on the hottest days.

Australia lost 2 for 19 on the first morning of the second Test, from 9 to 14 March at Bridgetown, Barbados, but were rescued by some resolute batting by the Chappell brothers. They had added 129 when Greg turned a ball down to fine leg for what looked a certain two. Ian ran like a hare and was well into the second run when Greg, slower to start, completed one. As he turned Greg saw that a fieldsman had the ball and was about to throw and immediately call "No". Ian was at full stretch and had to stop and turn. He had no hope of beating the throw and was run out. "Nice bloody call," said Ian as he departed for 72. Greg went on to 106, leaving it to the clubbing Marsh to take Australia past 300 with 78 very useful runs.

West Indies lost Greenidge at 19, lbw to Walker's inswinger without offering a stroke. Fredericks flashed away outside the off stump in his customary style and at 30 was dropped by Marsh off a nick from Hammond, and finally went two short of his century, lbw to Hammond. Kanhai (105) and Murray (90) took such care over their batting it was clear they realised the easy pitch promised only a draw, the 15th in the last 17 Tests played in the West Indies. Ian Chappell (106 not out) and Walters (102 not out) entertained when the match was dead.

Ian Chappell sprained his right ankle playing tennis two days before the third Test at Queen's Park, Port-of-Spain, from 23 to 28 March and should not have played. He remained in the slips and batted down the order, unable to go down the pitch to the spinners, but he was one of Australia's heroes in a memorable victory. The pitch took spin from the start and half an hour after the match began Gibbs bowled to three short-legs. Australia lost Stackpole to the third ball of the innings, but Redpath and Greg Chappell put on 107 before Chappell was out lunging forward in the last over before lunch.

Between lunch and tea Walters played the finest innings of the series, scoring 100 of the 130 runs made in the session. His 112 took 148 minutes, with 1 six and 16 fours. He was unrecognisable as the batsman who had averaged only 7.7 in Tests before he was dropped during the series against England a few months earlier. His driving was glorious and he repeatedly pulled away outside the leg stump and hammered the ball behind point.

An attractive half century by Kallicharran and another valuable knock by Murray (56) took the West Indies to within 52 of Australia's first innings of 332.

The ball turned a metre in Australia's second innings but Ian Chappell played a wonderful innings for 97 and Walters (32) and Redpath (44)

Keith Stackpole, injured while fielding in close, is led to the pavilion for treatment in the third Test at Port-of-Spain in 1973.

made handy runs. The innings should have ended quickly after Chappell was the seventh out at 231 but fighting batting by the tailenders produced a further 50 vital runs, including 33 for the last wicket by Walker and Hammond.

Left to score 334 on the turning pitch, the West Indies took advantage of wayward bowling by spinners O'Keeffe and Jenner to reach 4 for 268 at lunch on the last day. Kallicharran was in full flight on 91 and with only 66 needed, the West Indies looked certain winners. As the Australians were about to leave the lunch room, Ian Chappell sensed their dejected mood, turned in the doorway, and said: "You've been bowling like a bunch of sheilas. A quick wicket can change everything. We're going to win."

First ball after lunch, Kallicharran slashed at a Max Walker loosener and nicked a catch to Marsh. Immediately Ian Chappell moved in his

Lawrence Rowe is carried from the field after damaging ankle ligaments in the Port-of-Spain Test, which Australia won by 46 runs. Rowe did not bat in the match, and missed the rest of the series and the tour of England that followed.

fieldsmen, attacking, and hustled out the last West Indian batsmen for only 21 runs. O'Keeffe's accuracy was deadly as he collected three of the last five wickets to finish with 4 for 57. The West Indies were hampered by an injury to Rowe that prevented him batting in either innings but by a margin of only 44 runs this was a satisfying Australian victory.

The next match, against Guyana at Bridgetown on the South American mainland from 31 March to 3 April, saw the Australians in a careless mood following the celebrations of their Test win. Only a glorious 154 by Greg Chappell kept them in the match until the final day. Fredericks (158) and Lloyd (124) gave Guyana a first innings lead of 59, and another delightful innings of 77 from Greg Chappell meant that Guyana had to score 275 in 345 minutes to win. Fredericks made his second century of the match (118) but once he left Australia maintained a determined attack under which Guyana wilted. Massie's 7 for 52 won the match by 40 runs.

Clive Lloyd's true quality emerged in the fourth Test, at the Bourda ground in Georgetown from 6 to 11 April. Playing with care and patience, he rebuilt the West Indians' innings from 3 for 90, scoring 178 out of 366. Australia got to within 21 runs of this through a fine stand by Ian Chappell (109) and Greg Chappell (51), and another display of magical footwork against high-class spin by Walters (81). On a pitch on which 250 would have been enough to win, the West Indians recklessly threw their wickets away and were out for 109, their worst home total in 38 years. Demoralised by this batting failure, the West Indies offered little resistance as Stackpole and Redpath hit off the 135 needed to win.

With the series won, Australia had a thrilling last-ball win over the Windward Islands between 14 and 16 April at St George's, Grenada, thanks to a powerful 168 by Stackpole. They then wound up a happy, incident-free tour with a draw in the fifth Test at Queen's Park, Port-of-Spain, Trinidad, from 21 to 26 April. They were never in danger of defeat after scoring 8 for 419 in their first innings, Hammond and Walker again retaining control of the West Indian batsmen with their accurate line and length.

Walker, on his first tour, was the outstanding success in a team of stars, taking 41 first-class wickets at 20.48, 26 of them in the Tests in which his average slipped marginally to 20.73. Greg Chappell made most runs, 1110 at 69.37, but Walters finished ahead in the first-class batting averages with 69.50. Ian Chappell topped the Test batting averages with 77.42 compared to Walters' 77.00. Seven batsmen scored more than 500 runs on the tour for a team that made 12 centuries and had nine scored against them. The major difference between the teams was Ian Chappell's captaincy. After the tour ended it was disclosed that the Australian Board of Control had refused manager Jacobs' request for a replacement for Lillee when he broke down with back trouble, which at one stage left the side with only 12 fit players.

Lillee spent a long time in plaster after the Australians returned from the West Indies, with most critics tipping that the fractures in his back had finished his career. He had played in only five matches on the tour and taken five wickets at 47.60 apiece. He set out to cure his back problems with a herculean schedule of painful exercises, lifting weights and running on a treadmill which his Perth doctor said was the only way to restore his torso so that it could withstand the demands of pace bowling.

On the home front Western Australia had clinched their fourth Sheffield Shield win in the 1972-73 season despite the absence of Lillee, Marsh, Massie and Edwards in the West Indies, and without Graham McKenzie whom the selectors persistently ignored. Western Australia came with an impressive final surge, winning their last three games outright, completing their triumph between 3 and 6 March with a resounding win over South Australia in Perth by an innings and 47 runs.

Judy Chappell's first 13 months of marriage to Greg passed with him absent for eight months playing cricket in England and the West Indies. She did not mind because she sensed that her husband had rare leadership qualities, and a destiny to fulfill. Greg Chappell's biographer,

Adrian McGregor, said the Queensland Cricket Association recognised those qualities, too, when they invited Greg to switch states and play for Queensland, reputedly for $50,000 over three seasons. South Australia made surprisingly little effort to keep him and when his friend John Maclean phoned from Brisbane and offered to stand down for Greg as Queensland captain, that clinched the deal. Maclean said he preferred to be vice-captain in a side that could win under Greg's captaincy than captain in a losing side.

Lillee did not play in the three-Test series against New Zealand in the Australian summer of 1973-74, when Dell, Gilmour, Walker, Victorian right-hander Alan Hurst and Queensland left-hander Geoff Dymock were all tried in the opening bowling role. This rubber brought to an end Australia's neglect of New Zealand cricket. Matches between the countries dated back to 1878, when the first white Australian team to tour England visited New Zealand as part of their preparation. The pill-box hats and coloured sashes of the 1878 Australians were first seen at Invercargill, where Charles Bannerman made the initial century by an Australian against New Zealand.

Since then Australia had done little to foster New Zealand cricket, using short visits there as rewards for elderly players or as a proving trip for promising youngsters. Australia won the only Test against New Zealand in 1946-47 by an innings and 103 runs, although this was not officially recognised as a Test until 1948. The margin provided Australian administrators with a reason to delay the second official Test for 27 years.

On New Zealand's first major tour of Australia, Bevan Congdon's team had to play well enough to remove lingering Australian doubts about whether they were capable of taking their place among the Test nations. They arrived with a party of 14 players, badly chosen for Australian conditions in the lack of a wrist spinner and a genuinely fast bowler. All their opening bowlers were medium-pacers whose in-swing did not always work in clear, sunny conditions. This side was further handicapped by an injury to their vice-captain and star batsman Glenn Turner, who broke a finger attempting a slips catch. Jeremy Coney was flown over as a reinforcement, which in the long term proved a major gain for New Zealand cricket. The New Zealand team was B. E. Congdon (captain), 35, G. M. Turner, (vice-captain), 26, J. F. Morrison, 26, K. J. Wadsworth, 27, J. M. Parker, 22, B. F. Hastings, 33, B. Andrews, 28, D. R. Hadlee, 25, R. J. Hadlee, 22, D. R. O'Sullivan, 29, M. J. F. Shrimpton, 33, G. D. Alabaster, 33, K. O. Campbell, 30, B. L. Cairns, 24, and J. V. Coney, 21, with R. A. Vance as manager.

The New Zealanders were set to score 279 runs at 5.5 an over to win their first match from 30 November to 3 December against Victoria in Melbourne, but lost Turner and Congdon to fast bowler Hurst before a run was scored and settled for a draw. Turner broke a finger trying to catch a nick from Ron Crippin in the match against New South Wales in Sydney between 7 and 11 December, and could not bat in the second innings. Parker (130) and Shrimpton (100 not out) topscored in New Zealand's first innings of 7 for 400 declared, but the absence of Turner and some superb left-arm pace bowling by Gilmour saw New Zealand all out for 175 in their second innings. New South Wales lost only three wickets in scoring the 212 to win, thanks to a dashing stand of 132 in 85 minutes by Walters and Davis.

Greg Chappell, in his first international match for Queensland, set up a victory over New Zealand at the 'Gabba between 14 and 15 December with a magnificent innings of 165. Big Tony Dell took 6 for 40 and 6 for 23 to have New Zealand out for 100 and 161 and complete Queensland's win by an innings and two runs. The New Zealanders suffered their third successive defeat against South Australia in Adelaide from 21 to 24 December despite impressive bowling by Cairns and a century from Shrimpton (106). Mallett, in his first match after a bout of mumps, took 6 for 77 in New Zealand's first innings.

The disastrous sequence of defeats forced New Zealand to risk Turner for their initial Test on Australian soil in Melbourne from 29 December 1973 to 2 January 1974. They started badly when Shrimpton and Hastings collided trying to catch Stackpole from the sixth ball of the match. Stackpole, dropped four times before he reached 50, went on to 122 in a total of 8 for 462 declared. Turner was hit on the hand by Dell early in New Zealand's first innings, a blow which prevented him batting in the second innings. Forced on the defensive, New Zealand struggled to totals of 237 and 200 against a lively Australian attack and Australia won by an innings and 25 runs. Gilmour, replacing the injured Walker, made an impressive debut for Australia, scoring 52 and taking 4 for 75.

Australia were 425 runs behind with eight wickets left when rain prevented play on the fifth day of the second Test at Sydney from 5 to 10 January. The rain was a cruel blow to New Zealand who had led Australia by 150 runs on the first innings, thanks to an aggressive 108 from John Parker, who square drove brilliantly. Hampered by injuries to Walker, Gilmour and Walters, Ian Chappell found his attack could not prevent New Zealand pressing home their advantage in the second innings. This time John Morrison made 117, enabling Congdon to declare at 9 for 305. Richard Hadlee had dismissed Stackpole and Ian Chappell when the rain intervened.

Encouraged by this display and wins in Tasmania and Perth, New Zealand went into the third Test at Adelaide from 26 to 31 January heartened by Turner's return and the absence through injury of Walker and Gilmour from the Australian side. New Zealand suffered from the lack of a spinner to partner David O'Sullivan, a left-arm spinner with a jerky but effective action who had played for Hampshire.

After early problems against Cairns and Hadlee, Walters softened up the New Zealand attack with a powerful 94, which included a 100-run stand with Greg Chappell. Marsh took full advantage as New Zealand wilted in the heat to score his second Test century. His 132 included some memorable blows against Cairns, who was playing in his first Test. O'Sullivan's 5 for 148 from 35.5 overs was a gritty effort in a total of 477. The new Australian pace bowlers made early inroads in both New Zealand innings, with Mallett and O'Keeffe combining later to exploit the crumbling pitch. With Australia's team to tour New Zealand about to be picked, Dymock made sure of a berth by taking 2 for 44 and 5 for 58 in New Zealand's innings of 218 and 202, Australia winning by an innings and 57 runs to clinch the series 2–nil.

New Zealand won only 2 of their 9 first-class matches in Australia, lost 5 and had 2 drawn. Their batting was strong, with five batsmen scoring more than 400 runs, Shrimpton heading the tour averages with 426 runs at 42.60. They made ten first-class centuries on the tour and had four scored against them, with Brayshaw's 160 for Western Australia, in Perth, the top score against them. Their bowling was their undoing, with only two bowlers, Cairns (20 at 26.30) and Dayle Hadlee (26 at 34.92) taking 20 wickets on the trip. The loss of Turner and Wadsworth for important matches also handicapped the New Zealanders, who found Australia's batting depth too big an obstacle.

Queensland were unlucky not to receive a spectacular immediate dividend for their enterprise in signing Greg Chappell. They were superior to New South Wales and Victoria in their first two Shield matches but had to settle for draws. Had they won only one of these games they would have claimed the Shield for the first time in their history. Victoria, seven runs from

Kerry O'Keeffe, a key figure in Australia's matches against New Zealand in the 1973–74 season, during which he made his career highest score of 99 not out against Auckland.

defeat with Queensland three wickets in hand when bad light stopped play, won the Shield for the 22nd time largely because of the enterprising captaincy of Keith Stackpole, and the consistency of Redpath and Sheahan. Victoria's success was sadly marred by the car accident which confined young Bob Rose, hailed as a future international, to a wheelchair for the rest of his life.

Greg Chappell played in seven of Queensland's eight Shield matches and scored 1013 runs at 92.09. Queensland's other Test batsman, Majid Khan, began with centuries in his first two matches but failed to reach 20 in the five matches that followed. More consistent was Sam Trimble, who scored 596 runs at 37.25, a performance that took him at 39 into second place with 8286 runs behind Bradman (8926) among the highest-scoring Shield batsmen.

Queensland opening bowlers Dymock and Dell won their way into the Test team with some fine displays. Dymock was the summer's highest wicket-taker with 51 wickets at 19.88. Dell took 43 wickets at 23.65. They received strong support from Chappell with his slow-medium mixture of swing, off breaks and drift, and from the former Sri Lankan international Malcolm Francke. Francke bowled his way into Australian team consideration now that he had qualified by taking 39 wickets at 22.82, splendid figures for a leg spinner. Another spinner, 19-year-old left-arm tweaker Ray Bright, topped the Australian first-class averages with 32 wickets at 19.66.

This earned Bright a trip with the full-strength Australian team captained by Ian Chappell which visited New Zealand in the six weeks between the middle of February and the end of March 1974. The team played six first-class matches, including three Tests. The Australians showed the strain of a long first-class programme and there was an unhappy atmosphere on the field for several matches, culminating in a clash between Ian Chappell and Glenn Turner in the Christchurch Test. Drunken behaviour by New

Zealand spectators did nothing to improve the teams' relations. The Australian team picked by Neil Harvey, Sam Loxton and Phil Ridings was I. M. Chappell (captain), 30, K. R. Stackpole (vice-captain), 33, R. J. Bright, 19, G. S. Chappell, 25, I. C. Davis, 20, G. Dymock, 27, G. J. Gilmour, 22, A. A. Mallett, 28, R. W. Marsh, 26, K. J. O'Keeffe, 24, I. R. Redpath, 32, M. H. N. Walker, 25, K. D. Walters, 28, and A. J. Woodcock, 26, with Frank Bryant on his third trip to New Zealand as manager.

Experienced campaigners Dell and Sheahan were unavailable for business reasons, reflecting the players' difficulty in getting by on tour allowances, and Lillee was still unfit. Walker and Gilmour had to pass fitness tests before they were allowed to join the tour, which aroused so much interest the New Zealand Cricket Council showed a profit of $33,000 that year.

After a draw in the opening first-class match with Canterbury at Christchurch, Kerry O'Keeffe figured in a fine effort to win the match against Auckland in Auckland from 22 to 24 February. O'Keeffe made 99 not out and took 5 for 69 in Auckland's second innings but the Auckland tailenders held out for a draw. Ian Chappell (128) and Doug Walters (100 not out) were the big scorers at Hamilton against Northern Districts between 25 and 27 February. This allowed Australia to declare at 8 for 522. They then disposed of Northern Districts for 69 and 217 to win by an innings and 236 runs.

Australia had first use of a dead pitch in the first Test at Wellington from 1 to 6 March and with a powerful wind blowing down the ground for most of the match Congdon had trouble managing his bowling. The match belonged to the Chappell brothers. Greg batted with that elegant, imperious quality that became his trademark to set a world record by scoring 380 runs in a Test. His innings of 247 not out and 133 beat the previous record of 375 by Andy Sandham for England against the West Indies in 1929–30, when Sandham made 325 and 50. With

Ian, he provided only the second instance in all first-class cricket of brothers scoring centuries in both innings, matching the feat of R. E. and W. L. Foster who did it for Worcestershire against Hampshire in 1899 at Worcester.

In the first innings of 6 declared for 511, Ian matched Greg's power in a stand of 264 for the third wicket, which was only ended by wicket-keeper Ken Wadsworth's remarkable running catch. The Chappells accounted for 392 of Australia's 491 runs from the bat, Greg hitting 1 six and 30 fours. New Zealand responded with a score of 484, Congdon (132) and Hastings (101) both surviving early difficulties to play some splendid strokes. Redpath (93) helped Ian Chappell put on 141 for the second wicket in Australia's second innings, before Greg joined Ian in another good family partnership. This time they were only together for 44 minutes but managed to score 86 runs. Ian went to his third successive tour century (121) and Greg stayed to score 133. Between them they managed 646 runs in the match for three dismissals. The bowlers had little chance of forcing a result in a match that produced 1455 runs, still the highest total for any Test in New Zealand.

The second Test at Christchurch from 8 to 13 March 1974 was probably the most exciting ever staged in New Zealand. After the start was delayed by a drizzle, Australia had to bat first on a damp pitch but New Zealand failed to exploit the conditions until the score reached 2 for 101. Thereafter New Zealand fielded magnificently to have Australia out for 223. Walker and Dymock moved the ball about skilfully when New Zealand batted, with all their hopes resting on Turner. He was on 99 for 34 balls before completing his century and was out moments later. With New Zealand leading by 32 runs, Australia lost Stackpole and both Chappells in half an hour for only 33 runs.

Davis and Walters revived Australia's hopes with a stand of 106 for the fourth wicket, then the Hadlee brothers took charge. Richard

Richard Hadlee in action against Australia in New Zealand in 1974, when New Zealand held Australia to a 1–1 draw after three record-studded Tests.

dismissed Davis for 50 off a skied hook shot and Dayle completed an extraordinary caught and bowled diving full-length to take a heavily clubbed Marsh drive. The Australian innings closed at 259, Dayle Hadlee taking three of the last four wickets for 26 runs to finish with 4 for 75. Richard Hadlee had taken 4 for 71. Both brothers bowled at a lively pace and moved the ball sharply.

Set to score 228 to achieve their first victory over Australia in the six Tests played between the countries, New Zealand again relied on the cultured, pale-faced Turner. They began well with a stand of 51 for the first wicket but then Walker had Parker and Morrison out for four runs and Congdon was run out in a tragic mix-up. Turner remained calm, batting with faultless judgement, and found a plucky partner in Brian Hastings, who showed an admirable eagerness to attack. As the excitement mounted, Hastings hit a four which was signalled six by umpire R. L. Monteith. Turner turned at the non-striker's end to tell Monteith the ball had bounced before crossing the boundary, but before Monteith could correct his signal Ian Chappell ran up from the slips. Turner said he explained that the signal would be corrected but claimed that Chappell then addressed him in foul language. Later Turner and his team-mates asked for an apology but Chappell refused, saying that what happened on the field ended there.

Hastings was out in the last over of the fourth day, leaving New Zealand on 4 for 177 entering the final day. Australia attacked Coney tenaciously on the fifth morning, eager for a quick breakthrough, but Coney batted calmly for an hour while Turner moved to his second century of the match. Wadsworth came in at 6 for 206 and remained to hit the winning boundary through the covers off Greg Chappell. Turner's 110 not out may have taken 5 hours 38 minutes but it confirmed New Zealand's right to a place in international cricket. They had fought out a drawn series in the West Indies in 1972, had twice come close to victory over England in 1973, and in Sydney a few weeks earlier had been near to a win when rain intervened.

New Zealand had played 113 official Tests when they had their first win over Australia and while Ian Chappell's fierce will to win was frustrated, nobody could begrudge her moment of triumph to a country which had endured defeat in her first 44 Tests. The margin of five wickets was so complete nobody could attribute it to bad decisions, luck with the toss, or the other reasons beaten sides fall back on.

Australia reacted badly with a lacklustre display against Otago at Dunedin. The weather was as miserable as Australia's approach to the

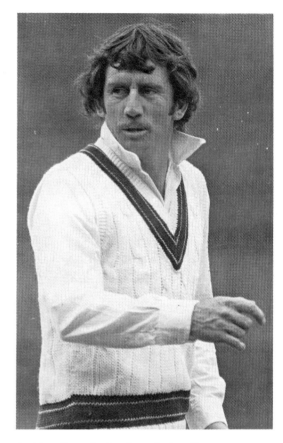

Ian Chappell soon after he took over the Australian captaincy from Bill Lawry.

match from 15 to 17 March, but their lack of interest was matched by the opposition and a draw was the only result possible.

Eighteen wickets fell on the first day of the third Test at Auckland from 22 to 24 March. The pitch was watered until just before play began and a heavy dew ensured it was still soft when Australia lost their first four wickets for 37. Only a brave century from Walters (104 not out) took Australia to 221. New Zealand were 8 for 85 in reply by the end of the first day. Ian Chappell blamed the pitch but the late swing achieved by Collinge and the Hadlees for New Zealand and by Walker and Gilmour for Australia had just as much to do with the regular fall of wickets.

Leading by 109, Australia lost Stackpole for a duck at two but sustained their policy of all-out attack, with 45 runs coming from the first six overs of their second innings. Redpath held up one end while the stroke-players Ian and Greg Chappell, and later the hitters Marsh and O'Keeffe, consolidated Australia's advantage. New Zealand wanted 456 to win and had scored 107 of them before a wicket fell, but once openers Turner (72) and Parker (34) went, Australia's bowlers wrapped up victory by 297 runs to level the series at a win apiece, with one drawn. Three limited-over matches completed a tour in which New Zealand cricket had come of age.

As heavily as the Chappell brothers had scored in the Tests, they could not match Turner's average of 100.75, which was a long way ahead of his next team-mate, Hastings, who averaged 33.40. Greg Chappell averaged 89.80 in the Tests, with Redpath in second place on 82.60 and Ian Chappell third on 59.83. Walker easily headed the Australian wicket-takers with 14 Test wickets, but his average of 19.07 was inferior to Gilmour's 7 wickets at 16.57. In all first-class matches, only Ian Chappell topped 500 runs, with 559 at 69.87 from 10 innings. The Australians won two of their six first-class matches, lost one, and had three drawn.

The major disappointment for Australia was Stackpole, who scored 50 runs in six Test innings, including "spectacles" in the final Test, and announced his retirement immediately the team arrived back in Australia. He had scored 2807 runs at 37.42 in 43 Tests and in 14 seasons of first-class cricket had made 10,100 runs at 39.29. He also took 148 wickets at 39.28 in first-class matches with his leg breaks and remains one of modern cricket's great entertainers, a batsman whose eagerness to hit the first delivery of a Test for four gave him heroic status when Test matches came to Melbourne. His retirement gave Australia a major headache to find a replacement opener for the 1974–75 rubber in Australia against England.

Frightening Twosome

England tours Australia 1974-75; domestic cricket 1974-75

When Greg Chappell suggested signing the Sydney pace bowler Jeff Thomson to play for Queensland, selectors Peter Burge and Ken Mackay were sceptical. Judged on his erratic debut for Australia against Pakistan in 1972–73, they doubted if Thomson could replace Dymock or Dell in the Queensland side, much less take wickets consistently for the State. Chappell backed his judgement. He had heard on the cricketers' grapevine of the hair-raising feats of Thomson and Len Durtanovich (later Pascoe) for the Bankstown club in Sydney and he knew that Thomson had suffered from a fractured foot when he played against Pakistan. Thomson was a bowler who terrorised batsmen, the fastest Greg had ever seen by quite a margin. "I don't care if he does spray them," said Chappell. "He'll frighten them out. They'll be so desperate to get down the other end when he's on they'll run themselves out."

Thomson had experienced difficulty regaining his place in the New South Wales team

The bowlers who thwarted England in 1974–75, Jeff Thomson (far right), who took 33 wickets, and Dennis Lillee, who had 25 victims. They were supported by brilliant catching and responsive pitches.

when he recovered from his foot injury and found Steve Bernard and David Colley taking wickets often enough to keep him out. When he replaced Bernard for the last match of the 1973–74 season against Queensland, his 7 for 85 included some alarming deliveries. Burge and Mackay accepted Chappell's opinion and Thomson moved to Queensland. In a Queensland team trial he bowled two of the fastest overs ever seen in Brisbane, which Chappell later described as "absolutely lethal—100 miles an hour in any direction".

Meanwhile in Perth Lillee had recovered from the back injury that forced him to spend weeks in a plaster cast after Australia's West Indian tour in 1972–73. Patiently following medical advice, he had seldom bowled in 1973–74, but worked hard on the exercises designed to strengthen the muscles used when he unleashed his faster ball. Everything he did on his return to big cricket was planned, from the gradual build-up as the summer progressed to the placement of his slips and the removal of his sweater.

Lillee and Thomson were an unpleasant shock to an England team chosen in the belief that Australia would not field a genuine fast bowler. At the pace they bowled it is doubtful if England's selectors could have done much to improve their team's showing, but only Alec Bedser of the panel that selected this thirty-first team to tour Australia was re-elected after the 1974–75 tour. The side included five fast bowlers and was led by the Scottish-born Kent batsman Mike Denness, who had captained the side to a 3-nil win over India, and a drawn series—three draws—against Pakistan in England in 1974. Ray Illingworth, whom Denness' had replaced, bitterly attacked Denness' leadership and the absence of John Snow. The team was: M. H. Denness (captain), 34, J. H. Edrich (vice-captain), 37, A. W. Greig, 28, A. P. E. Knott, 28, K. W. R. Fletcher, 30, D. Lloyd, 27, D. L. Amiss, 31, F. J. Titmus, 42, C. M. Old, 26,

R. G. D. Willis, 25, B. W. Luckhurst, 35, D. L. Underwood, 29, P. Lever, 34, M. Hendrick, 26, and G. G. Arnold, 30, with A. V. Bedser as manager, A. C. Smith as assistant manager and B. Thomas as masseur.

Boycott was in the original team but withdrew on the grounds that he was mentally unfit to tour and had to look after his ailing mother. Later he confessed to lacking any respect for Denness "as a captain and as a man". Boycott's decision annoyed the Yorkshire committee and even his fans were disappointed when he went off to South Africa on a tour organised by Derek Robins, while his England team-mates were being battered in Australia.

Cowdrey was flown out as a reinforcement, after six matches, for his sixth tour of Australia, which equalled Johnny Briggs' record between 1884–85 and 1897–98. There was intense interest among Australian cricket buffs in the appearance of the 2 metres tall England middle-order batsman Tony Greig, who had done so well for the World XI in Australia in 1971–72. Greig was given the credit for the fashion of batsmen facing oncoming deliveries with bats in the air, a technique dictated perhaps by Greig's height but copied by others who saw split-second advantages in its use.

Lillee and Thomson prepared for the Tests with moderate Sheffield Shield displays, Thomson taking 4 for 65 and 2 for 7 against New South Wales, and 2 for 46 and 0 for 50 against Western Australia; Lillee 4 for 82 and 3 for 40 against South Australia, 3 for 46 and 1 for 61 against Victoria, 2 for 102 and 2 for 69 against New South Wales, and 3 for 46 and 1 for 51 against Queensland. A better indication of the fireworks to come was the magazine interview given by Thomson in which he said he enjoyed hitting batsmen, and a book published by Lillee, *Back to the Mark*, in which he confessed that he aimed to hit batsmen with his bouncer.

England began in Adelaide with a draw against South Australia from 1 to 4 November despite a match bag of 7 for 127 by Underwood. They also had a draw in Melbourne against Victoria from 8 to 11 November despite an opening stand of 268 by Amiss (152) and Luckhurst (116). Greig set up a good win over New South Wales between 15 and 18 November in Sydney with 5 for 55 in New South Wales' second innings. Thomson was in second gear in the match between England and Queensland at the 'Gabba from 22 to 25 November, taking 1 for 22 and 1 for 29. Greg Chappell's first innings of 122 held up England temporarily but the English pace bowlers had no difficult taking their side to victory, dismissing Queensland for 161 in the final innings.

Brisbane's Lord Mayor Clem Jones, a novice in the art, prepared the pitch for the first Test at the 'Gabba from 29 November to 4 December. Jones, who had sacked the curator ten days before, had a difficult task when storms flooded the ground two days before play was due to begin. His pitch produced uneven bounce at the southern end where England lost 16 of their 20 wickets. On such a strip Thomson's unpredictable bowling proved an asset and his 38.5 overs included 3 wides and 13 no-balls. He took 3 for 59 and 6 for 46, bowling at tremendous speed in the second innings, repeatedly exploding the ball up around the chest, and occasionally producing what one team-mate dubbed his "throat ball". He broke Amiss's thumb in England's first innings.

Australia introduced Western Australian left-hander Wally Edwards to open the batting with Redpath, but he failed in both innings. Ian Chappell looked certain of a century when he was out for 90, but at 8 for 229 the last two Australian wickets added 80 runs. Walker followed his valuable 41 with the bat by taking 4 for 73 in England's first innings of 265. With the ball flying around his team-mates' ears and masseur Bernard Thomas working overtime on bruised torsos, Greig played a courageous innings, repeatedly driving straight past the bowlers on his way to 110. Chappell declared Australia's second innings at 5 for 288, giving England 333 to win in 400 minutes.

England appeared to have a strong chance of saving the match provided they could get through the first session on the final day without too much damage. But by lunch the match was virtually over, Thomson having completely blitzed England's top order. He had Edrich and Amiss out in successive overs and straight after lunch England slumped from 3 for 80 to 6 for 94. Greg Chappell had noticed that Greig wore soft, rubber-soled boots and suggested that Thomson might get through Greig's high backlift and hit him on the toes to slow down his footwork. Thomson was dead on target and thereafter this delivery became known as his "sandshoe crusher". Greig was one of the four batsmen he bowled as Australia cruised to victory by 166 runs.

England had little time to recover, for they were defeated by Western Australia in the next tour match at Perth from 7 to 10 December. Edrich had had confirmation of a broken hand just before play began and Cowdrey flew in as a reinforcement, arriving on the third day to find England in danger against a State that had not beaten them in 16 encounters. England led by 49 runs on the first innings thanks to a superb 167 not out by Greig, but Western Australia declared at 5 for 346 in their second innings in which Inverarity (99), Watson (86 not out), Langer (62 not out) and Laird (44) played vital roles. This gave England a target of 298 to win in four hours but once Greig was dismissed for 57 the innings collapsed for 177. Fletcher was unable to bat in either innings for England after a blow in the nets, but the English batsmen looked so inept against the leg spin of Paulsen (7 for 41) in the final innings it is doubtful if Fletcher's presence would have prevented their defeat by 120 runs. The win was all the more noteworthy as Marsh and Lillee rested before the second Test.

The hand injuries to Amiss and Edrich forced Cowdrey to play in the second Test between

*John Edrich, taking a stunning blow on the hand in the
Brisbane Test during the 1974–75 series: a blow that
broke a bone. Edrich was out in the following over.*

13 and 17 December at the WACA despite his
lack of match practice. He batted well before
falling to Thomson in both innings. England's
first innings of 208 was helped by a stubborn
51 from Knott. Great catching reduced England's
top order to tatters as Lillee and Thomson made
the ball fly, either bruising the batsmen or finding
an edge. Of the 14 catches offered in the slips
and gully area in the match, the Australians held
13. Greg Chappell took seven catches, a world
record for a fieldsman.

Australia consolidated their advantage by
scoring 481 in the first innings. All the top order
batted well, with Ross Edwards scoring 115, the
first Test century by a West Australian in Perth.
But Australia's batting hero was Walters, who
reached 97 and needed a six from the final ball
of the second day to complete 100 runs in the

tea-to-stumps session. Bets were laid in the
Australian dressing-room by Walters' supporters
who believed he could make it. Willis let go
a fast long hop which Walters exultantly hit into
the crowd who poured in over the square leg
boundary.

Fearing a burst of wisecracks from Walters,
all the Australians hid in the showers or toilets,
leaving him to share an empty dressing-room
with his triumph. They could not sustain it and
when the chuckling began they all burst out to
congratulate Dougie on a rare achievement.

England's slender chances of saving the match
vanished when Thomson dismissed Greig and
Denness in his first three overs and then saw
Fletcher edge his first ball to Marsh. Of the later
batsmen, only Titmus—in his 50th Test—got in
behind the ball and his 61 was an object lesson
to team-mates who hung the bat out well away
from their bodies. Thomson's 5 for 93 left
Australia to score only 21 to win and they got
them in four overs for the loss of Wally Edwards.

Three declarations failed to provide a result in England's next match, against South Australia between 21 and 23 December in Adelaide, even though an extra half hour was added to each day's play to compensate for the lack of a fourth day. Only 18 wickets fell in the three days and the match was drawn with England six short of the 216 required for victory. Cosier scored 75 and 48 for South Australia and took 3 for 41 in England's second innings.

Between 26 and 31 December, Australia and

Colin Cowdrey clean bowled by Jeff Thomson in 1974–75 four days after arriving in Perth to reinforce the injury-hit England team. Hand injuries to Amiss and Edrich forced England to play Cowdrey, who had not appeared in Tests since 1971.

England played out a thrilling draw in the third Test at Melbourne. Set to score 246 to win in the final innings, Australia appeared certain to get them at 2 for 106 after a third-wicket stand of 101 by Redpath and Greg Chappell, with Hendrick unable to bowl for England and Titmus suffering from a knee injury after a blow from Thomson. The last hour began with Australia still wanting 55 runs, but in seven overs from Titmus and Underwood they added only seven runs. The Englishmen thought Australia had settled for a draw and took the new ball to exploit Australia's unwillingness to play shots. Immediately Marsh hit out and nine runs came from Willis' opening over with the new ball. After Marsh went, Lillee and Walker attacked so effectively Australia were only 16 short of

victory with three overs left. With the 42,827 spectators shouting them home, the Australians could not find the balls to hit and only two runs came from an over by Greig. Underwood then bowled a maiden.

Denness caught Lillee from the fourth ball of the final over and a match watched by 250,721 spectators was left undecided because Australia was so concerned by possible defeat they refused to chase the eight runs needed to win. All four English bowlers deserved great credit for a final day that offered the Australians few loose deliveries.

Australia brought in McCosker for his Test debut as an opener in place of Wally Edwards for the fourth Test at Sydney from 4 to 9 January, but the headlines went to England captain Mike Denness who dropped himself through lack of form. His failures had become so regular Walters would watch him come through the gate with: "I'll be buggered—another two overs of Mike Denness".

McCosker quickly vindicated his selection with a fine 80 in the first innings, adding 96 for the first wicket with Redpath. The remaining Australians capitalised on this excellent start to take the total to 405, with Arnold taking 5 for 86 for England. Thomson took 4 for 74 in England's first innings of 295, only Edrich (50) and Knott (82) scoring freely. Redpath (105) and Greg Chappell (144) then figured in a record 220-run stand for the second wicket to press home Australia's advantage.

Australia's declaration at 4 for 289 set England to score 400 to win or bat for eight and a half hours to save the match. A thunderstorm cut 95 minutes from the fourth day, but on the fifth day the Lillee–Thomson combination once again demoralised England's batsmen. At 3 for 74 Lillee struck Edrich in the ribs and he went off to hospital for treatment, returning with the score on 6 for 156. Edrich defended for two and a half hours to finish undefeated on 33 not out. Only Amiss, caught off the glove avoiding a

Rick McCosker, whose selection, in the fourth Test against England in 1974–75, in place of Wally Edwards was vindicated with a fine first innings score of 80.

bouncer, and Fletcher, shaken by a blow on the forehead before he was caught off Thomson, were exempt from blame in England's collapse for 228.

Australia's win by 171 gave them the rubber 3–nil, with two to play, on the same ground on which they had surrendered the Ashes four years earlier, the end coming with Arnold caught at short leg off Mallett. This was Mallett's 100th wicket in 23 Tests. The attendance of 178,027 was a record for a match in Sydney.

The back-slapping and joyous hugging of bowlers and catchers that had begun with Benaud's teams intensified throughout this series. Home-made banners on which schoolboys spent hours of preparation became common in most stands. Many of the crowd on the Sydney Hill joined in the chant of "Lill . . . lee, Lill . . . lee", as the heavily-moustached Lillee moved smoothly in on his approach, spectators hushing just as he released the ball. *Wisden* commented that England's battered batsmen must have felt the same emotions as Christians awaiting the lions in the Colosseum.

England went off to Tasmania to recuperate with a draw and a win by an innings and 172 runs, the latter thanks to 157 not out from Denness, and then returned to the mainland to defeat New South Wales by 187 runs in Sydney, where Denness made 99 and Chris Old had 7 for 59 and 2 for 49. Denness returned to the English side for the fifth Test from 25 to 30 January, and put Australia in on a damp Adelaide pitch. England made a great start. Underwood went on after only three overs with a ring of close-in fieldsmen. For 50 valuable minutes Redpath and McCosker resisted before Underwood broke through to have Australia reeling at 5 for 84. Denness's failure to use Titmus's off spin at the other end early on puzzled experts and when the tail wagged furiously Australia's total rose to 304. The last five wickets added 220 in even time, Jenner contributing 74 as the pitch lost its bite.

Lillee and Thomson then fired England out for 172, with Mallett taking out the tailenders. Only Denness (51) and Fletcher (40) batted with any confidence but both were out trying to cut Thomson. Marsh's hands had to be specially strapped before he went out to keep wicket to them but the slips fieldsmen still heard frequent murmurs of pain from Marsh as the ball thudded into his gloves. Relief came unexpectedly when Thomson tore fibres in his right shoulder playing tennis on the rest day and could not bowl in England's second innings. To that stage Thomson had taken 33 wickets in the series, with his curious slinging action, bringing his hand up so fast from behind his back batsmen found it hard to pick up the ball.

Underwood again bowled cleverly in Australia's second innings, but fine team batting enabled Ian Chappell to declare at 5 for 272 and

Wicket-keeper Rodney Marsh shows the damage inflicted on his hands by 'keeping to Lillee and Thomson at their peak. Virtually every finger had to be reinforced with tape.

leave England to score 405 to win in 510 minutes. Underwood's match figures of 11 for 215 were the best by an Englishman in Australia since 1928–29. England's chances disappeared when they lost wickets in each of the first three overs. Amiss achieved spectacles when caught by Marsh off Lillee, Lloyd was taken at third slip off Walker, and Mallett held an unbelievable catch in the gully to dismiss Cowdrey. Greig and Denness followed to have England on 5 for 94 with a day to play.

Knott, who earlier had become the second wicket-keeper to complete 200 dismissals in Tests, gave England some compensation for a heavy defeat by batting for 225 minutes on the fifth day. His 106 not out was the second century by an English wicket-keeper against Australia, Les Ames having scored the first in 1934. Walker bowled beautifully in the absence of Thomson and, with Mallett and Jenner, sustained the pressure on England's batsmen originally applied by Lillee, who took eight wickets in the match. Australia's fourth win in the rubber was achieved by 163 runs and watched by just on 100,000 spectators.

The Melbourne ground staff helped England when they splashed water on the pitch for the sixth Test between 8 and 13 February as they removed the covers following overnight rain. This left a distinct damp patch on the southern end of the pitch. Ian Chappell gambled on Australia's overcoming this and the hot, oppressive conditions by batting when he won the toss. But the tall, lithe Essex left-arm fast bowler John Lever, who replaced the injured Willis, had other ideas, and his four wickets for five runs on the first morning proved too big a blow for Australia.

Australia were all out for 152 by tea, Lever finishing with 6 for 38, wonderful figures in a series that had seen England take such a hammering. Australia had England 2 for 18 in their first innings following Amiss's third successive duck, but Lillee badly bruised his heel and limped off with sock and boot in hand. This meant England had neither of their nemeses, Lillee or Thomson, to brood over and they took full advantage of the relief. A typically dour 70 from Edrich and centuries by Denness and Fletcher took England to 529 and a lead of 377. Denness's 188 was the highest Test score by an English captain in Australia, 15 more than Andrew Stoddart's 173 in 1894–95. Cowdrey's 7 extended his aggregate to 7624 runs at 44.06 in this his last and record 114th Test.

Australia had to score 377 runs to force England to bat again and that they failed to do so by only four runs was largely due to an opening

stand of 111 by Redpath and McCosker and six hours of stubborn batting by Greg Chappell, whose 102 was his best innings of the series. Though Australia lost by an innings, they had failed to hold catches which would have cut England's total in half; and Australia won the series 4–1, with one match drawn.

England's unlikely victory in the last Test could not conceal the mastery of Lillee and Thomson over all the England top order. Of the 14 scores over 50 in the rubber, eight came from Greig and Knott, who batted at number six and seven. There was scarcely a man in England's 17 tourists who was not unavailable through injury at some time on the trip. England won 6 of their 18 first-class matches, lost 5 and played 7 draws. They scored 12 centuries in these matches and had 7 scored against them.

Only one English batsman scored 400 runs in the six Tests, Greig heading the aggregates with 446 from 11 innings at 40.54, which gave him second place in England's Test averages behind Edrich's 43.33. Lever topped the Test bowling with seven wickets at 23.77 but the real workhorses were Willis (17 at 30.70), Underwood (17 at 35.00), Arnold (14 at 37.21) and Greig (17 at 40.05).

Greg Chappell topped Australia's Test batting averages with 608 runs at 55.27, Thomson the bowling averages with 33 wickets at 17.93. Six Australian batsmen averaged more than 40 runs per innings in Tests but only two Englishmen, Edrich and Greig, managed it. In all first-class matches only Greig (836 at 46.44) and Denness (896 at 44.80) managed more than 800 runs for England, and among England's bowlers only Underwood took 40 wickets in the first-class games. My overall impression was that Australia's superior athleticism, coupled with the magical enthusiasm Ian Chappell instilled in his team, gave Australia almost as important an advantage as the frightening pace of Lillee and Thomson.

Long before England's tour ended the one-sided Test series had been overshadowed by a Sheffield Shield competition that could have been won by any of the five teams with only three matches to be played. Queensland were a transformed side under Greg Chappell, whose assessment of Thomson's searing pace had proved so accurate. They led for most of the competition, only to suffer batting failures in the last crucial matches. New South Wales threatened after four successive centuries by McCosker, only to succumb to erratic batting displays. Victoria seemed likely to retain the Shield until they collapsed for 76 before a devastating performance from Thomson, following his recovery from the tennis injury that forced him to miss the final Test.

Lillee's return after recovering from the back

Leg-spinner Bob Paulsen. Big hopes were held for him but like other Australian spinners of the mid-1970s he had to take second place to the mighty twosome, Lillee and Thomson.

injury suffered in the West Indies proved as vital to Western Australia—the Shield winners—as it was to Australia. Lillee took 37 wickets in seven Shield matches and received admirable support from Brayshaw, Paulsen, and a new pace bowler, Mick Malone, from the Scarborough club. Wally Edwards may have failed for Australia but he continued to give Western Australia wonderful service, scoring 731 runs in all games. At Sydney, where Edwards made 153 against New South Wales, followed by 117 from Laird and 168 by Marsh, the 18-year-old pace bowler Terry Alderman overshadowed even Lillee by taking three wickets in his first over and finishing with 5 for 65 in the innings. Marsh set a Shield record for wicket-keeping by dismissing 45 batsmen. Opener Laird won a place in the Australian team to tour England by scoring two centuries towards the end of the season and finishing third in the first-class averages with 748 runs in all games at 44.00, behind Greg Chappell (1484 runs at 61.83) and McCosker (1254 at 54.42).

Thomson fully justified Greg Chappell's recommendation that Queensland sign him by taking 62 wickets at 19.37. Lillee also took 62 wickets but was slightly more costly at 25.15 apiece. The ever-reliable Mallett took 57 wickets at 22.05, 15 more than the next best spinner Jim Higgs, who took 42 wickets at 21.93.

By then the Gillette Cup limited-over knock-out competition had become part of the Australian season despite unimaginative camera-work by the ABC. But at the end of the season New Zealand informed the Australian Board of Control they no longer wished to go into the draw along with all the Australian States. New Zealand had won the Gillette Cup three times in the six years of its existence and taken away a significant proportion of the prizemoney but they probably were right in believing they should confine themselves to international matches.

Ian Chappell had moulded the Australian team into a side with a wonderful team spirit administrators more often than any player since Sid Barnes just after the Second World War. He was never willing to compromise and officials in his home State of South Australia had their hands full curbing his candid language. The South Australian Cricket Association carpeted him during the 1974–75 season and warned him that a recurrence of complaints from umpires about his bad language and the use of "protest" head-high full tosses would bring suspension.

Shortly afterwards in Brisbane Ian wore Adidas boots with three blue stripes instead of white stripes and was warned of the Australian Cricket Board's insistence on all-white gear. Despite these incidents the Australian Board did well to recognise the respect Ian commanded from his players by making him the first captain to be invited to their annual meeting. As a result of what he told the Board there was an increase in player payments and allowances. Richie Benaud wrote in *Wisden*:

> *Chappell himself would disclaim any suggestion of militant shop-steward style thinking but he has certainly livened things up in the four years of his captaincy, in a game where the top players have always been ridiculously underpaid.*

Ian Chappell's struggle for better pay for his players coincided with the arrival of a crop of talented young administrators in Australian cricket. David Richards took over from Jack Ledward as secretary of the Victorian Cricket Association in 1973, and in Sydney Alan Barnes took on a willing assistant in Bob Radford, who became secretary of the New South Wales Cricket Association in 1975 when Barnes became full-time secretary of the Australian Board of Control. Given the hold that cricket had won in the Australian community it seems absurd that for the first 70 years of its existence the Board operated with a part-time secretary. Barnes was an old-style administrator who believed in the secrecy the Board maintained over its operations but his capacity for work and devotion to his

The Dennis Lillee appealing style that became familiar to cricket fans throughout the world. He was never a bowler to hide his dislike of batsmen.

and a formidable desire to win. He did more to improve his players' lot than any previous Australian captain, and had quarrelled with job did much to re-shape the Board into an efficiently managed organisation.

The twenty-seventh Australian team to tour England in 1975 faced an itinerary that had to be worked out at the last moment by Barnes and his counterparts at Lord's. The advance tour calendar arrived at by the International Cricket Conference called for Australia's appearance only in the inaugural World Cup but such was the interest in Chappell's team—and particularly his fast bowlers Lillee and Thomson—the Australian Board agreed to let the team stay after the World Cup and play four Test matches. This was a tremendous favour to English cricket and committed the Australians to 15 first-class matches in ten weeks in addition to the World Cup games. The gates were frequently closed at grounds that could not hold the crowds which wanted to see them. The team chosen by Sam Loxton, Phil Ridings and Neil Harvey was at full-strength except for the unavailability for family reasons of Redpath, who was replaced by the New South Wales opener Alan Turner. The team was I. M. Chappell (captain), 31, G. S. Chappell (vice-captain), 26, R. Edwards, 32, G. J. Gilmour, 24, A. G. Hurst, 24, B. M. Laird, 24, D. K. Lillee, 25, R. B. McCosker, 28, A. A. Mallett, 29, R. W. Marsh, 27, R. D. Robinson, 29. J. R. Thomson, 24, A. Turner, 24, M. H. N. Walker, 26, K. D. Walters, 29, with Fred Bennett as manager, Dave Sherwood as scorer and David MacErlane as physiotherapist. J. D. Higgs, 25, and R. D. Robinson were not in the World Cup squad, which was limited to 14 players, but were added to the team for the matches that followed.

Only four of the 16 players, Higgs, Laird, Turner and the reserve wicket-keeper Richie Robinson, had not played in Tests. The team made an unusual stopover in Canada on their way to England, playing five one-day matches, one of which they lost, before they flew into London on 29 May. They were a powerful outfit judged on the standards of Test cricket but were generally regarded as amateurs at the limited-over game. Australia, in fact, had taken a long time to adjust to the strategies of the limited-over game, and even Ian Chappell's most fervent admirers did not expect his team to go far in the World Cup, which had attracted teams from eight nations, with South Africa still excluded. The sponsors had provided £100,000 in prizemoney for matches confined to 60 overs. It was difficult to see how Australia could get full value from their formidable duo Lillee and Thomson under conditions that restricted each bowler to 12 overs, the critics said. They underestimated the Australians' desire to take away a large slice of that prizemoney and the tremendous pride Ian Chappell had engendered in his players.

Inflicting Pain

World Cup 1975; twenty-seventh
Australian team to England 1975;
West Indies tours Australia 1975-76

On 25 February 1975, Lancashire fast bowler
Peter Lever moved into his approach run before
the team-mates who had been so badly battered
by Lillee and Thomson and decided to bowl a
bouncer at the New Zealand No. 11 batsman
Ewan Chatfield. Lever was well aware that
tradition decreed that he should not bowl
bouncers at tailenders but Chatfield, playing in
his first Test at Eden Park, Auckland, had put
on 44 runs with Geoff Howarth in a stand that
had taken the match into the fifth day.

The ball touched Chatfield's glove and flew
into his temple. He staggered from the crease
and fell, legs twitching, face turning purple. He
had sustained a hairline fracture of the skull. For
three or four seconds his heart stopped. Only
heart massage and mouth-to-mouth resuscitation
from St John's Ambulance officer John Hayland
and the English team's physiotherapist Bernard
Thomas saved his life. John Lever wept.

The match was awarded to England and
Chatfield was carried away to hospital, where

*West Indian fans race across the field at Lord's to
congratulate their team after they had beaten Australia by
17 runs in the final of the 1975 World Cup. Five
Australian run-outs helped.*

he regained consciousness an hour or so later. Lever wanted to retire then but was persuaded to play in the second Test a few days later at Christchurch. Chatfield watched from the stands, his chance of playing in the World Cup four months later in England gone, but he said he did not blame Lever.

Chatfield's narrow escape saw the world-wide introduction of helmets, but surprisingly brought no moves by administrators to prevent the bowling of bouncers at tailenders. John Snow had some excuse when he flattened Terry Jenner in the 1970–71 series in Australia, for Jenner was no novice with the bat, but since then umpires had repeatedly failed to intervene when batsmen of little ability were hit. Loaded with five fast bowlers, England had still taken a remorseless beating in Australia without umpires Tom Brooks or Robin Bailhache moving to reduce the bouncers or the foul language that had crept into the series.

The public's macabre fascination with pace bowlers and the pain their bouncers could inflict made Lillee and Thomson the big attractions of the World Cup. Lillee did not disappoint them when he took 5 for 34 in the Australians' first match on 7 June against Pakistan at Leeds. Free of all worries about his injured back, he bowled his 12 overs at whistling speed to provide Australia with victory by 73 runs. Australia scored 278 from their 60 overs, Ross Edwards contributing 80 not out, Pakistan 205 in a match that had the colourful Bill Alley as one of the umpires.

Thomson's first over included five no-balls and forced him to slacken his speed. There were 12 no-balls in his eight overs and his loss of rhythm and troubles with his approach run clearly concerned Ian Chappell. The little turn and soft-shoe shuffle in his run had gone away.

Alan Turner made the first pre-lunch century in the history of one-day internationals during Australia's second match on 11 June against Sri Lanka at The Oval. Turner's 101 out of 178 scored

while he was at the crease took 34 overs and enabled Australia to reach 328. This allowed Ian Chappell to give all his bowlers a solid workout but they lost admirers bowling too many high bouncers. The Sri Lankans bravely tried to get in behind the short deliveries and cut or hook them but against bowling of Thomson's pace even slight mistakes extracted heavy penalties. Tiny Duleep Mendis had to retire hurt when struck on the head. Sunil Wettimuny mis-hit a bouncer into his body. Forced to use a runner, he was hit on the instep from the very next ball and as he staggered in and out of his crease Thomson threw down the wicket. The run-out appeal was disallowed but both batsmen went to hospital. It was a brave effort by the Sri Lankans to get within 52 runs of Australia's big score.

Australia's third World Cup match against the West Indies at The Oval on 14 June made Englishmen feel like interlopers amid the hordes of excited West Indian and Australian fans. The match turned into a duel between two pace bowling batteries, with the West Indians Bernard Julien and Keith Boyce sweeping aside Australia's top order batsmen before Greenidge ran out Walters. At 5 for 61, Edwards and Marsh put on 99 but when Richards winkled out Edwards for 58, Marsh ran out of partners and he was left not out on 52.

Knowing that Lillee and Thomson had to make an early break-through, Fredericks gave them no chance to settle down, cutting and hooking brilliantly. Walker dismissed Greenidge at 29 but Fredericks and Kallicharran then gave Lillee and Thomson a hammering, their inspired shot-making arousing ecstasy among cheering supporters. Kallicharran hit 35 runs from ten deliveries by Lillee before he was caught for 78. Fredericks went for 58 with only 34 runs still needed, and Lloyd and Kanhai collected these at their leisure, leaving Australia outplayed on the day.

This setback meant that Australia had to defeat England at Leeds on 18 June to secure a place in the final against the West Indies. Gary Gilmour dominated this semi-final match by ripping through England's batting, with deliveries of a full length that swung in the heavy atmosphere and turned either way after pitching. His 12 overs included six maidens and yielded 6 for 14, by far the best bowling figures in international limited-over cricket to that stage.

Australia required only 94 to win but were in desperate trouble at 6 for 39 because of some splendid bowling by Snow, Arnold and Old. Gilmour then joined Walters and together they put on the 55 runs required, Gilmour finishing unbeaten on 28, Walters on 20. Both captains were critical of the Headingley pitch and a match scheduled for 120 overs finished in 65 overs.

The West Indian bowlers had too much firepower for New Zealand's batsmen in the other semi-final in which Kallicharran played another dazzling innings, this time for 72, to set up the final at Lord's on 21 June between the West Indies and Australia. Australia sent the West Indies in and kept them subdued until Lloyd arrived at 3 for 50. Kanhai became the anchor man as Lloyd attacked, reaching a century in 82 balls by hitting 2 sixes and 12 fours. Gilmour was again the star bowler, with 5 for 48 in the West Indian total of 291.

Australia batted defiantly but five run-outs proved too much for them to overcome. Kallicharran started their difficulties with an exhilarating slips catch to send McCosker back and twice threw down the stumps from backward square leg to cause dismissals. Then he returned the ball to Lloyd at the bowler's end quickly enough for Lloyd to break the wicket and run out Chappell. At 9 for 233, Lillee and Thomson hit out in thrilling fashion to take Australia to 274 and within 17 runs of victory, before Thomson's run out gave the West Indies the Cup.

The 15 World Cup matches attracted 158,000 spectators and overall takings of more than £200,000, with 26,000 at the final which drew £66,000 at the gate, a record for limited-over

cricket. The West Indies received £4000 for winning the final, Australia £2000 as runner-up. Each of the participating nations took 7½ per cent of the profits, England 10 per cent as the host.

The World Cup had shown that apart from Lillee and Thomson, Australia had outstanding pace bowlers in Walker, Gilmour and Hurst. When they were joined in the 15 first-class matches that followed the Cup by spinners Mallett and Higgs, they formed a balanced, effective attack. But most critics agreed that it was Australia's superior catching that proved the difference between the teams when Australia met England in the four Tests.

The Australians stumbled in their very first match from 25 to 27 June at Canterbury against Kent. Ian Chappell left Kent to score 354 in 315 minutes, which looked safe enough. Woolmer had to retire after scoring a smart 50 runs when he was struck on the elbow by Lillee. Cowdrey batted brilliantly while Woolmer received treatment and when he returned at the fall of the sixth wicket they formed a formidable partnership, scoring freely all round the wicket to give Kent their first win over Australia since 1899. Cowdrey's 151 not out was his 106th first-class century, and Woolmer's 71 not out brought him into Test consideration. Kent's four-wicket victory was accomplished despite an innings of 156 by Turner in Australia's first innings.

This sparkling cricket continued from 28 June to 1 July at Southampton, where Australia beat Hampshire by four wickets. Barry Richards scored 96 and was on 69 in his second innings when Thomson hit him in the groin and forced him to retire. Thomson then sent Turner off with a broken finger, but Hampshire still set Australia 255 to win in 180 minutes. They scored this for the loss of six wickets with only four balls remaining, thanks to a dashing knock of 127 by Ian Chappell, who hit 4 sixes and 16 fours.

Further good wins over the MCC at Lord's and Glamorgan at Swansea took the Australians

Alan Knott takes a boundary from Ashley Mallett's bowling in the Leeds Test in 1975. Gilmour is at short leg, just in front of 'keeper Marsh.

to the first Test at Edgbaston from 10 to 14 July in outstanding form. Lillee had taken 10 for 132 at Lord's and with Thomson repeatedly bruising his batsmen, Mike Denness postponed the confrontation with them by sending Australia in to bat when he won the toss. This was the tenth time in 215 Tests that England had done this and the move had brought only one victory.

McCosker and Turner put on 80 for the first wicket and later Ian Chappell, Edwards and

Marsh built on this foundation to produce a total of 359. Marsh showed obvious annoyance at his dismissal for 61, following a five-minute delay when a ball that had lost its shape after only eight overs was replaced. A thunderstorm delayed England's reply for 100 minutes, leaving 165 minutes of the second day when play resumed. In that period Australia took seven wickets for 83 runs, which included five wides and a no-ball from Thomson, who was so erratic Chappell replaced him with Walker after only two overs.

Australia took 25 minutes to complete England's rout for 101 early on the third morning, Lillee finishing with 5 for 15, Walker 5 for 48.

When England followed on, only two hold-ups for rain prolonged the agony as Thomson found his length and direction. Lillee struck Amiss such a painful blow on the elbow that the pain made him ill. Only Fletcher survived for long, mixing cuts over the slips with neat deflecting and glides until he miscued and Walters caught him at third slip for 51. Gooch, batting at No. 5 in his Test debut, scored a pair, surviving three balls in his first innings and seven in the second, when he received a nasty lifter from Thomson. Backed by superb catching, Thomson finished with 5 for 38. Only further rain delayed until the fourth morning England's defeat by an innings and 85 runs, England's first loss in 17 Tests at Edgbaston.

Between 16 and 18 July no less than six centuries were scored in Australia's match at Hove against Sussex, but even this prolific scoring—only 18 wickets fell for 1137 runs—took second place to discussion over captaincy. England's selectors had just announced the appointment of Tony Greig, Sussex's skipper, to replace the luckless Mike Denness for the second Test. Ian had handed over the Australian captaincy to his brother Greg, who upset Greig by using the final day against Sussex for batting practice instead of declaring.

Australia began with 7 for 402, McCosker (111), Greg Chappell (126) and Gilmour (102) scored centuries, Gilmour in 75 minutes of batting mayhem which included 5 sixes and 14 fours. Sussex responded with 6 for 401, Parsons (141) and Greig (129 not out) producing centuries. McCosker (115) then completed his second century of the match as Australia meandered to 5 for 334 with Greig awaiting the declaration that did not come. Greig was so angry he issued a written statement deploring the tame ending to the match, which he said denied spectators their right to "proper entertainment".

Ian Chappell batted superbly to set up Australia's win over Derbyshire by an innings and 38 runs from 19 to 22 July at Chesterfield. He took only two hours to make 114, hitting

Lillee traps John Snow leg before in the first Test at Edgbaston in 1975. Australia won the match by an innings and 85 runs, which clinched the series.

5 sixes and 10 fours. Thomson was typically wayward when Derbyshire set out after Australia's total of 9 declared for 398, but he took four wickets in their first innings of 184 and 3 for 6 in a fiery spell when they followed on. Richie Robinson kept wicket in Derbyshire's first innings, Marsh in the second.

After a rain-affected draw with Lancashire at Old Trafford, the Australians suffered another defeat at Leicester from 26 to 29 July. Brian Davison's 189 was the foundation of Leicestershire's first innings of 370, and McCosker's 120 the backbone of Australia's 4 for 313 in reply. With Greg Chappell leading the side despite the presence of his brother Ian, the Australian attack looked second-rate without Lillee and Thomson, allowing Leicestershire to declare at 2 for 217 in their second innings. Set to score 275 in 280 minutes, Australia were dismissed for 243 despite a fighting 102 not out by Walters, with Illingworth handling his attack in masterly fashion. This was the match in which Higgs was no-balled for' throwing and was bowled first ball, by the only delivery he faced on the entire tour.

England brought in the grey-haired, bespectacled David Steele at the age of 33, and Bob Woolmer at the age of 27, to bolster their batting for the second Test between 31 July and 5 August at Lord's, Tony Greig's first as England's captain. Greig went to the crease after Lillee had delivered ten overs for 33 runs and taken four wickets. This was one of Lillee's greatest spells, delivered with supreme control of that lovely high action, every ball considered and landing where he wanted. At the other end Thomson was so erratic he was no-balled 22 times and delivered four wides in between some devilishly fast deliveries.

From 4 for 49 Greig and Steele bravely restored England's innings, Greig using his extreme height to move into front-foot drives, Steele hooking and cutting Lillee's short balls. When Steele left for 50, Greig carried on with the perky Knott (69) until he reached 96. England's total of 315 represented an admirable fight-back, with Chappell persisting with six slips knowing that Thomson might suddenly emerge from his nightmarish lack of control and start finding edges.

Snow demonstrated how wrong England's selectors were in omitting him from the previous Australian tour by taking command of the first session of the second day, during which he dismissed Turner and the Chappell brothers. Lever supported him splendidly by accounting for McCosker and Walters and soon after lunch Australia were 7 for 81.

Australia's last three wickets put on 187 runs. Ross Edwards initiated the recovery with a magnificent 99, hitting 15 fours before he hit across a yorker from Woolmer and was leg-before. Lillee then produced a thrilling show of big hitting during which he connected with three

enormous blows for six and 8 fours, finishing unbeaten on 73 in Australia's total of 268.

Leading by 47 runs, England were far too slow in their second innings of 7 declared for 436. With Lillee bowling off a short run and Walker confined to the role of stock bowler, Edrich took 540 minutes to make 175 in stifling heat before a capacity crowd craving for excitement. Left to score 484 to win in 500 minutes, the Australians settled for a draw. McCosker batted 260 minutes for 79, Ian Chappell the same time for 86. A disappointing match that attracted 120,092 spectators and a gate of £119,692 was memorable mainly for the first appearance of a nude streaker at a Test, a male who risked all by hurdling both sets of stumps.

Walters' 103 paved the way to Australia's nine-wicket win over Somerset at Taunton from 6 to 8 August. Chasing Australia's 7 for 331 declared, Somerset collapsed for 106, with Viv Richards bowled for a duck by Lillee and 20-year-old Ian Botham scoring only eight in his first match against Australia. Following on, Somerset made 281, Mallett (4 for 70) and Higgs (5 for 96) accounting for Botham, Vivian Richards, Brian Close and the other Somerset batting stars. Left to score 57 to win, Australia lost Turner before a run was scored. Gilmour then clinched victory with 2 sixes and 7 fours in making 51 from 37 balls.

At Northampton from 9 to 12 August Australia defeated Northants by five wickets with a spectacular display of hitting on the last day after Ian Chappell had an angry clash with Pakistani Sarfraz Nawaz. Set to score 318 following a fine 102 from David Steele in Northants' second innings, the Australians reached their target in only 214 minutes. The Chappell brothers made 112 in an hour, then Marsh (65 not out) and Ian Chappell (116) added 107 in 54 minutes. Sarfraz, who believed Chappell was caught behind on four, was subjected to abuse and finger signs from Chappell before umpire Alan Whitehead told them to "cool it". This

Rival captains Tony Greig and Ian Chappell study the damage done by vandals to the Leeds pitch in 1975. The match was poised for a thrilling finish but play had to be abandoned.

was one of the matches in which Ian Chappell fielded in the outfield while brother Greg captained the side from the slips.

The third Test at Headingley from 14 to 19 August was abandoned as a draw after vandals, campaigning for the release of convicted criminal George Davis, sabotaged the pitch in the early hours of the fifth day. The culprits got underneath the covers and dug holes with knives near the popping crease and poured a gallon of crude oil in the area where good length balls would have

pitched. Davis was serving a 17-year sentence for his part in a £12,700 armed robbery in which a constable was wounded. Davis was eventually released but was subsequently convicted for another bank job.

The damage to the pitch deprived millions of people who had watched the match on television in Britain and Australia of what appeared certain to be an enthralling climax, with Australia on 3 for 220, chasing 445 to win. McCosker was then five runs short of his initial Test century. Rain which fell from noon until 4 p.m. probably would have produced the same result but the vandalism demonstrated that an overnight guard of one policeman was totally inadequate to protect Test pitches. The captains, Greig and Ian Chappell, considered other parts of the wicket square but could not find a suitable alternative pitch on which to complete the match.

The gates had to be closed for three of the days on which play was possible. Forced to find a place for the in-form Gilmour, Australia dropped Turner and promoted Marsh to open. England led by 153 on the first innings despite Gilmour's fine figures of 6 for 85. Edmonds took five wickets, including those of Ian Chappell and Ross Edwards with successive balls, in his Test debut.

Steele, who made 73 in the first innings, reached 92 in the second before Gilmour removed him. On the fourth day Australia fought hard to get back into the game, taking seven of England's wickets for 107 runs and then making an impressive start to the long chase for 445 runs. Ian Chappell put on 116 with McCosker, who was batting soundly with Walters when the match ended prematurely. Despite rain and the abandoned day, takings reached £54,466.

Laird (127), Edwards (101) and Turner (118) scored centuries in Australia's win over Essex by 98 runs between 23 and 26 August at Chelmsford, but were completely overshadowed by jovial, red-faced leg spinner Robin Hobbs. With Essex requiring 353 to win on the final day, Hobbs made 100 in 44 minutes, the second 50 in 12 minutes off 15 balls. Mallett and Higgs took a pasting as Hobbs hit 7 sixes and 12 fours in the fastest century scored in England for 55 years and the fourth-fastest of all time. Illness and injury prevented Edmeades and Fletcher batting in Essex's second innings and Hardie was left on 88 not out.

All chance of England sharing the series with a win virtually disappeared on the first day of the fourth Test at The Oval, scheduled for 28 August to 3 September. Australia were then 1 for 284 following Turner's dismissal with the score on seven. McCosker got the century he had been so unlucky to miss in the Third Test, his 127 playing a big part in a 277-run stand with Ian Chappell, who went on to 192, four short of his best Test score in this, his final Test as Australia's captain. Walters (65) and Edwards (44) were the best of the other Australian batsmen as the total climbed to 532.

The three-pronged Australian pace attack of Lillee, Thomson and Walker had England out for 191, only Steele (39) and Wood (32) staying for long. Following on 341 behind, England produced their highest-ever second innings total against Australia, but they made painfully slow work of it, taking 886 minutes to reach 538. Woolmer's 149 took him 396 minutes, the slowest century in England v. Australia Tests. Australia made no attempt to score the 198 required to win in 85 minutes, losing two wickets before the end, one of them Ross Edwards in his last Test appearance. The six days taken for this Test made it the longest ever played in England. Receipts were £63,704, attendance 78,000, with Australia taking home the Ashes through the sole win in the series.

Four months after the Australians left for home another Chappell, an Englishman and no relation, Peter Chappell, was jailed for 18 months at Birkenhead Crown Court for damaging the Headingley pitch. Three others who admitted helping him were given suspended sentences.

Chappell pleaded guilty to the damage and for this was sentenced to nine months imprisonment. He also admitted daubing the walls of a building, for which he received a three-month sentence. As he had breached two previous suspended sentences, his total jail term was lengthened to 18 months. Judge Frank Nance said to the four accused: "In this country we tolerate expression of set belief and campaigns provided behaviour is reasonable. But we live under the rule of law. We will not tolerate crime." In a letter read to the court Ian Chappell accepted an apology from the wife of prisoner George Davis for the Leeds vandalism and added: "I hope that in the end justice will prevail and that if your husband is not guilty he will be freed."

Despite the bruises they received, the English batsmen were fortunate that they encountered the Australian fast bowlers after 12 months of constant rain. They were never subjected to the pace off the pitch, nor the bounce, that the English players had to combat in the Australian summer of 1974–75. Nor were they subjected to the blood-curdling crowd noises Lillee and Thomson aroused in Australia.

On a tour that attracted huge crowds throughout a hot summer the presence of Lillee and Thomson ensured English cricket of a financial windfall, and the gates repeatedly had to be closed when they appeared. No spectator could have remained ignorant of why they had taken 95 England wickets within nine months. From a 19-pace approach run, Lillee had moulded a lovely high action through which he could apply a range of variations, with every delivery carefully considered. He easily headed both the Test and tour first-class wicket-takers, taking 41 wickets in all at 21.60, 21 of them in Tests at 21.90.

Thomson was just as exciting to watch, long fair hair flopping, his muscular bowling arm held back behind his thighs, the little stutter in his run-up preceding that unique full arm swing. Not for him the subtleties of swing and leg-cutters, though he could make the ball swerve. Generally, it was sheer pace and the limited available viewing time that accounted for his victims. He took 34 wickets on the tour at 31.14, 16 in the Tests at 28.56, and often bowled better when the shine had left the ball than when it was new.

Two Australians scored more than 1000 runs on the tour, but the side's consistency was shown in the fact that eight of the 15 players made more than 400 runs. Walters headed the first-class averages with 784 at 60.30, a feat often forgotten by his detractors, followed by McCosker with 1078 runs at 59.88 and Ian Chappell, 1022 at 53.79. McCosker, one of the major successes of the tour, scored four of the 18 centuries registered on the tour and headed the Test averages with 414 runs 82.80. Ian Chappell seldom batted better and also scored four tour centuries, finishing with 429 runs at 71.50 in the Tests. Jim Higgs managed to play eight first-class matches without scoring a run, losing his wicket to the only delivery he faced on tour.

Altogether, the twenty-seventh Australian team to tour England won 8 of their 15 first-class matches, drew 5 and lost 2—to Kent and Leicestershire. Walker (36 wickets at 29.88) and Gilmour (28 at 28.17) gave Lillee and Thomson admirable support. Higgs (27 at 32.92) and Mallett (31 at 39.51) provided the spin bowling required. The fielding was of a very high standard.

The tour attracted $89,000 in gatemoney and a profit of $78,000 for the Australian Cricket Board. But the players were out of pocket after receiving $2734 each, the equivalent of $182 a week for the 105-day tour. They complained that this was poor pay from such a successful tour to team manager Fred Bennett and Board chairman Tim Caldwell at a meeting in their London hotel, after which Bennett said: "The players feel $500 per Test for the series against the West Indies in 1975-76 would be reasonable, and that's the figure we will bring up at the next ACB meeting." The Board subsequently announced a payment of $400 per Test for the West Indies series, double the payment paid the previous season.

In stepping down from the Australian captaincy at 32, Ian Chappell left no doubt that his brother Greg should succeed him, fielding in county matches under Greg's leadership. Ian, whose teams had won 15 of his 30 Tests as captain, with 10 draws and only 5 losses, pre-empted the Board's formal appointment of Greg as captain. But just as his players never worried about his expletives on the field, nobody worried about Ian's indifference to protocol. The Australians felt pride in the Chappell family's achievements and Greg's advance to the captaincy was simply a justified honour for the family record. Greg had played 34 Tests in four countries and at the age of 27 had led Queensland to 11 wins in 21 matches and captained Australia in five matches in England.

Six weeks after the Australians arrived home from England, the West Indies began their fifth tour of Australia under Clive Lloyd's captaincy. The Australian Cricket Board had originally scheduled an Australian tour by South Africa for this summer, but when the Commonwealth ban on apartheid prevented this, the West Indies quickly offered to replace the South Africans and a six-Test series was arranged. Lloyd made a helicopter hop round the West Indies to display the World Cup before he sat down with Clyde Walcott, Joe Solomon and Andrew Ganteaume to pick a team. Lloyd and 11 of his players made a two-match appearance in Papua New Guinea in tribute to that country's independence before they opened their Australian visit in Adelaide. The team was C. H. Lloyd (captain), 31, D. L. Murray (vice-captain), 32, K. D. Boyce, 32, Inshan Ali, 26, L. Baichan, 29, R. C. Fredericks, 33, L. R. Gibbs, 41, C. G. Greenidge, 24, V. A. Holder, 30, M. A. Holding, 21, B. D. Julien, 25, A. I. Kallicharran, 26, David Murray, 25, A. L. Padmore, 28, I. V. A. Richards, 23, A. M. E. Roberts, 24, and L. G. Rowe, 26, with Esmond

West Indian captain Clive Lloyd slams a boundary in the final of the 1975 World Cup against Australia. Lloyd was to make five Australian tours.

Kentish as manager and Clyde Walcott as assistant manager.

The thrilling West Indies *v.* Australia match in the World Cup final ensured vast public support for a series between what were accepted as the world's two best teams. The West Indians brought Andy Roberts and Michael Holding to Australia for the first time to support Vanburn Holder, Keith Boyce and Bernard Julien in the forecast bouncer war against Lillee and Thomson. They also included the left-arm leg break and Chinaman bowler Inshan Ali as a backup for Gibbs' off spin.

England's captain Tony Greig also spent that 1975–76 summer in Australia after accepting $20,000 to be captain-coach for Sydney's Waverley club, whose total gate takings in 1974–75 had amounted to $38. Greig was hired solely for club cricket and local coaching and was unavailable for first-class matches. Waverley did not disclose how they raised the $20,000 to pay him.

The West Indies started badly. Undisciplined batting caused them to fight hard to escape defeat against South Australia in Adelaide, from 31 October to 3 November, and against Victoria in Melbourne from 7 to 10 November. Gary Cosier, who had moved to Adelaide from Melbourne, scored 137 against them for South Australia. At Melbourne Ian Redpath, unable to make the trip to England earlier in the year, hit 105 in the first of four centuries he was to make that summer against the West Indies.

Ian Chappell was cited to appear before the South Australian Cricket Association to explain his conduct in the match between 7 and 10 November against New South Wales. Chappell had dropped his trousers to adjust a thigh pad while batting and had bowled two overs of "beamers" or head-high full tosses at New South Wales batsmen. A sub-committee comprising Phil Ridings, Les Favell, Geff Noblet and Howard Mutton warned him that he faced suspension if he offended again.

Alan Turner scored 106 not out and 66 for New South Wales against the West Indies in Sydney from 14 to 17 November, but without the injured Walters his team-mates could not hold out against Michael Holding (6 for 60) in the fourth innings, losing by 52 runs. At Brisbane Inshan Ali bowled the West Indies to victory on a disgraceful pitch between 21 and 23 November against Queensland. Inshan Ali took 5 for 42 and 6 for 36, West Indies winning by an innings and 90 runs.

The Brisbane pitch for the first Test, from 28 November to 2 December, again angered the players. Clem Jones, the city's Lord Mayor, was still chief groundsman, and he endured deserved condemnation for the lack of work done on the Test strip. His covers proved hopelessly inadequate when two electrical storms burst over the 'Gabba four days before play began, but he did show originality in producing a hot air machine to help dry the pitch. Understandably, both teams included two spinners, Gibbs and Inshan Ali for the West Indies, Jenner and Mallett for Australia. The Australians badly missed Edwards, one of the best fieldsmen of his time, who had retired the previous season, and Walters, irrepressible all-rounder, out of the series because of a knee injury.

The West Indies virtually lost the match on the first morning, batting as if it were a limited-over game. They were 6 for 125 at lunch and only a spirited 66 from wicket-keeper Deryck Murray, who put on 72 with Holding, took the total to 214. Gilmour was the best Australian bowler with 4 for 42, with Lillee's 11 overs costing 84 runs, Thomson's 10 overs 69 runs.

Greg Chappell scored a century in each innings in his first Test as captain, an unprecedented feat, although he had previously achieved this under his brother's captaincy in a New Zealand Test in 1973–74. Australia used Ian Chappell in his customary role at first wicket down and he contributed knocks of 41 and 74. Lance Gibbs took 5 for 102 in Australia's first

Gary Gilmour, whose left-arm pace provided top quality support for Lillee and Thomson when they were in their prime. Here he lets one go during his impressive 1975 season.

innings of 366, Greg Chappell (123) adding 122 for the fifth wicket with Marsh (48).

The West Indies began their second innings disastrously, Gilmour sending back openers Fredericks and Greenidge with only 12 runs on the board. At 3 for 50, following the dismissal of nightwatchman Holding, Rowe and Kallicharran put on 198. Rowe, bowled by a no-ball from Thomson, reached 107, and Kallicharran 101, but when they left only Deryck Murray (55) held up Australia. Set to score 219 to win, Australia had to overcome a wonderful spell of off spin from Gibbs, whose 20 overs included eight maidens and cost only 48 runs. Ian Chappell decided to take as much of Gibbs' bowling as possible and his unbeaten 74 was just as important in Australia's eight-wicket win as Greg Chappell's 109 not out.

The brittleness of the West Indies' batting again showed in the match against Western Australia from 6 to 9 December in Perth. After Langer (96) and Brayshaw (100 not out) took Western Australia to 9 declared for 291, Fredericks (108), Richards (175) and Lloyd (105) batted brilliantly to give West Indies a lead of 188. The Western Australians then heavily punished all the West Indian bowlers to reach 520 in their second innings, Hughes producing a swashbuckling 102. Brayshaw's 62 not out gave him 162 unbeaten for the match. Left to score 333 in 220 minutes, the West Indies never tried to save the match but were victims of outstanding leg spin bowling from Paulsen, who took 8 for 71 in 13.1 overs, Western Australia winning by 115 runs.

Meanwhile Ian Chappell was in trouble again for his behaviour in the South Australia *v.* Victoria match in Melbourne. This time Chappell was cited for abusing umpires Jack Collins and Kevin Carmody. ACB chairman Bob Parish said Chappell had been severely reprimanded. The Board had taken into account Chappell's distinguished service to Australian cricket but warned him it could veto the selection of any player who breached the rules.

The second Test at Perth from 12 to 16 December was an amazing affair, studded with brilliant performances, on a fast, true pitch ideal for the West Indian bowlers. Australia began with an innings of 329, with Ian Chappell's 156 making him the fourth Australian after Bradman, Harvey and Lawry to score 5000 runs in Tests. Still fuming from his brush with the Board, Chappell hooked, drove and pulled delightfully as wickets fell at the other end, and after 5 wickets had fallen for 189 shared a stand of 88 with Gilmour (45). Holding bowled Chappell, Thomson and Mallett to finish off the innings in seven balls on the second morning, and ended with 4 for 88.

Fredericks hooked Lillee's second ball off the edge for six but thereafter his left-handed cuts,

Ian Chappell caught by wicket-keeper Deryck Murray, bowled Michael Holding for four in the Sydney Test in 1975–76.

pulls and drives were perfectly timed in a dazzling display of shot-making that brought 130 runs from the first 14 overs. His 169 took only 212 minutes and was scored off only 145 balls, with 27 fours and a six.

Kallicharran retired on 46 not out when a Lillee bouncer broke his nose. While he was absent Lloyd took his score to 149, going from 42 to 140 before lunch on the third day. Kallicharran returned at 7 for 522, going on to

57. Deryck Murray gave another useful display making 63. Australia's fielding was very sloppy and catches were dropped from all the main West Indian run-scorers in a total of 585. Leading by 256, the West Indies clinched an innings and 87-run win through a wonderful spell of pace bowling by phlegmatic Antiguan Andy Roberts, who dismissed the first seven Australian batsmen for 54 runs, relying on sheer speed instead of intimidatory bouncers, and his expressionless face scarcely acknowledging the congratulations or joy of his team-mates.

Both sides played a one-day international match of 40 overs apiece at Adelaide on 20 December. Ian Chappell won the Man of the Match award for his innings of 63 but I thought Max Walker had more influence on Australia's five-wicket win. The West Indies made 224 from 37.6 overs, Walker taking 4 for 19 off 6.6 overs, and Australia took only 31.5 overs to score the 225 needed to win.

The return match between South Australia and the West Indies was reduced to the three days from 21 to 23 December to fit in the one-day match, and this left insufficient time for a result. The West Indies made only 188 in their first innings, left-hander Leonard Baichan topscoring with 72. South Australia responded with 8 declared for 419, Cosier (107) scoring a century, as did Barry Curtin (101). Trailing South Australia by 231 on the first innings, the West Indies used the third day for batting practice, finishing on 4 for 289.

The exceptional pace of the Perth pitch was not repeated in the wicket for the third Test at Melbourne between 26 and 30 December. The MCG pitch did assist the seam bowlers on the first day while there was still moisture in it and it was in this period that Lillee and Thomson gave Australia the advantage they never surrendered. The West Indian bowlers could not match the lift and pace Thomson (5 for 62) achieved when Australia set out after the West Indian total of 224. Redpath had to duck and weave inside plenty of short deliveries, but he had little difficulty remaining for 315 minutes to reach 102. Later Cosier overcame early nervousness to make 109 in his Test debut. Greg Chappell and Marsh contributed half centuries that took Australia to a total of 485, 261 ahead.

The West Indies lost 3 for 48 in their second innings and never recovered, although Lloyd made 102. Steady, accurate bowling, coupled with excellent catching by Marsh, who held five catches in the innings and eight in the match, allowed Australia to wait for careless strokes and have the West Indies out for 312. Australia scored the 55 required to win for the loss of two wickets.

The West Indies made 355 in an eventful first innings of the fourth Test at Sydney, played from 3 to 7 January 1976. Julien fractured his thumb with the score on 15 and resumed at 6 for 259. Lloyd was struck on the jaw at 3 for 166 and resumed at 5 for 233. Holding was hit in the face at 6 for 286 from the last ball of the first day. When he tried to resume from the start next day, umpires Tom Brooks and Ray Ledwidge intervened; the law allows injured players to return only at the fall of a wicket.

At the end of the second day the West Indies appeared in an unassailable position with Australia on 4 for 164, and Greg Chappell struggling against Andy Roberts. On 11, Greg edged the ball to Keith Boyce at fourth slip and Boyce dropped the catch. Greg went on to 182 not out in an Australian total of 405 and thereafter Boyce's lapse was tagged as the turning point of the series.

With strong support from Cosier, Marsh and Gilmour, Greg Chappell brilliantly exploited his escape, scoring 77 from the first nine overs with the second new ball. Lloyd made six bowling changes in this hour, which rattled the confidence of his bowlers. Leading by 50 runs, Australia dismissed Fredericks, Kallicharran and Richards for 33 runs by the end of the third day to grab a winning position. In the absence of Lillee, who was suffering from pleurisy, Thomson bowled at great pace and with accuracy to take 6 for 50 and help bundle the West Indies out for 128. Australia then lost three wickets scoring the required 82 runs to take a 3–1 lead and win the Frank Worrell trophy. Walker in his 24th Test took his 100th Test wicket but all bowling honours went to Thomson for his match effort of 9 for 167.

Two matches against New South Wales country sides and two in Tasmania took the dispirited West Indian team to the Fifth Test at Adelaide from 23 to 28 January to face a now fit Lillee. Viv Richards opened the batting with Fredericks. Richards' promotion stemmed from

Ian Chappell and Clive Lloyd, rival captains on the West Indies 1975–76 Australian tour, share a beer at the end of a hard day

his performances, in the four lead-up matches, scoring two centuries and two nineties and starting the sequence in which he scored the most runs ever in a 12–month period. Over eight months he scored 1710 runs.

Australia lost Turner at 43 in Australia's first innings but Redpath then put on 128 for the second wicket with Yallop (47). Redpath's 103 included 2 sixes—his first in 66 Tests—and 6 fours. Gilmour made another handsome contribution near the end of the innings, with 95 in 139 minutes, to lift the total to 418.

Lillee was quite piqued when Greg Chappell gave the new ball to Gilmour and Thomson at the start of the West Indian innings and confessed later in his book, *Lillee, Over and Out*, that he deliberately bowled badly until a dressing-down from Marsh snapped him out of his sullen mood. He then took two wickets. Thomson, wanting to end the fuss over the new ball, told Greg Chappell he was ready to have second use of it and settled the argument.

Boyce saved the West Indies from following on with a fine 95 not out, but Australia, 144 ahead on the first innings, took a stranglehold on the match when Turner and Redpath put on 148 for the first wicket in the second innings.

Turner (136) batted for 280 minutes for his first Test hundred, which included 15 fours. This allowed Australia to set West Indies 490 to win in 645 minutes. Richards hit a dazzling 101 in three hours with 17 fours and Kallicharran (67) produced yet another splendid knock to take the match into the fifth day, when Boyce's 69 could not stop Australia winning by 190 runs.

Australia won the sixth Test, from 31 January to 5 February in Melbourne, by 165 runs, inflicting a fifth defeat on the West Indies for the first time. They got off to another fine start when Redpath made 101, his third century of the series. Redpath swung Gibbs to deep mid-wicket after reaching his century and Holding took the catch to give Gibbs his 308th Test wicket to pass Fred Trueman's world record. Greg Chappell (68) and Yallop (57) then took Australia to 351.

Lillee and Gilmour found Richards (50) and Lloyd (37) difficult to dislodge but, once they went, the two bowlers humbled the other West Indian batsmen. Leading by 191 on the first innings, Australia moved to 3 for 300 in the second innings thanks to 70 from Redpath, 109 not out by McCosker and 54 not out by Ian Chappell. This gave the West Indies the job of scoring 492 in 600 minutes to win, a task they never got near. Richards played marvellously well for 98 and Lloyd ended on 91 not out after some entertaining hitting on the final morning before the match finished with Australia winners by 165 runs. Lady Worrell, Sir Frank's widow, was on hand to present the Worrell Trophy to Greg Chappell. In the absence of the South Africans, Australian newspapers felt justified in acclaiming their side as the world champions, a title first Pakistan would have the chance to challenge in the 1976–77 season, and then England in the 1977 Centenary Test at Melbourne. Beaten 5–1, Clive Lloyd and Vivian Richards decided the way to international dominance for the West Indies was through fast bowlers like Lillee and Thomson who could inflict pain.

A Revolution

The birth of World Series Cricket; Pakistani team tours Australia 1976-77; Australia tours New Zealand 1977; Centenary Test 1977

The steady erosion of the ethical conduct that had once set cricket apart from other sports continued throughout the 1970s. Legislators failed to restrict the use of bouncers despite the near-death of a tailender in New Zealand. "Sledging", or onfield abuse of opponents, became more obscene and took on a bitterness that frayed tempers. Players left the field without seeking permission from opposing captains. Substitute fieldsmen took up catching positions. Team discipline virtually disappeared. Standards of dress deteriorated on and off the field. Very few batsmen walked any more when they were out.

None of these things were in themselves vital, but together they destroyed what had made cricket synonymous with the highest standards of behaviour. Cricket became a game even schoolboys had to play in helmets, a sport no schoolmaster could conscientiously promote among his pupils or give up spare time to teach.

Lindsay Hassett was one of the first to recognise the decline in the schools' interest in cricket in his role as a sports goods retailer.

Dennis Lillee bowling to nine slips in the Eden Park Test in Auckland against New Zealand in 1977. It has since been alleged Lillee did it to get a good cover picture for a book.

Orders fell off dramatically in the 1970s, with schools boasting 1000 pupils struggling to field two cricket teams. Pupils were offered everything from astronomy to mountain climbing, and in the playgrounds the boys' heroes were Australia's world surfing champions, not its cricketers. Falling standards unquestionably accelerated cricket's waning popularity.

Protective headgear had been in use since the 1870s when the Nottinghamshire star Richard Daft wore a towel round his head batting on a dangerous pitch at Lord's. In 1929, Patsy Hendren returned from Australia with a pith helmet he wore to protect his head, and in 1933 Hendren wore a cap made by his wife with sections lined in foam rubber that covered his ears and temples.

The need for this padding, that had been spurned by Victor Trumper, Joe Darling, Clem Hill and others, began in Australia with Gregory and McDonald and the tactic of using fast bowlers in tandem. Bodyline increased the trend through the expressed wish of Larwood and Voce to prevent shot-making, and down the years, Lindwall and Miller, Hall and Griffiths, Trueman and Statham, Roberts and Holding, Lillee and Thomson popularised short-pitched deliveries.

Mike Brearley wore a headpiece of his own design in 1973, and Sunil Gavaskar developed one that covered his forehead, ears and cheekbones. But it was not until Peter Lever fractured Ewan Chatfield's skull with a bouncer that designers really went to work on batsmen's headgear. The early helmets had bars across the face that interfered with the batsman's vision or side pieces that prevented him hearing calls and resulted in run-outs. As the market for them expanded so did the choice of designs for helmets, forearm, thigh and chestpads, and heavily reinforced batting gloves. Sadly, they were all just as necessary for tailenders as they were for top-order batsmen.

Jim Laker looked at this development with a bemused air and confessed that in all the years he batted near the bottom of the order for England Ray Lindwall never once bowled him a bouncer. "If the day ever came when I have to bowl bouncers at tailenders then I won't deserve to play for Australia," Lindwall said. Wes Hall in his 17 matches for Queensland in 1961 and 1962 had often refused to bowl bouncers at tailenders and even refused at first to bowl one at the Reverend David Sheppard. When his captain "Slasher" Mackay insisted, Hall reluctantly let loose a short pitched ball but in the process the gold cross he wore on a chain round his neck swung up and cut Hall's eyebrow. He took it as an omen and refused to bounce Sheppard again.

Oldtimers scoffed at all the increased protection. Denis Compton wrote that had helmets been in fashion when he went in to face Miller and Lindwall with five stitches in an eyebrow in 1948 he would have refused one because they insulted his manhood. Viv Richards refused to wear a helmet, preferring to face Lillee and Thomson in a cap, which some claimed made it easier for him to move his head quickly, but his team-mates Greenidge, Lloyd and Kallicharran all wore helmets. Brearley wrote that his helmet increased his confidence so much it proved a turning point in his career.

Ian Chappell retired from Test cricket having seldom worn a helmet and ensuring that his brother had a wonderful first season as Australia's captain. His presence in the side sustained the wonderful spirit he had built up since Australia's defeat by Ray Illingworth's English team in 1970–71. He was a great No. 3 batsman, repeatedly rescuing Australia after the early loss of an opener. He had played 72 Tests at the end of the 1975–76 Australian series against the West Indies when he retired to concentrate on club cricket in Adelaide.

Ian Redpath, Ross Edwards, Ashley Mallett and Terry Jenner also retired at the end of the series against the West Indies, unable to continue on the terms offered by the ACB, which seemed curiously unable to help leading players make the jump from part- to full-time professionalism. Their absence left big gaps in the Test team, but they could not be blamed for concentrating on other careers at a time when programmes were scheduling more and more international cricket.

Ian Chappell in his book *Chappelli*, published in 1976, said:

> The Board has a responsibility to see that leading Australian cricketers are satisfactorily rewarded. That means an annual salary for Test cricketers approaching $30,000, plus increases each year to cope with inflation. The figure will send Board money men scurrying for cover, but they should take a closer look at the situation and take into account what could be earned from sponsorships.

Chappell received only $470 from his Sheffield Shield matches in 1975–76, according to journalist Christopher Forsyth, who worked closely with him. This plus his Test appearance payments earned him $4800, less expenses, for the six matches played against the West Indies. Chappell called it "fish and chips money". Dennis Lillee calculated that he made around $150 a Test, after tax and deductions for expenses, which meant $30 a day for five-day matches.

The players explained their difficulties in dealing with the Australian Cricket Board to Bob Hawke at a dinner at Melbourne's Hilton Hotel during the sixth Test against the West Indies. Ian and Greg Chappell, Rod Marsh, Rick McCosker and the retired Test batsman Bob Cowper aired the problem between courses. Hawke, then president of the Australian Council of Trade Unions and president of the Australian Labor Party, agreed that the players had been badly treated over the years but advised them against using terms like "union" and "strike" in their discussions with the Board. The big development from the dinner was that Cowper agreed to become the players' liaison officer.

Apart from match payments and annual salaries for Test players, Cowper was asked to convey to the ACB the players' views on playing conditions, tour programmes, sponsorships and promotion. Sponsorships had got out of hand, with players signing individually to endorse products in opposition to those supported by the Board. Cowper's role was to meet twice a year with the five Sheffield Shield captains and, after a briefing, convey the consensus of their views to the controlling body. The Board refused to accept Cowper's appointment but did agree in September 1976 to set up a captains' committee to examine the players' grievances.

At that stage the former Perth journalist John Cornell, who had great success managing comedian Paul Hogan in the eastern States, became deeply interested in the players' case for more pay. Cornell became a major figure in the players' camp largely because of his access to Kerry Packer, for whom he had produced high-rating television shows starring Hogan. He gave Cowper a long hearing and introduced his former Western Australian journalistic colleague Austin Robertson jnr to the discussion. This culminated in Cowper writing to Ian Chappell that Packer was prepared to invest millions of dollars on big cricket, starting with the 1977–78 season.

In February 1976, Kerry Packer asked the ACB for an appointment so that he could bid for exclusive rights to televise Test and Sheffield Shield cricket. The ACB kept him waiting nearly four months during which time they completed negotiations with the ABC for $207,000 for television rights for three years. When Packer finally had a meeting with the ACB in Melbourne in June 1976, he offered $2.5 million for an exclusive five-year contract, but was told the Board had already signed with the ABC.

After describing this in his book *The Great Cricket Hijack*, Christopher Forsyth said:

> When Cornell went to Packer in late 1976 and suggested a series of one-day matches and Tests organised privately and played as an adjunct to, but

The man who revolutionised world cricket in the 1970s, Kerry Packer, takes block in a journalists' match at Harrogate in England, when his World Series Cricket venture was challenging traditional cricket for crowd support.

not necessarily in opposition to, the traditional game, it was the answer to a prayer for Packer, who said, 'Why not do the thing properly? Let's get the world's best to play Australia's best.'

Packer formed the company that became known as World Series Cricket (WSC) with 98 shares at $1. Austin Robertson received 16 shares and a directorship, Cornell 16 shares, Paul Hogan 16 shares, Kerry Packer 2 shares, with a Consolidated Press subsidiary, Publishing and Broadcasting Ltd, holding the major parcel of 48 shares. Following the instructions of Cowper

and Ian Chappell, Robertson made contact with the players they wanted, got their signatures on contracts, and paid out the signing-on cheques. Forsyth later became WSC's publicity director and Richie Benaud and his wife Daphne were hired as consultants to advise Packer on strategy, particularly in Packer's relations with the Board once the existence of WSC became known.

Freed of his responsibilities as Australia's captain, Ian Chappell led South Australia to win the Sheffield Shield in 1975–76 with a brand of aggressive, positive cricket that produced 5 wins and only 1 loss in 8 matches. Umpires were forced to intervene in several matches in the midst of churlish player outbursts. South Australia had finished last in the two previous competitions.

Well ahead on points, the entire South Australian team threatened to stand down from their last two matches in Sydney and Brisbane unless Brad Drewett, a regular team member, was reinstated to the side. Drewett had been replaced by Bob Blewett, a decision with which the team disagreed. After discussions with the SACA, all members of the team made themselves available and the SACA took no action against the players who had refused to go if Drewett were not included.

The South Australians owed their success to Ian Chappell's inspirational leadership, the experience of Mallett, Jenner and Woodcock and the success of two young batsmen, David Hookes and Ric Darling, who combined to fill the big gap left by Greg Chappell when he moved to Queensland. Wayne Prior proved the best young pace bowler in Australia and took a hat-trick and ten wickets in the match against New South Wales in Adelaide. Prior topped the Australian first-class bowling averages for the summer with 43 wickets at 19.67, and late in the season received handy support from Rodney Hogg, who had transferred from Melbourne to Adelaide.

The previous Sheffield Shield holders, Western Australia, suffered from the loss of their captain John Inverarity, who was in England teaching, but under their new captain Rodney Marsh finished third thanks to the success of youngsters Robbie Langer and Kim Hughes, who scored 119 and 60 against New South Wales in his initial Shield match. Queensland finished second because of the batting skills of Greg Chappell, David Ogilvie, Martin Kent, and the evergreen Sam Trimble, who was omitted from the side late in the season despite scoring 8647 runs in 123 Shield games, second only to Bradman's record of 8926 runs in 62 Shield matches.

Greg Chappell headed the first-class averages with 1547 runs at 85.94, a remarkable achievement considering his Test match responsibilities. Brother Ian was the only other batsman to score more than a thousand runs, with 1310 at 59.55. Lillee and Thomson finished level with 62 wickets apiece but Thomson shaded Lillee in the averages with 23.76 his average cost, compared with 24.03. The only other bowler who got near their bags was Mallett with 56 wickets at 27.52.

The Australian Cricket Board increased payments to the Test players' provident fund during the year but chose not to publicise this move, fearing that players might be compromised by the taxation department. This was an extremely gracious attitude by the Board, which deserved acclaim for replacing the impractical benefit match system with a scheme that rewarded players for their loyalty and long service.

The full effect of the retirements of Ian Chappell, Redpath, Edwards, Mallett and Jenner was quickly shown when the second Pakistani team arrived for a five-match tour, including three Tests, in December 1976. This proved an immensely entertaining tour despite the demand for higher tour pay by Pakistani professionals, who threatened not to come if they were not paid more. A team was announced and immediately scrapped and another selection committee appointed. All the best Pakistani

Martin Kent, the hard-hitting Queenslander whose Test debut was delayed by World Series Cricket. Injury prevented his career developing after the settlement with Packer.

players joined the team captained by Mushtaq Mohammad and a memorable vice-captain, Asif Iqbal, with Colonel Shuja-ud-Din as manager. The team was Mushtaq Mohammad (captain), Asif Iqbal (vice-captain), Zaheer Abbas, Sadiq Khan, Javed Miandad, Imran Khan, Sadiq Mohammad, Sarfraz Nawaz, Salim Altaf, Wasim Bari, Iqbal Qasim, Mudassar Nazar, Sikander Bakht, Asif Masood, and Haroon Rashid.

The Pakistanis agreed to a diabolical itinerary which allowed them only one first-class match against Western Australia on the fast WACA pitch before the first Test. Between 18 and 20 December 1976, Western Australia defeated them by six wickets on a strip ideally suited to the bowling of Lillee, Malone, Brayshaw and

Clark, supported by Paulsen's leg spin. Pakistan began splendidly, putting on 125 for the first wicket, thanks to the stroke-play of Majid Khan (75) and Majid Mohammad (60), but surrendered for a further 149 to an admirable attack. Western Australia declared at 7 for 261 in reply.

Zaheer Abbas's stylish 69 and an unbeaten century by Mushtaq (132) enabled Mushtaq to declare the Pakistan second innings at 5 for 319, which gave Western Australia 240 minutes to make 333 to win. Mushtaq's confidence in his bowlers on a hard, fast pitch turned out to be misplaced, for they took a hammering from Robbie Langer and Kim Hughes after taking 2 for 40. Hughes batted for 210 minutes to score 137 not out, which included 1 six and 14 fours, Langer hit 87 in 135 minutes, his first 50 including a six and 8 fours from only 44 balls.

The first Test at Adelaide Oval from 24 to 29 December ended in a draw but produced a disastrous blow for Australian cricket when Thomson, attempting to catch Zaheer off his own bowling, collided heavily with Alan Turner, who had moved to the catch from short leg. Both were knocked out. Turner was able to continue, but Thomson dislocated his shoulder and took no further part in the series. Thomson also missed the three-Test series that summer against New Zealand and the Centenary Test at Melbourne in March 1977, because of the injury.

On the last day Australia, with six wickets down, needed 57 runs to win in 70 minutes, but big-hitter Rodney Marsh stonewalled and his partnership with Cosier finished 23 runs short. Australian newspapers strongly criticised the home team for not chasing the runs, which suggested Greg Chappell was a more conservative captain than his brother Ian. Greg said he did not give Marsh any orders. Marsh had declined a similar challenge in the third Test with England in 1974–75 when he and Max Walker wanted 55 runs in the last hour but made only seven runs from the first seven overs in that hour.

Pakistan had begun the first Test with an innings of 272, Zaheer scoring 85. Australia's 454 in reply included an elegant maiden Test century from Ian Davis (105), who was supported by McCosker (65) and Greg Chappell (52). The Pakistanis were angry when Walters did not walk when he appeared to be caught behind on 35. The appeal was rejected and he continued on to 107, his 13th century in 58 Tests. Without Thomson's demoralising pace, Australia were further weakened when Lillee strained a thigh muscle and Gilmour was kept out of the attack by a foot injury. Zaheer (101) completed his third Test century and with Lillee and O'Keeffe sending down 65 of the 85 overs on the fourth day, Asif Iqbal batted for 270 minutes to score 152 not out in a total of 466. For Australia to finish 24 short of victory in such a match simply because they were afraid of losing rightly cost Marsh many of his fans.

Australia won the second Test at Melbourne from 1 to 6 January by 348 runs. They made 517 in their first innings through centuries by Greg Chappell (121) and Cosier (168) and took a 184-run lead by dismissing Pakistan for 333 after they had been 2 for 270, Sadiq (105) and Zaheer (90) top-scoring. Umpire Brooks warned Lillee for excessive use of the bouncer and then for taking too long to complete an over. Lillee's 6 for 82 included 5 for 30 with the second new ball. Davis (88) and McCosker (105) carried on after Lillee's splendid efforts with a stand of 175 which allowed Greg Chappell to declare at 8 for 315, leaving Pakistan to score 500 to win. Lillee took his match bag to 10 for 135 in Pakistan's second innings of 151, with O'Keeffe (4 for 38) supporting him well.

At Brisbane from 9 to 11 January Pakistan emerged with a draw against Queensland despite a brilliant innings by Vivian Richards, who hit 4 sixes and 18 fours in his 143 in two hours. Haroon Rashid responded with 1 six and 15 fours in an innings of 123 not out for Pakistan. The bat continued to dominate, Martin Kent scoring

122 not out in Queensland's second innings and Wasim Raja 108, which included 5 sixes and 11 fours, in Pakistan's second innings. Only 24 wickets fell in the three days of this drawn match, for 1204 runs.

All hope of Australia retaining world supremacy, despite the loss of half their team, disappeared when Pakistan won the third Test at Sydney from 14 to 18 January by eight wickets. Australia were out for 211 and 180 thanks to Imran Khan, who took 6 for 102 and 6 for 63. Asif Iqbal made 120 in Pakistan's first innings of 360 and they had to score only 32 in the final innings to achieve their first Test win in Australia.

Shaken by this defeat, Greg Chappell introduced early morning fitness runs when Australia went to New Zealand for a six-match tour that included two Tests. Doug Walters was last out on the first morning wearing a singlet advertising a new brand of cigarettes. On the second morning he wore a T-shirt bearing the slogan "Jogging Can Kill". On neither run was he sighted until the last 200 metres.

Australia's team for this one-month tour comprised G. S. Chappell (captain), 28, R. W. Marsh (vice-captain), 29, R. J. V. Bright, 22, G. J. Cosier, 23, I. C. Davis, 23, G. J. Gilmour, 25, K. J. Hughes, 23, A. G. Hurst, 26, D. K. Lillee, 27, R. B. McCosker, 30, K. J. O'Keeffe, 27, A. Turner, 26, M. H. N. Walker, 28, and K. D. Walters, 31, with Roger Wootton as manager and Syd Mackie as masseur.

The Australians defeated Northern Districts at Hamilton by 113 runs, Wellington at Wellington by 50 runs, Central Districts at Nelson by 65 runs, and Otago at Dunedin by 48 runs, in the first fortnight of February. In this period O'Keeffe took 29 wickets and Bright 25, on pitches that gave them assistance.

Walters had the last laugh, as he usually did, on critics of his early morning jogging by scoring 250 in the first innings of the first Test at Lancaster Park, Christchurch, between 18 and

Gary Cosier, one of the players whose opportunities increased because of World Series Cricket. He was not one of Australia's highest-scoring batsmen, against the weak New Zealand bowling, on the 1977 tour.

23 February. Australia were sent in on a pitch that had bite early but later became easy-paced. From 6 for 208, Walters and Gilmour put on 217, an Australian seventh wicket record against all countries. Gilmour's 101 was his first Test century. Walters took 390 minutes over his 250, his best score in Tests, which included 2 sixes and 30 fours.

New Zealand replied to Australia's 552 with 357, Mark Burgess contributing 66, Geoff Howarth 61. Chappell declared Australia's second innings at 4 for 154, setting New Zealand 350 in 330 minutes to win. At 3 for 203 New Zealand appeared likely winners but some outstanding defensive bowling by Walker and Chappell swung the match Australia's way and in the end New Zealand had to defend stubbornly to avoid defeat. Congdon's 107 not out, his seventh Test hundred, took 270 minutes.

Australia won the second Test at Eden Park, Auckland, from 25 February to 1 March by ten wickets. Australia led by 148 on the first innings after dismissing New Zealand for 229, Lillee taking 5 for 51. Lillee's second innings bag of 6 for 72 gave him a match analysis of 11 for 123 and his 150th wicket in 31 Tests. Hadlee's 81 forced Australia to bat a second time, but they made the 28 runs required without loss.

During this Auckland Test, World Series Cricket secured the signatures of Greg Chappell and Doug Walters. Greg became the highest paid player on the WSC books for a signing-on fee of $11,666 against a salary of $35,000 a year for five years, plus a $5,000 consultant and commentator's fee. WSC also bought his Brisbane house from him for $65,000. Walters signed for $25,000 a year for three years, with a signing-on fee of $8333.

With Robertson securing signatures on contracts and handing out deposit cheques once the contracts were ratified by Packer's legal adviser, WSC moved quickly. Lillee signed for $35,000 a year for three years, Ian Redpath for $16,500 for one year, with a further one-year option, Mick Malone for $19,000 a year for three years, with a two-year option.

Early in February 1977 while Robertson was still busy flying around the world to obtain players' signatures, Packer offered England's Test and County Cricket Board $118,000 for the exclusive rights to a live television relay of the five Tests due to be played between June and August in England. This easily topped the figure offered by the ABC. The offer was referred to the Australian Cricket Board, who said a decision was the prerogative of the TCCB but added that it hoped the support cricket had received over the years from the ABC would not be forgotten. The Board said a joint arrangement should be possible under which the ABC would not be totally excluded from TV coverage of the Tests. Packer was outraged at this and immediately doubled his original offer to $236,000, which won

him the rights he sought from the TCCB.

The Australian players received $2430 for the 35 days they were on tour in New Zealand. The presence of Cornell and Robertson at the Australians' matches made reporters suspicious but Cornell satisfied them by saying he had gone to New Zealand to sign Lillee to appear on Packer's TV show, "A Current Affair". But the WSC team took no chances, conducting their discussions with Walters in a dungeon-like tomb under the Auckland grandstand.

Walters headed the batting averages for the six first-class matches with 441 runs at 88.20, followed by McCosker with 415 runs at 59.28. Ray Bright topped the bowling averages with 25 wickets at 14.64, ahead of O'Keeffe with 35 wickets at 16.22. The Australians lost their two one-day matches but were unbeaten in the three-day games. The tour made a profit of $35,000 for New Zealand, for whom Richard Hadlee was the outstanding player.

The players returned home with ten days in which to prepare for the Centenary Test in Melbourne from 12 to 17 March, which with the tied Test in Brisbane and the first of all Tests in 1877 rates as the most spectacular cricket match ever held in Australia. The match was the idea of Hans Ebeling, who played two Tests for Australia in the 1930s. His idea of inviting all the survivors of 100 years of England *v.* Australia Tests worked superbly, with 244 former players accepting the Melbourne Cricket Club's invitation to attend. A further 26 players informed the club that they were too old and infirm to join what became the greatest reunion in cricket history.

Former Test captain Jack Ryder was Australia's oldest player present at the age of 87 and he died a month after the match ended. Percy Fender at 84 was the oldest of the English contingent. Fender was almost blind and brought his grandson to describe the events for him. The Lancashire left-hander Eddie Paynter, who in 1932–33 left his hospital bed in Brisbane to score what turned out a match-winning 83, was another who enjoyed the match immensely. He also died soon afterwards. The noted English critic John Arlott wrote:

> *The cumulative effect of all these men under the same roof, dining, lunching, watching the play, reminiscing, recalling old triumphs—and failures— across 40 or 50 years produced an atmosphere of almost unbelievable nostalgia. It was an historic triumph and, on a human level, unforgettably reassuring and stimulating for some fine cricketers who had thought themselves forgotten.*

The game matched the occasion and fully rewarded the years of planning Ebeling and the Melbourne Cricket Club put into it. England, captained by Tony Greig, won the toss and put Australia in. Lever, Willis, Underwood and Old bowled superbly, although Willis unfortunately broke McCosker's jaw with a ball that hit McCosker's glove. Only 40 by Greg Chappell and 28 by Rodney Marsh enabled Australia to reach 138. Old had 3 for 39, Underwood 3 for 16 and England fielded with a new-found athleticism.

England's first innings was even more disastrous and not one batsman reached 20. Lillee and Walker were at the peak of their considerable powers as they tumbled England out for 95. Lillee had 6 for 26, Walker 4 for 54, with four catches by 'keeper Marsh completing the rout, taking him past Wally Grout's Australian record of 187 dismissals. The crowd raised their chant of support for Lillee throughout his 13.3 overs. At that stage organisers discussed staging a limited-over match to ensure a crowd was present for the Queen's scheduled arrival on the fifth day.

Australia improved their position on the third day, which ended with Marsh on 95 not out, just short of the first Test century by an Australian 'keeper. David Hookes, the 22-year-old left-hander from the West Torrens club in Adelaide, made a blazing 56 in his Test debut, lifting spectators to a state of ecstasy with five successive drives to the boundary off Tony Greig. Ian Davis (68) and Walters (66) joined in the heavy scoring with some delightful strokes.

On the fourth morning, after Marsh had passed the century, McCosker went in with his shattered jaw heavily bandaged. Batting at No. 10, McCosker scored 25 in a thrilling partnership of 54 with Marsh which allowed Greg Chappell to declare at 9 for 419, leaving England to score 463 to win in 11 hours. Marsh remained unbeaten on 110. Old was the best English bowler with 4 for 104. By stumps on the fourth day England was on 2 for 191, with Randall on 87 not out.

There was a gradual build-up in excitement throughout the fifth day. Amiss and Randall put on 166 before Amiss was bowled by Chappell for 64. In the presence of the Queen and Prince Philip, who were warmly cheered when they drove around the ground, Randall batted with a jaunty, restless style, mixing audacious pulls with flowing drives. Lillee knocked him down with a bouncer but Randall captivated the crowd by bouncing straight up, grinning and rubbing his head. Another Lillee bouncer saw Randall weave away, doff his cap and bow to Lillee. Yet another Lillee bouncer drew a tennis shot from Randall, who hammered it to the midwicket fence.

Lillee's stamina in this battle was as engrossing as Randall's attitude. It created a happy atmosphere to which Marsh responded when umpire Tom Brooks gave Randall out caught. Marsh indicated he had not completed the catch before the ball bounced and after consultation Brooks called Randall back. He was then 161 and he added 13 more before he was brilliantly caught close in on the leg side by Cosier off O'Keeffe. His 174 had taken 446 minutes and included 21 fours, earned Randall $1600 as Man of the Match.

England batted on defiantly, with Knott (42) and Greig pushing the score closer to the target. After Greig became another victim of O'Keeffe, Lillee lifted himself for a final effort, sending

Rick McCosker, broken jaw heavily bandaged, goes out to bat with Rod Marsh in the Centenary Test. The runs they scored, despite McCosker's handicap, proved the difference for a thrilling Australian victory.

back Old and Knott to give Australia victory at 5.12 p.m. by 45 runs, the same margin of victory as in the first Test 100 years earlier. Lillee's team-mates chaired him from the field for his match-winning effort of 11 for 165. England's 417 was the highest fourth-innings total since Tests began.

Amongst all the distinguished old cricketers who pushed their way into the dressing-rooms to congratulate the players on a magnificent contest, Austin Robertson moved cautiously. He had $75,000 in signing-on cheques in his briefcase, each in an individually addressed envelope, and in full view of the members of the Australian Cricket Board and their guests from Lord's

Marylebone Cricket Club he handed them out, saying: "Hey, so-and-so, here's your theatre tickets", as they changed hands.

The day after the Centenary Test, Ross Edwards joined WSC and took his $8333 signing-on fee for a contract of $25,000 a year for two years. This completed the signing of the 28 players Ian Chappell had chosen from Australia. Robertson then turned his attention to signing 18 West Indians and 22 players for a Rest of the World team.

One of his targets was Tony Greig, who recalled:

After the Centenary Test I flew to Sydney to keep an appointment I had arranged to discuss a job with his television station. As I walked into Packer's office, I knew nothing about the plans for WSC. But after discussing a job that I hoped would make

my future after cricket secure, Mr Packer could not contain himself and told me about his World Series Cricket scheme. I was shocked but interested. I knew it needed a lot of thought because, whatever anyone might say, I was not happy to risk the captaincy of England. It took me a week of soul-searching and planning. When I finally signed, Mr Packer said he wanted me to help choose the World team and sign them.

Greig's contract, signed on 25 March 1977, was for $30,000 a year for three years. He was paid an initial fee of $10,000. Greig knew the scheme would not be welcomed by cricket authorities but the more he considered it, the more he believed it would help the players.

Back in England he broke the news to Alan Knott and Derek Underwood, who were stunned but excited by the idea of WSC. He left them to think it over while he flew to Trinidad to rendezvous with Robertson and John Kitto, Packer's legal adviser. They invited to the Trinidad Hilton the West Indian and Pakistani players they wanted among those who were then playing a five-Test series in the Caribbean.

Asif Iqbal signed on 3 April for $25,000 a year for three years. The following day Mushtaq Mohammad agreed to $25,000 a year for three years in what Chris Forsyth, who gave these figures in *The Great Cricket Hijack*, described as a coup for Packer because of Mushtaq's family traditions in big cricket. Imran Khan and Majid Khan followed for $25,000 a year each for three years. Clive Lloyd hesitated but finally signed for $30,000 a year for three years, judging WSC to be a way out of his problem with cartilage and knee injuries which appeared certain then to limit his career. On 5 April 1977 Vivian Richards accepted $25,000 a year for three years, followed the same day by Andy Roberts, on the same terms. On 6 April Michael Holding signed for $25,000 a year for three years on condition that the Jamaican government approved.

Now Greig turned his efforts to contracting

Austin Robertson, chief recruiting officer for Packer's World Series Cricket, a role often wrongly attributed to Tony Greig. Robertson handed out WSC contracts and cheques to Centenary Test players while unknowing officials congratulated them on their performances.

South Africans Eddie Barlow, Mike Procter, Garth Le Roux, Clive Rice and Barry Richards. After enduring isolation from big cricket, they welcomed the concept and agreed to meet Greig in London. Their absence from South Africa was noted and threatened WSC security momentarily, but the media's curiosity was satisfied by a story that a rebel tour of South Africa was planned. Greig wanted to be satisfied before signing the South Africans that the West Indies would be ready to play against them. The West Indians raised no objections and the South Africans were all signed up.

One of the most conscience-stricken of the players contracted by Packer was Derek Underwood, who finally accepted, with the South Africans, $25,000 a year (each) for three years. Underwood spent a restless month considering the proposal before he signed, agonising over his supporters' reactions, but realised he had no trade or profession to follow when his cricket career ended. "For me the security Packer offered was vital," Underwood said. "In one season I could double the income I collected in the tax year April 1976 to April 1977, when I played in a series against the West Indies, had a full season with Kent, and went on a four-month tour of India. Until I signed with Packer, I had been unable to save much money."

The signings went on until a few days before the twenty-eighth Australian team flew to London for a tour involving 22 first-class matches and five Tests. Thirteen of the 17 Australian players had joined Packer's WSC programme of matches from the start of the 1977–78 Australian season and most of them had Packer contracts in their bags when they arrived in London. He had signed 35 cricketers at that stage and later a total of 66. They were: *Australia* (28 players): Ian Chappell (captain), Greg Chappell, Trevor Chappell, Ray Bright, Ian Davis, Ross Edwards, Gary Gilmour, David Hookes, Martin Kent, Bruce Laird, Rob Langer, Dennis Lillee, Ashley Mallett, Mick Malone, Rod Marsh, Rick McCosker, Graham McKenzie, Kerry O'Keeffe, Len Pascoe, Wayne Prior, Ian Redpath, Richie Robinson, Jeff Thomson, Max Walker, Doug

Len Pascoe, Thomson's former bowling partner in Sydney club cricket, found his Test opportunities limited by the presence of the great Dennis Lillee. Pascoe still managed to play in 14 Tests.

Walters, Graeme Watson, Dennis Yagmich, and the former South African Kepler Wessels; *West Indies* (18 players): Clive Lloyd (captain), Jim Allen, Richard Austin, Colin Croft, Wayne Daniel, Roy Fredericks, Joel Garner, Gordon Greenidge, Desmond Haynes, David Holford, Michael Holding, Bernard Julien, Collis King, Deryck Murray, Albert Padmore, Vivian Richards, Andy Roberts and Lawrence Rowe; *Rest of the World* (20 players): Tony Greig (captain), Dennis Amiss, Alan Knott, John Snow, Derek Underwood, Bob Woolmer (England), Eddie Barlow, Garth Le Roux, Mike Procter, Clive Rice, Barry Richards (South Africa), Asif Iqbal, Imran Khan, Javed Miandad, Mushtaq

Mohammad, Sarfraz Nawaz, Haroon Rashid, Zaheer Abbas, Majid Khan (Pakistan), and Richard Hadlee (New Zealand).

Some of the signings were surprising. Dennis Yagmich, the South Australian wicket-keeper from the Kensington club in Adelaide, was offered a contract, for example, because in Ian Chappell's view WSC needed the safeguard of an additional wicket-keeper and he judged Yagmich to be the best after Marsh and Richie Robinson, who had held the Victorian captaincy from the start of the 1976–77 season. Robinson agreed that he cherished the captaincy but to him the decisive factor was that the contract guaranteed his two sons' future. Robinson said: "I knew people would say we had no loyalty. But loyalty would not get my sons a good education." Robinson signed for $22,500 for each of the three years, which made an intriguing comparison with the $35,000 a year for three years offered to Rod Marsh.

Lillee was unavailable for the tour of England. He said the reopening of the stress fracture in his back made it impossible. But all the other leading Australian players were available when Phil Ridings, Neil Harvey and Sam Loxton picked the side to tour. They asked for special fitness reports on McCosker, who was to have an operation on the jaw broken in the Centenary Test, and on the shoulder injury Thomson had sustained in the Adelaide Test against Pakistan. The chosen team all signed tour contracts with the Australian Cricket Board, although only Cosier, Dymock, Hughes and Serjeant had not signed with Packer. The team was Greg Chappell (captain), 28, R. W. Marsh (vice-captain), 29, R. J. Bright, 22, G. J. Cosier, 24, I. C. Davis, 23, K. J. O'Keeffe, 27, L. S. Pascoe, 27, R. D. Robinson, 31, G. Dymock, 30, D. W. Hookes, 22, K. J. Hughes, 23, R. B. McCosker, 30, M. F. Malone, 26, C. S. Serjeant, 25, J. R. Thomson, 26, M. H. N. Walker, 28, K. D. Walters, 31, with former Test wicket-keeper Len Maddocks as manager and Norm McMahon treasurer, Dave

Sherwood as scorer, and S. P. McRae as masseur.

According to Christopher Forsyth, Richie Benaud left Packer the draft of a letter to be sent to ACB chairman Bob Parish informing him of the plans for WSC. This letter left Packer's office on 5 May but because of an air strike did not reach Parish until after news of the WSC coup broke on Monday 9 May.

The Australians had begun their tour at the end of April and played draws at The Oval against Surrey and against Kent at Canterbury before their scheduled match against Tony Greig's team, Sussex, at Hove between 7 and 10 May. The match was abandoned because of rain but Greig invited the tourists and media to a party arranged by his wife Donna. Some of the reporters at the party had heard of the plans for WSC and were seeking confirmation. The *Age* reporter Peter McFarline and the *Adelaide News* writer Alan Shiell discovered at the party that Benaud's close friend Ian Wooldridge was about to publish the story in the London *Daily Mail*, so they decided not to wait any longer and filed the story to Australia.

The news of the formation of Kerry Packer's World Series Cricket broke around the world on 9 May 1977, with the clear intimation that the game would never be the same again. The establishment had clearly misjudged the players' desire for justice when the game's earnings were divided, and the few who understood it had waited too long.

In November 1976, Bob Simpson had negotiated a sponsorship deal with the Sydney brewer Toohey's, which provided for $15,000 in incentive payments to the New South Wales players from the start of the 1977–78 season. In January 1977, the Australian Cricket Board had accepted a deal from the Benson and Hedges cigarette company whereby the ACB would receive $350,000 over the following 15 months, $245,000 of it to go to the players. Both deals turned out to be too late to forestall the Packer revolt.

Night Cricket Arrives

Australia tours England 1977;
India in Australia 1977-78;
domestic cricket 1977-78;
"Super Tests" 1977-78;
Women's World Cup 1978

"World Series Cricket was foreign to all I had known about cricket. I understood why people were shocked, because that's how I felt when I first heard about it. For people to whom cricket was almost a religion we were heretics."

This was how Greg Chappell described his feelings about WSC to author Ray Robinson. He could have added that all the 35 players who originally signed for WSC imagined that their matches would be conducted in conjunction with those staged by the Australian Cricket Board. But Packer's delay in informing the Board of his plans meant they were completely stunned when the news broke and reacted bitterly. When Packer flew into London at the end of May, he told the rebels he still hoped their matches could be conducted with the co-operation of the ACB.

Formation of WSC was splashed so widely across the newspapers of the world, most of the

Kerry Francis Bullmore Packer, whose innovative cricket troupe caused the greatest upheaval in cricket history. And outside the law courts in London with defrocked England captain Tony Greig, who was wrongly labelled the instigator of World Series Cricket.

younger players realised for the first time the enormity of their action in signing for Packer. Page one headlines like the *Daily Mail*'s "World's Top Cricketers Turn Pirate" brought to them for the first time the realisation that their careers were in jeopardy. They looked for solace from their captain Greg Chappell but he could provide none. When Greg confronted the tour managers Len Maddocks and Norm McMahon they accused him of betraying the Board's trust. Letters he wrote giving reasons for the players' action failed to bring answers from Sir Donald Bradman and ACB chairman Bob Parish. When Parish arrived in London for the International Cricket Board conference, he refused to confer with Greg Chappell.

The tour proceeded against a background of angry establishment reprisals against the WSC signatories. Tony Greig was sacked as England's captain for his part in the formation of WSC. When he announced Greig's sacking Cricket Council chairman Freddie Brown said: "Greig's behaviour has inevitably impaired the trust which existed between cricket authorities and the captain of the England side." Richie Benaud found himself shunned by English Test players with whom he had been friendly for years and there was talk of barring him from Test grounds. Derek Underwood said: "It was a terrible time for me and my family. I sensed that people considered me disloyal, a traitor, a money-grabber and worse, when all I was trying to do was get a degree of security for my wife and daughters."

The tour weather was just as dismal as the atmosphere in the Australians' hotel. The match at Southampton with Hampshire, set to follow the game against Sussex at Hove, was washed out without a ball being bowled. Rain prevented play on the first day of the match against Glamorgan at Swansea and in the play that was possible the Australians had to fight desperately for a draw.

After five matches without a result or any decent practice, Somerset defeated the Australians at Bath between 18 and 20 May by seven wickets. Greg Chappell shrugged off his problems to score 99 by lunch on the first morning. Although he went on to 113, Australia scored only 232. Somerset took a 108-run lead through a century (110) by Brian Rose followed by some hefty hitting by Botham (59). A century by Hookes (108) failed to save Australia, and their second innings of 289 gave Somerset only 182 to win in 225 minutes, which they achieved for the loss of three wickets.

Twenty-two wickets fell for 289 runs on the first day of the match against Gloucestershire at Bristol, which Australia won before the end of the second day, 23 May. Gloucestershire's right-arm pace bowler Brian Brain took 7 for 51 in Australia's first innings of 154. Not to be outdone, Max Walker had 7 for 19 in bundling Gloucestershire out for 63. Greg Chappell's 102 took Australia to 251 in their second innings. Set to score 343 to win in a day and a half the home side were out for 169, giving Australia a 173-run win. To fill the blank final day Australia played a 45-over match on 24 May, which they won by six wickets.

Despite this win the Australians' morale continued at a low ebb, with reports that they might all be sent home still persisting. The unity of the team was not helped by the attitude of the four tourists who had not been offered Packer contracts, Cosier, Hughes, Dymock and Serjeant, who joked among themselves about which one might be the next Australian captain.

A 79-run win over MCC at Lord's from 25 to 27 May, and a draw against Worcestershire between 28 and 30 May at Worcester, where Chappell made another century (100 retired hurt), took the Australians into a series of three one-day matches for the 1977 Prudential Cup. England won the first at Manchester on 2 June by two wickets and the second at Birmingham on 4 June by 101 runs, with all the top-order Australian batsmen showing a lack of application.

Rodney Marsh, shown clubbing a huge six in the 1977 Prudential Cup match against England at Old Trafford, proved one of the major attractions of Packer's World Series Cricket.

Before the third limited-over match Greg Chappell called a team meeting to air his displeasure with the players' attitude. They had been outfielded by England and there was a general lack of concentration by batsmen and bowlers unable to sustain pressure on their opponents. At parties he adopted a schoolmasterly role, breaking up heated discussions, calling for music when arguments became noisy. On the field he carried Australia's batting, as he showed again in the third one-day international at Lord's on 6 June. Chasing England's 242, Australia got them for the loss of eight wickets thanks to 125 not out by Chappell.

Rodney Marsh hit 4 sixes and 15 fours in

his 124 in the drawn match with Essex between 11 and 13 June, but a blazing 100 not out by South African Ken McEwan showed up the limitations of the Australian attack. This was one of the matches Greg Chappell and Rod Marsh had in mind when they asked the Australian selectors to send the experienced medium-pacer Ian Brayshaw on the tour. Their suggestion was ignored.

The first Test at Lord's from 16 to 21 June 1977 was staged as a Jubilee Test to celebrate 25 years of Queen Elizabeth II's reign and produced a record gate of £220,384 and an aggregate attendance of 101,050. Australia removed Amiss and the new English captain Brearley for 13 runs, before Woolmer and Randall put on 98. After Randall went for 53, Woolmer prolonged his stay to 270 minutes and then he was smartly run out by Walters for 79, England finishing with 216. Australia took a first innings lead of 80 through solid batting by Chappell (66), Serjeant (81) and Walters (53). Willis sent back all the tailenders to finish with 7 for 78.

Woolmer was again the hero in England's second innings of 305, scoring 120, but the most attractive innings came from Greig, with 91. There were only 165 minutes left when Australia began their second innings needing 226 to win, after 5 hours 43 minutes had been lost to rain. They never seriously attempted the task after losing 2 for 5, and were on 6 for 114 when time expired. Australia's experiment in using wicket-keeper Robinson to open the batting with McCosker had failed in both innings, and although Thomson took eight wickets he suffered from the absence of Lillee.

There were 12 sixes and 73 fours in Australia's total of 531 against Nottinghamshire at Trent Bridge which paved the way to an innings and 98-run win in this match from 25 to 27 June. Serjeant made 159, Cosier 100, Kim Hughes 95, and Davis 72. Malone had match figures of 7 for 135. Draws against Derbyshire at Chesterfield

Mick Malone, the accurate, consistent Perth medium-pacer, was one of the 28 Australians who joined World Series Cricket. Family men found the rewards too high to reject.

and against Yorkshire at Scarborough took the Australians to the second Test at Old Trafford from 7 to 12 July with players still trying hard to justify the team's huge crowd support.

The pitch assisted spin as the match progressed and turned on an outstanding performance by WSC candidate Derek Underwood in Australia's second innings. Australia began with a score of 297, Walters missing his initial Test century in England by 12 runs. Another fine knock by Woolmer, this time for 137, gave England a lead of 140 runs following 79 from Randall and 76 from Greig, Australia fielding so badly that at tea on the second day Chappell gave his team a dressing-down. Australia's second innings developed into a long struggle between Underwood and the Australian batsmen, with only Chappell equal

to the task. Bowling with frustrating accuracy, at a speed too fast for batsmen to meet the ball on the half volley, Underwood invited the batsmen to take risks if they were to score.

Chappell went in to bat after the first wicket fell without a run on the board and stayed until the score reached 8 for 202. During that time he had to forget the regular fall of wickets at the other end in what turned out to be a gem of patience and skill. He was out to the one bad ball Underwood bowled all day, a delivery that pitched short and wide of the stumps. Chappell moved to dispatch it to the fence, got a bottom inside edge, and deflected it on to his stumps. His 112 was his 14th Test century and his sixth against England. Underwood dismissed Walker and Thomson to finish with 6 for 66 from 32.5 overs. Only two Australians apart from Chappell made more than 20 and England got the 79 runs needed at the cost of one wicket.

Meanwhile strange events were afoot in Sydney. Packer's WSC organisation applied on 17 May for the use of the Sydney Cricket Ground, and on 25 July the Sydney Cricket Ground Trust considered the application at length and rejected it. Packer had offered the Trust $260,000 for his programme of matches—$20,000 a day. On the day after they turned down WSC's application, the New South Wales government sacked the Trust and announced that it was to be reconstituted, a move the government said it had planned for some time. The New South Wales Cricket Association then instituted an action in the Equity Court challenging the Trust's right to let WSC use the ground on dates that were needed by the Association.

The Association's case turned on the relevance of the Sydney Cricket Ground and Sports Ground Amalgamation Act of 1951 which gave the Association the priority to use the ground during cricket seasons which it had enjoyed since the nineteenth century. The Trust had for many years sent the Association an annual cheque compensating it for the loss of gatemoney

Rick McCosker drops Geoff Boycott in the slips at Trent Bridge in the third Test against England in 1977. Boycott, who was then only 20, went on to score a century.

when the SCG members attended matches staged by the Association. Mr Justice Helsham decided in the Association's favour and ordered the Trust to give the Association the ground on the dates they required it. The Association's triumph was short-lived, however, for the Wran government simply introduced legislation in Parliament which stripped the Association of its traditional right, pushing through new laws in the middle of the night.

The opposition had it deferred long enough for Packer not to have the use of the Sydney Cricket Ground for the 1977–78 season, but Packer was given access to the ground for 1978–79, when the floodlight towers went up. In the Legislative Council the late Paul Landa said: "In the public interest this new attempt to get sparkle back into the cricket should be supported." Given the long history of laissez-faire in Australia's eastern States, cricket lovers could only ponder on the reasons behind the

sudden revisions to the Sydney Cricket Ground and Sports Ground Act.

While Packer was grappling with his problem of securing grounds where people were accustomed to watching cricket, Greg Chappell continued his magnificent form in England with 161 not out in the drawn match against Northants at Northampton from 16 to 19 July. Richie Robinson took the honours with 137 not out in Australia's 130-run win over Warwickshire at Birmingham between 20 and 22 July. But the batting failed against Leicestershire at Leicester from 23 to 25 July, only Walker's 7 for 45 in Leicestershire's first innings of 178 enabling a draw.

With relations between the players and team manager Maddocks worsening, Chappell called another team meeting. He told them the Packer venture was in the future and to concentrate on remaining united and defending the Ashes. Reports emerged of clashes bordering on violence between Marsh and Maddocks, with Marsh bitterly defending his pride in Australia's green cap.

England maintained their supremacy in the third Test of the rubber between 28 July and

2 August with their first win in a Test at Trent Bridge against Australia since 1930. The win was built on an impressive return to Test cricket after a self-imposed exile of 30 matches by Geoffrey Boycott, who scored 107 and 80 not out and by an impressive debut by a big, lumbering medium-pace bowler with a fondness for spitting, named Ian Botham, who took 5 for 74 in Australia's first innings. Knott gave valuable support by scoring 135 in England's first innings, which made him the first wicket-keeper to score 4,000 Test runs.

Australia made 243 and 309, McCosker scoring 107. England made 364 and knocked off the 189 required to win for the loss of three wickets, Brearley and Boycott making sure of victory with a 154-run opening partnership. Reporters covering the tour blamed Australia's miserable showing in this match on the fact that they had learned just before play began of an International Cricket Conference ban on Packer's players appearing in Test cricket.

From 6 to 8 August at Old Trafford Australia had one of the best wins of the tour, beating Lancashire by seven wickets. On a pitch that encouraged swing and pace early on and later provided bite for the spinners, Australia dismissed Lancashire for 215 and 202, Thomson, Malone and Dymock each taking three wickets in the first innings, Bright 5 for 67 and Chappell 3 for 45 in the second. Hughes topscored in Australia's first innings of 5 declared for 251 with a spirited 89 that included 4 sixes and 8 fours. After taking a rest in the first innings, Chappell made 70 not out in Australia's successful bid to score 167 in 140 minutes, Cosier contributing 66.

England regained the Ashes by winning the fourth Test at Headingley inside four days. Even England's most ardent followers felt it was a hollow victory because of the Australian team's problems with WSC, but there was no denying the completeness of Australia's defeat by an innings and 85 runs.

Before his home crowd Boycott batted on

Australian-born umpire Bill Alley, carefully watching Ray Bright's footwork in the England–Australia match at Headingley in 1977.

the first day as if his century was inevitable, going on to 191, to become the first player to complete his 100th first-class century in a Test match. Two other Yorkshiremen who made 100 centuries, Herbert Sutcliffe and Sir Leonard Hutton, watched him do it. Brearley went to the third ball of the match but Boycott proceeded at his own pace as partners came and went. Only Knott (57) reached a half century at the other end but Boycott's innings gave England a total of 436 and an ascendancy they never lost. Australia made 103 and 248 when they followed on, Botham taking 5 for 21 in the first innings, Hendrick 8 for 95 in the match. The fifth day, 16 August, was not required.

With only one batsman—Marsh (63)—scoring a half century in the fourth Test, the

Kerry Packer heads entrepreneur David Lord from the field in a journalists' cricket match in England.

Australians' morale was at a low ebb as they completed the tour with draws against Middlesex at Lord's between 20 and 22 August, and against England in the fifth Test at The Oval from 25 to 30 August. The Test was a gloomy affair, with almost 12 hours lost to rain, but Thomson's five wickets took him past 100 Test wickets and Malone celebrated his only Test appearance with five first innings wickets and 46 runs, his highest first-class score.

By the end of what must rank as the unhappiest of all tours involving Australian cricketers, Packer had launched an action for an injunction and damages against the International Cricket Conference for banning his players from all matches under their jurisdiction. A temporary injunction was granted against David Lord, claiming that Lord wrongly induced players for whom he acted as agent to break their contracts with Packer. This concerned Alvin Kallicharran, Vivian Richards and Jeff Thomson. By the time the London High Court gave its ruling the case had lasted 31 days. The judgment, covering 221 foolscap pages, took five and a half hours to deliver and found that any attempt to ban players from playing for Packer through changes in the ICC rules was an unreasonable restraint of trade.

So, too, were the proposed bans on Packer players appearing in Tests or county cricket. The costs of the action, estimated at £200,000, were awarded against the ICC and the Test and County Cricket Board.

Packer won a huge victory, but English cricket authorities could take comfort that they had received £150,000 from him for the television relay right to the 1977 England *v.* Australia Tests on Channel 9. As a result of Packer's intervention the massive Cornhill Insurance organisation moved to sponsor Test cricket in England for what was believed to be £1 million over five years.

The Australian tour ended with Greg Chappell announcing his retirement from Test cricket at the age of 29. He had headed Australia's first-class tour averages with 1182 runs at 59.10, which included five of the 11 centuries the Australians made on the tour. The team had ten centuries scored against them. They left behind one of the worst records of all time by winning only 5 of their 22 first-class matches and losing 4, with 13 draws. Max Walker was the only bowler to take 50 wickets on the tour, but his 53 dismissals at 22.33 gave him only third place in the bowling averages behind Bright (39 wickets at 20.35) and Pascoe (41 at 21.78). Thomson took most Test wickets, 23 at 25.34. A major blemish in their record was their defeat by Minor Counties in a second-class match on 4 and 5 August. Minor Counties dismissed them for 170 at Sunderland and scored at the rate of 8 runs an over in the final innings to win by six wickets.

Wisden found the 1977 team a colourless lot and regretted that the pride with which former Australian sides wore the green cap had disappeared. The reticence of commentators Richie Benaud and Ian Chappell, who refused in their Channel 9 broadcasts to condemn the appalling standard of play, was a poor start to the television coverage Packer had fought so hard to secure.

At the end of August 1977, Packer and Clive Lloyd flew to Jamaica for a conference arranged by Lloyd with Jamaican Prime Minister Michael Manley and his senior adviser D. K. Melhado. The Jamaicans said they had no intention of taking sides in Packer's dispute with cricket administrators but stressed they were concerned by his plans to use white cricketers resident in South Africa in his matches. Manley made it clear that the anti-apartheid struggle was held to be a "sacred responsibility". He saw no problems in Packer using South Africans such as Procter, Richards and Barlow who were appearing in English county cricket, but was worried that Packer might use Graeme Pollock and the spin bowler Hobson. Manley, in his book *A History of West Indies Cricket*, said Packer was told:

> *The Jamaican government would do everything in its power to lead the strongest possible Caribbean protest, and where possible, action, should the Packer organisation break the international understanding as a result of which South Africa was excluded from cricket and other forms of sport as long as the system of apartheid was maintained.*

Packer returned to Australia and telephoned the Jamaicans for further consultations during which he said he wanted to make an exception and use Graeme Pollock. He said Pollock was strongly opposed to apartheid and described a match in which Pollock refused to play in protest against apartheid. He was told that however decent Pollock was, no home-based South Africans should play in the Packer matches. Pollock took no part in Packer matches, but the terms of his compensation for Packer's failure to honour the original contract are unknown.

The ACB came up with an intriguing ploy in appointing a successor to Greg Chappell as Australian captain. Looking for a tough, seasoned cricketer with Test experience who could restore a sense of pride in the Australian dressing-room, they persuaded Bob Simpson to come out of retirement. Simpson had continued to play for Western Suburbs in the Sydney district competition after his retirement ten years earlier, with 52 Tests to his credit. He had been involved in the unsuccessful Double Wicket cricket venture in Australia and in 1965 was involved in a libel case with Ian Meckiff, who served a writ on him on the morning of a Test. He was 41 and taking a big risk in returning to big cricket but with India due to tour Australia for the ACB in 1977–78 he knew he would be facing the spin of Bishen Bedi and Chandrasekhar rather than the bouncer-laden pace attack usually seen in Australian summers.

The Board waited four months after the announcement of WSC's formation on 9 May to issue a statement outlining its side of the revolt, preferring to wait until the English tour was over rather than further damage the team's morale. The statement was largely devoted to disputing the payments the players claimed they had received. The Board said each player in the Centenary Test received $2,277 and not $300 as the WSC players alleged. The 17 players on the 1977 English tour received $10,890 and not $6,000 as claimed. The Board had paid the players as much as it could afford.

The WSC players quickly learned when they returned home the full extent of the administration's anger. Ray Bright was barred from playing grade cricket and had to appear for Footscray Technical College. Richie Robinson played on a malthoid pitch as captain–coach of North Alphington to get some cricket. Ian Chappell had to stand down as captain–coach of North Melbourne Cricket Club and Max Walker could not play for the Melbourne Cricket Club. Wayne Prior lost the driver's job secured for him by the South Australian Cricket Association. Bruce Laird and fellow West Australians in WSC were all barred from the WACA club competitions.

All the Australian WSC players met on 14 November 1977 at the Old Melbourne Motor Inn, where Ian Chappell supervised a discussion in which they laid down procedures all would follow. Christopher Forsyth recorded Chappell's comments this way:

Many people have had some cruel things to say about those of you who toured England this year, and a lot of you will be anxious to shove that criticism right down some extra large mouths. But I do want to remind you not to do anything or say anything that will give the press opportunity to have more goes at us. They've shown they don't like what we are doing, and they are only waiting to pounce so they can bury us. I suggest you don't discuss contracts with them. Your contract is your own business. You would not have signed unless you were happy with it. But if for any reason you are not happy with it discuss it with the WSC people and don't go blabbing to the press about it. That isn't professional.

The meeting discovered that places in the Australian team for WSC matches had to be earned, but players would be encouraged to help eliminate weaknesses in other WSC players' technique. Tracksuits were to be discarded for public appearances and slacks and blazers worn. But the speech that united the meeting came from Benaud, who said:

I want you to think about what it means to be called a 'disapproved person'. That's how the cricket establishment sees us—all of us. If you are a disapproved person on the racecourse, you are a person who is warned off. What right have they— because we accepted a retainer from a client—to call us disapproved people?

Over the years as a cricketer, captain, writer and sports consultant, I've done as much for the sport as most people, and perhaps as much as a lot of cricket administrators. I love the game and most of the people in it. Yet I can't adequately describe the feeling of despair I felt when I heard myself described in London as a disapproved person. It was very, very hard to take. I want you to think about it and what that means—it might help to strengthen your purpose and resolve in what we're doing in the months and years ahead.

Packer watching groundsmen install one of their prefabricated pitches in the season that he was banned from traditional cricket grounds. The success of these pitches shocked experts.

Packer lost heavily in the first season of WSC, but built a large, enthusiastic audience for his matches by the start of the second season. The public quickly saw that with most of the world's best fast bowlers in action against the cream of the world's batting talent the WSC matches were keenly competitive and not the exhibitions Ray Steele had in mind when he said he hoped nobody would watch WSC.

The establishment appeared to be winning the fight against Packer while they kept his matches away from traditional cricket venues, but they found him an innovative and resolute opponent. He introduced night cricket at VFL Park in north Melbourne and found the public enjoyed it. He hired the Woolloongabba Cricket

Ground curator John Maley to prepare artificial pitches on giant trays that could be moved to whatever grounds were available and slipped into place when there was not time to prepare conventional pitches. He brought in new rules for limited-over cricket forcing fieldsmen to field inside circles for the first 15 overs before retiring to the boundary.

Coloured clothing for players and umpires upset traditionalists but spectators loved it, just as television viewers found the use of field microphones improved their enjoyment of Channel 9's broadcast. But he did not invent the competitive spirit of the players and while WSC was in existence this spirit was what made it work. They played cricket of an extremely high standard and those who could not reach it were relegated to second team matches in the suburbs and to the schoolboy coaching classes Benaud devised as an adjunct to WSC.

The WSC matches did not affect crowds for the ACB's 1977–78 Indian tour matches. Only in Perth, the newest of Australia's Test venues, were the crowds disappointing. Simpson's rebuilt Australian side played lively, colourful cricket in a spirit Indian captain Bishen Bedi matched and spectators thoroughly enjoyed a series without frequent bouncers and protracted delays while pace bowlers walked out near the sightboards to begin their approach runs.

The Indians surprised even their closest fans by performing well above the form they had shown against England the previous season and with a little luck could have won the series. This was the team they brought for their third tour of Australia: B. S. Bedi (captain), 31, S. Venkataraghavan, 31, S. M. Gavaskar, 28, A. V. Mankad, 29, M. Amarnath, 27, S. M. H. Kirmani, 28, G. R. Vishwanath, 28, C. P. S. Chauhan, 30, D. B. Vengsarkar, 21, S. Amarnath, 29, B. P. Patel, 25, S. Madan Lal, 26, K. D. Ghavri, 26, E. A. S. Prasanna, 37, B. R. Reddy, 23, B. S. Chandrasekhar, 32. Surinder Amarnath was injured and had to return home halfway through

Bob Simpson completes a run after dropping his bat in the India v. New South Wales match in the 1977–78 summer.

the tour. A. D. Gaekwad, 25, replaced him for one match.

The Indians' tour began at Adelaide with the match against South Australia from 4 to 6 November. They achieved immediate success with their first win over a Sheffield Shield side. On a splendid batting strip their spinners had too much guile for South Australia, who were dismissed for 223 and 117. Bob Blewett's 72 in the first innings was the only South Australian score over 50. India struggled because of the bounce in the pitch compared with their home pitches, but managed innings of 168 and 4 for 173 to win by six wickets. Prasanna had 7 for 106, Bedi 8 for 61.

From 11 to 14 November in Melbourne the Indians sustained this form by beating Victoria by six wickets. Paul Hibbert made 100, Yallop 61, in Victoria's first innings of 8 declared for 246. Then India built up a 141-run first innings lead through a painful display by Chauhan, who batted for 525 minutes for 157. Chauhan put on 186 for the sixth wicket when India were struggling at 5 for 165 against the leg spin of Jim Higgs, who took 6 for 131. Trevor Laughlin's 88 not out was not enough to save Victoria, whose second innings of 270 gave India only 130 to win.

At Sydney between 18 and 21 November India defeated New South Wales by six wickets, with all their top-order batsmen scoring freely. New South Wales declared at 5 for 258 in their first innings, to which India replied with 5 for 386 declared, Mohinder Amarnath contributing 137. Bedi (5 for 87) and Venkat (3 for 103) restricted

New South Wales to 287 in their second knock, Simpson scoring 58 and 94 in his return to international cricket. India scored the 160 required to win for the loss of four wickets.

India completed their sequence of wins over all the Shield States except Western Australia when they beat Queensland at the 'Gabba by an innings and 123 runs between 25 and 27 November. They made 8 declared for 353 in their first innings, Vengsarkar scoring 63, Patel 54, Ashok Mankad 69 and Kirmani 59 not out. They then bundled Queensland out for 119 and 111. Bedi had another impressive match analysis, 10 for 73, and Chandra took 7 for 96. This run of wins over four States was a remarkable performance, considering India's lack of a single fast bowler.

The absence of the leading players with WSC gave the Australian selectors a chance to try six new players in the first Test at the 'Gabba from 2 to 6 December: Wayne Clark, Paul Hibbert, Tony Mann, David Ogilvie, Steve Rixon and Peter Toohey. The customary criticism of the pitch resulted in the groundsman over-watering it. This gave the Indian spinners an ideal surface on which to bowl when Australia batted, and only a brilliant 82 by Toohey enabled Australia to struggle to 166, Bedi taking 5 for 55. Toohey scored all of the 34 runs added for the last wicket when he ran out of partners.

Clark sent back Gavaskar with a ball that kicked viciously, but bad light prevented Australia exploiting the still-damp pitch late on the first day. Next day the pitch rolled out splendidly, but none of the Indian batsmen made any headway. Thomson, prevented from joining WSC by his commitment to a Queensland radio network, broke the only prolonged stand when he knocked Vengsarkar's cap off with a bouncer and the cap dislodged a bail. Vengsarkar (48) had put on 75 at that stage with Vishwanath (45).

Leading on the first innings by 13 runs, Australia started their second innings

Simpson square cuts India's Chandrasekhar for four. Simpson's form after ten years out of big cricket amazed all keen followers of the game, and delighted administrators.

disastrously, losing 3 for 7, but stubborn knocks from Simpson (89) and Toohey (57) and some hefty slogging by Thomson (41) and Hurst (26) at the end of the innings took Australia to 327. Following a fine 113 from Gavaskar, Simpson needed all his guile to vary his attack as he worked his way through the Indian batting, India finishing only 16 runs short of victory. Thomson took seven wickets in the match, Clark eight.

Western Australia demonstrated their great

winning by two wickets with 22 balls remaining. The free scoring of both sides was reflected in the aggregate of 1468 runs made in the match. Mohinder Amarnath made 90 and 100, Gavaskar a lovely 127 in the second innings, but Australia matched this with some pugnacious batting, Simpson scoring 176 in the first innings, Toohey 83 and Mann 105 in the second. Mann got his century after being sent in as a nightwatchman on the fourth evening. Bedi took five wickets in each innings, a feat he had accomplished 12 times, although never previously in a Test.

India had their first win in 12 Tests on Australian soil with the third Test at Melbourne from 30 December to 4 January 1978. Their victory was almost entirely due to the spin bowling of Chandrasekhar, who took 12 for 104. India made 256 and 343, Gavaskar scoring 118 in the second innings. Australia reached 213 in their first innings and collapsed for 164 when set to score 387 in the last innings.

By then the Indian spinners had a big psychological advantage over the inexperienced Australian youngsters and they exploited this in the fourth Test between 7 and 12 January in Sydney on a pitch that lacked preparation because of heavy rain. This time Australia managed 131 and 263 and India's first innings of 8 declared for 396 was enough to take the Test by an innings and two runs. Off spinner Erapally Anantharao Prasanna looked the best of a gifted bunch of bowlers, taking 5 for 65 in the match. Toohey's 85 in Australia's second innings included some memorable drives and pulls.

The deciding fifth Test in Adelaide between 28 January and 3 February was marred by Indian complaints over umpiring decisions. Australia began with an innings of 505, Yallop (121), Toohey (60), Simpson (100), and Darling (65 in his Test debut) scoring freely against a strangely inaccurate spin attack. Thomson bowled only 3.3 overs in the match but in that spell he dismissed Gavaskar for 7 and Amarnath for a duck, leaving the field with a torn hamstring. Despite a fighting

strength by beating India in Perth from 9 to 12 December by 150 runs. Charlesworth (95) and Hughes (99) hammered the Indian spinners but the batsman who caught the eye was Graeme Wood, a 20-year-old left-handed opener who made 40. India managed 238 in reply to Western Australia's 5 declared for 366. Western Australia pressed home their advantage with another fine batting display, declaring at 6 for 293 after Charlesworth and Wood put on 138. Set to make 422 in 430 minutes, India were out for 271, the left-arm fast bowler Sam Gannon taking 4 for 70.

The second Test at Perth from 16 to 21 December proved another thriller, with Australia

Gary Cosier hits Bishen Bedi for four in Melbourne.
Despite his Centenary Test century, Cosier's form was
erratic and he was not wanted for WSC matches.

89 from Vishwanath, India trailed by 236, but with six days allotted to the match Simpson did not enforce the follow-on.

Australia were unimpressive against a spin attack that had regained accuracy in their second innings, but the total of 256 gave India a target of 493 in over 14 hours. Without Thomson, the Australian attack looked mediocre. At 7 for 415, with Kirmani and Ghavri going along steadily, India had a chance but the third new ball allowed fast bowlers Callen and Clark to get Australia home by 47 runs.

Australia used 19 players in the five Tests and appeared to have discovered a batsman of rich promise in Peter Toohey, a 23-year-old right-hand batsman of rare power who was hailed as yet another discovery from bush cricket. Toohey came from the country town of Blayney

and learned his cricket at St Stanislaus, Bathurst. His 409 runs at 40.90 gave him second place in the Australian Test batting averages to Simpson, who made 539 runs at 53.90. Thomson headed the bowling averages with 22 wickets at 23.45, with Clark second on 28 wickets at 25.03 and it was in the bowling that Australia suffered most from the defection of so many players to WSC.

Unfortunately, the ACB chose this first season of WSC cricket as the year to introduce Tasmania to the Sheffield Shield competition. The decision to bring a sixth State into the Shield meant a surfeit of first-class cricket and nobody could have been surprised that Shield crowds were down on the previous year. The worst fall of all was in Perth, where there was a 34 per cent decline in attendance despite the fact that Western Australia retained the Shield. The attendance at 22 mainland Shield matches fell from 254,101 in 1976–77 to 179,228 in 1977–78 despite an additional two matches because of Tasmanian participation. In Tasmania 34,293 spectators attended the three matches, with the crowds in Launceston and Devonport higher than that in Hobart.

The Shield competition continued without players contracted to WSC, which had five players who had come out of retirement. This meant that 19 Shield players had to be replaced or one-third of the normal complement of Shield players in the mainland States. All the Shield players received higher match fees and payments to Test players were also lifted. The ACB said this was possible because of increased revenue from sponsors, but formation of WSC undoubtedly influenced the pay boost.

The entire season was conducted in an emotionally charged atmosphere with the supporters of establishment cricket and WSC sniping at each other. In all first-class matches players openly criticised umpires. There was deliberate slow play, over-aggressive fielding, excessive appeals, and post-match criticism by State and Australian captains.

In every State outstanding newcomers emerged. Apart from Wood, Western Australia included impressive performers in Sam Gannon, Bruce Yardley, who was a bowler who had reverted to off spin from medium pace, 19-year-old Geoff Marsh, Craig Serjeant, and Rodney Marsh's wicket-keeper replacement Kevin Wright. Queensland produced the season's highest run-getter in bearded David Ogilvie, who became one of the five batsmen to score 1000 runs in a Shield season and set a record even Bradman, Ponsford, Kippax and McCabe had not matched by scoring six centuries in a season.

Phil Carlson scored runs and took wickets regularly, Kallicharran in his six matches gave Queensland valuable service, and so did Trevor Hohns and wicket-keeper John Maclean who took over the captaincy in the absence of Greg Chappell. Thomson proved the best fast bowler in the country and was largely responsible for Queensland finishing second to Western Australia in the Shield competition.

Graham Yallop averaged 57.11 for Victoria, for whom Sri Lankan-born Davenell Whatmore, Jeff Moss and Julian Wiener, the powerful son of Austrian migrants, also topped 500 runs. South Australia recalled Barry Causby after an absence from the side of four years and he celebrated with a century. Ric Darling, a grand-nephew of Test captain Joe Darling, scored an impressive century for South Australia against Western Australia which won him a Test spot and a tour later to the West Indies. But South Australia were badly let down by their captain, all-rounder Bob Blewett, who engaged in uncalled-for criticism of umpires, Adelaide wickets and other State players.

New South Wales lost four of their first six matches outright and in that time used 15 players, blooding Bob Vidler, David Johnston, Geoff Lawson and Chris Beatty. Andrew Hilditch, 21, took over the New South Wales captaincy after only one season in first-class cricket when Bob Simpson was absent on Test duty. High hopes were held in Sydney for the knock-kneed left-arm spinner David Hourn, the season's leading wicket-taker with 48 victims.

Tasmania entered the Shield competition 126 years after staging Australia's initial first-class match with a restricted programme of five matches. They had substantial public and government financial support and were allowed to play three imported players. The Lancashire all-rounder Jack Simmons captained the side, which included Yorkshire's John Hampshire, and Dennis Baker, a fast bowler who had played regularly for Western Australia. Wicket-keeper Roger Woolley became the first batsman to score a Shield century for Tasmania by making 103 against Queensland at Launceston. Tasmania drew three and lost two of their five matches.

The first international cricket match staged in Australia outside the control of the Australian Cricket Board since 1905 began at VFL Park in the Melbourne suburb of Moorabbin on 16 November 1977, with a match between Australian WSC teams captained by Ian Chappell and Richie Robinson. Chappell's XI won by two runs despite an innings of 124 by Ian Davis, the first century in WSC cricket.

From then on three teams were involved, the Australian XI led by Ian Chappell, the World XI captained by Tony Greig, and the West Indian XI skippered by Clive Lloyd. The West Indian XI consisted of the finest players the West Indies could boast at the time except for Kallicharran, who had withdrawn.

Between 24 and 27 November at VFL Park, Melbourne, the Australian XI played a draw against the World XI. Ian Chappell—who had returned to the captaincy—made a pugnacious 118 in Australia's first innings of 8 declared for 276, and Ian Redpath a studious 152 in the second innings of 7 declared for 325. The World XI collapsed for 148 in their first innings, Prior, Bright and Walker each taking three wickets. The World XI were 2 for 100 in their second innings when time ran out.

VFL Park, home of Australian Rules football, to which Packer's troupe were banished in the first year of their breakaway from traditional cricket.

At Football Park, Adelaide, from 24 to 26 November, the West Indies defeated the World XI by ten wickets. Amiss topscored with 81 in the World XI's first innings of 7 declared for 334, but in their second innings Andy Roberts overwhelmed the World XI, taking 4 for 40 in an innings of 88. The West Indies' first innings of 369 featured a blazing 140 from Lloyd, and they made the 54 needed to win in their second innings without loss. From Adelaide the WSC teams moved to Geelong, where Australia beat the West Indies in a 40-over match, and to Rockhampton, where the World XI beat the Australian XI by 86 runs, Underwood taking a hat-trick in Australia's second innings failure of 143.

After the six preliminary matches selectors settled on their teams for six "Super Tests" in the capital cities. Players who missed selection for these games found themselves playing in virtual second-division matches in Bendigo, Adelaide, Albury, Melbourne, Canberra, Mildura, Geelong, Shepparton, Orange, Maitland, Lismore, Hamilton and Devonport.

From the start the "Super Tests" were conducted with an intensity and hostility Australian cricket followers had never seen before. The fierceness of the pace bowling in all three sides had to be seen to be believed as the months of pent-up anger at the jibes the players had received found expression on the field. Only a lunatic would have batted anywhere in the order in these matches without a helmet. The masseurs worked overtime, but WSC dressing-rooms during the "Super Tests" frequently resembled casualty wards at major hospitals.

At VFL Park, Melbourne, from 2 to 4 December 1977, in the first "Super Test", the West Indies beat Australia by three wickets. Australia began with a total of 256, with Roberts (3 for 52), Holding (4 for 60), and Daniel (2 for 52) at full bore. Lillee, Pascoe and Walker could not match this speed but were accurate enough to dismiss West Indies for 214. Then Roberts turned in one of his greatest displays to take 4 for 52 in Australia's second innings of 192, Walters contributing 63. Sound batting right down the order enabled the West Indies to score the 237 needed for the loss of seven wickets.

Richards' innings of 79 and 56 had proved decisive, and his batting was again the major factor when the West Indies beat Australia by nine wickets in the second "Super Test" on the Sydney Showground between 16 and 18 December. This match proved a triumph for John Maley, with players on both sides agreeing that the artificial pitch he dropped into the Showground a few days earlier was one of the best cricket wickets they had ever played on.

David Hookes topscored with 81 in Australia's first innings of 251 but Hookes paid a big price for the honour, retiring hurt when struck by a bouncer and playing no further part in the match. The West Indies replied with 336, Richards leading the way with a super 88. With Hookes unable to bat, Australia managed only 182 in their second innings, leaving the West

Burly Max Walker, one of the stars of WSC cricket, demonstrates the marvellous "wrong foot" action that made him an unrivalled crowd-pleaser.

Indies to score the 101 they required for victory for the loss of one wicket. Again the pace of Roberts (match figures 4 for 75), Holding (3 for 126), Daniel (3 for 86) and Garner (7 for 113) had contained the classy Australian batting lineup.

But Ian Chappell would not be contained in the third "Super Test" at Football Park, Adelaide, from 31 December to 4 January. His masterly 141, coupled with brother Greg's 90, took Australia to a first innings total of 388. Greg Chappell then took 5 for 20, including two caught and bowled, to rush the West Indies out for 145, Ian Chappell taking two smart catches off Bright. A fighting 106 by Bruce Laird pressed home Australia's advantage in the second innings of 8 declared for 267.

Facing a target of 511 to win, the West Indies were dismissed for 290 after Richards played another gem of an innings for 123. Ray Bright's 6 for 92 in the match played a major part in Australia's victory by 220 runs.

Back at the Sydney Showground between 14 and 19 January for the fourth "Super Test", Laird made another century (106) in Australia's first innings of 304, but Vivian Richards kept the World XI in touch with a breezy 119 in a total of 290. Andy Roberts then swung the match with 6 for 96 to have Australia all out for 128, Garner picking up 3 for 26 to finish the match with 6 for 97. Gilmour took 4 for 26 as Australia made the World XI fight grimly for the 145 needed to win by four wickets.

From 27 to 30 January at Gloucester Park, Perth, Australia did not take a wicket in the fifth "Super Test" until the World XI scored 369. Greenidge, who opened with Barry Richards, retired hurt at 234 and resumed with the score on 3 for 481. Barry Richards made 207, Vivian Richards 177 and Greenidge 140 in the first innings total of 625. Greg Chappell made 174, Ian Chappell 62, but Australia's first innings of 393 was not enough to prevent the follow-on. They were sent back for 159 in their second

Outstanding Australian all-rounder Sharon Tredrea pulls a ball to the boundary at Lord's. Umpire Dickie Bird said she bowled as fast as most men.

innings, leaving the World XI victors by an innings and 73 runs.

At Melbourne between 9 and 13 February in the final "Super Test" Australia defeated the World XI by 41 runs in a tense battle. Australia reached 6 declared for 538 in their first innings thanks to fine batting by Davis (84), McCosker (129), Greg Chappell (246 not out) and Hookes (57). The World XI's first innings yielded 434, Barry Richards scoring 76, Vivian Richards 170. Garner humbled Australia in their second innings, taking 5 for 52 in a total of 167. Set to score 272 to win, the World XI made 230, Walker's 5 for 62 and Lillee's 5 for 82 narrowly triumphing.

Given the high quality of the cricket, crowds for these WSC matches were a major disappointment to Packer and his staff. Packer's losses were estimated at between $10 million and $12 million in his first summer of WSC, with 25,000 for a night match at VFL Park at Moorabbin the biggest crowd. But all the Packer players were paid and with his staff now drilled to a highly professional standard he could afford to shrug off his losses and look forward confidently to a second season in which the New South Wales and Queensland governments had agreed to allow WSC to use Sydney and Brisbane cricket grounds. Everyone who followed that first WSC season knew that in night cricket Packer had a trump card, but a card best played at a traditional cricket ground.

Australia, runner-up to England in the inaugural women's World Cup in 1973 when five nations competed, was the surprise winner of the second World Cup in India early in 1978, against teams from England, New Zealand and India. Australia beat New Zealand at Jamshedpur on 2 January by 66 runs in their first match, by scoring 177 runs in 49.2 overs to 8 for 111 in 50 overs. The Australians followed with a comfortable win over India at Patna on 8 January, scoring 8 for 150 against India's 79, to win by 71 runs and take the World Cup. In the final at Hyderabad on 14 January, England managed only 8 for 96 in 50 overs, a score Australia easily overtook, finishing on 2 for 100 in only 31.3 overs to win by eight wickets.

Sharon Tredrea, whom English umpire Dickie Bird said was as fast as most men, was the star bowler of the series and also made more runs than any of her Australian team-mates. She could cut and swing the ball either way in a manner rare in women's cricket and made her runs quickly and powerfully.

At a meeting of the International Women's Cricket Council after the Cup had been decided the chairperson said that at a time of equality of the sexes she wondered how long it would be before there was a counterpart to Kerry Packer's operation. Packer's interest in women's cricket may have been aroused had he seen the crowd of 35,000 who watched the women's Cup match at Patna between India and Australia. This compared with the crowd of only 3000 who had watched the first women's cricket match at Lord's in 1976 between England and Australia.

Packer Prevails

Australia tours West Indies 1978;
England in Australia 1978-79;
"Super Tests" 1978-79;
Pakistan in Australia 1979

Although the defections to World Series Cricket seriously weakened the Australian team, the scheduled tour of the West Indies between February and May 1978 went ahead. Meanwhile the ramifications of Packer's venture had spread throughout the cricket nations, with Mr Justice Slade's "restraint of trade" High Court ruling creating confusion among officials and delight among most players.

The Kent and Hampshire county clubs found they had to reverse a decision not to engage professionals contracted to Packer. In the Caribbean, nations who were about to sponsor the anti-apartheid Gleneagles Agreement found themselves confronted with the problem of white South Africans playing alongside black players in WSC matches.

None of the WSC players were considered when selectors Neil Harvey, Sam Loxton and Phil Ridings picked the Australian team for the 11-match West Indian tour, although it was

A reunion of the unbeaten 1948 Australian team to England at the Cricketers' Club in Sydney brought this group together: (left to right) Bill Johnston, Ernie Toshack, Keith Miller and Ray Lindwall.

known that the West Indies intended to include their WSC players in the Test sides. At best, the Australian team which went to the West Indies was a third eleven. Only Simpson, Thomson and Cosier had any worthwhile Test experience and of these Thomson and Cosier were technically-deficient innocents in the game. Thomson still had days when he could not decide where to point the shiny side of the ball, and Cosier was still living off his Centenary Test century. Most Australian critics believed the Australian side was in for a shellacking but, as the tour unfolded, events off the field so dominated proceedings even the most statistically-minded West Indians today have trouble recalling what happened on the field.

There was some indecision about the vice-captaincy of the Australian team after Simpson had agreed to lead the side. Craig Serjeant and Graham Yallop were both named for the job before it went to Thomson, a reward for his long service to the game. David Ogilvie was flown in as a reinforcement when Hughes had an appendix operation and Toohey suffered a broken thumb. Ogilvie arrived at the start of the fifth tour match. The Australian squad was: R. B. Simpson (captain), 42, J. R. Thomson (vice-captain), 27, I. W. Callen, 22, W. M. Clark, 24, G. J. Cosier, 24, W. M. Darling, 20, J. D. Higgs, 27, K. J. Hughes, 24, T. Laughlin, 27, S. J. Rixon, 24, C. S. Serjeant, 26, P. M. Toohey, 23, G. M. Wood, 21, G. N. Yallop, 25, B. Yardley, 30, A. D. Ogilvie, 26, with Fred Bennett as manager.

Graeme Wood, the Perth university student, scored a polished century on his initial first-class appearance outside Australia when the tour began at Basseterre, St Kitts, with the match against the Leeward Islands from 17 to 20 February. Wood made 122, hitting 13 fours. Simpson (113) and burly Trevor Laughlin (60) built on Wood's impressive opening with a fifth-wicket stand of 119, to lift Australia to 9 declared for 431.

Jim Higgs also made a marvellous start, taking 6 for 91 and 6 for 71 in the Leeward Islands'

innings of 273 and 221. Leading by 158 on the first innings, Australia built this up to 404 with a second innings of 246. The Leeward Islands never looked likely to score so many against the spin of Higgs and Yardley, Australia winning by 183 runs.

The spinners also paved the way to Australia's six-wicket win over Trinidad and Tobago from 25 to 28 February at Port-of-Spain. Yardley took the honours with 4 for 51 and 5 for 89, Simpson chiming in with his leg spinners and top spinners for a match bag of 5 for 78. Darling's 105 helped Australia to a first-innings lead of 119 and when they dismissed Trinidad and Tobago for 297 in the second innings Australia had the relatively easy task of scoring 179 for a win.

Sent in to bat on a damp pitch in the first Test at Port-of-Spain between 3 and 5 March, the Australian youngsters were overwhelmed by the pace of the West Indies bowlers. Toohey looked confident until he was struck in the face trying to hook Roberts and had to be taken from the field to have the wound stitched. When he returned later, he had his thumb fractured by Roberts and took no further part in the match. Nine Australians contributed ten runs between them in the total of 90, the lowest Test score on the ground.

Desmond Haynes made 61, in his first Test, Kallicharran 127, Lloyd 86, in the West Indies' first innings of 405. Test newcomer Derek Parry was out first ball for a duck and bowled a wide with his first ball when given a bowl in Australia's second innings of 209, which gave the West Indies victory by an innings and 106 runs inside three days. Roberts had 2 for 26 and 5 for 56, Croft 4 for 15, Garner 3 for 35 and 2 for 39.

Serjeant (114) and Simpson (102) made centuries against Barbados between 11 and 14 March at Bridgetown, but a fighting 108 from wicket-keeper David Murray and a career-best 79 from Albert Padmore enabled Barbados to hold out for a draw.

The second Test at Bridgetown from 17 to

19 March was a repetition of the first, with the West Indian pace bowlers too much for the Australians. Garner had 8 for 121, Roberts 5 for 129, Croft 5 for 100 in the Australian innings of 250 and 178. The West Indies were all out for 288 in their first innings thanks to a fine display by Thomson (6 for 77), but lost only one wicket scoring the 141 needed in the second innings. Packer's West Indian players had upset their Board by demanding more pay just before the first Test, and from that point relations between them rapidly worsened. The players were angry when the West Indian Board relieved Deryck Murray, their spokesman, of the vice-captaincy. Similarly, the Board was upset when Richard Austin, Colin Croft and Desmond Haynes signed with Packer despite a verbal assurance that they would not do so. The showdown came when the Board omitted three Packer players—Austin, Haynes and Deryck Murray—from their third Test team. Clive Lloyd immediately protested and resigned the captaincy and within two days the rest of the Packer players joined him. Board chairman Jeff Stollmeyer called a meeting with the Packer players but when nothing was resolved a new West Indian team was announced and a ban imposed on the Packer players for the rest of the series.

The trouble reverberated throughout the Caribbean, with the Packer players' supporters calling for bans on the remaining Tests. The West Indian Board and their selectors were urged to resign. The Board countered that they had done everything possible to accommodate the Packer players, who refused to say if they were available for the forthcoming tour of India and Sri Lanka. WSC players had been dropped to allow team-building for that tour.

In the midst of the protests and counter-protests, Kerry Packer flew to the Caribbean to encourage his players, and he sent his personal jet around the islands to take them to his Barbados hotel to have dinner with him. Then Packer appeared on Caribbean television to speak of how

poorly paid West Indian Test players were, an approach that won wide sympathy for Lloyd and his WSC cohorts.

The Australians took a battering in the match against Guyana on the old coffee plantation known as the Bourda ground at Georgetown from 25 to 28 March. Ric Darling and Graham Yallop, batting without a helmet, put on 166 for the third wicket. Darling made 123, which included 1 six and 11 fours. Yallop was on 118 when he had his innings ended by a bouncer from Croft which struck him on the jaw as he tried to hook. An X-ray revealed a fracture and he could not play for three weeks. Yardley, affectionately known to team-mates as Kangaroo Dog, made the mistake of casting aspersions about the straightness of Croft's arm when he let loose his quicker ball. Croft, a huge hunk of a man who came off the shrimp boats to play Test cricket, gave Yardley a bouncer which thudded into the back of his head and opened a nasty wound. X-rays cleared Yardley of a fractured skull but the blood was still dripping from the wound when they stitched up his head in Georgetown Hospital.

Manager Fred Bennett issued a statement, after Yardley was carried away, objecting to Croft's over-use of the bouncer, which Bennett claimed was in "direct contravention of both the law and the tour conditions". Bob Simpson was on the field twice to complain to the umpires, and even called for a copy of the tour conditions to be brought on to the field for their scrutiny. The match petered out in a draw, with 1280 runs and four centuries scored, including a second-innings 114 not out from Cosier.

Freed from the ordeal of facing the West Indian pace bowlers, the Australians scraped home in the third Test from 31 March to 4 April at Georgetown by three wickets. The West Indian team included six players new to Test cricket and had only two men, Kallicharran and Parry, who had played in the earlier Tests. Facing the pace of Thomson and Clark, all the West

Indian batsmen except Alvin Greenidge, no relation to Gordon, and Sew Shivnarine, showed their inexperience.

After bowling the West Indies out for 205 on the first day, Australia stumbled. At 5 for 90, a plucky innings of 67 by Simpson, supported by Rixon (54) and Yardley (33), took Australia to 286, a lead of 81. Centuries by Basil Williams (100) and Larry Gomes (101), and useful knocks from Shivnarine (63) and Parry (51) boosted the West Indian total to 439.

Chasing 360 to win, more runs than either country had ever scored against the other in the fourth innings to win a Test, Australia lost 3 for 22, before a 251-run fourth-wicket stand by Wood and Serjeant swung the match their way. Serjeant's 124 included 18 fours and 1 six, Wood's 126 8 fours and 1 six. On the last day Australia required 69 to win with four wickets in hand, but the West Indies' lack of experience showed and Australia lost only one more wicket in scoring the runs. One week after being taken from the Bourda ground with his feet twitching, Yardley hit the winning boundary in a Test on the same field.

After beating the Windward Islands by 52 runs on a treacherous pitch that allowed Clark to take 12 for 71, the Australians flew to Port-of-Spain for the second time for the fourth Test, betweeen 15 and 18 April. Kallicharran won the toss and topscored with a clever innings of 92 in which he manipulated the strike after his side had lost 2 for 16. Basil Williams (87) continued in fine form and considering rain had leaked through the covers the West Indies were pleased with their score of 292. Australia fell just two runs short of this after Yallop (75), Toohey (40) and Serjeant (49) batted soundly. Bandy-legged Vanburn Holder finished with 6 for 28.

The West Indies' second innings of 290 was far more than it would have been had Australia held their catches. Set to score 293 to win, Australia collapsed for 94. Derek Parry, the right-arm off spinner from the tiny island of Nevis,

took five wickets, four of them bowled, turning the ball prodigiously to finish with 5 for 15, while Trinidadian Raphick Jumadeen took 3 for 34 at the other end with left-arm spinners. The West Indies' win by 198 runs was watched by less than 15,000 people over four days because of a boycott organised by a placard-carrying group supporting the sacked WSC players.

On the first day of Australia's match against Jamaica at Kingston, umpire Douglas Sang Hue twice no-balled Bruce Yardley for throwing. Yardley bowled off spinners with a leg spinner's grip at a brisk pace and could drift the ball away from right-handers or cut it back, but he was never again called for throwing in a career that covered 100 first-class matches. Operating exclusively from Sang Hue's end, he virtually won the match for Australia by taking 5 for 64 in Jamaica's second innings. Left to score 233 to win in the final innings, Australia reached their target with the ninth-wicket pair, Thomson and Yardley, together. Once again Yardley hit the winning runs.

The tour ended amid acrimony when Australia was denied victory in the fifth Test at Sabina Park, Kingston, where spectators rioted and invaded the field. Before a ball was bowled the Australians objected to Sang Hue, one of the West Indian Cricket Board's original choices to umpire. The West Indian Board agreed to a replacement, Wesley Malcolm, but expressed their faith in Sang Hue. A decision by Malcolm touched off the disturbance that ended the match.

Australia held the upper hand throughout. Toohey hit a maiden Test century that allowed Australia to recover from the loss of early wickets, his 122 including 10 fours. His stand of 133 with Yallop lifted Australia's total to 343. They then bowled the West Indies out for 280, despite a laborious 115 by Gomes. All the Australian top order made runs in their second innings of 3 declared for 305, Toohey reaching 97, Wood 90. This set the West Indies to score 369 to win. Kallicharran took 150 minutes to make

The fifth Test at Kingston in 1977–78 was typical of the troubles that dominated the tour. This shot shows police trying to restore order on the fifth day. The umpires refused to make up time with a sixth day.

his first 50 but scored the second in only 56 minutes on his way to 126.

Once Kallicharran fell lbw to Higgs, the West Indies floundered. When the eighth wicket fell at 242, Holder and Phillip gave up the chase for runs but dug in to save the match. With 6.2 overs of the mandatory final 20 overs remaining, umpire Malcolm ruled Holder caught behind by Rixon. Holder and Phillip stirred the crowd by showing angry disagreement, Holder at first refusing to leave. The crowd erupted, raining stones and debris onto the field. All attempts to complete the match that day were fruitless, although police chiefs and both captains appealed to spectators to retreat behind the fence. Next morning the West Indian Board offered to extend the match to make up the time lost but when they summoned umpire Ralph Gosein from his hotel he refused to continue.

The early finishes in the first two Tests, and the fourth Test crowd boycott turned the tour into a financial disaster for the West Indian Board, who estimated they lost more than £100,000. The Australian team lacked drawcards, with only Toohey and Wood emerging as potentially top-class players. Yallop headed the first-class averages with 660 runs at 55.00, but often appeared uneasy against pace bowling. Toohey made 567 runs at 51.54, Wood 779 at 41.00. Yardley and Higgs bowled more overs on the tour than any of the Australian bowlers, Yardley's 347.3 overs producing 41 wickets at 21.70, Higgs' 354 overs 42 wickets at 22.21.

Victorian Jim Higgs, who kept the art of leg spin alive through the 1970s and early 1980s producing several match-winning displays.

Yardley also topped the Test averages, with 15 wickets at 25.13.

The Australians won 5 of their 11 first-class matches, lost 3 and drew 3. They scored 11 centuries and had nine scored against them. Gomes made three of these but the classical batting in the series all came from Kallicharran, who made centuries in the first and fifth Tests. Only Vivian Richards compared with him.

Initially, the West Indies had been alone among the cricket nations in trying to field their strongest possible teams by picking Packer players. The rest were quite ready to take heavy defeats and big falls in their gate receipts rather than play Packer men. Pakistan took a thrashing in England in 1978 through excluding Zaheer Abbas, Asif Iqbal, Mushtaq Mohammad, Majid

Khan and Imran Khan, winning only one of their 16 first-class matches and losing the Tests 2–nil. Forced to visit India with a second-string team without WSC players, the West Indies lost the rubber 1–nil.

On his return from the unsuccessful tour of the West Indies, Bob Simpson asked the Australian Board of Control for a guarantee that he would be picked to play against England in 1978–79 if he continued in first-class cricket. The Board refused to agree to this and Simpson retired with 10 comeback Tests behind him, spared from the job of captaining the weakest side Australia had put into the field in 102 years of competition between the countries.

During his comeback Simpson took his total of Test catches past Ian Chappell's 103 to 110, which gave Simpson 383 first-class catches in his career. He finished with 21,029 first-class runs at 56.22, 4869 in 62 Tests at 46.81. In all first-class matches he made 60 centuries, a stubborn cricketer of copybook technique.

Packer's expenses for the first season of WSC had been increased by his failure to appoint a manager who could prevent wastage on newspaper advertising, eliminate disputes with unions whose members handled his prefabricated pitches, and prevent friction among his players. The World XI manager Mike Denness clashed repeatedly with Tony Greig, who assumed the right to run the World XI as he pleased. Neither did Greig get on well with Rudi Webster, the West Indian team manager, whose players had the best results and won more prizemoney in WSC's first summer, $78,375 compared with $61,699 by the Australians and $61,424 by the World XI. Webster was one of the first to recognise that WSC could provide permanent benefits for cricket.

Packer's first-year losses were offset by the success of WSC matches on television. Ratings proved they attracted excellent day and night audiences, and according to TV industry people like Christopher Forsyth, at a cost of $4346 an hour WSC cricket was far cheaper than first-run American TV dramas which cost $5000 an hour or the $28,000 an hour Packer paid Crawford Productions for Australian-produced drama like The Sullivans. The high public interest in the 51 days of televised WSC cricket was not lost on advertisers the second time around.

In its second season, with Andrew Caro as a cost-cutting managing director, a streamlined WSC easily won the duel with traditional cricket for public support. Banners even appeared at grounds bearing "Thanks, Mr Packer" messages and, though they had been able to attract increased support from sponsors, establishment cricket officials were a very worried lot long before the end of the summer.

Mike Brearley's twenty-third English team began their Australian tour early in November with a defeat in Adelaide by South Australia, for whom John Nash made 124 and Rodney Hogg took 6 for 72, including Boycott's wicket in both innings. A tame draw followed against Victoria in Melbourne, and although England revived to beat New South Wales by ten wickets in Sydney and Queensland by six wickets in Brisbane, the month passed with little public interest at the box office.

The problem was that most Australians were aware that Australia without its WSC stars would be no match for an English side which included tough, seasoned professionals and in Gower and Botham a touch of brilliance the home team lacked. The England party was: J. M. Brearley (captain), 36, R. G. D. Willis, 29, R. W. Tolchard, 32, D. W. Randall, 27, D. I. Gower, 21, G. Boycott, 28, G. Miller, 26, I. T. Botham, 23, G. A. Gooch, 25, R. W. Taylor, 37, P. H. Edmonds, 27, C. M. Old, 30, C. T. Radley, 34, J. E. Emburey, 26, J. K. Lever, 28, M. Hendrick, 30, with Alec Bedser as manager, Ken Barrington as assistant manager, and Bernard Thomas as physiotherapist.

On 28 November 1978, when Ian Chappell led the World Series Cricket Australians onto

Sydney Cricket Ground in Sydney's first match under lights, more than 50,000 attended. It was the night World Series Cricket was accepted and there is unlikely ever to be another to match it in Australian cricket. Packer campaigned hard in the days beforehand, appearing personally on commercial radio. On the morning of the match he predicted a crowd of 20,000 but said he would be content with 15,000.

The surge of people trying to get into the SCG was so great as the start of play approached Packer called to the gateman not to worry about collecting entrance money but to open the gates and let everyone in. There was the air of a big occasion around the ground. Phones were provided for every reporter and TV monitors, at that time an innovation, were set up at the back of the press box to provide instant replays. The dressing-room doors were open to all pressmen, even those the WSC players disliked. The players wrote what they liked about the game in newspapers and had their wives staying with them in the same hotel. At the meal break between innings the public were invited onto the ground, New Zealand style. Promotion of WSC's theme song "C'mon Aussies, c'mon" on the 9 Network took it to near the top of the charts.

The WSC players had begun their second season in New Zealand with a match between an Australian XI and a World XI from 4 to 6 November 1978, in Auckland. John Snow had joined WSC, but had to wait until Julien, Hadlee and Rice had a bowl before he got the ball. Australia began with a first innings of 184, made possible by a brilliant knock of 74 from Greg Chappell. The World XI replied with 128, finding Lillee in formidable form in taking 7 for 59. Greg Chappell was again the hero in Australia's second innings, scoring 89 out of a total of 196. Lillee was just as deadly in the World XI's second innings of 85, taking 5 for 30, leaving Australia comfortable winners by 167 runs.

Seven one-day matches followed in

Auckland, Tauranga, Wanganui, New Plymouth, Wellington, Hastings and Auckland, before the players flew to Perth to open their Australian programme with a limited-over match between Australia and a World XI on 23 November. Rivalry between the players intensified in one-day matches in Kalgoorlie, Bunbury and Perth, before they flew on to Sydney for that memorable opening night of cricket under lights.

There was no denying the popularity of one-day cricket, although traditionalists refused to watch it. Oldtimers like Test bowler Bill O'Reilly wrote in scathing terms of the "pyjama game", and attacked innovations like the coloured clothing and the white ball, but the matches brought a new audience to cricket, people eager for fast runs and a result in one day.

Cricket under lights had an eerie quality, with players brought somehow closer than they were by day to spectators who could see the beads of sweat on their faces as puffs of breath vaporised in the night air. Close finishes created an atmosphere English writers aptly compared to the Colosseum when the lions appeared. The sight of Colin Croft clubbing a mighty six into the Ladies' Stand with two runs to win off the final ball sent them home in a paroxysm of delight.

All the Packer players pre-recorded responses to a questionnaire covering every possible cricket occurrence. When Ian Chappell dropped a slips catch, up on the screen you would find his picture telling you how he felt about such an event. The concept worked well because Packer's panellists could find the appropriate part of the tape with amazing speed. To entertain spectators in the dinner break, a rock band circled the ground.

To match this, traditional cricket tried its hand at show business. When the first Test was played at the 'Gabba between 1 and 6 December the captains tossed with a special coin commemorating fifty years of Test cricket in Queensland, brought to them by skydivers who landed near the pitch. Yallop, captaining

Australia for the first time following Simpson's retirement, had a difficult choice but decided to bat in humid conditions. Under thick cloud cover, Willis, Old and Botham swung the ball at will and had Australia 6 for 26 and all out for 116.

The Australian team was seriously weakened by the absence of crowd favourite Jeff Thomson. After a 12-day court hearing Justice Kearney ruled that Thomson should honour his contract with the Australian Cricket Board and not play for WSC before April 1979. Thomson chose to retire temporarily, saying he would never play for Australia again.

Rodney Hogg, who topscored with 36, followed by taking 6 for 74, and Hurst bowled just as fast for his 4 for 93, but the ever-perky Randall helped England to a 170-run lead with a solid 75. Australia began their second innings by losing the wickets of Cosier and Toohey with only two runs on the board, and when Wood went at 49 it appeared unlikely England would need to bat again. But a defiant stand of 170 in 255 minutes made the score respectable. Yallop made 102, Hughes staying 90 minutes longer for 129, leaving England to score 170 to win. They achieved this for the loss of three wickets, Randall completing a fine double with 74 not out.

At Perth between 9 and 11 December England needed only half an hour longer than two days to defeat the Sheffield Shield champions Western Australia by 140 runs. Hendrick, Lever and Botham exploited the fast green pitch, low cloud cover and strong wind to bundle Western Australia out for 52, their lowest-ever score against an international side, and 78. Hendrick took 5 for 11 and 3 for 23 to finish with the remarkable figures of 8 for 34. Botham's match analysis was 8 for 53. England had similar problems but their greater experience of these conditions and a superb 61 not out in the first innings by Tolchard clinched the win.

Meanwhile in Melbourne WSC batsmen also struggled for runs in the first "Super Test" of

Alan Hurst leaps for joy as he successfully appeals for lbw against England in the 1978–79 series with England. Randall had made 13 on the Melbourne Ground, where he had triumphed two years earlier in the Centenary Test.

the 1978–79 season between Australia and a World XI at VFL Park from 8 to 11 December. The World XI found scoring difficult on an uneven pitch exposed to strong winds, only Miandad (59) surviving long in their first innings of 175, though Rice produced a valuable 41 near the end. Big Garth Le Roux's pace brought him 5 for 39 and had Australia out for 150 in reply.

Majid Khan (77), Mike Procter (66) and Zaheer Abbas (44) took the World XI to 257 in their second innings, leaving Australia to score 283 to win. They survived the opening onslaught from Le Roux and Procter, but folded for 180 before Imran Khan (4 for 30) and Underwood (4 for 59), despite a brilliant 81 from Greg Chappell.

England took a 2–nil lead in the establishment cricket series by beating Australia in Perth from 15 to 20 December by 166 runs. England laid the foundation for their success on the first day when Boycott batted seven and a half hours for 77 in which he hit only one four, and Gower scored 102 in exhilarating style. These contrasting innings took the total to 309, Hogg taking 5 for 65.

Willis responded with a similarly impressive display on the fast, well-grassed WACA pitch, taking 5 for 44 to send Australia back for 190.

Toohey's batting in his 81 not out deserved a century but he ran out of partners, only one of his team-mates passing 20. Hogg repeated his first-innings form with 5 for 57 in England's second innings, to give him 17 wickets in the two Tests, but England's 208 set Australia 328 to score for a win. England achieved an initial breakthrough, but with Australia 4 for 58 began spilling catches. This prolonged the innings to 161, Australia's last six wickets falling for the addition of only 20 runs.

Back at the SCG in Sydney from 21 to 23 December there was some glorious batting in the "Super Test" between a World XI and the West Indies. Zaheer Abbas confronted Holding, Roberts, Garner and King at full stretch with an array of dazzling strokes. When Zaheer left for 91, Clive Rice (83) and Mike Procter (56) had a stylish South African partnership before Asif Iqbal crowned it with a knock of 107. Chasing 471, the West Indies were all out for 217, Lawrence Rowe scoring 85. Following on, the West Indies managed 210 and were beaten by an innings and 44 runs.

In Adelaide at that time the official England team needed two runs from the last ball to defeat South Australia, but Geoff Miller managed only a single, leaving the match drawn. They then moved to Melbourne for the third Test between 29 December and 3 January on an MCG pitch that provoked criticism before a ball was bowled. Australia secured a big advantage by winning the toss and batting and a breezy opening stand of 65 delighted spectators. Tragedy struck when Darling was run out, but Wood went on to an even 100 and Australia reached 258.

With the pitch playing tricks from the second morning, England's batsmen made the mistake of playing back, exposing themselves to occasional low deliveries. Hogg relished the conditions and disposed of Boycott and Brearley for three runs. England's difficulties continued before splendid bowling by Dymock and when Hogg returned he took three more quick wickets

to have England out for 143.

Australia managed only 167 in their second innings but on such a sub-standard pitch the final innings target of 283 always was beyond England. Boycott (38), Gooch (40) and Gower (49) fought hard but Hogg's pace sealed an unexpected win for Australia by 103 runs. Hogg's 5 for 30 and 5 for 36 were outstanding figures in a Test in which Willis did not take a wicket. The Sydney left-hander Alan Border made 29 and a duck in his Test debut.

Melbourne fans were overjoyed at this victory, and altogether 128,758 people turned up to see it. But Packer was also drawing good crowds by exploiting the appeal of limited-over matches with his star players while the second-string players appeared in two-day matches in country centres. Between 30 December and 29 January, WSC played 15 limited-over matches, three in Brisbane, two in Sydney, one in Adelaide, three in Melbourne, one in Armidale, one in Sydney, three in Melbourne and one in Hamilton. In this period they also staged two-day matches in Bendigo, Tamworth, Orange, and Albury between teams labelled the Cavaliers and the World XI.

The mobility of John Maley's team of workers in moving pre-prepared pitches around to all these centres and providing splendid batting surfaces was astonishing. But the big advantage Packer enjoyed throughout the 1978-79 summer was that he could use both the Brisbane and Sydney cricket grounds, fields from which he had previously been ostracised. Sydney had the added advantage of floodlights, with night cricket a novelty everyone wanted to watch.

Brearley's team quickly recovered from the shock of their Melbourne defeat in the fourth Test at Sydney from 6 to 11 January. They were bowled out on the first day for 152, with Hurst generating considerable pace to take 5 for 28 and Higgs bowling straight at the stumps to finish with 3 for 42. At lunch on the second day Australia were 1 for 126 and seemed to have

A determined Rodney Hogg during the 1978–79 series against England. He had an unpredictable temperament.

complete control of the match, but from that point England staged an amazing comeback.

Hughes was caught off the first ball after lunch to end his 125-run stand with Darling. Although they lost Willis with a virus infection, England stuck to their task and had Australia out for 294, Darling contributing 91, Border 60 not out.

Hogg trapped Boycott lbw with the first ball of England's second innings, Boycott's first duck in 67 Test innings since 1969, but Brearley and Randall slowly restored England's position, adding 111 for the second wicket. Dropped at 113, 117 and 124, Randall went on to 150 for his best knock since his memorable 174 in the Centenary Test.

Despite Randall's gutsy effort in batting for 9 hours 49 minutes, Australia were left to score only 205 against an attack in which Willis and Botham were unwell. Brearley said it was a difficult target on such a pitch and set fields that kept most of his players in catching positions. The Australians obliged with a miserable batting display. Wood ran himself out for 27 and only Border (45 not out) resisted for long in a total of 111. The 93-run win gave England the Ashes and earned Brearley a place among England's finest captains.

While the official English team played in Newcastle against a Northern New South Wales Country XI, had a draw in Hobart against Tasmania, and appeared in three limited-over matches in Sydney, Launceston and Melbourne, WSC wound up their Australian programme with three "Super Tests", having kept their equivalent of traditional cricket's Test matches until the majority of the Australian population were on their annual holidays.

The first "Super Test" from 12 to 15 January at VFL Park, Melbourne, was drawn after Wessels (126) and Hookes (116) made centuries in Australia's first innings of 366. Lawrence Rowe, wearing contact lenses, then produced a sparkling 175 in the West Indian XI's 419 in reply. The Australians declared at 9 for 304 in their second innings, but time ran out with the West Indies on 2 for 126, chasing 252 to win.

Ray Bright gave the outstanding performance of his career to clinch the Australians' 10-wicket win over the West Indies in the next "Super Test", at Sydney between 21 and 24 January. The West Indies scored 163 in their first innings, with Bright bowling an impeccable line and length and drifting the ball subtly. Australia fared only marginally better against the West Indian pace men, Croft taking 5 for 65 in an innings of 185. Lillee then swept the West Indies aside with 7 for 23 in their second innings of 89. Australia then made the 68 needed to win without loss.

The final "Super Test" produced a five-wicket victory for the World XI against Australia in Sydney from 2 to 4 February. Australia were dismissed for 172, Le Roux taking 5 for 57, Procter 3 for 33. Lillee matched Le Roux's effort with

Kim Hughes narrowly escapes a run out following a fine return from Derek Randall in Sydney in the 1978–79 series.

5 for 51 in the World XI's reply of 168. After a brave 58 by Laird, Hookes lifted Australia to a winning position, but when he was run out for 96 their second innings collapsed for 219. Left to score 224 to win, the World XI got them for the loss of five wickets, thanks to a brilliant 101 not out by Barry Richards. A two-day match on 3 and 4 February at Devonport, in which Australia's Cavaliers beat a West Indian XI by 31, concluded the WSC season.

England showed just how weak Australia had become as a result of the WSC signings by winning the fifth Test in Adelaide by 205 runs between 27 January and 31 February and the sixth Test in Sydney, from 10 to 14 February, by nine wickets. This gave England an unprecedented 5–nil margin in the series and meant that in the space of 20 months since he took over the captaincy from Greig, Brearley's team had beaten Australia 8 times in 11 Tests and suffered only 1 defeat.

Australia had their chances in the fifth Test but let the match slip away from them in England's second innings when they allowed tailenders Miller (64) and Taylor to more than

double the England total. Taylor then added 69 more runs with Emburey, which gave England 204 runs while he was at the wicket. Taylor's 97 was his highest Test score and took six hours. He was so laborious in fact that he lost the Man of the Match award to Ian Botham, who followed his 74 in England's first innings of 169 with 4 for 42 in Australia's first innings of 164.

Hogg's seven wickets in the match took him past Arthur Mailey's record 36 victims in an England v. Australia series, set in 1920–21, but he gave his captain Graham Yallop plenty of problems. Hogg altered his field without referring the changes to Yallop and at one stage walked from the field saying he had breathing problems. Yallop later wrote that when he asked Hogg not to leave the field without his permission Hogg suggested they they survey the back of Adelaide Oval—"and I don't think Hogg had a tennis match in mind".

Yallop got some solace from a miserable season as Australia's captain by scoring 121 out of the first innings total of 198 in the sixth Test. England took a 110-run lead by scoring 308 in their first innings, Gooch (74) and Gower (65) punishing all bowlers. Australia virtually conceded the Test by making only 143 in their second innings, Yardley topscoring with 61 not out. England scored the 35 runs needed for the loss of Boycott's wicket, but not before a long argument in which Brearley protested against Australia opening a Test innings with an old ball.

Brearley had the Laws of the Game and the tour conditions on his side but umpires Weser and Crafter allowed him to be overruled. The argument delayed the start of the final innings for six minutes and caused a forgettable series to end amid acrimony. A lone trumpeter on the Sydney Hill greeted Australia's heavy defeat by sounding the Last Post. Only J. W. H. T. Douglas (1911–12), A. P. F. Chapman (1928–29) and D. R. Jardine (1932–33) achieved records comparable to Brearley's, by winning four Tests in a five-Test series.

Ian Botham's athleticism is clearly demonstrated as he dives to the left to catch Rodney Hogg close in off Emburey in the Sydney Test during England's 1978–79 Australian tour.

The entertainment provided by the official English and Australian teams was limited to the periods when Gower or Randall were batting or fielding, when Hogg decided he could breath well enough to let go a few really fast overs, or when the Australian openers were contriving to run each other out—they succeeded in losing a wicket this way in all six Tests. This was very dull fare compared with the drama of all the Packer matches, which had grown into something far more absorbing than administrators, in all the cricket nations, had imagined. The English critic Tony Lewis said this in a report to the London *Sunday Telegraph* from Sydney in January 1979:

The most dangerous act in the entertainment business these days is not balancing on the high wire or even putting a head in the lion's mouth. It is, without doubt, batting in Kerry Packer's Flying Circus. Fast bowling and repeated bouncers are destroying some of the best batsmen we have ever seen. I have never seen so many bouncers bowled in a session as by the World XI against the West Indies in a one-day game this week.

There was no quarter given and none asked. Joel Garner, batting with a broken left finger, was subjected to a fierce bouncer barrage from Clive Rice and had to leave the field when hit again on that finger. Tony Greig in the Sydney *Sun-Herald* said competition was so intense teams could not allow tailenders to hang around. Consequently the pace bowlers dished out bouncers to "the rabbits" and forced cricketers like Lillee and Le Roux to wear helmets.

Wisden said that WSC matches attracted 730,000 people through the gates in the 1978–79 season, compared to 580,000 who went through the turnstiles to watch traditional cricket. A higher advertising response and costs substantially lower than in its initial year produced substantial gains for Packer, whose JP Sports and Television Corporation Ltd showed a 26 per cent increase in profits. The Australian Board lost $445,000.

Immediately the Australian season concluded Packer sent his WSC players to the West Indies to play five "Super Tests", exploiting a lack of first-class cricket in the islands due to the absence in India and Sri Lanka of the West Indian national team. This venture helped rescue the financially endangered West Indian Cricket Board and territories it administered, each of whom received ground rental fees, plus a proportion of the gate above an agreed figure. The West Indian Board itself received an ex-gratia payment to compensate for any loss of interest in the islands' Shell Shield series.

Before he joined his players in the Caribbean, Packer had a secret meeting in America with International Cricket Conference chairman David Clark and MCC secretary Jack Bailey. He knew that members of Brearley's official England team, angered that their rates of pay were well below what Packer paid, wanted to push for a ban on Packer cricketers appearing in county teams at a coming meeting of the Cricketers' Association. He had threatened to take his WSC troupe to England if such a ban was passed and nobody doubted that he would get the grounds he needed in England to make this a success, as some ideal cricket fields were not owned by counties, but by city corporations in need of money.

The presence of WSC players in English county teams created widespread ill-feeling in the 1978 northern summer, with WSC men ignored on the field and forced to change in silence in the dressing-rooms. Alan Knott stood

down from the Kent side rather than submit to this treatment. Warwickshire decided not to renew Dennis Amiss's contract but changed their mind in discussions with the English Cricketers' Association.

The ICC officials, led by MCC chairman Charles Palmer, the former Leicestershire amateur batsman, refused to comment on their discussions with Packer but were known to have been impressed when he produced balance sheets showing that he could afford to continue for years with WSC. Later the Australian Cricket Board chairman Bob Parish and the treasurer Ray Steele said they had been advised to proceed unilaterally to a settlement with Packer for the sake of all international cricket.

After each side had had a win in limited-over warm-up matches, the "Super Tests" began at Kingston, Jamaica, from 23 to 26 February. Jeff Thomson, after spending the Australian summer fishing, opened the bowling with Dennis Lillee. The pace bowling from both sides again achieved undreamt-of fury, with bouncers galore. Lillee struck Lawrence Rowe on the temple with a ball which Rowe said he lost sight of in the background of the new George Headley Stand. The ball caused a depression in Rowe's helmet which fractured his temple.

Clive Lloyd won the match for the West Indies with a masterly knock of 197. West Indies made 188 and 481, Australia 106 and 194, with none of the Australians scoring 50 against the pace of Croft, Roberts, Holding and Daniel. The margin of victory was 369 runs.

The second "Super Test" at Bridgetown from 9 to 13 March was left unfinished after bottle-throwing spectators interrupted play on the second and fifth days when Fredericks and Greenidge showed disagreement with umpiring decisions. Australia scored 311 in their first innings, thanks to 61 from Greg Chappell and 78 by Martin Kent, and then gave themselves a splendid winning chance by dismissing the West Indies for 239 despite a dashing 89 by Fredericks.

They extended their advantage by scoring 294 in the second innings, Ian Chappell (86) and Greg Chappell (90) batting superbly. The West Indies were on 4 for 133, chasing 367 to win, when time ran out.

More bottle throwing united the Australians in the third "Super Test" at Port-of-Spain, Trinidad, between 16 and 20 March. They gave a magnificent display to win by 24 runs, after being 5 for 32 in their first innings. Bruce Laird made 122 in Australia's first innings total of 246, which saw Michael Holding (5 for 48) at his athletic best. West Indies found Thomson (5 for 78) equally troublesome in scoring 230. Greg Chappell then played what many consider the innings of his life to score 150 in Australia's second innings of 282, Padmore taking 6 for 81. Brilliant catching enabled Australia to dismiss the West Indies for 274.

The crowd violence reached its peak in the drawn fourth "Super Test" at Georgetown, Guyana, between 26 and 28 March. Greg Chappell produced another remarkable century (113) in an innings of 341, which Collis King (110) emulated in the West Indies' reply of 476. Heavy rain then flooded the outfield and although the pitch was covered conditions were impossible for cricket. Despite this, announcements were made at the ground and over local radio that play would begin on time and spectators were admitted to the ground. Frequent inspections by Lloyd and Ian Chappell only confirmed that no play was possible. Finally the lack of information stirred the big crowd to a riot. They wrecked the pavilion, destroyed club records, and forced players to cower in the changing rooms, wearing helmets as protection against missiles.

Ian Chappell apparently believed the West Indian official Vic Inshinali helped provoke the crowd's anger with his announcements that the match would continue. Chappell pleaded guilty later in court and was fined for "unlawful assault" on Inshinali.

The final "Super Test" at the recreation ground in St John's, Antigua, produced another draw and another superb century from Greg Chappell (104). He was run out in the second innings for 85. This time Rowe (135) was the West Indies' batting hero. Australia, 234 and 6 for 415, recovered bravely after trailing by 204 runs in the first innings. The hectic, often brilliant cricket rescued the West Indian Board's finances and produced further profits for Packer. Veteran cricket writer Phil Wilkins says the five "Super Tests" in the West Indies were the most fiercely contested cricket he has ever seen.

Back in Australia while these WSC matches were being played, Pakistan made a four-match end-of-season tour that included two Tests. Pakistan recognised the futility of fielding second-string teams and included all their eight WSC players. Five of them made centuries during the tour. Unfortunately, WSC player Asif Iqbal derided the quality of cricket provided in the England–Australia series that had just been completed. This led to ill-feeling and unsportsmanlike incidents in both Tests.

The first tour match against New South Wales from 3 to 4 March was set down for Sydney but was moved to Canberra when it was found that the towers that housed the lights for Packer's night matches caused a troublesome shadow on the SCG pitch. Rain in Canberra allowed only two hours play, during which Pakistan lost 4 for 53.

At Melbourne in the first Test from 10 to 15 March, Hogg (4 for 49) and Hurst (3 for 55) tumbled Pakistan out for 196, but Australia's batsmen failed dismally by scoring only 168 in reply. Hogg was run out by Miandad as he left his crease to inspect the pitch after playing a defensive stroke down the wicket. Although he was recalled by Mushtaq, umpire C. E. Harvey confirmed his decision. Hogg thereupon knocked down his stump with his bat.

Pakistan reached 9 declared for 353 in their second innings because of Majid's brilliant 108, his seventh Test century. Set to score 382 to win

Rodney Hogg, never one to hide his feelings, knocks down his stumps in disgust after being given out in Melbourne against Pakistan. He did the same thing in India in 1979 when no-balled.

in the final innings, Australia wanted only 77 runs with seven wickets in hand following sound batting by Hilditch (62), Border (105) and Whatmore (84), before Sarfraz Narwaz took an amazing seven wickets for one run off 33 deliveries to give his side victory by 71 runs. From 3 for 305, Australia were all out for 310. Sarfraz's 11 for 125 in the match could hardly be hailed as one of the great bowling feats, given the standard of the Australian team.

After a draw against South Australia in Adelaide, Pakistan started the second Test in Perth, from 24 to 29 March, strongly favoured to win. They justified this while Javed Miandad was at the crease scoring 129 not out in their first innings, but could total only 277. Australia

took a 50-run lead by scoring 327, Darling contributing 75, Border 85. Asif Iqbal made 134 not out in Pakistan's second innings but, like Miandad in the first innings, found support lacking. Pakistan's 285 left Australia to score 236 to win. The Pakistan innings ended when Hurst ran out Sikander at the bowler's end when Sikander backed up before Hurst let the ball go. Australia suffered from similarly unpleasant behaviour when Hilditch was given out "handled the ball" when he gathered a wayward return at the bowler's end and handed the ball to Sarfraz. Hilditch was, at the time, only the second batsman in Test history given out in this way. (South African Russell Endean was the first in 1956–57 against England at Cape Town.) Sarfraz's appeal left the umpire with no alternative.

Darling completed a fine double by scoring 79 before he was run out. Australia reached their target with Border on 66 not out and Moss on 38 not out to win by seven wickets and share an ill-tempered series one win apiece.

The shadow that had forced the move from the SCG to Canberra for Pakistan's match with New South Wales was not a problem in the Sheffield Shield, which in 1978–79 produced an evenly fought competition. Four States were in a position to win at one stage, but with Board of Control matches against two visiting countries and the WSC matches competing for attention, only 134,552 watched 25 Shield matches.

The Australian Cricket Board found itself offering higher pay to Shield cricketers who indulged in unnecessarily slow play, got involved in an increasing amount of sledging, and went round the country like undisciplined hobos, neglecting to shave, scorning team uniforms for thongs and brief shorts. Most Shield players received about $400 a match. Victoria had to use 19 players in the season but won the Shield for the first time since 1973–74 by winning four of their last five matches.

John Maclean retired as Queensland's captain

with a record 313 dismissals (289 caught, 24 stumped), which surpassed the career achievements of his famous predecessors, Don Tallon and Wally Grout. John Inverarity completed his last season for Western Australia before transferring to South Australia with his 23rd century. The remarkable all-rounder Ian Brayshaw also retired from the Western Australian team after 17 seasons in which he scored 4325 runs at 31.80 and took 178 wickets at 25.08. Andrew Hilditch was spoken of as a future Australian captain after his inspiring leadership of New South Wales. Tasmania, led by Lancashire professional Jack Simmons, had their first-ever Shield win by beating Western Australia at Devonport by four wickets. But the public showed little interest and officials in all States blamed Packer instead of looking at their own administrative efforts.

Richie Benaud's involvement in the Packer revolt and his memos advising Packer on how to handle establishment cricket saddened many of Benaud's admirers. Christopher Forsyth, publicity officer for the Channel 9 network in Melbourne, said in his book *The Great Cricket Hijack* that Benaud's company received $30,000 for their work in September 1977. Benaud defended his role, arguing that he was a sports consultant and as such free to accept assignments from any organisation, but right across the cricket world, from Denis Compton in London to Gerry Gomez in Trinidad, there were feelings of disgust and disbelief at the part he had played in WSC.

Packer had lost a lot of money in bringing world cricket to its knees. Attendances and income from WSC and traditional cricket had been split to the detriment of both sides. Some Australian State associations were close to bankruptcy and funds for Shield and junior cricket were rapidly disappearing. England was afraid some Counties would go broke if other nations continued to send second-rate teams to England. The West Indies were virtually insolvent with all their top players signed to WSC.

Although the cricket nations had agreed that no country should act unilaterally to end the Packer revolt, the International Cricket Conference sent a delegation to Australia, headed by ICC Chairman Charles Palmer, to consult with Packer. After the conferences the delegation gave the Australian Cricket Board signed permission to act unilaterally to end the dispute. Both sides wanted a settlement and in April 1979 a series of amicable discussions began in Melbourne, with Packer, his Finance Director Harry Chester and his PBL Marketing Manager Linton Taylor confronting Bob Parish, Ray Steele and Board Secretary Alan Barnes. Preliminary talks had already taken place with Tim Caldwell, the previous Australian Cricket Board Chairman, who was also a top executive in the Packer family's bank.

An Alarming Settlement

Australia in India 1979; England and West Indies in Australia 1979-80; domestic cricket 1979-80; Australia on tour 1980

Australia spoke for world cricket at the settlement conferences with Kerry Packer and his PBL Sports chief Lynton Taylor. Ostensibly they met in Melbourne to end an Australian problem, but in reality Packer's activities had created major problems throughout the cricket nations in the two years of WSC which everyone wanted to end.

The two men with this enormous responsibility were contrasting figures with long experience in cricket administration, Raymond Charles Steele, a dour solicitor whose family owned suburban hotels in Melbourne, and Robert John Parish, a tall, thin-faced Melbourne accountant, fond of practical jokes, but more aloof from the players than Steele.

Steele was educated at Melbourne's Scotch College and at Melbourne University where he won Blues for cricket and football. He was captain of Hawthorn–East Melbourne Cricket

A group of schoolboys at Beechworth, Victoria, take advantage of blue skies and a climate that is ideal for cricket for most of each year.

Club in 1948–49, president from 1957 to 1973, and had been the ACB treasurer since 1969. He captained the Victorian Amateur Australian Football team in 1939 and played VFL football for Richmond from 1940 to 1943. He had been a VCA delegate to the ACB since 1969 and began his long reign as president of the VCA in 1973. He had managed three Australian teams to England, in 1961, 1964 and 1972.

Parish, more outgoing but haughty in his dealing with players, played grade cricket for the Prahran club from 1935–36 to 1948–49 as a steady right-arm medium-pace bowler. He joined the Prahran committee in 1936–37, became president in 1954–55, and was appointed the club's delegate to the VCA in 1950–51. He managed the Australian team to the West Indies in 1965 and to England in 1968, and was in his second term as chairman of the ACB.

They faced Kerry Francis Bullmore Packer, chain-smoking teetotaller, the 42-year-old overweight son of the Sydney media baron Sir Douglas Frank Hewson Packer, who had died five years earlier. Kerry had inherited his father's empire after his elder brother Clyde accepted a cash settlement and went his own way. Kerry was inordinately proud of the Packer group and in one radio interview with David Frost recalled weeks when his father struggled desperately to pay the staff wages bill. From a scatterbrained youth who worked on the wharves clearing newsprint consignments for his father's newspapers and bounded up the stairs of the Packer building three at a time rather than take the lift, he had developed into a clever negotiator.

Kerry Packer was educated at Geelong Grammar, where he found sport an antidote to his dyslexia, then a little-understood condition. He was a grandson of Victor Trumper's doctor, Herbert Bullmore, and in building up the newspapers, magazines and television stations in the family chain to an organisation of great wealth, he had often shown his father's crudeness of speech, but he remained a man of his word.

Every cent he promised his WSC players was paid. Even Ian Redpath, who damaged an Achilles tendon practising before WSC's first matches, received his full contracted amount.

Some fancy footwork came from the "peace" conferences. The Board's representatives agreed that TV rights to Australian Cricket should go to the highest bidder. Channel 9, as the only bidder, was then given the rights and in the agreement accepted by the Trade Practices Commission PBL was to be the official promoter of Australian cricket for the following ten years. All Board members approved the deal for which both sides had made concessions. Packer agreed to cease all his independent promotion of cricket. The Board agreed to coloured clothing and use of the white ball in limited over matches. Nonetheless, when the settlement was disclosed widespread disgust among cricket fans remained.

When the ACB announced the deal on 30 May, no details of the amount PBL would pay for its ten years in control of the game were provided, nor was there any information on the distribution of profits. Only an inner group in the ACB knew the terms of the agreement and a decade later State officials like Alan Davidson had no idea of what it contained.

Packer agreed to disband WSC from 31 January 1980, but the ACB retained responsibility for the selection of teams and the deals with sponsors. Promotion and programming of all first-class cricket became the responsibility of Packer's company PBL Sports. The ACB's capitulation bewildered most cricket buffs, who spoke of treachery and accused Parish and Steele of selling out far too cheaply.

The 1978–79 England v. Australia Ashes matches had been the first since 1903–04 to lose money, but even that appeared small reason to hand over complete control of the game to a private company. However, prize-winning author Ric Sissons points out that the ACB's losses over the two years of WSC can be estimated at £445,000; and that the ICC/TCCB court case against Greig that they lost had cost £200,000.

The truth was that Parish and Steele lacked any bargaining tools and were compelled to settle as quickly as possible a dispute that had badly wounded all cricket. They had the authority of the International Cricket Conference to act for all cricket nations, but were powerless to achieve a better deal against a man who had all the best players under contract, had made a stunning financial coup with night cricket, and had won a major victory over the establishment in the English High Court.

Packer even won a concession for players involved in one-day matches to wear his WSC logo. The ACB further agreed to consider all the players who had played for WSC for the Australian teams in both limited over and Test matches. Characteristically Packer took little part in the discussions once he had secured 10 years exclusive television rights to Test cricket, all along his main objective. From then on he left details of the deal for Taylor to work out with Steele and Parish.

The only important concession Packer did not win in the settlement was for the 16 international matches played in the two years of WSC—10 in Australia, one in New Zealand, and five in the West Indies under the label of "Super Tests" —to be officially recognised as first-class. None of traditional cricket's statistical authorities has accepted these matches in assessing career records of the players involved, which seems to me a gross injustice that should now be corrected. The cricket involved in these 16 matches was of the highest quality, infinitely superior, say, to an average Oxford *v.* Cambridge match, which compares with Sydney third grade. Until performances in the 16 matches are accepted, Greg Chappell is deprived of 1578 runs and five magnificent centuries, Dennis Lillee is deprived of 79 wickets, and Rodney Marsh of 54 dismissals, achievements their career records should in all fairness include.

Australia made their final tour before the Packer settlement took effect with an 11-match visit to India in September–November 1979. The two countries had played seven rubbers over 31 years before this tour, with the results heavily in Australia's favour. Australia had won 19 Tests, India 5 and 5 had been left drawn. The poor quality of the Australian team without the WSC players was shown in the team's failure to win a single match. This wounded Australian pride but was not surprising considering that ten of the 15 tourists had never represented Australia overseas before. The tour was held early in the Indian monsoon season so that the Australians could get home in time for the first "twin" tour of Australia by England and the West Indies and this resulted in frequent interruptions by bad weather. Only outstanding efforts by the experienced Hughes, Border and Dymock kept the margin of defeat in the six Tests down to 2-nil.

The team was announced shortly after Australia returned from the disastrous tour of England and only players who had appeared in the previous season's Sheffield Shield matches were considered by selectors Ray Lindwall, Phil Ridings and Sam Loxton. The team was: K. J. Hughes (captain), 25, A. M. J. Hilditch (vice captain), 23, A. R. Border, 24, W. M. Darling, 22, G. Dymock, 33, J. D. Higgs, 29, R. M. Hogg, 28, A. G. Hurst, 29, G. D. Porter, 24, P. R. Sleep, 22, D. F. Whatmore, 25, G. M. Wood, 22, K. J. Wright, 25, G. N. Yallop, 26, B. Yardley, 32, with Bob Merriman manager. Wright was the only wicket-keeper chosen, with Yallop ready to deputise for him if needed.

The tour proceeded amid tight security, with armed police seldom far away, following threats to disrupt matches by the Jammu and Kashmir Liberation Front, based in Pakistan. A cordon of police met the team at Madras airport on their arrival and thereafter became a familiar part of the tour.

The matches against North Zone at Srinagar, South Zone at Hyderabad, the first Test at Madras, where Border made 162 and Hughes 100, the second Test at Bangalore, and the game with Central Zone at Nagpur during September were all drawn. In the second Test Hughes persuaded Hogg to apologise after Hogg who had been no-balled seven times in five overs, had kicked down the stumps. The first result of the tour came in the third Test at Kanpur from 2 to 7 October, when Australia were dismissed for 125 in the fourth innings when they needed 279 to win in 312 minutes. The pitch was grassy and fast early on but provided unpredictable bounce towards the end. Dymock took 5 for 99 and 7 for 67 for Australia, but only Yallop, with 89 in the first innings, impressed among Australia's batsmen.

The match against West Zone at Ahmedabad from 9 to 11 October, in which Hughes made an attractive 126, was drawn. Manager Merriman then called for a replacement for Hurst, whose back injury had failed to respond to treatment. Hurst flew home and 21-year-old Geoff Lawson was flown in.

At Delhi, in the fourth Test between 13 and 18 October, India were never in danger of defeat after running up 7 for 510 declared in their first innings. Gavaskar made 115 and Yashpal Sharma 100 not out, but the key innings came from Vishwanath, who provided the momentum whenever the Indian innings faltered by scoring 131. Australia followed on after Kapil Dev took 5 for 82 in an innings of 298, but stubborn batting by Hilditch (85), Whatmore (54) and Sleep (64) took them to a second innings total of 413 and saved them from defeat.

At Cuttack from 21 to 23 October East Zone, regarded as the weakest of the Indian provincial teams, defeated Australia by four wickets. Australia paid the penalty for trying to finish off the match quickly by declaring in both innings on a badly prepared pitch. Left to score 154 to win, East Zone found the Australian bowling lacking in accuracy and purpose.

Australia compiled their highest score of the series in the fifth Test at Calcutta between 26

Kim Hughes cutting. Many believed his loyalty to traditional cricket during the Packer revolts was not properly rewarded.

and 31 October. After losing Hilditch in the first over Yallop (167), Border (54) and Hughes (92) built up a promising total and although the tailenders failed, an aggressive 61 from Yardley took the score to 442. India's 347 in reply gave Australia a first-innings lead of 95. Hughes declared Australia's second innings closed at 6 for 151, which gave India 247 to score in 245 minutes to win. Only excellent left-arm pace bowling by Dymock, who took 4 for 63 from 25 overs, prevented India reaching the target, time running out with India on 4 for 200.

India clinched a first series win over Australia by winning the sixth Test at Bombay between 3 and 7 November by an innings and 100 runs with a day to spare. Yardley was unfit to play on a grassless pitch that would have suited him, and Yallop and Higgs continued under difficulty after suffering stomach trouble on the first day. India took a firm grip on the series by batting for most of the first two days and scoring 8 for 458 declared. Gavaskar (123) and Kirmani (101 not out) made centuries. Australia followed on after Doshi (5 for 43) and Yadav (4 for 40) had bundled them out for 160. Border (61) and Hughes (80) held up the Indian attack with a third wicket stand of 132 but after they departed none of the remaining batsmen reached double figures.

Taking the field for the first time in a decade without their three celebrated spinners, Bedi, Chandrasekar and Prasanna, India found splendid replacements in Doshi (24 wickets at 24.04) and Yadav (27 at 23.33), but their main wicket-taker was Kapil Dev, with 28 wickets at 22.32. Dymock was the only consistent Australian bowler, with 24 wickets at 24.16. Australia's major weakness, however, was the failure of various combinations to provide good starts to the batting. They scored five centuries on the tour and had seven made against them. Hughes, with 858 runs at 53.62, was the only batsman to average more than fifty in the first-class matches and he also headed the Test averages with 594 runs at 59.40.

The 1979–80 Australian season introduced twin tours, with domestic cricket swamped by Tests and one-day internationals in a programme designed by Packer's PBL Sports to ensure maximum television coverage. Show business took over Australian cricket to an extent that irritated lovers of traditional cricket. Australia's leading players finally received the financial rewards to which Ian Chappell had led them with a shop steward's toughness and were no longer forced to take jobs outside cricket.

Full-time professionalism brought with it a decline in discipline, frequent breaches in sportsmanship, but no improvement in playing skills. The players were paid improved fees for State and Australian team appearances and in most States qualified for career-end provident

funds after they had made a certain number of appearances. They played for $10,000 prizemoney in each Test, $6000 going to the winning side, $3000 to the loser, and $1000 to the Man of the Match. One-day matches provided $5000 in prizemoney, comprising $3000 for the winners, $1500 for the losers and $500 for the Man of the Match. The one-day finals, in which the leading teams played the best of three matches after Australia, England and the West Indies had met each other four times, carried $16,000 for the winners.

The Test and County Cricket Board refused to put the Ashes at stake in the three Tests with Australia and announced that no "abnormal conditions" would be acceptable. Both the England and West Indian teams arrived in Australia with their tour conditions still to be finalised. Mike Brearley immediately was cast in the role of a "whingeing Pom" when he said his players would not wear coloured clothing, refused to use a white ball, and rejected the idea of fines for slow over rates and excessive use of the bouncer. The thirty-fourth England team to tour Australia comprised: J. M. Brearley (captain), 37, D. I. Gower, 22, G. A. Gooch, 26, G. Boycott, 39, G. Miller, 27, I. T. Botham, 24, G. R. Dilley, 22, G. B. Stevenson, 24, P. Willey, 30, D. W. Randall, 28, R. W. Taylor, 38, W. Larkins, 26, J. E. Emburey, 27, J. K. Lever, 30, R. G. D. Willis, 30, and only one former WSC player, D. L. Underwood, 34. Alec Bedser, chairman of England's selectors, managed the team.

The sixth West Indian team to tour Australia included ten players who had appeared for WSC and nine who had endured the 5–1 defeat by Australia four years earlier. They knew that no West Indian side had ever triumphed in Australia. They went along with the Packer outfit's innovations, confident they were better prepared than any previous West Indian side, determined to get their hands on a major share of the huge prizemoney. The West Indian team was: C. H. Lloyd (captain), 35, A. I. Kallicharran, 30,

I. V. A. Richards, 27, H. A. Gomes, 26, D. L. Haynes, 23, C. G. Greenidge, 28, C. L. King, 28, L. G. Rowe, 30, D. L. Murray, 36, A. M. E. Roberts, 28, D. R. Parry, 24, J. Garner, 26, M. D. Marshall, 21, D. A. Murray, 29, M. A. Holding, 25, C. E. H. Croft, 26, with W. V. Rodriguez as manager. The West Indian selectors, C. L. Walcott, C. Wilkins, G. S. Camacho, and C. H. Lloyd, urged the West Indian Board to send a 17th player but were turned down.

England began their tour in Brisbane with the match against Queensland from 12 to 14 November after rain had washed out net practice in Sydney. Randall encouraged hopes that he would prove a successful opening partner for Boycott by scoring 97 in England's first innings of 176. England restricted Thomson to one wicket in two innings but found big, blond Carl Rackemann troublesome. Rackemann took 5 for 25 and 2 for 35, worrying all the Englishmen with his sharp lift, but the match finished in a tame draw. Hendrick broke down after only four overs and later returned home.

The itinerary then took England to two one-day matches in Newcastle against Northern New South Wales and a four-day match from 22 to 25 November in Adelaide against Combined Australian Universities, whose pace bowler Peter Clough felled Boycott and forced him to retire. Dirk Wellham batted for four hours for the Universities to score 95. The match was drawn, England scoring 179 and 8 for 411 declared against the Universities' 168 and 5 for 227.

The West Indies' tour began in Geelong from 11 to 13 November with a drawn match against Geelong and District. Haynes made two half centuries and Marshall took five wickets in a match designed to give the visitors match practice. Weak South Australian batting gave the West Indies victory by nine wickets between 16 and 18 November in Adelaide, where wicket-keeper Deryck Murray made 103. Rodney Hogg took 6 for 95 in the first innings but the West Indies had to score only 39 to win in the second.

The problems created by packed schedules were demonstrated in the West Indies' match against a Tasmanian Invitation XI from 23 to 25 November at Devonport. The home side was strengthened by the inclusion of mainland stars Ric Darling and Peter Sleep from South Australia and Gary Cosier from Queensland, but severely weakened by the absence of all Tasmania's leading players, who were involved in a McDonald's Cup match, the limited-over competition between the States, against Victoria in Melbourne. Richards (127) and Kallicharran (123) made centuries in the West Indies' first innings of 374 after which they rushed the Invitation XI out for 144. Clive Lloyd refused to enforce the follow-on to give his players batting practice, which Gomes (64) and Kallicharran (38) used to good effect in an unbroken fifth-wicket stand of 72. Only Knight (57) and Cosier (49) resisted for any length of time in the final innings, the West Indies winning by 260 runs.

This took the teams to the first official one-day international matches under floodlights in Sydney. Captained by Greg Chappell, who won the Man of the Match award with an innings of 74 not out, Australia won the first of these 50-over matches with a five-wicket win over West Indies, who succumbed for 193 to the speed of Pascoe (4 for 29) and the spin of Border (3 for 36). England won the second, which rain reduced to 47 overs, by two runs. Peter Willey was England's match-winner with an innings of 58 not out. With Croft needing three runs from the final ball, Brearley positioned all his fieldsmen, including wicket-keeper Bairstow, on the boundary. Botham bowled Croft to frustrate the West Indies.

Traditionalists were surprised by the appointment of Greg Chappell as Australia's captain for the first Test after the disappearance of World Series Cricket. Kim Hughes, who had led Australia under difficulty without the WSC players, was named as his deputy. The West

Indies gained an early advantage in this 'Gabba Test between 1 and 5 December through their fast bowlers, but in the end were denied victory on a placid pitch through their lack of a spinner. Trailing by 173 runs on the first innings after Richards' 140 took the West Indies to 441 compared with Australia's 268, Australia escaped defeat through steady batting in their second innings, with Greg Chappell (124) and Hughes (130 not out) handling the fast bowlers confidently. At 6 for 448, Chappell declared, giving the West Indies a meaningless 45 minutes batting.

Meanwhile England were involved in the south. They defeated Tasmania by 100 runs at Hobart from 30 November to 2 December thanks to Boycott's 101 not out in the first innings and a 10-wicket match haul by Underwood, who had 3 for 11 and 7 for 66. At Adelaide between 4 and 6 December they were subjected to a dose of Ian Chappell's cross-grained temperament. Making his return from a three-week suspension for using abusive language during his first match of the season for South Australia against Tasmania, Chappell again disputed an umpire's decision. When Brearley batted, Chappell put nine men on the leg side in an obvious move to show contempt for Brearley and England's distaste for restrictions on field placements.

The match petered out in a draw with the outstanding cricket on view overshadowed by Chappell's misbehaviour. Boycott scored 110 in England's first innings, the 117th century of his career, which equalled Bradman's achievement on Bradman's home ground. Despite Chappell's field placements, Brearley made 81 and had an opening stand of 174 with Boycott. Only 16 wickets fell in the three days.

England then flew to Melbourne, where they beat Australia by three wickets in a limited-over match on 8 December, and then watched the West Indies beat Australia the next day by 80 runs due to a dazzling 153 not out from Richards. On 11 December England beat Australia by 72

In the first England–Australia Test after the Packer settlement Dennis Lillee attracted headlines by using this aluminium bat. Play was stopped for ten minutes while he was persuaded to use the traditional willow.

runs in Sydney, Boycott's 105 and Willey's 64 lifting the 49-over total to 264 under floodlights. Australia managed only 192 in reply because of accurate bowling by Willis and Botham.

The West Indies flew to Launceston to defeat Tasmania by 61 runs thanks to centuries by Kallicharran (138) and Gomes (137 not out), while England met Australia at Perth in the first Test from 14 to 19 December. Lillee interrupted an enthralling match by trying to use an aluminium bat in Australia's first innings despite objections from Brearley, the umpires, M. G. O'Connell and D. G. Weser, and his captain, Greg Chappell. Play stopped for ten minutes before Lillee was persuaded to use the traditional willow.

Vastly strengthened by the return of the Packer rebels, Australia outplayed England in all three Tests. None of the Englishmen totalled 200 runs in these Tests and Botham and Underwood were the only English bowlers to take ten wickets. Australia won the Perth Test by 138 runs, with Dymock taking 9 for 86 in the match, Hughes scoring 99 and Border 115. Ian Chappell returned to Test cricket under his brother's captaincy for the second Test from 4 to 8 January in Sydney, where Australia won by six wickets with a day to spare. The bowling of Lillee (6 for 103 in the match) and Dymock (7 for 90) was again too strong for England, though Gower scored a splendid 98 not out in the second innings. Greg Chappell survived a confident appeal for caught behind off Dilley to score a match-winning 98 not out in the fourth innings. At Melbourne from 1 to 6 February Australia completed England's embarrassment by winning the third Test by eight wickets. This time Lillee, bowling with wonderful control without bouncing deliveries around the batsmen's heads, had match figures of 11 for 138, and Greg Chappell contributed 154 runs for once out.

Brearley found Greg Chappell a far tougher opposing captain than Yallop had been on his previous visit and had to endure frequent displays of disgraceful crowd abuse. After one demonstration in the Melbourne Test, Australian team manager John Edwards issued a statement in which he said he was ashamed to be an Australian. The crowds blamed Brearley for his objections to WSC innovations which Ian Chappell and Lillee claimed enhanced the spectacle. In Sydney spectators bombarded the Englishmen with an assortment of missiles.

The constant changing to limited over matches and back again to first-class games gave the Englishmen little chance to settle, and their batting remained extremely brittle throughout a thoroughly unpleasant tour in which special security measures had to be taken against drunken spectators. England lost 3 of their 8 first-class matches on the tour, and of the 12 non-first-class matches, won 7, drew 1, and lost 4. Gooch headed both the Test (172 runs at 43.00) and first-class (639 runs at 58.09) batting averages for the tour. Botham topped the Test (19 wickets at 19.52) and first-class (34 wickets at 15.64) bowling averages for the tour.

The Australians approached the three Tests against the West Indies with less confidence than they displayed against England and after the drawn first Test were heavily defeated in the other Tests. The West Indies won the second Test at Melbourne from 29 December to 1 January by ten wickets with a day to spare. Australia managed only 156 in their first innings against the pace bowling of Holding, Roberts, Croft and Garner and on 1 for 103 at stumps the West Indies had the game under control by the end of the first day. They passed Australia's score with only three batsmen out and led by 241 on the first innings. Australia's second innings was a repetition of the first, with the pace bowlers dominant and the West Indies were left to score only 22 in the last innings to win.

Western Australia provided the upset of the summer by defeating the West Indies by eight wickets with more than a day to spare between 5 and 7 January in Perth and they did it without Lillee, Hughes and Marsh, who were playing against England in the third Test. The West Indies collapsed for 169 against clever swing bowling by Alderman (5 for 47) and Malone (4 for 48). Western Australia lost 2 for 32 but then consolidated their position to score 6 declared for 396.

Burly left-hander Robbie Langer, one of the biggest hitters of his time, made 137 and South African right-hander Ken McEwan 112, adding 207 for the fourth wicket in 180 minutes. Facing a deficit of 227, the West Indies lost 6 for 103 to an attack shrewdly deployed by Tony Mann, before the tail rallied, Collis King's 92 ensuring that Western Australia batted again.

In the fortnight between 8 January and 22 January, the West Indies were unbeaten in seven one-day internationals in a programme that took them from Perth to Melbourne, Canberra,

Adelaide, Sydney and back to Melbourne. The last of these matches gave them a 2–nil victory over England in the best of three one-day finals and brought their total prizemoney to $86,000. Richards won awards for the best player in the Tests and limited-over matches, his prizes including a luxury car.

Australia gave a dispirited showing in the the third Test against the West Indies between 26 and 30 January in Adelaide. Put in to bat, the West Indies lost Greenidge at 11. Richards then hit 13 fours to lift the total to 1 for 115 at lunch. He fell to Lillee off the fourth ball after the interval, and Mallett, in his first Test in four years, dismissed Haynes and Kallicharran cheaply. Lloyd and Rowe faced this minor collapse with a defiant stand of 113 in even time. Lloyd was dropped twice on his way to 121, which included 17 fours. Lillee's 5 for 78 restricted the total to 328.

Australia never recovered from 3 for 26. The crucial wickets of the Chappell brothers fell to successive balls from Roberts, both nasty, kicking bouncers. Laird got his fourth half century (52) of the rubber and with plucky support from Hughes (34) and Border (54) against fiery pace bowling, lifted the score to 203, 125 in arrears.

Greenidge put on 48 with Haynes and 136 with Richards to lay the foundations for the West Indies' second innings total of 448, Kallicharran (106) carrying on the punishment of the Australian bowlers with his first century of the series and his 12th in Tests. Mindful of the humiliation Australians had inflicted on the West Indies in the past, Lloyd let his batsmen enjoy themselves and Australia were left to score 573. *Wisden* commented that none of Australia's batsmen had the will to make a fight of it in the final innings, when they were out for 165. The victory accounted for $24,000 of the West Indies' accumulated prizemoney.

The West Indies won 5 of their 7 first-class matches, lost 1, and drew 1. Of the 14 non-first-class matches on their tour, they won 8, lost 4

Allan Border, in one of his last appearances for New South Wales before transferring to Queensland, collects four from a characteristic cover drive in Sydney.

and drew 2, with one abandoned. Richards headed both the Test (386 runs at 96.50) and first-class (592 runs at 98.66) batting averages, and Garner topped both the Test (14 wickets at 21.50) and first-class (51 wickets at 18.21) bowling averages. The statistic that demonstrated the West Indies' superiority, however, was that they scored eight centuries in first-class matches and had only four scored against them. Five of their bowlers took 20 wickets or more in first-class matches. Their ground fielding and catching was a delight throughout the tour.

Bruce Laird (340 runs at 56.66), Kim Hughes (252 runs at 50.40) and Greg Chappell (270 runs at 45.00) performed well among Australian Test batsmen but nobody else averaged 20 or more. Only two Australian bowlers, Dymock with 11 wickets at 26.27, and Lillee, with 12 wickets at 30.41, took ten wickets or more.

For the promoters the biggest disappointment of this frenetic season, however, was Australia's failure to reach the finals of the one-day competition. Australia had a big advantage over both England and the West Indies who were restricted to the players they had brought on tour. Australia called on 20 players, but were unable to settle on the type of bowlers to play. The ACB needed to have Australia in the finals to attract crowds to help pay the heavy costs of twin tours.

The West Indians, many of them from impoverished homes, approached the task of winning prizemoney with an intense professionalism neither England nor Australia matched. The Englishmen knew their tour pay was guaranteed before they arrived and the Australians knew how well paid Sheffield Shield cricket was if they didn't make the national team.

In a season that included six Tests, 12 international one-day matches, nine first-class matches between the touring teams and State sides, and six other non-first-class matches between regional teams and the tourists, the programmers still managed to fit in 25 Sheffield Shield matches, each mainland State playing nine and Tasmania five, and the McDonald's Cup limited-over knockout one-day competition between the States. The packed itinerary meant that several leading players were seldom available for their States. Kim Hughes did not appear in a single Shield match for Western Australia owing to the late return of the Australian team from India. Alan Border played only once for New South Wales.

The Sheffield Shield competition was completely overshadowed by the Tests and one-day internationals, which had priority in Packer's television programming. Form shown in Shield matches no longer offered a reliable guide to Test selection, and despite the return of most of Australia's finest players after their two years

Plucky Western Australian opener Bruce Laird on his way to 117 in a Sheffield Shield match against New South Wales.

with WSC the State associations' losses on the 1979–80 summer totalled $125,000, leaving administrators searching desperately for a more practical Shield formula. Introduction of the six-ball over had failed to bring higher daily over rates and the dramatically improved financial rewards for players had not prevented Shield attendances falling even further.

The Melbourne *Age*'s Peter McFarline claimed that player misbehaviour had an adverse effect on attendances, but there was no evidence to prove people stayed away rather than watch Ian Chappell abuse umpires or adjust his trousers. The most obvious answer seemed the right one:

When Doug Walters bowled wide of the off stump to curb Ian Chappell's scoring rate in Sydney, Chappell obliged by moving the off stump. Administrators were not amused.

there was just too much cricket, most of it of poor quality.

The Victorians earned $70,000 by winning the Shield for the second successive season and adding the McDonald's Cup. This money came from prizemoney, sponsorship, and incentives for success. Victoria played eleven current or former internationals in the season so most of them also qualified for provident funds and appearance money. Left-hander Jeff Moss won the $10,000 bonus for the team's best batting performance for the second year running, scoring 711 runs at 50.78.

The Shield competition was decided by the last match, between South Australia and Victoria in Adelaide between 7 and 10 March. Play began with New South Wales at the top of the table, three points ahead of South Australia and five ahead of Victoria. After each side had completed their first innings, South Australia had secured nine bonus points, Victoria six, enough, it appeared, for South Australia to win. But in a dramatic recovery on the last afternoon leg spinner Jim Higgs spun out South Australia for 160, giving Victoria victory by 83 runs and the Shield. Among Higgs' five victims in the second innings was the season's highest run-scorer, Ian Chappell, who had made 112 in South Australia's first innings. Chappell made 713 runs in the season at 47.53, but Greg Chappell headed the Shield averages with 418 runs at 104.50 from his three matches.

Tasmania failed to win a match in their third season in the competition on a restricted basis. Their imported captain, Brian Davison, of Leicestershire and Rhodesia, hit a splendid 138 against Victoria but failed to sustain this form. Openers Bob ("Mutt") Jeffery and Gary Goodman, both former Sydney players, had a record opening stand of 194 against Queensland, and Jeffery stayed to reach 198, adding a further 142 for the third wicket with Davison. But Alan Border made the season's highest score with 200 for NSW against Queensland in his only Shield appearance.

Before the Shield competition was completed, the fourth Australian team to tour Pakistan flew to Karachi for five first-class matches, which included three Tests. The tour was in doubt until the Pakistanis, knowing cricket provided their best chance for international recognition, improved their guarantee from $94,000 to $150,000. The Australian Cricket Board did not allow the tour to proceed until manager Fred Bennett, after a flying visit to Pakistan, assured them that security arrangements were adequate. Ravaged by mullahs, corruption, drugs, and military power struggles, Pakistan brought incredible fervour to their cricket.

The Board named a squad of 18 players to prepare for the tour, but when Mallett withdrew with a shoulder injury Beard replaced him. Ian Chappell, Pascoe and McCosker were unavailable. Higgs, Hogg, Robinson and Whatmore were asked if they were available but were not chosen. The team was: G. S. Chappell (captain), 31, K. J. Hughes, 26, G. R. Beard, 29, A. R. Border, 24, R. J. Bright, 25, G. Dymock, 33, D. W. Hookes, 24, B. M. Laird, 29, G. F. Lawson, 22, D. K. Lillee, 29, M. F. Malone, 29, R. W. Marsh, 32, J. M. Wiener, 24, G. N. Yallop, 27.

The tour began with a match against the President's XI from 22 to 24 February at Rawalpindi. Australia looked in command at 5 for 210 but were out for 223. Bright took 5 for 93, helping to restrict the President's XI to 7 declared for 209 and after Australia had declared at 5 for 203, Bright took a further 6 for 29. Chasing 218 to win, the President's XI escaped with a draw when the last pair survived 35 balls, finishing on 9 for 81.

The spinners Tauseef Ahmad and Iqbal Qasim had Australia out for 225 in the first innings of the first Test at Karachi from 27 February to 2 March. Bright made things equally difficult for Pakistan in their first innings of 292, taking 7 for 87. But at their second attempt Australia

Victorian left-arm spinner Ray Bright produced the best performances of his career in Pakistan in 1980 on pitches the Australians claimed had been doctored to help Pakistan's spinners.

the third Test at Lahore from 18 to 23 March. Greg Chappell made 235, Yallop 172 in the Faisalabad Test. Border followed his 178 at Multan with innings of 150 not out and 153 in the Lahore Test, which brought up his 5000th Test run in his 60th Test.

The tour brought accusations of doctored pitches from the Australians, who were convinced the pitches had been prepared to assist spin and negate the pace of Lillee. But given Border's mastery of the spinners, a more disconcerting feature for the Australians was the constant appealing of the Pakistani players. Border scored 674 runs at an average of 112.33 in five matches and in the Tests averaged 131.66. Bright took 29 wickets at 19.24 in five matches, averaging 23.60 for his 15 Test wickets.

Between July and September 1980, a 14-man Australian team undertook a short tour to celebrate the centenary of Test cricket in England. The Ashes were not at stake. The team played three limited-over matches and five first-class matches, four of which were designed to prepare them for the reason behind the tour, the Centenary Test. Following the style of the remarkably successful Test in Melbourne three years earlier, organisers invited all the surviving English and Australian Test players, more than 200 of whom were fit enough to attend. The venue was switched to Lord's from The Oval, where Australia's first-ever Test in England was held, simply because Lord's had better grandstands and was better equipped to handle the vast crowds expected. The Australian team, chosen by Phil Ridings, Alan Davidson, Sam Loxton and Ray Lindwall, was: G. S. Chappell (captain), 32, K. J. Hughes, 26, A. R. Border, 25, R. J. Bright, 26, G. Dymock, 34, J. Dyson, 26, B. M. Laird, 29, D. K. Lillee, 31, A. A. Mallett, 35, R. W. Marsh, 32, L. S. Pascoe, 30, J. R. Thomson, 30, G. M. Wood, 23, G. N. Yallop, 27, with Ridings as manager and Dave Sherwood as scorer. Only Dyson had not visited England before in an Australian team.

had no answer to Tauseef and Qasim on a turning pitch and were spun out for 140 despite Border's 58 not out. Bright took three more wickets for match figures of 10 for 11 before Pakistan scored the 73 runs required to win.

Australia then played draws in the second Test at Faisalabad between 6 and 11 March, against the Governor of Punjab's XI at Multan from 13 to 15 March, and against Pakistan in

Rodney Marsh holds one of the catches that was to take him past Alan Knott's record as cricket's most successful 'keeper. Marsh ultimately took 355 wickets to Knott's 269.

In the three weeks before the Test, Australia defeated Hampshire by ten wickets from 6 to 8 August at Southampton, lost to Surrey by 59 runs at The Oval between 10 and 12 August, and played draws with Young England at Worcester on 14 August and with Lancashire at Old Trafford from 16 to 18 August. From the outset Lillee was the tourists' outstanding bowler but Pascoe bowled at a lively pace in taking 2 for 49 and 5 for 94 to clinch the win over Hampshire. Chappell made 86 against Hampshire and retired on 101 against Lancashire.

England won the first limited-over match on 20 August by 23 runs at The Oval thanks to a fine innings of 99 by Boycott and the second limited over match at Birmingham on 22 August by 47 runs because of Gooch's splendid innings of 108. The major disaster of the tour came at Trent Bridge from 23 to 25 August when Nottinghamshire inflicted the heaviest defeat this century by a county side over the Australians. The Australians scored 207 and 182, floundering from the start against the bowling of New Zealand's Richard Hadlee and the South African William Watson. Notts' innings of 462 included 90 from South African Clive Rice, Notts winning by an innings and 76 runs.

This led to a memorable week of nostalgia at Lord's interspersed by welcoming parties and dinners and the one evening takeover of a London theatre by the Test sponsors, Cornhill Insurance. When play began, Australia took a commanding position by scoring 5 declared for 385 in the first innings, with Wood (112) and Hughes (117) batting superbly before the capacity crowd.

Fifty minutes were lost to rain on the first day and all bar 75 minutes of the second day. On the third day 90 minutes rain in the early morning left sodden patches on the Tavern side of the ground. Umpires Bird and Constant, sole arbiters on when play should resume, upset spectators by conducting repeated inspections. Greg Chappell was keen to resume but England's captain Ian Botham was reluctant. After the fifth pitch inspection there was a scuffle which was shown to millions on TV between the umpires and angry MCC members as the umpires moved into the Long Room. Chappell and Botham moved in quickly to protect the umpires but the incident led to an MCC enquiry after which the culprits were disciplined and the club apologised to the captains and umpires.

England managed 205 runs in their first innings with only Boycott (62) and Gower (45) resisting for long against some magnificently controlled bowling by Lillee, who removed the first four batsmen, and some energetic bowling by Pascoe who finished the innings off with 5 for 15 off 32 balls. Leading by 180, Australia declared at 4 for 189 in their second innings after hammering 83 runs in an hour. Hughes this time made a brilliant 84, including a six onto the top deck of the pavilion where John Arlott was making his farewell broadcast.

England never attempted to chase the 370 wanted to win after Lillee removed Gooch and Pascoe sent back Athey with the score on 43. The insatiable Boycott went on to 128 not out when all interest had gone from the match, taking his Test aggregate to 7115 runs, ahead of Hutton and Bradman. This was his 19th Test century and his sixth against Australia. Hughes won the $1000 Man of the Match prize and the teams shared the prizemoney of $9000. Attendance for a drawn match which always lacked the tension of the Melbourne Centenary match was 84,938.

After the Centenary Test at Lord's Phil Ridings and Alan Barnes, secretary of the Australian Cricket Board since 1960, represented Australia at the International Cricket Conference meeting at Lord's. Ridings returned home to succeed Bob Parish as Board chairman at the ACB's October meeting. The following month Barnes, 64, had a stroke in his Sydney office. He stayed on the Board's payroll for another year but from the time of Barnes' illness David Richards, until then secretary of the Victorian Cricket Association, became the Board's chief executive and the day-to-day administration of Australian cricket moved from Sydney to Melbourne. With this move, the Board started to implement a series of major changes which the Packer experience had shown were sorely needed.

Exploiting the Prize

Twenty-ninth Australian team to England 1981; touring teams in Australia 1980-84; Australia on tour 1982-83

Profits for both Packer and the Australian Cricket Board reached record levels in the decade after the settlement of the Packer dispute. Advertisers strongly supported Packer's televised matches, which achieved very high ratings for 600 hours each season at a price far below what he would have paid for normal TV programmes. By bringing two overseas teams to Australia each summer, the Board made Australians familiar with the world's best players outside of South Africa. Cash distributions by the Board to the State associations were large enough for even vehemently anti-Packer delegates to accept that the settlement terms were justified.

Before the dispute the Board had been an old-fashioned, overworked and badly under-staffed body, lagging in even the simplest routine tasks. The idea of big firms sponsoring matches at cricket grounds had not yet been examined.

Terry Alderman winces in pain after breaking his shoulder attempting to tackle an intruder on the Perth ground in 1982. Alderman was out of cricket until the 1983–84 season.

Alan Barnes worked long hours trying to overcome his lack of staff until finally his health broke down but the truth was that few of the Board delegates recognised the scope or potential of the business they were running.

In the first eight years after the end of the Packer dispute, the ACB distributed $17,653,971 to the States, a figure that would have astounded delegates to the Board in the pre-Packer years. In 1987, the States received $2,397,836 and in 1988, $2,879,770. These handouts, together with sponsorships they organised themselves, allowed the States to expand their administrative staffs and embark on projects undreamt-of before Packer appeared.

At the centre of this financial renaissance of Australian cricket was a former Ringwood sub-district cricketer and university lecturer, David Lyle Richards, born in 1946, who had moved from a teaching job at Monash University, where he had taken his degree in economics, to become assistant secretary of the Victorian Cricket Association in 1973. When the ACB moved to Melbourne after Alan Barnes' stroke, Richards became its Executive Director. Behind him, in the formative years of the new-look Board from 1980–83, was ACB chairman Philip Lovett Ridings, one of four brothers who had played for the West Torrens club in Adelaide, a proficient right-hand batsman and right-arm medium-pace bowler who had 17 seasons in the South Australian team between 1936–37 and 1956–57. He was South Australia's captain for 12 summers and in 1952–53 won the Sheffield Shield without losing a match.

They made a happy combination. Richards had two years experience as the Board's marketing manager, drumming up support for traditional cricket with surprising success during the years of Packer's WSC. Ridings, whose younger brother Kenneth Lovett Ridings was spoken of as a future Australian captain before he was killed piloting a Sunderland over the Bay of Biscay in 1944, was one of seven men who

started Custom Credit in Australia. When he retired in 1980, Custom Credit had been built into an organisation with more than $100 million in assets.

The Board appointed Graham Wilfrid Halbish, a former Prahran minor grades stalwart whose cricket interest began at Murrumbeena High School, as its finance director. Halbish, a left-handed batsman who bowled right-hand medium-pacers, had a background in accountancy, and was encouraged by the Board to pursue his studies at Monash University, where he took an economics degree in 1986. Initially, Halbish prepared the Board's accounts, which had been done on a part-time basis by retired taxation official Alan Walsh when the Board's headquarters were in Sydney, but later Halbish worked on Kanga Cricket, an abridged form of the game for schoolboys, the founding of the Australian Cricket Academy in Adelaide, players' contracts when the ACB put up to 30 leading players on guaranteed annual salaries, and the players' provident fund. An in-house accountant took over the book-keeping.

The exposure the Packer settlement gave cricket helped the ACB and State associations to attract their own sponsors. Packer's hard-won exclusive TV cricket programmes also provided highly-paid careers for those who helped mastermind WSC. Tony Greig became the head of an insurance company partly-owned by Packer, and joined Richie Benaud and Ian Chappell in the TV commentary team. The pictures were outstanding but the commentators took some years to run into form. Many Australians in these years preferred to turn off Packer's sound and switch on Alan McGilvray's more polished ABC radio broadcasts as the accompaniment for the TV pictures.

The kaleidoscope of cricket that unfolded as Packer's programmers ruthlessly exploited their prize gave cricket followers little time to get to know the idiosyncrasies of players that have always enriched the game. Countries visiting

Australia always demanded return visits to their homeland and although these trips were not shown on television they added to the strain on Australia's playing resources.

India and New Zealand both toured Australia in the summer of 1980–81, playing three Tests each. New Zealand began their tour, comprising seven first-class matches and 22 limited-over matches, in October without their finest batsman, Glenn Turner, who could not be persuaded to make the trip. They were no match for Australia in the Tests, which they lost 2–nil, with one drawn. The fast bowling of Lillee, Pascoe and Hogg was too much for them, though John Wright and Bruce Edgar impressed as an opening pair. At Brisbane between 28 and 30 November 1980, Graeme Wood made 111 to help Australia to a ten-wicket win, Lillee taking 6 for 53 in the second innings. Australia won the second Test at Perth from 12 to 14 December by eight wickets, Lillee finishing with match figures of 7 for 77. The third Test at Melbourne from 26 to 30 December on a sub-standard pitch was drawn after Walters made 107.

India began their tour of eight first-class matches and 21 limited-over games in November. They shared the Test series, each side winning one, with the other drawn. An innings of 204 by Greg Chappell, who hit 27 fours, set up Australia's first Test win at Sydney from 2 to 4 January by an innings and four runs. Lillee took a further seven wickets for 165 runs. The second Test at Adelaide from 23 to 27 January was drawn. Following 125 from Wood, 213 from Hughes, and 174 from Patil, Australia were given four and a half hours in which to dismiss India for a win in the final innings. India hung on for a draw, the ninth-wicket pair surviving nine overs and two balls. India won the third Test from 7 to 11 February in Melbourne by 59 runs. Needing only 143 to win, Australia collapsed for 83, Kapil Dev taking the last five wickets for 28 runs. Lillee's 8 for 169 took his haul from the six Tests to 37 wickets for 697 runs, average 18.83.

Two incidents involving Greg Chappell created tremendous controversy in the limited-over finals with New Zealand after India had been eliminated from that competition. In the first at Melbourne on 1 February Chappell, then in the 50s, hit what looked a fair catch to Martin Sneddon off Cairns. Both umpires claimed they were unsighted. Captain Geoff Howarth supported Sneddon's claim that it was a fair catch but Chappell refused to believe them and continued to 90. Later the same day, with New Zealand needing six to win off the last ball, Chappell instructed his brother Trevor to bowl underarm to Brian McKechnie, New Zealand's No. 10. Although he was within the law in doing so, Trevor Chappell's underarm ball became one of the most infamous in cricket history. McKechnie blocked it and threw his bat down in disgust.

Chappell's instruction, which aroused a shout of "No, skip", from Rod Marsh on the field was universally deplored. New Zealand Prime Minister Robert ("Piggy") Muldoon called it an act of cowardice and said it was appropriate that the Australians were dressed in yellow. Richie Benaud said it was "a disgraceful happening", Don Bradman "totally disapproved" and Harold Larwood in Sydney said it was a "bloody stupid thing to do". A phone hook-up of ACB members agreed to change the law immediately so that underarm bowling was prohibited.

Exhausted by the dreadful schedule and pilloried on every side for his underarm ball instruction, Greg Chappell's hold on the Australian captaincy was in danger until he issued the following statement through the ACB:

I have always played cricket within the rules of the game. I took a decision which, whilst within the laws of cricket, in the cool light of day I recognise as not being within the spirit of the game. The decision was made whilst I was under pressure and in the heat of the moment. I regret the decision. It is something I would not do again.

Doug Walters turns to find he is out, stumped by Kirmani,
after missing an attempted drive against India in 1981.

Letters and telegrams poured into Australia's newspapers and to the Sydney hotel where the Australians gathered for the next match in the final series against New Zealand. Everybody from Prime Minister Malcolm Fraser ("contrary to the spirit of the game") to viewers in far off Madras had a strong view on Chappell's action. Tony Greig called for his sacking, Keith Miller said one-day cricket had died and Greg Chappell should be buried with it. But the comment that hurt Greg the most was his brother Ian's: "Fair dinkum, Greg, how much pride do you sacrifice to win $35,000?" This in turn distressed Martin and Jeanne Chappell, who attacked Ian for breaching family loyalty.

Two days after the underarm ball, Greg Chappell had to have a police escort to go out to the Sydney Cricket Ground for the next match in the series. He batted brilliantly for 87 and Australia won, to take the final series 3–1. Greg Chappell was named Man of the Match. Next day he announced he was unavailable for Australia's tour of England later in 1981. The tour involved 25 matches but eight of these were limited-over games, which enabled the ACB to reduce the side to 16 players. The team was: K. J. Hughes (captain), 27, R. W. Marsh, 33, T. M. Alderman, 25, M. F. Kent, 27, G. R. Beard, 30, G. F. Lawson, 23, A. R. Border, 25, R. J. Bright, 26, J. Dyson, 27, T. M. Chappell, 28, R. M. Hogg, 30, D. K. Lillee, 31, S. J. Rixon, 27, D. M. Wellham, 22, G. M. Wood, 24, G. N. Yallop, 28, with Fred Bennett as manager, Peter Philpott as coach, and Dave Sherwood on his seventh tour as scorer.

This twenty-ninth Australian team to England, chosen by Phil Ridings, Sam Loxton, Alan Davidson and Ray Lindwall, was notable for the omission of Doug Walters, who had received the unprecedented honour of being given 1980–81 as his benefit season by the New South Wales Cricket Association. Beloved of spectators, Walters had scored 781 runs, with two centuries, at an average of 48.81 in the Shield competition won by Western Australia. Walters had averaged 72.00 runs an innings in the three Tests against India and headed the batting averages with 181 runs at 45.25 against New Zealand. For him to be omitted on the ground that he did not perform well under English conditions was a blow to thousands of Walters' supporters.

Despite the absence of Greg Chappell, Australia outplayed England for most of this astounding series until the all-round brilliance of Ian Botham frustrated them. They went into the first Test at Trent Bridge from 18 to 21 June unbeaten in first-class matches against Hampshire, Somerset, Glamorgan, Gloucestershire, Derbyshire and Middlesex, having suffered defeat only in a Prudential Trophy one-day match with England, which they avenged by winning the trophy.

Australia held their catches, England dropped theirs, and on the fourth day Trevor Chappell, the youngest of the three brothers, hit the winning runs to give Australia a four-wicket win on the first Sunday of Test cricket in England. The second Test from 2 to 7 July at Lord's was drawn and having achieved a pair of spectacles in this match and after a fruitless year as England's captain, Botham resigned the captaincy. Lawson took 7 for 81 in England's first innings and Graeme Wood made 106 for once out, but rain and England's lack of urgency prevented a result.

England won the third Test at Headingley by 18 runs to become the first team this century to triumph after following on and only the second team to do so in the history of Test cricket.

Geoff Lawson leaps high as he nears his delivery stride in the 1981 Test against England at Headingley.

Australia scored 9 for 401 declared in their first innings, thanks to 102 by Dyson and 89 from Hughes. Lillee (4 for 49), Alderman (3 for 59) and Lawson (3 for 32) then bundled England out for 174, forcing England to bat again 227 behind. At 7 for 135 in their second innings, the Englishmen were still 92 behind, and their only hope of emerging from the match with honour lay in preventing an innings defeat. The England players had anticipated such a fate by checking out of their hotels. An unforgettable 149 not out from Botham transformed the match, taking it into the fifth day.

Australia remained firm favourites, needing only 130 to win, but Lillee and Marsh thought

Allan Border snaps up a superb catch close in to dismiss David Gower, with 'keeper Rod Marsh acclaiming the effort. This catch in the 1981 Test at Edgbaston did not prevent Australia losing the match.

the odds of 500-to-1 offered about England's chances in the betting tent on the ground astounding and invested £4 each. With Australia 1 for 56, their money appeared lost, but Willis then bowled like a man inspired to take 8 for 43, Australia's last nine wickets falling for 55 runs. The whole of Britain stopped work to watch the last hour on television and when Willis had achieved the apparently impossible the ground filled with spectators waving Union Jacks.

England performed the same magic in the fourth Test at Birmingham from 30 July to 2 August, winning by 29 runs after all appeared lost. Australia comfortably headed England's first innings of 189, in which Alderman took 5 for 42. Trailing by 69 runs, England were out for 219 in the second innings, leaving Australia to score 142 in two days for a win. Willis again gave England a fine start by dismissing Dyson

and Hughes for 19 runs.

Recalled to the England captaincy, Brearley was at his best, pressuring each batsman, making precise field changes, never allowing England to lose the initiative Willis's early breakthrough provided. Luck favoured England at 4 for 105, with only 45 needed, when a ball from Emburey lifted prodigiously to remove Border for 40, caught off his glove. Botham was reluctant when Brearley asked him to bowl, but he was right on target with every delivery, his 5 for 10 completing another remarkable victory, the last five Australian wickets falling for seven runs.

At Old Trafford between 13 and 17 August 1981, England won the fifth Test by 103 runs to take the series and the Ashes 3–1. Again it was Botham who swung the match. England, 101 ahead on the first innings, had squandered their advantage to be 5 for 104 in the second innings when Botham entered. He made 118 in 123 minutes, with 13 fours and 6 sixes, a record for England–Australia Tests. Botham hit three sixes off Lillee, all hook shots, and one off Alderman from an enormous pull to the back of the stands. He reached his century with a six from a sweep shot, and then struck Bright straight back over the sightscreen. Botham was caught by Marsh off Whitney from the 102nd ball he faced.

Whitney, a 22-year-old Sydney surfer with an Afro hairdo, was in England to gain experience with Fleetwood in League cricket, after appearing four times for New South Wales. His fast left-arm bowling impressed Gloucestershire selectors who promoted him to the county side. He was on his way to Cheltenham to play for Gloucestershire against Hampshire, his third county match, when the Australian management learned Lawson and Hogg were unfit and drafted Whitney into the Test team. He took 2 for 50 and 2 for 74 in a commendable debut, holding his place for the drawn sixth Test from 27 August to 1 September at The Oval.

Centuries by Border (106 not out) and Wellham (103 in his Test debut) and match figures of 11 for 159 by Lillee failed to produce a result because of Brearley's clever captaincy, Botham's 10 for 253 in the match, and Boycott's 137. Wellham was on 99 for 25 minutes. Picking himself up after falling in avoiding a bouncer, he heard Botham say: "You've done the hard work, so don't give it away". Marsh scored his 3000th Test run in this match and Alderman finished the series with 42 wickets at 21.26, ahead of Lillee's 39 wickets at 22.30. Border was the only Australian to average more than 50 in the Tests, with 533 runs at 29.22.

The Australians won only 3 of their 17 first-class matches, lost 3, and drew 11. They found county sides strengthened by overseas players tougher to beat than on previous tours and defeated only Sussex and Worcestershire. They won 4 of their 8 limited-over matches, lost 3, drew 1, and had one abandoned. They scored eight first-class centuries and had seven made against them. Border was the highest run-scorer on the tour with 807 first-class runs at 50.43 but Wellham finished ahead of him in the averages

with 497 runs at 55.22. Marsh, who completed 28 dismissals, finished the tour as the world's most successful wicket-keeper by passing Alan Knott's record of 263 Test victims.

The 1981 Tests in England will always—and rightly—be regarded as a tribute to Botham and his dazzling ability to rescue England from apparent defeat. But England's 3–1 triumph could just as easily be recorded as the aftermath of the underarm ball affair. The Australian Cricket Board's chief executive David Richards pressured Greg Chappell for an apology, in the precise words he believed were needed, but he also left Chappell feeling he lacked support among Australia's administrators. There was no attempt to reassure Chappell that this was not so nor was there any attempt to persuade him to tour. It seems inconceivable that Australia would have collapsed for the low scores it got in three innings, if a batsman of Chappell's mastery had been present.

In the Australian summer of 1981–82 Marsh broke Neil Harvey's Australian appearance record by playing in his 80th Test against Pakistan. The Pakistan tour, begun only a month after the Australians returned from England, involved eight first-class matches, including three Tests, plus a programme of limited-over matches, coinciding with a similar tour by the West Indies, who began their tour a month later. Australia won the Test series against Pakistan 3–1 and shared the Tests with the West Indies at 1–1, with the other Test drawn.

After Pakistan's warm-up matches with Western Australia, Queensland and Victoria, all of them drawn, at the end of October and early in November, Australia gave a miserable batting display in the first innings of the first Test in Perth from 13 to 17 November. Only Wood (37) reached 30 runs in Australia's 180. Lillee and Alderman had Pakistan on 8 for 26 in reply before the veteran Sarfraz, batting at No. 8, made 26 and helped lift the total to 62. Australia declared her second innings closed at 8 for 424 after a

*Terry Alderman sends Viv Richards' stump cartwheeling
in the 1981–82 Test in Melbourne. The spikes beside
the stumps are microphones.*

laborious 106 by Hughes, 85 in 298 minutes by
Laird and an aggressive 47 from Marsh. Set to
score 543 to win, Pakistan reached 3 for 96 when
one of the most undignified incidents in Test
history occurred.

Pakistan's captain Javed Miandad turned a
ball from Lillee to the leg side and as he completed
an easy single he was obstructed by Lillee. In
the fracas that followed Lillee kicked Miandad,
who responded by swinging back his bat and
shaping to hit Lillee with it. Lillee responded
by raising both fists. At this point umpire Tony
Crafter stepped between them and stopped what
appeared likely to develop into a brawl.

The Australian team, acting under an ACB
charter which allowed players to discipline team-
mates who misbehaved, fined Lillee $200 and
asked Miandad for an apology, but this was never
received. Umpires Crafter and Mel Johnson, who
had a close-up view of the affair, objected to
the penalty on the ground that it was too light
and Lillee was subsequently suspended for two
limited-over matches against Pakistan and West
Indies. Pakistan had made only 256 in the final
innings of the Test, Australia winning by 286
runs thanks to Yardley's 6 for 84.

Australia clinched the rubber by taking the
second Test by 10 wickets after further splendid
bowling by Lillee, who took 9 for 132 in the
match, and a copybook 201 by Greg Chappell.
A series of controversial umpiring decisions,
frequently replayed on Packer's TV programmes,
marred this and other matches in the summer.
Pakistan recovered to win the third Test by an

innings and 82 runs with excellent team batting, despite another fine display by Yardley, who took 7 for 186 off 66 overs, and 100 in 386 minutes by Wood.

The Pakistanis relied heavily on Miandad and Zaheer Abbas to score runs but their best player was Imran Khan who made handy runs and bowled splendidly, taking 28 wickets in the side's eight first-class matches, only two of which were won. The team won 6, lost 6 and drew 1 of their limited-over matches and failed to make the WSC finals.

The West Indies beat South Australia by 226 runs, New South Wales by nine wickets, played a draw with Tasmania, and beat Queensland by an innings and 92 runs before the first Test at Melbourne from 26 to 30 December. The West Indies encountered Greg Chappell in the midst of a sensational batting slump which saw him out for a duck seven times in the season. He had already made three successive ducks when he was out in the fifth over for his fourth.

Gloom for Greg Chappell fans contrasted sharply with the delight Lillee's admirers felt when he beat Lance Gibbs' world record in this match by taking his 310th Test wicket, a mark he would have reached far earlier had his "Super Test" wickets in the two years of WSC been accepted.

West Indies led by three runs on the first innings, but in the second innings Australia made the highest score of the match, 222, thanks to 66 by Border and a brave 64 by Laird. Left to score 220 to win, West Indies succumbed for 161, Australia winning by 58 runs. This was the last match before the old scoreboard was dismantled to make room for an electronic board that would carry millions of dollars worth of advertising.

At Sydney from 2 to 6 January Yardley prevented the West Indies getting a stranglehold on the second Test by taking 7 for 37 from 77 balls (final figures 7 for 98) when a huge score appeared likely in the tourists' second innings.

One of these wickets came from an astonishing catch on the boundary by Dyson, who sprinted 30 metres before leaping high to bring down an overhead catch that removed Clarke. Chasing 373 to win in the final innings, Australia were in trouble when Chappell was out for another duck. At 4 for 169, they appeared likely to fold before the West Indies fast bowlers until Dyson played a long (377 minutes) defensive innings for 127 to save the match.

Lynton Taylor, managing director of Packer's PBL Sports which marketed cricket in Australia, announced just before the third Test in Adelaide, from 30 January to 3 February, that he doubted if Test cricket could be saved. The players responded to this idiocy by providing a magnificent match in which the advantage swung back and forth for five days. Australia lost 4 for 17 before Chappell in his best innings for months made 61. Border's 78 and a plucky 39 from Marsh, after being flattened by a bouncer, lifted the total to 238. Gomes' second century of the series rescued the West Indies after they lost 4 for 92 and they finished with a lead of 151 on the first innings.

Australia made another disastrous start in the face of fiery pace bowling by Holding, Roberts, Croft and Garner. Border and Laird stayed together for four hours to add 166, Border reaching 126, Laird 78. Hughes carried on the good work with a fine 84 and at 4 for 341 they seemed likely to save the match and win the series. But on the final morning the Australians lost their last six wickets for 24 runs, big Joel Garner taking 4 for 5 in nine overs, leaving the West Indies to score 236 in 270 minutes to win. In a tense finish, Australia's dropped catches helped the West Indies get home with 17 balls to spare. Lloyd, 77 not out, was dropped three times.

The West Indies lost only one of their seven first-class matches and won 12 of their 17 limited-over matches. Larry Gomes, freed of worry about holding a Test spot, headed both the Test (393

Rodney Marsh clasps his face after having his helmet knocked off in the 1981–82 Test against the West Indies in Adelaide.

runs at 78.60) and first-class (712 runs at 89.00) averages. The bowling of Michael Holding overshadowed everything achieved by his team-mates, however, and in three Tests he took 24 wickets at 14.33. He was well supported by Garner, Roberts and Croft, but by contrast Lillee received little support from the declining Thomson. Border was Australia's batting hero with 336 runs at 67.20 in the Tests, with Dyson next best with 166 runs, scored in four innings, at 55.33.

The Australian selectors named Greg Chappell as captain of the Australian team to make a short tour of New Zealand during February and March 1982, before they picked the team. Chappell then helped Phil Ridings, Alan Davidson, Ray Lindwall and Len Maddocks pick the team, which was contrary to the normal custom of Board members selecting a captain from the chosen team. Chappell realised that

following the underarm incident in Melbourne he would be given a hostile reception. The programme was taken more seriously than previous New Zealand tours. Instead of choosing to "blood" aspiring youngsters, the selectors opted for the strongest possible team, but their squad was restricted to 13 players for the six-week tour. The team was: G. S. Chappell (captain), 33, K. J. Hughes, 28, T. A. Alderman, 25, A. R. Border, 26, R. J. Bright, 27, D. K. Lillee, 32, R. W. Marsh, 34, L. S. Pascoe, 32, J. Dyson, 27, B. M. Laird, 31, J. R. Thomson, 31, G. M. Wood, 25, B. Yardley, 35, with Alan Crompton as manager. The major absentee was Doug Walters, who had retired.

Just before the men's team arrived in New Zealand, Australia's women's team won the third World Cup by winning 11 of their 12 matches in New Zealand. The twelfth match was tied. In the 60-over final at Lancaster Park, Christchurch, a crowd of 3000 saw Australia beat England by three wickets. England batted first and had scored 5 for 151 against tight, accurate Australian bowling when their overs ran out.

Police show no mercy as they handcuff a spectator who invaded the field during the New Zealand–Australia one-day match in Auckland in 1982.

Australia reached 7 for 152 in 59 overs against a similarly accurate attack to win by three wickets. This exciting match received wide television coverage that delighted fans of women's cricket after a seven-week competition in both the north and south islands of New Zealand between four nations. Australia were the only unbeaten team.

The men's tour was the most successful ever made to New Zealand by an Australian side, with gate receipts, crowds and player behaviour reaching a new high. Chappell was a model of decorum before boisterous crowds that overflowed the grounds to see matches packed with incidents. One spectator rolled a lawn bowl onto the field while Chappell was batting—a reminder of the delivery he had ordered in Melbourne.

The first Test, from 26 February to 2 March 1982 at Wellington, was drawn, rain preventing

any chance of a result. The second Test, between 12 and 16 March in Auckland, produced New Zealand's second win in the matches between the countries. A magnificent 161 by opener Bruce Edgar enabled New Zealand to score 387 in their first innings and lead Australia by 177 runs. Richard Hadlee bowled superbly in Australia's second innings to take 5 for 63, restricting Australia to 280 despite an even 100 by Wood. Set to score 104 to win, New Zealand lost five wickets in doing so, with Lillee, Alderman and Yardley bowling defiantly.

At Christchurch from 19 to 22 March Australia won the third Test by eight wickets after Greg Chappell played one of the best innings of his career. Following a summer of unprecedented failures, he scored 176 out of Australia's 353, with 2 sixes and 23 fours. Lillee, Thomson and Alderman then dismissed New Zealand for 149. Following on, New Zealand struggled against the spin of Yardley and Border and were dismissed for 272, John Wright contributing 141. Australia made the 69 needed to win for the loss of two wickets, levelling the series. Greg Chappell was accidentally flattened by a spectator after scoring 108 in a one-day match, and in the Christchurch Test had his cap snatched from his head by a young spectator. There was no hint of complaint from the Australians over these incidents and paid attendances for the tour totalled more than 200,000 and the New Zealand Cricket Council made a profit of £NZ58,000 on the tour.

Greg Chappell averaged 78.33 in the Tests, the only Australian to average more than fifty. Yardley was the most successful Australian bowler, taking 13 wickets for 23.92 in the Tests and 17 wickets at 27.17 in all first-class matches. New Zealanders won £NZ14,000 and the Australians £NZ12,600 of the prizemoney on offer, Chappell taking the Sportsman of the Series award of £NZ1700.

While the Australian team was in New Zealand South Australia won the Sheffield Shield for the first time since 1975–76 with an exciting victory in the final match of the season, a victory that brought with it $56,000 in prizemoney. The competition had been conducted under a rule which required each team to bowl 100 balls an hour. The packed international programme meant that the States with several Test representatives were severely handicapped. To win the Shield, South Australia had to score maximum points in the last match against Victoria in Adelaide from 26 February to 1 March, which they achieved despite a splendid 116 by Wiener in Victoria's first innings. They led by 126 on the first innings thanks to 126 by Jeff Crowe. Victoria got the lead for the loss of only two wickets but thereafter disappointed, leaving South Australia only 161 for victory.

Pakistan, after a tough series against England during the southern winter, arrived home to meet an Australian side captained by Kim Hughes which was in match-hardened condition. Hughes' players left home as football competitions were ending and a brief training camp in Perth was their sole preparation. Greg Chappell was unavailable for business reasons, Lillee because of surgery to his right knee, and Pascoe for personal reasons. Marsh, who declined the vice-captaincy in favour of a younger man, arrived late because of the illness of his son. The Australian team was: K. J. Hughes (captain), 28, A. R. Border, 27, T. M. Alderman, 26, R. J. Bright, 28, I. W. Callen, 27, J. Dyson, 28, B. M. Laird, 31, G. F. Lawson, 24, R. W. Marsh, 34, W. B. Phillips, 24, G. M. Ritchie, 22, P. R. Sleep, 25, J. R. Thomson, 32, G. M. Wood, 25, B. Yardley, 35, with Col Egar as manager.

Australian newspapers largely ignored this six-week tour, concentrating on the Commonwealth Games in Brisbane. This was just as well for the team, which failed to win one of their nine games. Pakistan, astutely led by Imran Khan, won all three Tests and the two limited-over matches that were completed—the third was abandoned because of crowd disruption. The Australians were bamboozled by spinner Abdul Qadir, who took 22 wickets in the three Tests and proved the dominant personality of the series.

Qadir bowled a clever mixture of leg spin, top spin and googlies which, pitched into rough created by boot studs, destroyed the Australians' confidence. The Australians' frustration was compounded by unruly crowds and puzzling umpiring decisions. At Karachi in the first Test, from 22 to 27 September 1982, the Australians could scarcely believe it when umpire Mahboob Shah gave Mohsin Khan not out to a caught behind appeal. Mohsin scored a further 25 before he tried to brush a ball, from Lawson, away from his stumps with his hand and was given out "handled the ball".

On the first day spectators upset the players' concentration by setting alight a marquee and on the third day Hughes took his players from the field on two occasions when they were pelted with rocks, vegetables and other assorted missiles. Hughes threatened to end the tour and return immediately to Australia if any of his men were hurt by the stone-throwers. Australia lost this Test by nine wickets when Qadir took 5 for 19 to finish with 5 for 76 and seven wickets in the match. Qadir did even better in the second Test from 30 September to 5 October at Faisalabad, taking 4 for 76 and 7 for 142, Australia losing by an innings and three runs, despite 106 not out by Ritchie in the second innings.

Pakistan won the third Test at Lahore from 14 to 19 October by nine wickets after centuries by Mohsin Khan (135) and Javed Miandad (138). Australia increased their problems by dropping catches. This time it was Imran Khan's bowling that ended Australia's chances of saving the match after they trailed by 151 on the first innings. The tour ended unhappily after less than an hour's play in a limited-over match during which Lawson, Callen and Ritchie were struck on the leg and body by missiles. Hughes led his team from the field and they returned to their hotel. Violence erupted inside and outside the stadium.

Ritchie headed the Australian Test and first-class averages but the outstanding Australian on this ill-considered tour was Lawson, whose spirit remained undaunted in the face of his team-mates' failures. He took 15 wickets on the trip at 24.26, nine of them in the Tests at an average of 33.44 and his big-hitting often harassed the Pakistanis. Australia dropped 15 catches in the Tests, which ranks among the most dismal tours ever made by an Australian side.

By this time, cricket all round the world was being affected by politics. The Gleneagles Agreement signed at the Commonwealth Heads of Government Meeting in June, 1977, had caused tours to be cancelled, players to be suspended, and far too often had created opportunities for politicians with no interest in cricket to cheapen public debate. A Test had been cancelled in Guyana in 1981 because Robin Jackman, who had coached in South Africa, was in the England side. The West Indies Board of Control advised New Zealand they would not welcome a cricket team in 1982 because of a multi-racial South African Rugby tour of New Zealand. Mrs Gandhi, the Indian Prime Minister, tried to set an example when she said that although she continued her opposition to apartheid she would not ban English players from touring India if they had been to South Africa.

The Australians arrived home the day before the thirty-fifth English team began a tour of Australia which comprised 11 first-class matches and 12 limited-over matches. England did not consider the players who had toured in South Africa in 1982. They sadly missed Gooch and struggled throughout the tour to find an opening batsman to replace him. The crazy itinerary allowed England little time for acclimatisation and none at all for up-country matches, and meant that players who missed Test selection were idle for most of the tour. The English team was: R. G. D. Willis (captain), 33, D. W. Randall, 31, D. I. Gower, 25, A. J. Lamb, 28, G. Fowler, 25, E. E. Hemmings, 33, I. T. Botham, 27, D. R. Pringle, 24, C. J. Tavare, 28, G. Miller, 30, R. W. Taylor, 41, N. G. Cowans, 21, G. Cook, 31, with Doug Insole as manager, and Bernard Thomas, on his 11th successive tour, as physiotherapist.

All England's first-class matches were played before the start of the limited-over competition in which New Zealand joined. The Englishmen began badly when they lost by 171 runs to Queensland, the first time Queensland had defeated England since 1929–30. Kepler Wessels (103) and Greg Chappell (126) set up Queensland's victory with centuries in a second innings of 5 declared for 435, after Gower (100) and Lamb (117) made centuries in England's first innings. Both Chappell and Wessels were dropped and England had only their bad fielding to blame.

England recovered with a one-wicket win over Western Australia before the first Test on the WACA from 12 to 17 November. This tense match was marred by ugly crowd behaviour. Makeshift opener Chris Tavare batted all the first day for 66 out of England's total of 4 for 242. After having an appeal for caught behind against

Terry Alderman who badly injured his shoulder in an encounter with a spectator in Perth in the 1982–83 series against England.

Botham denied by the umpire at the bowler's end, Lawson appealed to the umpire at square leg, who gave Botham out. Botham walked off but indicated the ball had come off his pad.

When the English total passed the 400 mark, about a dozen spectators invaded the field brandishing Union Jacks. One of them cuffed Alderman across the back of the head. Alderman gave chase and executed a poor Rugby tackle on the intruder, pitching forward onto the point of his shoulder as he brought his man down. Lillee and Border rushed to Alderman's assistance and held the culprit until police arrived and took the man away in handcuffs. Alderman's shoulder was

quickly put back into place but the injury ended his season, at a high personal cost. Fights between English and Australian supporters, most of them the worse for alcohol, immediately broke out in the crowd and as other spectators invaded the field the police had a busy time restoring order. Chappell took the Australians from the field but they returned after 14 minutes to finish off England's innings for 411.

At 3 for 123 Chappell and Hughes added a further 141 in a display of outstanding driving that put the England dawdle to shame. Chappell hit 2 sixes and 11 fours in his 117, which gave Australia a lead of 13 runs. Reduced to three front-line bowlers by Alderman's injury, Australia were further handicapped when Lillee wrenched a knee in a crumbling foothold. At 5 for 151 England looked in danger of defeat but Australia lost their winning chance when they failed to remove nightwatchman Taylor. He stayed in for 90 minutes on the final morning and the match fizzled out in a draw after Randall (115) had made his third century in Australia.

Tavare was largely responsible for England's 26-run win over New South Wales at Sydney from 20 to 23 November, batting for six hours for 147. But he failed in both innings of the second Test at Brisbane in the following match, which Australia won by seven wickets after an outstanding debut by Wessels, with 162 and 46. Wessels was a controversial selection in the Australian team although he had married an Australian woman and bought a Brisbane newsagency. He was born in Bloemfontein in South Africa's Orange Free State and although he had served the qualifying period in the Queensland Sheffield Shield side, many experts doubted his loyalty to Australian cricket.

The depth of Australia's fast bowling talent shocked England in the third Test at Adelaide from 10 to 15 December. With Lillee and Alderman still unfit and Rackemann suffering from a groin strain, Lawson, Thomson and Hogg did a fine job in their place, taking 17 wickets between them to give Australia an eight-wicket win and a firm hold on the rubber. Greg Chappell made his second century of the series, 115. Gower's second innings 114 could not compensate for the damage Thomson's pace did to England's morale, although Lawson took most wickets, with 9 for 122 in the match.

With Australia leading 2–nil, England took the battle for the Ashes to the fifth Test with a thrilling three-run win in the fourth Test at Melbourne between 26 and 30 December. Australia wanted 292 to win in the final innings and appeared beaten when their ninth wicket fell at 218. Then Border and Thomson began a stand that had the whole of Australia watching on television. They were still together at the end of the fourth day, 37 runs short of victory. Although the match could have been over in a

few moments on the last day, 18,000 turned up to watch, all of them admitted free, and were rewarded with an enthralling finish.

Australia were only a boundary away from winning when Thomson sparred at a ball from Botham that was wide of the off stump. The ball flew to second slip from the edge of the bat to Tavare, who failed to get both hands to it. The ball struck his shoulder, bouncing over his head just within reach of Miller, fielding at first slip. Miller, reacting in an instant, held the catch near his knees. The only closer Tests were the ties between Australia and the West Indies and Australia and India. (In 1902, Australia beat England at Old Trafford, also by three runs.) The 18 overs bowled on the final morning were a fascinating tactical struggle, with Willis positioning all his fieldsman on the boundary when Border had strike, allowing easy singles and twos so that England could concentrate on dismissing Thomson. England showed unmistakable panic as Australia edged towards victory, every run cheered.

Australia regained the Ashes which had been held by England since 1977 when the fifth Test at Sydney from 2 to 7 January was drawn. Australia benefited from two umpiring decisions, the first allowing Dyson to continue to 79 when he was clearly run out before he scored, and the second permitting Hughes to carry on to 137 when he seemed to have been caught at short leg off Hemmings early on. But it was the dominance of the Australian fast bowlers, not umpiring, that decided the series. Lawson took 34 wickets in the rubber at 20.20, Thomson 22 at 18.68 and Hogg proved a fine substitute when Lillee was injured by taking 11 wickets at 27.45. None of England's bowlers reached 20 wickets, Willis finishing on top of the Test averages with 18 at 27.00. Largely because of the edges the pace men found, Marsh took 28 catches, a record for a five-Test series. Eight times in ten Test innings Australia's pace bowlers dismissed an opener before 15 runs had been scored.

*Mike Veletta plays a leg glance with the delicacy that
has made him a favourite of Perth fans.*

Greg Chappell handed over the Australian
captaincy to Hughes for the limited-over
competition which began two days after the Tests
concluded. England reluctantly agreed to wear
coloured clothing for this series and to use the
white ball needed at night, but with five players
unaccustomed to playing under floodlights, failed
to reach the finals, in which Australia beat New
Zealand 2–nil. England's tour was a big financial
success, with 554,142 watching the Tests and
451,098 the 17 limited-over matches. The
Australians shared more than $100,000 in
prizemoney, having helped to pull crowds of
84,153 and 71,393 in Melbourne.

Keen students of the game lamented the
inclusion of Wessels in the Australian side,
although he had taken out naturalisation papers.
They were also puzzled by the failure of Botham,
a match-winner in England, to produce a single
performance that influenced a match. His top
score with the bat was only 58 and his 18 Test
wickets came at a costly 40.50 apiece.

For the first time the Sheffield Shield was
decided by a final between the two leading States.
Tasmania competed as a full member for the first
time, with each State playing ten matches before
the finals. New South Wales won the Shield for
the first time in 17 seasons under the captaincy
of Rick McCosker. They defeated Western
Australia by 54 runs in the final at Perth from
4 to 8 March 1983, Trevor Chappell turning in
an outstanding all-round display. Tasmania had
the satisfaction of beating New South Wales

outright in Sydney and on the first innings in Hobart. Lillee was fined $600 for abusive language towards spectators in an Adelaide Shield match, Whitney received a small fine for aggressive behaviour in the final in Perth and Toohey missed a Shield match after disputing an umpire's decision in a Sydney grade match.

Australia did a lot to correct the drift away from cricket in schools by introducing in 1979 an all-States schoolboys carnival followed in the 1980s by tours for Young Australian teams. Dirk Wellham captained the first of these to Zimbabwe in 1982–83, and in August 1983 the Young Australian side captained by Mike Veletta beat Young England 2–1 in a three-"Test" series in England. Apart from Veletta, the Young Australian team included Craig McDermott, Tony Dodemaide and Ian Healy, who all played later for Australia. By 1988 it was calculated that 135 first-class players and 35 Test players began in the interstate schools carnival.

To help Sri Lanka build up for the 1983 World Cup in England, two Australian States played matches against a Sri Lankan touring team at the end of the 1982–83 home season. Both were drawn, the first against New South Wales in Sydney from 10 to 12 February after rain and bad light interrupted play, the second against Tasmania at Devonport from 14 to 16 February after Ratnayeke and Jeganathan made an impressive 140 for the eighth wicket. Two months later Greg Chappell took an Australian senior team to Sri Lanka for a tour comprising one Test, one three-day match, and four limited-over matches. Rod Marsh was unavailable and Roger Woolley replaced him, thus becoming the first Tasmanian to play for Australia since Laurie Nash in 1931–32. The Australian team was G. S. Chappell (captain), 34, D. W. Hookes, 28, A. R. Border, 27, T. G. Hogan, 26, R. M. Hogg, 32, D. K. Lillee, 33, J. N. Maguire, 26, S. B. Smith, 21, K. C. Wessels, 25, G. M. Wood, 26, R. D. Woolley, 28, G. N. Yallop, 30, B. Yardley, 35.

Sri Lanka had sensational wins in the first two limited-over matches, but were overwhelmed in the Test at Kandy from 22 to 26 April. Australia declared at 4 for 514 in the first innings after Wessels (141), Yallop (98), Chappell (66) and Hookes (143 not out) savaged the bowling. Sri Lanka were 3 for 9 in their first innings and 5 for 13 in their second innings, finishing with 271 and 205, giving Australia victory by an innings and 38 runs. The next two limited-over matches were drawn after rain.

Greg Chappell again showed his unwillingness to submit to the strain of limited-over cricket when he withdrew from Australia's team for the third World Cup in England in June 1983, and the captaincy again reverted to Hughes. Australia won only two of their six matches. They lost their opening match by 13 runs to Zimbabwe at Trent Bridge on 9 June, lost to the West Indies by 101 runs at Headingley on 11 and 12 June, beat India by 162 runs at Trent Bridge on 13 June, won against Zimbabwe by 32 runs at Southampton on 16 June, lost by seven wickets to the West Indies on 18 June, and in the match which would have taken them into the semi-finals had they won, succumbed to India by 118 runs at Chelmsford on June 20. None of the eight teams in the 60-over competition went without a win. The big surprise came when India beat the hot favourites, the West Indies, by 43 runs in a low-scoring final.

The Prudential Assurance Company put up £500,000 sponsorship, and with gate receipts totalling £1,195,712 the International Cricket Conference distributed more than £1 million to full and associate members. This was over and above the £53,900 paid in advance to full members like Australia and the £30,200 paid to Zimbabwe.

Pakistan erred in appointing Imran Khan captain of the team that toured Australia in 1983–84 after announcing that Zaheer Abbas would lead the side. Imran could not bowl on the tour because of a stress fracture to his left shin and was only able to bat in the last two of the five Tests.

Sarfraz Nawaz was left out of the original team and outspokenly condemned selectors for their incompetence. This drew a six-month suspension which had to be suddenly forgotten when Imran could not bowl and Sarfraz had to be flown in as his replacement. Abdul Qadir, who had destroyed Australia's batting in Pakistan the previous year, became prone to cussedness in the disunited team after Australia's selectors fielded as many as six left-handers against him to neutralise his googly. All those hoping to see him give a supreme exhibition of the leg-spinning skills were sadly disappointed.

Pakistan won only the matches against South Australia, Victoria and Tasmania in their 11 first-class matches. They lost twice to Australia in Tests, with the other three drawn, and were beaten by Western Australia. They lost eight and won four of their non-first-class matches, including four limited-over matches to Australia.

Australia's success stemmed from the dominance of their pace bowlers and little Qasim Omar won the admiration of spectators with his plucky batting against Lillee, Lawson, Hogg and Rackemann. He took nasty blows without flinching, in marked contrast to Zaheer and other senior batsmen in his team who appeared to lose their nerve against pace bowling.

Greg Chappell deliberately stage-managed his appearance in the fifth Test at Sydney from 2 to 6 January 1984. Having decided that this would be his last Test, he invited his parents over from Adelaide and brought his wife and children down from Brisbane, aware that he always performed best when there was heavy pressure on him. He did not disappoint either his family or his fans in an unforgettable final innings of 182, batting with his own imperious authority for 526 minutes, striking the on drive as well as it has ever been hit in an innings that produced 17 fours. On the way he passed Bradman's total of 6996 runs to become Australia's highest run-getter in Tests. When Pakistan batted, Chappell's two catches took him

Greg Chappell acknowledges the crowd's applause after reaching his century in his farewell Test innings in Sydney.

to 122 Test catches, two more than Cowdrey's world record.

Chappell announced his retirement in a television interview with his brother Ian at the end of the second day. Later that night Lillee also announced that this would be his last Test and his bag of eight wickets in the match took his total of Test wickets to 355, the exact number of Marsh's Test dismissals behind the stumps. Right to the end of a memorable career Lillee bowled with superb technique, his control a cricket wonder, throwing in a superb leg cutter to compensate for his drop in pace, never forgetting the position of the TV cameras nor neglecting a chance to fall into his special position for appeals, knees bent, both hands pointing skyward. He later played for Tasmania and Northants, and even at 40 kept a good line.

Shortly after this Test Rod Marsh also announced his retirement, removing a famous threesome from Australian cricket in the one season. All three had set world records, all three had incurred the wrath of the Australian Cricket Board and, even more, had angered traditionalists through their key roles in the success of Packer's new brand of cricket. Australian cricket was badly weakened by their departure and their absence created gaps in the Australian team it would take years to fill.

Greg Chappell, often in ill-health, batted with a talent and grace few Australians have matched. Between 1970 and 1984 he scored 74 first-class centuries, compiling 24,207 runs at an average of of 52.40, and held 371 catches. He captained Australia in 48 of his 88 Tests for 21 wins, 14 draws and 13 losses. He made 31 Test fifties and 24 centuries. He was sensitive, intelligent, and more than any other of the Packer players brooded over the strained friendships his WSC days had caused.

Lillee running in to bowl was one of the most exciting sights in Test cricket for more than a decade. Television gave him matinee idol status and even if there was a lot of the ham actor in him he had ideal equipment for TV stardom— big, dark, menacing, with an ability to make every ball a special experience. He took 861 wickets in first-class cricket at 23.13, 355 of them in Tests at 23.92, and if he had a weakness it was that he did not bowl as well to left-handers as he did to right-handers.

I have never agreed that Brian Taber deserved to be sacked for Marsh as Australia wicket-keeper, but once in the job there is no denying that Marsh gave it a unique combination of ebullience and competitiveness. The athleticism displayed as he overcame the physique of a wharf labourer to drag down catches with headlong dives was matched by power-hitting with the bat that was uplifting to see. With Lillee and Thomson to produce the nicks, he made 343 Test catches and 12 stumpings in 96 Tests and had five victims in an innings 12 times. He made three Test centuries and had four scores in the nineties. Altogether he made 11,607 first-class runs and dismissed 870 batsmen, 219 of them caught off Lillee's bowling, with only 65 of them stumped. Marsh's Test batting average should have been higher than 26.52, but he made only two fifties in his last 48 Test knocks, swinging across the ball too often instead of hitting straight.

Chappell, Lillee and Marsh began their Test careers together when Australia had just been comprehensively thrashed by South Africa. They were transformed from talented novices into tough, seasoned Test players by Ian Chappell and between them gave the Australian team strength that allowed them to take on and sometimes defeat the best cricket teams in the world.

The Captain's Hot Seat

Australia on tour 1983-88; the rebel tour 1985-86; touring teams in Australia 1984-88

Until the retirement of Rodney Marsh, Australia's selectors always gave their Test wicket-keepers lengthy periods in the job. They picked the 'keepers they ranked the best and stuck with them, and the role of Australian wicket-keeper became notoriously difficult to secure and even harder to lose. No other job in Australian sport aroused so many charges of unfair monopoly. Only 21 'keepers had been used in 107 years of Test cricket when Marsh quit after a run of 96 Tests. Seven of those 'keepers held their places for 30 or more Tests, and 14 of them held the job for at least ten Tests.

Marsh's retirement ushered in a period of puzzling selection indecision. Initially they tried Roger Woolley, the first player to appear for Australia direct from the Tasmanian Sheffield Shield team. Tall, good-looking, Woolley was born in Hobart in 1954 and went to school at New Town, from which he won selection in under-age teams and finally emerged from the local district club into Tasmania's Under-19 side.

Prime Minister Bob Hawke receives treatment after his glasses were shattered in an attempted hook shot in a Canberra match between parliamentarians and journalists.

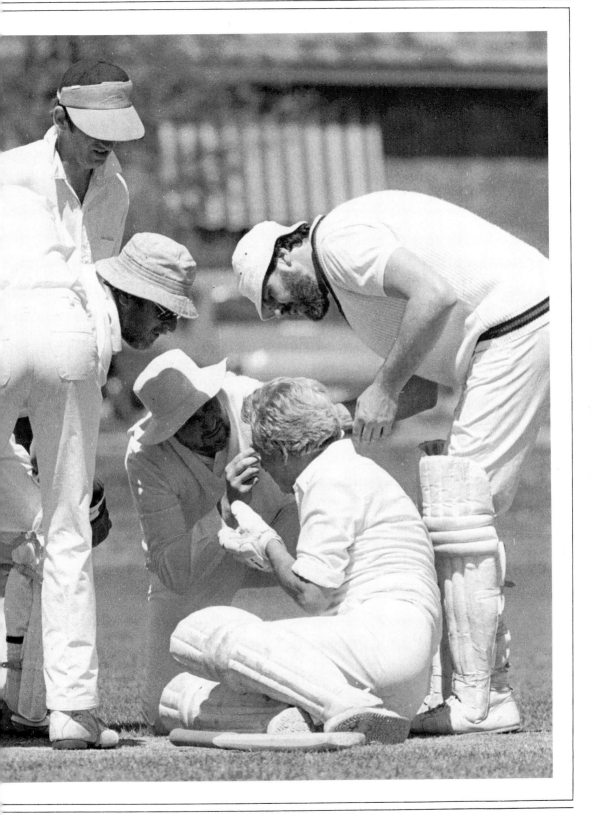

Consistently valuable displays as a middle order batsman won him a place in the Tasmanian side in 1977–78 when Bruce Doolan was the State's 'keeper. His 103 in his third Shield innings against Queensland at Launceston made him the first batsman to score a Shield century for Tasmania.

In 1978–79, Woolley and Jack Simmons put on 172 in an unbroken seventh-wicket stand which enabled Tasmania to beat Western Australia at Devonport and give Tasmania their first Shield win. In 1982–83, he became Tasmanian captain, with both Simmons and Brian Davison unavailable. His five catches in his Test debut at Kandy against Sri Lanka made him Marsh's logical successor, a position he consolidated by scoring 102 at Sydney in February 1984, to clinch Tasmania's fourth successive win over New South Wales.

Woolley was the only specialist 'keeper in the Australian team that toured the West Indies in 1983–84 under the captaincy of Kim Hughes. Wayne Phillips, who made 159 as Wessels' opening partner in his Test debut against Pakistan in Marsh's last season, was named as Woolley's understudy, although Kevin Wright held the 'keeping job for Phillips' State, South Australia. Yallop failed a fitness test on strained ligaments in his left knee six days before the team left for the West Indies and Dean Jones, a dashing right-hand batsman from the Melbourne club with only one season in the Victorian side behind him, took Yallop's place. Only Murray Bennett, the Sydney left-arm spinner, appeared unlucky not to be chosen for Australia's fifth tour of the West Indies. The team was: K. J. Hughes, 30, A. R. Border, 28, T. M. Alderman, 27, T. G. Hogan, 27, R. M. Hogg, 33, D. W. Hookes, 28, D. M. Jones, 22, G. F. Lawson, 26, J. N. Maguire, 28, G. R. J. Matthews, 24, W. B. Phillips, 26, C. G. Rackemann, 23, G. M. Ritchie, 24, S. B. Smith, 23, K. C. Wessels, 27, R. D. Woolley, 29, with Col Egar as manager, and Queenslander Geoff Dymock as coach.

Before the team left Australia the Australian Cricket Board faced a crisis when the players refused to sign tour contracts binding them without payment to play only for the ACB until May 1985. Board chairman Fred Bennett had discussions with the players and eventually a scheme guaranteeing the players' minimum payments was agreed on. Only two players who had appeared for Packer in the WSC years, Wessels and Hookes, were in the touring party. Most of the others had retired, and this left major weaknesses in the team. Col Egar had a difficult tour handling Hughes and Lawson, who were quick to challenge umpiring decisions, and his team became one of the most unpopular to visit the West Indies.

They played ten first-class matches, including five Tests, plus five one-day matches. They held out bravely for draws in the first two Tests but thereafter were crippled by injuries and were overwhelmed in the last three Tests and lost the one-day series 3–1, with one abandoned.

Wessels was forced to return home with a knee injury after the second Test and Graeme Wood was flown in to replace him. Wood began with innings of 76 against Barbados and 68 in the third Test before a ball from Garner broke an index finger and put him out of the tour. Steve Smith broke a finger in the fifth Test and could not bat in the second innings. Pace bowlers Hogg, Lawson and Rackemann were all forced to carry injuries into matches. Rackemann could not play for a month and was almost sent home for treatment, but in the end Egar decided not to fly in Rod McCurdy, on standby in Australia, to take his place. But the most controversial injury came in the second match against Guyana at Georgetown, when Woolley's finger was broken. Hughes called it a blessing in disguise, a comment which did not delight Woolley, who said:

The tour of the West Indies was a waste of time for me. I was really annoyed when I got back home and learned of the things Hughes had said about me. An

*Australian captain should be behind his players,
trying to build team spirit. I felt I was on the outer
from the start and my injury did not help.*

Woolley appeared in only one Test, the
fourth, at St John's, and made only six first-class
appearances on the tour. Opening batsman
Wayne Phillips was used in four Tests and in
other major matches on the tour and returned
home established as the team's No. 1 'keeper.
Woolley's problems with Hughes were unknown
to spectators who were regularly shown displays
of the Australians' petulance. Lawson was fined
£150 by the team management for angrily
snatching his hat from umpire D. J. Narine after
an appeal was disallowed in the first Test, which
was played from 2 to 7 March at Georgetown.
At Pointe-à-Pierre in the match against Trinidad
and Tobago, Hughes showed his annoyance at
the opposing captain's refusal to open up the
match with early declarations by refusing to take
easy runs, and patting back full tosses and half-
volleys while his partner Wayne Phillips sat on
the ground at the other end. Hughes made two
scoring strokes while 24 overs were bowled at
him. Phillips took his pads off and held them
under his arm while Hughes played out the final
over. Managers Egar and Dymock fined Hughes
£150 for this churlishness, which created
indignation among West Indians.

In the first innings of the first Test, Hogg
ignored Hughes' message to order Hogan to hit
out when Hogg joined him at the fall of the
ninth wicket. Instead Hogg batted for two and
a half hours and put on a record 97 for the last
wicket, Hogan contributing 42 not out, Hogg
52. Greenidge (120 not out) and Haynes (103 not
out) had an unbroken opening stand of 250 in
the final innings but fell 73 short of the 323 needed
to win.

Two heroic innings by Border saved Australia
from defeat in the second Test from 16 to 21
March at Port-of-Spain. In the first innings
Australia were 5 for 85, but Border batted for

*Wayne Phillips, who failed to reach the required standard
in an experimental period as Australia's 'keeper, certainly
did not lack class as a batsman and proved a splendid
timer of the ball.*

5 hours 49 minutes for 98 not out. In the second
innings, when Australia were headed for defeat
following a superb innings of 130 by Dujon,
Border batted for a further 4 hours 45 minutes
for 100 not out. He did not give a chance in
either innings.

Richards captained the West Indies in the
second Test while Lloyd flew to Melbourne to
fight a libel action against the Melbourne *Age*.
Lloyd was acting for the players in the West
Indian and Australian teams who figured in a
1981–82 one-day match where it was alleged that
the West Indies "threw" the match for financial

gain. Lloyd won $100,000 damages with costs after surviving an appeal to the Privy Council in London. All the players on both sides received $25,000 in out-of-court settlements following the Privy Council ruling in Lloyd's favour.

The third Test at Bridgetown from 30 March to 4 April was a curious affair. Neither side had gained a first innings advantage by lunch on the fourth day but by lunch on the fifth day the West Indies had won by 10 wickets. Australia made 429 thanks to a graceful 120 from Phillips. West Indies replied with 509, Haynes (145) and Richardson (131) adding 145 with the benefit of dropped catches. Lloyd, back from the Melbourne court, made 76. Australia then collapsed for 97, losing their last six wickets for 29 runs.

Three days later in the fourth Test at St John's Australia lost 2 for 14 in the first hour. Border propped up the innings with a stubborn 98 before Richardson (154) and Richards (178)—both playing at home in Antigua—put on 308 in a record third-wicket stand which carried West Indies to a total of 498 and a lead of 236. A spiritless Australian innings of 200 gave West Indies victory by an innings and 36 runs. By then the Australians were in disarray, unable to summon the fibre to resist Marshall, Garner and Holding at their fastest and the West Indies finished them off with a ten-wicket win in the fifth Test at Kingston. Australia had been outplayed in every department and in the five Tests West Indies did not lose a single second-innings wicket.

The statistics told a dismal story. Lawson was the highest Australian wicket-taker in the Tests with 12 wickets at a whopping 53.16 runs apiece. Four West Indian bowlers took ten wickets or more, Garner topping the list with 31 at 16.87, followed by Holding with 13 from three Tests at 18.84, and Marshall with 21 from four Tests at 22.85. Border made more runs than anybody on either side with 521 at 74.42, but no other Australian reached 300. Haynes (468 at 93.00), Richardson (327 at 81.75) and Greenidge (393 at

78.60) all exceeded 300 runs for the West Indies.

Matthews caused alarm among the team management when he was discovered smoking "funny cigarettes". No action was taken and this was treated as a minor indiscretion of a whole-hearted team member but it was recalled to his disadvantage by selectors years later.

While the Australian team toured the West Indies, Western Australia frustrated Queensland's hopes of winning the Sheffield Shield for the first time by winning the final in Perth from 9 to 13 March by four wickets. Thomson, captaining Queensland in Border's absence, allowed Queensland's first innings to meander on for more than 11 hours and when he declared at 7 for 431 Western Australia scored just as slowly. Geoff Marsh batted for four hours for 107 and when Marsh's stumps were scattered by Thomson, Rodney Marsh, at the non-striker's end, argued with the umpires that it was a no-ball. Thomson had, in fact, bowled 29 no-balls, but Marsh's plea for justice only won a place on the umpires' report for "showing dissent and hitting the pitch and throwing the bat". The players' committee gave Marsh a severe reprimand. Trailing by 68 on the first innings, Western Australia swung the match by dismissing Queensland for 154 in their second innings. Set to make 223 to win, Western Australia lost 6 for 199 before Marsh and Laird took them to a four-wicket win.

The season again demonstrated the futility of having Shield players sit in judgement on team-mates who misbehave. Between 27 and 30 January, Lillee, captaining Western Australia against Queensland in Brisbane, clashed with umpires firstly about taking a drinks break in a rain-interrupted session and later over their rejection of an appeal for a catch. Lillee was reported to the players' disciplinary committee, who exonerated him. The umpires then appealed to the ACB against the leniency of Lillee's treatment. Bob Merriman, co-ordinator of the ACB Cricket Committee, agreed with the

Geoffrey Lawson's determination is clear as he completes his long delivery stride. Injuries have hampered his career.

umpires and suspended Lillee for two matches.

Channel 9 televised none of this, but after showing 18 one-day matches between Australia, Pakistan and the West Indies, televised a further 8 one-day matches between the States for a trophy sponsored by a hamburger chain.

The West Indies were infuriated when, after winning the first final of the international one-day competition and playing a tie in the second, they were told a decider was necessary. They believed that in the event of a tie the team with the superior record in the qualifying rounds took the trophy, as happens in England.

But under the ACB regulations for this competition the third final had to be played, a decision greeted with anger in the West Indian

side. The West Indian Board of Control had to intervene and order their players to take the field. In an effort to placate the West Indians the ACB allocated an additional $18,000 in prizemoney for the winners of the third final. With Richards unfit to play, Lloyd did not appear at the MCG for the game, and Holding accepted the trophy when the West Indies won by six wickets. The interstate one-day competition went to South Australia for the first time, having somehow survived 15 seasons, despite regular screenings of defensive bowling and field placings. The boredom of watching great pace bowlers operate without slips and teams ready to concede singles to prevent boundaries apparently had not worried the sponsors.

Just before the Australian 1984–85 season began, Australia sent a team to India for a series of one-day internationals staged to celebrate the

Golden Jubilee of the Ranji Trophy, India's leading domestic competition. The trip was a goodwill gesture, but the activities of some of the Australian players produced yet another major crisis for Australian cricket.

The tour was significant to the Australian captain Kim Hughes, for he lost the support of several of his senior players and within a few weeks of his return home resigned the Australian captaincy in a tearful nationally televised press conference. After Australia had at last come to grips with the one-day game by winning the five match series 3–nil (the other two were abandoned), and after a magnificent gala dinner in Bombay, several of the Australians had their first serious discussions with representatives of the South African Cricket Union at Singapore on the way home.

Australia won the first one-day match at New Delhi on 28 September because of a gritty 107 by Wessels. The second at Trivandrum was washed out on 1 October, and the third at Jamshedpur on 3 October abandoned through rain after the truck carrying the Australians' gear arrived three hours late. Australia won the fourth match at Ahmedabad on 5 October by seven wickets, helped by 3 for 25 in 10 overs by Lawson, and then took the fifth match on 6 October at Indore by six wickets despite a steady 102 by Shastri. Rackemann impressed with his accuracy and hostility in all these matches and Phillips proved a neat and reliable 'keeper. The Australians donated most of their prizemoney of around $5000 to a home for crippled children in Ahmedabad.

The West Indies toured Australia for the fourth time in six seasons in 1984–85, and played their first full Test series against Australia since 1975–76, when they had suffered a demoralising 5–nil defeat. Lloyd, in his farewell tour, Richards, Greenidge and Holding were all that remained of that humiliated side and probably enjoyed the results of the tour more than their team-mates. They played 11 first-class matches, including 5

Tests, won 4, and drew 5, but the real joy of their programme for the veterans was the wide margins by which the West Indies won the first three Tests. This time it was Australia's turn to reel under the trauma of heavy defeat, with Lloyd going out after comfortable wins over India and a clean sweep over England, plus the emphatic victories over Australia in the West Indies. Not a bad year's work.

Australia contributed to their own problems by dropping 30 catches in the five Tests. Opposing an incessant battery of short-pitched deliveries at a time when gifted exponents of the hook shot, such as Kippax, McCabe and Richardson, did not exist, Australia tried 19 players, but the biggest disruption to the team was the resignation of Kim Hughes as captain after two Tests.

Hughes had become only a shadow of the batsman who had scored 24 first-class centuries. He scored 4 and 37, then 34 and 4, in the first two Tests of the West Indies tour and, instead of shrugging off the criticism by Ian Chappell and others, chose instead to demonstrate how valid Greg Chappell was when he warned the ACB of the immense strain involved in the Australian captaincy. Hughes was urged to reconsider but at a packed media conference began to read from a prepared statement, which said:

> The Australian captaincy is something I've held very dear to me. However, playing the game with the utmost enjoyment has always been of utmost importance. The constant speculation, criticism and innuendo from former players and sections of the media over the past four or five seasons have taken their toll. It is in the interests of the team and of myself that I have informed the ACB of my intention to stand down as Australian captain.

Hughes broke down towards the end of the statement and quit the room in tears, leaving team manager Bob Merriman to finish reading it. Hampered by Greg Chappell's habit of taking back the captaincy when he had rested, Hughes had led Australia in 28 Tests, for 4 wins, 11 draws

Skilful left-hander Graeme Wood, who took over the West Australian captaincy when Kim Hughes defaulted.

Western Australia by nine wickets in Perth from 2 to 4 November. Western Australia declared at 3 for 317 in their first innings, following a workmanlike century by Wood (141) and 97 by Shipperd, who was deprived of a century by a leg injury. West Indies got to within 15 runs of this total but the home team collapsed for 111 in their second innings, newcomer Courtney Walsh taking 5 for 60 to go with his first innings bag of 3 for 54.

The bouncy pitch at the WACA was tailor-made for the West Indies fast bowlers in the first Test from 9 to 12 November, with Holding at his awesome best, lightning fast, kicking the ball into the ribs, in a first innings coup of 6 for 21. With Australia out for 76 chasing 416, Holding could afford thereafter to concentrate on his racehorse betting, leaving Marshall, Garner and Walsh to take West Indies to an innings and 112-run win.

The West Indies' first defeat outside of Tests since 1980 followed between 16 and 19 November on a Sydney pitch responsive to spin. Bob Holland's right-arm leg spin and Murray Bennett's left-arm finger spin accounted for 15 West Indies wickets as New South Wales defeated the tourists by 71 runs. This began the theory that despite their expertise against fast bowling, the West Indians were vulnerable to spin, particularly wrist spin.

The Australian selectors failed to get the message that a spinner was needed at both ends and included only Holland for the second Test at Brisbane from 23 to 26 November. Holland, in his Test debut, impressed until Lloyd joined Richardson at 5 for 184. Lloyd (114) batted inspiringly and Richardson (138) lifted his stroke play in a stand of 152 in 122 minutes, which led to the West Indies winning by eight wickets.

Border took over as Australia's captain for the third Test at Adelaide from 7 to 11 December, which marked 100 years of Test cricket on that ground. The South Australian Cricket Association celebrated by inviting 22 captains

and 13 losses. He made 0 and 2 in the third Test at Adelaide and two ducks at Melbourne in the fourth Test and was dropped from the fifth in Sydney. He would have had ample opportunity to force his way back into the Australian side by scoring heavily in Shield matches for Western Australia but chose instead to drop out of first-class cricket.

After draws against Queensland and South Australia towards the end of October 1984, the West Indies defeated the Shield champions who had led their countries' teams there, and paraded them around Adelaide Oval in vintage cars. West Indies won by 191 runs but at no stage did the cricket fit the occasion. Lawson took 8 for 112 in the West Indies' first innings of 356 and followed with 3 for 69 in the second innings. Apart from Wessels' first innings of 98, the Australian batsmen looked impoverished.

Lloyd delayed his declaration in the fourth Test at Melbourne between 22 and 27 December until the second hour of the final day. Richards had given West Indies a big advantage by scoring 208 in their first innings of 479. Australia prevented the follow-on when Hilditch made 70, Wessels 90, in a total of 296, but when the West Indies batted again Lawson became the subject of an official West Indian protest over an incident with Greenidge. Lawson was fined $500 and put on a bond of $1500 for his future behaviour. Hilditch, after a break of five years from Test cricket, brought himself back into the limelight by scoring 113 in Australia's second innings, with Australia holding out against spirited bowling from Garner, Marshall and Walsh. Chasing 370 to win, Australia hung on to 8 for 198.

The West Indies entered the fifth Test from 30 December to 2 January at Sydney after 27 Tests without defeat, dating back to Melbourne in 1968–69. They were defeated by an innings and 55 runs, a result that delighted all lovers of spin bowling and proved that there were alternatives to the monotonous display of short-pitched bowling. Bennett and Holland, who had bowled New South Wales to victory earlier in the season, did it again.

Faced with deliveries that darted in or out from wrists or fingers they could not read, the West Indian batsmen, on a turning pitch, looked consistently uneasy. But the emphatic lesson of this upset was that spin bowlers need to bowl in tandem, with contrasting challenges at either end. Holland, born at Camperdown in Sydney but a product of Newcastle district cricket,

needed Murray Bennett to winkle batsmen out at the other end. Bennett, who bowled in dark glasses because of astigmatism, proved himself a thinking cricketer just short of Test quality, and was never the same bowler after Holland retired.

The West Indies contributed to their own defeat by omitting their one specialist spinner, Roger Harper, despite overwhelming evidence that the Sydney pitch favoured spin. Clive Lloyd in his 110th and last Test, 74 of those Tests as captain, fought hard in both innings to save his side. He took two hours to make 72 in the second innings and as he left the wicket the crowd gave him a standing ovation. Relations between the teams were strained throughout the series. Marshall, with 28 wickets at 19.78, was voted Man of the Series, but in hostility and accuracy he was little ahead of Garner, Walsh and Holding, all of them superb athletes and gutsy competitors.

The 1984–85 West Indian team under Lloyd reached a standard that few Australian teams have ever matched. Sir Donald Bradman, in an article in *Wisden*, said that only Armstrong's 1921 Australian team, his own 1948 side, and Joe Darling's 1902 team deserved comparison with the West Indies in 1984–85, whom he rated the best fielding team he had seen. The sole criticism of Lloyd's team was their low over-rate. They averaged only 74.4 overs a day in the Tests and, although a great side, attracted disappointing crowds with Australians perhaps unwilling to support their losing side.

Sri Lanka made their first full tour of Australia in 1984–85, competing in the one-day series against Australia and the West Indies, and in the World Championship Cup in Melbourne after Christmas. They proved they had classy batsmen in Duleep Mendis, Sidath Wettimuny and Ravindran Ratnayeke, but lacked strike bowlers.

Melbourne had endured months of acrimony as the Builders' Labourers Federation threatened to prevent the installation of floodlights for the

World Championship matches on the MCG to mark Victoria's 150th anniversary. All this was forgotten when the lights were switched on at sundown for the first floodlit cricket at the MCG with 82,494 spectators watching cricket's oldest rivals, England and Australia. The lights had cost $4 million to put up. They came on with Australia chasing England's 8 for 214, and to the delight of the crowd Robbie Kerr, 87 not out, and Dean Jones, 78 not out, produced a match-winning stand that took Australia to 3 for 215 and a seven-wicket win.

Both Australia and the West Indies missed a place in the final, Australia losing to Pakistan by 62 runs and to India by eight wickets, the West Indies going down to Pakistan in the semi-finals. India repeated her 1983 World Cup victory in England by defeating Pakistan by eight wickets in the final, an appropriate reward for Sunil Gavaskar, who captained India for the last time.

To celebrate fifty years of competition between the two countries, the Australian Women's Cricket Council invited England to make a tour of Australia in 1984–85 involving five Test matches and three one-day internationals. The Tests were played between December and February over four days in Perth, Adelaide, Brisbane, Gosford and Bendigo, the travelling and varying conditions fully testing the English players. The first and third Tests were drawn. England won a tension-packed match in Adelaide by five runs when Australia lost five wickets for six runs in the last 45 minutes. Australia won the fourth and fifth Tests by convincing margins. Jill Kennare scored 103 in the first Test and 104 in the fifth Test to pave the way for Australia's 2–1 victory, which was achieved despite the absence through injury of captain Sharon Tredrea. England's Janette Brittin won the Player of the Series award by averaging 42.90 compared with Kennare's 38.55.

Ignored yet again by the Channel 9 network, the Sheffield Shield competition produced a magnificent final for the second time in three

Dave Gilbert dives for a great close-in catch during a one-day international. He was one of the heroes of New South Wales' success in the 1985–86 Shield season.

years and provided cricket that was a great pleasure to watch after the dreary fare of the two limited-over tournaments. Queensland, as leaders on the Shield table, appeared all set for a final in Brisbane, a venue that would have suited them in their quest for their first-ever Shield win. But in the last round, New South Wales, aided by a Dave Gilbert hat-trick, beat Victoria by 25 runs. South Australia then surprisingly defeated Queensland in Adelaide to set up a Sydney final.

Border won the toss for Queensland but as his promising openers, Andrew Courtice and Robbie Kerr, went through the gates to start the Queensland innings, he must have regretted his luck with the toss. For the demolition contractor removing the Sheridan Stand chose

*Kim Hughes, who captained the Australians on two
rebel tours of South Africa, presents an Australian blazer
to South African captain Clive Rice.*

that moment to blow up the roof of the stand
and send it toppling to the ground. Queensland
were one wicket down for 12 and two for 18,
with both openers out. Jeff Thomson and Carl
Rackemann bowled their hearts out for
Queensland but in the final innings could not
break an epic last-wicket stand by Peter Clifford
and Dave Gilbert.

Needing 21 runs to win, Clifford took a nasty
blow on the head and another on the body. Gilbert
called him down the pitch for a conference.
"Don't stuff this up by getting out—I've waited
all season for this," said Gilbert. To that point
he had batted in 12 matches for 96 runs at an
average of 48, with 13 not outs. Now he scraped
together four more while Clifford provided the
stroke play at the other end. With the scores
level, Queensland had the chance of a tie, but
Gilbert gave New South Wales the Shield for
the 38th time by hacking Rackemann away for
a four. Packer's cameras were missing as
Rackemann came off in tears, the notion that
he was a gutless cream-puff of a bowler buried
forever.

Telecom, the Australian telephone service,
received more than 100,000 calls for scores during
this match. Radio announcers' voices quavered
through the excitement of it as they read the
scores. Clifford sat in the New South Wales
dressing-room amid the popping champagne
corks, content with 83 not out.

In March 1985, Australia sent a team to

Sharjah, at the invitation of the United Arab Emirates for a four-nation competition. The Australians found the Sharjah Cricket Ground had been built over a huge hole dug out of the desert by Arab businessman and cricket-lover Abdulrahman Bukhatir. All four matches, televised over Bukhatir's Dubai network, were sold out. Australia won their first match with a last-ball single against England, while India beat Pakistan in the other match. In the final India held their place as the world's best one-day cricket nation by easily passing Australia's total of 139.

Shortly after the Australians returned home the news leaked out that several players under contract to the ACB planned to join a rebel tour of South Africa in the summer of 1985–86. The ACB accepted immediately that it was unable to take action against the non-contracted players involved, Terry Alderman, Trevor Hohns, Rod McCurdy, Steve Rixon, Greg Shipperd and Michael Taylor. But the ACB decided to sue all the players who breached their ACB contracts by going to South Africa.

The South African Cricket Union had intended to wait until the thirtieth Australian team was in England before it announced the rebel players' venture. But the premature disclosure of the rebel tour plans created havoc with the ACB's English tour preparations. The Australian team for England was originally announced as A. R. Border, A. M. J. Hilditch, M. J. Bennett, W. B. Phillips, D. M. Wellham, G. M. Wood, T. M. Alderman, R. J. McCurdy, S. J. Rixon, G. R. J. Matthews, R. G. Holland, G. M. Ritchie, K. C. Wessels, G. F. Lawson, D. C. Boon, C. J. McDermott, and S. P. O'Donnell. But once the signatories to contracts for the South African tour became known, changes had to be made hurriedly.

The Federal Minister for Sport, John Brown, called on the ACB to take punitive action against players who went to South Africa. The former Australian opening batsman Bruce Francis, who

had acted as the South African Cricket Union's Australian agent in signing the rebel players, called this the most obnoxious request ever put to a sports organisation by the Australian government. Across Australia cricket writers took to checking with every likely Shield player whether they were going to South Africa. Public opinion polls were taken on the morality of the South African venture.

The ACB announced that every player who toured England would be asked to sign a statutory declaration that they would not tour South Africa. Kerry Packer helped the Board by persuading three of the best players who had agreed to go to South Africa—Dirk Wellham, Wayne Phillips and Graeme Wood—to change their minds and join his payroll. This was a smart move by Packer, who had a lot of money tied up in the television coverage of the English tour. Murray Bennett also withdrew from the South African visit when he realised his tour of England was at risk.

Part of Packer's deal with Wellham, Wood and Phillips was that he would pay their legal fees if they were sued for breach of contract by the South African Cricket Union. Prime Minister Bob Hawke offered similar support to those who had signed contracts with the SACU but now wished to withdraw from the agreements. But Hawke alienated adherents of fair play when he said players who went to South Africa would be subject to close taxation scrutiny. Most newspapers had by then fixed the payment to players making the South African tour as $300,000 apiece, but later information cut this to $200,000 for two tours, not one.

Terry Alderman, Rod McCurdy and Steve Rixon decided not to sign the ACB statutory declaration and withdraw from the English tour. The Board's selectors promptly replaced them with Carl Rackemann, John Maguire and Ray Phillips, only to find that Maguire and Rackemann had signed to go to South Africa. With the public utterly confused over who was left in the touring team, Jeff Thomson and Dave Gilbert were added to the side. There was no confusion in the thinking of Kim Hughes, however, and he grabbed the chance of captaining the rebel team in South Africa, adding that loyalty was worthless in Australian cricket. Hughes was clearly upset over missing selection in the side to go to England but on his form after resigning the Australian captaincy one could only agree with the selectors' view that he needed a rest.

Apart from coaxing Wellham, Wood and Phillips to dishonour their South African tour contracts, Packer's organisation further protected their interest by signing five aspiring youngsters to $45,000-a-year contracts. This money was a handy bonus on whatever Steve Waugh, Peter Clifford, Robbie Kerr, Dean Jones and Mike Veletta earned from their State and ACB contracts. The first year's money was paid so quickly Clifford was showing off his new car before the Australian team left for England.

The ACB began a Melbourne Supreme Court action against John Dyson, Rodney Hogg, Tom Hogan, John Maguire, Carl Rackemann, Steve Smith and Graham Yallop on 2 May 1985, and on 15 August began a similar breach of contract action against Kim Hughes. But the ACB did not proceed with actions that would have involved $300,000 in legal costs, and instead accepted settlement terms from the SACU. In return for $120,000 towards their legal costs to that time, the ACB agreed to release eight contracted players to tour South Africa. The SACU promised not to make any further approaches to contracted players.

Following the settlement, Tasmanian Peter Faulkner, a right-arm fast-medium bowler with a hat-trick in Shield cricket to his name, and South Australia's aspiring right-hand batsman Michael Haysman, joined the rebels, taking the South African touring party to 16 players, with Bruce Francis as manager. The ACB terminated its contracted payments to eight of the rebels

and declared all the rebels ineligible for payments from provident funds, which cost Hughes and Yallop a huge amount of money. The ACB also declared that none of the 16 rebels could play for their States for two years or for Australia for three years after the rebel tours ended, which effectively ended the Shield and Test prospects of several veterans.

The 16 players who went to South Africa on what proved to be two tours were: K. J. Hughes (captain), J. Dyson, S. B. Smith, G. N. Yallop, M. D. Haysman, M. D. Taylor, T. V. Hohns, S. J. Rixon, R. J. McCurdy, T. A. Alderman, C. G. Rackemann, J. N. Maguire, G. Shipperd, R. M. Hogg, T. G. Hogan, and P. I. Faulkner. Unlike the "Super Tests" conducted by Packer's WSC organisation, the rebels' matches have been accepted by the ICC as first-class where the appropriate conditions applied, and the players' records have been internationally credited with their figures during their two trips to South Africa.

Considering the crises that preceded the tour, Allan Border did a satisfactory job in England in 1985. He batted superbly, beginning with centuries in his first four first-class matches, and scoring eight centuries in his 1355 first-class runs at 71.31. He received only patchy support from his batsmen and his bowling resources were severely restricted by the absence of South African rebels Alderman, Hogg, Maguire and Rackemann. The presence in the side of Wellham and Phillips, who were known to have signed to go to South Africa, created tension within the team that even an astute management could not prevent. The team was: A. R. Border (captain), 30, A. M. J. Hilditch, 29, G. M. Ritchie, 25, W. B. Phillips, 27, K. C. Wessels, 28, G. M. Wood, 29, S. P. O'Donnell, 22, D. C. Boon, 24, G. F. Lawson, 28, R. B. Phillips, 31, C. J. McDermott, 20, R. G. Holland, 38, G. R. J. Matthews, 26, D. R. Gilbert, 24, D. M. Wellham, 26, M. J. Bennett, 29, J. R. Thomson, 35, with Bob Merriman as manager and Geoff

Simon O'Donnell batting in the Trent Bridge Test against England in 1985. At 22, he made a big impression as an allrounder of rich promise.

Dymock as assistant manager and coach.

Hookes, Kerr and the exciting Victorian Dean Jones were all rated unlucky not to have been included, but it was in pace bowling that Australia was weakest. The early batting got Australia off to good starts early in the tour, but once Hilditch began to regularly fall into Botham's trap by hooking straight into the hands of fieldsmen in the deep, the limitations of the openers became clear. Apart from Border, Ritchie was the only batsman to enhance his reputation, scoring 1097 runs at 54.85 on the tour and finishing second to Border in the Test averages with 422 runs at 42.20.

Australia beat Somerset by 233 runs from 8 to 10 May in the opening match of the tour after

Border (106) and Wessels (156) made centuries, and followed with draws against Worcestershire, Sussex, MCC, Derbyshire, Yorkshire and Leicestershire in the first-class matches preceding the first Test. They also beat England 2–1 in a limited-over series in this period.

At Headingley between 13 and 18 June, in the first Test, Hilditch made 119 and 80, batting from that curious stance of his with the bat held low and almost parallel to the pitch. Australia scored 331 and 324, respectable totals, but were beaten by five wickets. This was entirely due to the failure of the bowlers to contain the English batsmen. Robinson made 175 but all the thrills came from Botham's 60 off 51 balls in an hour. Phillips delayed the finish with a handsome 91, but England needed only 123 in the last innings to win. Australia did well to take five wickets before a disgraceful invasion of the pitch by spectators prevented Lawson from taking a catch from Lamb and stopping the winning run. The receipts of £321,250 broke all records for a Test outside London.

Holland, who had been omitted from the first Test, won a place in the second Test at Lord's between 27 June and 2 July by taking 5 for 51 against Hampshire three days before the Lord's Test. But it was the red-haired youngster Craig McDermott who gave Australia the early ascendancy by taking 6 for 70 in England's first innings of 290. Border exploited this advantage by scoring 196 and lifting Australia to 425. Ritchie gave him good support in an innings of 94.

Making his first appearance in a Test in England, Holland then bowled Australia to victory by taking 5 for 68 off 32 intelligent overs, pitching the ball into the rough created by the fast bowlers and mixing in an occasional googly. Australia lost six wickets scoring the 127 needed to win but their four-wicket triumph brought the series level at a win apiece. Border's 41 not out in Australia's second innings gave him 237 runs in the match, receipts for which were £668,312.

*Ian Botham congratulates Allan Border after he made
196 in the second Test at Lord's in 1985. Bowlers
McDermott and Holland helped clinch Australia's win.*

Thomson bowled 26 no-balls in the match
against Essex at Chelmsford from 6 to 9 July
but the main excitement came from a bomb scare.
Spectators moved onto the playing area while
police searched the ground. Boon's second innings
century (138) wiped off Essex's first-innings lead
of 130 and set Essex 204 to win. Gilbert gave
Australia a chance to win by taking 4 for 41
but the ninth-wicket pair, Foster and East,
survived the last 17 overs.

The third Test at Trent Bridge from 11 to
16 July fizzled out in a draw after Gower (166),
Wood (172) and Ritchie (146) made centuries.
At Neath from 20 to 22 July Javed Miandad (200

not out) and Younis Ahmed (118 not out) exposed
the weakness of Australia's bowling with an
unbroken partnership of 306 for the fourth
wicket, a record for the county and the highest
for any wicket against a touring side. Rain washed
out play when Australia reached 1 for 105 in
reply to Glamorgan's 3 for 409 declared.

Border (130) and Wellham (105) shared a
third-wicket stand of 236 at Bristol against
Gloucestershire between 24 and 26 July. This
paved the way for a 170-run win over a side
that batted a man short in each innings after
'keeper R. C. Russell broke a finger. Boon hit
a six and 28 fours in his 206 not out at
Northampton against Northants from 27 to 30
July, but again rain prevented a result.

Craig McDermott took 8 for 141 in England's
first innings at Old Trafford in the fourth Test

from 1 to 6 August, commendable figures given that Mike Gatting made 160 and the pitch resembled a sponge. Facing a 225-run first-innings deficit, Border organised a long defensive effort from Australia's middle order that saved the game. Phillips did not score for 50 balls and Border faced 334 balls in making 146 not out.

Wellham's 125 not out against Middlesex in the drawn match at Lord's from 10 to 13 August failed to win him a place in the team for the fifth Test. This was played at Edgbaston between 15 and 20 August. The first innings of the match, a dogged 335 by Australia, did not end until the third day and Australia should not have lost from that position. But by disgraceful bowling and a dramatic collapse in their second innings the Australians contrived to give England victory by an innings and 118 runs. England won despite frequent interruptions through rain because of the batting of Gower (215), Robinson (148) and Gatting (100 not out) and the brilliance of the Kent swing bowler Richard Ellison, who took 10 for 104 in the match.

Ellison troubled the Australians again in the following match, against Kent at Canterbury from 24 to 27 August, until Ritchie and Border produced an entertaining stand of 182. Ritchie hit 4 sixes and 18 fours in his 153, Border 13 fours in his 103. This drew a big effort from the Australian bowlers, who clinched victory by seven wickets by dismissing Kent for 126 in their second innings, McDermott taking 5 for 18.

England regained the Ashes, however, winning the sixth Test at The Oval from 29 August to 2 September by an innings and 94 runs. England rushed to 100 off the first 25 overs and thereafter Australia played without pride or spirit. Gooch made 196, Gower 157, in a total of 464, and Australia left out "Dutchy" Holland on a pitch ideal for him. Only Border showed any resolution in Australia's innings of 241 and 129, Ellison completing an impressive start in Tests with 5 for 46, to give England the series 3–1. The highlight of the series was England's

average of 60 runs per 100 balls, the fastest rate in the history of Tests between the two countries.

Australia won only 4 of their 20 first-class matches on the tour, lost 3, and played 13 draws. They won 5 of their 9 limited-over matches, lost 2 and drew 2. The weaknesses in the team created by the retirement of Chappell, Lillee and Marsh and the defections to South Africa were compounded by the failures of Thomson, at 35 but a shadow of his best, and Wessels, whose unattractive methods for once were ineffective. Matthews and Bennett were innocuous as spinners and the reluctance of Holland to use his googly after his success at Lord's deprived Australia of a morale-boosting weapon. McDermott was the bowling find of the tour and Ritchie was aptly described in *Wisden* as Australia's sole gain with the bat.

Border was shocked at how badly his team played under pressure. "We don't appear to be able to fight our way out of it when we are in trouble," he said. This was obvious in the series that followed in Australia against New Zealand. Richard Hadlee took 33 wickets in the three Tests to give New Zealand its first-ever win over Australia. Those who enjoyed criticising the ACB's coaching schemes could not resist deriding the faulty technique of the rising young Australian batsmen against Hadlee's "wicket-to-wicket" bowling.

New Zealand won the first Test at Brisbane from 8 to 12 November by an innings and 41 runs. Helped by a moist pitch and overcast conditions, Hadlee took 9 for 52 to bundle Australia out for 179. John Reid (108) and Martin Crowe (188) tightened the screws in a stand of 224 that lifted the New Zealand total to 7 for 553 declared, their highest score in Tests. Crowe's 188 came from 197 balls, with 16 fours and remains one of great displays of classical batting by a New Zealander.

Trailing by 373 runs, Australia slumped to 5 for 67 before Border and Matthews put on 197. Matthews, after undistinguished tours to the

Greg Matthews shows his elation after taking a wicket with an off-spinner. After two disappointing overseas tours he experienced a brief period as an Australian cricket idol.

to the crowd and drawing a big "M" for "Mumma" with his glove (for the benefit of his mother watching on television). After Matthews went for 115, Border continued to 152 not out, running out of partners. Hadlee had match figures of 15 for 123.

Matthews followed with another fine innings of 111 in New Zealand's drawn match in Sydney from 15 to 18 November against New South Wales. He was irrepressible. Another fighting 50 got Australia out of trouble at 5 for 71 in the first innings of the second Test on the SCG between 22 and 26 November. Trailing by 71 on the first innings, Australia won the match by four wickets by rushing New Zealand out for 193 in their second innings. Holland took 4 for 68, for match figures of 10 for 174. The third Test in Perth from 30 November to 4 December proved a further triumph for Hadlee, whose 11 for 155 gave New Zealand a six-wicket win and gave him a career total of 299 Test wickets.

The fifth Indian team to tour Australia for a Test series began their first-class programme immediately after the Tests with New Zealand. They were handicapped by rain, which interfered with four of their five first-class matches and they went into the first Test in Adelaide from 13 to 17 December on a completely inadequate preparation. By then Kepler Wessels had declared himself unavailable for the Australian team, refusing to accept a cut in pay from the ACB, who were aware of Wessels' role in recruiting players for the rebel South African tours. Wessels played out the rest of his contract with Queensland and joined the rebels in South Africa in 1986–87.

In mid-season, Australia experimented in the Tests with India, introducing seasoned Western Australian farmer Geoff Marsh, lanky, string-bean left-arm pace bowler Bruce Reid, tearaway fast bowler Merv Hughes and talented Sydney all-rounder Steve Waugh to Test cricket. In the third Test they successfully tried Marsh and Boon as openers. All three Tests were drawn in a series

West Indies and England, suddenly blossomed as a national hero. He had modified his haircut from his pony-tail days and no longer wore a jewel in his ear lobe. But there was no denying his joy as he lobbed the ball over the fence to reach his first Test century. He went into a dance of hip-wiggling jubilation, punching the air and sprinting halfway to the stands, throwing kisses

The unusual beanpole build of Western Australian left-arm pace bowler Bruce Reid, vividly shown in a 1986 match in Perth. Injuries have since upset his career.

enlivened by stylish batting from Gavaskar, who made 166 not out in Adelaide and 172 in Sydney, and Boon, who made 123 in Adelaide and 131 in Sydney. Border got the century (163) everyone expected from him in Melbourne, where Matthews made his second Test century (100 not out) of the season. Amarnath (138) and Srikkanth (116) also got centuries in Sydney, where India reached their first Test total of 600 on foreign soil.

The bowling from both teams looked pedestrian, with only Kapil Dev, who took 8 for 106 in the first innings of the first Test, showing the ability to run through a side, though the 2-metres tall Reid extracted exceptional bounce. Hughes, a country cricketer from Euroa in Victoria, was very fast but wild, an image

his heavy black moustache enhanced.

Boon and Marsh carried on their successful opening displays in January and February in the limited-over competition that followed the Tests. After all three teams had played ten matches Australia finished on top with six wins and a point from a washed-out match, India second with five wins, and New Zealand third with three wins. In the first final at Sydney on 5 February, Boon and Marsh put on 69 for the first wicket, which took Australia to 170 in a match reduced to 44 overs by rain. India managed 159 in reply, giving Australia victory by 11 runs. Australia then won the competition by dismissing India for 187 in 50 overs in the second final on 9 February in Melbourne, losing only three wickets to pass India's score.

On 16 February 1986, Australia began a six-week visit to New Zealand that included five first-class matches, three of them Tests, plus six one-day matches. The Australian team comprised: A. R. Border (captain), D. C. Boon, G. R. Marsh, G. M. Ritchie, G. R. J. Matthews, W. B. Phillips, B. A. Reid, T. J. Zoehrer, S. R. Waugh, R. J. Bright, C. J. McDermott, D. R. Gilbert, S. P. Davis. Without the players touring South Africa, hopes that they could reverse the 2–1 drubbing suffered early in the season proved fruitless, leaving New Zealanders amazed at their newly-won supremacy. Boon and Marsh again got away to a splendid start in the first Test at Wellington, between 21 and 25 February, putting on 104 for the first wicket. Matthews made his third Test century (130) of the season, but rain washed out the match on the fourth day just as Coney reached 101 not out.

Border and Hadlee produced further outstanding displays in the second Test at Christchurch from 1 to 4 March. Border made 140 and 114 not out, the second time he had scored two centuries in a Test. Hadlee had 9 for 163 in the match. New Zealand recovered from 4 for 48 in their first innings to score 339, thanks to 137 from Martin Crowe and 98 by Coney.

David Boon's elegant stroke play has brought him international recognition. Here he glances for four against New Zealand.

Australia collapsed for only 103 in their second innings in the third Test at Auckland from 13 to 17 March, giving New Zealand the series 1–nil. Off spinner John Bracewell won the match after Australia had led by 56 on the first innings (in which Marsh made 118) by taking 6 for 32, Boon batting right through the Australian innings for 58 not out. Four of Bracewell's victims were bowled. This gave New Zealand a victory over each of the cricket nations in seven seasons at home.

Meanwhile, back in Australia, Queensland were frustrated yet again in their bid to win the Sheffield Shield for the first time. They had to win the final against New South Wales in Sydney from 14 to 18 March to take the trophy but for the second successive year were foiled

by the New South Wales tailenders. Bennett and Holland batted through the last nine overs to save New South Wales from defeat and give New South Wales the Shield for the 39th time. Wessels, in his farewell match for Queensland, made 166. Glenn Trimble, son of Queensland's most prolific batsman Sam Trimble, hit his initial first-class century, 112. New South Wales only narrowly avoided following on. On the last day the crowd gave Jeff Thomson a standing ovation for his farewell appearance.

While Greg Matthews was becoming a national figure in the Tests and one-day matches that summer, the rebel tour of South Africa lost all public interest. Long before Kim Hughes' side had completed their itinerary, all the major Australian newspapers had withdrawn their reporters. None of the forecast demonstrations against the Australians eventuated. Crowds were down on expectations and even the disclosure towards the end of the tour that the South African government was funding most of the payments to the Australians aroused little public reaction in Australia.

Pace bowling decided the three-"Test" series, with 89 of the 95 wickets taken falling to fast stuff. Rackemann impressed with 28 wickets but both Alderman and Hogg were dogged by injury. The first two internationals resulted in evenly-fought draws and South Africa won the third at Johannesburg from 16 to 21 January by 188 runs, when the South Africans had the Australian XI out for 61 in their second innings. Dyson, Smith and Taylor batted with skill that would have won them Australian team places had they been available.

After the briefest of rests, the Australian team assembled for coaching under Bob Simpson before flying off to India in August 1986 for a tour comprising seven first-class matches, three of them Tests, and six limited-over games. Allan Border's first year as Australian captain had produced losses to the West Indies, England and New Zealand and he knew that on the dry, sun-parched pitches in India, before volatile crowds and inconsistent umpires, he had little chance of improving on that record.

The eleventh India v Australia Test series was planned as a preparation for the Ashes tour of Australia by England later in the summer and included six one-day matches and seven first-class matches, three of them Tests. The Australian team was A. R. Border (captain), D. C. Boon, D. R. Gilbert, G. C. Dyer, S. R. Waugh, D. M. Jones, G. R. J. Matthews, G. M. Ritchie, G. R. Marsh, T. J. Zoehrer, M. R. J. Veletta, C. J. McDermott, R. J. Bright, B. A. Reid, S. P. Davis, with Allan Compton as manager.

Ritchie made 124 in Gwalior in the drawn match against Bombay between 3 and 5 September, but on a feather-bed pitch the Australian bowlers made little headway. Australia declared at 8 for 525 and Bombay replied with 9 declared for 353. Matthews hit 72 of his 99 runs in boundaries, while Waugh (82) and Border (75) also punished the bowling. Pandit made 101 for Bombay. Ritchie was again in superb touch, with a knock of 95 against an Indian Under 25 XI at Chandigarh from 12 to 14 September, which was also drawn, but in the Test matches it was Dean Jones who impressed most.

Twenty-six years after the first tied Test at Brisbane, the Australians figured in the second tied Test at the Chidambaram Stadium in Madras. There was little hint of such a result on the first four days of this opening Test of the series. Boon gave Australia an excellent start with an innings of 122 on the first day, and on the second day Jones played one of the greatest of all Test innings, proceeding from his first Test century to Australia's initial double century against India. Jones faced 330 balls and batted for 8 hours and 23 minutes, fighting off nausea and leg cramps in stifling heat, dehydrating so badly he had to be rushed to hospital and placed on a drip when he was out for 210. He hit 2 sixes and 27 fours. Border's 106 enabled Australia to declare at 7 for 574.

Kapil Dev saved the follow-on for India with a free-flowing 119 off 109 balls but in reaching 397 India were still 177 behind. Matthews took 5 for 103. Border declared for the second time in the match with Australia's second innings on 5 for 170, which gave India 348 to win. When the final 20 overs began, India wanted 118 with seven wickets in hand. They moved steadily towards their target until only 18 were needed off the last 30 deliveries. Then Chetan Sharma, K. S. More, and Shivlal Yadav were dismissed, leaving India on 9 for 344 with 6 balls left.

Shastri blocked the first ball of the last over from Matthews, hit the second for two, and then stroked the third ball for a single to bring the scores level. Maninder Singh defended the fourth ball with some difficulty and next ball was given out off the second-last delivery of Matthews' over. All ten Indian wickets fell in the second innings to spin, Bright taking five and Matthews his second five-wicket haul in the match to finish with 10 for 249. In Australia, the fact that an Indian umpire, Vikram Raju, gave an lbw decision in Matthews' favour was met with amazement. The other two Tests ended in tame draws. Eighteen umpires were used in the three Tests and other matches but Australia's apprehension about umpiring proved groundless.

The young Australian batsmen did well to deny Kapil Dev a wicket in the Tests and, by sharing the series, disappointed Indian fans, who were already joyful at India's defeat of England in their previous series. Dean Jones topped the Test averages with 371 runs at 92.75, which underlined how unlucky he had been to miss the 1985 tour of England, adding 29, 35 and 73 not out, in the second and third Tests, to his double century in the first Test. David Boon topped the tour aggregates with 476 runs from six first-class innings at 68.00. Geoff Marsh and Boon proved highly efficient opening batsmen, Marsh scoring 101 in the third Test at Bombay between 15 and 19 October. Matthews thrived on long bowling spells and headed both Test and first-class bowling averages, taking 20 wickets at 30.05 on the tour. India won the limited-over internationals 3–2.

Mike Gatting's thirty-sixth England team to Australia arrived before Border's players got home for what looked a tussle for cricket's wooden spoon. England had not won any of their previous three series and had had eight defeats in Tests without a win. In 1986 England had taken an awful beating in the West Indies and their vice-captain, Mike Gatting, had had to return home to have a broken nose set midway through the tour. The England team to Australia was: M. W. Gatting (captain), 29, D. I. Gower, 29, N. A. Foster, 26, B. C. Broad, 29, I. T. Botham, 29, B. N. French, 27, A. J. Lamb, 32, J. J. Whitaker, 24, C. W. J. Athey, 29, C. J. Richards, 28, J. E. Emburey, 34, W. N. Slack, 32, P. A. J. DeFreitas, 20, G. R. Dilley, 27, G. C. Small, 25, and P. H. Edmonds, 25, with Peter Lush as manager and Micky Stewart as his assistant.

England were beaten by Queensland in Brisbane from 24 to 27 October by five wickets in the initial first-class match of the tour, thanks to an opening stand of 154 by Courtice (70) and Kerr (95) and hostile pace bowling by Frei, McDermott and Tazelaar. In the second match at Adelaide from 31 October to 3 November England's application improved and centuries from Lamb (105) and Whitaker (108) ended a sequence of 14 first-class matches without a win, England defeating South Australia by five wickets, despite centuries by Hookes (104) and Phillips (116). They were then outplayed by Western Australia in Perth between 7 and 10 November on the eve of the first Test. Burly left-arm pace bowler Chris Matthews helped lanky Bruce Reid dismiss England for 152 in three and a half hours after Geoff Marsh rescued Western Australia with an innings of 124.

Matthews' 4 for 30 persuaded the selectors to risk him in the first Test in Brisbane from 14 to 19 November after only one season in first-class cricket. Matthews' promise was obvious but

he showed the selectors had erred including him in the Test team so early in his career, by his lack of accuracy in both the first and second Tests.

Botham set up England's victory by seven wickets in Brisbane with a commanding innings of 138 in a total of 456, with Dilley's 5 for 68 and Emburey's 5 for 80 completing the job. The disappointing Australian totals were 248 and 282 (Marsh 110). The second Test at Perth between 28 November and 3 December was drawn, England dictating play after an opening stand of 223 from Athey (96) and Broad (162). Gower (136) and Richards (133) also hammered Australia's bowling to take England to 8 declared for 592. Australia saved the follow-on by 8 runs in scoring 401 and neither side appeared likely to win after that.

A lovely Adelaide pitch for the third Test

Steve Waugh, whose all-round talents proved invaluable in Australia's victory in the 1987 World Cup in India, did not have any luck when he edged this ball for a catch against India in Sydney.

from 12 to 16 December underlined the bowling poverty of both sides. Big Merv Hughes and leg-spinner Peter Sleep replaced Lawson and Matthews from the Perth Test line-up but the notable change in Australia's XI was Greg Dyer for Tim Zoehrer as wicket-keeper. The absence of Botham because of a rib injury gave Australia a chance to square the series but after the batsmen gave the side a splendid start, reaching 5 for 514 before Border declared, the bowlers were unable to press home the advantage. Boon and Marsh put on 113 for the first wicket, Boon going on to 103. Jones (93), Border (70), Greg Matthews (73 not out) and Waugh (79 not out) were all rewarded for their aggressive approach.

England were never in danger of following on after Broad and Athey added 112 for the first wicket. Broad and Gatting then put on 161 in a stand that gave England a chance of a big lead, but only Emburey (49), among the later batsmen, properly supported Broad's 116 and Gatting's 100. With Australia 59 ahead on the first innings, Border made his twenty-first Test century and his seventh against England before making a token declaration at 3 for 201. The attendance of only 46,720 for this Test, which ended in a draw, demonstrated the waning public interest in a lack-lustre series.

Gladstone Small became the first bowler on either side to rise above mediocrity in the fourth test at Melbourne between 26 and 28 December. Small's 5 for 48 and 2 for 40, coupled with Botham's 5 for 41 in the first innings, was enough to seal victory and the series for England. The crowds stayed away after Australia's dismal first innings of 141 on the first day, with Jones (59) the only batsman to pass 20. Broad batted sensibly for 112 as England took a lead of 208 on the first innings before another humiliating batting performance from Australia gave England victory by an innings and 14 runs. Two run-outs, one of them sending Marsh back for 60, deprived Australia of the will to fight on.

Greg Matthews had a miserable series with bat and ball before the selectors dropped him for the fifth Test at Sydney between 10 and 15 January. Australian cricket was at a low ebb, but Dean Jones started well by scoring 184 not out, his first Test century on Australian soil. This took Australia to 343, Jones surviving a supremely confident appeal for caught behind when he was five. Wicket-keeper Richards seemed to gather a leg glance but Jones was ruled not out. Trailing by 68 runs on the first innings, England looked likely to make the 320 needed to win in the last innings until Gatting was out for 96. Sleep bowled Emburey in the second last over to give Australia victory by 55 runs, her first Test success in more than a year, a triumph to which Peter Taylor, an off-spinner who had played only six first-class matches and only one that season, made a massive contribution.

Taylor's selection had been one of the most controversial of all time and earned him the soubriquet "Peter Who?", for few cricket followers had ever heard of him. Taylor turned out the hero of a memorable Test—a tall, red-haired, old-fashioned off-spinner with a kangaroo hop as he reached the delivery stride. He took eight wickets (6 for 78 and 2 for 76) and twice dismissed Botham cheaply (16 and 0) to salvage some honour from a sub-standard series.

Between July and September 1987, Australia's women cricketers flew to England for a tour that included three four-day Tests and three one-day internationals. Australia won the Test series 1–nil thanks to a patient 126 by Belinda Haggett in the first Test at Worcester. This innings set up victory by an innings and 21 runs with a day to spare. The Tests at Collingham and Hove were drawn. Linda Reeler (110) and Dawn Annetts (193) put on a record 309 for Australia for the third wicket at Collingham. Both sides had a win in the limited-over matches and the third was drawn.

After losing his place in the men's Test team, Greg Matthews fell further from grace on Australia's visit to Sharjah for the Sharjah Cup in April 1987. Australia was the only one of the four competing teams not to win a match and England took the Cup because of a superior run-rate to Pakistan, who finished level with England on the points table. During the tournament the Australian team management, comprising Border, Simpson and manager Ian McDonald, fined Matthews $1000 after he had an altercation with a chef. Matthews was lucky not to be sent home immediately.

Despite his sterling performance in the tied Test a year earlier, Matthews was not included in the Australian team for the World Cup in India and Pakistan in October and November 1987, the first World Cup conducted outside England. The Australians went into this competition as rank outsiders but caused an immediate upset at Madras by beating Cup holders India by one run on 9 October. They followed with wins over Zimbabwe by 96 runs and over New Zealand by three runs before they suffered their only loss of the tournament in the return against India at Delhi on 22 October, India winning by 56 runs.

Australia then repeated its victories over New Zealand and Zimbabwe to reach the semi-finals against Pakistan, which they won by 18 runs. In the final against England at Calcutta on 8 November, every top-order batsmen contributed to a total of 253. The tension was tremendous in the final ten overs as England moved closer to the target. Waugh bowled Lamb for 45 and then had DeFreitas caught at long on by Reid after DeFreitas hammered 15 from the 48th over. Seven runs were needed off the last over but Craig McDermott made certain England did not get them. Australia were the world champions.

This success came as great relief and sustained the Australians through an historic home season in 1987–88 and a 3–1 series defeat in 1988–89 by a bouncer-happy West Indies. In 1987 the ACB learnt that Kerry Packer had sold his Channel 9 network to Alan Bond for $1100 million. The ACB quickly organised a new five-year contract with Bond, which extended the PBL Sports control of Australian cricket until 1994 and left Australian cricket lovers stuck with the lopsided one-day format and Shield players without any foreseeable improvement in their competition. The deal made Packer the richest man in Australia but whether Australian cricket was any richer from his activities remains doubtful.

There probably would have been a players' revolt against the Australian Cricket Board in some form or other even without Packer. The ACB's failure to recognise the great assets they controlled and accept the justice in the players' pleas for higher pay inevitably ended in Australian cricket's wealth being shared with a media network, but the ACB and cricket were probably lucky someone with Packer's sporting instincts was involved. A tough, shrewd business-man maybe, but one who can take success or failure at the racetrack or on the polo field without bleating, and who has shown he can be trusted. He showed the State cricket associations how to make money by attracting their own sponsors.

The main problem arising from the Packer years is that they have led to over-saturation of home and overseas tour programmes and a lowering of playing standards that could lead to the public losing all interest in the game. The ACB has shown it is aware of this by initiating Kanga cricket, an abridged form of the game suitable for schoolkids; by establishing nation-wide age-group tournaments for teenagers; and in 1987–88 by setting up the Australian Cricket Academy in Adelaide. The academy began with 16 scholarship winners picked on their per-formances in the 1988 World Youth Cup. They were accommodated near Adelaide Oval and studied cricket technique for several hours a day under former international Jack Potter, also spending time on trade or scholastic courses.

The 1987–88 Australian season saw the first successes by academy graduates. Dirk Tazelaar, a fast-medium left-arm bowler, had an out-

Underestimated, low-profile boss of Packer's PBL Marketing, Linton Taylor. In ten years as chief promoter of Australian cricket, he won high ratings for one-day matches, completely neglected Sheffield Shield games, and forecast the demise of Test cricket by the year 2000.

standing season for Queensland, and with McDermott and Rackemann battling injuries, relished the role of strike bowler. With Botham in the Queensland side and all Australia's South African "rebels" available again, big crowds turned out right across the country for inter-State matches, encouraged in Brisbane by the flat $1 admission charge.

Queensland, still trying to get their name on the Sheffield Shield, started in exciting style with Botham in their side. But he failed to make a century, repeatedly losing his wicket swinging wildly, and did not capture more than three wickets in an innings. Botham was fined following a drinking session in Launceston with Dennis Lillee in which they allegedly caused heavy damage to a schoolroom. When Queensland flew to Perth for the Shield final against Western Australia, Botham was reported to have put a headlock on an airline passenger. Western Australia won by five wickets, and Botham's sponsors terminated his contract.

Captained by Graeme Wood, Western Australia won the Sheffield Shield for the eleventh time. Chris Matthews took 57 wickets for the second season in a row. Matthews' flair for scoring runs with a series of big, heavy swings was often very handy as only Wood, among Western Australia's top-order batsmen, was scoring consistently. Wood batted well enough to regain his Australian XI spot, scoring 1050 at 70.00. The Test selectors ignored his fine form, however, and the Test berth many felt he had earned went to Shield team-mate Mike Veletta, whose father Remo financed him, with earnings from his quarry near Perth, on three trips to England to improve his cricket.

New Zealand stopped off in Australia on their way home from the World Cup for a tour involving ten one-day matches and three Tests. The uncomfortable relations between the players that had grown up in 16 previous visits by New Zealand sides continued, but with their captain Jeff Crowe badly out of form the New Zealanders could not continue their recent good record against Australia.

They defeated Sheffield Shield holders Western Australia by an innings and 96 runs in Perth from 20 to 22 November thanks to centuries by Martin Crowe (119) and Dipak Patel (105). Richard Hadlee took five wickets in an innings for the 93rd time in his career. Then a shock defeat by South Australia in Adelaide at the end of November revealed the paucity of their bowling if Hadlee could not break through. David Hookes (128) and Glenn Bishop (123) helped South Australia to victory despite a New

Zealand first innings of 7 for 360 declared and a ten-wicket haul by John Bracewell.

At Brisbane, between 4 and 7 December, Australia made up for their defeat on the 'Gabba ground two years earlier. Only Patel, with a second innings of 62, gave Martin Crowe any support in New Zealand's scores of 186 and 212. David Boon, in wonderful form throughout the season, gave Australia the ascendancy with 143 in a total of 305. Hadlee beat the younger Australian batsmen so often that 3 for 95 was an unjust return from 31 overs. New Zealand struggled in the second innings, on a pitch that was slightly under-prepared because of heavy rain, and only a ninth-wicket stand of 52 in an hour by Patel and Morrison, who contributed just two runs, gave their total respectability. Australia made the 97 needed to win by nine wickets with a day to spare.

The second Test at Adelaide from 11 to 15 December attracted only 30,083 spectators over the five days. On a dead pitch neither side had the bowling strength to gain an advantage. Andrew Jones (150) and Martin Crowe (137) were mainly responsible for New Zealand's first innings total of 9 declared for 485. Border then made 205 in ten hours, which took him past Bradman's 6996 runs and Greg Chappell's 7110 runs for Australia and established him as Australia's highest run-getter and the seventh-best in the history of Test cricket. Australia led by 11 runs, Hadlee taking 5 for 68, his thirtieth five-wicket haul in Tests. New Zealand used the last hours of the match for practice, which left the third Test at Melbourne from 26 to 30 December, the twenty-fourth between the countries, to decide the rubber.

Dyer at that stage appeared to have earned a permanent place as Australia's wicket-keeper, having gone on the Indian tour in 1986–87 and in the World Cup in 1987–88, but just before tea on the first day of the Test with New Zealand came a decisive moment in his career. Andrew Jones edged a ball from McDermott and turned to see Dyer roll over and come up with the ball in his right hand, claiming a clean catch. The umpires conferred before Jones was given out but television replays showed the ball had bounced out of Dyer's hand onto the turf before he regathered it. Doubts arose over Dyer's sportsmanship and clearly sapped his confidence.

New Zealand were out for 317, which Australia passed by 40 runs, thanks to a solid 90 from Peter Sleep and an impressive 50 from Tony Dodemaide, a good-looking allrounder of French descent playing in his initial Test. Dodemaide followed this up by taking 6 for 58, swinging the ball about in a fashion that troubled all the New Zealanders. Left to score 247 to win, Australia got to within 31 runs of victory with 10 overs remaining. Bowling unchanged from 5.15 p.m. until 6.49 p.m., Hadlee took four wickets, leaving Michael Whitney, a self-confessed rabbit with the bat, to survive the last 4.5 overs with McDermott.

The crowd of 23,859 hushed, and across the nation Australians crowded round their television sets as Hadlee delivered the last over. Whitney held him out and when the exhausted Hadlee put an arm round Whitney and shook hands in a memorable gesture of sportsmanship, Australia had won her first home series in four seasons by a one–nil margin.

A fortnight later the Queensland wicket-keeper Peter Anderson fractured a thumb and was replaced by Ian Healy, a player officials had been watching following his success in teenagers' inter-State matches. Greg Dyer, who had inherited the New South Wales captaincy when Dirk Wellham retired, suddenly found himself under intense media scrutiny.

Dyer retained his place in the Test team for the much-publicised match against England, in Sydney from 29 January to 2 February 1988, staged as cricket's contribution to Australia's bicentenary celebrations. This match proved unworthy of the months of planning and staff work that preceded it, though it did permit a

Merv Hughes plays close attention to the hairdo that has helped make him an idol among young Australian cricket fans.

notable reunion of former Test players. England's batsmen showed a fear of getting out that was unfitting on such an occasion and dawdled to 2 for 221 on the first day. Only 103,831 spectators turned up for a five-day match which was expected to attract 200,000. Broad was fined $1200 for angrily knocking down his stumps when given out for 139. Australia got to within 12 runs of avoiding the follow-on, but their 214 in response to England's 425 was a very poor effort.

Any chance England had of preventing a draw evaporated when a total of 3 hours 30 minutes was lost through bad light. Boon, more disciplined and determined than in his previous displays against England, made 184 not out in Australia's second innings of 2 for 328, but against such mediocre bowling even his 14 fours failed to enthuse onlookers. The public showed more interest in a computer Test, scores for which were announced in the intervals, Australia defeating England by 37 runs. Two days after the Bicentenary Test ended, Australia won a one-day match against England in Melbourne before 54,159 spectators.

Australia dropped catches in both innings in the Test against Sri Lanka in Perth between 12 and 15 February. Although they won by an innings and 108 runs, Border, in his thirty-first successive Test as captain, condemned his team's lack of dedication. Dean Jones contributed 102, Border 88, in Australia's innings of 455, big Merv Hughes clinching the win for Australia by taking 5 for 67 in Sri Lanka's second innings. Dodemaide made certain of his place in the Australian team that toured Pakistan in September and October 1988 by taking 7 for 98 in the match.

The major surprise in the team for Pakistan was wicket-keeper Ian Healy, who was preferred to more experienced 'keepers Greg Dyer, Tim Zoehrer and the Victorian, Michael Dimattina, after only six first-class matches. Three spinners, Tim May, Peter Taylor and Peter Sleep, were included in the side, and Healy's skill against spin—demonstrated in his handling of Hohns and Henschell for Queensland—was reported to have won him his place.

The Australian team for the three-Test tour of Pakistan, which was undertaken in early summer heat and humidity—despite the 1982 recommendation of manager Col Egar that tours be moved to less taxing months—was: A. R. Border (captain), D. C. Boon, G. R. Marsh, A. I. C. Dodemaide, I. A. Healy, D. M. Jones, T. B. A. May, B. A. Reid, P. R. Sleep, P. L. Taylor, S. R. Waugh, G. M. Wood, C. J. McDermott, M. R. J. Veletta, and J. D. Siddons.

Australia maintained the record it had kept intact since 1975 by failing to win an overseas series. Only one of the six first-class matches brought a result, the first Test at Karachi from 15 to 20 September 1988. This match was marred by Australian complaints about the poor standard of the almost bare pitch and the umpiring of

Mahboob Shah. After Pakistan had lost 2 for 21, Shoaib Mohammad (94) and Javed Miandad (211) put on 196 for the third wicket. Javed batted 636 minutes to compile the highest score by a Pakistani against Australia, surviving chances at 126 and 186 and several confident lbw appeals.

Chasing Pakistan's 9 declared for 469, Australia found spinners Iqbal Qasim and Abdul Qadir virtually unplayable on the barren, grassless pitch and succumbed for 165 and 116, giving Pakistan victory by an innings and 188 runs. Australian manager Col Egar, a former Test umpire, protested to the Pakistan Board of Control over the umpiring of Mahboob Shah. Border expressed a strong desire to take his team home immediately and added that the match was "a conspiracy from the word go". The players agreed later, at a team meeting, to complete the tour.

Qasim took 5 for 35 and 4 for 49 in the match, Qadir 2 for 54 and 3 for 33. Peter Taylor, with 54 not out in Australia's first innings, was the only Australian to score more than 30 runs.

Dropped catches again cost Australia dearly in the second Test at Faisalabad between 23 and 28 September after Pakistan slumped to 4 for 25 early in the game. Ijaz Ahmed, just turned 20, rescued Pakistan by scoring 122, his maiden century in only his twelfth Test. Ijaz reached his century without offering a chance but Australia's bungled catches at the other end allowed Pakistan to reach 316. Border made 113 not out—his twenty-third Test century and fifty-ninth first-class century—in Australia's reply of 321. Border and Miandad had a heated argument over the dismissal of May, who was given out caught off Qadir. Miandad later survived a confident appeal for lbw off Reid when only 5, before going on to 107.

Play was held up late on the fourth day when spectators hurled bottles onto the field. Left to score 374 to win in 90 minutes plus 20 overs, Australia conceded the task was impossible and the match was called off before the mandatory final overs began.

Australia had a big chance to level the series in the third Test from 7 to 11 October at Lahore, where solid team batting gave them a first-innings lead of 107. Pakistan were asked to score 269 in 75 overs to win in the final innings and were 8 for 153 when time ran out. Iqbal Qasim and Tausif Ahmed defied the Australian attack for the last 26 minutes and 5.1 overs.

Reid's 20 wickets on the tour at an average of 20.35 was the best by an Australian bowler, though May impressed with 14 wickets at 30.71. None of the Australians took five wickets in an innings. Geoff Marsh easily headed the Australian batting averages with 475 runs at 67.86, with two centuries. Border, the other century-maker, averaged 66.50. Healy dismissed 12 batsmen in 11 innings in which he kept wicket. Nothing in Australia's displays on this tour suggested, however, that they could provide fair competition for the West Indies during the 1988–89 Australian summer. A team that could field four fast bowlers in every match and not worry about the no-balls they conceded as long as they sustained express pace, the West Indies were a formidable proposition.

The Ashes Regained

West Indies tour Australia 1988-89; Australia wins the Ashes 1989

Inter-territory cricket matches began in the West Indies in 1894 about the same time that Australia's Sheffield Shield competition got under way. By 1900 West Indians believed the game they first learned while working as labourers, on plantations opened up by British colonists, had improved enough for them to send their first team to England under the captaincy of "Plum" Warner's elder brother R. S. A. Warner. H. B. G. Austin had been first choice as captain but Warner took over when Austin was called up to fight in the Boer War. They won 5, lost 8 and drew 4 of their 17 matches.

Down the years regular exchanges of visits between English and West Indian teams lifted standards until the West Indies made their first tour of Australia in 1930–31. Despite the presence of brilliant players, they sustained some heavy defeats on this and succeeding Australian tours,

The Australian players show their elation on the balcony at Old Trafford as David Boon scores the winning runs to claim the Ashes. Border's side was the first since 1934 to regain The Ashes in England and only the third team this century to achieve the feat.

culminating in the 1975–76 tour when Australia overwhelmed them 5–1. Clive Lloyd said in his autobiography:

We had a lot of problems but the main one was that our batsmen were frequently exposed to Lillee and Thomson, still fresh and still raring to go with a relatively new ball. Our players were all put under constant pressure by sheer pace on some very quick wickets. Many of us were hit. I got hit on the jaw by Lillee in Perth and by Thomson in Sydney. Julien's thumb was broken, Kallicharran's nose was cracked by Lillee in Perth and everyone at some stage of the tour felt the discomfort and pain of a cricket ball being sent down at more than 90 miles an hour.

Lloyd and his deputy Vivian Richards came away from that tour convinced that a world-beating team could best be built around similarly intimidating fast bowling. Michael Manley in his *History of West Indian Cricket* clearly documents the manner in which Lloyd and Richards built their team's striking power around pace bowling. They were not content to include two speedsters, but added two more, who were just as fast, to go on when the openers tired. By the time the West Indians arrived in Australia for their tenth tour in 1988–89 they had become accustomed to touring without topline spinners. They had no place for a Ramadhin, Valentine or Gibbs.

The West Indian indifference to pleas for higher over-rates was apparent throughout their 10 weeks in Australia during which they played 23 matches, five of them Tests. Their team comprised: I. V. A. Richards (captain), C. E. L. Ambrose, K. L. T. Arthurton, W. K. M. Benjamin, I. R. Bishop, P. J. L. Dujon, C. G. Greenidge, R. A. Harper, D. L. Haynes, C. L. Hooper, A. L. Logie, M. D. Marshall, B. P. Patterson, R. B. Richardson, C. A. Walsh. D. Williams, with Clive Lloyd as manager.

The tour began at the end of October with defeats by Western Australia in a limited-over match and in a four-day match, both played in

Perth. Chris Matthews had match figures of 9 for 159 in the four-day match which Western Australia won by seven wickets because of strong batting by Veletta (81 not out) and Moody (78) in the second innings. The win was Western Australia's fifth in seven first-class matches against the West Indies, whose no-ball problems had emerged already, with 23 being called against their bowlers.

Greenidge scored his eighty-fourth first-class century, but only his first in Australia, by reaching 213 against South Australia at Adelaide from 4 to 7 November. He put on 169 for the first wicket with Haynes, 87 for the second wicket with Richardson, and 169 for the fourth wicket with Richards, whose 136 was his ninety-ninth first-class century. Peter Anderson, who had transferred to South Australia when Healy displaced him as Queensland's 'keeper, did not concede a bye in the West Indies total of 593 in 600 minutes.

Bundled out for 163 in their first innings, South Australia fared better in their second innings. Nobes topscored with 95, Hilditch contributed 64, Bishop 45 and Hookes 47, before they were all out 20 runs short of forcing the West Indies to bat again. Hookes scored his ten-thousandth first-class run in this match, which saw 10,705 people attend on the third day when admission was lowered to $1. Twenty-seven more no-balls took the West Indies' tour total to 50.

Mark Taylor, a stocky left-hander from the Northern Districts club in Sydney, showed his rich promise in an opening stand of 162 for New South Wales with John Dyson. This match, in Sydney from 11 to 14 November, produced Richards' hundredth first-class century, but on a placid pitch no result was possible for the first time since the teams first met, with New South Wales winning five and the West Indies four of their previous encounters. Dyson (100 not out) and Mark Waugh (103 not out) shared an unbroken stand of 193 in New South Wales' second innings of 1 for 261. When Dyer declared

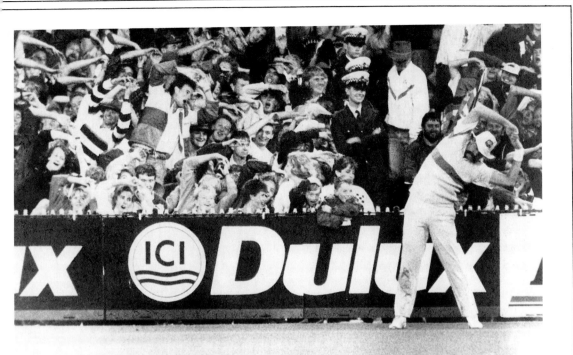

Merv Hughes's Melbourne fans copy his warm-up exercises during the 1988–89 series against the West Indies. Hughes has emerged as one of the greatest crowd-pleasers in recent cricket history.

the West Indies declined to chase the 334 runs wanted for victory from 50 overs.

The Australians had a torrid time against the West Indian speedsters on an under-prepared 'Gabba pitch in the first Test between 18 and 21 November. Curtly Ambrose lifted the ball alarmingly, often into the rib cage. Shrugging aside no-ball calls—37 in all were called against them—the West Indies ripped into the Australian batsmen, fully testing the effectiveness of their thigh, chest and forearm pads, and even bouncing occasional deliveries off their helmets. Richards marked his hundredth Test appearance by leading the West Indies to their fifth consecutive Test victory and in the process took his hundredth Test catch when he caught a skier from Dodemaide.

After managing only 167 in their first innings, Australia lost by nine wickets, Steve Waugh's

second innings of 90 providing their sole consolation. Walsh took a rare hat-trick, spread over two innings, for the West Indies. Chris Matthews, whom many hoped would provide a counter to the West Indian pace attack, bowled eight wides and six no balls in a forgettable display which mercifully ended when he broke down in the West Indies' second innings.

During the West Indies' MCG match from 25 to 28 November, chunky right-hander Wayne Phillips scored 111 on debut for Victoria, but all the headlines went to umpire Robin Bailhache for warning Winston Benjamin for intimidatory bowling. Benjamin had bowled seven bouncers in a row. The third day was washed out and prevented a result.

The second Test in Perth between 2 and 6 December saw the development of Merv Hughes into a remarkable crowd-pleaser, who showed all the menace of a rampaging bull. Wild-eyed Merv in his eighth Test took the nineteenth Test hat-trick, the first by an Australian for 31 years, and the first to be split over three overs. Hughes dismissed Ambrose with the last ball of his thirty-sixth over, and Patterson with the first ball of his thirty-seventh over, in the West Indies' first innings of 449. Then in the West Indies' second innings, Hughes had Greenidge lbw with his first ball to complete an unlikely hat-trick.

Hughes' 13 wickets for 217 runs was the best ever by an Australian against the West Indies and the best by an Australian in Perth, and although this performance did not save the match for Australia, it won Hughes the Man-of-the-Match award. In a match that bristled with magnificent individual efforts, Richards made 146, including a 163-run fifth-wicket stand with Logie (93). Boon (80), Wood (111) and Steve Waugh (91) took Australia to within 54 runs of the West Indies before the Australian innings ended in chaos.

Ambrose knocked Lawson unconscious with a bouncer that struck him a sickening blow on the face. The ball deflected onto the stumps, but Lawson was incorrectly ruled "retired hurt" as he was carried away to hospital. Border then declared the innings closed on 395 before the last man, Hughes, later to prove a very useful batsman, could go to the crease. X-rays showed Lawson had sustained a fractured jaw and he took no further part in the series. A level century from Haynes, who appeared to be unlucky to be given out caught behind, helped the West Indies to 9 for 349 declared in their second attempt.

Umpire Bailhache officially warned Patterson for intimidatory bowling in Australia's second innings of 234, the West Indies winning by 169 runs. Despite this handsome victory the West Indies lost many admirers because of their tedious over rate. With all four pace bowlers operating from unnecessarily long approach runs, they bowled an amazing 72 no-balls in the match. Worse still, they made no attempt to bowl the 90 overs a day laid down in the tour conditions of play. This meant that, attractive as they were while they were batting, the West Indies were a very boring team to watch in the field, with

the four fast bowlers walking leisurely out near the sight-screens before they delivered each ball. No amount of brilliant fielding could compensate for the tedium this inflicted on the game.

The West Indies made certain of retaining the Frank Worrell trophy with another big win in the third Test at Melbourne from 24 to 29 December. This time their bowling on a green pitch on the last day was absolutely ferocious. Australia had done well for four days, getting to within 38 runs of the West Indies' first innings of 280, but a fine 122 by Richardson took the West Indies to a 399-run lead with a day to play. Batting for a draw, the Australians took a fearful battering. Jones' chest was badly bruised, Healy was twice hit in the groin and the others spent most of their brief time at the crease taking blows on the arms and ribs and ducking under bouncers. A further 19 no-balls were called against the West Indies for over-stepping, but there was no hint of them ending the barrage until Patterson swept through the tail to take 4 for 4 in 13 balls and give his team a 285-run win. With Greenidge recovering from a blow in the face that sent him to hospital and Logie suffering from a broken nose, the dressing rooms were like casualty clearing stations.

The fourth Test at Sydney produced a shock reversal on a dry, grassless pitch that suited spin bowling from the start. Mark Taylor and Trevor Hohns were brought into the Australian side for the first time, clearly with the English tour, later in the year, in mind. Taylor's selection meant splitting the successful Boon and Marsh opening pairing in the hope his left-handed style would upset the bowlers' line. Hohns, at 35 a seasoned leg-spinner with more than 200 victims to his credit, impressed with his economy when given a long bowl in each innings.

Border introduced spin in the seventh over of this 26 to 30 January match and, after Peter Taylor had Greenidge caught, went on himself to produce an astonishing collapse with his orthodox left-arm spinners. From 2 for 144, the

West Indies were all out for 224, Border taking 7 for 46. There were clear signs of panic among the West Indian batsmen as they swung wildly across the ball instead of playing straight.

Determined not to let this advantage slip, Border batted for 310 minutes for 50 when Australia batted, surviving until he was 75. Boon made his third Test century in succession in Sydney to consolidate Australia's position, 149 in 499 minutes, and Steven Waugh chimed in with 55 not out to take Australia to 401, 177 runs ahead. With the pitch providing sharp turn, the West Indians' technique deserted them. Haynes alone remained calm, batting 316 minutes for a chanceless 143, but at the other end persistent West Indian mis-hits won applause that increased the pressure. Hohns took the vital wickets of Hooper, Richards and Logie before Border dismissed the last four batsmen to become the first Australian captain ever to take ten wickets in a match. His 11 for 96 left Australia to score only 81 to win, which they achieved for the loss of three wickets.

Australia were never in danger of defeat in the fifth Test at Adelaide from 3 to 7 February after Dean Jones made 216, his highest Test score, mixing some classical strokeplay with speedy running between wickets. He did not give a chance until he was 135, when he survived a run-out appeal, and was finally out attempting a quick single. Big Merv Hughes produced the major surprise of the Australian innings by scoring 72 not out, submitting most of his body to bruising by short-pitched deliveries. Australia's 515 was its first score in excess of 500 against the West Indies for 20 years.

Whitney, who had replaced the injured Alderman, had his career-best analysis of 7 for 89 in the West Indies' first innings of 369, repeatedly moving his left-arm deliveries across right-handed batsmen to provide behind-the-stumps catches. Border declared Australia's second innings closed at 4 for 224, setting the West Indies the task of scoring 371 in 95 overs

on the last day. Greenidge's 104, his maiden Test century in Australia, made a draw inevitable.

By defeating the West Indies in the fourth Test, and playing an honourable draw in the fifth, Australia showed promise of doing very well in England in 1989. The West Indies had overwhelmed England four-nil in 1988 in England and although their obsession with the short-pitched ball was unpopular, they were acknowledged as the world's best team. Further, England were in disarray following the dismissal of Mike Gatting, captain since 1968, over allegations of his relations with a barmaid during a Test match.

The umpires called 362 no-balls during the five Australia *v* West Indies Tests, 247 of them against West Indian bowlers. Only 54 of these were scored from, while a high percentage hit batsmen. Australia was responsible for 115 no-balls, 19 of which were scored from. The Australian Cricket Board fined the West Indies $22,500 for falling 37 overs short of the agreed daily minimum of 90 overs during the five Tests. The fine was deducted from the $27,000 prizemoney won in the Tests, which left $4800 for the players. Captain Vivian Richards said he was not unhappy over the fine as his players were well paid and placed winning before money.

Both Haynes and Richardson scored more than 500 runs in the Tests, a record for West Indian teams in Australia. Haynes made 537 runs at 59.67, Richardson 528 at 58.67. Curtly Ambrose topped the Test bowling with 26 wickets at 21.46, followed by 17 at 28.71 by Malcolm Marshall and 17 at 29.41 by Courtney Walsh. Marshall, who was twice disciplined for disputing umpires' decisions, took his three-hundredth Test wicket on the tour, which the West Indies completed by winning their fifth one-day competition in Australia.

Dean Jones headed Australia's Test batting averages with 321 runs at 64.20, with David Boon next on 397 at 44.11. The only other batsman to average more than 40 was Steve Waugh, with

A dramatic demonstration of the all-out effort Michael Whitney brings to his left-arm fast-medium bowling. Whitney has a big following among Sydney fans who admire his gutsy efforts at the end of long hot days.

331 runs at 41.38. Merv Hughes took most wickets in the Tests, 14 at 35.93, but Allan Border was the most economical with 11 wickets at 11.00. A ninth-wicket stand of 114 by Jones and Hughes in the fifth Test at Adelaide during which Hughes hit Walsh for six was the highlight of the series.

Pakistan toured Australia in December 1988, playing nine limited-over matches against the West Indies and Australia and one first-class match against New South Wales, before their one-day matches and a three-Test series in New Zealand. They were captained by Imran Khan, who had declined to play in the matches against Australia three months earlier in Pakistan. At Sydney between 19 and 21 December, Aaqib Javed became the youngest player to appear for a touring side in Australia when he turned out against New South Wales, aged 16 years and 136 days. Batting at No. 11 he did not score,

but he took 2 for 28 with the ball. Rain curtailed the match, the fourth draw between the teams. Whitney's match figures of 9 for 100 gave him 58 wickets at a handy 23.62 for the first-class season, ten wickets more than the next-highest wicket-taker Terry Alderman, who took one of his wickets against the visiting Indian state side Tamil Nadu. The English County team Worcestershire also visited Australia in 1988–89, Ian Botham joining their lineup in two one-day matches against Queensland. The first match was drawn, the second won by Queensland.

Western Australia won their third successive Sheffield Shield competition and their twelfth since joining the competition in 1947–48. Western Australia lost three matches during the season, one to South Australia and two to New South Wales, but their overall strength, competent management and the captaincy of Graeme Wood prevailed. They compiled their highest-ever score against South Australia (535) in the final at Perth between 25 and 29 March, Moody's 162, his third century of the summer, virtually assuring him of an English tour spot. Just to make sure of it, he made 155 in the second innings, after a fine 146 not out from Peter Sleep lifted South Australia to 494. The New South Wales batsman Mark Taylor headed the season's run-scorers with 1241 runs at 49.64.

Apart from Whitney, all the outstanding performers in this eventful summer were rewarded when the thirty-first Australian team to tour England was named by selectors John Benaud, Jim Higgs, Lawrie Sawle and Bob Simpson. The team was A. R. Border (captain), G. R. Marsh, T. M. Alderman, D. C. Boon, G. D. Campbell, I. A. Healy, T. V. Hohns, M. G. Hughes, D. M. Jones, G. F. Lawson, T. B. A. May, T. M. Moody, C. G. Rackemann, M. A. Taylor, M. R. J. Veletta, S. R. Waugh, T. J. Zoehrer, with L. M. Sawle as manager, R. B. Simpson as coach and M. K. Walsh as scorer. The choice of Tasmanian Greg Campbell, a medium-pace bowler with no international experience, ahead of Whitney was the only surprise in the side. Whitney's 58 wickets in the 1988–89 Australian season included nine in the fifth Test against the West Indies, a display that seemed certain to have earned him a tour.

Lawrie "The Colonel" Sawle invited Border to sit in on the final selection meeting and give his views on players the panel were not "certain about". Border left this first meeting with 14 names confirmed including Campbell, a unanimous selection. Merv Hughes was among the last three chosen at a second meeting, going in ahead of Whitney, whose omission caused a justified uproar in Sydney. Judged on his fitness, team spirit and gutsy end-of-the-day displays, Whitney could not be faulted, whereas Hughes appeared a wayward clown of a bowler, more intent on luring crowds into mimicking his warm-up exercises than on taking wickets.

The tour started badly, with defeat in two days by Worcestershire at Worcester where the pitch was below first-class standard. After a series of social matches, starting at Dartmouth on 5 May, against the League Cricket Conference, followed by games at Arundel, Hove and Lord's, the Australians were desperately keen for an outing on a good pitch under first-class conditions. The match scheduled for 13 to 15 May with Worcestershire was a bitter disappointment to them, with the locals claiming victory by three wickets on the second day.

Duncan Fearnley, the bat-maker boss at Worcester, was irate when the Australians refused to play a limited-over match to compensate for the lost day. Sawle ignored threats of press criticism and simply refused to play an unscheduled one-day match. Botham, who had scored 39 and 42, attracted the headline: "Fans fume as Aussies duck Both". Australia had made 103 and 205, Worcestershire 146 and 7 for 163.

With English commentators still talking about Border leading the worst side ever to tour England, the Australians played a draw against Somerset at Taunton between 17 and 19 May. The significance of Mark Taylor's innings of 97 and 58 was missed by critics who concentrated on the Australian bowlers' inability to prevent Peter Roebuck scoring 100 not out.

At Lord's from 20 to 22 May, Australia had their first win, beating a strong Middlesex side by three wickets. Middlesex began with 245, Gatting contributing 65, Rackemann 4 for 85. Marsh was on 100 not out and Moody 60 not out when Australia declared at 2 for 233. They then bowled Middlesex out for 227, despite Gatting's 79, Lawson taking 5 for 48. Boon (86) and Border (77) made light work of taking the total to 7 for 243.

Most writers believed Australia had a better chance of beating England in the tour's limited-over matches than in the Tests. They were proved wrong when England won the first one-day match at Old Trafford on 25 May by 95 runs and then took the series with a tie at Trent Bridge on 27 May. Both sides scored 226, but England were awarded the match through losing only five wickets compared with eight by Australia. At

Lord's on 29 May England made 7 for 278, but Marsh (111 not out), Border (53) and Waugh (35) allowed Australia to overtake that total with three balls to spare. It was just the tonic Australian morale needed.

After a draw against Warwickshire at Edgbaston, where Jones made 248, a career-best, Australia began a winning sequence by defeating Derbyshire at Derby by 11 runs in a cliff-hanger. All the bowlers were running into form, except Rackemann who had a damaged knee and required a cartilage operation. Unusually hot weather buoyed the Australians' spirits.

Mark Taylor's consistency could not be denied and in picking him to open with Marsh in the first Test at Headingley from 8 to 13 June, the Australians settled on a deliberate policy of upsetting the accuracy of England's bowlers with left-handers Taylor and Border at No. 2 and No. 4 respectively. They could have opted for another left-hander, Hohns, later in the order but after long consideration omitted him for Campbell and his medium-pacers.

Every detail in the team's approach was considered. Border took a tougher, less genial approach when he went out to toss with England captain David Gower and his down-to-earth demeanour rubbed off on his players. In considering field placements for each England batsman, Border decided on a shortish mid-on for Gooch, instead of a bat-pad, as he had noticed Gooch's habit of occasionally hitting on drives in the air.

Gower and England's manager Micky Stewart tried hard to warn supporters that Australia were a well-chosen, thoughtfully prepared team who were a big threat to England's Ashes hopes. English newspapers would have none of it, reminding readers Australia had fallen in a heap when beaten 3–1 in 1985 and had won only five of the 30 Tests they had played since then, losing nine. Tony Greig called Border's men "pussy-cats" and labelled Alderman a "straight-up-and-down bowler". With the aristocratic, intelligent

Generously built Mark Taylor, who gave Australia consistently lavish starts throughout the six-Test series in England in 1989.

Ted Dexter in charge, English fans looked forward to a resounding series triumph.

On the pitch where they had failed in 1985, Australia moved to 3 for 207 on the first day, with Taylor 96 not out at stumps. Border enlivened play by hitting a short, kicking ball outside the off stump over backward point for six, on his way to 66. Next day Taylor set up a big total by carrying his score to 136 and when he went at 273, Steve Waugh joined Dean Jones in a stand that delighted the purists. Tom Graveney said it should have been videotaped for every cricket coach in England. Jones was out for 79 but Waugh's steady flow of off drives and cuts continued. Healy supported him until the total reached 441, leaving Australian

England's Graham Gooch batting against Alderman to a keen, alert Australian slips field in the first Test at Headingley in 1989.

supporters hoping for 500.

Merv Hughes had no notion of stopping there and notched up a blustering innings of 71, joining Waugh in a flood of runs that had Gower desperately moving fieldsmen in an effort to stop it. Waugh hit 24 fours. Hughes, whose first scoring shot was a six, also hit six fours. Hughes was out at 558, leaving Lawson to join the run-spree until Australia reached 7 for 601 and Border declared. It was a record score at Leeds in 20 England–Australia Tests, and Waugh's 177 not out was acclaimed as one of the finest in all those matches.

Faced with scoring 402 to avoid the follow-on, England lost Gooch for 13 and Broad for 37, Hughes producing a surprise leg-break. Kim Barnett and Allan Lamb made the Australian bowling look threadbare until Alderman trapped Barnett lbw at 195. Barnett's departure for 80 from 118 balls left Lamb (125) to take England past the follow-on mark, with support from Gower (26), Robin Smith (66) and Newport (36). The innings finished at 430, with Alderman taking 5 for 107.

By the end of the fourth day Australia led by 329, having built on their first innings lead of 171 in commanding fashion, 72 runs coming in 10 overs during a Jones–Border stand of 101. This allowed Border to declare at 3 for 230 and set England 402 runs to win in 83 overs. Given the placid pitch, a draw appeared certain.

England looked safe at 1 for 67 but lost two wickets at 134 and two more at 153, all of them to deliveries, in line with the stumps, that moved slightly off the crumbling pitch. Fine slips catching by Border and Taylor, energetic work by 'keeper Healy, and Boon at bat-pad sustained the collapse until Hughes found the edge of Russell's bat and clean-bowled DeFreitas to end the innings at 191, giving Australia victory by 210 runs, its ninety-eighth victory over England.

Alderman's 5 for 44 gave him 10 for 151 in the match, but only narrowly earned him the man-of-the-match award in front of Waugh and Taylor. The takings were an all-time record for Leeds—in excess of $1 million Australian. Australia last won at Leeds in 1964 when the present coach, Bob Simpson, was captain.

Australia did not allow this big psychological advantage to slip and after a nine-wicket win over Lancashire at Manchester (where Campbell's 5 for 54 impressed), and a 272-run

*The Australians congratulate Merv Hughes after he had
'keeper Jack Russell caught by Healy in the first Test at
Headingley in 1989. Australia were then only one wicket
away from victory.*

victory over Northants at Northampton (where
Border scored 135), they went into the second
Test at Lord's from 22 to 27 June oozing
confidence. Hohns replaced Campbell, which
gave the bowling more variety, and brought in
another left-handed batsman to upset the England
bowlers' direction.

On a splendid Lord's pitch Australia restricted
England to 286 by sticking to their astute plans
for each top-order batsman. Gooch made 60,
Gower 57, but only 'keeper Jack Russell really
frustrated the Australians with his unbeaten 64.
Hughes' pace and periodic bouncers unsettled the
batsmen but he bowled too many balls wide of
the leg stump to support comparison with the

great Australian pace bowlers.

Australia's first innings of 528 was a model
of solid team batting, and by Saturday night,
24 June, Australia's Ashes-winning supremacy
was clear to the sell-out crowd. After losing
Marsh at six, Boon and Taylor added 145. Boon
went for 94, Taylor for 62 and when Border
and Boon failed to exploit their promising starts,
Waugh played another classic knock, for 152.
Hughes, Hohns and Lawson supported him
admirably. The 130-run Waugh-Lawson
partnership for the ninth wicket set up the match-
winning lead and a total of 528, with England
conceding 263 runs in taking the last four wickets.
At 4 for 84 in England's second innings, Gower
shared a 139 stand with Smith. One had to admire
the defiance and sheer brilliance of his stroke-
play as he moved to 106 with 16 boundaries.
Hughes then delivered England a staggering
blow, by lifting a ball into Gower's ribs that
deflected to Border in the gully. Four short of

his 100, Smith was bowled by Alderman, having also hit 16 fours.

England's second innings of 359 brought Alderman his seventh five-wicket coup in eight Tests in England. Left to score 118 to win on the last day, Australia lost four wickets achieving this, Boon steering them to a six-wicket win and a two–nil lead in the series with a craftsmanlike 58 not out. Not many Englishmen shared the optimism of David Gower, who said England could still win the series, and when he walked out of the press conference after this defeat the critics unanimously condemned him.

The third Test at Edgbaston saw Marsh and Taylor give Australia a splendid start with an opening stand of 88. Three wickets then fell for 17 runs but Dean Jones remained uninhibited in his stroke-play, taking the attack up to Emburey, the bowler Australians feared most. Botham had regained his place in the England side amid controversy about his fitness. Former selector Alec Bedser strongly opposed the view that Botham could lift the confidence of England's players and was proved correct as Jones hammered Botham and the other England bowlers on his way to a chanceless century. Jones' 157, with 17 fours, followed his 248 scored on the same ground earlier on the tour.

Angus Fraser made a highly impressive Test debut, taking 4 for 63 from 33 overs, including the wicket of Steve Waugh, whose stumps he scattered when Waugh was 43. Waugh's average for the series then stood at 393. Botham had Marsh lbw and bounced Border first ball, but the swing and nip from the pitch and subtle changes of pace were gone. England replied to Australia's 424 with a disappointing 242, the top order turning in yet another woeful display, and they only prevented the follow-on with last man Jarvis at the crease. Interruptions for rain forced a draw with Australia 2 for 158 and 340 ahead in the second innings.

Australia prepared for the fourth Test at Old Trafford between 27 July and 1 August with a

trip to Scotland where Veletta and Moody made 101 apiece in a 97-run win over Scotland; followed by a draw with Hampshire at Southampton where Waugh (122) and Boon (103) made centuries; and a handsome innings and 146-run victory over Gloucestershire at Bristol, where Lawson had 10 for 77 and Jones (167 not out) and Taylor (141) contributed hundreds.

Lawson's bowling had lacked rhythm in the first three Tests but now at Old Trafford he returned to his splendidly controlled best, taking 6 for 72 in England's first innings of 260, which Robin Smith adorned with a magnificent 143. With partners falling at the other end, Smith hit 15 glorious fours. Botham missed with a wild swing and was bowled by Hohns for a duck, a sad figure as he passed into the pavilion shadows.

Marsh and Taylor gave Australia a further splendid start by putting on 135 for the first wicket. Taylor made 85 before he was stumped. Marsh scored 47. Border (80), Jones (69), and Waugh (92) kept the momentum of the innings going with crowd-pleasing shot-making, seldom failing to punish bad deliveries, running superbly between wickets, continually taking the attack to the bowling, to give Australia a 187-run lead on the first innings.

Alderman and Lawson then whipped through England's batting in such an efficient manner that Merv Hughes was left to fill a mere supporting role. It was not until England's top order had again been disposed of that plucky little 'keeper Jack Russell counter-attacked. Russell hit 14 fours in notching up a wonderful 124 that took the score from 6 for 59 to 201. With support from Emburey (64), he saved face for England by forcing Australia to bat again, but the Australians had little trouble scoring the 81 runs needed to regain the Ashes 3–nil with a nine-wicket victory. It was Australia's hundredth Test win in England and the two-hundredth in all Tests.

Border's team thus became only the third team this century to regain the Ashes in England, emulating the feat of Bill Woodfull's 1930 and

David Boon leads his Australian team-mates in a victory song during the 1989 tour of England. The players' elation after being written off as one of the worst sides to visit England is obvious.

1934 sides. English newspapers, the next day, discounted the excellence of the Australians' cricket and devoted their headlines to bitter attacks on Gower and his players. Ian Todd wrote in the London *Sun*: "England achieved the impossible. They got even worse." The *London Daily Express* said: "There is nowhere left for English cricket to hide."

Australia's recovery of the Ashes did not get the press it deserved because of the announcement, on the final morning, of Mike Gatting's decision to take a team to South Africa. Border read the papers in partial disbelief for he could not believe that his players had not defeated a very "impressive bunch of England cricketers",

all of whom had sound records.

Australian openers Marsh and Taylor set up an Australian win and a four–nil series lead by batting throughout the first day of the fifth Test at Trent Bridge. Their unbroken stand of 301 in six hours took Marsh to 125 not out and Taylor to 141 not out. The next day Marsh went for 138, but Taylor continued to 219, which, with 73 from Boon and 65 from Border, enabled Australia to declare at 6 for 602. Alderman stunned England with an opening spell of 3 for 12. Compelled to follow on with a first innings total of 255, 101 of which had come from Robin Smith, England succumbed for 167 in the second innings, giving Australia a winning margin of an innings and 180 runs.

Just before the sixth Test, in the last County match of the tour, the Australians were involved in another record when twins Steve and Mark Waugh scored centuries, Steve for Australia, Mark for Essex, both reaching 100 not out. The spectacle of Mark bowling to Steve mesmerised spectators.

Australia compiled their eighth successive total in excess of 400 at The Oval in the sixth Test between 24 and 29 August, when only rain and poor light saved England from further humiliation. Dean Jones scored his sixth Test century (122), to topscore in another fine display of team batting that took Australia to 468. Gower made 79 to help England prevent the follow on, but Gladstone Small (59) was the only other batsman to score in excess of 40 in England's 285. Having failed to force the follow-on, Australia batted on to 4 for 219 in the second innings before Border declared. England were 4 for 67, needing 403 to win, when Robin Smith's bright 77 prevented another collapse. The draw gave Australia an unbeaten record in the Tests, a feat only previously achieved by the 1948 and 1921 teams.

Alderman's 41 Test wickets gave him a career total of 127 victims at 27.38. His success attracted world-wide attention to his methods. The experts found that: he bowled straight; he released the ball close to the stumps at the bowler's end, which gave him more chance of earning lbw decisions; and he relied on the green English wickets to occasionally deviate the ball off the seam by just enough to elude the bat and hit stumps or pads. The myth that he had lost his ability to swing the ball after he broke his shoulder, trying to clobber a hoodlum who invaded the field in 1982 at Perth, had finally been buried.

Alderman was Man of the Series, but Geoff Lawson gave him skilful support by taking 29 wickets at 27.28 and taking his career total to 177 Test wickets. Hughes bowled a lot of wayward balls down the leg side but his 19 Test victims at 32.37 and his belligerent batting satisfied his fans. But I am one of those who believes Whitney would have done better.

At a time of nationwide economic woes, the Australian cricket team's 1989 success enthralled the nation. Border was hailed as an embattled captain who had not allowed disappointments to lessen his belief that the team would eventually triumph. There was hardly a failure in the team, never a suggestion of tantrums or misbehaviour, and all 17 players were rewarded with some unforgettable functions when they returned home.

The Australian Cricket Board staged a special dinner for them in Melbourne. In Sydney they were given a tickertape parade through the streets which was watched by more than 100,000 people and was topped by lunch with 1800 well-wishers who maintained their applause for several minutes as the players entered the Darling Harbour banquet room. The sincerity of this welcome home was deeply moving.

Nobody could say for sure if the 1989 team was better than the 1948 side, which went through England unbeaten, or the 1921 team that won the Ashes inside three days in their first three Tests. But they had certainly done as much as any of the great sides for Australian cricket.

After 187 years of cricket in Australia the game was controlled by a Board that did not own a ground or have plans for establishing one. The State associations were left to negotiate as best they could with parliaments and city councils for the hire of capital city venues. This worked with varying degrees of success, but the controllers of the major grounds have not always been ready to co-operate with cricket administrators.

The Woolloongabba ground in Brisbane is administered by a government appointed Trust, whose three main tenants are the Queensland Cricket Association, the 'Gabba Greyhound Racing Club, and the Queensland Cricketers' Club. The Sydney Cricket Ground is administered by a 14-member government-appointed Trust, in which only two of the members are elected by the ground's 20,000 members. In 1986–87 the New South Wales Cricket Association negotiated a seven-year lease

The Sydney Cricket Ground, where State cricket authorities have won important concession, including cash payments for revenue lost when ground members and not "gate-payers" attend Test cricket.

under which the Trust agreed to pay the Association $150,000 a year compensation for lost gate receipts when ground members attend cricket at the SCG and a share of catering, fence and scoreboard advertising. The Melbourne Cricket Ground is controlled by 20 government-appointed trustees who leave management of the ground to the Melbourne Cricket Club. In 1987–88 the club paid the Victorian Cricket Association $208,000 for the loss of revenue when club members watched cricket on the MCG. Adelaide Oval is controlled by 16 members of the South Australian Cricket Association, whose lease on the ground expires in 2035. The Western Australian Cricket Association is unique among State associations in that it fully controls the WACA ground on a 999-year lease that began in 1889.

The arrangements are satisfactory although in Sydney cricket officials have nasty memories of how the SCG Trust betrayed traditional cricket, and according to Justice Helsham broke the law, when Packer's WSC breakaway occurred. The SCG Trust has developed the ground without a master plan, erecting stands that have no relation to each other as funds became available. The light towers are an eyesore and the electronic scoreboard's erection on the **Hill instead of at the back of the ground severely** limits the ground capacity. At a time when the MCG (which got its big boost by staging the 1956 Olympics), has begun work on a $100 million grandstand that will lift capacity by 10,000 to 110,000 seats, the SCG is restricted to a capacity of 45,000.

Although the matches it stages attract millions of dollars in gate receipts, the Australian

Cricket Board is not the fabulously wealthy organisation of popular belief. The Board retains enough of its annual profits to support its operation in the Melbourne suburb of Jolimont but distributes the rest to the six State associations who form its membership. Distributions to the States since the Packer dispute show how the game has prospered despite the poor performance of the Test team. These are the amounts handed to the States since the Packer settlement:

1980	$891,932	1985	$2,527,538
1981	$1,166,907	1986	$2,323,307
1982	$1,537,106	1987	$2,397,836
1983	$1,907,510	1988	$2,879,770
1984	$2,022,065	Total:	$17,653,971

Until June 1989 the distribution was divided into 14 parts—New South Wales, Victoria, and South Australia received three fourteenths each as the foundation States, Queensland and Western Australia received two fourteenths, and Tasmania one fourteenth. The Board recognised the limitations of this distribution and from 1990, as a new five year agreement with the Bond network began, a fairer, more equitable allocation, acceptable to all States, applied. Queensland had tried unsuccessfully to improve its share for 75 years and recently Western Australia has sought a better split as the State that has dominated the Sheffield Shield and provided so many Test players. Western Australia and Queensland argued that they deserve a higher share as they take cricket to vastly bigger geographical areas than New South Wales, Victoria and South Australia, who in turn countered that they look after more players. Tasmania's one fourteenth share looked paltry to a State that seeks inclusion in the Test roster.

Given the higher receipts from the ACB, and a big inflow of cash from sponsors New South Wales cricket officials began in the mid-1980s to look for possible sites for their own ground. Desperate to retain major sports for the SCG following the departure of Rugby Union to Concord, the Sydney Cricket Ground Trust lifted the annual payment to the Association to compensate for the loss of revenue when members watch cricket.

Back in 1929–30 the Sydney Cricket Ground Trust paid the NSWCA £1172. In 1952–53 this was lifted to £3506, and in 1973–74 the figure was $7500. When the Association successfully took the Trust to court in 1974–75 in an effort to retain its priority use of the ground following the Packer revolt, the Trust paid the Association $9763. No further payments were received until the Association's new lease on the ground was negotiated in 1986–87, but the $150,000 a year (with increases linked to the Consumer Price Index) now paid by the Trust represents a complete change of face, especially as the Association has advertising concessions when cricket is played on the ground. The Victorian Cricket Association's annual payment of $208,000 from the Melbourne Cricket Club does not give the VCA advertising rights for cricket on the MCG.

Australian cricket has achieved unprecedented financial prosperity in the decade since the settlement with Packer against a background of declining standards of conduct among players. With the exception of the 1989 tour to England, the game's high standards of discipline, sportsmanship and ethical behaviour have not been models for schoolboys to copy.

Back in 1931 Lord Harris, when he was the major power at Lord's, wrote a letter to *The Times* about cricket in which he said:

> *You do well to love it, for it is more free from anything sordid, anything dishonourable, than any game in the world. To play it keenly, honourably, generously, self-sacrificingly is a moral lesson in itself, and the classroom is God's air and sunshine. Foster it, my brothers, so that it may attract all who can find the time to play it; protect it from all who would sully it, so that it may be in favour with all men.*

Lord Harris believed cricket was a major factor in linking the countries of the British Empire and in two world wars Australians who enjoyed their cricket probably supported that view.

An increasingly cosmopolitan Australia accepts Packer's success as an inevitable part of the country's cricket history, given that cricketers all round the world were so badly paid before he came along. The revolt he underwrote has helped Australia maintain its position as the world's most successful cricket nation. Even if the current team is not No. 1 in the world, it rates among the best Australian XIs. Australia has defeated each of the cricket nations more often than any of them has inflicted defeat on it. As the accompanying table shows, only Pakistan has come close to Australia's success on a wins for and against basis:

Australian Tests

Opponent	Played	Won	Lost	Drawn	Tied
England	269	101	88	80	—
West Indies	67	28	22	16	1
South Africa	53	29	11	13	—
India	45	20	8	16	1
Pakistan	31	11	9	11	—
New Zealand	21	9	5	7	—
Sri Lanka	1	1	—	—	—
Total	487	199	143	143	2

The margins of Australian supremacy vary, but there is little doubt that Australia has performed well on the world's cricket fields. The teams that went to England in 1884, 1902, 1921, 1948 and 1989 achieved results that set them apart from other touring teams.

Bradman's 1948 side is still the only touring outfit with an unbeaten record, a performance that earned its comparisons with Armstrong's 1921 side, which won the first three Tests and the Ashes inside three days and lost only two matches at the end of the tour. Armstrong,

though, always said of the 1902 side, which had the same record as his 1921 outfit: "The 1902 side could have played 22 of my 1921 blokes and given them a beating."

The 1902 team was blessed with an incomparable batsman—Victor Trumper—and the 1948 side had a batsman of similar genius in Don Bradman. On hard wickets the 1948 side has often been rated unbeatable, but Trumper and his team-mates had more practice on damp pitches which would have made the outcome close when rain was about.

According to my figures, 86 Australian teams have appeared in first-class matches overseas. That figure includes two Services teams, which helped revive cricket after the First and Second World Wars; the two Australian teams that toured the United States; one which went to Sri Lanka; and one to Zimbabwe.

Allan Border's 1989 Australian team, the thirty-first to tour England, had its deficiencies. The spin bowling was weak and there was no left-arm bowler of consequence, but they achieved a few records that even the distinguished teams, which challenge their record, could not match. They established a world record by scoring more than 400 in eight successive Tests and they became the first team to bat through a day without losing a wicket, with the 301 opening-day stand at Trent Bridge by Taylor and Marsh. They also achieved a record number of lbw decisions by bowling straight. Some of the sides led by Richie Benaud in the early 1960s and by Ian Chappell, when Thomson and Lillee were at their peak, achieved a superb standard but none of them could claim to have done as much for cricket, since 1948, as Border's side did by playing consistently aggressive and entertaining cricket.

Australian cricket entered the 1990s with the changes the Packer revolt brought in 1977 still dominating the conduct and promotion of the game. Crowds for Test matches and Sheffield Shield matches remain a worry, though there are signs this could be altered with stronger promotion. The big money in the game comes from the one-day matches Packer initiated and even at Test matches, the atmosphere he created governs crowd behaviour. From the hundreds of banners, to the imitations of players' warm-up routines and the recently adopted Mexican wave the audience participation Packer encouraged is a major part of big matches. PBL Sports, the company Packer founded, remains the sole promoter of Australian cricket with a strong influence on tour itineraries and which cities overseas teams visit. No individual in the long history of Australian cricket has so thoroughly shaken the foundations of the game as Packer has done.

Appendix

Australia's Mainland Test Cricket Grounds

	THE 'GABBA	SCG	MCG	ADELAIDE OVAL	THE WACA
Members	3000	14,156	44,000	9300	9800
Waiting list	200	25,000	75,000	8000	400
Waiting time	3 years	10 years	16 years	10 years	1 year
Joining fee	$150	$500	$200	$100	$285
Annual sub.	$95	$225/$125	$133	$105	$170
Women members	101	424	75	300	600
Lights	no	yes	yes	no	yes
Seating capacity	21,000	45,000	110,000	30,000	29,500

ADDITIONAL NOTES

The 'Gabba ground membership does not include 6000 members of the Queensland Cricketers' Club.

Current seating capacity in Brisbane is 15,000, but by seating people on the dog track that circles the ground this has lifted capacity to a record 21,000.

SCG membership should not be confused with Gold Membership, which costs $5000 plus $200 per year and provides dual membership of both the SCG and the Sydney Football Stadium.

SCG members pay $125 per annum, plus a further $100-a-year for a lady's ticket—7029 ladies tickets were issued in 1988–89.

MCG membership comprises 28,000 voting members and 16,000 restricted members.

Restricted membership of the MCG is offered after 16 years and after a further 12 years voting rights are granted.

The Melbourne Cricket Club is enlarging the public grandstand to include a complex for 25,000 (included in the total shown above) Victorian Football League members at football matches. The VFL will share the cost of the new stand and has agreed to play the VFL grand final and preliminary final on the MCG for 30 years. VFL membership now carries access to reserved seats at both the MCG and VFL Park.

Bibliography

Alley, Bill, *My Incredible Innings*, Pelham, London, 1969

Arlott, John, *The Great Ones*, Pelham, London, 1967
The Great Captains Pelham, London, 1971

Arnold, Peter and Peter Wynne-Thomas, *The Illustrated History of the Test Match,* Guild Books, London, 1988

Bailey, Philip, Philip Thorn, and Peter Wynne-Thomas, *Who's Who of Cricketers*, Newnes Books, London, 1984

Barnes, Sid, *It Isn't Cricket*, William Kimber, London, 1953
Eyes on the Ashes, William Kimber, London, 1953
The Ashes Ablaze, William Kimber, London, 1955

Benaud, Richie, *A Tale of Two Tests*, Hodder & Stoughton, London, 1962
Way of Cricket, Hodder & Stoughton, London, 1961
On Reflection, William Collins, London, 1984

Bouman, Richard, *Glorious Innings*, Hutchinson Australia, Melbourne, 1987

Bowen, Rowland, *Cricket: A History*, Eyre & Spottiswood, London, 1970

Boycott, Geoffrey, *The Autobiography*, Macmillan, Melbourne, 1987

Brearley, Michael and Dudley Doust, *The Ashes Retained*, Hodder & Stoughton, London, 1979
The Art of Captaincy, Hodder & Stoughton, London, 1985

Brooke, Robert, *The Collins Who's Who of English First-Class Cricket*, William Collins, London 1985

Butler, Keith, *Howzat*, William Collins, Sydney, 1979

Caro, Andrew, *With A Straight Bat*, The Sales Machine, Hong Kong, 1979

Cashman, Richard, *'Ave A Go, Yer Mug!*, William Collins, Sydney, 1984

Chappell, Ian, *Chappelli*, Hutchinson Australia, Melbourne, 1976

Cheetham, Jack, *Caught By the Springboks*, Howard Timmins, Cape Town, 1953

Davidson, Alan, *Fifteen Paces*, Souvenir Press, London, 1963

Dunstan, Keith, *The Paddock That Grew* (revised edition), Macmillan, Melbourne, 1988

Favell, Les, *By Hook Or By Cut*, Investigator Press, Adelaide, 1970

Fingleton, Jack, *Brightly Fades The Don*, Collins, London, 1949
Brown And Company, William Collins, London, 1951
The Greatest Test Of All, William Collins, London, 1961

Forsyth, Christopher, *The Great Cricket Hijack*, Widescope, Melbourne, 1978

Frindall, Bill, *The Wisden Book of Cricket Records* Queen Anne Press, London, 1981
The Wisden Book of Test Cricket 1877–1984, Macdonald & Jane, London, 1986

Green, Benny, *Cricket Archive*, Pavilion Library Edition London, 1985
  Wisden Anthology, Macdonald Queen Anne Press, London, 1979
  A History of Cricket, Macdonald Queen Anne Press, London, 1988
Grout, Wally, *My Country's 'Keeper*, Pelham, London, 1965
Hall, Wes, *Pace Like Fire*, Pelham, London, 1965
Harte, Chris, *Cricket Rebels*, Horwitz Grahame, Sydney, 1985
  Two Tours and Pollock, Sports Marketing, Adelaide, 1988
Harvey, Neil, *My World of Cricket*, Hodder & Stoughton, London, 1963
James, Alfred, *Averages & Results of Australian First-Class Cricket 1918–1958*, A. B. M. James, Sydney, 1987
James, C. R. L., *Beyond a Boundary*, Stanley Paul, London, 1963
Johnson, Ian, *Cricket At the Crossroads*, Cassell, London, 1957
Lemmon, David, *Great One Day Cricket Matches*, Allen & Unwin, Sydney, 1982
Lillee, Dennis, *My Life In Cricket*, Methuen, Australia, 1982
McCool, Colin, *Cricket is a Game*, Stanley Paul, London, 1961
McFarline, Peter, *A Game Divided*, Hutchinson Australia, Melbourne, 1977
  A Testing Time, Hutchinson Australia, Melbourne, 1979
McGregor, Adrian, *Greg Chappell*, William Collins, Sydney, 1987
McHarg, Jack, *Stan McCabe*, William Collins, Sydney, 1987
Mackay, Ken, *Slasher Opens Up*, Pelham, London, 1964
Manley, Michael, *A History of West Indies Cricket*, Andre Deutsch, London, 1988
Marsh, Rodney, *You'll Keep*, Hutchinson Australia, Melbourne, 1975
Marshall, Michael, *Gents & Players*, Grafton Books, London, 1987
Meckiff, Ian (with Ian McDonald), *Thrown Out*, Stanley Paul, London, 1961
Miller, Keith and R. S. Whitington, *Gods And Flannelled Fools* Macdonald, London, 1954
Morris, Arthur (with Pat Landsberg), *Operation Ashes*, Hale, London, 1956
Moyes, A. G., *With the West Indies In Australia 1951–52*, Angus & Robertson, Sydney, 1952
  and Tom Goodman, *With the MCC In Australia 1962–63*, Angus & Robertson, Sydney, 1963
O'Reilly, Bill, *Cricket Conquest*, T. Werner Laurie, London, 1949
Page, Michael, *Bradman*, Macmillan, Melbourne, 1984
Pollard, Jack, *Australian Cricket—The Game And The Players* (revised), Angus & Robertson, Sydney, 1988
  (ed.), *Middle & Leg*, Macmillan, Melbourne, 1988
Redpath, Ian, *Always Ready*, Garry Sparkes & Associates, Melbourne, 1976
Robinson, Ray, *The Wildest Tests*, Pelham, London, 1972
  On Top Down Under, Cassell, Australia, 1975
Rowan, Lou, *The Umpire's Story*, Jack Pollard, Sydney, 1972
Sissons, Ric, *The Players*, Pluto Press, Sydney, 1988
Smith, Rick, *Prominent Tasmanian Cricketers*, Foot & Playstead, Launceston, 1985
Swanton, E. W., George Plumptre and John Woodcock, *Barclay's World of Cricket*, Willow Books, London, 1986
  Gubby Allen—Man of Cricket, Hutchinson/Stanley Paul, London, 1984

Thomson, A. A., *Cricket My Pleasure*, Museum Press, London, 1953

Tyson, Frank, *History of the Richmond Cricket Club*, Richmond Cricket Club, Melbourne, 1987

Walker, Max, *Tangles*, Gary Sparkes & Associates, Melbourne, 1976
   Back To Bay 13, Gary Sparkes & Associates, Melbourne, 1980

Ward, Kirwan, *Put Lock On!* Robert Hale, London, 1972

Wellings, E. M., *Dexter* v. *Benaud*, Bailey Bros & Swinfen, London, 1963

Whitington, R. S. *The Quiet Australian*, Heinemann, London, 1962
   The Golden Nugget, Rigby, Adelaide, 1981

Wisden's *Cricketer Almanack*, Macdonald & Jane, London

Wynne-Thomas, Peter, *Cricket in Conflict*, Newnes Books, London, 1984
   Cricket Tours at Home and Abroad, Guild Publishing, London, 1989
   Who's Who of Cricketer's, Newnes Books, London, 1984

Picture Credits

The author and publishers gratefully acknowledge the following people and organisations who gave permission to reproduce photographs and illustrations on the pages noted. Every effort has been made to trace copyright holders and apology is made for any unintended infringement. Pictures not listed come from the author's collection.

Associated Press, 13, 15

Australian Picture Library, 410–1

Bell Publishing Group Pty Ltd, 110

Central Press, 5, 170, 215

Courier Mail (Brisbane), 20–1, 183, 231, 253, 299

Patrick Eagar, 246, 248, 267, 276, 289, 298, 308, 309, 314, 315, 367, 376, 418, 419, 420, 422, 424

Herald & Weekly Times, 53, 171, 174, 176, 234, 339, 344, 366, 370, 372, 387, 407, 413

John Fairfax & Sons, 38, 177, 305

Ken Kelly, 7, 62–3, 68, 101, 214, 244, 261, 263, 282, 288, 306, 311, 312, 313, 360, 368, 376, 395

Keystone Press Agency Ltd, 69

Milton Wordley, 283

Mirror Australia Telegraph Publications, 405

News Ltd, 2–3, 8, 10, 12, 17, 18, 29, 30, 34–5, 42, 43, 44–5, 51, 85, 90–1, 94, 172–3, 236–7, 255, 257, 258, 290–1, 301, 304, 319, 320–1, 333, 340, 341, 355, 356, 357, 359, 391, 398, 402, 416

New South Wales Cricket Association, 126

New Zealand Herald, 294–5

Qantas, 118–9

Sport & General, 104–5

Sunday Times Library, 378, 385, 389, 400

The Age (Melbourne), 24, 26, 130, 202, 211, 346–7

West Australian Newspapers Ltd, 353, 362–3

A. Wilkes & Son, 159

Index

AN ANGUS & ROBERTSON BOOK

First published in Australia in 1990 by
Collins/Angus & Robertson Publishers Australia

Collins/Angus & Robertson Publishers Australia
A division of HarperCollins Publishers (Australia) Pty Ltd
Unit 4, Eden Park, 31 Waterloo Road, North Ryde
NSW 2113, Australia
William Collins Publishers Ltd
31 View Road, Glenfield, Auckland 10, New Zealand
Angus & Robertson (UK)
16 Golden Square, London W1R 4BN, United Kingdom

National Library of Australia
Cataloguing-in-Publication data:

Pollard, Jack 1926-
    From Bradman to Border: Australian Cricket 1948-89.

    Bibliography.
    Includes index.
    ISBN 0 207 16124 0.

    1. Cricket–Australia–History–20th century.
    2.Cricket players–Australia–History–20th century.
    I.Title.

796.3580994

Typeset in 9pt Bembo
Printed in Singapore

5 4 3 2 1
95 94 93 92 91 90